The Oxford Book
of English Verse

The Oxford Book of English Verse, 1250–1900, edited by Arthur Quiller-Couch, appeared in 1900 (revised 1939), and *The New Oxford Book of English Verse, 1250–1950*, edited by Helen Gardner, in 1972.

The
Oxford Book of
English Verse

❁

Edited by

Christopher Ricks

OXFORD

UNIVERSITY PRESS

OXFORD
UNIVERSITY PRESS

Great Clarendon Street, Oxford OX2 6DP

Oxford University Press is a department of the University of Oxford.
It furthers the University's objective of excellence in research, scholarship,
and education by publishing worldwide in

Oxford New York

Athens Auckland Bangkok Bogotá Buenos Aires Calcutta
Cape Town Chennai Dar es Salaam Delhi Florence Hong Kong Istanbul
Karachi Kuala Lumpur Madrid Melbourne Mexico City Mumbai
Nairobi Paris São Paulo Singapore Taipei Tokyo Toronto Warsaw

and associated companies in Berlin Ibadan

Oxford is a registered trade mark of Oxford University Press
in the UK and certain other countries

Published in the United States
by Oxford University Press Inc., New York

British Library Cataloguing in Publication Data

Data available

Library of Congress Cataloging in Publication Data
The Oxford book of English verse / edited by Christopher Ricks.
Includes indexes.
1. English poetry. I. Ricks, Christopher B.
PR1175.O897 1999
821.008—dc21 99–20831

ISBN 0–19–214182–1

1 3 5 7 9 10 8 6 4 2

Typeset by Jayvee, Trivandrum, India
Printed in Great Britain
on acid-free paper by
The Bath Press.
Bath, Somerset

CONTENTS

PREFACE: THE OXFORD BOOK

'Here is God's plenty': so it was that a great poet in the seventeenth century, John Dryden, paid tribute to the father of English poetry, Geoffrey Chaucer. God's plenty has proved to be mankind's too. Any anthologist of the unparagoned achievement that is English poetry must enjoy the pleasure, privilege, and responsibility of being for a while the master of its ceremonies. Or of being, at any rate, in the rueful Americanism, kinda humble and kinda proud.

Gratitude for the delights, the inspirations, the consolations, of English poetry is happily widespread. Each of us remembers what, once upon a time, an anthology did for her or him. I shall not myself ever forget the anthologies that—an age ago—gave young me such pleasure, and affably trained me to find new pleasures for myself. Gratitude is in order, then, and on this occasion my further gratitude for the invitation not only to attend this banquet but to select the food, the drink, and the honoured guests. Or rather some of the honoured ones, the writers, since there are others, the readers.

The Oxford Book of English Verse established itself—one hundred years ago in the hands of Arthur Quiller-Couch, and thirty years ago in those of Helen Gardner—as the foremost celebration of English poetry and all its lasting powers. A worthy successor to the supreme Victorian anthology *The Golden Treasury*, it was more capacious than Palgrave in historical amplitude and in the kinds of poem that it relished and proffered. To Palgrave's full title, *The Golden Treasury of the Best Songs and Lyrical Poems in the English Language*, there came an amiable retort from *The Oxford Book of English Verse*: for *the Best Songs and Lyrical Poems*, read *the Best Poems*.

Now the enterprise has been undertaken anew. As one day it will again be undertaken yet once more, since English poetry—having a life of its own—is forever being supplemented, complemented, culled, and found fresh. The anthologist had better not repine at the thought of his or her future departure.

> And slowly answered Arthur from the barge:
> 'The old order changeth, yielding place to new . . .'

*   *   *

> Dust hath closed Helen's eye . . .

*   *   *

> You did late review my lays,
>   Crusty Christopher . . .

Historical Range

Like its predecessors, this *Oxford Book of English Verse* launches itself on the wings of medieval lyric. Medieval poets, for instance Chaucer and Langland, are then given a greater representation than they formerly enjoyed, and others—notably Gower—appear for the first time. The poets proceed in the order of their dates of birth. Their names are given in the form they chose. At our hither end, the span—which in Helen Gardner was 1250–1950—is extended to poetry of the last fifty years, and arrives finally at its particular pause in the progress of poetry with Seamus Heaney.

My decision to rest at Heaney acknowledges a conjunction of felicities: his being of Ireland both North and South; his having been born in 1939 just prior to the blood-dimmed watershed of the Second World War; his being a Nobel Laureate; and his having proved welcome to so many readers as a truly open poet, this being one of the ways—though certainly only one—in which poetry may realize itself.

There is moreover a caveat: the experienced conviction that most of us are not good at appreciating the poetry of those appreciably younger than we are. Recency might not of itself be disabling, and I have included recent poems not only by Heaney but by Thom Gunn and Geoffrey Hill, yet life tells us that often the young idea, even just the younger idea, shoots past its seniors. Heaney, the only poet represented here who is younger than I am (by five years and seven months, but who's counting?), can reasonably constitute a terminus for this particular selector. With more than seven centuries to cover, or not to pretend to cover exactly, I have thought it right not to grant pages— pages are scarce, about a page per year—to recent decades and to those younger poets who are presently before the public eye and who stand in no need of reinstatement.

Kinds and Excerpts

Represented here as usual, in their lasting freshness, are the various kinds: lyric (which has come in, at the very head, as 'Sumer is icumen in'), satire, hymn, ode, epistle, elegy, ballad, nonsense verse ... Plus a challenge to our categorizing, the prose poem, in the diverse accents of Synge and T. S. Eliot. Newly figuring are the dear daily kinds of verse: nursery rhymes (a loved glory of English culture), limericks, and clerihews. No poem is given other than in its entirety without this being made clear at the head. Several of the greatest long poems are here in full, among them Wordsworth's 'Tintern Abbey', Coleridge's 'The Rime of the Ancient Mariner', Christina G. Rossetti's 'Goblin Market', and Hopkins's 'The Wreck of the Deutschland'.

An anthologist, naturally enough, cannot but be aware of what in the end could not, sadly, be included, and of what had to be reduced to an excerpt. This awareness is salutary for him or her, but should not be passed on as a sadness to the reader, who has wonderfully more than enough to be getting on with. Excerpting assuredly beats the alternative: entire loss. But excerpting is not merely a form of damage-control but can be discriminatingly positive. Fortunately, too, there can often be the choice of an autonomous section, such as a distinct movement from Tennyson's *Maud*. Another favourable opportunity has been taken, seizing an opening: so the reader of this anthology on many occasions meets what any reader of a poet's complete works would meet, the beginning of a work—that of *The Canterbury Tales*, for instance, of *Piers Plowman*, of Shakespeare's *Richard III*, and of *Paradise Lost*. An opening passage will incite, excite, entice.

A complementary effect has been gained, it is hoped, by including on occasion the conclusion of a poem, again with this fact made clear; see, and hear, the agonized quittance of Marlowe's *Doctor Faustus*, or the faithful elegy that concludes *Samson Agonistes*, or the rippling coda to Arnold's 'Sohrab and Rustum' and to 'The Scholar-Gipsy'. Such endings make friends with—or pointedly refuse to make friends with—the necessity of dying.

One small innovation has been to include two versions of half a dozen poems. A valuable insistence within literary criticism and literary history during the last decades has been the reminder that we don't always know just what we mean by, say, *The Prelude*, or *The Dunciad*, or 'The Rime of the Ancient Mariner'. For they changed, the poets changed them. Nor is this just a point of philosophical exquisiteness. Revision makes us ask when a version becomes a different poem, pondering imaginative gains and losses. Without being able to make room for dual versions of poems on the great scale, I have included variant versions of short poems by Blake, Wordsworth, Yeats, Edward Thomas, and Graves. A reader would not have to narrow the eyes or the mind to find the differences intriguing and moving. We should stay beneficially aware of the ways in which other poems too may be tentative entities.

Translation

The twentieth century, thanks in part to the passion of Ezra Pound, has restored the truth that a translation of a poem can be as great a poem as any other. Much of the supreme poetry in our language has always been translation, repaying with generous interest a debt to other languages, other societies and worlds. So now gaining admission to *The Oxford Book of English Verse*, which had mostly limited itself to such fine imitations as Wyatt's Petrarchan sonnets or Johnson's Juvenalian satire, are many feats of translation that are sheer poetry: Chapman's Homer (bringing in its happy wake Keats's 'On First Looking into Chapman's Homer'), Milton's Horace, Dryden's Lucretius, down through the ages to the vital translations of our days, arriving at Heaney's Dante. These are complemented by Gavin Douglas's Virgil and Tom Scott's Villon—translations not into English but into Scots, the tongue that English is blessed to have as its audibly frictive neighbour.

Here, then, are new creations from languages classical and modern, western and eastern. Though this is no conspectus of world poetry, there is gratifying delight in hearing how resourcefully the English poets have responded to so wide a range. The signal instances of translation and imitation, as against the ubiquitous promptings of influence, are given salience here with the subscription to a poem of the formula '[after the Latin of Martial]' or '[after the French of Racine]'. An index of the foreign poets represented has been supplied, as convenient and revelatory.

Drama, Song, and Hymn

In the past, dramatic verse was excluded despite its supremacy and despite its fecundating so much else within the liveliest English poetry. Helen Gardner, explaining why she followed Quiller-Couch in excluding it, said 'Here context is all-important'. One knows what she means, but context is often of no less importance in epic poetry such as *Paradise Lost*, in allegorical romance such as *The Faerie Queene*, and in such a verse-tale as Crabbe's 'Peter Grimes', and these are all kinds admitted by Helen Gardner as by Quiller-Couch.

The nub is not context but medium, it being true that the medium of drama (Pound again) is not words but people moving about on a stage using words—a mixed medium. But here too there has been a traditional inconsistency, since both songs and hymns, which are likewise constituted not of words alone, have always been admitted. William Blake, graphic artist and poet, has traditionally found a place even when his visual embodiments have not been reproduced; there are even those of us who believe that 'The Tyger' is the better for lacking Blake's weirdly unconvincing picture of the beast.

So it is best to continue to represent such irreplaceable instances (the songs of Shakespeare, Campion, and Burns, the hymns of Watts, Smart, and Cowper, the unique hauntings of Blake and of Stevie Smith), but to add to them, as no more anomalous in an anthology of verse, the accomplishments of Elizabethan and Jacobean theatre: some momentous Shakespeare, and the feats of his inaugurator Marlowe, of his competitor Ben Jonson, and of his successors Webster and Tourneur.

English and British

This anthology does not seek to be a book of Anglophone verse, of verse in the English language whatever its provenance. But until the political independence that created the United States of America in the 1770s, Americans claimed, with good cause, to take part in the making of English literature. So American poetry until the 1770s, most notably Edward Taylor and Anne Bradstreet, is here accorded its rightful and rewarding place.

The word English is on occasion resented or resisted elsewhere in the British Isles (as is the word American in the Americas), but people do not as yet say that they love or study British literature (or that they work in British departments), and this is not only because the language's name is English. Without going in for as drastic a devolution as some would honourably seek, I have sought to do right by poetry from the British Isles. Some of it is Scots: Henryson and MacDiarmid, for example, belatedly join Dunbar and Burns. Irish poetry is represented also—thanks to the courtesy of Austin Clarke's art—by translation from Gaelic into English. The Republic of Ireland does bring home an anomaly, but to have excluded poetry in English that comes from the Republic would have been to gain political consistency at the cost of

poetical distortion and diminution.*The British Isles may be taken as a
concept that is not on every occasion empty or unjust.

And the poetry of the British Empire or the British Commonwealth? I faced
a usual dilemma. On the one hand, I judged that political independence
should constitute the cut-off point, in its establishing a distinct claim to
the artistically national. But on the other, I judged reluctantly that pre-
independence poetry had not achieved poetic independence (freedom from
diluted fashion), had not given to the world such poetic accomplishments as
would constitute a claim to the pages of an anthology of the best in English
poetry. Fortunately, like Scottish and Irish poetry, the more recently
independent poetry of Canada, of Australia, of New Zealand, of South Africa,
and of other English-speaking cultures such as India, can claim their own
national anthologies, other Oxford Books.

Texts

To these differences of editorial principle must be added my decision not to
modernize the texts but to retain in the appearance of the poems some sense
of the passing centuries, of auld lang syne.

There are always inconsistencies in such matters. So an editor who claims
not to modernize will usually make an exception for the u/v i/j conventions
and for the long s, while an editor who claims to modernize will make an
exception for *The Faerie Queene*.

I have weighed the gains and losses differently from my predecessors here.
While it is true that there is a loss of immediate accessibility in this retaining of
old spelling (including old capitalization, punctuation, italicizing of names,
and other conventions), it is not necessarily a bad thing for a reader to be mildly
slowed down. And there is after all a different kind of accessibility gained by not
modernizing, in that a duller page—and modernizing does have a dulling
effect, a bland levelling—has its own quietly powerful way of being inaccessible.

Moreover, modernizing creates its own anomalies; for instance it makes
Spenser, who is always left unmodernized, look a thousand times more
bizarrely ancient than he can be seen to be once his text is alongside an
*un*modernized Sidney or Shakespeare. Hopkins looks even more idiosyn-
cratic than he was, since the idiosyncrasies of earlier ages have been ironed out.
Medieval poems, semi-modernized as they often are, may be neither one thing
nor the other. Scottish poems, and dialect poems such as the poignancies of
the great Dorset poet William Barnes, these traditionally all being left as they
originally stood, come out looking particularly eccentric once they are set in
the company of nothing but standardized modern-looking matter. And if you
are modernizing, do you take it right through to Heaney, or stop doing it at a
particular point or period? Modernize Pope, but not Keats?

---

* An absence. Patrick Kavanagh (1904–1967) was to have been represented by four poems: 'The
Great Hunger', 'Sanctity', 'Epic', and 'Come Dance with Kitty Stobling'; but the Estate of Patrick
Kavanagh and his brother Peter Kavanagh are at odds as to who has the right to be credited.

Again, archaisms deliberately adopted by later poets, such as Eliot, have their nature changed if no earlier archaisms survive. Furthermore, since a poem when modernized is designed to look as if it might have been created in our day, a reader is more likely to fall into the trap of supposing that its words have exactly the same force and nuance as they would have today. A salutary persistent warning, visibly there on the page, has been withdrawn, withheld. And with all this, there disappears the sense of the passing of years and centuries as one achievement gives way to another within the long traditions and developments of English poetry.

Still, an anthology such as this should not set much store by textual invulnerability. Despite my not modernizing, I have made minor changes to the texts on occasion, to help the modern reader not to be momentarily misled. If the word means 'here', but was spelt in the original 'hear', and if there is not enough in the immediate context to make this promptly clear, I have amended 'hear' to 'here'. But there remains the valuable complication of puns, suggestivenesses, that ought not to escape us; so I have for instance retained Sidney's 'hart' ('My true love hath my hart, and I have his') even though the main sense is manifestly 'heart'; for the manifestness of the meaning 'heart' could be missed only by someone not bothering to read alertly, whereas the punning secondary sense of 'hart' (deer) was given salience by Sidney. So 'hart' is retained there, despite my 'here'/'hear' instance, because its secondariness, along with the rarity these days of the word 'hart', is just what might make it escape even an alert reader's notice.

I have not recorded textual changes, and I must stress that although I hope this book is not textually irresponsible, it makes no claim to textual authority. Each such small local change is itself something open to contest and worthwhile discussion, but art is long, life is short, and a bound book is price-bound. I should like to think that I have removed, by my occasional local tinkering, unnecessary stumbling-blocks for the reader, while not reducing the terrain to slippery effortless conveyance, for I have borne in mind the reader who enjoys among other things the fascination of what's difficult, or at any rate of what's not been made unmindfully easy.

I have similarly amended the punctuation sometimes, but only slightly. We have learned from the scholars of punctuation (notably Malcolm Parkes and John Lennard) about two systems or emphases in punctuation: the earlier rhetorical punctuation, such as gives visual instruction to the reader on how the poems should be breathed and phrased as spoken aloud, and syntactic punctuation, which clarifies the syntactic relations within the sentence. It is the latter to which we are now used, but the former, in Wyatt for instance as given here, offers its own form of aid.

Nursery rhymes have been left in the modernized form in which those fine scholars the Opies give them; this, because otherwise there is too complicatedly messy a textual history, with no clear crystallization. And occasionally there is a poet of whom no unmodernized text has been published; William Alabaster is the notable case.

I follow my predecessors' practice of deleting stanza numbering. No titles of my own have been supplied. Within square brackets, on a few occasions, there is given the title by which a poem has long been known (e.g. 'A Lament for the Makars', of Dunbar). Glosses are supplied only for medieval, Scottish, and dialect poems. The Scottish qu has been changed to w.

Since nothing is more important than being able to hear the rhythms and cadences of a poem, I have given a little help with pronunciation. First, I have marked the sounded e (é) in some medieval poems. (But the reader should be warned that scholars continue to dispute the sounded e, even apart from the question of particular instances.) Second, I have marked, though only where I judge that it might otherwise be misheard, the difference between the sounded and the unsounded ed. Until sometime in the nineteenth century, the cadence of the line can often make the distinction clear. The form 'd is always unsounded ('swoon'd' as one syllable). But the form ed was not always to be sounded, so I have added a grave accent to indicate the sounded form èd on occasions that might otherwise be doubtful ('swoonèd' as two syllables). Once the elision with the apostrophe ('swoon'd') mostly disappears from the page, the form with ed can be assumed to have its modern pronunciation, 'swooned' being one syllable.

Third, I have added an acute accent when the archaic pronunciation of a word might make the reader mis-hear the line; hence 'revénue', to show the stress on the second syllable, not as for us on the first (révenue); and 'Máhomét', with stresses on the first and third syllable, not as we now say it, Mahómet. These small intrusions on the text are not obtrusive, and they may forestall the mangling of a lovely or a telling line. The movement of poetry moves us, and this asks that we hear it truly. For as Matthew Arnold understood, 'The superior character of truth and seriousness, in the matter and substance of the best poetry, is inseparable from the superiority of diction and movement marking its style and manner.'

INTRODUCTION: OF ENGLISH VERSE

Poems in an anthology are best left to do what poems are particularly good at: speaking for themselves. But criticism, provided that it knows its place, has its place. So these few pages of introduction will follow a tip from one of our poet-critics, Matthew Arnold, and try to fix 'what the French, taking an expression from the builder's business, call *points de repère*—points which stand as so many natural centres, and by returning to which we can always find our way again' ('Johnson's Lives', 1878). The *points de repère* here are points of principle enunciated by the supreme poet-critics as to poetry itself, how to seize it and be seized by it. The poets never forget, though, that the greatest criticism takes the form not of criticism at all, but of subsequent creation, a poem itself.

In the tributes that it gives and receives, English verse has proved to be age-long and world-wide, well beyond the reach of a survey. Samuel Johnson opened *The Vanity of Human Wishes* (1749) with a vista that in due course the poem comes to acknowledge as in itself a vain wish:

> Let Observation with extensive View,
> Survey Mankind, from *China* to *Peru*.

Such an aspiration makes breathless even Observation itself. But then just the local hope would be inordinate: to survey our precious stones from Land's End to John o'Groats, leave alone the emerald of Ireland.

Nations may gain the arts that they deserve but they do not gain any one art equally, nor does one nation equally gain all of the arts. No sane Briton supposes that the architecture of these islands is by and large a glory, even though pride is to be taken in Sir Christopher Wren (who wins in these pages the serious tribute of a comical clerihew). British music, for all our Purcell and even our immigrant Handel, is not held to hold a candle to German or Austrian music. Some cultural commentators have maintained that the standing of the arts reflects nothing more than a bending of knees before imperial and economic power. But someone would then need to explain why no amount of such power was ever able to gain wide or lasting credit for, say, British sculpture or British cuisine. The poetry, on the other hand, has been acknowledged throughout the world as one of the golden treasuries. Helen Gardner invoked and evoked in her anthology 'the richest and most continuously lively poetic tradition in the world'.

In 1913, in *Patria Mia*, Ezra Pound—at home nowhere, the American who needed Italian, the spectator to see most of the game—ventured to identify the quiddity of English poetry. He returned to the earliest English poems, earlier even than the English language as we and the *Oxford English Dictionary* know it.

I trust in the national chemical, or, if the reader be of Victorian sensibility, let us say the 'spirit' or the 'temper' of the nation.

I have found in 'The Seafarer' and in 'The Wanderer' trace of what I should call the English national chemical. In those early Anglo-Saxon poems I find expression of that quality which seems to me to have transformed the successive arts of poetry that have been brought to England from the south. For the art has come mostly from the south, and it has found on the island something in the temper of the race which has strengthened it and given it fibre. And this is hardly more than a race conviction that words scarcely become a man.

We should do well to distrust Pound's reiterated word 'race', given what became of the political Pound, but we should value the paradox that catches the light: alive within so much of English poetry, an art of words, there has long been a principled dubiety about words, a conviction that words scarcely become a man. This 'English keynote', 'the Anglo-Saxon objection to speaking at all', Pound contrasted with the American keynote, which includes 'a willingness to stand exposed'.

Yet the strength of both peoples is just here; that one undertakes to keep quiet until there is something worth saying, and the other will undertake nothing in its art for which it will not be in person responsible.

Whereupon Pound descended from his flight: 'This is, of course, the high ideal, not the standard or average of practice.'

The poets have proved to be the best critics. Ben Jonson may have overstated the truth when he said that 'To judge of poets is only the faculty of poets; and not of all poets, but the best', yet the truth was there for Jonson to overstate, and the line of English poet-critics bears it out: Jonson himself, Dryden, Johnson, Coleridge, Arnold, and Eliot.

Jonson, our first great man of letters, speaks out. At once, here in his criticism as in his poems, is a man speaking to men and to women. One of the delights of his criticism, most manifest in the conversations recorded by William Drummond of Hawthornden, is its summary justice. 'That Shakespeare wanted art.' 'He cursed Petrarch for redacting verses to sonnets, which he said were like that tyrant's bed, where some who were too short were racked, others too long cut short.' 'That Sidney did not keep a decorum in making everyone speak as well as himself.' In these accents, combative, emulous, generous, we hear speaking Jonson himself, responding not only to poets as people but to poems as though they were people too, open to our human and humane judgement.

Jonson loves judgement, the exercise of it. 'He esteemeth John Donne the first poet in the world, in some things.' This is due discrimination. And the reservations? 'That Donne, for not keeping of accent, deserved hanging.' 'That Donne himself, for not being understood, would perish.' It is characteristic of Jonson's authority that these crisp caveats should raise points of principle. True, Donne's rhythmical audacities, and his courting of witty arcaneness, are—whatever Jonson may say—glorious. But, whatever we may say, they are costly too, a price is paid for them, and how refreshing it is to hear growling away like this a great contemporary of Donne's. Are there not, should there not be, days on which any one of us, reading Donne, feels some such Jonsonian impatience within our admiration?

For Jonson, it was imperative to hold to an ancient faith: the impossibility of anyone's being a good poet without first being a good man or a good woman. The sceptic in us may rightly remember the daily lives of the poets, their vanities and envies and irritabilities, and so be puzzled by Jonson's confidence. Yet does not some such truth hold? Realized in the very words of a true poem, there has to be a new sensitivity to consciousness and to conscience, and where could this come from but somewhere good? If we cannot acquiesce in Jonson's assurance, we might accede to Henry James's oblique form of it.

> There is one point at which the moral sense and the artistic sense lie very near together; that is in the light of the very obvious truth that the deepest quality of a work of art will always be the quality of the mind of the producer. In proportion as that intelligence is fine will the novel, the picture, the statue partake of the substance of beauty and truth. ('The Art of Fiction', 1884)

The novel, the picture, the statue—and the poem, pondering for ever what truth may live in the hope that 'Beauty is truth, truth beauty'.

For Dryden, the judicious poet-critic of succeeding times, truth lived in a political world. The Popish Plot was conspiracy practice, not just conspiracy theory.

> Some Truth there was, but dash'd and brew'd with Lyes;
> To please the Fools, and puzzle all the Wise.
> Succeeding times did equal folly call,
> Believing nothing, or believing all.
> ('Absalom and Achitophel')

For Dryden, what had been in Jonson an emphasis upon the quality of the individually human poet turns towards the quality of the age, or (more circumscribedly) of the society, or (yet more so) of Society. The quality of poetry, Dryden believed, its strain, might be improved.

> If natural causes be more known now than in the time of Aristotle, because more studied, it follows that poesy and other arts may, with the same pains, arrive still nearer to perfection. (Eugenius speaking, in Dryden's *Essay on Dramatic Poesy*, 1665)

This flies in the face of the belief, very dear to us, that one characteristic of artistic achievement is its never being superseded, its eluding or eschewing the march of progress. Whereas in the sciences . . .

Yet there must be some truth in Jonson's claim about the good poet's relation to goodness somewhere within, and the same is true of Dryden's claim for the possibility of improvement in poetry. Dramatic poetry, for instance, 'though a limited art, yet might be capable of receiving some innovations for the better' (*Discourse of Satire*, 1693). After all, when we praise something as excellent, we ought to respect the root-sense of the word, which is not just a synonym for very good but means excelling. The excellent excels. That which has been excelled may be a recent or an ancient achievement that was in its way in competition. To be excelled must mean relegation, and may come to mean oblivion.

The Critical Opinions of John Dryden, compiled by John Aden, boasts two columns of citations headed 'Progress'. But belief in progress does not enjoy a monopoly of complacency, and Dryden's welcoming the possibility of poetic improvement, far from being smug, is and was a challenge. Laurels are not for resting on.

What mostly saves Dryden from servility to his age is his respectful understanding of inheritance, of poetic lineage, of what is owed, not only as debt but as tribute, to past poets, ever-present.

Milton was the poetical son of Spenser, and Mr. Waller of Fairfax; for we have our lineal descents and clans as well as other families. Spenser more than once insinuates, that the soul of Chaucer was transfused into his body; and that he was begotten by him two hundred years after his decease. Milton has acknowledged to me, that Spenser was his original.   (Preface to *Fables Ancient and Modern*, 1700)

These lineal descents have a comic side but they foster piety.

Paradoxes teasingly remain. If Chaucer is to be venerated as 'the father of English poetry' (Preface to *Fables*), how exactly is this to be reconciled with the insistence that Chaucer's imperfect versification should be forgiven as infantine? 'We can only say, that he lived in the infancy of our poetry, and that nothing is brought to perfection at the first.' Dryden is a very skilled negotiator. Within the art of prose-dialogue, he grants his spokesman a paradoxical truth about the great predecessors (who valuably exhausted so many of the possibilities): 'that not only we shall never equal them, but they could never equal themselves, were they to rise and write again' (*Essay on Dramatic Poesy*). Within the art of poetry, he turns his point so that both its edges glint, a boast and an admission:

> Well then; the promis'd hour is come at last;
> The present Age of Wit obscures the past:
> Strong were our Syres; and as they Fought they Writ,
> Conqu'ring with force of Arms, and dint of Wit;
> Theirs was the Gyant Race, before the Flood.
>   ('To My Dear Friend Mr. Congreve')

That last line is the best of postdiluvian tributes. Even when too pleased with what his times have effected, Dryden can be trusted to writhe honestly. 'I may safely say it of this present age, that if we are not as great wits as Donne, yet certainly we are better poets' (*Discourse of Satire*, 1693). Certainly the case, no, but certainly a case that may engagingly, enlargingly for us, be put.

Given the rarity of universal acknowledgement, we famously suspect of irony a novel—especially one by Jane Austen—that begins with the words 'It is a truth universally acknowledged, that . . .' Conversely, we might suspect of insufficient irony a commentator such as Dryden who (admittedly characterizing friends in argument) can unmisgivingly invoke every one:

every one was willing to acknowledge how much our poesy is improved by the happiness of some writers yet living; who first taught us to mould our thoughts into easy and significant words; to retrench the superfluities of expression, and to make our rhyme so properly a part of the verse, that it should never mislead the sense, but itself be led and governed by it. (*Essay on Dramatic Poesy*)

Yet there will always remain some truth to this claim, and readers who delight in the 'happiness' of Dryden's own poetry, and of many other Augustan poets, are relishing some such relation of wording to thinking, of rhyme to reason, of sensibility to sense.

'The happiness of some writers yet living': Johnson, the poet-critic of the succeeding period, found a particular place for the happiness of writing, not as a blithe spirit but as writing's falling out so happily. His predecessor Jonson had specified as one of the hiding places of poetry's power the individual probity of the poet, and Dryden had located certain poetical powers elsewhere: in what the age and a society had realized by way of advance. For Johnson, poetic powers of mind were in some respects both less individual and less social, more a matter of being open to that which is not exactly—or rather is exactly not—of man's making.

Poetic achievement then becomes, under one aspect, a grace; for grace, which is not ours for the asking, has to be recognized and asked to stay if it is to prove ours. Johnson, who valued reason as highly as is reasonable, and who set immense store by will-power, nevertheless delighted in poetry's ability to profit profoundly from what could neither be reasoned into nor willed into existence, from what just happened to be the case, from hap, from happiness. In Pope's epitaph on Simon Harcourt, Johnson extolled

the artful introduction of the name, which is inserted with a peculiar felicity, in which chance must concur with genius, which no man can hope to attain twice, and which cannot be copied but with servile imitation. (Life of Pope)

The term 'felicity' is itself felicitous, catching the way in which something happily happened. Such praise has the virtue of chastening in a poet what would be the wrong sort of pride in his work. For the proud, then, read the propitious. As when Johnson praised Denham's superb quatrain on the Thames in 'Cooper's Hill', 'O could I flow like thee . . .':

It has beauty peculiar to itself, and must be numbered among those felicities which cannot be produced at will by wit and labour, but must arise unexpectedly in some hour propitious to poetry. (Life of Denham)

How much more is won by the Augustan 'felicity' than by the dour modernist word for the throw of the dice, the 'aleatory'.

Since, like the rest of us, Johnson often gets hold of the wrong end of the stick, his example can be very heartening. Humbling, too, in that what we do feebly, he does forcibly. So his notorious complaint about 'Lycidas', in the life of Milton, that 'Where there is leisure for fiction there is little grief', puts unignorably a central question about any pastoral elegy and about the nature of the grief that it understands.

Johnson is a true critic in this, that whatever judgement he may make of the phenomenon, he has assuredly grasped it anew. What he seizes will then, as often in art and in criticism, be seen to be not a direction but an axis, amenable to traffic in either direction. In *The Rambler* (no. 168, 1751), Johnson is profoundly provocative in his vexation at a soaring speech from *Macbeth*, 'Come thick Night . . .'. He thrillingly insisted that 'In this passage is exerted all the force of poetry, that force which calls new powers into being, which embodies sentiment, and animates matter'—yet nevertheless he judged the speech all but vitiated by the contrariety between the damnation of determined wickedness and the language of daily doings, 'knife' and 'peep' and 'blanket' all so at odds with Heaven's high surveillance. But is this contrariety, so well remarked by Johnson, ridiculous or sublime? A mindless or a mindful discrepancy?

Mindlessness exists, though, and Johnson is never more wittily accurate than when a passage of poetry invites reproach for discrepancy that is in no way the point. Johnson regretted that the poetry of Addison 'has not often those felicities of diction which give lustre to sentiments'. It was one of Addison's infelicities, a 'broken metaphor', that incited Johnson's forensic attention:

> Fir'd with that name—
> I bridle in my struggling muse with pain,
> That longs to launch into a nobler strain.

To *bridle a goddess* is no very delicate idea; but why must she be *bridled*? Because she *longs to launch*: an act which was never hindered by a *bridle*: and whither will she *launch*? into a nobler *strain*. She is in the first line a *horse*, in the second a *boat*; and the care of the poet is to keep his *horse* or his *boat* from *singing*.   (Life of Addison)

With what happy dexterity is the unhappiness of Addison's metaphorical muddle laid bare. There is no substitute for sense, even though a true felicity may soar beyond the reach of the reasonable.

For Coleridge, Johnson's successor as the poet-critic among the Romantics, poetry is of yet higher origins. Johnson, as the central proponent of sheer acumen, had set limits to his admiration even for great poetry, and of religious or devotional poetry he says roundly:

Poetry loses its lustre and its power, because it is applied to the decoration of something more excellent than itself. . . . The ideas of Christian theology are too simple for eloquence, too sacred for fiction, and too majestic for ornament; to recommend them by tropes and figures, is to magnify, by a concave mirror, the sidereal hemisphere.
                                        (Life of Waller)

But to Coleridge's eyes, the poetic imagination is itself divine.

The primary IMAGINATION I hold to be the living Power and prime Agent of all human Perception, and as a representation in the finite mind of the eternal act of creation in the infinite I AM.   (*Biographia Literaria*, 1817, ch. 13)

An author is such only by courtesy of the Author of our being.

Can this cosmic insight be brought down to the particulars of poetic criticism? It can, but only because Coleridge builds a bridge that can link this highest claim for the imagination to specifiable feats within particular works of imagination.

The poet, described in *ideal* perfection, brings the whole soul of man into activity, with the subordination of its faculties to each other, according to their relative worth and dignity. He diffuses a tone, and spirit of unity, that blends, and (as it were) *fuses*, each into each; by that synthetic and magical power, to which we have exclusively appropriated the name of imagination. This power, first put in action by the will and understanding, and retained under their irremissive, though gentle and unnoticed, controul (*laxis effertur habenis*) reveals itself in the balance or reconciliation of opposite or discordant qualities: of sameness, with difference; of the general, with the concrete; the idea, with the image; the individual, with the representative; the sense of novelty and freshness, with old and familiar objects; a more than usual state of emotion, with more than usual order; judgement ever awake and steady self-possession, with enthusiasm and feeling profound or vehement; and while it blends and harmonizes the natural and the artificial, still subordinates art to nature; the manner to the matter; and our admiration of the poet to our sympathy with the poetry.   (ch. 14)

The mysteries of poetry and of the imagination have never been more lucidly, specifically, and gratefully limned. Coleridge himself effects the very reconciliation of opposite or discordant qualities that he celebrates. No one has ever paid a nobler tribute to the art. The wonder is that Coleridge is the master not only of such high vistas but also of well-grounded particularities. Such as how to hear the rhythms of the poets. 'To read Dryden, Pope &c, you need only count syllables'—(how *could* you, Coleridge? But then at once there comes a contrastive illumination)—'but to read Donne you must measure *Time*, & discover the *Time* of Each word by the Sense & Passion.' 'If you would teach a Scholar in the highest form, how to *read*, take Donne, and of Donne this Satire [III]. When he has learnt to read Donne, with all the force & meaning which are involved in the Words—then send him to Milton—& he will stalk on, like a Master, *enjoying* his Walk.'

His conversational powers were legendary. Like other legends, they have been viewed sceptically. See Max Beerbohm's caricature in *The Poets' Corner*, 'Samuel Taylor Coleridge, table-talking', Coleridge depicted as wont to set the table on a snore. Or hear Thomas Carlyle, recalling what it was like to be spouted at by Coleridge in full flood (a touchstone for biography, these pages):

I have heard Coleridge talk, with eager musical energy, two stricken hours, his face radiant and moist, and communicate no meaning whatsoever to any individual of his hearers,—certain of whom, I for one, still kept eagerly listening in hope; the most had long before given up, and formed (if the room were large enough) secondary humming groups of their own. He began anywhere . . .   (*The Life of John Sterling*, 1851)

An unparalleled conversationalist *on the page*, Coleridge engaged in conversation the authors themselves. Plying his mind in the margins of his books, he gave us the most central Marginalia ever.

It was with Matthew Arnold, Coleridge's successor as poet-critic, that 'centrality' emerged as an essential critical concept. Arnold was deeply adept in judging social centralities and daily duties. The Inspector of Schools, the Professor of Poetry at Oxford, was a true teacher. There is no better introduction to an anthology (but then Arnold was a genius) than his to the first volume of *The English Poets*, edited by Thomas Humphry Ward (1880). After more than a century, 'The Study of Poetry' stands as the most challenging succinct account of tradition and development in English poetry, from Chaucer to Burns. Stopping short of the Romantics, whom Arnold treats individually elsewhere, and of his contemporaries, the far-sighted conspectus is happy to anticipate objection, especially as to its disparagement of Augustan poetry. But it formulates so much, and so shrewdly (even creating room for the most memorable summing-up of the development of English *prose*), as to leave it still without a competitor.

Above all, Arnold wished to be of service, not only to poems but to the reader of poems. His advice has not been bettered, partly because he succeeds in offering advice in such a way as to make one happy to take it. What could be more idealistic and at the same time more practical than his asking us to bear in mind a touchstone, to test our experience against his touchstones and in due course to come to select our own?

Indeed there can be no more useful help for discovering what poetry belongs to the class of the truly excellent, and can therefore do us most good, than to have always in one's mind lines and expressions of the great masters, and to apply them as a touchstone to other poetry. Of course we are not to require this other poetry to resemble them; it may be very dissimilar. But if we have any tact we shall find them, when we have lodged them well in our minds, an infallible touchstone for detecting the presence or absence of high poetic quality, and also the degree of this quality, in all poetry which we may place beside them. Short passages, even single lines, will serve our turn quite sufficiently.

Ever willing to give hostages, eager even, Arnold immediately adduces compacted glories from Homer, from Dante, from Shakespeare, and from Milton, confident that these 'are enough even of themselves to keep clear and sound our judgments about poetry, to save us from fallacious estimates of it, to conduct us to a real estimate'.

That Arnold's taste was narrower, not than ours, but than we should like to think ours is, this is true, for his cult of 'high seriousness' came between him and any respect for such poetry as is duly comic, satirical, or searchingly light. It was moments of noble resistance to fate or to force, resistance realized in wording of unillusioned dignity, that most drew his admiring love. But the concept of touchstones, as Arnold was the first to acknowledge, is wider, more widely useful, than any one person's sensibility or set. Henry James's advice to the novelist was dramatize, dramatize; Arnold's advice to the reader, and not only of poetry, was particularize, particularize.

Critics give themselves great labour to draw out what in the abstract constitutes the characters of a high quality of poetry. It is much better simply to have recourse to concrete examples;—to take specimens of poetry of the high, the very highest quality, and to say: The characters of a high quality of poetry are what is expressed *there*. They are far better recognised by being felt in the verse of the master, than by being perused in the prose of the critic.

It took the master-critic so to subordinate (the opposite of demean) the claims of criticism.

We may widen—not deepen—the application of touchstones if we judge that the finest moments in criticism too can serve as touchstones. Unforgettable criticism may help us to detect elsewhere the presence or absence of high critical quality. There is always to hand, for instance, the revelatory precision of another poet-critic, Donald Davie, on *Paradise Lost* (III. 37–40):

> Then feed on thoughts, that voluntarie move
> Harmonious numbers; as the wakeful Bird
> Sings darkling, and in shadiest Covert hid
> Tunes her nocturnal Note.

If any arrangement of language is a sequence of verbal events, here syntax is employed so as to make the most of each word's eventfulness, so as to make each key-word, like each new episode in a well-told story, at once surprising and just. The eventfulness of language comes out for instance in 'Then feed on thoughts that voluntarie move', where at the line-ending 'move' seems intransitive, and as such wholly satisfying; until the swing on to the next line, 'Harmonious numbers', reveals it (a little surprise, but a wholly fair one) as transitive. This flicker of hesitation about whether the thoughts move only themselves, or something else, makes us see that the numbers aren't really 'something else' but are the very thoughts themselves, seen under a new aspect; the placing of 'move', which produces the momentary uncertainty about its grammar, ties together 'thoughts' and 'numbers' in a relation far closer than cause and effect.

> (1960; *Older Masters*, 1992)

And from Arnold himself? A critical touchstone from the man who gave currency to the poetic touchstone? For me, it would be a passage by him in what is still the best book on translation, his *On Translating Homer* (1861–2).

If blank verse is used in translating Homer, it must be a blank verse of which English poetry, naturally swayed much by Milton's treatment of this metre, offers at present hardly any examples. . . . It must not be Mr. Tennyson's blank verse.

> Yet all experience is an arch wherethro'
> Gleams that untravell'd world, whose margin fades
> For ever and for ever when I move.
> ['Ulysses', correcting Arnold's misquotations . . .]

It is no blame to the thought of those lines, which belongs to another order of ideas than Homer's, but it is true, that Homer would certainly have said of them, 'It is to consider too curiously to consider so'. It is no blame to their rhythm, which belongs to another order of movement than Homer's, but it is true that these three lines by themselves take up nearly as much time as a whole book of the *Iliad*.

The point could not be better put, or the mysterious evocation of time-taking be more precisely figured.

T. S. Eliot, of the twentieth century the central poet-critic, preferred the dry, well-nigh clinical, term *practitioner*. Not for him the Romantic notion of the bard. 'Hear the voice of the Bard! | Who present, past, and future sees'? No, hear the voice of the practitioner.

Eliot's achievement reminds us how much goes to the making of a true critic, crystallizing as the gift (in the lovely phrase of Dr Johnson) of improving opinion into knowledge. The list of apt qualities is long, and it includes the ability to synthesize as well as to analyse, along with the percipience that not only notices things that escaped the rest of us but can then put the whole undertaking through another round of imaginative engagement, by noticing relations between the things noticed. There is no method—Eliot remarked in passing, not arrogantly though dauntingly—except to be very intelligent.

Critical intelligence in Eliot may alight upon the unexpected comparison, or may quote unerringly, as when he heard—and gave us the opportunity to hear—the profound poignancy in Jasper Heywood's translation from Seneca ('The persons addressed are the dead children of Hercules, whom he has just slain in his madness'):

> Go hurtless soules, whom mischiefe hath opprest
> Even in first porch of life but lately had,
> And father's fury goe unhappy kind
> O little children, by the way ful sad
> Of journey knowen.
> Goe see the angry kynges.

Nothing can be said of such a translation except that it is perfect. It is a last echo of the earlier tongue, the language of Chaucer, with an overtone of that Christian piety and pity which disappears with Elizabethan verse.   (1927; *Selected Essays*, 1932, 1951)

Nothing need be said of such criticism except that it is perfect.

Eliot manifests the poet-critic's feeling not only for words as alive (odd, quick to breed, as much a writer's master as servant), but for all the ways in which words can miraculously be brought to acknowledge everything in life that is not a matter of words or of wording, however perfect.

True, there is no substitute for wits, and for having them about you. But there is no substitute for knowledge either—a lasting poet-critic such as Eliot is effective partly by dint of hard-won, lightly-worn learning. Not knowledge only, though, but wisdom, social or political, sacred or secular, moral or spiritual.

The true critic, like the true poet, refuses to permit any blank antithesis of literature and life, as if reading or writing were for some reason less a part of life than, say, selling vegetables. When, in 1923, Eliot had inaugurated his cosmopolitan journal *The Criterion*, he enunciated this truth:

It is the function of a literary review to maintain the autonomy and disinterestedness of literature, and at the same time to exhibit the relations of literature—not to 'life', as something contrasted to literature, but to all the other activities, which, together with literature, are the components of life.

The poet is aware that there is more to life than literature, and more to literature than poetry. These acknowledgements themselves then prove to be something that poetry can transform into its art. For among the things that words can catch is the conviction, of which we need to be aware sometimes but not all the time, that words scarcely become a man.

> I sometimes hold it half a sin
>   To put in words the grief I feel;
>   For words, like Nature, half reveal
> And half conceal the Soul within.
>
> But, for the unquiet heart and brain,
>   A use in measur'd language lies;

> The sad mechanic exercise,
> Like dull narcotics, numbing pain.
>
> In words, like weeds, I'll wrap me o'er,
>   Like coarsest clothes against the cold:
>   But that large grief which these enfold
> Is given in outline and no more.
>
> (*In Memoriam*, V)

Tennyson, acknowledging at once the indispensability and the inadequacy of giving an outline, chose to bring to an end this poem with the enfolded words 'and no more': no more than an outline, and now no more of this my outline.

Elizabeth Barrett, reviewing in 1842 an anthology over the centuries, *The Book of the Poets*, praised 'the Tennysons and the Brownings' of her day. She was free to do so, not yet being Elizabeth Barrett Browning. Her words do right by the books of the poets:

It is advantageous for us all, whether poets or poetasters, or talkers about either, to know what a true poet is, what his work is, and what his patience and successes must be, so as to raise the popular idea of these things, and either strengthen or put down the individual aspiration. 'Art', it was said long ago, 'requires the whole man', and 'Nobody', it was said later, 'can be a poet who is any thing else'; but the present idea of Art requires the segment of a man, and everybody who is any thing at all, is a poet in a parenthesis. And our shelves groan with little books over which their readers groan less metaphorically; there is a plague of poems in the land apart from poetry; and many poets who live and are true, do not live by their truth, but hold back their full strength from Art because they do not *reverence* it fully; and all booksellers cry aloud and do not spare, that poetry will not sell; and certain critics utter melancholy frenzies, that poetry is worn out forever—as if the morning star was worn out from heaven, or 'the yellow primrose' from the grass.

ANONYMOUS

[THIRTEENTH CENTURY]

1
Sumer is icumen in—
Lhude sing, cuccu!
Groweth sed and bloweth med
And springth the wude nu.
Sing, cuccu!   5

Awe bleteth after lomb,
Lhouth after calve cu,
Bulluc sterteth, bucke verteth.
Murie sing, cuccu!
Cuccu, cuccu,   10
Wel singes thu, cuccu!
Ne swik thu naver nu!

Sing, cuccu, nu! Sing, cuccu!
Sing, cuccu! Sing, cuccu, nu!

[FOURTEENTH CENTURY]

2
Ich am of Irlaunde
Ant of the holy londe of irlande
Gode sir pray ich ye
For of saynte charite
Come ant daunce wyt me
In irlaunde.

3
Maiden in the mor lay,
　　In the mor lay,
Sevenyst fulle, sevenist fulle,
Maiden in the mor lay,
　　In the mor lay,   5
Sevenistes fulle ant a day.

Welle was hire mete;
　　Wat was hire mete?

1: 6 *Awe*] ewe   7 *Lhouth*] lows   8 *verteth*] farts   12 *swik*] leave off
3: 1 *mor*] moor   *lay*] dwelt   3 *Sevenyst*] seven nights   7 *mete*] food

The primerole ant the,—
The primerole ant the,—   10
Welle was hire mete;
Wat was hire mete?—
The primerole ant the violet.

Welle was hire dryng;
Wat was hire dryng?   15
The chelde water of the welle-spring.

Welle was hire bour;
Wat was hire bour?
The rede rose an te lilie flour.

JOHN GOWER

1330?–1408

4   from *Confessio Amantis* [Book Four, lines 371–423]

I finde hou whilom ther was on,
Whos namé was Pymaleon,
Which was a lusti man of yowthe:
The werkés of entaile he cowthe
Above alle othre men as tho;   5
And thurgh fortune it fell him so,
As he whom lové schal travaile,
He made an ymage of entaile
Lich to a womman in semblance
Of feture and of contienance,   10
So fair yit neveré was figure.
Riht as a lyvés creature
Sche semeth, for of yvor whyt
He hath hire wroght of such delit,
That sche was rody on the cheke   15
And red on bothe hire lippés eke;
Whereof that he himself beguileth.
For with a goodly lok sche smyleth,
So that thurgh pure impression
Of his ymaginacion   20
With al the herte of his corage
His love upon this faire ymage

9 *primerole*] primrose   14 *dryng*] drink   16 *chelde*] cold

4: 1 *whilom*] formerly   *on*] one   4 *entaile*] sculpture   5 *as tho*] then
7 *travaile*] trouble   12 *lyvés*] living   13 *yvor*] ivory   21 *corage*] spirit

He sette, and hire of lové preide;
Bot sche no word ayeinward seide.
The longé day, what thing he dede,   25
This ymage in the samé stede
Was evere bi, that até mete
He wolde hire serve and preide hire ete,
And putte unto hire mowth the cuppe;
And whan the bord was taken uppe,   30
He hath hire into chambre nome,
And after, whan the nyht was come,
He leide hire in his bed al nakid.
He was forwept, he was forwakid,
He keste hire coldé lippés ofte,   35
And wissheth that thei weren softe,
And ofte he rouneth in hire Ere,
And ofte his arm now hier now there
He leide, as he hir wolde embrace,
And evere among he axeth grace,   40
As thogh sche wisté what he mente:
And thus himself he gan tormente
With such desese of lovés peine,
That noman mihte him moré peine.
Bot how it were, of his penance   45
He madé such continuance
Fro dai to nyht, and preith so longe,
That his preiere is underfonge,
Which Venus of hire grace herde;
Be nyhte and whan that he worst ferde,   50
And it lay in his nakede arm,
The colde ymage he fieleth warm
Of fleissh and bon and full of lif.

WILLIAM LANGLAND
1330?–1386?

5–6   from *Piers Plowman*

5   [*Prologue*, lines 1–45]

In a somer seson whan soft was the sonne
I shope me in shroudes as I a shepe were;

---

23 *preide*] prayed   31 *nome*] taken   34 *forwept*] worn out with weeping
37 *rouneth*] whispers   41 *wisté*] knew   48 *underfonge*] accepted   50 *ferde*] fared
    5: 2 *shope*] dressed   *shroudes*] outer garments

In habite as an heremite unholy of workes
Went wyde in this world wondres to here.
Ac on a May mornynge on Malverne hulles   5
Me befel a ferly, of fairy me thoughte:
I was wery forwandred and went me to reste
Under a brode banke bi a bornes side,
And as I lay and lened and loked in the wateres,
I slombred in a slepyng, it sweyved so merye.   10

   Than gan I to meten a merveilouse swevene,
That I was in a wildernesse, wist I never where.
As I bihelde into the est, an hiegh to the sonne,
I seigh a toure on a toft trielich ymaked;
A deep dale binethe, a dongeon thereinne   15
With depe dyches and derke and dredful of sight.
A faire felde ful of folke fonde I there bytwene,
Of alle maner of men, the mene and the riche,
Worchyng and wandryng as the worlde asketh.
Some putten hem to the plow, pleyed ful selde,   20
In settyng and in sowyng swonken ful harde,
And wonnen that wastours with glotonye destruyeth.

   And some putten hem to pruyde, apparailed hem thereafter,
In contenaunce of clothyng comen disgised.

   In prayers and in penance putten hem manye,   25
Al for love of owre Lorde lyveden ful streyte,
In hope forto have heveneriche blisse;
As ancres and heremites that holden hem in here selles,
And coveiten nought in contre to kairen aboute,
For no likerous liflode her lykam to plese.   30

   And somme chosen chaffare; they cheven the bettere,
As it semeth to owre syght that suche men thryveth;
And somme murthes to make as mynstralles conneth,
And geten gold with here glee giltless, I leve.
Ac japers and jangelers, Judas chylderen,   35
Feynen hem fantasies and foles hem maketh,
And han here witte at wille to worche, yif they sholde;
That Paule precheth of hem I nel nought preve it here;
Qui turpiloquium loquitur etc. is Luciferes hyne.

6 *ferly . . . thoughte*] marvel, seemingly of the supernatural realm   7 *forwandred*]
gone astray   8 *bornes*] brook's   10 *sweyved*] sounded   11 *meten*] dreamed
swevene] dream   12 *wist*] knew   14 *seigh*] saw   *toft*] hillock   *trielich*] choicely
20 *selde*] seldom   21 *settyng*] planting   *swonken*] worked   22 *wonnen that*] effected
that which   23 *putten hem to pruyde*] devoted themselves to fine array   *thereafter*] accord-
ingly   24 *contenaunce*] display   26 *streyte*] strictly   28 *ancres*] anchorites
here] their (as below)   29 *kairen*] travel   30 *likerous lifelode*] pleasurable means of
life   *her*] their (as below)   *lykam*] body   31 *chaffare*] trade   *cheven*] succeeded
33 *murthes*] entertainment   *conneth*] know   34 *glee*] music   *leve*] believe   35 *japers
and jangelers*] jesters and tale-tellers   36 *Feynen*] invent   *fantasies*] tricks   37 *And . . .
sholde*] And had intelligence enough to work if they had to   38 *nel nought preve*] will not
attest   39 *Qui . . . hyne*] He who slanders is Lucifer's servant

Bidders and beggeres fast about yede 40
Woth her bely and her bagge of bred ful ycrammed;
Fayteden for here fode, foughten atte ale;
In glotonye, God it wote, gon hij to bedde,
And risen with ribaudye, tho roberdes knaves;
Slepe and sori sleuthe seweth hem evre. 45

6 [Passus I, lines 140–88]

'It is a kynde knowyng,' quod she, 'that kenneth in thine herte
For to lovye thi Lorde lever than thiselve;
No dedly synne to do, dey though thou sholdest:
This I trowe be treuthe; who can teche the better,
Loke thow suffre hym to sey and sithen lere it after. 5
For thus witnesseth his worde, worche thou thereafter:
For Trewthe telle that love is triacle of hevene;
May no synne be on him sene that useth that spise,
And alle his werkes he wroughte with love, as him liste,
And lered it Moises for the levest thing and moste like to hevene, 10
And also the plante of pees, moste precious of vertues.
For hevene myghte noughte holden it, it was so hevy of hymself,
Tyl it hadde of the erthe yeten his fylle.
And whan it haved of this folde flesshe and blode taken
Was nevere leef upon lynde lighter thereafter, 15
And portatyf and persant as the poynt of a nedle,
That myghte non armure it lette ne none heigh walles.
Forthi is love leder of the lordes folke of hevene,
And a mene, as the maire is bitwene the kyng and the comune;
Right so is love a ledere and the lawe shapeth; 20
Upon man for his mysdedes the merciment he taxeth.
And, for to knowe it kyndely, it comseth bi myght,
And in the herte there is the hevede and the heigh welle;
For in kynde knowynge in herte there a myghte bigynneth,
And that falleth to the fader that formed us alle, 25
Loked on us with love and lete his sone deye
Mekely for owre mysdedes, to amende us alle.

---

40 *Bidders and beggeres*] those who made a trade of begging   *yede*] went   42 *Fayteden*]
shammed   43 *wote*] knows   *hij*] they   44 *tho roberdes*] those robbers
45 *sleuthe*] sloth   *seweth*] follows

6: 2 *lever*] dearer   3 *dey*] die   5 *sithen*] since   *lere*] teach   6 *worche*]
perform   7 *triacle*] balm   8 *spise*] spice (figuratively)   10 *lered it Moises*] taught
it (love) to Moses   11 *pees*] peace   13 *yeten*] eaten   14 *haved*] had   *folde*] earth
15 *lynde*] linden tree   16 *portatyf and persant*] quick and piercing   17 *lette*] hinder
19 *mene*] intermediary   *maire*] mayor   *comune*] commonalty   21 *merciment he taxeth*]
fine he assesses   22 *knowe . . . myght*] recognize it (love) by instinct, it springs up in the heart
by divine power   23 *hevede*] source   25 *falleth*] appertains

And yet wolde he hem no woo that wrought hym that peyne,
But mekelich with mouthe mercy he bisoughte
To have pite of that poeple that peyned hym to deth.   30
  Here myghtow see ensamples in hymselve one,
That he was mightful and meke and mercy gan graunte
To hem that hongen him an heigh and his herte thirled.
  Forthi I rede yow riche: haveth reuthe of the pouere;
Though ye be myghtful to mote, beth meke in yowre werkes.   35
For the same mesures that ye mete, amys other elles,
Ye shullen ben weyen therewyth whan ye wende hennes:
    Eadem mensura qua mensi fueritis, remecietur vobis.
  For though ye be treewe of yowre tongue and trewliche wynne,
And as chaste as a childe that in cherche wepeth,   40
But if ye loved lelliche and lende the poure,
Such good as God yow sent godelich parteth,
Ye ne have na more meryte in masse ne in houres
Than Malkyn of here maydenhode that no man desireth.
  For James the gentil jugged in his bokes   45
That faith without the faite is righte no thinge worthi,
And as ded as a dore-tree but if the dedes folwe:
    Fides sine operibus mortua est, etc.
  Forthi chastite withoute charite worth cheyned in helle;
It is as lewed as a laumpe that no lighte is inne.'   50

GEOFFREY CHAUCER
1343?–1400

7–10   from *The Canterbury Tales*

7   [*General Prologue*, lines 1–18]

Whan that Aprill with his shourés soote
The droghte of March hath perced to the roote,
And bathed every veyne in swich licour
Of which vertu engendred is the flour;

---

28 *wolde . . . woo*] wished them no harm   30 *pite*] pity   31 *one*] alone
33 *thirled*] pierced   34 *rede*] advise   *reuthe*] pity   35 *mote*] summon to a law
court   36 *amys other elles*] amiss or otherwise   37 *weyen*] weighed   *hennes*]
hence   38 *Eadem . . . vobis*] with what measure ye mete, it shall be measured to you again
39 *trewliche wynne*] make honest profit   41 *But if*] unless (as below)   *lelliche*] faithfully
lende] give   42 *parteth*] share with each other   43 *houres*] the daily services of the
church   46 *faite*] action   47 *dore-tree*] door-post   48 *Fides . . . est*] faith without
works is dead   49 *worth*] is going to be   50 *lewed*] useless

  7: 1 *soote*] sweet   3 *licour*] juice

Whan Zephirus eek with his sweeté breeth   5
Inspired hath in every holt and heeth
The tendre croppés, and the yongé sonne
Hath in the Ram his halvé cours yronne,
And smalé fowelés maken melodye,
That slepen al the nyght with open ye   10
(So priketh hem nature in hir corages);
Thanne longen folk to goon on pilgrimages,
And palmerés for to seken straunge strondes,
To ferné halwes, kowthe in sondry londes;
And specially from every shires ende   15
Of Engelond to Caunterbury they wende,
The hooly blisful martir for to seke,
That hem hath holpen whan that they were seeke.

8   *[The Wife of Bath's Prologue, lines 1–34]*

'Experience, though noon auctoritee
Were in this world, is right ynogh for me
To speke of wo that is in mariage;
For, lordynges, sith I twelve yeer was of age,
Thonked be God that is eterne on lyve,   5
Housbondes at chirché dore I have had fyve,—
If I so ofte myghte have ywedded bee,—
And alle were worthy men in hir degree.
But me was toold, certeyn, nat longe agoon is,
That sith that Crist ne wente neveré but onis   10
To weddyng, in the Cane of Galilee,
That by the same ensample taughte he me
That I ne sholdé wedded be but ones.
Herkne eek, lo, which a sharp word for the nones,
Biside a wellé, Jhesus, God and man,   15
Spak in repreeve of the Samaritan:
"Thou hast yhad fyve housbondés," quod he,
"And that ilké man that now hath thee
Is noght thyn housbonde," thus seyde he certeyn.
What that he mente therby, I kan nat seyn;   20
But that I axe, why that the fifthé man
Was noon housbonde to the Samaritan?
How manye myghte she have in mariage?
Yet herde I nevere tellen in myn age
Upon this nombre diffinicioun.   25

11 *priketh . . . corages*] nature spurs them in their hearts' desires   14 *ferné halwes, kowthe*]
distant shrines, known   18 *seeke*] sick

8: 5 *on lyve*] alive   10 *sith*] since   14 *nones*] occasion   21 *axe*] ask

Men may devyne and glosen, up and doun,
But wel I woot, expres, withouté lye,
God bad us for to wexe and multiplye;
That gentil text kan I wel understonde.
Eek wel I woot, he seyde myn housbonde　　　　　　30
Sholde leté fader and mooder, and take to me.
But of no nombre mencion made he,
Of bigamye, or of octogamye;
Why sholdé men thanne speke of it vileynye?'

9　　　　　[*The Pardoner's Tale*, lines 711–49]

Whan they han goon nat fully half a mile,
Right as they wolde han troden over a stile,
An oold man and a povré with hem mette.
This oldé man ful mekely hem grette,
And seydé thus, 'Now, lordés, God yow see!'　　　　　5
The proudeste of thisé riotourés three
Answerde agayn, 'What, carl, with sory grace!
Why artow al forwrapped save thy face?
Why lyvestow so longe in so greet age?'
This oldé man gan looke in his visage,　　　　　　10
And seydé thus: 'For I ne kan nat fynde
A man, though that I walked into Ynde,
Neither in citee ne in no village,
That woldé chaunge his youthé for myn age;
And therfore moot I han myn agé stille,　　　　　15
As longé tyme as it is Goddés wille.
Ne Deeth, allas! ne wol nat han my lyf.
Thus walke I, lyk a restélees kaityf,
And on the ground, which is my moodres gate,
I knokké with my staf, bothe erly and late,　　　　20
And seyé "Leevé mooder, leet me in!
Lo how I vanysshe, flessh, and blood, and skyn!
Allas! whan shul my bonés been at reste?
Mooder, with yow wolde I chaungé my cheste
That in my chambre longé tyme hath be,　　　　　25
Ye, for an heyré clowt to wrappe in me!"
But yet to me she wol nat do that grace,
For which ful pale and welked is my face.

---

26 *glosen*] comment　　　30 *woot*] know　　　31 *leté*] forsake

9: 3 *povré*] poor　　　5 *see*] look upon　　　6 *riotourés*] revellers　　　7 *carl*] churl
17 *han*] have, take　　　18 *kaityf*] wretch　　　19 *moodres*] mother's　　　21 *Leevé*] dear
24 *cheste*] coffer containing valuables　　26 *heyré clowt*] hair clout, cloth　　28 *welked*] withered

But, sires, to yow it is no curteisye
To speken to an old man vileynye,   30
But he trespasse in word, or elles in dede.
In Hooly Writ ye may yourself wel rede:
"Agayns an oold man, hoor upon his heed,
Ye sholde arise;" wherfore I yeve yow reed,
Ne dooth unto an oold man noon harm now,   35
Namoore than that ye woldé men did to yow
In age, if that ye so longe abyde.
And God be with yow, where ye go or ryde!
I moot go thider as I have to go.'

10   from *Troilus and Criseyde* [line 1800–end]

The wrath, as I bigan yow for to seye,
Of Troilus the Grekis boughten deere.
For thousandés his hondés maden deye,
As he that was withouten any peere,
Save Ector, in his tyme, as I kan heere.   5
But weilawey, save only Goddés wille!
Despitously hym slough the fierse Achille.

And whan that he was slayn in this manere,
His lighté goost ful blisfully is went
Up to the holughnesse of the eighthé spere,   10
In convers letyng everich element;
And ther he saugh, with ful avysement,
The erratik sterrés, herkenyng armonye
With sownés ful of hevenyssh melodie.

And down from thennés faste he gan avyse   15
This litel spot of erthe, that with the se
Embraced is, and fully gan despise
This wrecched world, and held al vanite
To respect of the pleyn felicite
That is in hevene above; and at the laste,   20
Ther he was slayn, his lokyng down he caste.

And in hymself he lough right at the wo
Of hem that wepten for his deth so faste;
And dampned al oure werk that foloweth so

31 *But*] unless   33 *Agayns*] in the presence of (respectfully)   34 *yeve yow reed*] advise you

10: 7 *slough*] slew   11 *convers letyng*] leaving on the other side   12 *avysement*] observation   13 *herkenyng*] attentively listening to   22 *lough*] laughed   24 *dampned*] damned

The blyndé lust, the which that may nat laste,   25
And sholden al oure herte on heven caste.
And forth he wenté, shortly for to telle,
Ther as Mercurye sorted hym to dwelle.

Swich fyn hath, lo, this Troilus for love!
Swich fyn hath al his greté worthynesse!   30
Swich fyn hath his estat real above,
Swich fyn his lust, swich fyn hath his noblesse!
Swych fyn hath falsé worldés brotelnesse!
And thus bigan his lovyng of Criseyde,
As I have told, and in this wise he deyde.   35

O yongé, fresshé folkes, he or she,
In which that love up groweth with youre age,
Repeyreth hom fro worldly vanyte,
And of youre herte up casteth the visage
To thilké God that after his ymage   40
Yow made, and thynketh al nys but a faire
This world, that passeth soone as floures faire.

And loveth hym, the which that right for love
Upon a crois, oure soulés for to beye,
First starf, and roos, and sit in hevene above;   45
For he nyl falsen no wight, dar I seye,
That wol his herte al holly on hym leye.
And syn he best to love is, and most meke,
What nedeth feynede lovés for to seke?

Lo here, of payens corsed oldé rites,   50
Lo here, what alle hire goddés may availle;
Lo here, thise wrecched worldés appetites;
Lo here, the fyn and guerdoun for travaille
Of Jove, Appollo, of Mars, of swich rascaille!
Lo here, the forme of oldé clerkis speche   55
In poetrie, if ye hire bokés seche.

O moral Gower, this book I directe
To the and to the, philosophical Strode,
To vouchen sauf, ther nede is, to correcte,
Of youre benignites and zelés goode.   60
And to that sothefast Crist, that starf on rode,
With al myn herte of mercy evere I preye,
And to the Lord right thus I speke and seye:

29 *fyn*] end   33 *brotelnesse*] frailty   44 *beye*] ransom   45 *starf*] died   *roos*]
rose   46 *falsen*] prove false to   50 *payens*] pagans   61 *sothefast*] firm to the truth
rode] cross

Thow oon, and two, and thre, eterne on lyve,
That regnest ay in thre, and two, and oon, 65
Uncircumscript, and al maist circumscrive,
Us from visible and invisible foon
Defende, and to thy mercy, everichon,
So make us, Jesus, for thi mercy digne,
For love of mayde and moder thyn benigne. 70
    Amen.

JOHN LYDGATE

1370?–1449/50

11   from *The Daunce of Death* [stanzas LXIII–LXIV]

Dethe to the Mynstralle

O thow Minstral that cannest so note and pipe
Un-to folkes for to do plesaunce
By the right honde anoone I shal thee gripe
With these other to go up-on my daunce
Ther is no scape nowther a-voydaunce 5
On no side to contrarie my sentence
For yn musik be crafte and accordaunce
Who maister is shew his science.

The Mynstral answereth

This newe daunce is to me so straunge
Wonder dyverse and passyngli contrarie 10
The dredful fotyng dothe so ofte chaunge
And the mesures so ofte sithes varie
Whiche now to me is no thyng necessarie
If hit were so that I myght asterte
But many a man if I shal not tarie 15
Ofte daunceth but no thynge of herte.

[after the French]

---

67 *foon*] foes

11: 1 *note*] make musical notes   5 *nowther*] nor   12 *sithes*] times   14 *asterte*]
escape   16 *no thynge of herte*] not with all his heart

ANONYMOUS

ANONYMOUS

[FIFTEENTH CENTURY]

12   Adam lay ibowndyn, bowndyn in a bond,
      Fowre thowsand wynter thowt he not to long.

      And al was for an appil, an appil that he tok,
      As clerkes fyndyn wretyn in here book.

      Ne hadde the appil take ben, the appil take ben,   5
      Ne hadde never our Lady a ben hevene qwen.

      Blyssid be the tyme that appil take was,
      Therfore we mown syngyn '*Deo gracias!*'

13   *The Corpus Christi Carol*

          Lully, lulley; lully, lulley;
          The fawcon hath born my mak away.

      He bare hym up, he bare hym down;
      He bare hym into an orchard brown.

      In that orchard ther was an hall,   5
      That was hangid with purpill and pall.

      And in that hall ther was a bede;
      Hit was hangid with gold so rede.

      And yn that bed ther lythe a knyght,
      His wowndes bledyng day and nyght.   10

      By that bedes side ther kneleth a may,
      And she wepeth both nyght and day.

      And by that beddes side ther stondith a ston,
      '*Corpus Christi*' wretyn theron.

12: 1 *ibowndyn*] bound   4 *here*] their   8 *mown*] may   *Deo gracias*] Thanks be
to God
13: 2 *mak*] mate   11 *may*] maiden   14 *Corpus Christi*] the body of Christ

14
I syng of a mayden that is makeles,
Kyng of alle kynges to here sone che ches.

He cam also stylle ther his moder was
As dew in Aprylle that fallyt on the gras.

He cam also stylle to his moderes bowr
As dew in Aprille that fallyt on the flour.

He cam also stylle ther his moder lay
As dew in Aprille that fallyt on the spray.

Moder and maydyn was never non but che—
Wel may swych a lady Godes moder be!

15
A Lyke Wake Dirge

This ae nighte, this ae nighte,
—Every nighte and alle,
Fire and fleet and candle-lighte,
And Christe receive thy saule.

When thou from hence away art past,
—Every nighte and alle,
To Whinny-muir thou com'st at last;
And Christe receive thy saule.

If ever thou gavest hosen and shoon,
—Every nighte and alle,
Sit thee down and put them on;
And Christe receive thy saule.

If hosen and shoon thou ne'er gav'st nane
—Every nighte and alle,
The whinnes sall prick thee to the bare bane;
And Christe receive thy saule.

From Whinny-muir when thou may'st pass,
—Every nighte and alle,
To Brig o' Dread thou com'st at last;
And Christe receive thy saule.

From Brig o' Dread when thou may'st pass,
—Every nighte and alle,
To Purgatory fire thou com'st at last;
And Christe receive thy saule.

14: 1 *makeles*] without a mate, matchless   2 *ches*] chose   3 *also*] as   *ther*] where
15: *title*] the watch kept at night over a dead body   1 *ae*] one   3 *Fire and fleet*] expression occurring in wills (*flet*, house-room)   7 *Whinny-muir*] furze-moor   15 *whinnes*] thorns   19 *Brig*] bridge

If ever thou gavest meat or drink,   25
—*Every nighte and alle,*
The fire sall never make thee shrink;
And Christe receive thy saule.

If meat or drink thou ne'er gav'st nane,
—*Every nighte and alle,*   30
The fire will burn thee to the bare bane;
And Christe receive thy saule.

This ae nighte, this ae nighte,
—*Every nighte and alle,*
Fire and fleet and candle-lighte,   35
And Christe receive thy saule.

16   Westron wynde when wyll thow blow,
          The smalle rayne downe can rayne—
          Cryst, yf my love wer in my armys
          And I yn my bed agayne!

ROBERT HENRYSON
1424?–1506?

17   from *The Testament of Cresseid* [line 484–end]

          That samin tyme, of Troy the garnisoun,
          Whilk had to chiftane worthie Troylus,
          Throw jeopardie of weir had strikken doun
          Knichtis of Grece in number mervellous;
          With greit tryumphe and laude victorious   5
          Agane to Troy richt royallie thay raid
          The way whair Cresseid with the lipper baid.

          Seing that companie, all with ane stevin
          Thay gaif ane cry, and schuik coppis gude speid,
          'Worthie lordis, for Goddis lufe of hevin,   10
          To us lipper part of your almous deid!'
          Than to thair cry nobill Troylus tuik heid,
          Having pietie, neir by the place can pas
          Whair Cresseid sat, not witting what scho was.

17: 1 *garnisoun*] garrison   3 *Throw*] through   5 *laude*] praise   6 *raid*]
rode   7 *lipper baid*] lepers lived   8 *stevin*] voice   9 *schuik...speid*] rattled their
bowls briskly   11 *part*] some (as noun), or give a share (verb)   *almous deid*] alms-giving
13 *can pas*] passed   14 *what*] who

Than upon him scho kest up baith hir ene,   15
And with ane blenk it come into his thocht
That he sumtime hir face befoir had sene,
Bot scho was in sic plye he knew hir nocht;
Yit than hir luik into his mynd it brocht
The sweit visage and amorous blenking   20
Of fair Cresseid, sumtyme his awin darling.

Na wonder was, suppois in mynd that he
Tuik hir figure sa sone, and lo, now why:
The idole of ane thing in cace may be
Sa deip imprentit in the fantasy   25
That it deludis the wittis outwardly,
And sa appeiris in forme and lyke estait
Within the mynd as it was figurait.

Ane spark of lufe than till his hart culd spring
And kendlit all his bodie in ane fyre;   30
With hait fevir, ane sweit and trimbling
Him tuik, whill he was reddie to expyre;
To beir his scheild his breist began to tyre;
Within ane whyle he changit mony hew;
And nevertheles not ane ane uther knew.   35

For knichtlie pietie and memoriall
Of fair Cresseid, ane gyrdill can he tak,
Ane purs of gold, and mony gay jowall,
And in the skirt of Cresseid doun can swak;
Than raid away and not ane word he spak,   40
Pensive in hart, whill he come to the toun,
And for greit cair oft syis almaist fell doun.

The lipper folk to Cresseid than can draw
To se the equall distributioun
Of the almous, bot when the gold thay saw,   45
Ilk ane to uther prevelie can roun,
And said, 'Yone lord hes mair affectioun,
How ever it be, unto yone lazarous
Than to us all; we knaw be his almous.'

'What lord is yone,' quod scho, 'haue ye na feill,   50
Hes done to us so greit humanitie?'

---

15 *ene*] eyes   18 *plye*] plight   22 *suppois*] if   23 *Tuik her figure*] recognized her
24 *idole*] image   31 *hait fevir*] hot fever   39 *can swak*] tossed (it)   42 *oft syis*]
oft-times   46 *prevelie can roun*] whispered in private   49 *knaw*] recognize, know this
50 *feill*] knowledge

'Yes,' quod a lipper man, 'I knaw him weill;
Schir Troylus it is, gentill and fre.'
When Cresseid understude that it was he,
Stiffer than steill thair stert ane bitter stound   55
Throwout hir hart, and fell doun to the ground.

When scho ovircome, with siching sair and sad,
With mony cairfull cry and cald ochane:
'Now is my breist with stormie stoundis stad,
Wrappit in wo, ane wretch full will of wane!'   60
Than fel in swoun full oft or ever scho fane,
And ever in hir swouning cryit scho thus,
'O fals Cresseid and trew knicht Troylus!

'Thy lufe, thy lawtie, and thy gentilnes
I countit small in my prosperitie,   65
Sa efflated I was in wantones,
And clam upon the fickill wheill sa hie.
All faith and lufe I promissit to the
Was in the self fickill and frivolous:
O fals Cresseid and trew knicht Troilus!   70

'For lufe of me thow keipt continence,
Honest and chaist in conversatioun;
Of all wemen protectour and defence
Thou was, and helpit thair opinioun;
My mynd in fleschelie foull affectioun   75
Was inclynit to lustis lecherous:
Fy, fals Cresseid; O trew knicht Troylus!

'Lovers be war and tak gude heid about
Whome that ye lufe, for whome ye suffer paine.
I lat yow wit, thair is richt few thairout   80
Whome ye may traist to have trew lufe agane;
Preif when ye will, your labour is in vaine.
Thairfoir I reid ye tak thame as ye find,
For thay ar sad as widdercok in wind.

'Becaus I knaw the greit unstabilnes,   85
Brukkill as glas, into my self, I say—
Traisting in uther als greit unfaithfulnes,
Als unconstant, and als untrew of fay—

55 *stound*] pang   57 *ovircome*] came to   *siching*] sighing   58 *cald ochane*] chilling
lament (alas)   59 *stad*] beset   60 *full . . . wane*] entirely hopeless   61 *or . . . fane*]
before she ceased   64 *lawtie*] loyalty   66 *efflated*] puffed up   67 *clam . . . wheill*]
climbed upon the untrustworthy wheel   72 *conversatioun*] conduct, dealings   80 *lat
yow wit*] would have you know   82 *Preif*] put it to the test   83 *reid*] advise
84 *sad*] steadfast   86 *Brukkill*] brittle   87 *Traisting in uther*] expecting in others
88 *fay*] faith

Thocht sum be trew, I wait richt few ar thay;
Wha findis treuth, lat him his lady ruse; 90
Nane but my self as now I will accuse.'

When this was said, with paper scho sat doun,
And on this maneir maid hir testament:
'Heir I beteiche my corps and carioun
With wormis and with taidis to be rent; 95
My cop and clapper, and myne ornament,
And all my gold the lipper folk sall have,
When I am deid, to burie me in grave.

'This royall ring, set with this rubie reid,
Whilk Troylus in drowrie to me send, 100
To him agane I leif it when I am deid,
To mak my cairfull deid unto him kend.
Thus I conclude schortlie and mak ane end:
My spreit I leif to Diane, whair scho dwellis,
To walk with hir in waist woddis and wellis. 105

'O Diomeid, thou hes baith broche and belt
Whilk Troylus gave me in takning
Of his trew lufe', and with that word scho swelt.
And sone ane lipper man tuik of the ring,
Syne buryit hir withouttin tarying; 110
To Troylus furthwith the ring he bair,
And of Cresseid the deith he can declair.

When he had hard hir greit infirmitie,
Hir legacie and lamentatioun,
And how scho endit in sic povertie, 115
He swelt for wo and fell doun in ane swoun;
For greit sorrow his hart to brist was boun;
Siching full sadlie, said, 'I can no moir;
Scho was untrew and wo is me thairfoir.'

Sum said he maid ane tomb of merbell gray, 120
And wrait hir name and superscriptioun,
And laid it on hir grave whair that scho lay,
In goldin letteris, conteining this ressoun:
'Lo, fair ladyis, Cresseid of Troy the toun,
Sumtyme countit the flour of womanheid, 125
Under this stane, lait lipper, lyis deid.'

89 *Thocht*] though 90 *ruse*] praise 94 *beteiche*] bequeath *corps and carioun*]
dead body 95 *taidis*] toads 96 *clapper*] clap-dish's lid, to give warning of approach
and to receive alms 102 *deid*] death *kend*] known 107 *takning*] token
108 *swelt*] died 116 *swelt*] swooned 117 *brist was boun*] about to break
123 *ressoun*] declaration 126 *lait lipper*] formerly a leper

Now, worthie wemen, in this ballet schort,
Maid for your worschip and instructioun,
Of cheritie, I monische and exhort,
Ming not your lufe with fals deceptioun: 130
Beir in your mynd this sore conclusioun
Of fair Cresseid, as I have said befoir.
Sen scho is deid I speik of hir no moir.

WILLIAM DUNBAR

1456?–1513?

18   Done is a battell on the dragon blak;
        Our campioun Chryst confoundit hes his force:
        The yettis of hell ar brokin with a crak,
        The signe triumphall rasit is of the croce,
        The divillis trymmillis with hiddous voce,   5
        The saulis ar borrowit and to the bliss can go,
        Chryst with his blud our ransonis dois indoce:
        Surrexit Dominus de sepulchro.

        Dungin is the deidly dragon Lucifer,
        The crewall serpent with the mortall stang,   10
        The auld kene tegir with his teith on char
        Whilk in a wait hes lyne for us so lang
        Thinking to grip us in his clowis strang:
        The mercifull lord wald nocht that it wer so;
        He maid him for to felye of that fang: 15
        Surrexit Dominus de sepulchro.

        He for our saik that sufferit to be slane
        And lyk a lamb in sacrifice wes dicht
        Is lyk a lyone rissin up agane
        And as a gyane raxit him on hicht;   20
        Sprungin is Aurora radius and bricht,
        On loft is gone the glorius Appollo,
        The blisfull day depairtit fro the nycht:
        Surrexit Dominus de sepulchro.

---

127 *ballet*] ballad, poem   130 *Ming*] mingle

18: 3 *yettis*] gates   5 *trymmillis*] tremble   6 *borrowit*] redeemed   7 *indoce*]
endorse   8 *Surrexit . . . sepulchro*] The Lord is risen from the tomb   9 *Dungin*]
beaten down   11 *tegir*] tiger   *on char*] bared   12 *wait*] ambush   *lyne*] lain
13 *clowis*] claws   15 *felye*] fail   *fang*] prey   18 *dicht*] killed   20 *raxit*]
raised   21 *radius*] radiant   22 *On loft*] aloft

The grit victour agane is rissin on hicht   25
That for our querrell to the deth wes woundit;
The sone that wox all paill now schynis bricht,
And dirknes clerit, our fayth is now refoundit;
The knell of mercy fra the hevin is soundit,
The Cristin ar deliverit of thair wo,   30
The Jowis and thair errour ar confoundit:
Surrexit Dominus de sepulchro.

The fo is chasit, the battell is done ceis,
The presone brokin, the jevellouris fleit and flemit;
The weir is gon, confermit is the peis,   35
The fetteris lowsit and the dungeoun temit,
The ransoun maid, the presoneris redemit;
The feild is win, ourcumin is the fo,
Dispulit of the tresur that he yemit:
Surrexit Dominus de sepulchro.   40

19   *[The Lament for the Makars]*

I that in heill wes and gladnes
Am trublit now with gret seiknes
And feblit with infermite:
Timor mortis conturbat me.

Our plesance heir is all vane glory,   5
This fals warld is bot transitory,
The flesch is brukle, the Fend is sle:
Timor mortis conturbat me.

The stait of man dois change and vary,
Now sound, now seik, now blith, now sary,   10
Now dansand mery, now like to dee:
Timor mortis conturbat me.

No stait in erd heir standis sickir;
As with the wynd wavis the wickir
Wavis this warldis vanite: 15
Timor mortis conturbat me.

---

27 *wox*] waxed   28 *clerit*] cleared   31 *Jowis*] Jews   34 *jevellouris fleit and flemit*] gaolers frightened to flight   36 *lowsit*] loosed   *temit*] cleared   38 *ourcumin*] overcome   39 *Dispulit*] despoiled   *yemit*] guarded

19: 1 *heill*] health   4 *Timor . . . me*] The fear of death greatly disturbs me   5 *heir*] here   7 *brukle*] fragile   *sle*] cunning   11 *like to dee*] likely to die   13 *in erd*] on earth   *sickir*] secure   14 *wavis the wickir*] waves the willow

On to the ded gois all estatis,
Princis, prelotis and potestatis,
Baith riche and pur of al degre:
Timor mortis conturbat me.   20

He takis the knychtis in to feild
Anarmyt undir helme and scheild,
Victour he is at all melle:
Timor mortis conturbat me.

That strang unmercifull tyrand   25
Takis on the moderis breist sowkand
The bab full of benignite:
Timor mortis conturbat me.

He takis the campion in the stour,
The capitane closit in the tour,   30
The lady in bour full of bewte:
Timor mortis conturbat me.

He sparis no lord for his piscence,
Na clerk for his intelligence;
His awfull strak may no man fle: 35
Timor mortis conturbat me.

Art magicianis and astrologgis,
Rethoris, logicianis and theologgis—
Thame helpis no conclusionis sle:
Timor mortis conturbat me.   40

In medicyne the most practicianis,
Lechis, surrigianis and phisicianis,
Thame self fra ded may not supple:
Timor mortis conturbat me.

I se that makaris amang the laif   45
Playis heir ther pageant, syne gois to graif;
Sparit is nought ther faculte:
Timor mortis conturbat me.

He has done petuously devour
The noble Chaucer of makaris flour,   50

22 *Anarmyt*] armoured   23 *all melle*] every combat   26 *sowkand*] sucking
27 *bab*] babe   29 *stour*] battle   33 *piscence*] power   34 *clerk*] learned man
35 *strak*] stroke   38 *Rethoris*] skilled speakers   42 *Lechis*] doctors   43 *supple*]
extricate   45 *makaris*] poets   *laif*] rest   46 *syne gois to graif*] then go to the grave
49 *petuously*] pitiably   50 *of makaris flour*] the flower of poets

The monk of Bery, and Gower, all thre:
Timor mortis conturbat me.

The gud Syr Hew of Eglintoun
And eik Heryot and Wyntoun
He has tane out of this cuntre: 55
Timor mortis conturbat me.

That scorpion fell has done infek
Maister Johne Clerk and James Afflek
Fra balat making and trigide:
Timor mortis conturbat me. 60

Holland and Barbour he has berevit;
Allace that he nought with us levit
Schir Mungo Lokert of the Le:
Timor mortis conturbat me.

Clerk of Tranent eik he has tane 65
That maid the anteris of Gawane;
Schir Gilbert Hay endit has he:
Timor mortis conturbat me.

He has Blind Hary and Sandy Traill
Slane with his schour of mortall haill 70
Whilk Patrik Johnestoun myght nought fle:
Timor mortis conturbat me.

He has reft Merseir his endite
That did in luf so lifly write,
So schort, so quyk, of sentence hie: 75
Timor mortis conturbat me.

He has tane Roull of Aberdene
And gentill Roull of Corstorphin—
Two bettir fallowis did no man se:
Timor mortis conturbat me. 80

In Dunfermelyne he has done roune
With Maister Robert Henrisoun;
Schir Johne the Ros enbrast has he:
Timor mortis conturbat me.

---

57 *done infek*] poisoned   61 *berevit*] bereaved (us of)   62 *Allace*] alas
63 *Schir*] sir   66 *anteris*] adventures   67 *endit*] ended   73 *reft*] snatched from
endite] power to write   81 *done roune*] whispered

And he has now tane last of aw   85
Gud gentill Stobo and Quintyne Schaw
Of wham all wichtis has pete:
Timor mortis conturbat me.

Gud Maister Walter Kennedy
In poynt of dede lyis veraly—   90
Gret reuth it wer that so suld be:
Timor mortis conturbat me.

Sen he has all my brether tane
He will naught lat me lif alane;
On forse I man his nyxt pray be: 95
Timor mortis conturbat me.

Sen for the ded remeid is none
Best is that we for dede dispone
Eftir our deid that lif may we:
Timor mortis conturbat me.   100

JOHN SKELTON
1460?–1529

20   [Skelton Laureat, uppon a deedmans hed, that was sent to hym from an
     honorable Jentyllwoman for a token, Devysyd this gostly medytacyon
     in Englysh: Covenable in sentence, Comendable, Lamentable, Lacry-
     mable, Profytable for the soule.]

Youre ugly tokyn
My mynd hath brokyn
From worldly lust;
For I have dyscust
We ar but dust,   5
And dy we must.
    It is generall
To be mortall:
I have well espyde
No man may hym hyde   10
From deth holow-eyed,
With synnews wyderyd,
With bonys shyderyd,

---

87 *wichtis has pete*] people have pity   90 *In poynt of dede lyis veraly*] lies truly at the point of
death   91 *reuth*] pity   93 *Sen*] since   95 *On forse I man*] needs be I must
pray] prey   97 *remeid*] remedy   98 *dispone*] dispose ourselves   99 *lif*] live
    20: 12 *wyderyd*] withered   13 *shyderyd*] shattered

With hys worme-etyn maw
And hys gastly jaw   15
Gaspyng asyde,
Nakyd of hyde,
Neyther flesh nor fell.
    Then by my councell,
Loke that ye spell   20
Well thys gospell;
For wherso we dwell,
Deth wyll us quell
And with us mell.
    For all oure pamperde paunchys,   25
There may no fraunchys
Nor worldly blys
Redeme us from this.
Oure days be datyd
To be chekmatyd,   30
With drawttys of deth
Stoppyng oure breth;
Oure eyen synkyng,
Oure bodys stynkyng,
Oure gummys grynnyng,   35
Oure soulys brynnyng!
To whom then shall we sew
For to have rescew,
But to swete Jesu
On us then for to rew?   40
    O goodly chyld
Of Mary mylde,
Then be oure shylde!
That we be not exylyd
To the dyne dale   45
Of boteles bale,
Nor to the lake
Of fendys blake.
    But graunt us grace
To se thy face,   50
And to purchace
Thyne hevenly place
And thy palace,
Full of solace,
Above the sky   55
That is so hy,

24 *mell*] meddle   26 *fraunchys*] immunity   31 *drawttys*] chess-moves   36 *bryn-*
nyng] burning   37 *sew*] make a petition   45 *dyne*] gloomy   46 *boteles bale*]
torment without remedy   48 *fendys*] fiends

Eternally
To beholde and se
The Trynyte!
    Amen.   60
Myrres vous y.

21   from *The Bowge of Courte* [lines 197–217]

SUSPYCYON

'Ye remembre the gentylman ryghte nowe
That commaunde with you, me thought, a praty space?
Beware of him, for, I make God avowe,
He wyll begyle you and speke fayre to your face.
Ye never dwelte in suche an other place,   5
For here is none that dare well other truste;
But I wolde telle you a thynge, and I durste.

Spake he, a fayth, no worde to you of me?
I wote, and he dyde, ye wolde me telle.
I have a favoure to you, wherof it be   10
That I must shewe you moche of my counselle—
But I wonder what the devyll of helle
He sayde of me, whan he with you dyde talke—
By myne avyse use not with him to walke.

The soveraynst thynge that ony man maye have   15
Is lytyll to saye, and moche to here and see;
For, but I trusted you, so God me save,
I wolde noo thynge so playne be.
To you oonly, me thynke, I durste shryve me;
For now am I plenarely dysposed   20
To shewe you thynges that may not be disclosed.'

22   *Calliope*

[Why were ye Calliope, embrawdred with letters of golde?
Skelton Laureate, *Orator Regius*, maketh this aunswere etc.]

    Calliope,
    As ye may se,
    Regent is she,
    Of poetes al,

61 *Myrres vous y*] look upon yourself herein
  21: 20 *plenarely*] fully

Whiche gave to me
The high degre
Laureat to be
 Of fame royall;

Whose name enrolde
With silke and golde
I dare be bolde
 Thus for to were.
Of her I holde
And her housholde;
Though I waxe olde
 And somdele sere,

Yet is she fayne,
Voyde of disdayn,
Me to retayne
 Her serviture.
With her certayne
I wyll remayne
As my soverayne
 Moost of pleasure.

23–4   from *A Garland or Chapelet of Laurell*

23   *To mastres Margery Wentworthe*

With margerain jentyll,
The flowre of goodlyhede,
Enbrowdred the mantill
Is of your maydenhede.

Plainly, I can not glose,
Ye be, as I devyne,
The praty primrose,
The goodly columbyne.

With margerain jantill,
The flowre of goodlyhede,
Enbrawderyd the mantyll
Is of yowre maydenhede.

Benynge, corteise, and meke,
With wordes well devysid;
In you, who list to seke,
Be vertus well comprysid.

With margerain jantill,
The flowre of goodlyhede,
Enbrawderid the mantill
Is of yowr maydenhede.

24   *To maystres Margaret Hussey*

Mirry Margaret,
As mydsomer flowre,
Jentill as fawcoun
Or hawke of the towre;

With solace and gladnes,
Moche mirthe and no madnes,
All good and no badnes,
So joyously,
So maydenly,
So womanly
Her demenyng
In every thynge,
Far, far passynge
That I can endyght,
Or suffice to wryght
Of mirry Margarete,
As mydsomer flowre,
Jentyll as fawcoun
Or hawke of the towre,

As pacient and as styll,
And as full of good wyll,
As fayre Isaphill;
Colyaunder,
Swete pomaunder,
Good Cassaunder;
Stedfast of thought,
Wele made, wele wrought;
Far may be sought
Erst that ye can fynde
So corteise, so kynde
As mirry Margarete,
This midsomer flowre,
Jentyll as fawcoun
Or hawke of the towre.

GAVIN DOUGLAS
1475?–1522

25   from Virgil's *Eneados* [Book VI, cap. V, lines 7–40]

Thir riveris and thir watteris kepit war
By ane Charon, a grislie ferriar,
Terrible of schap, and sluggert of array:
Apon his chin feill cannos haris gray,
Lyart feltat tatis; with birnand ene reid,   5
Like tua fire blesis fixit in his heid.
His smotterit habit, our his schulderis lidder,
Hang prevagely knyt with a knot togiddir.
Hymself the cobil did with his bolm furth schow,
And, when hym list, halit up salis fow.   10
This ald hasard careis our fludis hoit
Spretis and figuris in his irn hewit boit,
Allthocht he eildit was, or step in age,
Als fery and als swippir as a page;
For in a god the age is fresche and grene,   15
Infatigable and immortale as thai mene.
    Thiddir to the bray swarmit all the rout
Of deid gaistis, and stud the bank about;
Baith matrouns, and thair husbandis, all yferis,
Ryall princis, and nobill chevaleris,   20
Small childrin, and young damicellis unwed,
And fair springaldis laitlie deid in bed,
In fader and in moderis presens laid on beir.
Als gret number thiddir thikkit in feir,
As in the first frost eftir hervist tyde,   25
Levis of treis in the wod doith slyde;
Or birdis flokkis our the fludis gray,
Onto the land seikand the nerrest way,
Whom the cald sesoun cachis our the see,
Into sum benar realm and warm countre.   30

25: 1 *Thir*] these   4 *feill*] many   *cannos*] hoary   5 *Lyart feltat tatis*] grey matted locks   *ene*] eyes   6 *tua*] two   *blesis*] blazes   7 *smotterit*] spattered   *lidder*] loose   8 *prevagely*] carelessly   9 *cobil*] boat   *bolm*] pole   *schow*] shove 10 *halit*] hauled   *fow*] full   11 *hasard...hoit*] dotard carries over hot floods   12 *irn hewit*] iron-coloured   13 *step*] advanced   14 *Als . . . swippir*] as strong and nimble 16 *mene*] destine   17 *bray*] bank   19 *yferis*] together   22 *springaldis*] youths 24 *thikkit in feir*] crowded together   29 *cachis our*] hastens over   30 *benar*] kinder

Thair stud thai praying sum support to gett,
That thai mycht with the formast our be sett,
And gan uphevin petuuslie handis tuay,
Langing to be apon the forthir bray.

[after the Latin of Virgil]

SIR THOMAS WYATT

1503–1542

26   The longe love, that in my thought doeth harbar
  And in myn hert doeth kepe his residence
  Into my face preseth with bold pretence,
  And therin campeth, spreding his baner.
She that me lerneth to love and suffre
  And will that my trust, and lustes negligence
  Be reinèd by reason, shame, and reverence
  With his hardines taketh displeasure.
Wherewithall, unto the hertes forrest he fleith,
  Leving his entreprise with payne and cry
  And there him hideth and not appereth.
What may I do when my maister fereth,
  But, in the felde, with him to lyve and dye?
  For goode is the liff, ending faithfully.

[after the Italian of Petrarch]

27   Who so list to hounte I know where is an hynde;
  But as for me, helas, I may no more:
  The vayne travaill hath weried me so sore,
  I ame of theim that farthest cometh behinde;
Yet may I by no meanes my weried mynde
  Drawe from the Diere: but as she fleeth afore
  Faynting I folowe; I leve off therefore,
  Sithens in a nett I seke to hold the wynde.
Who list her hount I put him owte of dowbte,
  As well as I may spend his tyme in vain:
  And graven with Diamondes in letters plain
There is written her faier neck rounde abowte:
  'Noli me tangere for Cesars I ame,
  And wylde for to hold though I seme tame'.

[after the Italian of Petrarch]

33 *petuuslie*] piteously *tuay*] two

28
    Farewell, Love, and all thy lawes for ever;
      Thy bayted hookes shall tangill me no more;
      Senec and Plato call me from thy lore,
      To perfaict welth my wit for to endever.
    In blynde errour when I did perséver,
      Thy sherpe repulce that pricketh ay so sore
      Hath taught me to sett in tryfels no store
      And scape forth syns libertie is liefer.
    Therefore, farewell; goo trouble yonger hertes
      And in me clayme no more authoritie;
      With idill yeuth goo use thy propertie
    And theron spend thy many britill dertes:
      For hetherto though I have lost all my tyme,
      Me lusteth no lenger rotten boughes to clyme.

29
    My galy chargèd with forgetfulnes
      Thorrough sharpe sees in wynter nyghtes doeth pas
      Twene Rock and Rock; and eke myn ennemy, Alas,
      That is my lorde, sterith with cruelnes;
    And every houre a thought in readines,
      As tho that deth were light in suche a case;
      An endles wynd doeth tere the sayll a pace
      Of forcèd sightes and trusty ferefulnes.
    A rayn of tearis, a clowde of derk disdain
      Hath done the wearied cordes great hinderaunce,
      Wrethèd with errour and eke with ignoraunce.
    The starres be hid that led me to this pain;
      Drownèd is reason that should me confórt,
      And I remain dispering of the port.

        [after the Italian of Petrarch]

30
    They fle from me that sometyme did me seke
    With naked fote stalking in my chambre.
    I have sene theim gentill tame and meke
    That nowe are wyld and do not remembre
    That sometyme they put theimself in daunger
    To take bred at my hand; and nowe they raunge
    Busely seking with a continuell chaunge.

    Thanckèd be fortune, it hath ben othrewise
    Twenty tymes better; but once in speciall
    In thin arraye after a pleasaunt gyse

When her loose gowne from her shoulders did fall,
And she me caught in her armes long and small;
Therewithall swetely did me kysse,
And softely said 'dere hert, how like you this?'

It was no dreme: I lay brode waking.
But all is tornèd thorough my gentilnes
Into a straunge fasshion of forsaking;
And I have leve to goo of her goodeness,
And she also to use new fangilnes.
But syns that I so kyndely ame servèd,
I would fain knowe what she hath deservèd.

31   My lute, awake! perfourme the last
       Labour that thou and I shall waste
       And end that I have now begon;
       For when this song is sung and past,
       My lute be still, for I have done.

       As to be heard where ere is none,
       As leade to grave in marbill stone,
       My song may perse her hert as soone;
       Should we then sigh, or syng, or mone?
       No, no, my lute, for I have done.

       The Rokkes do not so cruelly
       Repulse the waves continuelly
       As she my suyte and affection,
       So that I ame past remedy,
       Whereby my lute and I have done.

       Prowd of the spoyll that thou hast gott
       Of simple hertes thorough loves shot,
       By whome, unkynd, thou hast theim wone,
       Thinck not he haith his bow forgot,
       All tho my lute and I have done.

       Vengeaunce shall fall on thy disdain
       That makest but game on ernest pain;
       Thinck not alone under the sonne
       Unquit to cause thy lover's plain,
       All tho my lute and I have done.

       Perchaunce thee lye wetherèd and old,
       The wynter nyghtes that are so cold,
       Playnyng in vain unto the moone;
       Thy wisshes then dare not be told;
       Care then who lyst, for I have done.

And then may chaunce thee to repent
The tyme that thou hast lost and spent,
To cause thy lover's sigh and swoune;
Then shalt thou knowe beautie but lent
And wisshe and want as I have done.

Now cesse, my lute; this is the last
Labour that thou and I shall waste,
And ended is that we begon;
Now is this song boeth sung and past;
My lute, be still, for I have done.

32   So unwarely was never no man cawght
      With stedefast loke apon a goodly face,
      As I of late; for sodenly me thowght
      My hart was torne owte of hys place.

      Thorow myn eye the strock frome hers dyd slyde,
      Dyrectly downe unto my hert ytt ranne;
      In helpe wherof the blood therto dyd glyde,
      And left my face both pale and wanne.

      Then was I leke a manne for woe amasyd,
      Or leke the byrde that flyeth in to the fyer;
      For whyll that I upon her beautie gazyd
      The more I burnt in my desyre.

      Anon the blowd stert in my face agayne,
      Enflamde with hete that yt had att my hart,
      And browght therwith thorowt in every vayne
      A quakyng hete with plesaunt smert.

      Then was I leke the strawe whan that the flame
      Ys drevyn therin by force and rage of wynd;
      I can nott tell, alas, what I shall blame,
      Nor what to seke, nor what to fynd.

      But wele I wote the grieffe holdes me so sore
      In hete and cold betwyxt hope and drede,
      That but her helpe to helth doth me restore
      Thys restles lyff I may nott lede.

33   Dyverse dothe use as I have heard and kno,
         Whan that to chaunge ther ladies do beginne
         To mourne and waile and never for to lynne
         Hoping therbye to 'pease ther painefull woe.

And some therbe that whan it chansith soo
    That women change and hate where love hath bene,
    Thei call them fals and think with woordes to wynne
The hartes of them wich otherwhere dothe gro.
But as for me though that by chaunse indede
    Change hath outworne the favour that I had,
    I will not wayle, lament, nor yet be sad,
Nor call her fals that falsley ded me fede,
    But let it passe and think it is of kinde
    That often chaunge doth plese a womans minde.

34   The piller pearisht is whearto I lent,
    The strongest staye of myne unquyet mynde;
    The lyke of it no man agayne can fynde
From East to west still seking though he went.
To myne unhappe, for happe away hath rent
    Of all my joye the verye bark and rynde;
    And I (alas) by chaunce am thus assynde
Dearlye to mourne till death do it relent.
But syns that thus it is by destenye
    What can I more but have a wofull hart,
    My penne in playnt, my voyce in wofull crye,
My mynde in woe, my bodye full of smart,
    And I my self my self alwayes to hate
    Till dreadfull death do ease my dolefull state?

                      [after the Italian of Petrarch]

35   Stond who so list upon the Slipper toppe
Of courtes estates, and lett me here rejoyce;
And use me quyet without lett or stoppe,
Unknowen in courte, that hath suche brackish joyes.
In hidden place, so lett my dayes forthe passe,
That when my yeares be done, withouten noyse,
I may dye agèd after the common trace.
For hym death greep'th right hard by the croppe
That is moche knowen of other, and of him self alas,
Doth dye unknowen, dazèd with dreadfull face.

                      [after the Latin of Seneca]

36   *Psalm 130. De profundis clamavi*

From depth of sinn and from a diepe dispaire,
    From depth of deth, from depth of hertes sorow,

From this diepe Cave of darknes diepe repayre,
Thee have I cald o lord to be my borow;
  Thou in my voyce o lord perceyve and heare
  My hert, my hope, my plaint, my overthrow,
My will to ryse, and let by graunt apere
  That to my voyce, thine eares do well entend.
No place so farr that to thee it is not nere;
No depth so diepe that thou ne maist extend
  Thine eare therto; here then my wofull plaint.
For, lord, if thou do observe what men offend
And putt thi natyff mercy in restraint,
  If just exaction demaund recompense,
  Who may endure o lord? who shall not faynt
At such acompt? dred, and not reverence,
  Shold so reigne large. But thou sekes rather love,
  For in thi hand is mercys resedence,
By hope wheroff thou dost our hertes move.
  I in thee, lord, have set my confydence;
  My sowle such trust doth evermore approve
Thi holy word of eterne excellence,
  Thi mercys promesse, that is alway just,
  Have bene my stay, my piller and pretence;
My sowle in god hath more desyrus trust
  Than hath the wachman lokyng for the day,
  By the releffe to quenche of slepe the thrust.
Let Israell trust unto the lord alway,
  For grace and favour arn his propertie;
  Plenteus rannsome shall com with hym, I say,
And shall redeme all our iniquitie.

  [after the Hebrew of the Psalms]

HENRY HOWARD, EARL OF SURREY

1517?–1547

37   The soote season, that bud and blome furth bringes,
    With grene hath clad the hill and eke the vale;
    The nightingale with fethers new she singes;
    The turtle to her make hath tolde her tale.
    Somer is come, for every spray nowe springes;
    The hart hath hong his olde hed on the pale;
    The buck in brake his winter cote he flinges;
    The fishes flote with newe repairèd scale;
    The adder all her sloughe awaye she slinges;
    The swift swalow pursueth the flyes smale;

The busy bee her honye now she minges;
Winter is worne that was the flowers bale.
And thus I see among these pleasant thinges
Eche care decayes, and yet my sorow springes.

38   Alas, so all thinges nowe doe holde their peace,
Heaven and earth disturbèd in nothing;
The beastes, the ayer, the birdes their song doe cease;
The nightes chare the starres aboute dothe bring.
Calme is the sea, the waves worke lesse and lesse;
So am not I, whom love alas doth wring,
Bringing before my face the great encrease
Of my desires, whereat I wepe and syng
In joye and wo as in a doutfull ease.
For my swete thoughtes sometyme doe pleasure bring,
But by and by the cause of my disease
Geves me a pang that inwardly dothe sting,
    When that I thinke what griefe it is againe
    To live and lacke the thing should ridde my paine.

ALEXANDER SCOTT

1520?–1590?

39   [*A Rondel of Luve*]

Lo! what it is to lufe,
Lerne ye, that list to prufe,
Be me, I say, that no wayis may
The grund of greif remufe,
Bot still decay, both nycht and day: 5
Lo! what it is to lufe.

Lufe is ane fervent fyre,
Kendillit without desyre:
Schort plesour, lang displesour;
Repentence is the hyre;   10
Ane pure tressour without mesour:
Lufe is ane fervent fyre.

To lufe and to be wyiss,
To rege with gud advyiss,

39: 2 *prufe*] proof   3 *Be*] by   4 *remufe*] remove   14 *rege*] rage   *advyiss*]
consideration

Now thus, now than, so gois the game,   15
    Incertane is the dyiss:
Thair is no man, I say, that can
    Both lufe and to be wyiss.

    Fle alwayis frome the snair;
    Lerne at me to be ware;   20
It is ane pane and dowbill trane
    Of endless wo and cair;
For to refrane that denger plane,
    Fle alwayis frome the snair.

RICHARD EDWARDES

1523–1566

40   *Amantium iræ amoris redintigratia est*

In goyng to my naked bedde, as one that would have slept,
I heard a wife syng to her child, that long before had wept:
She sighèd sore and sang full sore, to bryng the babe to rest,
That would not rest but crièd still, in suckyng at her brest.
She was full wearie of her watche, and grevèd with her child,
She rockèd it and rated it, untill on her it smilde:
Then did she saie now have I founde, the proverbe true to prove,
The fallyng out of faithfull frends, is the renewing of love.

Then tooke I paper, penne and ynke, this proverbe for to write,
In regester for to remaine, of suche a worthie wight:
As she proceded thus, in song unto her little bratte,
Muche matter utterèd she of waight, in place whereas she satte.
And proved plaine, there was no beast, nor creature bearyng life,
Could well be knowne to live in love, without discorde and strife:
Then kissèd she her little babe, and sware by God above,
The fallyng out of faithfull frends, is the renewing of love.

She saied that neither kyng ne prince, ne lorde could live aright,
Untill their puissance thei did prove, their manhode and their might.
When manhode shalbe matchèd so, that feare can take no place,
Then wearie works makes warriours eche other to embrace.
And leave their forse that failèd them, whiche did consume the rout,
That might before have lived their tyme, and nature out:
Then did she syng as one that thought, no man could her reprove,
The fallyng out of faithfull frendes, is the renewing of love.

16 *dyiss*] dice

She saied she sawe no fishe ne foule, nor beast within her haunt,
That mett a straunger in their kinde, but could geve it a taunt:
Since fleshe might not indure, but reste must wrathe succede,
And forse the fight to fall to plaie, in pasture where thei feede.
So noble nature can well ende the works she hath begone,
And bridle well that will not cease her tragedy in some:
Thus in her songe she oft reherst, as did her well behove,
The fallyng out of faithfull frends, is the renewing of love.

I mervaile muche pardy quoth she, for to beholde the route,
To see man, woman, boy and beast, to tosse the worlde about:
Some knele, some crouch, some beck, some check, and some can smothly
    smile,
And some embrace others in armes, and there thinke many a wile.
Some stande aloufe at cap and knee, some humble and some stout,
Yet are thei never frends indeede, untill thei once fall out:
Thus ended she her song, and saied before she did remove,
The fallyng out of faithfull frends, is the renewing of love.

SIR HENRY LEE

1530–1610

[formerly attributed to GEORGE PEELE]

41   His Golden lockes, Time hath to Silver turn'd,
O Time too swift, ô Swiftnesse never ceasing:
His Youth gainst Time and Age hath ever spurn'd
But spurn'd in vain, Youth waineth by increasing.
    Beauty Strength, Youth, are flowers, but fading seen,
    Dutie, Faith, Love are roots, and ever greene.

His Helmet now, shall make a hive for Bees,
And Lovers Sonets, turn'd to holy Psalmes:
A man at Armes must now serve on his knees,
And feede on praiers, which are Age his almes.
    But though from Court to Cottage he depart,
    His Saint is sure of his unspotted heart.

And when he saddest sits in homely Cell,
Heele teach his Swaines this Carroll for a Song,
Blest be the heartes that wish my Soveraigne well,
Curst be the soules that thinke her any wrong.
    Goddesse, allow this agèd man his right,
    To be your Beads-man now, that was your Knight.

ARTHUR GOLDING
1536?–1605

42   from *Ovid's Metamorphosis*
                [The Seventh Book, lines 253–89]

The moysting Ayre was whist: no leafe ye could have moving sene.
The starres alonly faire and bright did in the welkin shine.
To which she lifting up hir handes did thrise hirselfe encline,
And thrice with water of the brooke hir haire besprincled shee:
And gasping thrise she opte hir mouth: and bowing downe hir knee
Upon the bare hard ground, she said: O trustie time of night
Most faithfull unto privities, O golden starres whose light
Doth jointly with the Moone succeede the beames that blaze by day
And thou three headed *Hecaté* who knowest best the way
To compasse this our great attempt and art our chiefest stay:
Ye Charmes and Witchcrafts, and thou Earth which both with herbe
      and weed
Of mightie working furnishest the Wizardes at their neede:
Ye Ayres and windes: ye Elves of Hilles, of Brookes, of Woods alone,
Of standing Lakes, and of the Night approche ye everychone.
Through helpe of whom (the crooked bankes much wondring at the thing)
I have compellèd streames to run cleane backward to their spring.
By charmes I make the calme Seas rough, and make the rough Seas plaine
And cover all the Skie with Cloudes, and chase them thence againe.
By charmes I rayse and lay the windes, and burst the Vipers jaw,
And from the bowels of the Earth both stones and trees doe drawe.
Whole woods and Forestes I remove: I make the Mountaines shake,
And even the Earth it selfe to grone and fearfully to quake.
I call up dead men from their graves: and thee O lightsome Moone
I darken oft, though beaten brasse abate thy perill soone
Our Sorcerie dimmes the Morning faire, and darkes the Sun at Noone.
The flaming breath of firie Bulles ye quenchèd for my sake.
And causèd their unwieldie neckes the bended yoke to take.
Among the Earthbred brothers you a mortall war did set
And brought a sleepe the Dragon fell whose eyes were never shet.
By meanes whereof deceiving him that had the golden fleece
In charge to keepe, you sent it thence by *Jason* into *Greece*.
Now have I neede of herbes that can by vertue of their juice
To flowring prime of lustie youth old withred age reduce.
I am assurde ye will it graunt. For not in vaine have shone
These twincling starres, ne yet in vaine this Chariot all alone
By draught of Dragons hither comes. With that was fro the Skie
A Chariot softly glauncèd downe, and stayèd hard thereby.

                              [after the Latin of Ovid]

ALEXANDER MONTGOMERIE
1545?–1610?

43   *A Description of Tyme*

Tak tyme in tym, or tym will not be tane;
Thairfor tak tent how thou this tyme suld tak:
Sho hes no hold, to hold hir by, bot ane;
A toppe befor, bot beld behind hir bak.
Let thou hir slippe, or slipperly grow slak,   5
Thou gettis no grippe agane fra sho be gane.
If thou wald speid, remember what I spak;
Tak tyme in tyme, or tym will not be tane.

For I haif hard in adagies of auld,
That tyme dois waist and weir all things away;   10
Then trow the taill that trew men oft hes tauld—
A turne in tyme is ay worth other tway.
Siklyk, I haif hard oft-tymis suith men say,
That negligence yit nevir furtherit nane;
Als, seindle tymis luck folowes long delayis.   15
Tak tyme in tyme, or tyme will not be tane.

EDMUND SPENSER
1552?–1599

44–6   from *The Faerie Queene*

44   [Book I, Canto ix, stanzas 35–40]

That darkesome cave they enter, where they find
    That cursèd man, low sitting on the ground,
    Musing full sadly in his sullein mind;
    His griesie lockes, long growen, and unbound,
    Disordred hong about his shoulders round,
    And hid his face; through which his hollow eyne
    Lookt deadly dull, and stared as astound;
    His raw-bone cheekes through penurie and pine,
Were shronke into his jawes, as he did never dine.

43: 2 *tent*] care   4 *toppe*] forelock   *beld*] bald   5 *slipperly*] insecurely
15 *seindle tymis*] seldom

His garment nought but many ragged clouts,
  With thornes together pind and patchèd was,
  The which his naked sides he wrapt abouts;
  And him beside there lay upon the gras
  A drearie corse, whose life away did pas,
  All wallowd in his owne yet luke-warme blood,
  That from his wound yet wellèd fresh alas;
  In which a rustie knife fast fixèd stood,
And made an open passage for the gushing flood.

Which piteous spectacle, approving trew
  The wofull tale that *Trevisan* had told,
  When as the gentle *Redcrosse* knight did vew,
  With firie zeale he burnt in courage bold,
  Him to avenge, before his bloud were cold,
  And to the villein said, Thou damnèd wight,
  The author of this fact, we here behold,
  What justice can but judge against thee right,
With thine owne bloud to price his bloud, here shed in sight?

What franticke fit (quoth he) hath thus distraught
  Thee, foolish man, so rash a doome to give?
  What justice ever other judgement taught,
  But he should die, who merites not to live?
  None else to death this man despayring drive,
  But his owne guiltie mind deserving death.
  Is then unjust to each his due to give?
  Or let him die, that loatheth living breath?
Or let him die at ease, that liveth here uneath?

Who travels by the wearie wandring way,
  To come unto his wishèd home in haste,
  And meetes a flood, that doth his passage stay,
  Is not great grace to helpe him over past,
  Or free his feet, that in the myre sticke fast?
  Most envious man, that grieves at neighbours good,
  And fond, that joyest in the woe thou hast,
  Why wilt not let him passe, that long hath stood
Upon the banke, yet wilt thy selfe not passe the flood?

He there does now enjoy eternall rest
  And happie ease, which thou doest want and crave,
  And further from it daily wanderest:
  What if some litle paine the passage have,
  That makes fraile flesh to feare the bitter wave?
  Is not short paine well borne, that brings long ease,
  And layes the soule to sleepe in quiet grave?
  Sleepe after toyle, port after stormie seas,
Ease after warre, death after life does greatly please.

45 [Book II, Canto XII, stanzas 70–8]

Eftsoones they heard a most melodious sound,
   Of all that mote delight a daintie eare,
   Such as attonce might not on living ground,
   Save in this Paradise, be heard elswhere:
   Right hard it was, for wight, which did it heare,
   To read, what manner musicke that mote bee:
   For all that pleasing is to living eare,
   Was there consorted in one harmonee,
Birdes, voyces, instruments, windes, waters, all agree.

The joyous birdes shrouded in chearefull shade,
   Their notes unto the voyce attempred sweet;
   Th'Angelicall soft trembling voyces made
   To th'instruments divine respondence meet:
   The silver sounding instruments did meet
   With the base murmure of the waters fall:
   The waters fall with difference discreet,
   Now soft, now loud, unto the wind did call:
The gentle warbling wind low answerèd to all.

There, whence that Musick seemèd heard to bee,
   Was the faire Witch her selfe now solacing,
   With a new Lover, whom through sorceree
   And witchcraft, she from farre did thither bring:
   There she had him now layd a slombering,
   In secret shade, after long wanton joyes:
   Whilst round about them pleasauntly did sing
   Many faire Ladies, and lascivious boyes,
That ever mixt their song with light licentious toyes.

And all that while, right over him she hong,
   With her false eyes fast fixèd in his sight,
   As seeking medicine, whence she was stong,
   Or greedily depasturing delight:
   And oft inclining downe with kisses light,
   For feare of waking him, his lips bedewd,
   And through his humid eyes did sucke his spright,
   Quite molten into lust and pleasure lewd;
Wherewith she sighèd soft, as if his case she rewd.

The whiles some one did chaunt this lovely lay;
   Ah see, who so faire thing doest faine to see,
   In springing flowre the image of thy day;
   Ah see the Virgin Rose, how sweetly shee
   Doth first peepe forth with bashfull modestee,

That fairer seemes, the lesse ye see her may;
Lo see soone after, how more bold and free
Her bared bosome she doth broad display;
Loe see soone after, how she fades, and falles away.

So passeth, in the passing of a day,
  Of mortall life the leafe, the bud, the flowre,
  Ne more doth flourish after first decay,
  That earst was sought to decke both bed and bowre,
  Of many a Ladie, and many a Paramowre:
  Gather therefore the Rose, whilest yet is prime,
  For soone comes age, that will her pride deflowre:
  Gather the Rose of love, whilest yet is time,
Whilest loving thou mayst lovèd be with equall crime.

He ceast, and then gan all the quire of birdes
  Their diverse notes t'attune unto his lay,
  As in approvance of his pleasing words.
  The constant paire heard all, that he did say,
  Yet swarvèd not, but kept their forward way,
  Through many covert groves, and thickets close,
  In which they creeping did at last display
  That wanton Ladie, with her lover lose,
Whose sleepie head she in her lap did soft dispose.

Upon a bed of Roses she was layd,
  As faint through heat, or dight to pleasant sin,
  And was arayd, or rather disarayd,
  All in a vele of silke and silver thin,
  That hid no whit her alablaster skin,
  But rather shewd more white, if more might bee:
  More subtile web *Arachne* cannot spin,
  Nor the fine nets, which oft we woven see
Of scorchèd deaw, do not in th'aire more lightly flee.

Her snowy brest was bare to readie spoyle
  Of hungry eies, which n'ote therewith be fild,
  And yet through languour of her late sweet toyle,
  Few drops, more cleare than Nectar, forth distild,
  That like pure Orient perles adowne it trild,
  And her faire eyes sweet smyling in delight,
  Moystenèd their fierie beames, with which she thrild
  Fraile harts, yet quenchèd not; like starry light
Which sparckling on the silent waves, does seeme more bright.

46   **[Book III, Canto VI, stanzas 39–42]**

Great enimy to it, and to all the rest,
   That in the *Gardin* of *Adonis* springs,
   Is wicked *Time*, who with his scyth addrest,
   Does mow the flowring herbes and goodly things,
   And all their glory to the ground downe flings,
   Where they doe wither, and are fowly mard:
   He flyes about, and with his flaggy wings
   Beates downe both leaves and buds without regard,
Ne ever pittie may relent his malice hard.

Yet pittie often did the gods relent,
   To see so faire things mard, and spoylèd quight:
   And their great mother *Venus* did lament
   The losse of her deare brood, her deare delight:
   Her hart was pierst with pittie at the sight,
   When walking through the Gardin, them she spyde,
   Yet no'te she find redresse for such despight.
   For all that lives, is subject to that law:
All things decay in time, and to their end do draw.

But were it not, that *Time* their troubler is,
   All that in this delightfull Gardin growes,
   Should happie be, and have immortall blis:
   For here all plentie, and all pleasure flowes,
   And sweet love gentle fits emongst them throwes,
   Without fell rancor, or fond gealosie;
   Franckly each paramour his leman knowes,
   Each bird his mate, ne any does envie
Their goodly meriment, and gay felicitie.

There is continuall spring, and harvest there
   Continuall, both meeting at one time:
   For both the boughes doe laughing blossomes beare,
   And with fresh colours decke the wanton Prime,
   And eke attonce the heavy trees they clime,
   Which seeme to labour under their fruits lode:
   The whiles the joyous birdes make their pastime
   Emongst the shadie leaves, their sweet abode,
And their true loves without suspition tell abrode.

47   *Prothalamion*

Calme was the day, and through the trembling ayre,
Sweete breathing *Zephyrus* did softly play

A gentle spirit, that lightly did delay
Hot *Titans* beames, which then did glyster fayre:
When I whom sullein care,
Through discontent of my long fruitlesse stay
In Princes Court, and expectation vayne
Of idle hopes, which still doe fly away,
Like empty shaddowes, did aflict my brayne,
Walkt forth to ease my payne
Along the shoare of silver streaming *Themmes*,
Whose rutty Bancke, the which his River hemmes,
Was paynted all with variable flowers,
And all the meades adornd with daintie gemmes,
Fit to decke maydens bowres,
And crowne their Paramours,
Against the Brydale day, which is not long:
    Sweete *Themmes* runne softly, till I end my Song.

There, in a Meadow, by the Rivers side,
A Flocke of *Nymphes* I chauncèd to espy,
All lovely Daughters of the Flood thereby,
With goodly greenish locks all loose untyde,
As each had bene a Bryde,
And each one had a little wicker basket,
Made of fine twigs entraylèd curiously,
In which they gatherèd flowers to fill their flasket:
And with fine Fingers, cropt full feateously
The tender stalkes on hye.
Of every sort, which in that Meadow grew,
They gatherèd some; the Violet pallid blew,
The little Dazie, that at evening closes,
The virgin Lillie, and the Primrose trew,
With store of vermeil Roses,
To decke their Bridegromes posies,
Against the Brydale day, which was not long:
    Sweete *Themmes* runne softly, till I end my Song.

With that, I saw two Swannes of goodly hewe,
Come softly swimming downe along the Lee;
Two fairer Birds I yet did never see:
The snow which doth the top of *Pindus* strew,
Did never whiter shew,
Nor *Jove* himselfe when he a Swan would be
For love of *Leda*, whiter did appeare:
Yet *Leda* was they say as white as he,
Yet not so white as these, nor nothing neare;
So purely white they were,
That even the gentle streame, the which them bare,
Seem'd foule to them, and bad his billowes spare

To wet their silken feathers, least they might
Soyle their fayre plumes with water not so fayre,
And marre their beauties bright,
That shone as heavens light,
Against their Brydale day, which was not long:
   Sweete *Themmes* runne softly, till I end my Song.

Eftsoones the *Nymphes*, which now had Flowers their fill,
Ran all in haste, to see that silver brood,
As they came floating on the Christal Flood.
Whom when they sawe, they stood amazèd still,
Their wondring eyes to fill,
Them seem'd they never saw a sight so fayre,
Of Fowles so lovely, that they sure did deeme
Them heavenly borne, or to be that same payre
Which through the Skie draw *Venus* silver Teeme,
For sure they did not seeme
To be begot of any earthly Seede,
But rather Angels or of Angels breede:
Yet were they bred of *Somers-heat* they say,
In sweetest Season, when each Flower and weede
The earth did fresh aray,
So fresh they seem'd as day,
Even as their Brydale day, which was not long:
   Sweete *Themmes* runne softly, till I end my Song.

Then forth they all out of their baskets drew,
Great store of Flowers, the honour of the field,
That to the sense did fragrant odours yeild,
All which upon those goodly Birds they threw,
And all the Waves did strew,
That like old *Peneus* Waters they did seeme,
When downe along by pleasant *Tempes* shore
Scattred with Flowres, through *Thessaly* they streeme,
That they appeare through Lillies plenteous store,
Like a Brydes Chamber flore:
Two of those *Nymphes*, meane while, two Garlands bound,
Of freshest Flowres which in that Mead they found,
The which presenting all in trim Array,
Their snowie Foreheads therewithall they crownd,
Whil'st one did sing this Lay,
Prepar'd against that Day,
Against their Brydale day, which was not long:
   Sweete *Themmes* runne softly, till I end my Song.

Ye gentle Birdes, the worlds faire ornament,
And heavens glorie, whom this happie hower

Doth leade unto your lovers blisfull bower,
Joy may you have and gentle hearts content
Of your loves couplement:
And let faire *Venus*, that is Queene of love,
With her heart-quelling Sonne upon you smile,
Whose smile they say, hath vertue to remove
All Loves dislike, and friendships faultie guile
For ever to assoile.
Let endlesse Peace your steadfast hearts accord,
And blessèd Plentie wait upon your bord,
And let your bed with pleasures chast abound,
That fruitfull issue may to you afford,
Which may your foes confound,
And make your joyes redound,
Upon your Brydale day, which is not long:
　　Sweete *Themmes* run softlie, till I end my Song.

So ended she; and all the rest around
To her redoubled that her undersong,
Which said, their bridale daye should not be long.
And gentle Eccho from the neighbour ground,
Their accents did resound.
So forth those joyous Birdes did passe along,
Adowne the Lee, that to them murmurde low,
As he would speake, but that he lackt a tong
Yeat did by signes his glad affection show,
Making his streame run slow.
And all the foule which in his flood did dwell
Gan flock about these twaine, that did excell
The rest, so far, as *Cynthia* doth shend
The lesser starres. So they enrangèd well,
Did on those two attend,
And their best service lend,
Against their wedding day, which was not long:
　　Sweete *Themmes* run softly, till I end my song.

At length they all to mery *London* came,
To mery London, my most kyndly Nurse,
That to me gave this Lifes first native sourse:
Though from another place I take my name,
An house of auncient fame.
There when they came, whereas those bricky towres,
The which on *Themmes* brode agèd backe doe ryde,
Where now the studious Lawyers have their bowers
There whylome wont the Templer Knights to byde,
Till they decayd through pride:

Next whereunto there standes a stately place,
Where oft I gaynèd giftes and goodly grace
Of that great Lord, which therein wont to dwell,
Whose want too well now feeles my freendles case:
But Ah here fits not well
Olde woes but joyes to tell
Against the bridale daye, which is not long:
    Sweete *Themmes* runne softly, till I end my Song.

Yet therein now doth lodge a noble Peer,
Great *Englands* glory and the Worlds wide wonder,
Whose dreadfull name, late through all *Spaine* did thunder,
And *Hercules* two pillors standing neere,
Did make to quake and feare:
Faire branch of Honor, flower of Chevalrie,
That fillest *England* with thy triumphs fame,
Joy have thou of thy noble victorie,
And endlesse happinesse of thine owne name
That promiseth the same:
That through thy prowesse and victorious armes,
Thy country may be freed from forraine harmes:
And great *Elisaes* glorious name may ring
Through al the world, fil'd with thy wide Alarmes,
Which some brave muse may sing
To ages following,
Upon the Brydale day, which is not long:
    Sweete *Themmes* runne softly, till I end my Song.

From those high Towers, this noble Lord issuing,
Like Radiant *Hesper* when his golden hayre
In th'*Ocean* billowes he hath Bathèd fayre,
Descended to the Rivers open vewing,
With a great traine ensuing.
Above the rest were goodly to bee seene
Two gentle Knights of lovely face and feature
Beseeming well the bower of anie Queene,
With gifts of wit and ornaments of nature,
Fit for so goodly stature:
That like the twins of *Jove* they seem'd in sight,
Which decke the Bauldricke of the Heavens bright.
They two forth pacing to the Rivers side,
Receivèd those two faire Brides, their Loves delight,
Which at th'appointed tyde,
Each one did make his Bryde,
Against their Brydale day, which is not long:
    Sweete *Themmes* runne softly, till I end my Song.

FULKE GREVILLE, LORD BROOKE
1554–1628

48   I with whose colors *Myra* drest her head,
I, that ware posies of her owne hand making,
I, that mine owne name in the chimnies read
By *Myra* finely wrought ere I was waking:
    Must I looke on? in hope time comming may
    With change bring backe my turne againe to play.

I, that on Sunday at the Church-stile found,
A Garland sweet, with true-love knots in flowers,
Which I to weare about mine arme was bound,
That each of us might know that all was ours:
    Must I now lead an idle life in wishes?
    And follow *Cupid* for his loaves, and fishes?

I, that did weare the ring her Mother left,
I, for whose love she gloried to be blamèd,
I, with whose eyes her eyes committed theft,
I, who did make her blush when I was namèd;
    Must I lose ring, flowers, blush, theft and go naked,
    Watching with sighs, till dead love be awakèd?

I, that when drowsie *Argus* fell asleep,
Like Jealousie o'rewatchèd with desire,
Was even warnèd modestie to keepe,
While her breath speaking kindled Natures fire:
    Must I looke on a-cold, while others warme them?
    Doe *Vulcans* brothers in such fine nets arme them?

Was it for this that I might *Myra* see?
Washing the water with her beauties, white,
Yet would she never write her love to me;
Thinks wit of change while thoughts are in delight?
    Mad Girles must safely love, as they may leave,
    No man can print a kisse, lines may deceive.

49   Downe in the depth of mine iniquity,
That ugly center of infernall spirits;
Where each sinne feeles her owne deformity,
In these peculiar torments she inherits,
    Depriv'd of humane graces, and divine,
    Even there appeares this *saving God* of mine.

And in this fatall mirrour of transgression,
Shewes man as fruit of his degeneration,
The errours ugly infinite impression,
Which beares the faithlesse downe to desperation;
    Depriv'd of humane graces and divine,
    Even there appeares this *saving God* of mine.

In power and truth, Almighty and eternall,
Which on the sinne reflects strange desolation,
With glory scourging all the Spr'its infernall,
And uncreated hell with unprivation;
    Depriv'd of humane graces, not divine,
    Even there appeares this *saving God* of mine.

For on this sp'rituall Crosse condemnèd lying,
To paines infernall by eternall doome,
I see my Saviour for the same sinnes dying,
And from that hell I fear'd, to free me, come;
    Depriv'd of humane graces, not divine,
    Thus hath his death rais'd up this soule of mine.

50   from *Mustapha*

                          Chorus Sacerdotum

Oh wearisome Condition of Humanity!
Borne under one Law, to another bound:
Vainely begot, and yet forbidden vanity,
Created sicke, commanded to be sound:
What meaneth Nature by these diverse Lawes?
Passion and Reason, selfe-division cause:
Is it the marke, or Majesty of Power
To make offences that it may forgive?
Nature herselfe, doth her owne selfe defloure,
To hate those errors she her selfe doth give.
For how should man thinke that, he may not doe
If Nature did not faile, and punish too?
Tyrant to others, to her selfe unjust,
Onely commands things difficult and hard.
Forbids us all things, which it knowes is lust,
Makes easie paines, unpossible reward.
If Nature did not take delight in blood,
She would have made more easie waies to good.
We that are bound by vowes, and by Promotion,
With pompe of holy Sacrifice and rites,

To teach beleefe in good and still devotion,
To preach of Heavens wonders, and delights:
Yet when each of us, in his owne heart lookes,
He findes the God there, farre unlike his Bookes.

SIR PHILIP SIDNEY

1554–1586

51–2   from *The Countess of Pembroke's Arcadia*

51   My true love hath my hart, and I have his,
              By just exchange, one for the other giv'ne.
              I holde his deare, and myne he cannot misse:
              There never was a better bargaine driv'ne.

              His hart in me, keepes me and him in one,
              My hart in him, his thoughtes and senses guides:
              He loves my hart, for once it was his owne:
              I cherish his, because in me it bides.

              His hart his wound receavèd from my sight:
              My hart was wounded, with his wounded hart,
              For as from me, on him his hurt did light,
              So still me thought in me his hurt did smart:
                  Both equall hurt, in this change sought our blisse:
                  My true love hath my hart and I have his.

52   *Strephon.* Yee Gote-heard Gods, that love the grassie mountaines,
                  Yee Nimphes which haunt the springs in pleasant vallies,
                  Ye Satyrs joyde with free and quiet forrests,
                  Vouchsafe your silent eares to playning musique,
                  Which to my woes gives still an early morning:
                  And drawes the dolor on till wery evening.

      Klaius. O *Mercurie,* foregoer to the evening,
                  O heavenlie huntresse of the savage mountaines,
                  O lovelie starre, entitled of the morning,
                  While that my voice doth fill these wofull vallies,
                  Vouchsafe your silent eares to plaining musique,
                  Which oft hath *Echo* tir'd in secrete forrests.

      Strephon. I that was once free-burges of the forrests,
                  Where shade from Sunne, and sporte I sought in evening,

I that was once esteem'd for pleasant musique,
Am banisht now among the monstrous mountaines
Of huge despaire, and foule affliction's vallies,
Am growne a shrich-owle to my selfe each morning.

Klaius. I that was once delighted every morning,
Hunting the wilde inhabiters of forrests,
I that was once the musique of these vallies,
So darkenèd am, that all my day is evening,
Hart-broken so, that molehilles seeme high mountaines,
And fill the vales with cries in steed of musique.

Strephon. Long since alas, my deadly Swannish musique
Hath made it selfe a crier of the morning,
And hath with wailing strength clim'd highest mountaines:
Long since my thoughts more desert be than forrests:
Long since I see my joyes come to their evening,
And state throwen downe to over-troden vallies.

Klaius. Long since the happie dwellers of these vallies,
Have praide me leave my strange exclaiming musique,
Which troubles their daye's worke, and joyes of evening:
Long since I hate the night, more hate the morning:
Long since my thoughts chase me like beasts in forrests,
And make me wish my selfe layd under mountaines.

Strephon. Me seemes I see the high and stately mountaines,
Transforme themselves to lowe dejected vallies:
Me seemes I heare in these ill-changèd forrests,
The Nightingales doo learne of Owles their musique:
Me seemes I feele the comfort of the morning
Turnde to the mortall sérene of an evening.

Klaius. Me seemes I see a filthie clowdie evening,
As soon as Sunne begins to clime the mountaines:
Me seemes I feele a noysome scent, the morning
When I doo smell the flowers of these vallies:
Me seemes I heare, when I doo heare sweete musique,
The dreadfull cries of murdred men in forrests.

Strephon. I wish to fire the trees of all these forrests;
I give the Sunne a last farewell each evening;
I curse the fidling finders out of Musicke:
With envie I doo hate the loftie mountaines;
And with despite despise the humble vallies:
I doo detest night, evening, day, and morning.

Klaius. Curse to my selfe my prayer is, the morning:
My fire is more, than can be made with forrests;

My state more base, than are the basest vallies:
I wish no evenings more to see, each evening;
Shamèd I hate my selfe in sight of mountaines,
And stoppe mine eares, lest I growe mad with Musicke.

Strephon. For she, whose parts maintainde a perfect musique,
Whose beawties shin'de more than the blushing morning,
Who much did passe in state the stately mountaines,
In straightnes past the Cedars of the forrests,
Hath cast me, wretch, into eternall evening,
By taking her two Sunnes from these darke vallies.

Klaius. For she, with whom compar'd, the Alpes are vallies,
She, whose least word brings from the spheares their musique,
At whose approach the Sunne rase in the evening,
Who, where she went, bare in her forhead morning,
Is gone, is gone from these our spoylèd forrests,
Turning to desarts our best pastur'de mountaines.

Strephon. These mountaines witnesse shall, so shall these vallies,
Klaius. These forrests eke, made wretched by our musique,
Our morning hymne this is, and song at evening.

53   Thou blind man's marke, thou foole's selfe chosen snare,
Fond fancie's scum, and dregs of scattred thought,
Band of all evils, cradle of causelesse care,
Thou web of will, whose end is never wrought;

Desire, desire I have too dearely bought,
With price of mangled mind thy worthlesse ware,
Too long, too long asleepe thou hast me brought,
Who should my mind to higher things prepare.

But yet in vaine thou hast my ruine sought,
In vaine thou madest me to vaine things aspire,
In vaine thou kindlest all thy smokie fire;

For vertue hath this better lesson taught,
Within my selfe to seeke my onelie hire:
Desiring nought but how to kill desire.

54–7   from *Astrophil and Stella*

54   Loving in truth, and faine in verse my love to show,
That the deare She might take some pleasure of my paine:
Pleasure might cause her reade, reading might make her know,
Knowledge might pitie winne, and pitie grace obtaine,
   I sought fit words to paint the blackest face of woe,

Studying inventions fine, her wits to entertaine:
Oft turning others' leaves, to see if thence would flow
Some fresh and fruitfull showers upon my sunne-burn'd braine.
   But words came halting forth, wanting Invention's stay,
Invention, Nature's child, fled step-dame Studie's blowes,
And others' feete still seem'd but strangers in my way.
Thus great with child to speake, and helplesse in my throwes,
   Biting my trewand pen, beating my selfe for spite,
   Foole, said my Muse to me, looke in thy heart and write.

55   With how sad steps, ô Moone, thou climb'st the skies,
        How silently, and with how wanne a face,
        What, may it be that even in heav'nly place
     That busie archer his sharpe arrowes tries?
Sure, if that long with *Love* acquainted eyes
        Can judge of *Love*, thou feel'st a Lover's case;
        I reade it in thy lookes, thy languisht grace,
To me that feele the like, thy state descries.
        Then ev'n of fellowship, ô Moone, tell me
Is constant *Love* deem'd there but want of wit?
Are Beauties there as proud as here they be?
Do they above love to be lov'd, and yet
        Those Lovers scorne whom that *Love* doth possesse?
        Do they call *Vertue* there ungratefulnesse?

56   Come sleepe, ô sleepe, the certaine knot of peace,
        The baiting place of wit, the balme of woe,
        The poore man's wealth, the prisoner's release,
     Th'indifferent Judge betweene the high and low;
        With shield of proofe shield me from out the prease
Of those fierce darts, dispaire at me doth throw:
O make in me those civill warres to cease;
I will good tribute pay if thou do so.
        Take thou of me smooth pillowes, sweetest bed,
A chamber deafe to noise, and blind to light:
A rosie garland, and a wearie hed:
And if these things, as being thine by right,
        Move not thy heavy grace, thou shalt in me,
        Livelier than else-where, *Stella's* image see.

57   Who will in fairest booke of Nature know,
        How Vertue may best lodg'd in beautie be,
        Let him but learne of *Love* to reade in thee,
Stella, those faire lines, which true goodnesse show.

There shall he find all vices' overthrow,
  Not by rude force, but sweetest soveraigntie
  Of reason, from whose light those night-birds flie;
That inward sunne in thine eyes shineth so.
  And not content to be Perfection's heire
Thy selfe, doest strive all minds that way to move,
  Who marke in thee what is in thee most faire.
So while thy beautie drawes the heart to love,
  As fast thy Vertue bends that love to good:
  But ah, Desire still cries, give me some food.

JOHN LYLY

1554?–1606

58   from *Campaspe* [Act I, scene ii]

Song

Granichus. O for a Bowle of fatt Canary,
          Rich Palermo, sparkling Sherry,
          Some Nectar else, from *Juno's* Daiery,
          O these draughts would make us merry.

Psyllus. O for a wench, (I deale in faces,
          And in other dayntier things,)
          Tickled am I with her Embraces,
          Fine dancing in such Fairy Ringes.

Manes. O for a plump fat leg of Mutton,
          Veale, Lambe, Capon, Pigge, and Conney, ·
          None is happy but a Glutton,
          None an Asse but who wants money.

Chorus. Wines (indeed,) and Girles are good,
          But brave victuals feast the bloud,
          For wenches, wine, and Lusty cheere,
          Jove would leape down to surfet heere.

SIR WALTER RALEGH

1554?–1618

59   As you came from the holy land
              Of Walsinghame
          Mett you not with my true love
              By the way as you came.

How shall I know your trew love
That have mett many one
As I went to the holy lande
That have come, that have gone.

She is neyther whyte nor browne
Butt as the heavens fayre
There is none hathe a forme so divine
In the earth or the ayre.

Such an one did I meet, good Sir,
Suche an Angelyke face,
Who lyke a queene, lyke a nymph, did appere
By her gait, by her grace.

She hath lefte me here all alone,
All allone as unknowne,
Who somtymes did me lead with her selfe,
And me lovde as her owne.

Whats the cause that she leaves you alone
And a new waye doth take;
Who loved you once as her owne
And her joye did you make.

I have lovde her all my youth,
Butt now ould, as you see,
Love lykes not the fallyng frute
From the wythered tree.

Know that love is a careless chylld
And forgets promyse past,
He is blynd, he is deaff when he lyste
And in faythe never faste.

His desyre is a dureless contente
And a trustless joye
He is wonn with a world of despayre
And is lost with a toye.

Of women kynde suche indeed is the love
Or the word Love abused
Under which many chyldysh desyres
And conceytes are excusde.

Butt true Love is a durable fyre
In the mynde ever burnynge;
Never sycke, never ould, never dead,
From itt selfe never turnynge.

60   *The Lie*

Goe soule the bodies guest
    Upon a thankelesse arrant,
Feare not to touch the best
    The truth shall be thy warrant.
Goe since I needs must die,
    And give the world the lie.

Say to the Court it glowes
    And shines like rotten wood,
Say to the Church it showes
    What's good, and doth noe good.
If Church and Court reply
    Then give them both thc lie.

Tell Potentates they live
    Acting by others action,
Not loved unlesse they give,
    Not strong but by affection:
If Potentates reply
    Give Potentates the lie.

Tell men of high condition,
    That manage the estate,
Their purpose is ambition,
    Their practise only hate,
And if they once reply
    Then give them all the lie.

Tell them that brave it most,
    They beg for more by spending
Who in their greatest cost
    Seek nothing but commending.
And if they make reply,
    Then give them all the lie.

Tell zeale it wants devotion
    Tell love it is but lust,
Tell time it meets but motion,
    Tell flesh it is but dust.
And wish them not reply
    For thou must give the lie.

Tell age it daily wasteth,
    Tell honor how it alters.
Tell beauty how she blasteth
    Tell favour how it falters
And as they shall reply,
    Give every one the lie.

Tell wit how much it wrangles
   In tickle points of nycenesse,
Tell wisedome she entangles
   Her selfe in over wisenesse.
And when they do reply
   Straight give them both the lie.

Tell Phisick of her boldnes,
   Tell skill it is prevention
Tell charity of coldnes,
   Tell Law it is contention,
And as they doe reply
   So give them still the lie.

Tell Fortune of her blindnesse,
   Tell nature of decay,
Tell friendship of unkindnesse,
   Tell Justice of delay.
And if they wil reply,
   Then give them all the lie.

Tell Arts they have no soundnes,
   But vary by esteeming,
Tell schooles they want profoundnes
   And stand too much on seeming.
If Arts and schooles reply,
   Give arts and schooles the lie.

Tell faith it's fled the Citie,
   Tell how the country erreth
Tell manhood shakes off pitty
   Tell vertue least preferreth,
And if they doe reply,
   Spare not to give the lie.

So when thou hast as I
   Commanded thee, done blabbing,
Although to give the lie,
   Deserves no lesse than stabbing,
Stab at thee, he that will,
   No stab thy soule can kill.

61   Even such is tyme which takes in trust
Our yowth, our Joyes, and all we have,
And payes us butt with age and dust:
Who in the darke and silent grave

When we have wandred all our wayes
Shutts up the storye of our dayes.
And from which earth and grave and dust
The Lord shall rayse me up I trust.

GEORGE PEELE

1556–1596

62–3   from *The Old Wives Tale*

62   When as the Rie reach to the chin,
And chopcherrie chopcherrie ripe within,
Strawberries swimming in the creame,
And schoole boyes playing in the streame:
Then O, then O, then O my true love said,
Till that time come againe,
Shee could not live a maid.

63   *Voice.* Gently dip: but not too deepe;
For feare you make the goulden beard to weepe.

[*A head comes up with eares of Corne, and she combes
them in her lap.*]

Faire maiden white and red,
Combe me smoothe, and stroke my head:
And thou shalt have some cockell bread.
Gently dippe, but not too deepe,
For feare thou make the goulden beard to weep.

[*A head comes up full of golde, she combes it into her lap.*]

Faire maiden, white, and redde,
Combe me smooth, and stroke my head;
And every haire, a sheave shall be,
And every sheave a goulden tree.

64   from *David and Fair Bethsabe*

Hot sunne, coole fire, temperd with sweet aire,
Black shade, fair nurse, shadow my white haire.
Shine sun, burne fire, breathe aire, and ease mee,
Black shade, fair nurse, shroud me and please me.

Shadow (my sweet nurse) keep me from burning,
Make not my glad cause, cause of mourning.
Let not my beauties fire,
Enflame unstaied desire,
Nor pierce any bright eye,
That wandreth lightly.

CHIDIOCK TICHBORNE

1558?–1586

65   My prime of youth is but a froste of cares:
        My feaste of joy, is but a dishe of payne:
        My cropp of corne, is but a field of tares:
        And all my good is but vaine hope of gaine:
        The daye is gone, and yet I sawe no sonn:
        And nowe I live, and nowe my life is donn.

        The springe is past, and yet it hath not sprong
        The frute is deade, and yet the leaves are greene
        My youth is gone, and yet I am but yonge
        I sawe the woorld, and yet I was not seene
        My threed is cutt, and yet it was not sponn
        And nowe I lyve, and nowe my life is donn.

        I saught my death, and founde it in my wombe
        I lookte for life, and sawe it was a shade.
        I trode the earth and knewe it was my Tombe
        And nowe I die, and nowe I am but made
        The glasse is full, and nowe the glass is run
        And nowe I live, and nowe my life is donn.

GEORGE CHAPMAN

1559?–1634

66   from *Homer's Iliads: The Twelfth Book* [lines 308–32]

So far'd divine Sarpedon's mind, resolv'd to force his way
Through all the fore-fights and the wall. Yet, since he did not see
Others as great as he in name, as great in mind as he,
He spake to Glaucus: 'Glaucus, say why are we honord more
Than other men of Lycia in place—with greater store
Of meates and cups, with goodlier roofes, delightsome gardens, walks,
More lands and better, so much wealth that Court and countrie talks

Of us and our possessions and every way we go
Gaze on us as we were their Gods? This where we dwell is so:
The shores of Xanthus ring of this: and shall not we exceed
As much in merit as in noise? Come, be we great in deed
As well as looke, shine not in gold but in the flames of fight,
That so our neat-arm'd Lycians may say: "See, these are right
Our kings, our Rulers: these deserve to eate and drinke the best;
These governe not ingloriously; these thus exceed the rest,
Do more than they command to do." O friend, if keeping backe
Would keepe backe age from us, and death, and that we might not wracke
In this life's humane sea at all, but that deferring now
We shund death ever—nor would I halfe this vaine valour show,
Nor glorifie a folly so, to wish thee to advance:
But, since we must go though not here, and that, besides the chance
Proposd now, there are infinite fates of other sort in death
Which (neither to be fled nor scap't) a man must sinke beneath—
Come, trie we if this sort be ours and either render thus
Glorie to others or make them resigne the like to us.'

[after the Greek of Homer]

67–8   from *Achilles' Shield*

67   [lines 139–75]

        This said, the smith did to his bellowes goe,
    Set them to fire and made his Cyclops blow.
    Full twentie paire breathd through his furnace holes
    All sorts of blastes t'enflame his temperd coles,
    Now blusterd hard and now did contrarise
    As Vulcan would, and, as his exercise
    Might with perfection serve the dame's desire,
    Hard brasse and tinne he cast into the fire,
    High-prisèd gold and silver, and did set
    Within the stocke an anvile bright and great.
    His massie hammer then his right hand held,
    His other hand his gasping tonges compeld.
        And first he forgde a huge and solid Shield
    Which every way did variant artship yeeld,
    Through which he three ambitious circles cast,
    Round and refulgent; and, without, he plac't
    A silver handle. Fivefold proofe it was,
    And in it many thinges with speciall grace
    And passing arteficiall pompe were graven.
    In it was earthe's greene globe, the sea and heaven,

Th'unwearied Sunne, the Moone exactly round
And all the starres with which the skie is crownd,
The Pleiades, the Hyads and the force
Of great Orion, and the Beare, whose course
Turnes her about his Sphere observing him
Surnam'de the Chariot, and doth never swimme
Upon the unmeasur'de Ocean's marble face
Of all the flames that heaven's blew vayle enchace.
    In it two beautious Citties he did build
Of divers-languag'd men. The one was fild
With sacred nuptialles and with solemne feastes
And through the streetes the faire officious guests
Lead from their brydall chambers their faire brides
With golden torches burning by their sides.
Hymen's sweet triumphes were abundant there
Of youthes and damzels dauncing in a Sphere,
Amongst whom masking flutes and harps were heard.

68   [lines 233–94]

    He carvde besides a soft and fruitfull field,
Brode and thrice new tild in that heavenly shield,
Where many plowmen turnd up here and there
The earth in furrowes, and their soveraigne neere
They striv'd to worke: and, every furrow ended,
A bowle of sweetest wine hee still extended
To him that first had done: then turnde they hand,
Desirous to dispatch that peece of land,
Deep and new ear'de; black grew the plough with mould,
Which lookt like blackish earth, though forgd of gold,
And this he did with miracle adorne.
Then made he grow a field of high-sprung corne,
In which did reapers sharpned sickles plie:
Others their handfulles, falne confusedly,
Laid on the ridge together: others bound
Their gatherd handfulles to sheaves hard and round.
Three binders were appointed for the place
And at their heeles did children gleane apace
Whole armefulles, to the binders ministring.
Amongst all these, all silent stood their king
Upon a balke, his Scepter in his hand,
Glad at his heart to see his yeeldie land.
The herraldes then the harvest feast prepare
Beneath an Oke far off, and for their fare
A mightie Oxe was slaine, and women drest
Store of white cakes and mixt the labourers' feast.

In it, besides, a vine yee might behold
Loded with grapes; the leaves were all of gold;
The bunches blacke and thicke did through it growe
And silver props sustainde them from below.
About the vine an azure dike was wrought
And about it a hedge of tinne he brought.
One path went through it, through the which did passe
The vintagers, when ripe their vintage was.
The virgines then and youthes (childishly wise)
For the sweet fruit did painted cuppes devise
And in a circle bore them dauncing round,
In midst whereof a boy did sweetly sound
His silver harpe and with a piercing voyce
Sung a sweete song, when each youth with his choice,
Triumphing over earth, quicke daunces treades.
    A heard of Oxen, thrusting out their heades
And bellowing, from their stalles rushing to feed
Neere a swift flood, raging and crownd with reed,
In gold and tinne he carvèd next the vine,
Foure golden heardsmen following, heard-dogs nine
Waiting on them: in head of all the heard
Two Lyons shooke a Bull, that, bellowing, rearde
In desperate horror and was dragde away:
The dogs and youthes pursude, but their slaine pray
The Lions rent out of his spacious hide
And in their entrailes did his flesh divide,
Lapping his sable blood: the men to fight
Set on their dogges in vaine, that durst not byte
But barckt and backewards flew. He forgde beside,
In a faire vale, a pasture sweete and wide
Of white-fleest sheepe, in which he did impresse
Sheepecotes, sheepfolds and coverd cottages.
    In this rare Shield the famous Vulcan cast
A dauncing maze, like that in ages past
Which in brode Cnossus Dædalus did dresse
For Ariadne with the golden tresse.

                [after the Greek of Homer]

69   from *Homer's Odysses: The Fifth Book* [lines 560–614]

                        While this discourse he held,
            A curst Surge gainst a cutting rocke impeld
            His naked bodie, which it gasht and tore,
            And had his bones broke, if but one sea more

Had cast him on it. But she prompted him
That never faild, and bade him no more swim
Still off and on, but boldly force the shore
And hug the rocke that him so rudely tore.
Which he with both hands sigh'd and claspt till past
The billowes' rage was; which scap't backe, so fast
The rocke repulst it, that it reft his hold,
Sucking him from it, and farre backe he rould.
And as the Polypus that (forc't from home
Amidst the soft sea, and neare rough land come
For shelter gainst the stormes that beate on her
At open sea, as she abroad doth erre)
A deale of gravill and sharpe little stones
Needfully gathers in her hollow bones:
So he forc't hither (by the sharper ill
Shunning the smoother), where he best hop't, still
The worst succeeded: for the cruell friend,
To which he clingd for succour, off did rend
From his broad hands the soken flesh so sore
That off he fell and could sustaine no more.
Quite under water fell he, and, past Fate,
Haplesse Ulysses there had lost the state
He held in life, if (still the grey-eyd Maid
His wisedome prompting) he had not assaid
Another course and ceast t'attempt that shore,
Swimming, and casting round his eye, t'explore
Some other shelter. Then the mouth he found
Of faire Callicoe's flood, whose shores were crownd
With most apt succors—rocks so smooth they seemd
Polisht of purpose, land that quite redeemd
With breathlesse coverts th'other's blasted shores.
The flood he knew, and thus in heart implores:
'King of this River, heare! Whatever name
Makes thee invokt, to thee I humbly frame
My flight from Neptune's furies. Reverend is
To all the ever-living Deities
What erring man soever seekes their aid.
To thy both flood and knees a man dismaid
With varied sufferance sues. Yeeld then some rest
To him that is thy suppliant profest.'
    This (though but spoke in thought) the Godhead heard,
Her Current strait staid, and her thicke waves cleard
Before him, smooth'd her waters, and just where
He praid, halfe drownd, entirely sav'd him there.
    Then forth he came, his both knees faltring, both
His strong hands hanging downe, and all with froth

His cheeks and nosthrils flowing, voice and breath
Spent to all use; and downe he sunke to Death.
The sea had soakt his heart through: all his vaines
His toiles had rackt t'a labouring woman's paines.
Dead wearie was he.

[after the Greek of Homer]

SIR JOHN HARINGTON
1560–1612

70   from Ariosto's *Orlando Furioso*
          [The Twenty-Eighth Book, stanzas 55–65]

The masters go abrod to vew the towne
And first the Churches for devotions sake
And then the monuments of most renowne
As travellers a common custome take.
The girle within the chamber sate her downe,
The men are busied, some the beds do make,
Some care to dresse their wearide horse, and some
Make readie meat against their masters come.

In this same house the girle a Greeke had spide
That in her fathers house a boy had been
And slept full often sweetlie by her side,
And much good sport had passèd them between;
Yet fearing least their love should be discride,
In open talke they durst not to be seen,
But when by hap the pages downe were gone,
Old love renewd, and thus they talke thereon.

The Greeke demaunds her whither she was going
And which of these two great estates her keeps.
She told them all, she needs no further wooing,
And how a night between them both she sleeps.
Ah (quoth the Greeke) thou tellest my undoing,
My deare *Fiametta*, and with that he weeps;
With these two Lords wilt thou from Spaine be banishèd?
Are all my hopes thus into nothing vanishèd?

My sweet designments turnèd are to sour,
My service long finds litle recompence.
I made a stock according to my power
By hoording up my wages and the pence

That guests did give that came in luckie hower.
I ment ere long to have departed hence
And to have askt thy sires goodwill to marry thee,
And that obtain, unto a house to carrie thee.

The wentch of her hard fortune doth complaine
And saith that now she doubts he sues too late.
The Greeke doth sigh and sob and part doth faine,
And shall I dye (quoth he) in this estate?
Let me enjoy thy sweetnes once againe
Before my dayes draw to their dolfull date.
One small refreshing ere we quite depart
Will make me dye with more contented hart.

The girle with pittie movèd thus replies:
Thinke not (quoth she) but I desire the same,
But hard it is among so many eyes
Without incurring punishment and shame.
Ah (quoth the Greeke) some means thou wouldst devise,
If thou but felt a quarter of my flame,
To meet this night in some convenient place
And be togither but a litle space.

Tush (aunswerd she) you sue now out of season,
For ev'ry night I lye betwixt them two,
And they will quicklie feare and find the treason,
Sith still with one of them I have to do.
Well (quoth the Greek) I could refute that reason
If you would put your helping hand thereto.
You must (said he) some pretie 'scuse devise
And finde occasion from them both to rise.

She first bethinks her selfe, and after bade
He should return when all were sound a sleepe,
And learnèd him, who was thereof right glad,
To go and come, what order he should keepe.
Now came the Greeke, as he his lesson had,
When all was husht, as soft as he could creepe,
First to the dore, which opend when he pushèd,
Then to the chamber which was softlie rushèd.

He takes a long and leysurable stride,
And longest on the hinder foote he staid;
So soft he treads, although his stepps were wide,
As though to tread on eggs he were affraid;
And as he goes, he gropes on either side
To find the bed with hands abroad displaid,
And having found the bottom of the bed,
He creepeth in, and forward go'th his head.

Betweene *Fiamettas* tender thighes he came
That lay upright as readie to receave.
At last they fell unto their merry game,
Embracing sweetly now to take their leave.
He rodc in post, ne can he bait for shame;
The beast was good and would not him deceave:
He thinks her pace so easie and so sure
That all the night to ride he could endure.

Jocundo and the King do both perceave
The bed to rock as oft it comes to passe,
And both of them one error did deceave,
For either thought it his companion was.
Now hath the Greeke taken his latter leave,
And as he came he back againe doth passe,
And Phebus beames did now to shine begin;
Fiametta rose and let the pages in.

[after the Italian of Ariosto]

71   *Of Treason*

Treason doth never prosper, what's the reason?
For if it prosper, none dare call it Treason.

MARY HERBERT, COUNTESS OF PEMBROKE
1561–1621

72   *Psalm 117. Laudate Dominum*

P raise him that ay
R emaines the same:
A ll tongues display
I ehovas fame.
S ing all that share
T his earthly ball:
H is mercies are
E xpos'd to all:
L ike as the word
O nce he doth give,
R old in recórd,
D oth tyme outlive.

[after the Hebrew of the Psalms]

73   *Psalm 120. Ad Dominum*

As to th'Eternall often in anguishes
Erst have I callèd, never unanswerèd,
Againe I call, againe I calling
Doubt not againe to receave an answer.

Lord ridd my soule from treasonous eloquence
Of filthy forgers craftily fraudulent:
And from the tongue where lodg'd resideth
Poison'd abuse, ruine of beleevers.

Thou that reposest vainly thy confidence
In wily wronging; say by thy forgery
What good to thee? what gaine redoundeth?
What benefitt from a tongue deceitfull?

Though like an arrow strongly deliverèd
It deeply pierce, though like to a Juniper
It coales doe cast, which quickly firèd,
Flame very hott, very hardly quenching?

Ah God! too long heere wander I banishèd,
Too long abiding barbarous injury:
With Kedar and with Mesech harbour'd,
How? in a tent, in a howslesse harbour.

Too long, alas, too long have I dwellèd here
With frendly peaces furious enemies:
Who when to peace I seeke to call them,
Faster I find to the warre they arme them.

[after the Hebrew of the Psalms]

ANONYMOUS

1604

[formerly attributed to SIR WALTER RALEGH]

74   *The passionate mans Pilgrimage*

Supposed to be Written by One at the Point of Death

Give me my Scallop shell of quiet,
My staffe of Faith to walke upon,
My Scrip of Joy, Immortall diet,
My bottle of salvation:

My Gowne of Glory, hopes true gage,
And thus Ile take my pilgrimage.

Blood must be my bodies balmer,
No other balme will there be given
Whilst my soule like a white Palmer
Travels to the land of heaven,
Over the silver mountaines,
Where spring the Nectar fountaines:
And there Ile kisse
The Bowle of blisse,
And drink my eternall fill
On every milken hill.
My soule will be a-dry before,
But after it, will nere thirst more.

And by the happie blisfull way
More peacefull Pilgrims I shall see,
That have shooke off their gownes of clay,
And goe appareld fresh like mee.
Ile bring them first
To slake their thirst,
And then to tast those Nectar suckets
At the cleare wells
Where sweetnes dwells,
Drawne up by Saints in Christall buckets.

And when our bottles and all we,
Are fill'd with immortalitie:
Then the holy paths we'll travell
Strewde with Rubies thicke as gravell,
Ceilings of Diamonds, Saphire floores,
High walles of Corall and Pearle Bowres.

From thence to heavens Bribeless hall
Where no corrupted voyces brall,
No Conscience molten into gold,
Nor forg'd accusers bought and sold,
No cause deferd, nor vaine spent Journey,
For there Christ is the Kings Atturney:
Who pleades for all without degrees,
And he hath Angells, but no fees.

When the grand twelve million Jury,
Of our sinnes and sinfull fury,
Gainst our soules blacke verdicts give,
Christ pleades his death, and then we live,

Be thou my speaker taintless pleader,
Unblotted Lawyer, true proceeder,
Thou movest salvation even for almes:
Not with a bribèd Lawyers palmes.

And this is my eternall plea,
To him that made Heaven, Earth and Sea,
Seeing my flesh must die so soone,
And want a head to dine next noone,
Just at the stroke when my vaines start and spred
Set on my soule an everlasting head.
Then am I readie like a palmer fit,
To tread those blest paths which before I writ.

ST ROBERT SOUTHWELL

1561–1595

75   *The burning Babe*

As I in hoarie Winters night stoode shivering in the snow,
Surpris'd I was with sodaine heate, which made my hart to glow;
And lifting up a fearefull eye, to view what fire was neare,
A pretty Babe all burning bright did in the ayre appeare;
Who scorchèd with excessive heate, such floods of teares did shed,
As though his floods should quench his flames, which with his teares
        were fed:
Alas (quoth he) but newly borne, in fierie heates I frie,
Yet none approach to warme their harts or feele my fire, but I;
My faultlesse breast the furnace is, the fuell wounding thornes:
Love is the fire, and sighs the smoake, the ashes, shame and scornes;
The fewell Justice layeth on, and Mercie blowes the coales,
The mettall in this furnace wrought, are mens defilèd soules:
For which, as now on fire I am to worke them to their good,
So will I melt into a bath, to wash them in my blood.
With this he vanisht out of sight, and swiftly shrunk away,
And straight I callèd unto minde, that it was Christmasse day.

76   *The Nativitie of Christ*

Beholde the father, is his daughters sonne:
The bird that built the nest, is hatched therein:
The olde of yeares, an houre hath not out runne:
Eternall life, to live doth now beginne.
The word is dumme: the mirth of heaven doth weepe:
Might feeble is: and force doth faintly creepe.

O dying soules, beholde your living spring:
O dasled eyes, behold your sonne of grace:
Dull eares, attend what word this word doth bring:
Up heavie hartes: with joye your joye embrace.
From death, from darke, from deafenesse, from dispaires:
This life, this light, this word, this joy repaires.

Gift better than himselfe, God doth not know:
Gift better than his God, no man can see:
This gift doth here the gever geven bestow:
Gift to this gift let each receiver bee.
God is my gift, himselfe he freely gave me:
Gods gift am I, and none but God shall have me.

Man altered was by sinne from man to beast:
Beastes foode is haye, haye is all mortall flesh:
Now God is flesh, and lies in Manger prest:
As haye, the brutest sinner to refresh.
O happie fielde wherein this fodder grew,
Whose tast, doth us from beasts to men renew.

77 *A childe my Choyce*

Let folly praise that fancie loves, I praise and love that child,
Whose hart, no thought: whose tong, no word: whose hand no deed
   defiled.
I praise him most, I love him best, all praise and love is his:
While him I love, in him I live, and cannot live amisse.

Loves sweetest mark, Laudes highest theme, mans most desired
   light:
To love him, life: to leave him, death: to live in him, delight.
He mine, by gift: I his, by debt: thus each, to other due:
First friend he was: best friend he is: all times will try him true.

Though young, yet wise: though smal, yet strong: though man, yet
   God he is:
As wise, he knowes: as strong, he can: as God, he loves to blisse.
His knowledge rules: his strength, defends: his love, doth cherish all:
His birth, our Joye: his life, our light: his death, our end of thrall.

Alas, he weepes, he sighes, he pants, yeat doo his Angels sing:
Out of his teares, his sighes and throbs, doth bud a joyfull spring.
Almightie babe, whose tender armes can force all foes to flie:
Correct my faultes, protect my life, direct me when I die.

MARK ALEXANDER BOYD
1563–1601

78   *Sonet*

Fra banc to banc fra wod to wod I rin
Ourhailit with my feble fantasie
Lyc til a leif that fallis from a trie
Or til a reid ourblawin with the wind.
Twa gods gyds me, the ane of tham is blind,   5
Ye and a bairn brocht up in vanitie.
The nixt a wyf ingenrit of the se,
And lichter nor a dauphin with hir fin.
Unhappie is the man for evirmaire
That teils the sand and sawis in the aire,   10
Bot twyse unhappier is he I lairn
That feidis in his hairt a mad desyre,
And follows on a woman throw the fyre
Led be a blind and teichit be a bairn.

ANONYMOUS
[formerly attributed to QUEEN ELIZABETH]

79   He was the Word that spake it,
Hee tooke the bread and brake it;
And what that Word did make it,
I doe beleeve and take it.

SAMUEL DANIEL
1563–1619

80   Care-charmer sleepe, sonne of the Sable night,
Brother to death, in silent darknes borne:
Relieve my languish, and restore the light,
With darke forgetting of my cares returne.
And let the day be time enough to morne
The shipwrack of my ill-adventred youth:
Let waking eyes suffice to wayle theyr scorne,
Without the torment of the nights untruth.

Cease dreames, th'ymagery of our day desires,
To modell foorth the passions of the morrow:
Never let rysing Sunne approve you lyers,
To adde more griefe to aggravat my sorrow.
  Still let me sleepe, imbracing clowdes in vaine;
  And never wake, to feele the dayes disdayne.

81   *Ulisses and the Syren*

Syren. Come worthy Greeke, *Ulisses* come
         Possesse these shores with me:
         The windes and Seas are troublesome,
         And heere we may be free.
           Here may we sit, and view their toile
         That travaile in the deepe,
         And joy the day in mirth the while,
         And spend the night in sleepe.

Ulisses. Faire Nimph, if fame, or honor were
         To be attaynd with ease
         Then would I come, and rest me there,
         And leave such toyles as these.
           But here it dwels, and here must I
         With danger seeke it forth,
         To spend the time luxuriously
         Becomes not men of worth.

Syren. *Ulisses*, O be not deceiv'd
         With that unreall name:
         This honour is a thing conceiv'd,
         And rests on others fame.
           Begotten onely to molest
         Our peace, and to beguile
         (The best thing of our life) our rest,
         And give us up to toile.

Ulisses. Delicious Nimph, suppose there were
         Nor honour, nor report,
         Yet manlines would scorne to weare
         The time in idle sport.
           For toyle doth give a better touch,
         To make us feele our joy;
         And ease findes tediousnesse as much
         As labour yeelds annoy.

Syren. Then pleasure likewise seemes the shore,
         Whereto tends all your toyle,
         Which you forgo to make it more,
         And perish oft the while.

Who may disporte them diversly,
Finde never tedious day,
And ease may have varietie,
As well as action may.

Ulisses. But natures of the noblest frame
These toyles, and dangers please,
And they take comfort in the same,
As much as you in ease.
    And with the thought of actions past
Are recreated still;
When pleasure leaves a touch at last,
To shew that it was ill.

Syren. That doth opinion onely cause,
That's out of custome bred,
Which makes us many other lawes
Than ever Nature did.
    No widdowes waile for our delights,
Our sportes are without bloud,
The world we see by warlike wights
Receives more hurt than good.

Ulisses. But yet the state of things require
These motions of unrest,
And these great Spirits of high desire,
Seeme borne to turne them best.
    To purge the mischiefes that increase,
And all good order mar:
For oft we see a wicked peace
To be well chang'd for war.

Syren. Well, well *Ulisses* then I see,
I shall not have thee heere,
And therefore I will come to thee,
And take my fortunes there.
    I must be wonne that cannot win,
Yet lost were I not wonne:
For beauty hath created bin,
T'undoo, or be undonne.

MICHAEL DRAYTON

1563–1631

82   Since ther's no helpe, Come let us kisse and part,
Nay, I have done: You get no more of Me,
And I am glad, yea glad with all my heart,
That thus so cleanly, I my Selfe can free.

Shake hands for ever, Cancell all our Vowes,
And when We meet at any time againe,
Be it not seene in either of our Browes,
That We one jot of former Love retayne;
Now at the last gaspe, of Loves latest Breath,
When his Pulse fayling, Passion speechlesse lies,
When Faith is kneeling by his bed of Death,
And Innocence is closing up his Eyes,
    Now if thou would'st, when all have given him over,
    From Death to Life, thou might'st him yet recover.

CHRISTOPHER MARLOWE
1564–1593

83   *The Passionate Shepherd to His Love*

Come live with mee, and be my love,
And we will all the pleasures prove,
That Vallies, groves, hills and fieldes,
Woods, or steepie mountaine yeeldes.

And wee will sit upon the Rocks,
Seeing the Sheepheards feede theyr flocks,
By shallow Rivers, to whose falls,
Melodious byrds sing Madrigalls.

And I will make thee beds of Roses,
And a thousand fragrant posies,
A cap of flowers, and a kirtle,
Imbroydred all with leaves of Mirtle.

A gowne made of the finest wooll,
Which from our pretty Lambes we pull,
Fayre linèd slippers for the cold:
With buckles of the purest gold.

A belt of straw, and Ivie buds,
With Corall clasps and Amber studs,
And if these pleasures may thee move,
Come live with mee, and be my love.

The Sheepheards Swaines shall daunce and sing,
For thy delight each May-morning.
If these delights thy minde may move;
Then live with mee, and be my love.

84–5   from *Hero and Leander*

84   [Sestiad I, lines 61–90]

His bodie was as straight as *Circes* wand,
Jove might have sipt out *Nectar* from his hand.
Even as delicious meat is to the tast,
So was his necke in touching, and surpast
The white of *Pelops* shoulder. I could tell ye,
How smooth his brest was, and how white his bellie,
And whose immortall fingars did imprint
That heavenly path, with many a curious dint,
That runs along his backe, but my rude pen,
Can hardly blazon foorth the loves of men,
Much lesse of powerfull gods. Let it suffise,
That my slacke muse, sings of *Leanders* eies,
Those orient cheekes and lippes, exceeding his
That leapt into the water for a kis
Of his owne shadow, and despising many,
Died ere he could enjoy the love of any.
Had wilde *Hippolitus, Leander* seene,
Enamourèd of his beautie had he beene,
His presence made the rudest paisant melt,
That in the vast uplandish countrie dwelt,
The barbarous *Thratian* soldier moov'd with nought,
Was moov'd with him, and for his favour sought.
Some swore he was a maid in mans attire,
For in his lookes were all that men desire,
A pleasant smiling cheeke, a speaking eye,
A brow for Love to banquet roiallye,
And such as knew he was a man would say,
Leander, thou art made for amorous play:
Why art thou not in love, and lov'd of all?
Though thou be faire, yet be not thine owne thrall.

85   [Sestiad II, lines 263–324]

And as her silver body downeward went,
With both her hands she made the bed a tent,
And in her owne mind thought her selfe secure,
O'recast with dim and darksome coverture.
And now she lets him whisper in her eare,
Flatter, intreat, promise, protest and sweare,

Yet ever as he greedily assayd
To touch those dainties, she the *Harpey* playd,
And every lim did as a soldier stout,
Defend the fort, and keep the foe-man out.
For though the rising yv'rie mount he scal'd,
Which is with azure circling lines empal'd,
Much like a globe, (a globe may I tearme this,
By which love sailes to regions full of blis,)
Yet there with *Sysiphus* he toyld in vaine,
Till gentle parlie did the truce obtaine.
Wherein *Leander* on her quivering brest,
Breathlesse spoke some thing, and sigh'd out the rest;
Which so prevail'd, as he with small ado,
Inclos'd her in his armes and kist her too.
And everie kisse to her was as a charme,
And to *Leander* as a fresh alarme.
So that the truce was broke, and she alas,
(Poore sillie maiden) at his mercie was.
Love is not ful of pittie (as men say)
But deaffe and cruell, where he meanes to prey.
Even as a bird, which in our hands we wring,
Foorth plungeth, and oft flutters with her wing,
She trembling strove, this strife of hers (like that
Which made the world) another world begat,
Of unknowne joy. Treason was in her thought,
And cunningly to yeeld her selfe she sought.
Seeming not woon, yet woon she was at length,
In such warres women use but halfe their strength.
Leander now like Theban *Hercules*,
Entred the orchard of *Th'esperides*,
Whose fruit none rightly can describe, but hee
That puls or shakes it from the golden tree:
And now she wisht this night were never done,
And sigh'd to thinke upon th'approching sunne,
For much it greev'd her that the bright day-light,
Should know the pleasure of this blessèd night,
And them like *Mars* and *Ericine* displayd,
Both in each others armes chaind as they layd.
Againe she knew not how to frame her looke,
Or speake to him who in a moment tooke
That which so long so charily she kept,
And faine by stealth away she would have crept,
And to some corner secretly have gone,
Leaving *Leander* in the bed alone.
But as her naked feet were whipping out,
He on the suddaine cling'd her so about,

That Meremaid-like unto the floore she slid,
One halfe appear'd, the other halfe was hid.
Thus neere the bed she blushing stood upright,
And from her countenance behold ye might,
A kind of twilight breake, which through the haire,
As from an orient cloud, glymse here and there.
And round about the chamber this false morne,
Brought foorth the day before the day was borne.
So *Heroes* ruddie cheeke, *Hero* betrayd,
And her all naked to his sight displayd.

from *Ovid's Elegies*

86 ## [Book I, Elegia 5]

Corinnæ concubitus

In summers heate, and midtime of the day,
To rest my limbes, uppon a bedde I lay,
One window shut, the other open stood,
Which gave such light, as twincles in a wood,
Like twilight glimps at setting of the sunne,
Or night being past, and yet not day begunne.
Such light to shamefaste maidens must be showne,
Where they may sport, and seeme to be unknowne.
Then came *Corinna* in a long loose gowne,
Her white necke hid with tresses hanging downe,
Resembling faire *Semiramis* going to bed,
Or *Layis* of a thousand wooers sped.
I snatcht her gowne: being thin, the harme was small,
Yet strivde she to be coverèd therewithall,
And striving thus as one that would be cast,
Betrayde her selfe, and yeelded at the last.
Starke naked as she stood before mine eie,
Not one wen in her bodie could I spie,
What armes and shoulders did I touch and see,
How apt her breasts were to be prest by me,
How smoothe a bellie, under her waste sawe I,
How large a legge, and what a lustie thigh?
To leave the rest, all likt me passing well,
I clingèd her naked bodie, downe she fell,
Judge you the rest, being tyrde she bad me kisse.
Jove send me more such afternoones as this.

[after the Latin of Ovid]

87   from *The Second Part of Tamburlaine the Great*
                    [Act II, scene iv, lines 1–38]

[*The Arras is drawn and* Zenocrate *lies in her bed of state,* Tamburlaine *sitting by her: three Physicians about her bed, tempering potions.* Theridamas, Techelles, Usumcasane, *and the three sonnes.*]

    Tamburlaine. Blacke is the beauty of the brightest day,
    The golden balle of heavens eternal fire,
    That danc'd with glorie on the silver waves,
    Now wants the fewell that enflamde his beames:
    And all with faintnesse and for foule disgrace,
    He bindes his temples with a frowning cloude,
    Ready to darken earth with endlesse night:
    Zenocrate that gave him light and life,
    Whose eies shot fire from their Ivory bowers,
    And temperèd every soule with lively heat,
    Now by the malice of the angry Skies,
    Whose jealousie admits no second Mate,
    Drawes in the comfort of her latest breath
    All dasled with the hellish mists of death.
    Now walk the angels on the walles of heaven,
    As Centinels to warne th'immortall soules,
    To entertaine devine *Zenocrate.*
    Apollo, Cynthia, and the ceaslesse lamps
    That gently look'd upon this loathsome earth,
    Shine downwards now no more, but deck the heavens
    To entertaine divine *Zenocrate.*
    The christall springs whose taste illuminates
    Refinèd eies with an eternall sight,
    Like trièd silver runs through Paradice
    To entertaine divine *Zenocrate.*
    The Cherubins and holy Seraphins
    That sing and play before the king of kings,
    Use all their voices and their instruments
    To entertaine divine *Zenocrate.*
    And in this sweet and currious harmony,
    The God that tunes this musicke to our soules,
    Holds out his hand in highest majesty
    To entertaine divine *Zenocrate.*
    Then let some holy trance convay my thoughts,
    Up to the pallace of th'imperiall heaven:
    That this my life may be as short to me
    As are the daies of sweet *Zenocrate*:
    Physicians, wil no phisicke do her good?

88   from *Doctor Faustus* [Act V, scene ii, lines 1926–82]

[*The Clock strikes eleven.*]

Faustus. Ah *Faustus,*
Now hast thou but one bare houre to live,
And then thou must be damn'd perpetually.
Stand still you ever moving Spheares of heaven,
That time may cease, and midnight never come.
Faire natures eye, rise, rise againe and make
Perpetuall day: or let this houre be but
A yeare, a month, a weeke, a naturall day,
That *Faustus* may repent, and save his soule.
O lente lente currite noctis equi:
The Stars move still, Time runs, the Clocke will strike,
The devill will come, and *Faustus* must be damn'd.
O I'le leape up to my God: who puls me downe?
See see where Christs bloud streames in the firmament,
One drop would save my soule, halfe a drop, ah my Christ.
Rend not my heart, for naming of my Christ,
Yet will I call on him: O spare me *Lucifer.*
Where is it now? 'tis gone. And see where God
Stretcheth out his Arme, and bends his irefull Browes:
Mountaines and Hils, come, come, and fall on me,
And hide me from the heavy wrath of God.
No, no?
Then will I headlong run into the earth:
Gape earth; O no, it will not harbour me.
You Starres that raign'd at my nativity,
Whose influence hath allotted death and hell;
Now draw up *Faustus* like a foggy mist,
Into the entrals of yon labouring cloud,
That when you vomite forth into the aire,
My limbes may issue from your smoky mouthes,
So that my soule may but ascend to heaven.
[*The Watch strikes.*]
Ah halfe the houre is past: 'twill all be past anone:
O God, if thou wilt not have mercy on my soule,
Yet for Christs sake, whose bloud hath ransom'd me,
Impose some end to my incessant paine:
Let *Faustus* live in hell a thousand yeares,
A hundred thousand, and at last be sav'd.
No end is limited to damnèd soules.
Why wert thou not a creature wanting soule?
Or why is this immortall that thou hast?
Ah *Pythagoras Metemsycosis*; were that true,

This soule should flie from me, and I be chang'd
Unto some brutish beast.
All beasts are happy, for when they die,
Their soules are soone dissolv'd in elements,
But mine must live still to be plagu'd in hell.
Curst be the parents that ingendred me;
No *Faustus*, curse thy selfe, curse *Lucifer*,
That hath depriv'd thee of the joies of heaven.
                         [*The clocke striketh twelve.*]
It strikes, it strikes; now body turne to aire,
Or *Lucifer* will beare thee quicke to hell.
O soule be chang'd into little water drops,
And fall into the Ocean, ne're be found.
                    [*Thunder, and enter the devils.*]
My God, my God, looke not so fierce on me;
Adders and serpents, let me breathe a while:
Ugly hell gape not; come not *Lucifer*,
I'le burne my bookes; ah *Mephostophilis*.
                              [*Exeunt with him.*]

WILLIAM SHAKESPEARE

1564–1616

89   *The Phœnix and Turtle*

Let the bird of lowdest lay,
On the sole *Arabian* tree,
Herauld sad and trumpet be:
To whose sound chaste wings obay.

But thou shriking harbinger,
Foule precurrer of the fiend,
Augour of the fevers end,
To this troupe come thou not neere.

From this Session interdict
Every foule of tyrant wing,
Save the Eagle feath'red King,
Keepe the obsequie so strict.

Let the Priest in Surples white,
That defunctive Musicke can,
Be the death-devining Swan,
Lest the *Requiem* lacke his right.

And thou treble dated Crow,
That thy sable gender mak'st,
With the breath thou giv'st and tak'st,
Mongst our mourners shalt thou go.

Here the Antheme doth commence,
Love and Constancie is dead,
Phœnix and the *Turtle* fled,
In a mutuall flame from hence.

So they loved as love in twaine,
Had the essence but in one,
Two distincts, Division none,
Number there in love was slaine.

Hearts remote, yet not asunder;
Distance and no space was seene,
Twixt this *Turtle* and his Queene;
But in them it were a wonder.

So betweene them Love did shine,
That the *Turtle* saw his right,
Flaming in the *Phœnix* sight;
Either was the others mine.

Propertie was thus appallèd,
That the selfe was not the same:
Single Natures double name,
Neither two nor one was callèd.

Reason in it selfe confounded,
Saw Division grow together,
To themselves yet either neither,
Simple were so well compounded.

That it cried, how true a twaine,
Seemeth this concordant one,
Love hath Reason, Reason none,
If what parts, can so remaine.

Whereupon it made this *Threne*,
To the *Phœnix* and the *Dove*,
Co-supremes and starres of Love,
As *Chorus* to their Tragique Scene.

THRENOS

Beautie, Truth, and Raritie,
Grace in all simplicitie,
Here enclosde, in cinders lie.

Death is now the *Phœnix* nest,
And the *Turtles* loyall brest,
To eternitie doth rest.

Leaving no posteritie,
Twas not their infirmitie,
It was married Chastitie.

Truth may seeme, but cannot be,
Beautie bragge, but tis not she,
Truth and Beautie buried be.

To this urne let those repaire,
That are either true or faire,
For these dead Birds, sigh a prayer.

90–100   from the *Sonnets*

90   *Sonnet 18*

Shall I compare thee to a Summers day?
Thou art more lovely and more temperate:
Rough windes do shake the darling buds of Maie,
And Sommers lease hath all too short a date:
Sometime too hot the eye of heaven shines,
And often is his gold complexion dimm'd,
And every faire from faire some-time declines,
By chance, or natures changing course untrim'd:
But thy eternall Sommer shall not fade,
Nor lose possession of that faire thou ow'st,
Nor shall death brag thou wandr'st in his shade,
When in eternall lines to time thou grow'st,
    So long as men can breathe or eyes can see,
    So long lives this, and this gives life to thee.

91   *Sonnet 53*

What is your substance, whereof are you made,
That millions of strange shaddowes on you tend?
Since every one, hath every one, one shade,
And you but one, can every shaddow lend:
Describe *Adonis* and the counterfet
Is poorely immitated after you,

On *Hellens* cheeke all art of beautie set,
And you in *Grecian* tires are painted new:
Speake of the spring, and foison of the yeare,
The one doth shaddow of your beautie show,
The other as your bountie doth appeare,
And you in every blessèd shape we know.
   In all externall grace you have some part,
   But you like none, none you for constant heart.

92   *Sonnet 55*

Not marble, nor the guilded monuments
Of Princes shall out-live this powrefull rime,
But you shall shine more bright in these conténts
Than unswept stone, besmeer'd with sluttish time.
When wastefull warre shall *Statues* over-turne,
And broiles roote out the worke of masonry,
Nor *Mars* his sword, nor warres quick fire shall burne
The living record of your memory.
Gainst death, and all oblivious enmity
Shall you pace forth, your praise shall stil finde roome,
Even in the eyes of all posterity
That weare this world out to the ending doome.
   So til the judgement that your selfe arise,
   You live in this, and dwell in lovers eies.

93   *Sonnet 60*

Like as the waves make towards the pibled shore,
So do our minuites hasten to their end,
Each changing place with that which goes before,
In sequent toile all forwards do contend.
Nativity once in the maine of light
Crawles to maturity, wherewith being crown'd,
Crooked eclipses gainst his glory fight,
And time that gave, doth now his gift confound.
Time doth transfixe the florish set on youth,
And delves the paralels in beauties brow,
Feedes on the rarities of natures truth,
And nothing stands but for his sieth to mow.
   And yet to times in hope, my verse shall stand
   Praising thy worth, dispight his cruell hand.

94   *Sonnet 73*

That time of yeeare thou maist in me behold,
When yellow leaves, or none, or few doe hange
Upon those boughes which shake against the cold,
Bare ruin'd quiers, where late the sweet birds sang.
In me thou seest the twi-light of such day,
As after Sun-set fadeth in the West,
Which by and by blacke night doth take away,
Deaths second selfe that seals up all in rest.
In me thou seest the glowing of such fire,
That on the ashes of his youth doth lye,
As the death bed, whereon it must expire,
Consum'd with that which it was nurrisht by.
      This thou percev'st, which makes thy love more strong,
      To love that well, which thou must leave ere long.

95   *Sonnet 86*

Was it the proud full saile of his great verse,
Bound for the prize of (all too precious) you,
That did my ripe thoughts in my braine inhearse,
Making their tombe the wombe wherein they grew?
Was it his spirit, by spirits taught to write,
Above a mortall pitch, that struck me dead?
No, neither he, nor his compiers by night
Giving him ayde, my verse astonishèd.
He nor that affable familiar ghost
Which nightly gulls him with intelligence,
As victors of my silence cannot boast,
I was not sick of any feare from thence.
      But when your countinance fild up his line,
      Then lackt I matter, that infeebled mine.

96   *Sonnet 94*

They that have power to hurt, and will doe none,
That doe not do the thing, they most do showe,
Who moving others, are themselves as stone,
Unmoovèd, cold, and to temptation slow:

They rightly do inherrit heavens graces,
And husband natures ritches from expence,
They are the Lords and owners of their faces,
Others, but stewards of their excellence:
The sommers flowre is to the sommer sweet,
Though to it selfe, it onely live and die,
But if that flowre with base infection meete,
The basest weed out-braves his dignity:
　　For sweetest things turne sowrest by their deedes,
　　Lillies that fester, smell far worse than weeds.

97　　　　　　*Sonnet 116*

Let me not to the marriage of true mindes
Admit impediments, love is not love
Which alters when it alteration findes,
Or bends with the remover to remove.
O no, it is an ever fixèd marke
That lookes on tempests and is never shaken;
It is the star to every wandring barke,
Whose worths unknowne, although his heigth be taken.
Lov's not Times foole, though rosie lips and cheeks
Within his bending sickles compasse come,
Love alters not with his breefe houres and weekes,
But beares it out even to the edge of doome:
　　If this be error and upon me proved,
　　I never writ, nor no man ever loved.

98　　　　　　*Sonnet 129*

Th'expence of Spirit in a waste of shame
Is lust in action, and till action, lust
Is perjurd, murdrous, blouddy full of blame,
Savage, extreame, rude, cruell, not to trust,
Injoyd no sooner but dispisèd straight,
Past reason hunted, and no sooner had
Past reason hated as a swollowèd bayt,
On purpose layd to make the taker mad.
Mad in pursut and in possession so,
Had, having, and in quest to have extreame,
A blisse in proofe and prov'd a very wo,
Before a joy proposd, behind a dreame,
　　All this the world well knowes yet none knowes well,
　　To shun the heaven that leads men to this hell.

99   *Sonnet 130*

My Mistres eyes are nothing like the Sunne,
Corrall is farre more red, than her lips red,
If snow be white, why then her brests are dun:
If haires be wiers, black wiers grow on her head:
I have seene Roses damaskt, red and white,
But no such Roses see I in her cheekes,
And in some perfumes is there more delight,
Than in the breath that from my Mistres reekes.
I love to heare her speake, yet well I know,
That Musicke hath a farre more pleasing sound:
I graunt I never saw a goddesse goe,
My Mistres when shee walkes treads on the ground.
    And yet by heaven I thinke my love as rare,
    As any she beli'd with false compare.

100   *Sonnet 138*

When my love sweares that she is made of truth,
I do beleeve her though I know she lyes,
That she might thinke me some untuterd youth,
Unlearnèd in the worlds false subtilties.
Thus vainely thinking that she thinkes me young,
Although she knowes my dayes are past the best,
Simply I credit her false speaking tongue,
On both sides thus is simple truth supprest:
But wherefore sayes she not she is unjust?
And wherefore say not I that I am old?
O loves best habit is in seeming trust,
And age in love, loves not t'have yeares told.
    Therefore I lye with her, and she with me,
    And in our faults by lyes we flatterèd be.

101   from *Love's Labour's Lost* [Act V, scene ii]

                           [*Spring*]
When Dasies pied, and Violets blew,
And Cuckow-buds of yellow hew:
And Ladie-smockes all silver white,
Do paint the Medowes with delight:
The Cuckow then on everie tree,
Mockes married men, for thus sings he,

Cuckow.
Cuckow, Cuckow: O word of feare,
Unpleasing to a married eare.

When Shepheards pipe on Oaten strawes,
And merrie Larkes are Ploughmens clockes:
When Turtles tread, and Rookes and Dawes,
And Maidens bleach their summer smockes:
The Cuckow then on everie tree
Mockes married men; for thus sings he,
Cuckow.
Cuckow, Cuckow: O word of feare,
Unpleasing to a married eare.

[*Winter*]

When Isicles hang by the wall,
And Dicke the Shepheard blowes his naile;
And Tom beares Logges into the hall,
And Milke comes frozen home in paile:
When blood is nipt, and waies be fowle
Then nightly sings the staring Owle
Tu-whit to-who.
   A merrie note,
   While greasie Joane doth keele the pot.

When all aloud the winde doth blow,
And coffing drownes the Parsons saw:
And birds sit brooding in the snow,
And Marrians nose lookes red and raw:
When roasted Crabs hisse in the bowle,
Then nightly sings the staring Owle,
Tu-whit to who:
   A merrie note,
   While greasie Joane doth keele the pot.

102–3   from *Twelfth Night*

102   [Act II, scene iii]

Feste. O Mistris mine where are you roming?
        O stay and heare, your true loves coming,
        That can sing both high and low.
        Trip no further prettie sweeting.
        Journeys end in lovers meeting,
        Every wise mans sonne doth know.

What is love, tis not heereafter,
Present mirth, hath present laughter:
What's to come, is still unsure.
In delay there lies no plentie,
Then come kisse me sweet and twentie:
Youths a stuffe will not endure.

103   [Act V, scene i]

Feste. When that I was and a little tiny boy,
    With hey, ho, the winde and the raine:
A foolish thing was but a toy,
    For the raine it raineth every day.

But when I came to mans estate,
    With hey ho, the winde and the raine:
Gainst Knaves and Theeves men shut their gate,
    For the raine it raineth every day.

But when I came alas to wive,
    With hey ho, the wind and the raine:
By swaggering could I never thrive,
    For the raine it raineth every day.

But when I came unto my beds,
    With hey ho, the winde and the raine:
With tosspottes still had drunken heades,
    For the raine it raineth every day.

A great while ago the world begun,
    Hey ho, the winde and the raine:
But that's all one, our Play is done,
    And wee'l strive to please you every day.

104   from *Measure for Measure* [Act IV, scene i]

Mariana. Take, oh take those lips away,
    That so sweetly were forsworne,
And those eyes: the breake of day,
    Lights that doe mislead the Morne;
But my kisses bring againe, bring againe,
Seales of love, but seal'd in vaine, seal'd in vaine.

105   from *Cymbeline* [Act IV, scene ii]

Guiderius. Feare no more the heate o'th'Sun,
        Nor the furious Winters rages,
        Thou thy worldly task hast don,
        Home art gon, and tane thy wages.
        Golden Lads, and Girles all must,
        As Chimney-Sweepers come to dust.

Arviragus. Feare no more the frowne o'th'Great,
        Thou art past the Tirants stroake,
        Care no more to cloath and eate,
        To thee the Reede is as the Oake:
        The Scepter, Learning, Physicke must,
        All follow this and come to dust.

Guiderius. Feare no more the Lightning flash.
Arviragus. Nor th'all-dreaded Thunderstone.
Guiderius. Feare not Slander, Censure rash.
Arviragus. Thou hast finish'd Joy and mone.
    Both. All Lovers young, all Lovers must,
        Consigne to thee and come to dust.
Guiderius. No Exorcisor harme thee,
Arviragus. Nor no witch-craft charme thee.
Guiderius. Ghost unlaid forbeare thee.
Arviragus. Nothing ill come neere thee.
    Both. Quiet consumation have,
        And renownèd be thy grave.

106   from *The Tempest* [Act I, scene ii]

Ariel. Full fadom five thy Father lies,
        Of his bones are Corrall made:
        Those are pearles that were his eies,
        Nothing of him that doth fade,
        But doth suffer a Sea-change
        Into something rich, and strange:
        Sea-Nimphs hourly ring his knell.
                [Burthen: ding dong.]
        Harke now I heare them, ding-dong bell.

107   from *Richard III* [Act I, scene i, lines 1–41]

[*Enter Richard Duke of Gloster, solus.*]
Now is the Winter of our Discontent,
Made glorious Summer by this Son of Yorke:
And all the clouds that lowr'd upon our house
In the deepe bosome of the Ocean buried.
Now are our browes bound with Victorious Wreathes,
Our bruisèd armes hung up for Monuments;
Our sterne Alarums chang'd to merry Meetings;
Our dreadfull Marches, to delightfull Measures.
Grim-visag'd Warre, hath smooth'd his wrinkled Front:
And now, in stead of mounting Barbèd Steeds,
To fright the Soules of fearfull Adversaries,
He capers nimbly in a Ladies Chamber,
To the lascivious pleasing of a Lute.
But I, that am not shap'd for sportive trickes,
Nor made to court an amorous Looking-glasse:
I, that am Rudely stampt, and want loves Majesty,
To strut before a wonton ambling Nymph:
I, that am curtail'd of this faire Proportion,
Cheated of Feature by dissembling Nature,
Deform'd, un-finish'd, sent before my time
Into this breathing World, scarse halfe made up,
And that so lamely and unfashionable,
That dogges barke at me, as I halt by them:
Why I (in this weake piping time of Peace)
Have no delight to passe away the time,
Unlesse to see my Shadow in the Sunne,
And descant on mine owne Deformity.
And therefore, since I cannot prove a Lover,
To entertaine these faire well spoken dayes,
I am determinèd to prove a Villaine,
And hate the idle pleasures of these dayes.
Plots have I laide, Inductions dangerous,
By drunken Prophesies, Libels, and Dreames,
To set my Brother *Clarence* and the King
In deadly hate, the one against the other:
And if King *Edward* be as true and just,
As I am Subtle, False, and Treacherous,
This day should *Clarence* closely be mew'd up:
About a Prophesie, which sayes that G,
Of *Edwards* heyres the murtherer shall be.
Dive thoughts downe to my soule, here *Clarence* comes.

108   from *Romeo and Juliet* [Act I, scene iv, lines 50–96]

Romeo. I dreampt a dreame to night.
Mercutio.   And so did I.
Romeo. Well what was yours?
Mercutio.   That dreamers often lye.
Romeo. In bed a sleep while they do dreame things true.
Mercutio. O then I see Queene Mab hath beene with you:
  She is the Fairies Midwife, and she comes
  In shape no bigger than an Agat-stone
  On the fore-finger of an Alderman,
  Drawne with a teeme of little Atomies,
  Over mens noses as they lie asleepe:
  Her Waggon Spokes made of long Spinners legs:
  The Cover of the wings of Grashoppers,
  Her Traces of the smallest Spiders web,
  Her collars of the Moonshines watry Beames,
  Her Whip of Crickets bone, the Lash of Film,
  Her Waggoner, a small gray-coated Gnat,
  Not halfe so bigge as a round little Worme,
  Prickt from the Lazie-finger of a maid.
  Her Chariot is an emptie Haselnut,
  Made by the Joyner Squirrel or old Grub,
  Time out o'mind, the Faries Coach-makers:
  And in this state she gallops night by night,
  Through Lovers braines: and then they dreame of Love.
  On Courtiers knees, that dreame on Curtsies strait:
  Ore Lawyers fingers, who strait dreame on Fees,
  Ore Ladies lips, who strait on kisses dreame,
  Which oft the angry Mab with blisters plagues,
  Because their breath with Sweet meats tainted are.
  Sometime she gallops ore a Courtiers nose,
  And then dreames he of smelling out a sute:
  And somtime comes she with a Tithe pigs tail,
  Tickling a Parsons nose as a lies asleepe,
  Then he dreames of another Benefice.
  Sometime she driveth ore a Souldiers necke,
  And then dreames he of cutting Forraine throats,
  Of Breaches, Ambuscados, Spanish Blades:
  Of Healths five Fadome deepe, and then anon
  Drums in his eares, at which he startes and wakes;
  And being thus frighted, sweares a prayer or two
  And sleepes againe: this is that very Mab
  That plats the manes of Horses in the night:
  And bakes the Elflocks in foule sluttish haires,
  Which once untangled, much misfortune bodes,

This is the hag, when Maides lie on their backs,
That presses them, and learnes them first to beare,
Making them women of good carriage:
This is she—
Romeo.   Peace, peace, *Mercutio* peace,
Thou talk'st of nothing.
Mercutio.   True, I talke of dreames.

109   from *Richard II* [Act II, scene i, lines 40–68]

John of Gaunt. This royall Throne of Kings, this sceptred Isle,
This earth of Majesty, this seate of Mars,
This other Eden, demy paradise,
This Fortresse built by Nature for her selfe,
Against infection, and the hand of warre:
This happy breed of men, this little world,
This precious stone, set in the silver sea,
Which serves it in the office of a wall,
Or as a Moate defensive to a house,
Against the envy of lesse happier Lands,
This blessèd plot, this earth, this Realme, this England,
This Nurse, this teeming wombe of Royall Kings,
Fear'd by their breed, and famous for their birth,
Renownèd for their deeds, as farre from home,
For Christian service, and true Chivalrie,
As is the sepulcher in stubborne *Jewry*
Of the Worlds ransome, blessèd *Maries* Sonne.
This Land of such deere soules, this deere-deere Land,
Deere for her reputation through the world,
Is now Leas'd out (I dye pronouncing it)
Like to a Tenement or pelting Farme.
England bound in with the triumphant sea,
Whose rocky shore beates backe the envious siedge
Of watery Neptune, is now bound in with shame,
With Inky blottes, and rotten Parchment bonds.
That England, that was wont to conquer others,
Hath made a shamefull conquest of it selfe.
Ah! would the scandall vanish with my life,
How happy then were my ensuing death?

110   from *A Midsummer Night's Dream* [Act V, scene i, lines 1–27]

Hippolita. 'Tis strange my *Theseus*, that these lovers speake of.
Theseus. More strange than true. I never may beleeve

These anticke fables, nor these Fairy toyes,
Lovers and mad men have such seething braines,
Such shaping phantasies, that apprehend more
Than coole reason ever comprehends.
The Lunaticke, the Lover, and the Poet,
Are of imagination all compact.
One sees more divels than vaste hell can hold;
That is the mad man. The Lover, all as franticke,
Sees *Helens* beauty in a brow of *Egipt*.
The Poets eye in a fine frenzy rolling,
Doth glance from heaven to earth, from earth to heaven.
And as imagination bodies forth
The forms of things unknowne, the Poets pen
Turnes them to shapes, and gives to aire nothing,
A locall habitation, and a name.
Such tricks hath strong imagination,
That if it would but apprehend some joy,
It comprehends some bringer of that joy.
Or in the night, imagining some feare,
How easie is a bush suppos'd a Beare?
Hippolita. But all the storie of the night told over,
And all their minds transfigur'd so together,
More witnesseth than fancies images,
And growes to something of great constancie;
But howsoever, strange, and admirable.

111   from *The Merchant of Venice* [Act IV, scene i, lines 180–203]

Portia.   Then must the Jew be mercifull.
Shylock. On what compulsion must I? Tell me that.
Portia. The quality of mercy is not strain'd,
   It droppeth as the gentle raine from heaven
   Upon the place beneath. It is twice blest,
   It blesseth him that gives, and him that takes,
   'Tis mightiest in the mightiest, it becomes
   The thronèd Monarch better than his Crowne.
   His Scepter shewes the force of temporall power,
   The attribute to awe and Majestie,
   Wherein doth sit the dread and feare of Kings:
   But mercy is above this sceptred sway,
   It is enthronèd in the hearts of Kings,
   It is an attribute to God himselfe;
   And earthly power doth then shew likest Gods
   When mercie seasons Justice. Therefore Jew,
   Though Justice be thy plea, consider this,
   That in the course of Justice, none of us

Should see salvation: we do pray for mercie,
And that same prayer, doth teach us all to render
The deeds of mercie. I have spoke thus much
To mittigate the justice of thy plea:
Which if thou follow, this strict course of Venice
Must needes give sentence 'gainst the Merchant there.

112   from *Julius Cæsar* [Act III, scene ii, lines 73–107]

Mark Antony. Friends, Romans, Countrymen, lend me your ears:
    I come to bury *Cæsar*, not to praise him:
    The evill that men do, lives after them,
    The good is oft enterrèd with their bones,
    So let it be with *Cæsar*. The Noble *Brutus*,
    Hath told you *Cæsar* was Ambitious:
    If it were so, it was a greevous Fault,
    And greevously hath *Cæsar* answer'd it.
    Heere, under leave of *Brutus*, and the rest
    (For *Brutus* is an Honourable man,
    So are they all; all Honourable men)
    Come I to speake in *Cæsars* Funerall.
    He was my Friend, faithfull, and just to me;
    But *Brutus* sayes, he was Ambitious,
    And *Brutus* is an Honourable man.
    He hath brought many Captives home to Rome,
    Whose Ransomes, did the generall Coffers fill:
    Did this in *Cæsar* seeme Ambitious?
    When that the poore have cry'de, *Cæsar* hath wept:
    Ambition should be made of sterner stuffe,
    Yet *Brutus* sayes, he was Ambitious:
    And *Brutus* is an Honourable man.
    You all did see, that on the *Lupercall*,
    I thrice presented him a Kingly Crowne,
    Which he did thrice refuse. Was this Ambition?
    Yet *Brutus* sayes, he was Ambitious:
    And sure he is an Honourable man.
    I speake not to disproove what *Brutus* spoke,
    But heere I am, to speake what I do know;
    You all did love him once, not without cause,
    What cause with-holds you then, to mourne for him?
    O Judgement! thou art fled to brutish Beasts,
    And Men have lost their Reason. Beare with me,
    My heart is in the Coffin there with *Cæsar*,
    And I must pawse, till it come backe to me.

113   from *As You Like It* [Act II, scene vii, lines 136–66]

Duke Senior. Thou seest, we are not all alone unhappie:
This wide and universall Theater
Presents more wofull Pageants than the Sceane
Wherein we play in.
Jaques.   All the world's a stage,
And all the men and women, meerely Players;
They have their *Exits* and their Entrances,
And one man in his time playes many parts,
His Acts being seven ages. At first the Infant,
Mewling, and puking in the Nurses armes:
Then, the whining Schoole-boy with his Satchell
And shining morning face, creeping like snaile
Unwillingly to schoole. And then the Lover,
Sighing like Furnace, with a wofull ballad
Made to his Mistresse eye-brow. Then, a Soldier,
Full of strange oaths, and bearded like the Pard,
Jelous in honor, sodaine, and quicke in quarrell,
Seeking the bubble Reputation
Even in the Canons mouth: And then, the Justice
In faire round belly, with good Capon lin'd,
With eyes severe, and beard of formall cut,
Full of wise sawes, and moderne instances,
And so he playes his part. The sixt age shifts
Into the leane and slipper'd Pantaloone,
With spectacles on nose, and pouch on side,
His youthfull hose well sav'd, a world too wide,
For his shrunke shanke, and his bigge manly voice,
Turning againe toward childish trebble, pipes
And whistles in his sound. Last Scene of all,
That ends this strange eventfull historie,
Is second childishnesse, and meere oblivion,
Sans teeth, sans eyes, sans taste, sans every thing.

114   from *Twelfth Night* [Act I, scene i, lines 1–15]

Duke. If Musicke be the food of Love, play on,
Give me excesse of it: that surfetting,
The appetite may sicken, and so dye.
That straine agen, it had a dying fall:
O, it came ore my eare, like the sweet sound
That breathes upon a banke of Violets;
Stealing, and giving Odour. Enough, no more,

'Tis not so sweet now, as it was before.
O spirit of Love, how quicke and fresh art thou,
That notwithstanding thy capacitie,
Receiveth as the Sea. Nought enters there,
Of what validity, and pitch so ere,
But falles into abatement, and low price
Even in a minute; so full of shapes is fancie,
That it alone, is high fantasticall.

115   from *Hamlet* [Act III, scene i, lines 56–88]

Hamlet. To be, or not to be, that is the Question:
    Whether 'tis Nobler in the minde to suffer
    The Slings and Arrowes of outragious Fortune,
    Or to take Armes against a Sea of troubles,
    And by opposing end them: to dye, to sleepe,
    No more; and by a sleepe, to say we end
    The Heart-ake, and the thousand Naturall shockes
    That Flesh is heyre to? 'Tis a consummation
    Devoutly to be wish'd. To dye, to sleepe,
    To sleepe, perchance to Dreame; ay, there's the rub,
    For in that sleepe of death, what dreames may come,
    When we have shufflel'd off this mortall coile,
    Must give us pawse. There's the respect
    That makes Calamity of so long life:
    For who would beare the Whips and Scornes of time,
    The Oppressors wrong, the proud mans Contumely,
    The pangs of dispriz'd Love, the Lawes delay,
    The insolence of Office, and the Spurnes
    That patient merit of the unworthy takes,
    When he himselfe might his *Quietus* make
    With a bare Bodkin? Who would these Fardles beare
    To grunt and sweat under a weary life,
    But that the dread of something after death,
    The undiscovered Countrey, from whose Bourne
    No Traveller returnes, Puzzels the will,
    And makes us rather beare those illes we have,
    Than flye to others that we know not of.
    Thus Conscience does make Cowards of us all,
    And thus the Native hew of Resolution
    Is sicklied o're, with the pale cast of Thought,
    And enterprizes of great pith and moment,
    With this regard their Currents turne awry,
    And lose the name of Action.

116   from *Measure for Measure* [Act III, scene i, lines 116–32]

Isabella. What saies my brother?
Claudio.   Death is a fearefull thing.
Isabella. And shamèd life, a hatefull.
Claudio. Ay, but to die, and go we know not where,
    To lie in cold obstruction, and to rot,
    This sensible warme motion, to become
    A kneaded clod; And the delighted spirit
    To bath in fierie floods, or to reside
    In thrilling Region of thicke-ribbèd Ice,
    To be imprison'd in the viewlesse windes
    And blowne with restlesse violence round about
    The pendant world: or to be worse than worst
    Of those that lawlesse and incertaine thought
    Imagine howling, 'tis too horrible.
    The weariest, and most loathèd worldly life
    That Age, Ache, penury, and imprisonment
    Can lay on nature, is a Paradise
    To what we feare of death.

117   from *Othello* [Act V, scene ii, lines 1–23]

                    [*Enter Othello, and Desdemona in her bed.*]
        Othello. It is the Cause, it is the Cause (my Soule)
            Let me not name it to you, you chaste Starres,
            It is the Cause. Yet Ile not shed her blood,
            Nor scarre that whiter skin of hers, than Snow,
            And smooth as Monumentall Alablaster:
            Yet she must dye, else shee'l betray more men:
            Put out the Light, and then put out the Light:
            If I quench thee, thou flaming Minister,
            I can againe thy former light restore,
            Should I repent me. But once put out thy Light,
            Thou cunning'st Patterne of excelling Nature,
            I know not where is that *Promethæan* heate
            That can thy Light re-Lume.
            When I have pluck'd thy Rose,
            I cannot give it vitall growth againe,
            It needs must wither. Ile smell thee on the Tree.
            Oh Balmy breath, that dost almost perswade
            Justice to breake her Sword. One more, one more:
            Be thus when thou art dead, and I will kill thee,
            And love thee after. One more, and that's the last.

So sweet, was ne're so fatall. I must weepe,
But they are cruell Teares: This sorrow's heavenly,
It strikes, where it doth love. She wakes.

118   from *King Lear* [Act IV, scene v, lines 11–25]

Edgar.   Come on Sir,
   Heere's the place: stand still: how fearefull
   And dizie 'tis, to cast ones eyes so low,
   The Crowes and Choughes, that wing the midway ayre
   Shew scarce so grosse as Beetles. Halfe way downe
   Hangs one that gathers Sampire: dreadfull Trade:
   Me thinkes he seemes no bigger than his head.
   The Fishermen, that walk'd upon the beach
   Appeare like Mice: and yond tall Anchoring Barke,
   Diminish'd to her Cocke: her Cocke, a Buoy
   Almost too small for sight. The murmuring Surge,
   That on th'unnumbred idle Pebble chafes
   Cannot be heard so high. Ile lookc no more,
   Least my braine turne, and the deficient sight
   Topple downe headlong.

119   from *Macbeth* [Act V, scene v, lines 8–29]

                           [*A Cry within of Women.*]
Seyton. It is the cry of women, my good Lord.
Macbeth. I have almost forgot the taste of Feares:
   The time ha's beene, my sences would have cool'd
   To heare a Night-shrieke, and my Fell of haire
   Would at a dismall Treatise rowze, and stirre
   As life were in't. I have supt full with horrors,
   Direnesse familiar to my slaughterous thoughts
   Cannot once start me. Wherefore was that cry?
Seyton. The Queene (my Lord) is dead.
Macbeth. She should have dy'de heereafter;
   There would have beene a time for such a word:
   To morrow, and to morrow, and to morrow,
   Creepes in this petty pace from day to day,
   To the last Syllable of Recorded time:
   And all our yesterdayes, have lighted Fooles
   The way to dusty death. Out, out, breefe Candle,
   Life's but a walking Shadow, a poore Player,
   That struts and frets his houre upon the Stage,

And then is heard no more. It is a Tale
Told by an Ideot, full of sound and fury
Signifying nothing.   [*Enter a Messenger.*]
Thou com'st to use thy Tongue: thy Story quickly.

120   from *Antony and Cleopatra* [Act II, scene ii, lines 190–218]

Enobarbus.   I will tell you,
The Barge she sat in, like a burnisht Throne
Burnt on the water: the Poope was beaten Gold,
Purple the Sailes: and so perfúmèd that
The Windes were Love-sicke with them: the Oars were Silver,
Which to the tune of Flutes kept stroke, and made
The water which they beate, to follow faster;
As amorous of their strokes. For her owne person,
It beggerd all discription, she did lye
In her Pavillion, cloth of Gold, of Tissue,
O're-picturing that Venus, where we see
The fancie out-worke Nature. On each side her,
Stood pretty Dimpled Boyes, like smiling Cupids,
With divers coulour'd Fannes whose winde did seeme,
To glow the delicate cheekes which they did coole,
And what they undid did.
Agrippa.   Oh rare for *Anthony.*
Enobarbus. Her Gentlewomen, like the Nereides,
So many Mer-maides tended her i'th'eyes,
And made their bends adornings. At the Helme
A seeming Mer-maide steeres: The Silken Tackle
Swell with the touches of those Flower-soft hands,
That yarely frame the office. From the Barge
A strange invisible perfume hits the sense
Of the adjacent Wharfes. The Citty cast
Her people out upon her: and *Anthony*
Enthron'd i'th'Market-place, did sit alone,
Whisling to'th'ayre: which but for vacancie,
Had gone to gaze on *Cleopater* too,
And made a gap in Nature.
Agrippa.   Rare Egiptian.

121   from *The Tempest* [Act IV, scene i, lines 146–63]

Prospero. You doe looke (my son) in a mov'd sort,
As if you were dismaid: be cheerefull Sir,
Our Revels now are ended: These our actors,

(As I foretold you) were all Spirits, and
Are melted into Ayre, into thin Ayre,
And like the baselesse fabricke of this vision
The Clowd-capt Towres, the gorgeous Pallaces,
The solemne Temples, the great Globe it selfe,
Yea, all which it inherit, shall dissolve,
And like this insubstantiall Pageant faded
Leave not a racke behinde: we are such stuffe
As dreames are made on; and our little life
Is rounded with a sleepe: Sir, I am vext,
Beare with my weakenesse, my old braine is troubled:
Be not disturb'd with my infirmitie,
If you be pleas'd, retire into my Cell,
And there repose. A turne or two, Ile walke
To still my beating minde.
Ferdinand and Miranda.   We wish your peace.

THOMAS BASTARD

1566–1618

122   *De puero balbutiente*

Me thinkes tis pretie sport to heare a childe,
Rocking a worde in mouth yet undefiled.
The tender racket rudely playes the sound,
Which weakly handied cannot backe rebound,
And the soft ayre the softer roofe doth kisse,
With a sweet dying and a pretie miss,
Which heares no answere yet from the white ranke
Of teeth, not risen from their corall banke.
The alphabet is searcht for letters soft,
To trye a worde before it can be wrought,
And when it slideth forth, it goes as nice,
As when a man does walke upon the yce.

THOMAS CAMPION

1567–1620

123   Followe thy faire sunne, unhappy shadowe,
Though thou be blacke as night,
And she made all of light,
Yet follow thy faire sun, unhappie shadowe.

Follow her whose light thy light depriveth,
Though here thou liv'st disgrac't,
And she in heaven is plac't,
Yet follow her whose light the world reviveth.

Follow those pure beames whose beautie burneth,
That so have scorchèd thee,
As thou still blacke must bee,
Til her kind beames thy black to brightnes turneth.

Follow her while yet her glorie shineth:
There comes a luckless night,
That will dim all her light;
And this the black unhappie shade devineth.

Follow still since so thy fates ordainèd;
The Sunne must have his shade,
Till both at once doe fade,
The Sun still proud, the shadow still disdainèd.

124   Harke, al you ladies that do sleep;
      The fayry queen Proserpina
Bids you awake and pitie them that weep.
     You may doe in the darke
What the day doth forbid;
     Feare not the dogs that barke,
      Night will have all hid.

But if you let your lovers mone,
      The Fairie Queene Proserpina
Will send abroad her Fairies ev'ry one,
     That shall pinch blacke and blew
Your white hands and faire armes
     That did not kindly rue
      Your Paramours harmes.

In Myrtle Arbours on the downes
      The Fairie Queene Proserpina,
This night by moone-shine leading merrie rounds
     Holds a watch with sweet love,
Downe the dale, up the hill;
     No plaints or groanes may move
      Their holy vigill.

All you that will hold watch with love,
      The Fairie Queene Proserpina
Will make you fairer than Dione's dove;

Roses red, Lillies white,
And the cleare damaske hue,
   Shall on your cheekes alight:
   Love will adorne you.

All you that love, or lov'd before,
   The Fairie Queene Proserpina
Bids you encrease that loving humour more:
   They that yet have not fed
On delight amorous,
   She vowes that they shall lead
   Apes in Avernus.

125   When thou must home to shades of under ground,
And there ariv'd, a newe admired guest,
The beauteous spirits do ingirt thee round,
White Iope, blith Hellen, and the rest,
To heare the stories of thy finisht love
From that smoothe toong whose musicke hell can move;

Then wilt thou speake of banqueting delights,
Of masks and revels which sweete youth did make,
Of Turnies and great challenges of knights,
And all these triumphes for thy beauties sake:
When thou hast told these honours done to thee,
Then tell, O tell, how thou didst murther me.

126   Rose-cheekt *Lawra*, come
Sing thou smoothly with thy beawties
Silent musick, either other
      Sweetely gracing.

Lovely formes do flowe
From concent devinely framèd;
Heav'n is musick, and thy beawties
      Birth is heavenly.

These dull notes we sing
Discords neede for helps to grace them;
Only beawty purely loving
      Knowes no discord,

But still mooves delight,
Like cleare springs renew'd by flowing,
Ever perfet, ever in them-
      selves eternall.

127   Kinde are her answeres,
             But her performance keeps no day;
           Breaks time, as dancers
             From their own Musicke when they stray:
             All her free favors and smooth words,
           Wing my hopes in vaine.
           O did ever voice so sweet but only fain?
             Can true love yeeld such delay,
             Converting joy to pain?

             Lost is our freedome,
             When we submit to women so:
           Why doe wee neede them,
             When in their best they worke our woe?
             There is no wisedome
           Can alter ends, by Fate prefixt.
           O why is the good of man with evill mixt?
             Never were days yet call'd two,
             But one night went betwixt.

128   Now winter nights enlarge
             The number of their houres;
           And clouds their stormes discharge
             Upon the ayrie towres.
           Let now the chimneys blaze
             And cups o'erflow with wine,
           Let well-tun'd words amaze
             With harmonie divine.
           Now yellow waxen lights
             Shall waite on hunny Love
           While youthfull Revels, Masks, and Courtly sights,
             Sleepes leaden spels remove.

             This time doth well dispence
             With lovers long discourse;
           Much speech hath some defence,
             Though beauty no remorse.
           All doe not all things well;
             Some measures comely tread;
           Some knotted Ridles tell;
             Some Poems smoothly read.
           The Summer hath his joyes,
             And Winter his delights;
           Though Love and all his pleasures are but toyes,
             They shorten tedious nights.

THOMAS NASHE
1567–1601

129–30   from *Summer's Last Will and Testament*

129   Spring, the sweete spring, is the yeres pleasant King,
Then bloomes eche thing, then maydes daunce in a ring,
Cold doeth not sting, the pretty birds doe sing,
Cuckow, jugge, jugge, pu we, to witta woo.

The Palme and May make countrey houses gay,
Lambs friske and play, the Shepherds pype all day,
And we heare aye birds tune this merry lay,
Cuckow, jugge, jugge, pu we, to witta woo.

The fields breathe sweete, the dayzies kisse our feete,
Young lovers meete, old wives a sunning sit;
In every streete, these tunes our eares doe greete,
Cuckow, jugge, jugge, pu we, to witta woo.
    Spring, the sweete spring.

130   Adieu, farewell earths blisse,
This world uncertaine is,
Fond are lifes lustfull joyes,
Death proves them all but toyes,
None from his darts can flye;
I am sick, I must dye:
    Lord, have mercy on us.

Rich men, trust not in wealth,
Gold cannot buy you health;
Phisick himselfe must fade.
All things to end are made,
The plague full swift goes bye;
I am sick, I must dye:
    Lord, have mercy on us.

Beauty is but a flowre,
Which wrinckles will devoure,
Brightnesse falls from the ayre,
Queenes have died yong and faire,
Dust hath closde *Helens* eye.
I am sick, I must dye:
    Lord, have mercy on us.

Strength stoopes unto the grave,
Wormes feed on *Hector* brave,
Swords may not fight with fate,
Earth still holds ope her gate.
Come, come, the bells do crye.
I am sick, I must dye:
    Lord, have mercy on us.

Wit with his wantonnesse
Tasteth deaths bitternesse:
Hels executioner
Hath no eares for to heare
What vaine art can reply.
I am sick, I must dye:
    Lord, have mercy on us.

Haste therefore eche degree,
To welcome destiny:
Heaven is our heritage,
Earth but a players stage,
Mount wee unto the sky.
I am sick, I must dye:
    Lord, have mercy on us.

WILLIAM ALABASTER
1568–1640

131   What should there be in Christ to give offence?
His corded hands, why they for thee were bound,
His mangled brows, why they for thee were crown'd,
His piercèd breast, thy life did flow from thence.
What though some arrows glance with violence
From him to thee, shall this thy friendship wound?
What though some stones upon thee do rebound,
Shall such small fillips break thy patience?
Those shafts which raze thy skin, ran through his heart;
Those stones which touch thy hands, first broke his head;
But those small drops of pain he doth impart
To show what he did bear, what thou hast fled.
And yet we grieve to suffer for his sake:
'Tis night, or else how could we so mistake?

132   from *Upon the Ensigns of Christ's Crucifying*

Ego Sum Vitis

Now that the midday heat doth scorch my shame
With lightning of fond lust, I will retire
Under this vine whose arms with wandering spire
Do climb upon the Cross, and on the same
Devise a cool repose from lawless flame,
Whose leaves are intertwist with love entire,
That envy's eye cannot transfuse her fire,
But is rebated on the shady frame;
And youthful vigour from the leavèd tier,
Doth stream upon my soul a new desire.
List, list, the ditties of sublimèd fame,
Which in the closet of those leaves the choir
Of heavenly birds do warble to his name.
O where was I that was not where I am?

SIR HENRY WOTTON

1568–1639

133   *On his Mistress, the Queen of Bohemia*

You meaner *Beauties* of the *Night*,
That poorly satisfie our *Eyes*
More by your *number*, than your *light*,
You *Common people* of the *Skies*;
    What are you when the *Sun* shall rise?

You curious Chanters of the Wood,
That warble forth *Dame Natures* layes,
Thinking your *Voices* understood
By your weak *accents*; what's your praise
    When *Philomel* her voice shall raise?

You *Violets*, that first appear,
By your *pure purple mantles* known,
Like the proud *Virgins* of the *year*,
As if the *Spring* were all your own;
    What are you when the *Rose is blown*?

So, when *my Mistress* shall be *seen*
In *Form* and *Beauty* of her *mind*,

By *Vertue* first, then *Choice a Queen,*
Tell me, if *she* were not design'd
Th' *Eclipse* and *Glory* of her kind?

134   *Upon the sudden Restraint of the Earl of*
        Somerset, then falling from favour

Dazzled thus with height of place,
Whilst our Hopes our wits Beguile,
No man marks the narrow space
'Twixt a Prison and a Smile.

Then since Fortunes favours fade,
You that in her arms do sleep,
Learn to swim and not to wade;
For the Hearts of Kings are deep.

But if Greatness be so blind,
As to trust in Towers of *Air,*
Let it be with Goodness lin'd,
That at least the Fall be fair.

Then though darkened you shall say,
When Friends fail and Princes frown,
Vertue is the roughest way,
But proves at night a *Bed of Down.*

135   *The Character of a Happy Life*

How *happy* is he born and taught,
That serveth not anothers *will*?
Whose *armour* is his *honest thought,*
And simple *truth* his utmost *skill*?

Whose *passions* not his *masters* are,
Whose *soul* is still prepar'd for *death*;
Unti'd unto the *World* by care
Of *publick fame,* or *private breath.*

Who *envies* none that *chance* doth *raise,*
Nor *vice* hath ever understood;
How deepest wounds are giv'n by *praise,*
Nor rules of *State,* but rules of *good.*

Who hath his *life* from *rumours freed*,
Whose *conscience* is his strong *retreat*:
Whose *state* can neither *flatterers feed*,
Nor *ruine* make *Oppressors* great.

Who *God* doth late and early pray,
More of his *grace* than *gifts* to lend:
And entertains the harmless day
With a *Religious Book*, or Friend.

This man is freed from servile bands,
Of hope to rise, or *fear* to fall:
Lord of himself, though not of *Lands*,
And having *nothing*, yet hath *all*.

[after the Latin of Martial]

136   *Upon the death of Sir Albert Morton's Wife*

He first deceas'd; She for a little tri'd
To live without him: lik'd it not, and di'd.

EDWARD FAIRFAX
1568?–1635

137   from *The fourth booke of Godfrey of Bulloigne* [Tasso's
       Gerusalemme Liberata] [stanzas 87–93]

All wilie sleights, that subtile women know,
Howrely she us'd, to catch some lover new.
None kend the bent of her unstedfast bow,
For with the time her thoughts her lookes renew,
From some she cast her modest eies below,
At some her gazing glances roaving flew,
    And while she thus pursewd her wanton sport,
    She spurd the slow, and rein'd the forward short.

If some, as hopelesse that she would be wonne,
Forbore to love, because they durst not move her,
On them her gentle lookes to smile begonne,
As who say, she is kinde, if you dare prove her:
On everie hart thus shone this lustfull sonne,
All strove to serve, to please, to woo, to love her,
    And in their harts that chaste and bashfull were,
    Her eies hot glance dissolv'd the frost of feare.

On them, who durst with fingring bold assay
To touch the softnes of her tender skin,
She lookt as coy, as if she list not play,
And made as things of worth were hard to win;
Yet tempred so her deignfull lookes alway,
That outward scorne shew'd store of grace within:
　　Thus with false hope their longing harts she fired,
　　For hardest gotten things, are most desired.

Alone sometimes she walkt in secret where,
To ruminate upon her discontent,
Within her eie-lids sat the swelling teare,
Not pourèd forth, though sprong from sad lament;
And with this craft a thousand soules welneare,
In snares of foolish ruth and love she hent,
　　And kept as slaves, by which we fitly prove,
　　That witlesse pitie, breedeth fruitlesse love.

Sometimes, as if her hope unloosèd had
The chaines of griefe, wherein her thoughts lay fetterèd,
Upon her minions lookt she blithe and glad,
In that deceitfull lore so was she letterèd;
Not glorious *Titan*, in his brightnes clad,
The sun-shine of her face in luster betterèd:
　　For when she list to cheare her beauties so,
　　She smil'd away the cloudes of griefe and wo.

Her double charme of smiles and sugred words,
Lullèd on sleepe the vertue of their sences,
Reason small aide gainst those assaults affords,
Wisedome no warrant from those sweet offences,
Cupids deepe rivers, have their shallow fordes,
His griefes, bring joyes; his losses recompences;
　　He breedes the sore, and cures us of the paine:
　　Achilles lance that wounds and heales againe.

While thus she them torments twixt frost and fire,
Twixt joy and griefe, twixt hope and restlesse feare,
The slie enchantresse, felt her gaine the nigher,
These were her flockes that golden fleeces beare:
But if some one durst utter his desire,
And by complaining make his grieves appeare,
　　He laborèd hard rocks with plaints to move,
　　She had not learn'd the Gamut then of love.

　　　　　　　　[after the Italian of Tasso]

SIR JOHN DAVIES
1569–1626

138   from *Orchestra: or a Poeme of Dauncing* [stanzas 1–6]

Where lives the man that never yet did heare
Of chast *Penelope, Ulisses* Queene?
Who kept her faith unspotted twenty yeere
Till he returnd that far away had beene,
And many men, and many townes had seene:
    Ten yeere at siedge of *Troy* he lingring lay,
    And ten yeere in the *Midland-sea* did stray.

Homer, to whom the Muses did carouse,
A great deepe cup with heavenly Nectar filld
The greatest, deepest cup in *Joves* great house,
(For *Jove* himselfe had so expresly willd)
He dranke off all, ne let one drop be spilld;
    Since when, his braine that had before been dry,
    Became the welspring of all Poetry.

Homer doth tell in his aboundant verse,
The long laborious travailes of the *Man*,
And of his Lady too he doth reherse,
How shee illudes with all the Art she can,
Th'ungratefull love which other Lords began;
    For of her Lord false Fame long since had sworne,
    That *Neptunes* Monsters had his carcasse torne.

All this he tells, but one thing he forgot,
One thing most worthy his eternall song,
But he was old, and blind, and saw it not,
Or else he thought he should *Ulisses* wrong,
To mingle it, his Tragick acts among.
    Yet was there not in all the world of things,
    A sweeter burden for his Muses wings.

The Courtly love *Antinous* did make,
Antinous that fresh and jolly Knight,
Which of the gallants that did undertake
To win the Widdow, had most wealth and might,
Wit to perswade, and beautie to delight.
    The Courtly love he made unto the Queene,
    Homer forgot as if it had not beene.

Sing then *Terpsichore*, my light Muse sing
His gentle Art and *cunning curtesie*:
You, Lady, can remember every thing,
For you are daughter of Queene Memorie,
But sing a plaine and easie Melodie:
   For the soft meane that warbleth but the ground,
   To my rude eare doth yield the sweetest sound.

THOMAS DEKKER

1572?–1632

139   from *Patient Grissil* [Act IV, scene ii]

Golden slumbers kisse your eyes,
Smiles awake you when you rise:
Sleepe pretty wantons doe not cry,
And I will sing a lullabie,
Rocke them rocke them lullabie.

Care is heavy therefore sleepe you,
You are care and care must keep you:
Sleepe pretty wantons doe not cry,
And I will sing a lullabie,
Rocke them rocke them lullabie.

JOHN DONNE

1572–1631

140   *The good-morrow*

I wonder by my troth, what thou, and I
Did, till we lov'd? were we not wean'd till then?
But suck'd on countrey pleasures, childishly?
Or snorted we in the seaven sleepers den?
T'was so; But this, all pleasures fancies bee.
If ever any beauty I did see,
Which I desir'd, and got, t'was but a dreame of thee.

And now good morrow to our waking soules,
Which watch not one another out of feare;
For love, all love of other sights controules,
And makes one little roome, an every where.

Let sea-discoverers to new worlds have gone,
Let Maps to other, worlds on worlds have showne,
Let us possesse one world, each hath one, and is one.

My face in thine eye, thine in mine appeares,
And true plain hearts doe in the faces rest,
Where can we finde two better hemispheares
Without sharpe North, without declining West?
What ever dyes, was not mixt equally;
If our two loves be one, or, thou and I
Love so alike, that none doe slacken, none can die.

141   *Song*

    Goe, and catche a falling starre,
      Get with child a mandrake roote,
    Tell me, where all past yeares are,
      Or who cleft the Divels foot,
    Teach me to heare Mermaides singing,
    Or to keep off envies stinging,
        And finde
        What winde
    Serves to advance an honest minde.

    If thou beest borne to strange sights,
      Things invisible to see,
    Ride ten thousand daies and nights,
      Till age snow white haires on thee,
    Thou, when thou retorn'st, wilt tell mee
    All strange wonders that befell thee,
        And sweare
        No where
    Lives a woman true, and faire.

    If thou findst one, let mee know,
      Such a Pilgrimage were sweet;
    Yet doe not, I would not goe,
      Though at next doore wee might meet,
    Though shee were true, when you met her,
    And last, till you write your letter,
        Yet shee
        Will bee
    False, ere I come, to two, or three.

142   *A nocturnall upon S. Lucies day,*
                  Being the shortest day

Tis the yeares midnight, and it is the dayes,
Lucies, who scarce seaven houres herself unmaskes,
   The Sunne is spent, and now his flasks
   Send forth light squibs, no constant rayes;
     The worlds whole sap is sunke:
The generall balme th'hydroptique earth hath drunk,
Whither, as to the beds-feet, life is shrunke,
Dead and enterr'd; yet all these seeme to laugh,
Compar'd with mee, who am their Epitaph.

Study me then, you who shall lovers bee
At the next world, that is, at the next Spring:
   For I am every dead thing,
   In whom love wrought new Alchimie.
     For his art did expresse
A quintessence even from nothingnesse,
From dull privations, and leane emptinesse:
He ruin'd mee, and I am re-begot
Of absence, darknesse, death; things which are not.

All others, from all things, draw all that's good,
Life, soule, forme, spirit, whence they beeing have;
   I, by loves limbecke, am the grave
   Of all, that's nothing. Oft a flood
     Have wee two wept, and so
Drownd the whole world, us two; oft did we grow
To be two Chaosses, when we did show
Care to aught else; and often absences
Withdrew our soules, and made us carcasses.

But I am by her death, (which word wrongs her)
Of the first nothing, the Elixer grown;
   Were I a man, that I were one,
   I needs must know; I should preferre,
     If I were any beast,
Some ends, some means; Yea plants, yea stones detest,
And love; All, all some properties invest;
If I an ordinary nothing were,
As shadow, a light, and body must be here.

But I am None; nor will my Sunne renew.
You lovers, for whose sake, the lesser Sunne
   At this time to the Goat is runne
   To fetch new lust, and give it you,

Enjoy your summer all;
Since shee enjoyes her long nights festivall,
Let mee prepare towards her, and let mee call
This houre her Vigill, and her Eve, since this
Both the yeares, and the dayes deep midnight is.

143   *A Valediction: forbidding mourning*

As virtuous men passe mildly away,
   And whisper to their soules, to goe,
Whilst some of their sad friends doe say,
   The breath goes now, and some say, no:

So let us melt, and make no noise,
   No teare-floods, nor sigh-tempests move,
T'were prophanation of our joyes
   To tell the layetie our love.

Moving of th'earth brings harmes and feares,
   Men reckon what it did and meant,
But trepidation of the spheares,
   Though greater farre, is innocent.

Dull sublunary lovers love
   (Whose soule is sense) cannot admit
Absence, because it doth remove
   Those things which elemented it.

But we by a love, so much refin'd,
   That our selves know not what it is,
Inter-assurèd of the mind,
   Care lesse, eyes, lips, and hands to misse.

Our two soules therefore, which are one,
   Though I must goe, endure not yet
A breach, but an expansion,
   Like gold to ayery thinnesse beate.

If they be two, they are two so
   As stiffe twin compasses are two,
Thy soule the fixt foot, makes no show
   To move, but doth, if the'other doe.

And though it in the center sit,
   Yet when the other far doth rome,
It leanes, and hearkens after it,
   And growes erect, as that comes home.

Such wilt thou be to mee, who must
   Like th'other foot, obliquely runne;
Thy firmnes makes my circle just,
   And makes me end, where I begunne.

144   *The Extasie*

Where, like a pillow on a bed,
   A Pregnant banke swel'd up, to rest
The violets reclining head,
   Sat we two, one anothers best.
Our hands were firmely cimented
   With a fast balme, which thence did spring,
Our eye-beames twisted, and did thred
   Our eyes, upon one double string;
So to'entergraft our hands, as yet
   Was all the meanes to make us one,
And pictures in our eyes to get
   Was all our propagation.
As 'twixt two equal Armies, Fate
   Suspends uncertaine victorie,
Our soules, (which to advance their state,
   Were gone out,) hung 'twixt her, and mee.
And whil'st our soules negotiate there,
   Wee like sepulchrall statues lay;
All day, the same our postures were,
   And wee said nothing, all the day.
If any, so by love refin'd,
   That he soules language understood,
And by good love were growen all minde,
   Within convenient distance stood,
He (though he knew not which soule spake,
   Because both meant, both spake the same)
Might thence a new concoction take,
   And part farre purer than he came.
This Extasie doth unperplex
   (We said) and tell us what we love,
Wee see by this, it was not sexe,
   Wee see, we saw not what did move:
But as all severall soules containe
   Mixture of things, they know not what,
Love, these mixt soules doth mixe againe,
   And makes both one, each this and that.
A single violet transplant,
   The strength, the colour, and the size,

(All which before was poore, and scant,)
   Redoubles still, and multiplies.
When love, with one another so
   Interinanimates two soules,
That abler soule, which thence doth flow,
   Defects of lonelinesse controules.
Wee then, who are this new soule, know,
   Of what we are compos'd, and made,
For, th'Atomies of which we grow,
   Are soules, whom no change can invade.
But O alas, so long, so farre
   Our bodies why doe wee forbeare?
They'are ours, though they'are not wee, Wee are
   The intelligences, they the spheare.
We owe them thankes, because they thus,
   Did us, to us, at first convay,
Yeelded their forces, sense, to us,
   Nor are drosse to us, but allay.
On man heavens influence workes not so,
   But that it first imprints the ayre,
Soe soule into the soule may flow,
   Though it to body first repaire.
As our blood labours to beget
   Spirits, as like soules as it can,
Because such fingers need to knit
   That subtile knot, which makes us man:
So must pure lovers soules descend
   T'affections, and to faculties,
Which sense may reach and apprehend,
   Else a great Prince in prison lies.
To'our bodies turne wee then, that so
   Weake men on love reveal'd may looke;
Loves mysteries in soules doe grow,
   But yet the body is his booke.
And if some lover, such as wee,
   Have heard this dialogue of one,
Let him still marke us, he shall see
   Small change, when we'are to bodies gone.

145   *Elegy: To his Mistris Going to Bed*

Come, Madam, come, all rest my powers defie,
Until I labour, I in labour lie.
The foe oft-times having the foe in sight,
Is tir'd with standing though he never fight.

Off with that girdle, like heavens Zone glittering,
But a far fairer world incompassing.
Unpin that spangled breastplate which you wear,
That th'eyes of busie fooles may be stopt there.
Unlace your self, for that harmonious chyme,
Tells me from you, that now it is bed time.
Off with that happy busk, which I envíe,
That still can be, and still can stand so nigh.
Your gown going off, such beautious state reveals,
As when from flowry meads th'hills shadow steales.
Off with that wyerie Coronet and shew
The haiery Diademe which on you doth grow:
Now off with those shooes, and then safely tread
In this loves hallow'd temple, this soft bed.
In such white robes, heaven's Angels us'd to be
Receavd by men; Thou Angel bringst with thee
A heaven like Máhométs Paradise; and though
Ill spirits walk in white, we easly know,
By this these Angels from an evil sprite,
Those set our hairs, but these our flesh upright.
    Licence my roaving hands, and let them go,
Before, behind, between, above, below.
O my America! my new-found-land,
My kingdome, safeliest when with one man man'd,
My Myne of precious stones, My Emperie,
How blest am I in this discovering thee!
To enter in these bonds, is to be free;
Then where my hand is set, my seal shall be.
    Full nakedness! All joyes are due to thee,
As souls unbodied, bodies uncloth'd must be,
To taste whole joyes. Gems which you women use
Are like Atlanta's balls, cast in mens views,
That when a fools eye lighteth on a Gem,
His earthly soul may covet theirs, not them.
Like pictures, or like books gay coverings made
For lay-men, are all women thus array'd;
Themselves are mystick books, which only wee
(Whom their imputed grace will dignifie)
Must see reveal'd. Then since that I may know;
As liberally, as to a Midwife, shew
Thy self: cast all, yea, this white lynnen hence,
There is no pennance due to innocence.
    To teach thee, I am naked first; why than
What needst thou have more covering than a man.

146–7   from *Holy Sonnets*

146   At the round earths imagin'd corners, blow
               Your trumpets, Angells, and arise, arise
               From death, you numberlesse infinities
               Of soules, and to your scattred bodies goe,
               All whom the flood did, and fire shall o'erthrow,
               All whom warre, dearth, age, agues, tyrannies,
               Despaire, law, chance, hath slaine, and you whose eyes,
               Shall behold God, and never tast deaths woe.
               But let them sleepe, Lord, and mee mourne a space,
               For, if above all these, my sinnes abound,
               'Tis late to aske abundance of thy grace,
               When wee are there; here on this lowly ground,
               Teach mee how to repent; for that's as good
               As if thou'hadst seal'd my pardon, with thy blood.

147   Death be not proud, though some have callèd thee
               Mighty and dreadfull, for, thou art not soe,
               For, those, whom thou think'st, thou dost overthrow,
               Die not, poore death, nor yet canst thou kill mee;
               From rest and sleepe, which but thy pictures bee,
               Much pleasure, then from thee, much more must flow,
               And soonest our best men with thee doe goe,
               Rest of their bones, and soules deliverie.
               Thou'art slave to Fate, chance, kings, and desperate men,
               And dost with poyson, warre, and sicknesse dwell,
               And poppie,'or charmes can make us sleepe as well,
               And better than thy stroake; why swell'st thou then?
               One short sleepe past, wee wake eternally,
               And death shall be no more; death, thou shalt die.

148   *A Hymne to God the Father*

                    Wilt thou forgive that sinne where I begunne,
                         Which was my sin, though it were done before?
                    Wilt thou forgive that sinne; through which I runne,
                         And do run still: though still I do deplore?
                         When thou hast done, thou hast not done,
                              For, I have more.

                    Wilt thou forgive that sinne which I have wonne
                         Others to sinne? and, made my sinne their doore?

Wilt thou forgive that sinne which I did shunne
A yeare, or two: but wallowed in, a score?
  When thou hast done, thou hast not done,
    For I have more.

I have a sinne of feare, that when I have spunne
My last thred, I shall perish on the shore;
But sweare by thy selfe, that at my death thy sonne
Shall shine as he shines now, and heretofore;
  And, having done that, Thou hast done,
    I feare no more.

BEN JONSON
1572?–1637

149   *Epitaph on S[alomon] P[avy] a child of*
             Q. Elizabeths Chappel

Weepe with me all you that read
  This little storie:
And know, for whom a teare you shed,
  Death's selfe is sorry.
'Twas a child, that so did thrive
  In grace, and feature,
As *Heaven* and *Nature* seem'd to strive
  Which own'd the creature.
Yeeres he numbred scarse thirteene
  When *Fates* turn'd cruell,
Yet three fill'd *Zodiackes* had he beene
  The stages jewell;
And did act (what now we mone)
  Old men so duely,
As, sooth, the *Parcæ* thought him one,
  He plai'd so truely.
So, by error, to his fate
  They all consented;
But viewing him since (alas, too late)
  They have repented.
And have sought (to give new birth)
  In bathes to steepe him;
But, being so much too good for earth,
  Heaven vowes to keepe him.

150   *On my First Sonne*

Farewell, thou child of my right hand, and joy;
　My sinne was too much hope of thee, lov'd boy,
Seven yeeres thou'wert lent to me, and I thee pay,
　Exacted by thy fate, on the just day.
O, could I lose all father, now. For why
　Will man lament the state he should envíe?
To have so soone scap'd worlds, and fleshes rage,
　And, if no other miserie, yet age?
Rest in soft peace, and, ask'd, say here doth lye
　BEN. IONSON his best piece of *poetrie*.
For whose sake, hence-forth, all his vowes be such,
　As what he loves may never like too much.

151–2   from *Volpone*

151   [Act I, scene i, lines 1–29]

Volpone. Good morning to the day; and, next, my gold:
　Open the shrine, that I may see my *saint*.
　Haile the worlds soule, and mine. More glad than is
　The teeming earth, to see the long'd-for sunne
　Peepe through the hornes of the celestiall *ram*,
　Am I, to view thy splendor, darkening his:
　That, lying here, amongst my other hoords,
　Shew'st like a flame, by night; or like the day
　Strooke out of *chaos*, when all darkenesse fled
　Unto the center. O, thou sonne of SOL,
　(But brighter than thy father) let me kisse,
　With adoration, thee, and every relique
　Of sacred treasure, in this blessèd roome.
　Well did wise Poets, by thy glorious name,
　Title that age, which they would have the best;
　Thou being the best of things: and far transcending
　All stile of joy, in children, parents, friends,
　Or any other waking dreame on earth.
　Thy lookes, when they to VENUS did ascribe,
　They should have giv'n her twentie thousand CUPIDS;
　Such are thy beauties, and our loves! Deare *saint*,
　Riches, the dumbe god, that giv'st all men tongues:
　That canst doe nought, and yet mak'st men doe all things;
　The price of soules; even hell, with thee to boot,

Is made worth heaven! Thou art vertue, fame,
Honour, and all things else! Who can get thee,
He shall be noble, valiant, honest, wise—
Mosca. And what he will, sir. Riches are in fortune
A greater good, than wisedome is in nature.

152 [Act III, scene i, lines 1–33]

Mosca. I feare, I shall begin to grow in love
With my deare selfe, and my most prosp'rous parts,
They doe so spring, and burgeon; I can feele
A whimsey i' my bloud: (I know not how)
Successe hath made me wanton. I could skip
Out of my skin, now, like a subtill snake,
I am so limber. O! Your Parasite
Is a most precious thing, dropt from above,
Not bred 'mong'st clods, and clot-poules, here on earth.
I muse, the mysterie was not made a science,
It is so liberally profest! almost
All the wise world is little else, in nature,
But Parasites, or Sub-parasites. And, yet,
I meane not those, that have your bare towne-arte,
To know, who's fit to feede 'hem; have no house,
No family, no care, and therefore mould
Tales for mens eares, to bait that sense; or get
Kitchin-invention, and some stale receipts
To please the belly, and the groine; nor those,
With their court-dog-tricks, that can fawne, and fleere,
Make their revénnue out of legs, and faces,
Eccho my-Lord, and lick away a moth:
But your fine, elegant rascall, that can rise,
And stoope (almost together) like an arrow;
Shoot through the aire, as nimbly as a starre;
Turne short, as doth a swallow; and be here,
And there, and here, and yonder, all at once;
Present to any humour, all occasion;
And change a visor, swifter, than a thought!
This is the creature, had the art borne with him;
Toiles not to learne it, but doth practise it
Out of most excellent nature: and such sparkes,
Are the true Parasites, others but their *Zanies*.

153   *Song*
                           To Celia

          Come my CELIA, let us prove,
          While we may, the sports of love;
          Time will not be ours, for ever:
          He, at length, our good will sever.
          Spend not then his guifts in vaine.
          Sunnes, that set, may rise againe:
          But if once we lose this light,
          'Tis, with us, perpetuall night.
          Why should we deferre our joyes?
          Fame, and rumor are but toyes.
          Cannot we delude the eyes
          Of a few poore houshold spyes?
          Or his easier eares beguile,
          So removèd by our wile?
          'Tis no sinne, loves fruit to steale,
          But the sweet theft to reveale:
          To be taken, to be seene,
          These have crimes accounted beene.

                  [after the Latin of Catullus]

154   *Song*
                           To Celia

          Drinke to me, onely, with thine eyes,
             And I will pledge with mine;
          Or leave a kisse but in the cup,
             And Ile not looke for wine.
          The thirst, that from the soule doth rise,
             Doth aske a drinke divine:
          But might I of JOVE'S *Nectar* sup,
             I would not change for thine.
          I sent thee, late, a rosie wreath,
             Not so much honoring thee,
          As giving it a hope, that there
             It could not withered bee.
          But thou thereon did'st onely breathe,
             And sent'st it backe to mee:
          Since when it growes, and smells, I sweare,
             Not of it selfe, but thee.

               [after the Greek of Philostratus]

155   from *The Key Keeper*

Song

If to your ear it wonder bring
To hear Apollo's statue sing
'Gainst nature's law,
Ask this great King
And his fair Queen, who are the proper cause.
It is not wisdom's power alone
Or beauty's that can move a stone,
But both so high
In this great King
And his fair Queen do strike the harmony,
Which harmony hath power to touch
The dullest earth, and make it such
As I am now.
To this great King
And his fair Queen, whom none to praise knows how
Except with silence which indeed
Doth truest Admiration breed
And that came I
To this best King
And his best Queen in my last note and die.

156   from *The Alchemist* [Act II, scene ii, lines 41–87]

Mammon. I will have all my beds, blowne up; not stuft:
Downe is too hard. And then, mine oval roome,
Fill'd with such pictures, as TIBERIUS tooke
From ELEPHANTIS: and dull ARETINE
But coldly imitated. Then, my glasses,
Cut in more subtill angles, to disperse,
And multiply the figures, as I walke
Naked betweene my *succubæ*. My mists
I'le have of perfume, vapor'd 'bout the roome,
To lose our selves in; and my baths, like pits
To fall into: from whence, we will come forth,
And rowle us drie in gossamour, and roses.
(Is it arriv'd at *ruby?*)— Where I spie
A wealthy citizen, or rich lawyer,
Have a sublim'd pure wife, unto that fellow
I'll send a thousand pound, to be my cuckold.

Face. And I shall carry it?
Mammon.   No. I'll ha' no bawds,
  But fathers, and mothers. They will doe it best.
  Best of all others. And, my flatterers
  Shall be the pure, and gravest of Divines,
  That I can get for money. My mere fooles,
  Eloquent burgesses, and then my poets,
  The same that writ so subtly of the *fart*,
  Whom I will entertaine, still, for that subject.
  The few, that would give out themselves, to be
  Court, and towne-stallions, and, each where, belye
  Ladies, who' are knowne most innocent, for them;
  Those will I begge, to make me *eunuchs* of:
  And they shall fan me with ten estrich tailes
  A piece, made in a plume, to gather wind.
  We will be brave, *Puffe*, now we ha' the *med'cine*.
  My meat, shall all come in, in *Indian* shells,
  Dishes of agate, set in gold, and studded,
  With emeralds, saphyres, hiacynths, and rubies.
  The tongues of carpes, dormice, and camels heeles,
  Boil'd i' the spirit of SOL, and dissolv'd pearle,
  (APICIUS diet, 'gainst the *epilepsie*)
  And I will eate these broaths, with spoones of amber,
  Headed with diamant, and carbuncle.
  My foot-boy shall eate phesants; calverd salmons,
  Knots, godwits, lamprey's: I my selfe will have
  The beards of barbels, serv'd, in stead of sallades;
  Oild mushromes; and the swelling unctuous paps
  Of a fat pregnant sow, newly cut off,
  Drest with an exquisite, and poynant sauce;
  For which, Ile say unto my cooke, there's gold,
  Goe forth, and be a knight.

157   Doing, a filthy pleasure is, and short;
       And done, we straight repent us of the sport:
       Let us not then rush blindly on unto it,
       Like lustfull beasts, that onely know to doe it:
       For lust will languish, and that heat decay.
       But thus, thus, keeping endlesse Holy-day,
       Let us together closely lie, and kisse,
       There is no labour, nor no shame in this;
       This hath pleas'd, doth please, and long will please; never
       Can this decay, but is beginning ever.

         [after the Latin of a fragment formerly attributed to Petronius]

158   *To Penshurst*

Thou art not, PENSHURST, built to envious show,
    Of touch, or marble; nor canst boast a row
Of polish'd pillars, or a roofe of gold:
    Thou hast no lantherne, whereof tales are told;
Or stayre, or courts; but stand'st an ancient pile,
    And these grudg'd at, art reverenc'd the while.
Thou joy'st in better markes, of soyle, of ayre,
    Of wood, of water: therein thou art faire.
Thou hast thy walkes for health, as well as sport:
    Thy *Mount*, to which the *Dryads* doe resort,
Where PAN, and BACCHUS their high feasts have made,
    Beneath the broad beech, and the chest-nut shade;
That taller tree, which of a nut was set,
    At his great birth, where all the *Muses* met.
There, in the writhèd barke, are cut the names
    Of many a SYLVANE, taken with his flames.
And thence, the ruddy *Satyres* oft provoke
    The lighter *Faunes*, to reach thy *Ladies oke*.
Thy copp's, too, nam'd of GAMAGE, thou hast there,
    That never failes to serve thee season'd deere,
When thou would'st feast, or exercise thy friends.
    The lower land, that to the river bends,
Thy sheepe, thy bullocks, kine, and calves doe feed:
    The middle grounds thy mares, and horses breed.
Each banke doth yeeld thee coneyes; and the topps
    Fertile of wood, ASHORE, and SYDNEY's copp's,
To crowne thy open table, doth provide
    The purpled pheasant, with the speckled side:
The painted partrich lyes in every field,
    And, for thy messe, is willing to be kill'd.
And if the high-swolne *Medway* faile thy dish,
    Thou hast thy ponds, that pay thee tribute fish,
Fat, agèd carps, that runne into thy net.
    And pikes, now weary their owne kinde to eat,
As loth, the second draught, or cast to stay,
    Officiously, at first, themselves betray.
Bright eeles, that emulate them, and leape on land,
    Before the fisher, or into his hand.
Then hath thy orchard fruit, thy garden flowers,
    Fresh as the ayre, and new as are the houres.
The earely cherry, with the later plum,
    Fig, grape, and quince, each in his time doth come:
The blushing apricot, and woolly peach
    Hang on thy walls, that every child may reach.

And though thy walls be of the countrey stone,
    They'are rear'd with no mans ruine, no mans grone,
There's none, that dwell about them, wish them downe;
    But all come in, the farmer, and the clowne:
And no one empty-handed, to salute
    Thy lord, and lady, though they have no sute.
Some bring a capon, some a rurall cake,
    Some nuts, some apples; some that thinke they make
The better cheeses, bring 'hem; or else send
    By their ripe daughters, whom they would commend
This way to husbands; and whose baskets beare
    An embleme of themselves, in plum, or peare.
But what can this (more than expresse their love)
    Adde to thy free provisions, farre above
The neede of such? whose liberall boord doth flow,
    With all, that hospitalitie doth know!
Where comes no guest, but is allow'd to eate,
    Without his feare, and of thy lords owne meate:
Where the same beere, and bread, and selfe-same wine,
    That is his Lordships, shall be also mine.
And I not faine to sit (as some, this day,
    At great mens tables) and yet dine away.
Here no man tells my cups; nor, standing by,
    A waiter, doth my gluttony envý:
But gives me what I call, and lets me eate,
    He knowes, below, he shall finde plentie of meate,
Thy tables hoord not up for the next day,
    Nor, when I take my lodging, need I pray
For fire, or lights, or livorie: all is there;
    As if thou, then, wert mine, or I raign'd here:
There's nothing I can wish, for which I stay.
    That found King JAMES, when hunting late, this way,
With his brave sonne, the Prince, they saw thy fires
    Shine bright on every harth as the desires
Of thy *Penates* had beene set on flame,
    To entertayne them; or the countrey came,
With all their zeale, to warme their welcome here.
    What (great, I will not say, but) sodayne cheare
Did'st thou, then, make 'hem! and what praise was heap'd
    On thy good lady, then! who, therein, reap'd
The just reward of her high huswifery;
    To have her linnen, plate, and all things nigh,
When shee was farre: and not a roome, but drest,
    As if it had expected such a guest!
These, PENSHURST, are thy praise, and yet not all.
    Thy lady's noble, fruitfull, chaste withall.

His children thy great lord may call his owne:
A fortune, in this age, but rarely knowne.
They are, and have beene taught religion: Thence
Their gentler spirits have suck'd innocence.
Each morne, and even, they are taught to pray,
With the whole houshold, and may, every day,
Reade, in their vertuous parents noble parts,
The mysteries of manners, armes, and arts.
Now, PENSHURST, they that will proportion thee
With other edifices, when they see
Those proud, ambitious heaps, and nothing else,
May say, their lords have built, but thy lord dwells.

ANONYMOUS

1603

159

Weepe you no more sad fountaines,
What need you flowe so fast,
Looke how the snowie mountaines,
Heav'ns sunne doth gently waste.
But my sunnes heav'nly eyes
View not your weeping,
That nowe lies sleeping
Softly now softly lies sleeping.

Sleepe is a reconciling,
A rest that peace begets:
Doth not the sunne rise smiling,
When faire at ev'n he sets,
Rest you, then rest sad eyes,
Melt not in weeping,
While she lies sleeping
Softly now softly lies sleeping.

CYRIL TOURNEUR

1575?–1626

160–1

from *The Revenger's Tragedy*

160

[Act I, scene i, lines 1–49]

Vindice. Duke: royall letcher; goe, gray hayrde adultery,
And thou his sonne, as impious steept as hee:
And thou his bastard true-begott in evill:

And thou his Dutchesse that will doe with Divill,
Foure exlent Characters—O that marrow-lesse age,
Would stuffe the hollow Bones with damnd desires,
And stead of heate kindle infernall fires,
Within the spend-thrift veynes of a drye Duke,
A parcht and juicelesse luxur. O God! one
That has scarce bloud inough to live upon.
And hee to ryot it like a sonne and heyre?
O the thought of that
Turnes my abusèd heart-strings into fret.

                                        [*to the skull*]
Thou sallow picture of my poysonèd love,
My studies ornament, thou shell of Death,
Once the bright face of my betrothèd Lady,
When life and beauty naturally filld out
These ragged imperfections;
When two-heaven-pointed Diamonds were set
In those unsightly Rings;—then 'twas a face
So farre beyond the artificiall shine
Of any womans bought complexion
That the uprightest man, (if such there be,
That sinne but seaven times a day) broke custome
And made up eight with looking after her.
Oh she was able to ha' made a Usurers sonne
Melt all his patrimony in a kisse,
And what his father fiftie yeares told
To have consumde, and yet his sute beene cold:
But oh accursèd Pallace!
Thee when thou wert appareld in thy flesh,
The old Duke poyson'd,
Because thy purer part would not consent
Unto his palsey-lust, for old men lust-full
Do show like young men angry, eager violent,
Out-bid like their limited performances—
O ware an old man hot, and vicious
'Age as in gold, in lust is covetous.'
Vengence thou murder's Quit-rent, and whereby
Thou showst thy selfe Tennant to Tragedy,
Oh keepe thy day, houre, minute, I beseech,
For those thou hast determind: hum: who ere knew
Murder unpayd? faith give Revenge her due
She'has kept touch hetherto—be merry, merry,
Advance thee, O thou terror to fat folkes
To have their costly three-pilde flesh worne off
As bare as this—for banquets, ease and laughter,
Can make great men, as greatnesse goes by clay,
But wise men little are more great than they.

161   [Act III, scene v, lines 53–97]

               [*Vindice, with the skull of his love drest up in Tires*]

Vindice. Art thou beguild now? tut, a Lady can,
    At such all hid, beguile a wiser man.
    Have I not fitted the old surfetter
    With a quaint peice of beauty? age and bare bone
    Are e'er allied in action; here's an eye,
    Able to tempt a greatman—to serve God,
    A prety hanging lip, that has forgot now to dissemble;
    Me thinkes this mouth should make a swearer tremble,
    A drunckard claspe his teeth, and not undo 'em,
    To suffer wet damnation to run through 'em.
    Heres a cheeke keepes her colour; let the winde go whistle,
    Spout Raine, we feare thee not, be hot or cold
    Alls one with us; and is not he absurd,
    Whose fortunes are upon their faces set,
    That feare no other God but winde and wet?
Hippolite. Brother y'ave spoke that right;
    Is this the forme that living shone so bright?
Vindice. The very same,
    And now me thinkes I could e'en chide my selfe,
    For doating on her beauty, tho her death
    Shall be revengd after no common action;
    Do's the Silke-worme expend her yellow labours
    For thee? for thee dos she undoe herselfe?
    Are Lord-ships sold to maintaine Lady-ships
    For the poore benefit of a bewitching minute?
    Why dos yon fellow falsify hie-waies
    And put his life betweene the Judges lippes,
    To refine such a thing, keepes horse and men
    To beate their valours for her?
    Surely wee're all mad people, and they
    Whome we thinke are, are not; we mistake those,
    Tis we are mad in sense, they but in clothes.
Hippolite. Faith and in clothes too we, give us our due.
Vindice. Dos every proud and selfe-affecting Dame
    Camphire her face for this? and grieve her Maker
    In sinfull baths of milke,—when many an infant starves,
    For her superfluous out-side, all for this?
    Who now bids twenty pound a night, prepares
    Musick, perfumes, and sweete-meates? all are husht,
    Thou maist lie chast now! it were fine me thinkes,
    To have thee seene at Revells, forgetfull feasts,

And uncleane Brothells; sure twould fright the sinner
And make him a good coward, put a Reveller
Out of his Antick amble
And cloye an Epicure with empty dishes.

JOHN WEBSTER
1575?–1634 or 1638?

162   from *The White Devil* [Act V, scene iv]

Call for the Robin-Red-brest and the wren,
Since ore shadie groves they hover,
And with leaves and flowres doe cover
The friendlesse bodies of unburied men.
Call unto his funerall Dole
The Ante, the field-mouse, and the mole
To reare him hillockes, that shall keepe him warme,
And (when gay tombes are robb'd) sustaine no harme,
But keepe the wolfe far thence, that's foe to men,
For with his nailes hee'l dig them up agen.

163–6   from *The Duchess of Malfi*

163   [Act II, scene ii, lines 18–36]

Duchess. Do'st thou thinke we shall know one an other,
   In th'other world?
Cariola. Yes, out of question.
Duchess. O that it were possible we might
   But hold some two dayes conference with the dead,
   From them I should learne somewhat, I am sure
   I never shall know here: I'll tell thee a miracle,
   I am not mad yet, to my cause of sorrow.
   Th'heaven ore my head, seemes made of molton brasse,
   The earth of flaming sulphure, yet I am not mad:
   I am acquainted with sad misery,
   As the tan'd galley-slave is with his Oare,
   Necessity makes me suffer constantly,
   And custome makes it easie. Who do I looke like now?
Cariola. Like to your picture in the gallery,
   A deale of life in shew, but none in practise:

Or rather like some reverend monument
Whose ruines are even pittied.
Duchess.   Very proper:
And Fortune seemes onely to have her eie-sight,
To behold my Tragedy.

164   [Act IV, scene ii]

Hearke, now every thing is still,
The Schritch-Owle, and the whistler shrill,
Call upon our Dame, aloud,
And bid her quickly don her shrowd:
Much you had of Land and rent,
Your length in clay's now competent.
A long war, disturb'd your minde,
Here your perfect peace is sign'd,
Of what is't, fooles make such vaine keeping?
Sin their conception, their birth, weeping:
Their life, a generall mist of error,
Their death, a hideous storme of terror.
Strew your haire, with powders sweete:
Don cleane linnen, bath your feete,
And (the foule feend more to checke)
A crucifixe let blesse your necke,
'Tis now full tide, 'tweene night, and day,
End your groane, and come away.

165   [Act IV, scene ii, lines 194–224]

Duchess. What death?
Bosola.   Strangling, here are your Executioners.
Duchess. I forgive them:
      The apoplexie, cathar, or cough o'th'loongs,
      Would do as much as they do.
Bosola. Doth not death fright you?
Duchess.   Who would be afraid on't?
      Knowing to meete such excellent company
      In th'other world.
Bosola.   Yet, me thinkes,
      The manner of your death should much afflict you,
      This cord should terrifie you?
Duchess.   Not a whit,
      What would it pleasure me, to have my throate cut
      With diamonds? or to be smotherèd

With Cassia? or to be shot to death, with pearles?
I know death hath ten thousand severall doores
For men, to take their *Exits*: and 'tis found
They go on such strange geometricall hinges,
You may open them both wayes: any way, (for God sake)
So I were out of your whispering. Tell my brothers,
That I perceive death, (now I am well awake)
Best guift is, they can give, or I can take:
I would faine put off my last womans-fault,
I'l'd not be tedious to you.
Executioners.   We are ready.
Duchess. Dispose my breath, how please you, but my body
    Bestow upon my women, will you?
Executioners.   Yes.
Duchess. Pull, and pull strongly, for your able strength
    Must pull downe heaven upon me:
    Yet stay, heaven gates are not so highly arch'd
    As Princes pallaces, they that enter there
    Must go upon their knees. [*kneels*] Come violent death,
    Serve for *Mandragora*, to make me sleepe;
    Go tell my brothers, when I am laid out,
    They then may feede in quiet.

166   [Act V, scene v, lines 91–104]

Malateste. Thou wretched thing of blood,
    How came *Antonio* by his death?
Bosola. In a mist: I know not how,
    Such a mistake, as I have often seene
    In a play: Oh, I am gone.
    We are onely like dead wals, or vaulted graves,
    That ruin'd, yeildes no eccho: Fare you well,
    It may be paine, but no harme to me to die,
    In so good a quarrell: Oh this gloomy world,
    In what a shadow, or deepe pit of darknesse,
    Doth (womanish, and fearefull) mankind live?
    Let worthy mindes, nere stagger in distrust
    To suffer death, or shame for what is just:
    Mine is an other voyage.

RICHARD CORBETT
1582–1635

167   *A Proper New Ballad Intituled The Faeryes*
      Farewell: Or God-a-Mercy Will:

To be sung or whistled to the Tune of the Meddow Brow by
the Learned; by the unLearned; To the Tune of FORTUNE

Farewell, Rewards and *Faeries*,
   Good Houswives now may say;
For now foule Slutts in Dairies
   Doe fare as well as they;
And though they sweepe theyr Hearths no less
   Than Maydes were wont to doe,
Yet who of late for Cleaneliness
   Finds *sixe-pence* in her Shoe?

Lament, lament, old Abbies,
   The *Faries* lost Command:
They did but change Priests *Babies*,
   But some have changd your *Land*;
And all your Children sprung from thence
   Are now growne *Puritanes*:
Who live as *Changelings* ever since
   For love of your Demaines.

At Morning and at Evening both
   You merry were and glad,
So little Care of Sleepe or Sloth
   These Prettie ladies had.
When *Tom* came home from labour,
   Or *Ciss* to Milking rose,
Then merrily, merrily went theyre Tabor,
   And nimbly went theyre Toes.

Wittness those Rings and Roundelayes
   Of theirs, which yet remaine,
Were footed in Queene *Maries* dayes
   On many a Grassy Playne;
But, since of late *Elizabeth*,
   And later *James*, came in,
They never daunc'd on any heath
   As *when the Time hath bin.*

By which wee note the *Faries*
  Were of the old Profession;
Theyre Songs were *Ave Maryes*,
  Theyre Daunces were *Procession*.
But now, alas, they all are dead,
  Or gone beyond the Seas,
Or Farther for Religion fled,
  Or elce they take theyre Ease.

A Tell-tale in theyre Company
  They never could endure,
And who-so kept not secretly
  Theyre Mirth, was punisht sure.
It was a just and Christian Deed
  To pinch such blacke and blew.
O, how the Common welth doth need
  Such Justices as you!

Now they have left our Quarters
  A *Register* they have,
Who looketh to theyre Charters,
  A Man both *Wise* and *Grave*;
An hundred of theyre merry Prancks
  By one that I could name
Are kept in Store, conn twenty Thanks
  To *William* for the same.

I marvell who his Cloake would turne
  When *Puck* had led him round,
Or where those Walking Fires would burne,
  Where *Cureton* would be found;
How *Broker* would appeare to be,
  For whom this Age doth mourne;
But that theyre Spiritts live in Thee,
  In Thee, old *William Chourne*.

To *William Chourne* of Stafford Shire
  Give Laud and Prayses due,
Who every Meale can mend your Cheare
  With Tales both old and true.
To *William* all give Audience,
  And pray yee for his Noddle,
For all the *Faries* Evidence
  Were lost, if that were Addle.

EDWARD, LORD HERBERT OF CHERBURY
1582–1648

168　　　*An Ode upon a Question moved, Whether*
　　　　　Love should continue for ever?

Having interr'd her Infant-birth,
　　The watry ground that late did mourn,
　　Was strew'd with flow'rs for the return
Of the wish'd Bridegroom of the earth.

The well accorded Birds did sing
　　Their hymns unto the pleasant time,
　　And in a sweet consorted chime
Did welcom in the chearful Spring.

To which, soft whistles of the Wind,
　　And warbling murmurs of a Brook,
　　And vari'd notes of leaves that shook,
An harmony of parts did bind.

While doubling joy unto each other,
　　All in so rare concent was shown,
　　No happiness that came alone,
Nor pleasure that was not another.

When with a love none can express,
　　That mutually happy pair,
　　Melander and *Celinda* fair,
The season with their loves did bless.

Walking thus towards a pleasant Grove,
　　Which did, it seem'd, in new delight
　　The pleasures of the time unite,
To give a triumph to their love,

They stay'd at last, and on the Grass
　　Reposèd so, as o'r his breast
　　She bow'd her gracious head to rest,
Such a weight as no burden was.

While over eithers compass'd waist
　　Their folded arms were so compos'd,
　　As if in straitest bonds inclos'd,
They suffer'd for joys they did taste.

Long their fixt eyes to Heaven bent,
　　Unchangèd, they did never move,
　　As if so great and pure a love
No Glass but it could represent.

When with a sweet, though troubled look,
    She first brake silence, saying, Dear friend,
    O that our love might take no end,
Or never had beginning took!

I speak not this with a false heart,
    (Wherewith his hand she gently strain'd)
    Or that would change a love maintain'd
With so much faith on either part.

Nay, I protest, though Death with his
    Worst Counsel should divide us here,
    His terrors could not make me fear,
To come where your lov'd presence is.

Only if loves fire with the breath
    Of life be kindlèd, I doubt,
    With our last air 'twill be breath'd out,
And quenchèd with the cold of death.

That if affection be a line,
    Which is clos'd up in our last hour;
    Oh how 'twould grieve me, any pow'r
Could force so dear a love as mine!

She scarce had done, when his shut eyes
    An inward joy did represent,
    To hear *Celinda* thus intent
To a love he so much did prize.

Then with a look, it seem'd, deny'd
    All earthly pow'r but hers, yet so,
    As if to her breath he did ow
This borrow'd life, he thus repli'd;

O you, wherein, they say, Souls rest,
    Till they descend pure heavenly fires,
    Shall lustful and corrupt desires
With your immortal seed be blest?

And shall our Love, so far beyond
    That low and dying appetite,
    And which so chast desires unite,
Not hold in an eternal bond?

Is it, because we should decline,
    And wholly from our thoughts exclude
    Objects that may the sense delude,
And study only the Divine?

No sure, for if none can ascend
 Ev'n to the visible degree
 Of things created, how should we
The invisible comprehend?

Or rather since that Pow'r exprest
 His greatness in his works alone,
 B'ing here best in his Creatures known,
Why is he not lov'd in them best?

But is't not true, which you pretend,
 That since our love and knowledge here,
 Only as parts of life appear,
So they with it should take their end.

O no, Belov'd, I am most sure,
 Those vertuous habits we acquire,
 As being with the Soul intire,
Must with it evermore endure.

For if where sins and vice reside,
 We find so foul a guilt remain,
 As never dying in his stain,
Still punish'd in the Soul doth bide,

Much more that true and real joy,
 Which in a vertuous love is found,
 Must be more solid in its ground,
Than Fate or Death can e'r destroy.

Else should our Souls in vain elect,
 And vainer yet were Heavens laws,
 When to an everlasting Cause
They gave a perishing Effect.

Nor here on earth then, nor above,
 Our good affection can impair,
 For where God doth admit the fair,
Think you that he excludeth Love?

These eyes again then, eyes shall see,
 And hands again these hands enfold,
 And all chast pleasures can be told
Shall with us everlasting be.

For if no use of sense remain
 When bodies once this life forsake,
 Or they could no delight partake,
Why should they ever rise again?

And if every imperfect mind
   Make love the end of knowledge here,
   How perfect will our love be, where
All imperfection is refin'd?

Let then no doubt, *Celinda*, touch,
   Much less your fairest mind invade,
   Were not our souls immortal made,
Our equal loves can make them such.

So when one wing can make no way,
   Two joynèd can themselves dilate,
   So can two persons propagate,
When singly either would decay.

So when from hence we shall be gone,
   And be no more, nor you, nor I,
   As one anothers mystery,
Each shall be both, yet both but one.

This said, in her up-lifted face,
   Her eyes which did that beauty crown,
   Were like two starrs, that having faln down,
Look up again to find their place:

While such a moveless silent peace
   Did seize on their becalmèd sense,
   One would have thought some Influence
Their ravish'd spirits did possess.

AURELIAN TOWNSHEND

1583?–1651?

169   Your smiles are not as other womens bee
Only the drawing of the mouth awrye,
For breasts and cheekes and forehead wee may see,
Parts wanting motion, all stand smiling by.
    Heaven hath noe mouth, and yet is sayd to smile
           After your style;
    Noe more hath Earth, yet that smyles too,
           Just as you doe.

Noe sympering lipps nor lookes can breed
Such smyles, as from your Face proceed.
    The sunn must lend his goulden beames,
    Soft windes their breath, green trees their shade,

Sweete fields their flowers, cleare springs their streams,
Ere such another smyle bee made.
But these concurring, wee may say,
Soe smiles the spring, and soe smyles lovely Maye.

170   *A Dialogue betwixt Time and a Pilgrime*

Pilgrim.   Agèd man, that mowes these fields.
Time.   Pilgrime speak, what is thy will?
Pilgrim. Whose soile is this that such sweet Pasture yields?
            Or who art thou, whose Foot stands never still?
                Or where am I?   *Time.* In love.
Pilgrim.   His Lordship lies above?
Time.   Yes and below, and round about,
                Wherein all sorts of flow'rs are growing,
                Which as the early Spring puts out,
                    Time falls as fast a mowing.
Pilgrim.   If thou art Time, these Flow'rs have Lives,
                    And then I fear,
                Under some Lilly, she I love
                    May now be growing there.
Time.   And in some Thistle or some spyre of grasse
            My syth thy stalk, before hers come, may passe.
Pilgrim. Wilt thou provide it may.   *Time.* No.   *Pilgrim.* Alleage
            the cause.
Time. Because Time cannot alter but obey Fates laws.

Chorus. Then happy those whom Fate, that is the stronger,
            Together twists their threads, and yet draws hers the longer.

171   from *Albion's Triumph*

            Song

            Mercury

What mak's me so unnimbly ryse,
    That did descend so fleete?
There is no up-hill in the skyes;
    Clouds stay not featherèd feete.

            Chorus

Thy wings are sing'd: and thou canst fly
But slowly now, swift MERCURY.

Mercury

Some Lady heere, is sure to blame
That from Loves starry skyes,
Hath shot some Beame, or sent some flame,
Like Lightning, from her Eyes.

Chorus

Taxe not the Starrs, with what the Sunne,
Too neere aproch't (insens't) hath done.

Mercury

I'le rowle me in Auroras Dew,
Or lye in Tethis bed;
Or from coole Iris begge a few
Pure Opale showrs new shed.

Chorus

Nor Dew, nor showers, nor sea can slake
Thy quenchlesse heate, but Lethes lake.

WILLIAM DRUMMOND
1585–1649

172   *For the Baptiste*

The last and greatest Herauld of Heavens King,
Girt with rough Skinnes, hyes to the Desarts wilde,
Among that savage brood the Woods foorth bring,
Which hee than Man more harmlesse found and milde:
His food was Blossomes, and what young doth spring,
With Honey that from virgine Hives distil'd;
Parcht Bodie, hollow Eyes, some uncouth thing
Made him appeare, long since from Earth exilde.
There burst hee foorth; All yee, whose Hopes relye
On GOD, with mee amidst these Desarts mourne,
Repent, repent, and from olde errours turne.
Who listned to his voyce, obey'd his crye?
   Onelie the Ecchoes which hee made relent,
   Rung from their Marble Caves, repent, repent.

LADY MARY WROTH
1587?–1652?

173   *Song*

Love a child is ever crying,
    Please him, and hee straite is flying,
    Give him hee the more is craving
    Never satisfi'd with having;

His desires have noe measure,
    Endles folly is his treasure,
    What hee promiseth hee breaketh
    Trust nott one word that hee speaketh;

Hee vowes nothing butt faulse matter,
    And to cousen you hee'l flatter,
    Lett him gaine the hand hee'll leave you,
    And still glory to deceive you;

Hee will triumph in your wayling,
    And yett cause bee of your fayling,
    These his vertus are, and slighter
    Are his guiftes, his favours lighter,

Feathers are as firme in staying
    Woulves noe fiercer in theyr preying.
    As a child then leave him crying
    Nor seeke him soe giv'n to flying.

GEORGE WITHER
1588–1667

174   Shall I wasting in Dispaire,
                     Dye because a *Womans* faire?
                     Or make pale my cheekes with care,
                     Cause anothers Rosie are?
                     Be shee fairer than the Day,
                     Or the Flowry Meads in May;
                         If She be not so to me,
                         What care I how faire shee be.

                     Should my heart be grievd or pin'd,
                     Cause I see a *Woman* kind?

Or a well disposèd Nature,
Joynèd with a lovely Feature?
Be shee meeker, kinder, than
Turtle-Dove, or *Pelican*:
　If shee be not so to me,
　What care I, how kind she be.

Shall a *Womans* Virtues move
Me, to perish for her love?
Or, her well-deserving knowne,
Make me quite forget mine owne?
Be shee with that Goodnesse blest,
Which may gaine her, name of *Best*:
　If she be not such to me,
　What care I, how good she be.

Cause her Fortune seemes too high,
Shall I play the foole, and dye?
Those that beare a Noble minde,
Where they want of Riches find,
Thinke, what with them, they would doe,
That without them, dare to wooe.
　And, unlesse that mind I see,
　What care I, though Great she be.

Great, or *Good*, or *Kind*, or *Faire*,
I will ne'er the more dispaire,
If She love me, this beleeve;
I will die, ere she shall grieve.
If she slight me, when I wooe;
I can scorne, and let her goe.
　For, if shee be not for me,
　What care I, for whom she be.

ROBERT HERRICK

1591–1674

175　　　　*Delight in Disorder*

A sweet disorder in the dresse
Kindles in cloathes a wantonnesse:
A Lawne about the shoulders thrown
Into a fine distraction:
An erring Lace, which here and there
Enthralls the Crimson Stomacher:

A Cuffe neglectfull, and thereby
Ribbands to flow confusedly:
A winning wave (deserving Note)
In the tempestuous petticote:
A carelesse shooe-string, in whose tye
I see a wilde civility:
Doe more bewitch me, than when Art
Is too precise in every part.

176   *Corinna's going a Maying*

Get up, get up for shame, the Blooming Morne
Upon her wings presents the god unshorne.
　　See how *Aurora* throwes her faire
　　Fresh-quilted colours through the aire:
　　Get up, sweet-Slug-a-bed, and see
　　The Dew-bespangling Herbe and Tree.
Each Flower has wept, and bow'd toward the East,
Above an houre since; yet you not drest,
　　Nay! not so much as out of bed?
　　When all the Birds have Mattens seyd,
　　And sung their thankfull Hymnes: 'tis sin,
　　Nay, profanation to keep in,
When as a thousand Virgins on this day,
Spring, sooner than the Lark, to fetch in May.

Rise; and put on your Foliage, and be seene
To come forth, like the Spring-time, fresh and greene;
　　And sweet as *Flora*. Take no care
　　For Jewels for your Gowne, or Haire:
　　Feare not; the leaves will strew
　　Gemms in abundance upon you:
Besides, the childhood of the Day has kept,
Against you come, some *Orient Pearls* unwept:
　　Come, and receive them while the light
　　Hangs on the Dew-locks of the night:
　　And *Titan* on the Eastern hill
　　Retires himselfe, or else stands still
Till you come forth. Wash, dresse, be briefe in praying:
Few Beads are best, when once we goe a Maying.

Come, my *Corinna*, come; and comming, marke
How each field turns a street; each street a Parke
　　Made green, and trimm'd with trees: see how
　　Devotion gives each House a Bough,
　　Or Branch: Each Porch, each doore, ere this,
　　An Arke a Tabernacle is

Made up of white-thorn neatly enterwove;
As if here were those cooler shades of love.
　　Can such delights be in the street,
　　And open fields, and we not see't?
　　Come, we'll abroad; and let's obay
　　The Proclamation made for May:
And sin no more, as we have done, by staying;
But my *Corinna*, come, let's goe a Maying.

There's not a budding Boy, or Girle, this day,
But is got up, and gone to bring in May.
　　A deale of Youth, ere this, is come
　　Back, and with *White-thorn* laden home.
　　Some have dispatcht their Cakes and Creame,
　　Before that we have left to dreame:
And some have wept, and woo'd, and plighted Troth,
And chose their Priest, ere we can cast off sloth:
　　Many a green-gown has been given;
　　Many a kisse, both odde and even:
　　Many a glance too has been sent
　　From out the eye, Loves Firmament:
Many a jest told of the Keyes betraying
This night, and Locks pickt, yet w'are not a Maying.

Come, let us goe, while we are in our prime;
And take the harmlesse follie of the time.
　　We shall grow old apace, and die
　　Before we know our liberty.
　　Our life is short; and our dayes run
　　As fast away as do's the Sunne:
And as a vapour, or a drop of raine
Once lost, can ne'r be found againe:
　　So when or you or I are made
　　A fable, song, or fleeting shade;
　　All love, all liking, all delight
　　Lies drown'd with us in endlesse night.
Then while time serves, and we are but decaying;
Come, my *Corinna*, come, let's goe a Maying.

177　　　*To the Virgins, to make much of Time*

　　Gather ye Rose-buds while ye may,
　　　Old Time is still a flying:
　　And this same flower that smiles to day,
　　　To morrow will be dying.

The glorious Lamp of Heaven, the Sun,
   The higher he's a getting;
The sooner will his Race be run,
   And neerer he's to Setting.

That Age is best, which is the first,
   When Youth and Blood are warmer;
But being spent, the worse, and worst
   Times, still succeed the former.

Then be not coy, but use your time;
   And while ye may, goe marry:
For having lost but once your prime,
   You may for ever tarry.

178   *The comming of good luck*

So Good-luck came, and on my roofe did light,
Like noyse-lesse Snow; or as the dew of night:
Not all at once, but gently, as the trees
Are, by the Sun-beams, tickel'd by degrees.

179   *To Anthea, who may command him any thing*

Bid me to live, and I will live
   Thy Protestant to be:
Or bid me love, and I will give
   A loving heart to thee.

A heart as soft, a heart as kind,
   A heart as sound and free,
As in the whole world thou canst find,
   That heart Ile give to thee.

Bid that heart stay, and it will stay,
   To honour thy Decree:
Or bid it languish quite away,
   And't shall doe so for thee.

Bid me to weep, and I will weep,
   While I have eyes to see:
And having none, yet I will keep
   A heart to weep for thee.

Bid me despaire, and Ile despaire,
   Under that *Cypresse* tree:
Or bid me die, and I will dare
   E'en Death, to die for thee.

Thou art my life, my love, my heart,
    The very eyes of me:
And hast command of every part,
    To live and die for thee.

180   *Upon Julia's Clothes*

When as in silks my *Julia* goes,
Then, then (me thinks) how sweetly flowes
That liquefaction of her clothes.

Next, when I cast mine eyes and see
That brave Vibration each way free;
O how that glittering taketh me!

181   *To his ever-loving God*

Can I not come to Thee, my God, for these
So very-many-meeting hindrances,
That slack my pace; but yet not make me stay?
Who slowly goes, rids (in the end) his way.
Cleere Thou my paths, or shorten Thou my miles,
Remove the barrs, or lift me o're the stiles:
Since rough the way is, help me when I call,
And take me up; or els prevent the fall.
I kenn my home; and it affords some ease,
To see far off the smoaking Villages.
Fain would I rest; yet covet not to die,
For feare of future-biting penurie:
No, no, (my God) Thou know'st my wishes be
To leave this life, not loving it, but Thee.

HENRY KING

1592–1669

182   *An Exequy To his Matchlesse never to be*
                forgotten Freind

Accept, thou Shrine of my Dead Saint!
Instead of Dirges this Complaint;
And, for sweet flowres to crowne thy Hearse,
Receive a strew of weeping verse

From thy griev'd Friend; whome Thou might'st see
Quite melted into Teares for Thee.
    Deare Losse! since thy untimely fate
My task hath beene to meditate
On Thee, on Thee: Thou art the Book,
The Library whereon I look
Though almost blind. For Thee (Lov'd Clay!)
I Languish out, not Live the Day,
Using no other Exercise
But what I practise with mine Eyes.
By which wett glasses I find out
How lazily Time creepes about
To one that mournes: This, only This
My Exercise and bus'nes is:
So I compute the weary howres
With Sighes dissolvèd into Showres.
    Nor wonder if my time goe thus
Backward and most præposterous;
Thou hast Benighted mee. Thy Sett
This Eve of blacknes did begett,
Who wast my Day, (though overcast
Before thou hadst thy Noon-tide past)
And I remember must in teares,
Thou scarce hadst seene so many Yeeres
As Day tells Howres. By thy cleere Sunne
My Love and Fortune first did run;
But Thou wilt never more appeare
Folded within my Hemispheare:
Since both thy Light and Motion
Like a fledd Starr is fall'n and gone;
And 'twixt mee and my Soule's deare wish
The Earth now interposèd is,
Which such a straunge Ecclipse doth make
As ne're was read in Almanake.
    I could allow Thee for a time
To darken mee and my sad Clime,
Were it a Month, a Yeere, or Ten,
I would thy Exile live till then;
And all that space my mirth adjourne,
So Thou wouldst promise to returne,
And putting off thy ashy Shrowd
At length disperse this Sorrowe's Cloud.
    But woe is mee! the longest date
Too narrowe is to calculate
These empty hopes. Never shall I
Be so much blest, as to descry

A glympse of Thee, till that Day come
Which shall the Earth to cinders doome,
And a fierce Feaver must calcine
The Body of this World, like Thine,
(My Little World!) That fitt of Fire
Once off, our Bodyes shall aspire
To our Soules' blisse: Then wee shall rise,
And view our selves with cleerer eyes
In that calme Region, where no Night
Can hide us from each other's sight.
    Meane time, thou hast Hir, Earth: Much good
May my harme doe thee. Since it stood
With Heaven's will I might not call
Hir longer Mine; I give thee all
My short liv'd right and Interest
In Hir, whome living I lov'd best:
With a most free and bounteous grief,
I give thee what I could not keep.
Be kind to Hir: and prethee look
Thou write into thy Doomsday book
Each parcell of this Rarity,
Which in thy Caskett shrin'd doth ly:
See that thou make thy reck'ning streight,
And yeeld Hir back againe by weight;
For thou must Auditt on thy trust
Each Grane and Atome of this Dust:
As thou wilt answere Him, that leant,
Not gave thee, my deare Monument.
    So close the ground, and 'bout hir shade
Black Curtaines draw, My Bride is lay'd.
    Sleep on (my Love!) in thy cold bed
Never to be disquieted.
My last Good-night! Thou wilt not wake
Till I Thy Fate shall overtake:
Till age, or grief, or sicknes must
Marry my Body to that Dust
It so much loves; and fill the roome
My heart keepes empty in Thy Tomb.
Stay for mee there: I will not faile
To meet Thee in that hollow Vale.
And think not much of my delay;
I am already on the way,
And follow Thee with all the speed
Desire can make, or Sorrowes breed.
Each Minute is a short Degree
And e'ry Howre a stepp towards Thee.

At Night when I betake to rest,
Next Morne I rise neerer my West
Of Life, almost by eight Howres' sayle,
Than when Sleep breath'd his drowsy gale.
  Thus from the Sunne my Bottome steeres,
And my Daye's Compasse downward beares.
Nor labour I to stemme the Tide,
Through which to Thee I swiftly glide.
  'Tis true; with shame and grief I yeild.
Thou, like the Vann, first took'st the Field,
And gotten hast the Victory
In thus adventuring to Dy
Before Mee; whose more yeeres might crave
A just præcédence in the Grave.
But hark! My Pulse, like a soft Drum
Beates my Approach, Tells Thee I come;
And, slowe howe're my Marches bee,
I shall at last sitt downe by Thee.
  The thought of this bids mee goe on,
And wait my dissolution
With Hope and Comfort. Deare! (forgive
The Crime) I am content to live
Divided, with but half a Heart,
Till wee shall Meet and Never part.

183   Tell mee no more how faire shee is;
           I have no mind to heare
       The Story of that distant Blisse
           I never shall come neere.
         By sad experience I have found
         That Hir perfection is my wound.

       And tell mee not how fond I am
           To tempt a daring Fate,
       From whence no triumph ever came
           But to repent too late.
         There is some hope ere long I may
         In silence dote my self away.

       I aske no Pitty (Love!) from thee,
           Nor will thy Justice blame;
       So that thou wilt not envy mee
           The glory of my Flame:
         Which crownes my Heart, when e're it dyes,
         In that it falles Hir Sacrifice.

GEORGE HERBERT
1593–1633

184   [*Easter*]

I got me flowers to straw thy way;
I got me boughs off many a tree:
But thou wast up by break of day,
And brought'st thy sweets along with thee.

The Sunne arising in the East,
Though he give light, and th' East perfume;
If they should offer to contest
With thy arising, they presume.

Can there be any day but this,
Though many sunnes to shine endeavour?
We count three hundred, but we misse:
There is but one, and that one ever.

185   *Redemption*

Having been tenant long to a rich Lord,
    Not thriving, I resolvèd to be bold,
    And make a suit unto him, to afford
A new small-rented lease, and cancell th' old.
In heaven at his manour I him sought:
    They told me there, that he was lately gone
    About some land, which he had dearly bought
Long since on earth, to take possession.
I straight return'd, and knowing his great birth,
    Sought him accordingly in great resorts;
    In cities, theatres, gardens, parks, and courts:
At length I heard a ragged noise and mirth
    Of theeves and murderers: there I him espied,
    Who straight, *Your suit is granted*, said, and died.

186   *Prayer* (1)

Prayer the Churches banquet, Angels age,
    Gods breath in man returning to his birth,
    The soul in paraphrase, heart in pilgrimage,
The Christian plummet sounding heav'n and earth;

Engine against th' Almightie, sinners towre,
    Reversèd thunder, Christ-side-piercing spear,
    The six-daies world transposing in an houre,
A kinde of tune, which all things heare and fear;
Softnesse, and peace, and joy, and love, and blisse,
    Exalted Manna, gladnesse of the best,
    Heaven in ordinarie, man well drest,
The milkie way, the bird of Paradise,
    Church-bels beyond the starres heard, the souls bloud,
    The land of spices; something understood.

187   *Jordan* (1)

Who sayes that fictions onely and false hair
Become a verse? Is there in truth no beautie?
Is all good structure in a winding stair?
May no lines passe, except they do their dutie
    Not to a true, but painted chair?

Is it no verse, except enchanted groves
And sudden arbours shadow course-spunne lines?
Must purling streams refresh a lovers loves?
Must all be vail'd, while he that reades, divines,
    Catching the sense at two removes?

Shepherds are honest people; let them sing:
Riddle who list, for me, and pull for Prime:
I envie no mans nightingale or spring;
Nor let them punish me with losse of rime,
    Who plainly say, *My God, My King.*

188   *Vertue*

Sweet day, so cool, so calm, so bright,
The bridall of the earth and skie:
The dew shall weep thy fall to night;
        For thou must die.

Sweet rose, whose hue angrie and brave
Bids the rash gazer wipe his eye:
Thy root is ever in its grave,
        And thou must die.

Sweet spring, full of sweet dayes and roses,
A box where sweets compacted lie;
My musick shows ye have your closes,
        And all must die.

Onely a sweet and vertuous soul,
Like season'd timber, never gives;
But though the whole world turn to coal,
      Then chiefly lives.

189   *The Pearl*

Matth. 13. 45

I know the wayes of Learning; both the head
And pipes that feed the presse, and make it runne;
What reason hath from nature borrowèd,
Or of it self, like a good huswife, spunne
In laws and policie; what the starres conspire,
What willing nature speaks, what forc'd by fire;
Both th' old discoveries, and the new-found seas,
The stock and surplus, cause and historie:
All these stand open, or I have the keyes:
      Yet I love thee.

I know the wayes of Honour, what maintains
The quick returns of courtesie and wit:
In vies of favours whether partie gains,
When glorie swells the heart, and moldeth it
To all expressions both of hand and eye,
Which on the world a true-love-knot may tie,
And bear the bundle, wheresoe're it goes:
How many drammes of spirit there must be
To sell my life unto my friends or foes:
      Yet I love thee.

I know the wayes of Pleasure, the sweet strains,
The lullings and the relishes of it;
The propositions of hot bloud and brains;
What mirth and musick mean; what love and wit
Have done these twentie hundred yeares, and more:
I know the projects of unbridled store:
My stuffe is flesh, not brasse; my senses live,
And grumble oft, that they have more in me
Than he that curbs them, being but one to five:
      Yet I love thee.

I know all these, and have them in my hand:
Therefore not sealèd, but with open eyes
I flie to thee, and fully understand
Both the main sale, and the commodities;
And at what rate and price I have thy love;
With all the circumstances that may move:

Yet through these labyrinths, not my groveling wit,
But thy silk twist let down from heav'n to me,
Did both conduct and teach me, how by it
         To climbe to thee.

190   *The Quip*

         The merrie world did on a day
         With his train-bands and mates agree
         To meet together, where I lay,
         And all in sport to jeere at me.

         First, Beautie crept into a rose,
         Which when I pluckt not, Sir, said she,
         Tell me, I pray, Whose hands are those?
         But thou shalt answer, Lord, for me.

         Then Money came, and chinking still,
         What tune is this, poore man? said he:
         I heard in Musick you had skill.
         But thou shalt answer, Lord, for me.

         Then came brave Glorie puffing by
         In silks that whistled, who but he?
         He scarce allow'd me half an eie.
         But thou shalt answer, Lord, for me.

         Then came quick Wit and Conversation,
         And he would needs a comfort be,
         And, to be short, make an Oration.
         But thou shalt answer, Lord, for me.

         Yet when the houre of thy designe
         To answer these fine things shall come;
         Speak not at large; say, I am thine:
         And then they have their answer home.

191   *Hope*

         I gave to Hope a watch of mine: but he
                   An anchor gave to me.
         Then an old prayer-book I did present:
                   And he an optick sent.

With that I gave a viall full of tears:
        But he a few green eares.
Ah Loyterer! I'le no more, no more I'le bring:
        I did expect a ring.

192   *The Flower*

    How fresh, O Lord, how sweet and clean
Are thy returns! ev'n as the flowers in spring;
      To which, besides their own demean,
The late-past frosts tributes of pleasure bring.
        Grief melts away
        Like snow in May,
    As if there were no such cold thing.

    Who would have thought my shrivel'd heart
Could have recover'd greennesse? It was gone
      Quite under ground; as flowers depart
To see their mother-root, when they have blown;
        Where they together
        All the hard weather,
    Dead to the world, keep house unknown.

    These are thy wonders, Lord of power,
Killing and quickning, bringing down to hell
      And up to heaven in an houre;
Making a chiming of a passing-bell.
        We say amisse,
        This or that is:
    Thy word is all, if we could spell.

    O that I once past changing were,
Fast in thy Paradise, where no flower can wither!
      Many a spring I shoot up fair,
Offring at heav'n, growing and groning thither:
        Nor doth my flower
        Want a spring-showre,
    My sinnes and I joining together.

    But while I grow in a straight line,
Still upwards bent, as if heav'n were mine own,
      Thy anger comes, and I decline:
What frost to that? what pole is not the zone,
        Where all things burn,
        When thou dost turn,
    And the least frown of thine is shown?

    And now in age I bud again,
After so many deaths I live and write;

I once more smell the dew and rain,
And relish versing: O my onely light,
It cannot be
That I am he
On whom thy tempests fell all night.

These are thy wonders, Lord of love,
To make us see we are but flowers that glide:
Which when we once can finde and prove,
Thou hast a garden for us, where to bide.
Who would be more,
Swelling through store,
Forfeit their Paradise by their pride.

193   *Love* (III)

Love bade me welcome: yet my soul drew back,
Guiltie of dust and sinne.
But quick-ey'd Love, observing me grow slack
From my first entrance in,
Drew nearer to me, sweetly questioning,
If I lack'd any thing.

A guest, I answer'd, worthy to be here:
Love said, You shall be he.
I the unkinde, ungratefull? Ah my deare,
I cannot look on thee.
Love took my hand, and smiling did reply,
Who made the eyes but I?

Truth Lord, but I have marr'd them: let my shame
Go where it doth deserve.
And know you not, sayes Love, who bore the blame?
My deare, then I will serve.
You must sit down, sayes Love, and taste my meat:
So I did sit and eat.

THOMAS CAREW
1594?–1640

194   *Epitaph on the Lady Mary Villers*

The Lady *Mary Villers* lyes
Under this stone; with weeping eyes

The Parents that first gave her birth,
And their sad Friends, lay'd her in earth:
If any of them (Reader) were
Knowne unto thee, shed a teare,
Or if thyselfe possesse a gemme,
As deare to thee, as this to them;
Though a stranger to this place,
Bewayle in theirs, thine owne hard case;
For thou perhaps at thy returne
Mayest find thy Darling in an Urne.

195   *A Song*

Ask me no more where *Jove* bestowes,
When *June* is past, the fading rose:
For in your beauties orient deep,
These Flowers as in their causes sleep.

Ask me no more whither doe stray
The golden Atomes of the day:
For in pure love heaven did prepare
Those powders to inrich your hair.

Ask me no more whither doth hast
The Nightingale, when *May* is past:
For in your sweet dividing throat
She winters, and keeps warm her note.

Ask me no more where those starres light,
That downwards fall in dead of night:
For in your eyes they sit, and there,
Fixèd, become as in their sphere.

Ask me no more if East or West,
The Phenix builds her spicy nest:
For unto you at last she flyes,
And in your fragrant bosome dies.

JAMES SHIRLEY
1596–1666

196   The glories of our blood and state,
                 Are shadows, not substantial things,
              There is no armour against fate,
                 Death lays his icy hand on Kings,

Scepter and Crown,
Must tumble down,
And in the dust be equal made,
With the poor crooked sithe and spade.

Some men with swords may reap the field,
And plant fresh laurels where they kill,
But their strong nerves at last must yield,
They tame but one another still;
Early or late,
They stoop to fate,
And must give up their murmuring breath,
When they pale Captives creep to death.

The Garlands wither on your brow,
Then boast no more your mighty deeds,
Upon Deaths purple Altar now,
See where the Victor-victim bleeds,
Your heads must come,
To the cold Tomb,
Onely the actions of the just
Smell sweet, and blossom in their dust.

WILLIAM HABINGTON
1605–1654

197   *Nox nocti indicat Scientiam*

When I survey the bright
Cœlestiall spheare:
So rich with jewels hung, that night
Doth like an Æthiop bride appear,

My soule her wings doth spread
And heaven-ward flies,
Th' Almighty's Mysteries to read
In the large volumes of the skies.

For the bright firmament
Shootes forth no flame
So silent, but is eloquent
In speaking the Creators name.

No unregarded star
Contracts its light
Into so small a Character,
Remov'd far from our humane sight:

But if we stedfast looke,
     We shall discerne
In it as in some holy booke,
How man may heavenly knowledge learne.

It tells the Conqueror,
     That farre-stretcht powre
Which his proud dangers traffique for,
Is but the triumph of an houre.

That from the farthest North,
     Some Nation may
Yet undiscoverèd issue forth,
And o'er his new got conquest sway.

Some Nation yet shut in
     With hills of ice
May be let out to scourge his sinne
'Till they shall equall him in vice.

And then they likewise shall
     Their ruine have,
For as your selves your Empires fall,
And every Kingdome hath a grave.

Thus those Celestiall fires,
     Though seeming mute,
The fallacie of our desires
And all the pride of life confute.

For they have watcht since first
     The World had birth:
And found sinne in itselfe accurst,
And nothing permanent on earth.

SIR WILLIAM DAVENANT

1606–1668

198   *Song*

The Lark now leaves his watry Nest
     And climbing, shakes his dewy Wings;
He takes this Window for the East;
     And to implore your Light, he Sings,
Awake, awake, the Morn will never rise,
Till she can dress her Beauty at your Eies.

The Merchant bowes unto the Seamans Star,
   The Ploughman from the Sun his Season takes;
But still the Lover wonders what they are,
   Who look for day before his Mistress wakes.
Awake, awake, break through your Vailes of Lawne!
Then draw your Curtains, and begin the Dawne.

199   *The Philosopher and the Lover; to a Mistress dying*

Song

Lover

Your Beauty, ripe, and calm, and fresh,
   As Eastern Summers are,
Must now, forsaking Time and Flesh,
   Add light to some small Star.

Philosopher

Whilst she yet lives, were Stars decay'd,
   Their light by hers, relief might find:
But Death will lead her to a shade
   Where Love is cold, and Beauty blinde.

Lover

Lovers (whose Priests all Poets are)
   Think ev'ry Mistress, when she dies,
Is chang'd at least into a Starr:
   And who dares doubt the Poets wise?

Philosopher

But ask not Bodies doom'd to die,
   To what abode they go;
Since Knowledge is but sorrows Spy,
   It is not safe to know.

EDMUND WALLER

1606–1687

200   *Song*

Go lovely Rose,
   Tell her that wastes her time and me,
   That now she knows

When I resemble her to thee
How sweet and fair she seems to be.

Tell her that's young,
And shuns to have her graces spy'd
That hadst thou sprung
In desarts where no men abide,
Thou must have uncommended dy'd.

Small is the worth
Of beauty from the light retir'd;
Bid her come forth,
Suffer her self to be desir'd,
And not blush so to be admir'd.

Then die that she,
The common fate of all things rare
May read in thee;
How small a part of time they share,
That are so wondrous sweet and fair.

201   *Of the Last Verses in the Book* [*Divine Poems*]

When we for Age could neither read nor write,
The Subject made us able to indite.
The Soul with Nobler Resolutions deckt,
The Body stooping, does Herself erect:
No Mortal Parts are requisite to raise
Her, that Unbody'd can her Maker praise.
    The Seas are quiet, when the Winds give o're;
So calm are we, when Passions are no more:
For then we know how vain it was to boast
Of fleeting Things, so certain to be lost.
Clouds of Affection from our younger Eyes
Conceal that emptiness, which Age descries.
    The Soul's dark Cottage, batter'd and decay'd,
Let's in new Light thrô chinks that time has made.
Stronger by weakness, wiser Men become
As they draw near to their Eternal home:
Leaving the Old, both Worlds at once they view,
That stand upon the Threshold of the New.

—*Miratur Limen Olympi.*
Virgil.

SIR RICHARD FANSHAWE
1608–1666

202   *A Great Favorit Beheaded*

The bloudy trunck of him who did possesse
　　Above the rest a haplesse happy state,
　　This little Stone doth Seale, but not depresse,
　　And scarce can stop the rowling of his fate.

Brasse Tombes which justice hath deny'd t'his fault,
　　The common pity to his vertues payes,
　　Adorning an Imaginary vault,
　　Which from our minds time strives in vaine to raze.

Ten yeares the world upon him falsly smild,
　　Sheathing in fawning lookes the deadly knife
　　Long aymèd at his head; That so beguild
　　It more securely might bereave his Life;

Then threw him to a Scaffold from a Throne.
Much Doctrine lyes under this little Stone.

　　　　　　[after the Spanish of Góngora]

JOHN MILTON
1608–1674

203   from *Ode on the Morning of Christ's Nativity:*
　　　　　　The Hymn [stanzas I–IX]

It was the Winter wilde,
While the Heav'n-born-childe,
　　All meanly wrapt in the rude manger lies;
Nature in aw to him
Had doff't her gawdy trim,
　　With her great Master so to sympathize:
It was no season then for her
To wanton with the Sun her lusty Paramour.

Only with speeches fair
She woo's the gentle Air
　　To hide her guilty front with innocent Snow,

And on her naked shame,
Pollute with sinfull blame,
    The Saintly Vail of Maiden white to throw,
Confounded, that her Makers eyes
Should look so neer upon her foul deformities.

But he her fears to cease,
Sent down the meek-eyd Peace,
    She crown'd with Olive green, came softly sliding
Down through the turning sphear
His ready Harbinger,
    With Turtle wing the amorous clouds dividing,
And waving wide her mirtle wand,
She strikes a universall Peace through Sea and Land.

No War, or Battails sound
Was heard the World around,
    The idle spear and shield were high up hung;
The hookèd Chariot stood
Unstain'd with hostile blood,
    The Trumpet spake not to the armèd throng,
And Kings sate still with awfull eye,
As if they surely knew their sovran Lord was by.

But peacefull was the night
Wherin the Prince of light
    His raign of peace upon the earth began:
The Windes with wonder whist,
Smoothly the waters kist,
    Whispering new joyes to the milde Ocean,
Who now hath quite forgot to rave,
While Birds of Calm sit brooding on the charmèd wave.

The Stars with deep amaze
Stand fixt in stedfast gaze,
    Bending one way their pretious influence,
And will not take their flight,
For all the morning light,
    Or *Lucifer* that often warn'd them thence;
But in their glimmering Orbs did glow,
Untill their Lord himself bespake, and bid them go.

And though the shady gloom
Had given day her room,
    The Sun himself with-held his wonted speed,
And hid his head for shame,
As his inferiour flame,
    The new enlightn'd world no more should need;
He saw a greater Sun appear
Than his bright Throne, or burning Axletree could bear.

The Shepherds on the Lawn,
Or ere the point of dawn,
 Sate simply chatting in a rustick row;
Full little thought they than,
That the mighty *Pan*
 Was kindly com to live with them below;
Perhaps their loves, or els their sheep,
Was all that did their silly thoughts so busie keep.

When such musick sweet
Their hearts and ears did greet,
 As never was by mortall finger strook,
Divinely-warbled voice
Answering the stringèd noise,
 As all their souls in blisfull rapture took:
The Air such pleasure loth to lose,
With thousand echo's still prolongs each heav'nly close.

204   from *Arcades*

      Song

 Nymphs and Shepherds dance no more
  By sandy *Ladons* Lillied banks.
 On old *Lycæus* or *Cyllene* hoar,
  Trip no more in twilight ranks,
 Though *Erymanth* your loss deplore,
  A better soyl shall give ye thanks.
 From the stony *Mænalus*,
 Bring your Flocks, and live with us,
 Here ye shall have greater grace,
 To serve the Lady of this place.
  Though *Syrinx* your *Pans* Mistres were,
  Yet *Syrinx* well might wait on her.
   Such a rural Queen
   All *Arcadia* hath not seen.

205   *Lycidas*

In this Monody the Author bewails a learned Friend, unfortunatly drown'd in his Passage from *Chester* on the *Irish* Seas, 1637. And by occasion foretels the ruine of our corrupted Clergy then in their height.

 Yet once more, O ye Laurels, and once more
 Ye Myrtles brown, with Ivy never-sear,

I com to pluck your Berries harsh and crude,
And with forc'd fingers rude,
Shatter your leaves before the mellowing year.
Bitter constraint, and sad occasion dear,
Compels me to disturb your season due:
For *Lycidas* is dead, dead ere his prime
Young *Lycidas*, and hath not left his peer:
Who would not sing for *Lycidas*? he knew
Himself to sing, and build the lofty rhyme.
He must not flote upon his watry bier
Unwept, and welter to the parching wind,
Without the meed of som melodious tear.
　　Begin then, Sisters of the sacred well,
That from beneath the seat of *Jove* doth spring,
Begin, and somwhat loudly sweep the string.
Hence with denial vain, and coy excuse,
So may som gentle Muse
With lucky words favour my destin'd Urn,
And as he passes turn,
And bid fair peace be to my sable shrowd.
For we were nurst upon the self-same hill,
Fed the same flock, by fountain, shade, and rill.
　　Together both, ere the high Lawns appear'd
Under the opening eye-lids of the morn,
We drove a field, and both together heard
What time the Gray-fly winds her sultry horn,
Batt'ning our flocks with the fresh dews of night,
Oft till the Star that rose, at Ev'ning, bright
Toward Heav'ns descent had slop'd his westering wheel.
Mean while the Rural ditties were not mute,
Temper'd to th'Oaten Flute;
Rough *Satyrs* danc'd, and *Fauns* with clov'n heel,
From the glad sound would not be absent long,
And old *Damœtas* lov'd to hear our song.
　　But O the heavy change, now thou art gon,
Now thou art gon, and never must return!
Thee Shepherd, thee the Woods, and desert Caves,
With wilde Thyme and the gadding Vine o'regrown,
And all their echoes mourn.
The Willows, and the Hazle Copses green,
Shall now no more be seen,
Fanning their joyous Leaves to thy soft layes.
As killing as the Canker to the Rose,
Or Taint-worm to the weanling Herds that graze,
Or Frost to Flowers, that their gay wardrop wear,
When first the White thorn blows;
Such, *Lycidas*, thy loss to Shepherds ear.

Where were ye Nymphs when the remorseless deep
Clos'd o're the head of your lov'd *Lycidas*?
For neither were ye playing on the steep,
Where your old *Bards*, the famous *Druids* ly,
Nor on the shaggy top of *Mona* high,
Nor yet where *Deva* spreads her wisard stream:
Ay me, I fondly dream!
Had ye bin there—for what could that have don?
What could the Muse her self that *Orpheus* bore,
The Muse her self, for her inchanting son
Whom Universal nature did lament,
When by the rout that made the hideous roar,
His goary visage down the stream was sent,
Down the swift *Hebrus* to the *Lesbian* shore.
Alas! What boots it with uncessant care
To tend the homely slighted Shepherds trade,
And strictly meditate the thankles Muse,
Were it not better don as others use,
To sport with *Amaryllis* in the shade,
Or with the tangles of *Neæra's* hair?
Fame is the spur that the clear spirit doth raise
(That last infirmity of Noble mind)
To scorn delights, and live laborious dayes;
But the fair Guerdon when we hope to find,
And think to burst out into sudden blaze,
Comes the blind *Fury* with th'abhorrèd shears,
And slits the thin spun life. But not the praise,
Phœbus repli'd, and touch'd my trembling ears;
Fame is no plant that grows on mortal soil,
Nor in the glistering foil
Set off to th'world, nor in broad rumour lies,
But lives and spreds aloft by those pure eyes,
And perfet witnes of all judging *Jove*;
As he pronounces lastly on each deed,
Of so much fame in Heav'n expect thy meed.
O Fountain *Arethuse*, and thou honour'd floud,
Smooth-sliding *Mincius*, crown'd with vocall reeds,
That strain I heard was of a higher mood:
But now my Oate proceeds,
And listens to the Herald of the Sea
That came in *Neptune's* plea,
He ask'd the Waves, and ask'd the Fellon winds,
What hard mishap hath doom'd this gentle swain?
And question'd every gust of rugged wings
That blows from off each beakèd Promontory,
They knew not of his story,
And sage *Hippotades* their answer brings,

That not a blast was from his dungeon stray'd,
The Ayr was calm, and on the level brine,
Sleek *Panope* with all her sisters play'd.
It was that fatall and perfidious Bark
Built in th'eclipse, and rigg'd with curses dark,
That sunk so low that sacred head of thine.

   Next *Camus*, reverend Sire, went footing slow,
His Mantle hairy, and his Bonnet sedge,
Inwrought with figures dim, and on the edge
Like to that sanguine flower inscrib'd with woe.
Ah; Who hath reft (quoth he) my dearest pledge?
Last came, and last did go,
The Pilot of the *Galilean* lake,
Two massy Keyes he bore of metals twain,
(The Golden opes, the Iron shuts amain)
He shook his Miter'd locks, and stern bespake,
How well could I have spar'd for thee, young swain,
Anow of such as for their bellies sake,
Creep and intrude, and climb into the fold?
Of other care they little reck'ning make,
Than how to scramble at the shearers feast,
And shove away the worthy bidden guest.
Blind mouthes! that scarce themselves know how to hold
A Sheep-hook, or have learn'd ought els the least
That to the faithfull Herdmans art belongs!
What recks it them? What need they? They are sped;
And when they list, their lean and flashy songs
Grate on their scrannel Pipes of wretched straw,
The hungry Sheep look up, and are not fed,
But swoln with wind, and the rank mist they draw,
Rot inwardly, and foul contagion spread:
Besides what the grim Woolf with privy paw
Daily devours apace, and nothing sed,
But that two-handed engine at the door,
Stands ready to smite once, and smite no more.

   Return *Alpheus*, the dread voice is past,
That shrunk thy streams; Return *Sicilian* Muse,
And call the Vales, and bid them hither cast
Their Bels, and Flourets of a thousand hues.
Ye valleys low where the milde whispers use,
Of shades and wanton winds, and gushing brooks,
On whose fresh lap the swart Star sparely looks,
Throw hither all your quaint enameld eyes,
That on the green terf suck the honied showres,
And purple all the ground with vernal flowres.
Bring the rathe Primrose that forsaken dies.
The tufted Crow-toe, and pale Gessamine,

The white Pink, and the Pansie freakt with jeat,
The glowing Violet.
The Musk-rose, and the well attir'd Woodbine.
With Cowslips wan that hang the pensive hed,
And every flower that sad embroidery wears:
Bid *Amaranthus* all his beauty shed,
And Daffadillies fill their cups with tears,
To strew the Laureat Herse where *Lycid* lies.
For so to interpose a little ease,
Let our frail thoughts dally with false surmise.
Ay me! Whilst thee the shores, and sounding Seas
Wash far away, where ere thy bones are hurld,
Whether beyond the stormy *Hebrides*,
Where thou perhaps under the whelming tide
Visit'st the bottom of the monstrous world;
Or whether thou to our moist vows deny'd,
Sleep'st by the fable of *Bellerus* old,
Where the great vision of the guarded Mount
Looks toward *Namancos* and *Bayona's* hold;
Look homeward Angel now, and melt with ruth.
And, O ye *Dolphins*, waft the haples youth.
    Weep no more, woful Shepherds weep no more,
For *Lycidas* your sorrow is not dead,
Sunk though he be beneath the watry floar,
So sinks the day-star in the Ocean bed,
And yet anon repairs his drooping head,
And tricks his beams, and with new spangled Ore,
Flames in the forehead of the morning sky:
So *Lycidas* sunk low, but mounted high,
Through the dear might of him that walk'd the waves
Where other groves, and other streams along,
With *Nectar* pure his oozy Lock's he laves,
And hears the unexpressive nuptiall Song,
In the blest Kingdoms meek of joy and love.
There entertain him all the Saints above,
In solemn troops, and sweet Societies
That sing, and singing in their glory move,
And wipe the tears for ever from his eyes.
Now *Lycidas* the Shepherds weep no more;
Hence forth thou art the Genius of the shore,
In thy large recompense, and shalt be good
To all that wander in that perilous flood.
    Thus sang the uncouth Swain to th'Okes and rills,
While the still morn went out with Sandals gray,
He touch'd the tender stops of various Quills,
With eager thought warbling his *Dorick* lay:

And now the Sun had stretch'd out all the hills,
And now was dropt into the Western bay;
At last he rose, and twitch'd his Mantle blew:
To morrow to fresh Woods, and Pastures new.

206–7   from *Comus*

206   *Song*

   Sabrina fair
     Listen where thou art sitting
  Under the glassie, cool, translucent wave,
    In twisted braids of Lillies knitting
  The loose train of thy amber-dropping hair,
     Listen for dear honour's sake,
     Goddess of the silver lake,
          Listen and save.

207   [*Song*]

   By the rushy-fringèd bank,
  Where grows the Willow and the Osier dank,
    My sliding Chariot stayes,
  Thick set with Agat, and the azurn sheen
  Of Turkis blew, and Emrauld green
    That in the channell strayes,
  Whilst from off the waters fleet
  Thus I set my printless feet
  O're the Cowslips Velvet head,
    That bends not as I tread,
  Gentle swain at thy request
    I am here.

208   *The Fifth Ode of Horace*

                          Lib. I

Quis multa gracilis te puer in Rosa, *Rendred almost word for word without*
Rhyme according to the Latin Measure, as near as the Language will permit.

  What slender Youth bedew'd with liquid odours
  Courts thee on Roses in some pleasant Cave,
    Pyrrha for whom bind'st thou
    In wreaths thy golden Hair,

Plain in thy neatness; O how oft shall he
On Faith and changèd Gods complain: and Seas
    Rough with black winds and storms
      Unwonted shall admire:
Who now enjoyes thee credulous, all Gold,
Who alwayes vacant, always amiable
    Hopes thee; of flattering gales
      Unmindfull. Hapless they
To whom thou untry'd seem'st fair. Me in my vow'd
Picture the sacred wall declares t' have hung
    My dank and dropping weeds
      To the stern God of Sea.

    [after the Latin of Horace]

209   *On the late Massacher in Piemont*

Avenge O Lord thy slaughter'd Saints, whose bones
    Lie scatter'd on the Alpine mountains cold,
    Ev'n them who kept thy truth so pure of old
    When all our Fathers worship't Stocks and Stones,
Forget not: in thy book record their groanes
    Who were thy Sheep and in their antient Fold
    Slayn by the bloody *Piemontese* that roll'd
    Mother with Infant down the Rocks. Their moans
The Vales redoubl'd to the Hills, and they
    To Heav'n. Their martyr'd blood and ashes sow
    O're all th'*Italian* fields where still doth sway
The triple Tyrant: that from these may grow
    A hunder'd-fold, who having learnt thy way
    Early may fly the *Babylonian* wo.

210   When I consider how my light is spent,
    E're half my days, in this dark world and wide,
    And that one Talent which is death to hide,
    Lodg'd with me useless, though my Soul more bent
To serve therewith my Maker, and present
    My true account, least he returning chide,
    Doth God exact day-labour, light deny'd,
    I fondly ask; But patience to prevent
That murmur, soon replies, God doth not need
    Either man's work or his own gifts, who best
    Bear his milde yoak, they serve him best, his State
Is Kingly. Thousands at his bidding speed
    And post o're Land and Ocean without rest:
    They also serve who only stand and waite.

211–13   from *Paradise Lost*

211   [Book I, lines 1–26]

    Of Mans First Disobedience, and the Fruit
Of that Forbidden Tree, whose mortal tast
Brought Death into the World, and all our woe,
With loss of *Eden*, till one greater Man
Restore us, and regain the blissful Seat,
Sing Heav'nly Muse, that on the secret top
Of *Oreb*, or of *Sinai*, didst inspire
That Shepherd, who first taught the chosen Seed,
In the Beginning how the Heav'ns and Earth
Rose out of *Chaos*: or if *Sion* Hill
Delight thee more, and *Siloa's* Brook that flow'd
Fast by the Oracle of God; I thence
Invoke thy aid to my adventrous Song,
That with no middle flight intends to soar
Above th' *Aonian* Mount, while it pursues
Things unattempted yet in Prose or Rhime.
And chiefly Thou O Spirit, that dost prefer
Before all Temples th' upright heart and pure,
Instruct me, for Thou know'st; Thou from the first
Wast present, and with mighty wings outspread
Dove-like satst brooding on the vast Abyss
And mad'st it pregnant: What in me is dark
Illumine, what is low raise and support;
That to the highth of this great Argument
I may assert Eternal Providence,
And justifie the wayes of God to men.

212   [Book III, lines 1–55]

    Hail holy light, ofspring of Heav'n first-born,
Or of th' Eternal Coeternal beam
May I express thee unblam'd? since God is light,
And never but in unapproachèd light
Dwelt from Eternitie, dwelt then in thee,
Bright effluence of bright essence increate.
Or hear'st thou rather pure Ethereal stream,
Whose Fountain who shall tell? before the Sun,
Before the Heavens thou wert, and at the voice
Of God, as with a Mantle didst invest

The rising world of waters dark and deep,
Won from the void and formless infinite.
Thee I re-visit now with bolder wing,
Escap't the *Stygian* Pool, though long detain'd
In that obscure sojourn, while in my flight
Through utter and through middle darkness borne
With other notes than to th' *Orphean* Lyre
I sung of *Chaos* and *Eternal Night*,
Taught by the heav'nly Muse to venture down
The dark descent, and up to reascend,
Though hard and rare: thee I revisit safe,
And feel thy sovran vital Lamp; but thou
Revisit'st not these eyes, that rowle in vain
To find thy piercing ray, and find no dawn;
So thick a drop serene hath quencht thir Orbs,
Or dim suffusion veild. Yet not the more
Cease I to wander where the Muses haunt
Cleer Spring, or shadie Grove, or Sunnie Hill,
Smit with the love of sacred song; but chief
Thee *Sion* and the flowrie Brooks beneath
That wash thy hallowd feet, and warbling flow,
Nightly I visit: nor somtimes forget
Those other two equal'd with me in Fate,
So were I equal'd with them in renown,
Blind *Thamyris* and blind *Mæonides*,
And *Tiresias* and *Phineus* Prophets old.
Then feed on thoughts, that voluntarie move
Harmonious numbers; as the wakeful Bird
Sings darkling, and in shadiest Covert hid
Tunes her nocturnal Note. Thus with the Year
Seasons return, but not to me returns
Day, or the sweet approach of Ev'n or Morn,
Or sight of vernal bloom, or Summers Rose,
Or flocks, or herds, or human face divine;
But cloud in stead, and ever-during dark
Surrounds me, from the chearful waies of men
Cut off, and for the Book of knowledg fair
Presented with a Universal blanc
Of Natures works to mee expung'd and ras'd,
And wisdome at one entrance quite shut out.
So much the rather thou Celestial light
Shine inward, and the mind through all her powers
Irradiate, there plant eyes, all mist from thence
Purge and disperse, that I may see and tell
Of things invisible to mortal sight.

213   [Book IX, lines 1–47]

No more of talk where God or Angel Guest
With Man, as with his Friend, familiar us'd
To sit indulgent, and with him partake
Rural repast, permitting him the while
Venial discourse unblam'd: I now must change
Those Notes to Tragic; foul distrust, and breach
Disloyal on the part of Man, revolt,
And disobedience: On the part of Heav'n
Now alienated, distance and distaste,
Anger and just rebuke, and judgement giv'n,
That brought into this World a world of woe,
Sinne and her shadow Death, and Miserie
Deaths Harbinger: Sad task, yet argument
Not less but more Heroic than the wrauth
Of stern *Achilles* on his Foe pursu'd
Thrice Fugitive about *Troy* Wall; or rage
Of *Turnus* for *Lavinia* disespous'd,
Or *Neptun*'s ire or *Juno*'s, that so long
Perplex'd the *Greek* and *Cytherea*'s Son;
If answerable style I can obtaine
Of my Celestial Patroness, who deignes
Her nightly visitation unimplor'd,
And dictates to me slumbring, or inspires
Easie my unpremeditated Verse:
Since first this Subject for Heroic Song
Pleas'd me long choosing, and beginning late;
Not sedulous by Nature to indite
Warrs, hitherto the onely Argument
Heroic deem'd, chief maistrie to dissect
With long and tedious havoc fabl'd Knights
In Battels feign'd; the better fortitude
Of Patience and Heroic Martyrdom
Unsung; or to describe Races and Games,
Or tilting Furniture, emblazon'd Shields,
Impreses quaint, Caparisons and Steeds;
Bases and tinsel Trappings, gorgious Knights
At Joust and Torneament; then marshal'd Feast
Serv'd up in Hall with Sewers, and Seneshals;
The skill of Artifice or Office mean,
Not that which justly gives Heroic name
To Person or to Poem. Mee of these
Nor skilld nor studious, higher Argument
Remaines, sufficient of it self to raise
That name, unless an age too late, or cold

Climat, or Years damp my intended wing
Deprest, and much they may, if all be mine,
Not Hers who brings it nightly to my Ear.

214   from *Samson Agonistes* [line 1745–end]

Chorus. All is best, though we oft doubt,
What th' unsearchable dispose
Of highest wisdom brings about,
And ever best found in the close.
Oft he seems to hide his face,
But unexpectedly returns
And to his faithful Champion hath in place
Bore witness gloriously; whence *Gaza* mourns
And all that band them to resist
His uncontroulable intent,
His servants he with new acquist
Of true experience from this great event
With peace and consolation hath dismist,
And calm of mind all passion spent.

SIR JOHN SUCKLING
1609–1641

215   Oh! for some honest Lovers ghost,
Some kind unbodied post
Sent from the shades below.
I strangely long to know
Whether the nobler Chaplets wear,
Those that their mistresse scorn did bear,
Or those that were us'd kindly.

For what-so-e're they tell us here
To make those sufferings dear,
'Twill there I fear be found,
That to the being crown'd,
T'have lov'd alone will not suffice,
Unlesse we also have been wise,
And have our Loves enjoy'd.

What posture can we think him in,
That here unlov'd agen

Departs, and's thither gone
Where each sits by his own?
Or how can that *Elizium* be
Where I my Mistresse still must see
Circled in others Armes?

For there the Judges all are just,
And *Sophonisba* must
Be his whom she held dear;
Not his who lov'd her here:
The sweet *Philoclea* since she dy'de
Lies by her *Pirocles* his side,
Not by *Amphialus.*

Some Bayes (perchance) or Myrtle bough
For difference crowns the brow
Of those kind souls that were
The noble Martyrs here;
And if that be the onely odds,
(As who can tell) ye kinder Gods,
Give me the Woman here.

216   *The constant Lover*

Out upon it, I have lov'd
Three whole days together;
And am like to love three more,
If it hold fair weather.

Time shall moult away his wings
Ere he shall discover
In the whole wide world agen
Such a constant Lover.

But a pox upon't, no praise
There is due at all to me:
Love with me had made no stay,
Had it any been but she.

Had it any been but she
And that very very Face,
There had been at least ere this
A dozen dozen in her place.

217 *Song*

Why so pale and wan fond Lover?
            Prithee why so pale?
Will, when looking well can't move her,
            Looking ill prevaile?
            Prithee why so pale?

Why so dull and mute young Sinner?
            Prithee why so mute?
Will, when speaking well can't win her,
            Saying nothing doo't?
            Prithee why so mute?

Quit, quit, for shame, this will not move,
            This cannot take her;
If of her selfe shee will not Love,
            Nothing can make her,
            The Devill take her.

SIDNEY GODOLPHIN

1610–1643

218   Lord when the wise men came from Farr
       Ledd to thy Cradle by A Starr,
       Then did the shepheards too rejoyce,
       Instructed by thy Angells voyce,
       Blest were the wisemen in their skill,
       And shepheards in their harmelesse will.

       Wisemen in tracing Natures lawes
       Ascend unto the highest cause,
       Shepheards with humble fearefulnesse
       Walke safely, though their light be lesse,
       Though wisemen better know the way
       It seemes noe honest heart can stray:

       Ther is noe merrit in the wise
       But love, (the shepheards sacrifice)
       Wisemen all wayes of knowledge past,
       To 'th shepheards wonder come at last,
       To know, can only wonder breede,
       And not to know, is wonders seede.

A wiseman at the Alter Bowes
And offers up his studied vowes
And is received, may not the teares,
Which spring too from a shepheards feares,
And sighs upon his fraylty spent,
Though not distinct, be eloquent.

Tis true, the object sanctifies
All passions which within us rise,
But since noe creature comprehends
The cause of causes, end of ends,
Hee who himselfe vouchsafes to know
Best pleases his creator soe.

When then our sorrowes wee applye
To our owne wantes and poverty,
When wee looke up in all distresse
And our owne misery confesse
Sending both thankes and prayers above
Then though wee doe not know, we love.

219   Thou Joy of my Life
               First love of my youth
               Thou safest of pleasures
               And fullest of trueth,
               Thou purest of Nimphs
               And never more fayre
               Breathe this way and coole mee
               Thou pittying ayre,
               Come hither and hover
               On every parte
               Thou life of my sense
               And joy of my hart.

JAMES GRAHAM, MARQUIS OF MONTROSE

1612–1650

220   My dear and only Love, I pray
                   This noble World of thee,
               Be govern'd by no other Sway
                   But purest Monarchie.
               For if Confusion have a Part,
                   Which vertuous Souls abhor,
               And hold a Synod in thy Heart,
                   I'll never love thee more.

Like *Alexander* I will reign,
  And I will reign alone,
My Thoughts shall evermore disdain
  A Rival on my Throne.
He either fears his Fate too much,
  Or his Deserts are small,
That puts it not unto the Touch,
  To win or lose it all.

But I must rule and govern still,
  And always give the Law,
And have each Subject at my Will,
  And all to stand in awe.
But 'gainst my Battery if I find
  Thou shun'st the Prize so sore,
As that thou set'st me up a Blind,
  I'll never love thee more.

Or in the Empire of thy Heart,
  Where I should solely be,
Another do pretend a Part,
  And dares to Vie with me,
Or if Committees thou erect,
  And goes on such a Score,
I'll sing and laugh at thy Neglect,
  And never love thee more.

But if thou wilt be constant then,
  And faithful of thy Word,
I'll make thee glorious by my Pen,
  And famous by my Sword.
I'll serve thee in such noble Ways,
  Was never heard before:
I'll crown and deck thee all with Bays,
  And love thee evermore.

ANNE BRADSTREET

1612–1672

221   from *In Honour of that High and Mighty Princess
       Queen Elizabeth of Happy Memory: Her Epitaph*

Here sleeps THE *Queen*, this is the royall bed
Of th' Damask Rose, sprung from the white and red,

Whose sweet perfúme fills the all-filling air,
This Rose is withered, once so lovely faire,
On neither tree did grow such Rose before,
The greater was our gain, our losse the more.

222   *To my Dear and loving Husband*

If ever two were one, then surely we.
If ever man were lov'd by wife, then thee;
If ever wife was happy in a man,
Compare with me ye women if you can.
I prize thy love more than whole Mines of gold,
Or all the riches that the East doth hold.
My love is such that Rivers cannot quench,
Nor aught but love from thee, give recompence.
Thy love is such I can no way repay,
The heavens reward thee manifold I pray.
Then while we live, in love lets so perséver,
That when we live no more, we may live ever.

CLEMENT PAMAN

1612–1663

[probably Paman's; formerly attributed to JOHN CLEVELAND]

223   *Epitaph on the Earl of Strafford*

Here lies Wise and Valiant Dust,
Huddled up 'twixt Fit and Just:
STRAFFORD, who was hurried hence
'Twixt Treason and Convenience.
He spent his Time here in a Mist;
A *Papist*, yet a *Calvinist*.
His Prince's nearest Joy, and Grief.
He had, yet wanted all Reliefe.
The Prop and Ruine of the State;
The People's violent Love, and Hate:
One in extreames lov'd and abhor'd.
Riddles lie here; or in a word,
Here lies Blood; and let it lie
Speechlesse still, and never crie.

RICHARD CRASHAW
1612/13–1649

224   from *A Hymn to the Name and Honor of the*
              Admirable Sainte Teresa [lines 1–64]

Love, thou art Absolute sole lord
Of LIFE and DEATH. To prove the word,
Wee'l now appeal to none of all
Those thy old Souldiers, Great and tall,
Ripe Men of Martyrdom, that could reach down
With strong armes, their triumphant crown;
Such as could with lusty breath
Speak lowd into the face of death
Their Great LORD's glorious name, to none
Of those whose spatious Bosomes spread a throne
For LOVE at larg to fill: spare blood and sweat;
And see him take a private seat,
Making his mansion in the mild
And milky soul of a soft child.

     Scarse has she learn't to lisp the name
Of Martyr; yet she thinks it shame
Life should so long play with that breath
Which spent can buy so brave a death.
She never undertook to know
What death with love should have to doe;
Nor has she e're yet understood
Why to show love, she should shed blood
Yet though she cannot tell you why,
She can LOVE, and she can DY.

     Scarse has she Blood enough to make
A guilty sword blush for her sake;
Yet has she'a HEART dares hope to prove
How much lesse strong is DEATH than LOVE.

     Be love but there; let poor six yeares
Be pos'd with the maturest Feares
Man trembles at, you straight shall find
LOVE knowes no nonage, nor the MIND.
'Tis LOVE, not YEARES or LIMBS that can
Make the Martyr, or the man.

     LOVE touch't her HEART, and lo it beates
High, and burnes with such brave heates;
Such thirsts to dy, as dares drink up
A thousand cold deaths in one cup.

Good reason. For she breathes All fire.
Her weake brest heaves with strong desire
Of what she may with fruitles wishes
Seek for amongst her MOTHER's kisses.
    Since 'tis not to be had at home
She'l travail to a Martyrdom.
No home for hers confesses she
But where she may a Martyr be.
    She'l to the Moores; And trade with them,
For this unvalued Diadem.
She'l offer them her dearest Breath,
With CHRIST's Name in't, in change for death.
She'l bargain with them; and will give
Them GOD; teach them how to live
In him: or, if they this deny,
For him she'l teach them how to DY.
So shall she leave amongst them sown
Her LORD's Blood; or at lest her own.
    FAREWEL then, all the world! Adieu.
TERESA is no more for you.
Farewell, all pleasures, sports, and joyes,
(Never till now esteemèd toyes)
Farewell what ever deare may bee,
MOTHER's armes or FATHER's knee
Farewell house, and farewell home!
SHE's for the Moores, and MARTYRDOM.

SAMUEL BUTLER

1613–1680

225   from *Hudibras* [First Part, Canto I, lines 187–216]

            For his *Religion* it was fit
            To match his Learning and his Wit:
            'Twas *Presbyterian* true blew,
            For he was of that stubborn Crew
            Of Errant Saints, whom all men grant
            To be the true Church *Militant*:
            Such as do build their Faith upon
            The holy Text of *Pike* and *Gun*;
            Decide all Controversies by
            Infallible *Artillery*;
            And prove their Doctrine Orthodox
            By Apostolick *Blows* and *Knocks*;

Call Fire and Sword and Desolation,
A *godly-thorough-Reformation*,
Which alwayes must be carry'd on,
And still be doing, never done:
As if Religion were intended
For nothing else but to be mended.
A Sect, whose chief Devotion lies
In odde perverse Antipathies;
In falling out with that or this,
And finding somewhat still amiss:
More peevish, cross, and spléenatick,
Than Dog distract, or Monky sick:
That with more care keep holy-day
The wrong, than others the right way:
Compound for Sins, they are inclin'd to,
By damning those they have no mind to;
Still so perverse and opposite,
As if they worshipp'd God for spight.

ANONYMOUS

1641

226   *Interrogativa Cantilena*

If all the world were paper,
And all the Sea were Inke;
If all the Trees were bread and cheese,
How should we do for drink?

If all the World were sand'o,
Oh then what should we lack'o;
If as they say there were no clay,
How should we take Tobacco?

If all our vessels ran'a,
If none but had a crack'a;
If Spanish Apes eat all the Grapes,
How should we do for Sack'a?

If Fryers had no bald pates,
Nor Nuns had no Dark Cloysters,
If all the Seas were Beans and Pease,
How should we do for Oysters?

If there had been no projects,
Nor none that did great wrongs;
If Fidlers shall turn Players all,
How should we do for songs?

If all things were eternal,
And nothing their end bringing;
If this should be, then how should we,
Here make an end of singing?

SIR JOHN DENHAM

1615–1669

227   from *Cooper's Hill* [lines 159–92]

My eye descending from the Hill, surveys
Where *Thames* amongst the wanton vallies strays.
Thames, the most lov'd of all the Oceans sons,
By his old Sire to his embraces runs,
Hasting to pay his tribute to the Sea,
Like mortal life to meet Eternity.
Though with those streams he no resemblance hold,
Whose foam is Amber, and their Gravel Gold;
His genuine, and less guilty wealth t' explore,
Search not his bottom, but survey his shore;
Ore which he kindly spreads his spacious wing,
And hatches plenty for th' ensuing Spring.
Nor then destroys it with too fond a stay,
Like Mothers which their Infants overlay.
Nor with a sudden and impetuous wave,
Like profuse Kings, resumes the wealth he gave.
No unexpected inundations spoyl
The mowers hopes, nor mock the plowmans toyl:
But God-like his unwearied Bounty flows;
First loves to do, then loves the Good he does.
Nor are his Blessings to his banks confin'd,
But free, and common, as the Sea or Wind;
When he to boast, or to disperse his stores
Full of the tributes of his grateful shores,
Visits the world, and in his flying towers
Brings home to us, and makes both *Indies* ours;
Finds wealth where 'tis, bestows it where it wants,
Cities in deserts, woods in Cities plants.

So that to us no thing, no place is strange,
While his fair bosom is the worlds exchange.
O could I flow like thee, and make thy stream
My great example, as it is my theme!
Though deep, yet clear, though gentle, yet not dull,
Strong without rage, without ore-flowing full.

ABRAHAM COWLEY

1618–1667

228 *Drinking*

The thirsty *Earth* soaks up the *Rain*,
And drinks, and gapes for drink again.
The *Plants* suck in the *Earth*, and are
With constant drinking fresh and fair.
The *Sea* it self, which one would think
Should have but little need of *Drink*,
Drinks ten thousand *Rivers* up,
So fill'd that they or'eflow the *Cup*.
The busie *Sun* (and one would guess
By's drunken fiery face no less)
Drinks up the *Sea*, and when h'as done,
The *Moon* and *Stars* drink up the *Sun*.
    They drink and dance by their own light,
They drink and revel all the night.
Nothing in *Nature's Sober* found,
But an eternal *Health* goes round.
Fill up the *Bowl* then, fill it high,
Fill all the *Glasses* there, for why
Should every creature drink but *I*,
Why, *Man* of *Morals*, tell me why?

[after the Greek of Anacreon]

RICHARD LOVELACE
1618–1657/8

229   *To Lucasta, Going to the Warres*

Tell me not (Sweet) I am unkinde,
    That from the Nunnerie
Of thy chaste breast, and quiet minde,
    To Warre and Armes I flie.

True; a new Mistresse now I chase,
    The first Foe in the Field;
And with a stronger Faith imbrace
    A Sword, a Horse, a Shield.

Yet this Inconstancy is such,
    As you too shall adore;
I could not love thee (Deare) so much,
    Lov'd I not Honour more.

230   *To Althea, from Prison*

When Love with unconfinèd wings
    Hovers within my Gates;
And my divine *Althea* brings
    To whisper at the Grates:
When I lye tangled in her haire,
    And fetterd to her eye;
The *Gods* that wanton in the Aire,
    Know no such Liberty.

When flowing Cups run swiftly round
    With no allaying *Thames*,
Our carelesse heads with Roses bound,
    Our hearts with Loyall Flames;
When thirsty griefe in Wine we steepe,
    When Healths and draughts go free,
Fishes that tipple in the Deepe,
    Know no such Libertie.

When (like committed Linnets) I
    With shriller throat shall sing
The sweetnes, Mercy, Majesty,
    And glories of my KING;

When I shall voyce aloud, how Good
    He is, how Great should be;
        Inlargèd Winds that curle the Flood,
        Know no such Liberty.

Stone Walls doe not a Prison make,
    Nor I'ron bars a Cage;
Mindes innocent and quiet take
    That for an Hermitage;
If I have freedome in my Love,
    And in my soule am free;
Angels alone that sore above,
    Injoy such Liberty.

231   *La Bella Bona Roba*

I cannot tell who loves the Skeleton
Of a poor Marmoset, nought but boan, boan.
Give me a nakednesse with her cloath's on.

Such whose white-sattin upper coat of skin,
Cut upon Velvet rich Incarnadin,
Ha's yet a Body (and of Flesh) within.

Sure it is meant good Husbandry in men,
Who do incorporate with Aëry leane,
T' repair their sides, and get their Ribb agen.

Hard hap unto that Huntsman that Decrees
Fat joys for all his swet, when as he sees,
After his 'Say, nought but his Keepers Fees.

Then Love I beg, when next thou tak'st thy Bow,
Thy angry shafts, and dost Heart-chasing go,
Passe *Rascall Deare*, strike me the largest Doe.

232   *Another*

                [*A Black patch on Lucasta's Face*]

As I beheld a Winters Evening Air,
Curl'd in her court false locks of living hair,
Butter'd with Jessamine the Sun left there,

Galliard and clinquant she appear'd to give,
A Serenade or Ball to us that grieve,
And teach us *A la mode* more gently live.

But as a *Moor*, who to her Cheeks prefers
White Spots t'allure her black Idolaters,
Me thought she look'd all ore bepatch'd with Stars;

Like the dark front of some *Ethiopian* Queen,
Vailèd all ore with Gems of Red, Blew, Green;
Whose ugly Night seem'd maskèd with days Skreen;

Whilst the fond people offer'd Sacrifice
To Saphyrs 'stead of Veins and Arteries,
And bow'd unto the Diamonds, not her Eyes.

Behold *Lucasta*'s Face, how't glows like Noon!
A Sun intire is her complexion,
And form'd of one whole Constellation.

So gently shining, so serene, so cleer,
Her look doth Universal Nature cheer;
Only a cloud or two hangs here and there.

ANDREW MARVELL

1621–1678

233   *The Definition of Love*

My Love is of a birth as rare
As 'tis for object strange and high:
It was begotten by despair
Upon Impossibility.

Magnanimous Despair alone
Could show me so divine a thing,
Where feeble Hope could ne'r have flown
But vainly flapt its Tinsel Wing.

And yet I quickly might arrive
Where my extended Soul is fixt,
But Fate does Iron wedges drive,
And alwaies crouds it self betwixt.

For Fate with jealous Eye does see
Two perfect Loves; nor lets them close:
Their union would her ruine be,
And her Tyrannick pow'r depose.

And therefore her Decrees of Steel
Us as the distant Poles have plac'd,
(Though Loves whole World on us doth wheel)
Not by themselves to be embrac'd.

Unless the giddy Heaven fall,
And Earth some new Convulsion tear;
And, us to joyn, the World should all
Be cramp'd into a *Planisphere*.

As Lines so Loves *oblique* may well
Themselves in every Angle greet:
But ours so truly *Paralel*,
Though infinite can never meet.

Therefore the Love which us doth bind,
But Fate so enviously debarrs,
Is the Conjunction of the Mind,
And Opposition of the Stars.

234   *To his Coy Mistress*

Had we but World enough, and Time,
This coyness Lady were no crime.
We would sit down, and think which way
To walk, and pass our long Loves Day.
Thou by the *Indian Ganges* side
Should'st Rubies find: I by the Tide
Of *Humber* would complain. I would
Love you ten years before the Flood:
And you should if you please refuse
Till the Conversion of the *Jews*.
My vegetable Love should grow
Vaster than Empires, and more slow.
An hundred years should go to praise
Thine Eyes, and on thy Forehead Gaze.
Two hundred to adore each Breast:
But thirty thousand to the rest.
An Age at least to every part,
And the last Age should show your Heart.
For Lady you deserve this State;
Nor would I love at lower rate.
    But at my back I alwaies hear
Times wingèd Charriot hurrying near:
And yonder all before us lye
Desarts of vast Eternity.
Thy Beauty shall no more be found;
Nor, in thy marble Vault, shall sound
My ecchoing Song: then Worms shall try
That long preserv'd Virginity:
And your quaint Honour turn to dust;
And into ashes all my Lust.

The Grave's a fine and private place,
But none I think do there embrace.
  Now therefore, while the youthful hew
Sits on thy skin like morning dew,
And while thy willing Soul transpires
At every pore with instant Fires,
Now let us sport us while we may;
And now, like am'rous birds of prey,
Rather at once our Time devour,
Than languish in his slow-chapt pow'r.
Let us roll all our Strength, and all
Our sweetness, up into one Ball:
And tear our Pleasures with rough strife,
Thorough the Iron gates of Life.
Thus, though we cannot make our Sun
Stand still, yet we will make him run.

235 ## *An Horatian Ode upon Cromwel's Return from Ireland*

The forward Youth that would appear
Must now forsake his *Muses* dear,
    Nor in the Shadows sing
    His Numbers languishing.
'Tis time to leave the Books in dust,
And oyl th' unusèd Armours rust:
    Removing from the Wall
    The Corslet of the Hall.
So restless *Cromwel* could not cease
In the inglorious Arts of Peace,
    But through adventrous War
    Urgèd his active Star.
And, like the three-fork'd Lightning, first
Breaking the Clouds where it was nurst,
    Did thorough his own Side
    His fiery way divide.
For 'tis all one to Courage high
The Emulous or Enemy;
    And with such to inclose
    Is more than to oppose.
Then burning through the Air he went,
And Pallaces and Temples rent:
    And *Cæsars* head at last
    Did through his Laurels blast.

'Tis Madness to resist or blame
The force of angry Heavens flame:
   And, if we would speak true,
   Much to the Man is due.
Who, from his private Gardens, where
He liv'd reservèd and austere,
   As if his highest plot
   To plant the Bergamot,
Could by industrious Valour climbe
To ruine the great Work of Time,
   And cast the Kingdome old
   Into another Mold.
Though Justice against Fate complain,
And plead the antient Rights in vain:
   But those do hold or break
   As Men are strong or weak.
Nature that hateth emptiness,
Allows of penetration less:
   And therefore must make room
   Where greater Spirits come.
What Field of all the Civil Wars,
Where his were not the deepest Scars?
   And *Hampton* shows what part
   He had of wiser Art.
Where, twining subtile fears with hope,
He wove a Net of such a scope,
   That *Charles* himself might chase
   To *Caresbrooks* narrow case.
That thence the *Royal Actor* born
The *Tragick Scaffold* might adorn:
   While round the armèd Bands
   Did clap their bloody hands.
He nothing common did or mean
Upon that memorable Scene:
   But with his keener Eye
   The Axes edge did try:
Nor call'd the *Gods* with vulgar spight
To vindicate his helpless Right,
   But bow'd his comely Head,
   Down as upon a Bed.
This was that memorable Hour
Which first assur'd the forcèd Pow'r.
   So when they did design
   The *Capitols* first Line,
A bleeding Head where they begun,
Did fright the Architects to run;

And yet in that the *State*
Foresaw it's happy Fate.
And now the *Irish* are asham'd
To see themselves in one Year tam'd:
So much one Man can do,
That does both act and know.
They can affirm his Praises best,
And have, though overcome, confest
How good he is, how just,
And fit for highest Trust:
Nor yet grown stiffer with Command,
But still in the *Republick's* hand:
How fit he is to sway
That can so well obey.
He to the *Commons Feet* presents
A *Kingdome*, for his first years rents:
And, what he may, forbears
His Fame to make it theirs:
And has his Sword and Spoyls ungirt,
To lay them at the *Publick's* skirt.
So when the Falcon high
Falls heavy from the Sky,
She, having kill'd, no more does search,
But on the next green Bow to pearch;
Where, when he first does lure,
The Falckner has her sure.
What may not then our *Isle* presume
While Victory his Crest does plume!
What may not others fear
If thus he crown each Year!
A *Cæsar* he ere long to *Gaul*,
To *Italy* an *Hannibal*,
And to all States not free
Shall *Clymacterick* be.
The *Pict* no shelter now shall find
Within his party-colour'd Mind;
But from this Valour sad
Shrink underneath the Plad:
Happy if in the tufted brake
The *English Hunter* him mistake;
Nor lay his Hounds in near
The *Caledonian* Deer.
But thou the Wars and Fortunes Son
March indefatigably on;
And for the last effect
Still keep thy Sword erect:

Besides the force it has to fright
The Spirits of the shady Night,
The same *Arts* that did *gain*
A *Pow'r* must it *maintain*.

236 *The Garden*

How vainly men themselves amaze
To win the Palm, the Oke, or Bayes;
And their uncessant Labours see
Crown'd from some single Herb or Tree.
Whose short and narrow vergèd Shade
Does prudently their Toyles upbraid;
While all Flow'rs and all Trees do close
To weave the Garlands of repose.

Fair quiet, have I found thee here,
And Innocence thy Sister dear!
Mistaken long, I sought you then
In busie Companies of Men.
Your sacred Plants, if here below,
Only among the Plants will grow.
Society is all but rude,
To this delicious Solitude.

No white nor red was ever seen
So am'rous as this lovely green.
Fond Lovers, cruel as their Flame,
Cut in these Trees their Mistress name.
Little, Alas, they know, or heed,
How far these Beauties Hers exceed!
Fair Trees! where s'eer your barkes I wound,
No Name shall but your own be found.

When we have run our Passions heat,
Love hither makes his best retreat.
The *Gods*, that mortal Beauty chase,
Still in a Tree did end their race.
Apollo hunted *Daphne* so,
Only that She might Laurel grow.
And *Pan* did after *Syrinx* speed,
Not as a Nymph, but for a Reed.

What wond'rous Life in this I lead!
Ripe Apples drop about my head;
The Luscious Clusters of the Vine
Upon my Mouth do crush their Wine;

The Nectaren, and curious Peach,
Into my hands themselves do reach;
Stumbling on Melons, as I pass,
Insnar'd with Flow'rs, I fall on Grass.

Mean while the Mind, from pleasure less,
Withdraws into its happiness:
The Mind, that Ocean where each kind
Does streight its own resemblance find;
Yet it creates, transcending these,
Far other Worlds, and other Seas;
Annihilating all that's made
To a green Thought in a green Shade.

Here at the Fountains sliding foot,
Or at some Fruit-trees mossy root,
Casting the Bodies Vest aside,
My Soul into the boughs does glide:
There like a Bird it sits, and sings,
Then whets, and combs its silver Wings;
And, till prepar'd for longer flight,
Waves in its Plumes the various Light.

Such was that happy Garden-state,
While Man there walk'd without a Mate:
After a Place so pure, and sweet,
What other Help could yet be meet!
But 'twas beyond a Mortal's share
To wander solitary there:
Two Paradises 'twere in one
To live in Paradise alone.

How well the skilful Gardner drew
Of flow'rs and herbes this Dial new;
Where from above the milder Sun
Does through a fragrant Zodiack run;
And, as it works, th' industrious Bee
Computes its time as well as we.
How could such sweet and wholsome Hours
Be reckon'd but with herbs and flow'rs!

237   *A Dialogue between the Soul and Body*

Soul

O who shall, from this Dungeon, raise
A Soul inslav'd so many wayes?
With bolts of Bones, that fetter'd stands
In Feet; and manacled in Hands.

Here blinded with an Eye; and there
Deaf with the drumming of an Ear.
A Soul hung up, as 'twere, in Chains
Of Nerves, and Arteries, and Veins.
Tortur'd, besides each other part,
In a vain Head, and double Heart.

Body

O who shall me deliver whole,
From bonds of this Tyrannic Soul?
Which, stretcht upright, impales me so,
That mine own Precipice I go;
And warms and moves this needless Frame:
(A Fever could but do the same.)
And, wanting where its spight to try,
Has made me live to let me dye.
A Body that could never rest,
Since this ill Spirit it possest.

Soul

What Magick could me thus confine
Within anothers Grief to pine?
Where whatsoever it complain,
I feel, that cannot feel, the pain.
And all my Care its self employes,
That to preserve, which me destroys:
Constrain'd not only to indure
Diseases, but, whats worse, the Cure:
And ready oft the Port to gain,
Am Shipwrackt into Health again.

Body

But Physick yet could never reach
The Maladies Thou me dost teach;
Whom first the Cramp of Hope does Tear:
And then the Palsie Shakes of Fear.
The Pestilence of Love does heat:
Or Hatred's hidden Ulcer eat.
Joy's chearful Madness does perplex:
Or Sorrow's other Madness vex.
Which Knowledge forces me to know;
And Memory will not foregoe.
What but a Soul could have the wit
To build me up for Sin so fit?
So Architects do square and hew,
Green Trees that in the Forest grew.

238   *The Mower to the Glo-Worms*

Ye living Lamps, by whose dear light
The Nightingale does sit so late,
And studying all the Summer-night,
Her matchless Songs does meditate;

Ye Country Comets, that portend
No War, nor Princes funeral,
Shining unto no higher end
Than to presage the Grasses fall;

Ye Glo-worms, whose officious Flame
To wandring Mowers shows the way,
That in the Night have lost their aim,
And after foolish Fires do stray;

Your courteous Lights in vain you waste,
Since *Juliana* here is come,
For She my Mind hath so displac'd
That I shall never find my home.

239   *Bermudas*

Where the remote *Bermudas* ride
In th' Oceans bosome unespy'd,
From a small Boat, that row'd along,
The listning Winds receiv'd this Song.
    What should we do but sing his Praise
That led us through the watry Maze,
Unto an Isle so long unknown,
And yet far kinder than our own?
Where he the huge Sea-Monsters wracks,
That lift the Deep upon their Backs.
He lands us on a grassy Stage;
Safe from the Storms, and Prelat's rage.
He gave us this eternal Spring,
Which here enamells every thing;
And sends the Fowl's to us in care,
On daily Visits through the Air.
He hangs in shades the Orange bright,
Like golden Lamps in a green Night.
And does in the Pomgranates close,
Jewels more rich than *Ormus* show's.
He makes the Figs our mouths to meet;
And throws the Melons at our feet.

But Apples plants of such a price,
No Tree could ever bear them twice.
With Cedars, chosen by his hand,
From *Lebanon*, he stores the Land.
And makes the hollow Seas, that roar,
Proclaime the Ambergris on shoar.
He cast (of which we rather boast)
The Gospels Pearl upon our Coast.
And in these Rocks for us did frame
A Temple, where to sound his Name.
Oh let our Voice his Praise exalt,
Till it arrive at Heavens Vault:
Which thence (perhaps) rebounding, may
Eccho beyond the *Mexique Bay*.
Thus sung they, in the *English* boat,
An holy and a chearful Note,
And all the way, to guide their Chime,
With falling Oars they kept the time.

HENRY VAUGHAN

1621–1695

240   *The Retreate*

Happy those early dayes! when I
Shin'd in my Angell-infancy.
Before I understood this place
Appointed for my second race,
Or taught my soul to fancy ought
But a white, Celestiall thought,
When yet I had not walkt above
A mile, or two, from my first love,
And looking back (at that short space,)
Could see a glimpse of his bright-face;
When on some *gilded Cloud*, or *flowre*
My gazing soul would dwell an houre,
And in those weaker glories spy
Some shadows of eternity;
Before I taught my tongue to wound
My Conscience with a sinfull sound,
Or had the black art to dispence
A sev'rall sinne to ev'ry sence,
But felt through all this fleshly dresse
Bright *shootes* of everlastingnesse.

O how I long to travell back
And tread again that ancient track!
That I might once more reach that plaine,
Where first I left my glorious traine,
From whence th' Inlightned spirit sees
That shady City of Palme trees;
But (ah!) my soul with too much stay
Is drunk, and staggers in the way.
Some men a forward motion love,
But I by backward steps would move,
And when this dust falls to the urn
In that state I came return.

241   *Peace*

My Soul, there is a Countrie
    Far beyond the stars,
Where stands a wingèd Centrie
    All skilfull in the wars,
There above noise, and danger
    Sweet peace sits crown'd with smiles,
And one born in a Manger
    Commands the Beauteous files,
He is thy gracious friend,
    And (O my Soul awake!)
Did in pure love descend
    To die here for thy sake,
If thou canst get but thither,
    There growes the flowre of peace,
The Rose that cannot wither,
    Thy fortresse, and thy ease;
Leave then thy foolish ranges;
    For none can thee secure,
But one, who never changes,
    Thy God, thy life, thy Cure.

242   *The World*

I saw Eternity the other night
Like a great *Ring* of pure and endless light,
    All calm, as it was bright,
And round beneath it, Time in hours, days, years
    Driv'n by the spheres

Like a vast shadow mov'd, In which the world
    And all her train were hurl'd;
The doting Lover in his queintest strain
    Did there Complain,
Neer him, his Lute, his fancy, and his flights,
    Wits sour delights,
With gloves, and knots the silly snares of pleasure
    Yet his dear Treasure
All scatter'd lay, while he his eys did pour
    Upon a flowr.

The darksome States-man hung with weights and woe
Like a thick midnight-fog mov'd there so slow
    He did nor stay, nor go;
Condemning thoughts (like sad Ecclipses) scowl
    Upon his soul,
And Clouds of crying witnesses without
    Pursued him with one shout.
Yet dig'd the Mole, and lest his ways be found
    Workt under ground,
Where he did Clutch his prey, but one did see
    That policie,
Churches and altars fed him, Perjuries
    Were gnats and flies,
It rain'd about him bloud and tears, but he
    Drank them as free.

The fearfull miser on a heap of rust
Sate pining all his life there, did scarce trust
    His own hands with the dust,
Yet would not place one peece above, but lives
    In feare of theeves.
Thousands there were as frantick as himself
    And hug'd each one his pelf,
The down-right Epicure plac'd heav'n in sense
    And scornd pretence
While others slipt into a wide Excesse
    Said little lesse;
The weaker sort slight, triviall wares Inslave
    Who think them brave,
And poor, despisèd truth sate Counting by
    Their victory.

Yet some, who all this while did weep and sing,
And sing, and weep, soar'd up into the *Ring*,
    But most would use no wing.
O fools (said I,) thus to prefer dark night
    Before true light,

To live in grots, and caves, and hate the day
    Because it shews the way,
The way which from this dead and dark abode
    Leads up to God,
A way where you might tread the Sun, and be
    More bright than he.
But as I did their madnes so discusse
    One whisper'd thus,
This Ring the Bride-groome did for none provide
    But for his bride.

243   They are all gone into the world of light!
    And I alone sit lingring here;
Their very memory is fair and bright,
    And my sad thoughts doth clear.

It glows and glitters in my cloudy brest
    Like stars upon some gloomy grove,
Or those faint beams in which this hill is drest,
    After the Sun's remove.

I see them walking in an Air of glory,
    Whose light doth trample on my days:
My days, which are at best but dull and hoary,
    Meer glimering and decays.

O holy hope! and high humility,
    High as the Heavens above!
These are your walks, and you have shew'd them me
    To kindle my cold love,

Dear, beauteous death! the Jewel of the Just,
    Shining nowhere, but in the dark;
What mysteries do lie beyond thy dust;
    Could man outlook that mark!

He that hath found some fledg'd birds nest, may know
    At first sight, if the bird be flown;
But what fair Well, or Grove he sings in now,
    That is to him unknown.

And yet, as Angels in some brighter dreams
    Call to the soul, when man doth sleep:
So some strange thoughts transcend our wonted theams,
    And into glory peep.

If a star were confin'd into a Tomb
    Her captive flames must needs burn there;
But when the hand that lockt her up, gives room,
    She'l shine through all the sphære.

O Father of eternal life, and all
    Created glories under thee!
Resume thy spirit from this world of thrall
    Into true liberty.

Either disperse these mists, which blot and fill
    My pérspective (still) as they pass,
Or else remove me hence unto that hill,
    Where I shall need no glass.

244   *The Night*

                         John 2. 3

        Through that pure *Virgin-shrine,*
That sacred vail drawn o'r thy glorious noon
That men might look and live as Glo-worms shine,
        And face the Moon:
    Wise *Nicodemus* saw such light
    As made him know his God by night.

        Most blest believer he!
Who in that land of darkness and blinde eyes
Thy long expected healing wings could see,
        When thou didst rise,
    And what can never more be done,
    Did at mid-night speak with the Sun!

        O who will tell me, where
He found thee at that dead and silent hour!
What hallow'd solitary ground did bear
        So rare a flower,
    Within whose sacred leafs did lie
    The fulness of the Deity.

        No mercy-seat of gold,
No dead and dusty *Cherub,* nor carv'd stone,
But his own living works did my Lord hold
        And lodge alone;
    Where *trees* and *herbs* did watch and peep
    And wonder, while the *Jews* did sleep.

        Dear night! this worlds defeat;
The stop to busie fools; cares check and curb;
The day of Spirits; my souls calm retreat
        Which none disturb!
    Christs progress, and his prayer time;
    The hours to which high Heaven doth chime.

Gods silent, searching flight:
When my Lords head is fill'd with dew, and all
His locks are wet with the clear drops of night;
His still, soft call;
His knocking time; The souls dumb watch,
When Spirits their fair kinred catch.

Were all my loud, evil days
Calm and unhaunted as is thy dark Tent,
Whose peace but by some *Angels* wing or voice
Is seldom rent;
Then I in Heaven all the long year
Would keep, and never wander here.

But living where the Sun
Doth all things wake, and where all mix and tyre
Themselves and others, I consent and run
To ev'ry myre,
And by this worlds ill-guiding light,
Erre more than I can do by night.

There is in God (some say)
A deep, but dazling darkness; As men here
Say it is late and dusky, because they
See not all clear;
O for that night! where I in him
Might live invisible and dim.

PATRICK CARY

1623/4–1657

245   For God's sake marcke that *Fly*:
See what a poore, weake, little Thing itt is.
When Thou hast marck'd, and scorn'd itt; know that This,
This little, poore, weake *Fly*
Has killed a *Pope*; can make an *Emp'rour* dye.

Behold yon *Sparcke of Fire*:
How little hott! how neare to nothing 'tis!
When thou has donne despising, know that this,
This contemn'd *Sparcke of Fire*
Has burn't whole Townes; can burne a World entire.

That crawling *Worme* there see:
Ponder how ugly, filthy, vild Itt is.
When Thou hast seene and loath'd itt, know that This
This base *Worme* Thou doest see,
Has quite devour'd thy Parents; shall eate Thee.

Honour, the *World*, and *Man*,
What Trifles are they! Since most true itt is
That this poore *Fly*, this little *Sparckle*, this
Soe much abhorr'd *Worme*, can
Honour destroy; burne *Worlds*; devoure up *Man*.

JOHN BUNYAN

1628–1688

246   Who would true Valour see,
             Let him come hither;
             One here will Constant be,
             Come Wind, come Weather.
             There's no *Discouragement*,
             Shall make him once *Relent*,
             His first avow'd *Intent*,
             To be a Pilgrim.

             Who so beset him round,
             With dismal *Stories*,
             Do but themselves Confound;
             His Strength the *more is*.
             No *Lyon* can him fright,
             He'l with a *Gyant Fight*,
             But he will have a right,
             To be a Pilgrim.

             Hobgoblin, nor foul *Fiend*,
             Can *daunt* his Spirit:
             He knows, he *at the end*,
             Shall Life Inherit.
             Then Fancies fly away,
             He'll fear not what men say,
             He'll labour Night and Day,
             To be a Pilgrim.

CHARLES COTTON

1630–1687

247   *Evening Quatrains*

             The Day's grown old, the fainting Sun
             Has but a little way to run,
             And yet his Steeds, with all his skill,
             Scarce lug the Chariot down the Hill.

With Labour spent, and Thirst opprest,
Whilst they strain hard to gain the West,
From Fetlocks hot drops melted light,
Which turn to Meteors in the Night.

The Shadows now so long do grow,
That Brambles like tall Cedars show,
Mole-hills seem Mountains, and the Ant
Appears a monstrous Elephant.

A very little little Flock
Shades thrice the ground that it would stock;
Whilst the small Stripling following them,
Appears a mighty *Polypheme.*

These being brought into the Fold,
And by the thrifty Master told,
He thinks his Wages are well paid,
Since none are either lost, or stray'd.

Now lowing Herds are each-where heard,
Chains rattle in the Villeins Yard,
The Cart's on Tayl set down to rest,
Bearing on high the Cuckolds Crest.

The hedg is stript, the Clothes brought in,
Nought's left without should be within,
The Bees are hiv'd, and hum their Charm,
Whilst every House does seem a Swarm.

The Cock now to the Roost is prest:
For he must call up all the rest;
The Sow's fast pegg'd within the Sty,
To still her squeaking Progeny.

Each one has had his Supping Mess,
The Cheese is put into the Press,
The Pans and Bowls clean scalded all,
Rear'd up against the Milk-house Wall.

And now on Benches all are sat
In the cool Air to sit and chat,
Till *Phœbus,* dipping in the West,
Shall lead the World the way to Rest.

JOHN DRYDEN
1631–1700

248–9   from *Absalom and Achitophel*

248   [lines 150–74]

Of these the false *Achitophel* was first:
A Name to all succeeding Ages Curst.
For close Designs, and crooked Counsels fit;
Sagacious, Bold, and Turbulent of wit:
Restless, unfixt in Principles and Place;
In Power unpleas'd, impatient of Disgrace.
A fiery Soul, which working out its way,
Fretted the Pigmy Body to decay:
And o'r inform'd the Tenement of Clay.
A daring Pilot in extremity;
Pleas'd with the Danger, when the Waves went high
He sought the Storms; but for a Calm unfit,
Would Steer too nigh the Sands, to boast his Wit.
Great Wits are sure to Madness near ally'd;
And thin Partitions do their Bounds divide:
Else, why should he, with Wealth and Honour blest,
Refuse his Age the needful hours of Rest?
Punish a Body which he coud not please;
Bankrupt of Life, yet Prodigal of Ease?
And all to leave, what with his Toyl he won,
To that unfeather'd, two Leg'd thing, a Son:
Got, while his Soul did hudled Notions try;
And born a shapeless Lump, like Anarchy.
In Friendship False, Implacable in Hate:
Resolv'd to Ruine or to Rule the State.

249   [lines 543–62]

Some of their Chiefs were Princes of the Land:
In the first Rank of these did *Zimri* stand:
A man so various, that he seem'd to be
Not one, but all Mankinds Epitome.
Stiff in Opinions, always in the wrong;
Was every thing by starts, and nothing long:
But, in the course of one revolving Moon,
Was Chymist, Fidler, States-Man, and Buffoon:

Then all for Women, Painting, Rhiming, Drinking;
Besides ten thousand freaks that dy'd in thinking.
Blest Madman, who coud every hour employ,
With something New to wish, or to enjoy!
Rayling and praising were his usual Theams;
And both (to shew his Judgment) in Extreams:
So over Violent, or over Civil,
That every man, with him, was God or Devil.
In squandring Wealth was his peculiar Art:
Nothing went unrewarded, but Desert.
Begger'd by Fools, whom still he found too late:
He had his Jest, and they had his Estate.

250   from *Mac Flecknoe* [lines 1–50]

All humane things are subject to decay,
And, when Fate summons, Monarchs must obey:
This *Fleckno* found, who, like *Augustus*, young
Was call'd to Empire, and had govern'd long:
In Prose and Verse, was own'd, without dispute
Through all the Realms of *Non-sense*, absolute.
This agèd Prince now flourishing in Peace,
And blest with issue of a large increase,
Worn out with business, did at length debate
To settle the succession of the State:
And pond'ring which of all his Sons was fit
To Reign, and wage immortal War with Wit;
Cry'd, 'tis resolv'd; for Nature pleads that He
Should onely rule, who most resembles me:
Sh—— alone my perfect image bears,   [*Shadwell*]
Mature in dullness from his tender years.
Sh—— alone, of all my Sons, is he
Who stands confirm'd in full stupidity.
The rest to some faint meaning make pretence,
But Sh—— never deviates into sense.
Some Beams of Wit on other souls may fall,
Strike through and make a lucid intervall;
But Sh——'s genuine night admits no ray,
His rising Fogs prevail upon the Day:
Besides his goodly Fabrick fills the eye,
And seems design'd for thoughtless Majesty:
Thoughtless as Monarch Oakes, that shade the plain,
And, spread in solemn state, supinely reign.
Heywood and *Shirley* were but Types of thee,
Thou last great Prophet of Tautology:

Even I, a dunce of more renown than they,
Was sent before but to prepare thy way;
And coursly clad in *Norwich* Drugget came
To teach the Nations in thy greater name.
My warbling Lute, the Lute I whilom strung
When to King *John* of *Portugal* I sung,
Was but the prelude to that glorious day,
When thou on silver *Thames* did'st cut thy way,
With well tim'd Oars before the Royal Barge,
Swell'd with the Pride of thy Celestial charge;
And big with Hymn, Commander of an Host,
The like was ne'er in *Epsom* Blankets tost.
Methinks I see the new *Arion* Sail,
The Lute still trembling underneath thy nail.
At thy well sharpned thumb from Shore to Shore
The Treble squeaks for fear, the Bases roar:
Echoes from *Pissing-Ally, Sh*—— call,
[*Aston*]   And *Sh*—— they resound from *A*—— *Hall.*
About thy boat the little Fishes throng,
As at the Morning Toast, that Floats along.

251   *To the Memory of Mr. Oldham*

Farewel, too little and too lately known,
Whom I began to think and call my own;
For sure our Souls were near ally'd; and thine
Cast in the same Poetick mould with mine.
One common Note on either Lyre did strike,
And Knaves and Fools we both abhorr'd alike:
To the same Goal did both our Studies drive,
The last set out the soonest did arrive.
Thus *Nisus* fell upon the slippery place,
While his young Friend perform'd and won the Race.
O early ripe! to thy abundant store
What could advancing Age have added more?
It might (what Nature never gives the young)
Have taught the numbers of thy native Tongue.
But Satyr needs not those, and Wit will shine
Through the harsh cadence of a rugged line.
A noble Error, and but seldom made,
When Poets are by too much force betray'd.
Thy generous fruits, though gather'd ere their prime ⎫
Still shew'd a quickness; and maturing time   ⎬
But mellows what we write to the dull sweets of Rime. ⎭

Once more, hail and farewel; farewel thou young,
But ah too short, *Marcellus* of our Tongue;
Thy Brows with Ivy, and with Laurels bound;
But Fate and gloomy Night encompass thee around.

252   from *Lucretius: The Fourth Book, Concerning*
the Nature of Love [lines 35–98]

When Love its utmost vigour does imploy,
Ev'n then, 'tis but a restless wandring joy:
Nor knows the Lover, in that wild excess,
With hands or eyes, what first he wou'd possess:
But strains at all; and fast'ning where he strains,
Too closely presses with his frantique pains:
With biteing kisses hurts the twining fair,
Which shews his joyes imperfect, unsincere:
For stung with inward rage, he flings around,
And strives t' avenge the smart on that which gave the wound.
But love those eager bitings does restrain,
And mingling pleasure mollifies the pain.
For ardent hope still flatters anxious grief,
And sends him to his Foe to seek relief:
Which yet the nature of the thing denies;
For Love, and Love alone of all our joyes
By full possession does but fan the fire,
The more we still enjoy, the more we still desire.
Nature for meat, and drink provides a space;
And when receiv'd they fill their certain place;
Hence thirst and hunger may be satisfi'd,
But this repletion is to Love deny'd:
Form, feature, colour, whatsoe're delight
Provokes the Lovers endless appetite,
These fill no space, nor can we thence remove
With lips, or hands, or all our instruments of love:
In our deluded grasp we nothing find,
But thin aerial shapes, that fleet before the mind.
As he who in a dream with drought is curst,
And finds no real drink to quench his thirst,
Runs to imagin'd Lakes his heat to steep,
And vainly swills and labours in his sleep;
So Love with fantomes cheats our longing eyes,
Which hourly seeing never satisfies;
Our hands pull nothing from the parts they strain,
But wander o're the lovely limbs in vain:

Nor when the Youthful pair more clossely joyn,
When hands in hands they lock, and thighs in thighs they twine;
Just in the raging foam of full desire,
When both press on, both murmur, both expire,
They gripe, they squeeze, their humid tongues they dart,
As each wou'd force their way to t'others heart:
In vain; they only cruze about the coast,
For bodies cannot pierce, nor be in bodies lost:
As sure they strive to be, when both engage,
In that tumultuous momentary rage,
So 'tangled in the Nets of Love they lie,
Till Man dissolves in that excess of joy.
Then, when the gather'd bag has burst its way,
And ebbing tydes the slacken'd nerves betray,
A pause ensues; and Nature nods a while,
Till with recruited rage new Spirits boil;
And then the same vain violence returns,
With flames renew'd th' erected furnace burns.
Agen they in each other wou'd be lost,
But still by adamantine bars are crost;
All wayes they try, successeless all they prove,
To cure the secret sore of lingring love.
    Besides—
They waste their strength in the venereal strife,
And to a Womans will enslave their life;
Th' Estate runs out, and mortgages are made,   ⎫
All Offices of friendship are decay'd;   ⎬
Their fortune ruin'd, and their fame betray'd. ⎭

[after the Latin of Lucretius]

253–4   from *The Sixth Satyr of Juvenal*

253   [lines 1–35]

In *Saturn*'s Reign, at Nature's Early Birth,
There was that Thing call'd Chastity on Earth;
When in a narrow Cave, their common shade,
The Sheep the Shepherds and their Gods were laid:
When Reeds and Leaves, and Hides of Beasts were spread   ⎫
By Mountain Huswifes for their homely Bed,   ⎬
And Mossy Pillows rais'd, for the rude Husband's head.   ⎭
Unlike the Niceness of our Modern Dames
(Affected Nymphs with new Affected Names:)
The *Cynthia's* and the *Lesbia's* of our Years,
Who for a Sparrow's Death dissolve in Tears.

Those first unpolisht Matrons, Big and Bold,
Gave Suck to Infants of Gygantick Mold;
Rough as their Savage Lords who Rang'd the Wood,
And Fat with Akorns Belcht their windy Food.
For when the World was Bucksom, fresh, and young,
Her Sons were undebauch'd, and therefore strong;
And whether Born in kindly Beds of Earth,
Or strugling from the Teeming Oaks to Birth,
Or from what other Atoms they begun,
No Sires they had, or if a Sire the Sun.
Some thin Remains of Chastity appear'd
Ev'n under *Jove*, but *Jove* without a Beard:
Before the servile *Greeks* had learnt to Swear
By Heads of Kings; while yet the Bounteous Year
Her common Fruits in open Plains expos'd,
E're Thieves were fear'd, or Gardens were enclos'd:
At length uneasie Justice upwards flew,
And both the Sisters to the Stars withdrew;
From that Old *Æra* Whoring did begin,
So Venerably Ancient is the Sin.
Adult'rers next invade the Nuptial State,
And Marriage-Beds creak'd with a Foreign Weight;
All other Ills did Iron times adorn;
But Whores and Silver in one Age were Born.

254   [lines 416–46]

   What care our Drunken Dames to whom they spread?
Wine, no distinction makes of Tail or Head.
Who lewdly Dancing at a Midnight-Ball,
For hot Eringoes, and Fat Oysters call:
Full Brimmers to their Fuddled Noses thrust;
Brimmers the last Provocatives of Lust.
When Vapours to their swimming Brains advance,
And double Tapers on the Tables Dance.
   Now think what Bawdy Dialogues they have,
What *Tullia* talks to her confiding Slave;
At Modesty's old Statue: when by Night,
They make a stand, and from their Litters light;
The Good Man early to the Levee goes,
And treads the Nasty Paddle of his Spouse.
   The Secrets of the Goddess nam'd the Good,
Are ev'n by Boys and Barbers understood:
Where the Rank Matrons, Dancing to the Pipe,
Gig with their Bums, and are for Action ripe;

With Musick rais'd, they spread abroad their Hair;
And toss their Heads like an enamour'd Mare:
Laufella lays her Garland by, and proves
The mimick Leachery of Manly Loves.
Rank'd with the Lady, the cheap Sinner lies;
For here not Blood, but Virtue gives the prize.
Nothing is feign'd, in this Venereal Strife;
'Tis downright Lust, and Acted to the Life.
So full, so fierce, so vigorous, and so strong;
That, looking on, wou'd make old *Nestor* Young.
Impatient of delay, a general sound,
An universal Groan of Lust goes round;
For then, and only then, the Sex sincere is found.

[after the Latin of Juvenal]

255   from *The First Book of Virgil's Æneis* [lines 1–49]

Arms, and the Man I sing, who, forc'd by Fate,
And haughty *Juno's* unrelenting Hate;
Expell'd and exil'd, left the *Trojan* Shoar:
Long Labours, both by Sea and Land he bore;
And in the doubtful War, before he won
The *Latian* Realm, and built the destin'd Town:
His banish'd Gods restor'd to Rites Divine,
And setl'd sure Succession in his Line:
From whence the Race of *Alban* Fathers come,
And the long Glories of Majestick *Rome.*
        O Muse! the Causes and the Crimes relate,
What Goddess was provok'd, and whence her hate:
For what Offence the Queen of Heav'n began
To persecute so brave, so just a Man!
Involv'd his anxious Life in endless Cares,
Expos'd to Wants, and hurry'd into Wars!
Can Heav'nly Minds such high resentment show;
Or exercise their Spight in Human Woe?
        Against the *Tiber's* Mouth, but far away,
An ancient Town was seated on the Sea:
A *Tyrian* Colony; the People made
Stout for the War, and studious of their Trade.
Carthage the Name, belov'd by *Juno* more
Than her own *Argos,* or the *Samian* Shoar.
Here stood her Chariot, here, if Heav'n were kind,
The Seat of awful Empire she design'd.
Yet she had heard an ancient Rumour fly,
(Long cited by the People of the Sky;)

That times to come shou'd see the *Trojan* Race
Her *Carthage* ruin, and her Tow'rs deface:
Nor thus confin'd, the Yoke of Sov'raign Sway,
Should on the Necks of all the Nations lay.
She ponder'd this, and fear'd it was in Fate;
Nor cou'd forget the War she wag'd of late,
For conq'ring *Greece* against the *Trojan* State.
Besides long Causes working in her Mind,
And secret Seeds of Envy lay behind.
Deep graven in her Heart, the Doom remain'd
Of partial *Paris*, and her Form disdain'd:
The Grace bestow'd on ravish'd *Ganimed*,
Electra's Glories, and her injur'd Bed.
Each was a Cause alone, and all combin'd
To kindle Vengeance in her haughty Mind.
For this, far distant from the *Latian* Coast,
She drove the Remnants of the *Trojan* Hoast:
And sev'n long Years th' unhappy wand'ring Train,
Were toss'd by Storms, and scatter'd through the Main.
Such Time, such Toil requir'd the *Roman* Name,
Such length of Labour for so vast a Frame.

[after the Latin of Virgil]

256   from *The Secular Masque*

[*Enter Janus.*]
Janus.   *Chronos, Chronos,* mend thy Pace,
         An hundred times the rowling Sun
         Around the Radiant Belt has run
         In his revolving Race.
         Behold, behold, the Goal in sight,
         Spread thy Fans, and wing thy flight.

*   *   *

Janus.   Then our Age was in it's Prime,
Chronos. Free from Rage.
Diana.   And free from Crime.
Momus.   A very Merry, Dancing, Drinking,
         Laughing, Quaffing, and unthinking Time.
Chorus of all.   *Then our Age was in it's Prime,*
         Free from Rage, and free from Crime,
         A very Merry, Dancing, Drinking,
         Laughing, Quaffing, and unthinking Time.

*   *   *

             Momus.   All, all, of a piece throughout;
[*Pointing to Diana.*]   Thy Chase had a Beast in View;
       [*To Mars.*]   Thy Wars brought nothing about;
      [*To Venus.*]   Thy Lovers were all untrue.
             Janus.   'Tis well an Old Age is out,
           Chronos.   And time to begin a New.
    Chorus of all.   *All, all, of a piece throughout;*
                       Thy Chase had a Beast in View;
                       Thy Wars brought nothing about;
                       Thy Lovers were all untrue.
                       'Tis well an Old Age is out,
                       And time to begin a New.

KATHERINE PHILIPS
1632–1664

257   *To my Excellent Lucasia, on our Friendship*

        I did not live until this time
            Crown'd my felicity,
        When I could say without a crime,
            I am not thine, but Thee.

        This Carcass breath'd, and walkt, and slept,
            So that the World believ'd
        There was a Soul the Motions kept;
            But they were all deceiv'd.

        For as a Watch by art is wound
            To motion, such was mine:
        But never had *Orinda* found
            A Soul till she found thine;

        Which now inspires, cures and supplies,
            And guides my darkned Breast:
        For thou art all that I can prize,
            My Joy, my Life, my Rest.

        No Bridegrooms nor Crown-conquerors mirth
            To mine compar'd can be:
        They have but pieces of this Earth,
            I've all the World in thee.

        Then let our Flames still light and shine,
            And no false fear controul,
        As innocent as our Design,
            Immortal as our Soul.

258 *The Enquiry*

If we no old historian's name
 Authentique will admitt,
And thinke all said of friendship's fame
 But poetry and wit:
Yet what's revered by minds so pure
Must be a bright Idea, sure.

But as our immortalitie
 By inward sense we find,
Judging that if it could not be,
 It would not be design'd:
So here how could such copyes fall,
If there were no originall?

But if truth be in auncient song,
 Or story we beleive,
If the inspir'd and greater throng
 Have scornèd to deceive;
There have been hearts whose friendship gave
Them thoughts at once both soft and brave.

Among that consecrated few,
 Some more seraphick shade
Lend me a favourable clew,
 Now mists my eyes invade,
Why, having fill'd the world with fame,
Left you so little of your flame?

Why is't so difficult to see
 Two bodyes and one minde?
And why are those who else agree
 So differently kind?
Hath nature such fantastique art,
That she can vary every heart?

Why are the bands of friendship tyed
 With so remisse a knot,
That by the most it is defyed,
 And by the rest forgot?
Why do we step with so slight sense
From friendship to indifference?

If friendship sympathy impart,
 Why this illshuffled game,
That heart can never meet with heart,
 Or flame encounter flame?
What doth this crueltie create?
Is it th' intrigue of love or fate?

Had friendship nere been known to men,
    (The ghost at last confest)
The world had been a stranger then
    To all that Heav'n possess'd.
But could it all be here acquir'd,
Not heaven it selfe would be desir'd.

THOMAS TRAHERNE

1637–1674

259   *Wonder*

How like an Angel came I down!
    How Bright are all Things here!
When first among his Works I did appear
    O how their GLORY me did Crown?
The World resembled his *Eternitie*,
    In which my Soul did Walk;
And evry Thing that I did see,
    Did with me talk.

The Skies in their Magnificence,
    The Lively, Lovely Air;
Oh how Divine, how soft, how Sweet, how fair!
    The Stars did entertain my Sence,
And all the Works of GOD so Bright and pure,
    So Rich and Great did seem,
As if they ever must endure,
    In my Esteem.

A Native Health and Innocence
    Within my Bones did grow,
And while my GOD did all his Glories shew,
    I felt a Vigour in my Sence
That was all SPIRIT. I within did flow
    With Seas of Life, like Wine;
I nothing in the World did know,
    But 'twas Divine.

Harsh ragged Objects were conceald,
    Oppressions Tears and Cries,
Sins, Griefs, Complaints, Dissentions, Weeping Eys,
    Were hid: and only Things reveald,
Which Heav'nly Spirits, and the Angels prize.
    The State of Innocence
And Bliss, not Trades and Poverties,
    Did fill my Sence.

The Streets were pavd with Golden Stones,
    The Boys and Girles were mine,
Oh how did all their Lovly faces shine!
    The Sons of Men were Holy Ones.
Joy, Beauty, Welfare did appear to me,
      And evry Thing which here I found,
    While like an Angel I did see,
      Adornd the Ground.

Rich Diamond and Pearl and Gold
    In evry Place was seen;
Rare Splendors, Yellow, Blew, Red, White and Green,
    Mine Eys did evrywhere behold,
Great Wonders clothd with Glory did appear,
    Amazement was my Bliss.
That and my Wealth was evry where:
    No Joy to this!

Cursd and Devisd Proprieties,
    With Envy, Avarice
And Fraud, those Feinds that Spoyl even Paradice,
    Fled from the Splendor of mine Eys.
And so did Hedges, Ditches, Limits, Bounds,
    I dreamd not ought of those,
    But wanderd over all mens Grounds,
    And found Repose.

Proprieties themselvs were mine,
    And Hedges Ornaments;
Walls, Boxes, Coffers, and their rich Contents
    Did not Divide my Joys, but shine.
Clothes, Ribbans, Jewels, Laces, I esteemd
    My Joys by others worn;
For me they all to wear them seemd
    When I was born.

260   *The Apostacy*

One Star
Is better far
Than many Precious Stones:
One Sun, which is abov in Glory seen,
    Is worth ten thousand Golden Thrones:
    A juicy Herb, or Spire of Grass,
    In useful Virtu, native Green,
      An Em'rald doth surpass;
Hath in't more Valu, tho less seen.

No Wars,
Nor mortal Jars,
Nor bloody Feuds, nor Coin,
Nor Griefs which they occasion, saw I then;
Nor wicked Thievs which this purloin:
I had no Thoughts that were impure;
Esteeming both Women and Men
God's Work, I was secure,
And reckon'd Peace my choicest Gem.

As *Eve*
I did believ
My self in *Eden* set,
Affecting neither Gold, nor Ermin'd Crowns,
Nor ought els that I need forget;
No Mud did foul my limpid Streams,
No Mist eclypst my Sun with frowns;
Set off with hev'nly Beams,
My Joys were Meadows, Fields, and Towns.

Those things
Which *Cherubins*
Did not at first behold
Among God's Works, which *Adam* did not see;
As Robes, and Stones enchas'd in Gold,
Rich Cabinets, and such like fine
Inventions; could not ravish me:
I thought not Bowls of Wine
Needful for my Felicity.

All Bliss
Consists in this,
To do as *Adam* did;
And not to know those superficial Joys
Which were from him in *Eden* hid:
Those little new-invented Things,
Fine Lace and Silks, such Childish Toys
As Ribbans are and Rings,
Or worldly Pelf that Us destroys.

For God,
Both Great and Good,
The Seeds of Melancholy
Created not: but only foolish Men,
Grown mad with customary Folly
Which doth increase their Wants, so dote
As when they elder grow they then
Such Baubles chiefly note;
More Fools at Twenty Years than Ten.

> But I,
> I knew not why,
> Did learn among them too
> At length; and when I once with blemisht Eys
> Began their Pence and Toys to view,
> Drown'd in their Customs, I became
> A Stranger to the Shining Skies,
> Lost as a dying Flame;
> And Hobby-horses brought to prize.

> The Sun
> And Moon forgon,
> As if unmade, appear
> No more to me; to God and Heven dead
> I was, as tho they never were:
> Upon som useless gaudy Book,
> When what I knew of God was fled,
> The Child being taught to look,
> His Soul was quickly murtherèd.

> O fine!
> O most divine!
> O brave! they cry'd; and shew'd
> Som Tinsel thing whose Glittering did amaze,
> And to their Cries its beauty ow'd;
> Thus I on Riches, by degrees,
> Of a new Stamp did learn to gaze;
> While all the World for these
> I lost: my Joy turn'd to a Blaze.

SIR CHARLES SEDLEY

1639?–1701

261   *A Song to Celia*

> Not *Celia*, that I juster am
>   Or better than the rest,
> For I would change each Hour like them,
>   Were not my Heart at rest.

> But I am ty'd to very thee,
>   By every Thought I have,
> Thy Face I only care to see,
>   Thy Heart I only crave.

All that in Woman is ador'd,
  In thy dear self I find,
For the whole Sex can but afford,
  The Handsome and the Kind.

Why then should I seek farther Store,
  And still make Love anew;
When Change it self can give no more,
  'Tis easie to be true.

262   *Song*

Love still has something of the Sea,
  From whence his Mother rose;
No time his Slaves from Doubt can free,
  Nor give their Thoughts repose:

They are becalm'd in clearest Days,
  And in rough Weather tost;
They wither under cold Delays,
  Or are in Tempests lost.

One while they seem to touch the Port,
  Then straight into the Main,
Some angry Wind in cruel sport
  The Vessel drives again.

At first Disdain and Pride they fear,
  Which if they chance to 'scape,
Rivals and Falsehood soon appear
  In a more dreadful shape.

By such Degrees to Joy they come,
  And are so long withstood,
So slowly they receive the Sum,
  It hardly does them good.

'Tis cruel to prolong a Pain;
  And to defer a Joy,
Believe me, gentle *Celemene*,
  Offends the wingèd Boy.

An hundred thousand Oaths your Fears
  Perhaps would not remove;
And if I gaz'd a thousand Years
  I could no deeper love.

APHRA BEHN
1640?–1689

263   *Love Arm'd*

Love in Fantastique Triumph satt,
Whilst Bleeding Hearts a round him flow'd,
For whom Fresh paines he did Create,
And strange Tyranick power he show'd;
From thy Bright Eyes he took his fire,
Which round about, in sport he hurl'd;
But 'twas from mine, he took desire,
Enough to undo the Amorous World.

From me he took his sighs and tears,
From thee his Pride and Crueltie;
From me his Languishments and Feares,
And every Killing Dart from thee;
Thus thou and I, the God have arm'd,
And sett him up a Deity;
But my poor Heart alone is harm'd,
Whilst thine the Victor is, and free.

EDWARD TAYLOR
1642?–1729

264   *Meditation. Cant. 6. 11*

I went down into the Garden of Nuts, to see the fruits etc.

Oh that I was the Bird of Paradise!
    Then in thy Nutmeg Garden, Lord, thy Bower
Celestiall Musick blossom should my voice
    Enchanted with thy gardens aire and flower.
    This Aromatick aire would so enspire
    My ravisht Soule to sing with angells Quire.

What is thy Church, my Lord, thy Garden which
    Doth gain the best of Soils? Such Spots indeed
Are Choicest Plots empalde with Palings rich
    And set with slips, herbs best, and best of seed.
    As th' Hanging Gardens rare of Babylon
    And Palace Garden of King Solomon.

But that which doth excell all gardens here
   Was Edens Garden: Adams Palace bright.
The Tree of Life, and knowledge too were there
   Sweet herbs and sweetest flowers all sweet Delight
     A Paradise indeed of all Perfúme
     That to the Nose, the Eyes and Eares doth tune.

But all these Artificiall Gardens bright
   Enamelèd with bravest knots of Pincks
And flowers enspangld with black, red and White
   Compar'd with this are truely stincking sincks.
     As Dunghills reech with stinking sents that dish
     Us out, so these, when balancèd with this.

For Zions Paradise, Christs Garden Deare
   His Church, enwalld, with Heavenly Crystall fine
Hath every Bed beset with Pearle all Cleare
   And Alleys Opald with Gold, and Silver Shrine.
     The shining Angells are its Centinalls
     With flaming Swords Chaunting out Madrigalls.

The Sparkling Plants, Sweet Spices, Herbs and Trees,
   The glorious Shews of aromatick Flowers,
The pleasing beauties soakt in sweet breath lees
   Of Christs rich garden ever upward towers.
     For Christ Sweet Showers of Grace makes on it fall.
     It therefore bears the bell away from all.

The Nut of evry kinde is found to grow big,
   With food, and Physick, lodgd within a tower
A Wooden Wall with Husky Coverlid,
   Or Shell flesht ore, or in an Arching bower
     Beech, Hazle, Wallnut, Coco, Almond brave
     Pistick or Chestnut in its prickly Cave.

These all as meate, and med'cine, emblems choice
   Of Spirituall Food, and Physike are which sport
Up in Christs Garden. Yet the Nutmeg's Spice
   A leathern Coate wares, and a Macie Shirt,
     Doth far excell them all. Aromatize
     My Soule therewith, my Lord, and spirituall wise.

Oh! Sweet Sweet Paradise, Whose Spicèd Spring
   Will make the lips of him asleep to tune
Heart ravishing tunes, sweet Musick for our king
     In Aromatick aire of blesst perfúme
     Open thy garden doore: mee entrance give
     And in thy Nut tree garden make me live.

If, Lord, thou opst, and in thy garden bring
    Mee, then thy little Linet sweetly Will
Upon thy Nut tree sit and sweetly sing
    Will Crack a Nut and eat the kirnell still.
    Thou wilt mine Eyes, my Nose, and Palate greet
    With Curious Flowers, Sweet Odors, Viands Sweet.

Thy Gardens Odorif'rous aire mee make
    Suck in, and out t'aromatize my lungs.
That I thy garden, and its Spicie State
    May breathe upon with such ensweetned Songs.
    My Lungs and Breath ensweetend thus shall raise
    The Glory of thy garden in its praise.

265   *The Preface* [to *Gods Determinations*]

      Infinity, when all things it beheld
In Nothing, and of Nothing all did build,
Upon what Base was fixt the Lath, wherein
He turn'd this Globe, and riggalld it so trim?
Who blew the Bellows of his Furnace Vast?
Or held the Mould wherein the world was Cast?
Who laid its Corner Stone? Or whose Command?
Where stand the Pillars upon which it stands?
Who Lac'de and Fillitted the earth so fine,
With Rivers like green Ribbons Smaragdine?
Who made the Sea's its Selvedge, and it locks
Like a Quilt Ball within a Silver Box?
Who Spread its Canopy? Or Curtains Spun?
Who in this Bowling Alley bowld the Sun?
Who made it always when it rises set
To go at once both down, and up to get?
Who th'Curtain rods made for this Tapistry?
Who hung the twinckling Lanthorns in the Sky?
Who? who did this? or who is he? Why, know
Its Onely Might Almighty this did doe.
His hand hath made this noble worke which Stands
His Glorious Handywork not made by hands.
Who spake all things from nothing; and with ease
Can speake all things to nothing, if he please.
Whose Little finger at his pleasure Can
Out mete ten thousand worlds with halfe a Span:
Whose Might Almighty can by half a looks
Root up the rocks and rock the hills by th'roots.
Can take this mighty World up in his hande,
And shake it like a Squitchen or a Wand.

Whose single Frown will make the Heavens shake
Like as an aspen leafe the Winde makes quake.
Oh! what a might is this Whose single frown
Doth shake the world as it would shake it down?
Which All from Nothing fet, from Nothing, All:
Hath All on Nothing set, lets Nothing fall.
Gave All to nothing Man indeed, whereby
Through nothing man all might him Glorify.
In Nothing then imbosst the brightest Gem
More pretious than all pretiousness in them.
But Nothing man did throw down all by Sin:
And darkenèd that lightsom Gem in him.
　　　That now his Brightest Diamond is grown
　　　Darker by far than any Coalpit Stone.

266   *Let by rain*

Ye Flippering Soule,
　　Why dost between the Nippers dwell?
Not stay, nor goe. Not yea, nor yet Controle.
　　Doth this doe well?
　　　　Rise journy'ng when the skies fall weeping Showers.
　　　　Not o're nor under th'Clouds and Cloudy Powers.

Not yea, nor noe:
　　On tiptoes thus? Why sit on thorns?
Resolve the matter: Stay thyselfe or goe.
　　Be n't both wayes born.
　　　　Wager thyselfe against thy surplice, see,
　　　　And win thy Coate: or let thy Coate Win thee.

Is this th'Effect,
　　To leaven thus my Spirits all?
To make my heart a Crabtree Cask direct?
　　A Verjuicte Hall?
　　　　As Bottle Ale, whose Spirits prisond nurst
　　　　When jog'd, the bung with Violence doth burst?

Shall I be made
　　A sparkling Wildfire Shop
Where my dull Spirits at the Fireball trade
　　Do frisk and hop?
　　　　And while the Hammer doth the Anvill pay,
　　　　The fireball matter sparkles evry way.

One sorry fret,
　An anvill Sparke, rose higher
And in thy Temple falling almost set
　The house on fire.
　　Such fireballs droping in the Temple Flame
　　Burns up the building: Lord forbid the same.

267　　　　*Upon a Spider Catching a Fly*

Thou sorrow, venom Elfe.
　Is this thy play,
To spin a web out of thyselfe
　To Catch a Fly?
　　For Why?

I saw a pettish wasp
　Fall foule therein.
Whom yet thy Whorle pins did not clasp
　Lest he should fling
　　His sting.

But as affraid, remote
　Didst stand hereat
And with thy little fingers stroke
　And gently tap
　　His back.

Thus gently him didst treate
　Lest he should pet,
And in a froppish, waspish heate
　Should greatly fret
　　Thy net.

Whereas the silly Fly,
　Caught by its leg
Thou by the throate tookst hastily
　And 'hinde the head
　　Bite Dead.

This goes to pot, that not
　Nature doth call.
Strive not above what strength hath got
　Lest in the brawle
　　Thou fall.

This Frey seems thus to us.
    Hells Spider gets
His intrails spun to whip Cords thus
    And wove to nets
        And sets.

To tangle Adams race
    In's stratigems
To their Destructions, spoil'd, made base
    By venom things
        Damn'd Sins.

But mighty, Gracious Lord
    Communicate
Thy Grace to breake the Cord, afford
    Us Glorys Gate
        And State.

We'l Nightingaile sing like
    When pearcht on high
In Glories Cage, thy glory, bright,
    And thankfully,
        For joy.

268   *Upon a Wasp Child with Cold*

The Bear that breathes the Northern blast
Did numb, Torpedo like, a Wasp
Whose stiffend limbs encrampt, lay bathing
In Sol's warm breath and shine as saving,
Which with her hands she chafes and stands
Rubbing her Legs, Shanks, Thighs, and hands.
Her petty toes, and fingers ends
Nipt with this breath, she out extends
Unto the Sun, in greate desire
To warm her digits at that fire.
Doth hold her Temples in this state
Where pulse doth beate, and head doth ake.
Doth turn, and stretch her body small,
Doth Comb her velvet Capitall.
As if her little brain pan were
A Volume of Choice precepts cleare.
As if her sattin jacket hot
Contained Apothecaries Shop
Of Natures recepts, that prevails
To remedy all her sad ailes,

As if her velvet helmet high
Did turret rationality.
She fans her wing up to the Winde
As if her Pettycoate were lin'de,
With reasons fleece, and hoises sails
And hu'ming flies in thankfull gails
Unto her dun Curld palace Hall
Her warm thanks offering for all.

    Lord cleare my misted sight that I
May hence view thy Divinity.
Some sparkes whereof thou up dost hasp
Within this little downy Wasp
In whose small Corporation wee
A school and a schoolmaster see
Where we may learn, and easily finde
A nimble Spirit bravely minde
Her worke in ev'ry limb: and lace
It up neate with a vitall grace,
Acting each part though ne'er so small
Here of this Fustian animall.
Till I enravisht Climb into
The Godhead on this Ladder doe.
Where all my pipes inspir'de upraise
An Heavenly musick furrd with praise.

JOHN WILMOT, EARL OF ROCHESTER
1647–1680

269   *Seneca's Troas.*

Act 2. Chorus

  After Death, nothing is, and nothing Death,
    The utmost Limit of a gaspe of Breath;
Let the Ambitious Zealot, lay aside
His hopes of Heav'n, (whose faith is but his Pride)
    Let Slavish Soules lay by their feare;
    Nor be concern'd which way, nor where,
  After this Life they shall be hurl'd;
Dead, wee become the Lumber of the World,
And to that Masse of matter shall be swept,
Where things destroy'd, with things unborne, are kept.
    Devouring tyme, swallows us whole.
Impartiall Death, confounds, Body, and Soule.

For Hell, and the foule Fiend that Rules
Gods everlasting fiery Jayles
(Devis'd by Rogues, dreaded by Fooles)
With his grim griezly Dogg, that keepes the Doore,
Are senselesse Storyes, idle Tales
Dreames, Whimseys, and noe more.

[after the Latin of Seneca]

270   *A Song*

Absent from thee I languish still,
    Then ask me not, when I return?
The straying Fool 'twill plainly kill,
    To wish all Day, all Night to Mourn.

Dear; from thine Arms then let me flie,
    That my Fantastick mind may prove
The Torments it deserves to try,
    That tears my fixt Heart from my Love.

When wearied with a world of Woe,
    To thy safe Bosom I retire
Where Love and Peace and Truth does flow,
    May I contented there expire.

Lest once more wandring from that Heav'n
    I fall on some base heart unblest;
Faithless to thee, False, unforgiv'n,
    And lose my Everlasting rest.

271   *A Song of a young Lady*

                    To her Ancient Lover

                           1

Ancient Person, for whom I,
All the flattering Youth defy;
Long be it e're thou grow Old,
Aking, shaking, Crazy Cold.
But still continue as thou art,
Ancient Person of my Heart.

                           2

On thy withered Lips and dry,
Which like barren Furrows lye;

Brooding Kisses I will pour,
Shall thy youthful Heat restore.
Such kind Show'rs in Autumn fall,
And a second Spring recall:
Nor from thee will ever part,
Antient Person of my Heart.

3

Thy Nobler part, which but to name
In our Sex wou'd be counted shame,
By Ages frozen grasp possest,
From his Ice shall be releast:
And, sooth'd by my reviving hand,
In former Warmth and Vigor stand.
All a Lover's wish can reach,
For thy Joy my Love shall teach:
And for thy Pleasure shall improve,
All that Art can add to Love.
Yet still I love thee without Art,
Antient Person of my Heart.

272–3   from *Satyr* [*A Satyr against Mankind*]

272   [lines 1–45]

Were I (who to my cost already am
One of those strange prodigious Creatures *Man*)
A Spirit free, to choose for my own share,
What Case of Flesh, and Blood, I pleas'd to weare,
I'd be a *Dog*, a *Monkey*, or a *Bear*,
Or any thing but that vain *Animal*,
Who is so proud of being rational.
The senses are too gross, and he'll contrive
A Sixth, to contradict the other Five;
And before certain instinct, will preferr
Reason, which Fifty times for one does err.
Reason, an *Ignis fatuus*, in the *Mind*,
Which leaving light of *Nature*, sense behind;
Pathless and dang'rous wandring ways it takes,
Through errors Fenny *Boggs*, and Thorny *Brakes*;
Whilst the misguided follower, climbs with pain,
Mountains of Whimseys, heap'd in his own *Brain*:
Stumbling from thought to thought, falls headlong down,
Into doubts boundless Sea, where like to drown,

Books bear him up awhile, and make him try,
To swim with Bladders of *Philosophy*;
In hopes still t'oretake th'escaping light,
The *Vapour* dances in his dazling sight,
Till spent, it leaves him to eternal Night.
Then Old Age, and experience, hand in hand,
Lead him to death, and make him understand,
After a search so painful, and so long,
That all his Life he has been in the wrong;
Hudled in dirt, the reas'ning *Engine* lyes,
Who was so proud, so witty, and so wise.
Pride drew him in, as *Cheats*, their *Bubbles* catch,
And makes him venture, to be made a *Wretch*.
His wisdom did his happiness destroy,
Aiming to know that *World* he shou'd enjoy;
And *Wit*, was his vain frivolous pretence,
Of pleasing others, at his own expence.
For *Witts* are treated just like common *Whores*,
First they're enjoy'd, and then kickt out of *Doores*:
The pleasure past, a threatning doubt remains,
That frights th'enjoyer, with succeeding pains:
Women and *Men* of *Wit*, are dang'rous Tools,
And ever fatal to admiring *Fools*.
Pleasure allures, and when the *Fopps* escape,
'Tis not that they're belov'd, but fortunate,
And therefore what they fear, at heart they hate.

273   [lines 123–58]

You see how far *Mans* wisedom here extends,
Look next, if humane Nature makes amends;
Whose Principles, most gen'rous are, and just,
And to whose *Moralls*, you wou'd sooner trust.
Be judge your self, I'le bring it to the test,
Which is the basest *Creature Man*, or *Beast*?
Birds, feed on *Birds*, *Beasts*, on each other prey,
But Savage *Man* alone, does *Man*, betray:
Prest by necessity, they Kill for Food,
Man, undoes *Man*, to do himself no good.
With Teeth, and Claws, by Nature arm'd they hunt,
Natures allowance, to supply their want.
But *Man*, with smiles, embraces, Friendships, praise,
Unhumanely his Fellows life betrays;
With voluntary pains, works his distress,
Not through necessity, but wantonness.

For hunger, or for Love, they fight, or tear,
Whilst wretched *Man*, is still in Arms for fear;
For fear he armes, and is of Armes afraid,
By fear, to fear, successively betray'd.
Base fear, the source whence his best passion came,
His boasted Honor, and his dear bought Fame.
That lust of *Pow'r*, to which he's such a *Slave*,
And for the which alone he dares be brave:
To which his various Projects are design'd,
Which makes him gen'rous, affable, and kind.
For which he takes such pains to be thought wise,
And screws his actions, in a forc'd disguise:
Leading a tedious life in Misery,
Under laborious, mean *Hypocrisie*.
Look to the bottom, of his vast design,
Wherein *Mans* Wisdom, Pow'r, and Glory joyn;
The good he acts, the ill he does endure,
'Tis all for fear, to make himself secure.
Meerly for safety, after Fame we thirst,
For all Men, wou'd be *Cowards* if they durst.

274   *Plain Dealings Downfall*

Long time plain dealing in the Hauty Town,
Wandring about, though in thread-bare Gown,
At last unanimously was cry'd down.

When almost starv'd, she to the Countrey fled,
In hopes, though meanly she shou'd there be fed,
And tumble Nightly on a Pea-straw Bed.

But Knav'ry knowing her intent, took post,
And Rumour'd her approach through every Coast,
Vowing his Ruin that shou'd be her host.

Frighted at this, each *Rustick* shut his door,
Bid her be gone, and trouble him no more,
For he that entertain'd her must be poor.

At this grief seiz'd her, grief too great to tell,
When weeping, sighing, fainting, down she fell,
Whil's Knavery Laughing, Rung her passing Bell.

275   God bless our good and gracious King
             Whose promise none relyes on
           Who never said A foolish thing
             Nor ever did A wise one.

276   *Love and Life: a Song*

    All my past life is mine noe more
       The flying Houres are gon
    Like transitory Dreames giv'n ore
    Whose Images are kept in Store
       By Memory alone.

    What ever is to come is not
       How can it then be mine,
    The present Moment's all my Lott
    And that as fast as it is got
       Phillis is wholy thine.

    Then talke not of Inconstancy,
       False Hearts, and broken Vows,
    If I, by Miracle can be,
    This live-long Minute true to thee,
       Tis all that Heav'n allows.

277   *Upon Nothing*

Nothing thou Elder Brother even to Shade
Thou hadst a being ere the world was made
And (well fixt) art alone of ending not afraid.

Ere Time and Place were, Time and Place were not
When Primitive Nothing, somthing straight begott
Then all proceeded from the great united what—

Somthing, the Generall Attribute of all
Severed from thee its sole Originall
Into thy boundless selfe must undistinguisht fall.

Yet Somthing did thy mighty power command
And from thy fruitfull Emptinesses hand
Snatcht, Men, Beasts, birds, fire, water, Ayre, and land.

Matter, the Wickedst offspring of thy Race
By forme assisted flew from thy Embrace
And Rebell-Light obscured thy Reverend dusky face.

With forme and Matter, Time and Place did joyne
Body thy foe with these did Leagues combine
To spoyle thy Peaceful Realme and Ruine all thy Line.

But Turncote-time assists the foe in vayne
And brib'd by thee destroyes their short liv'd Reign
And to thy hungry wombe drives back thy slaves again.

Though Misteries are barr'd from Laick Eyes
And the Divine alone with warrant pries
Into thy Bosome, where thy truth in private lyes

Yet this of thee the wise may truly say
Thou from the virtuous Nothing doest delay
And to be part of thee the wicked wisely pray.

Great Negative how vainly would the wise
Enquire, define, distinguish, teach, devise,
Didst Thou not stand to poynt their blind Phylosophies.

Is or is not, the two great Ends of Fate
And true or false the Subject of debate
That pérfect or destroy the vast designes of State—

When they have wrackt the Politicians Brest
Within thy Bosome most Securely rest
And when reduc't to thee are least unsafe and best.

But (Nothing) why does Somthing still permitt
That Sacred Monarchs should at Councell sitt
With persons highly thought, at best for nothing fitt,

Whilst weighty Somthing modestly abstaynes
From Princes Coffers and from Statesmens braines
And nothing there like Stately nothing reignes?

Nothing who dwell'st with fooles in grave disguise
For whom they Reverend Shapes and formes devise
Lawn-sleeves and Furrs and Gowns, when they like thee looke wise:

French Truth, Dutch Prowess, Brittish policy
Hibernian Learning, Scotch Civility
Spaniards Dispatch, Danes witt, are Mainly seen in thee;

The Great mans Gratitude to his best freind
Kings promises, Whores vowes towards thee they bend
Flow Swiftly into thee, and in thee ever end.

CHARLES MORDAUNT, EARL OF PETERBOROUGH

1658–1735

278   I said to my Heart, between sleeping and waking,
Thou wild Thing, that ever art leaping or aching,
For the Black, for the Fair: In what Clime, in what Nation,
Hast thou not felt a Fit of Pitapatation?

Thus accus'd, the wild Thing gave this serious Reply;
See the Heart without Motion, tho' *Celia* pass by;
Not the Beauty she has, nor the Wit that she borrows,
Gives the Eye any Joys, or the Heart any Sorrows.

When our *Sappho* appears, whose Wit's so refined,
I am forced to admire with the rest of Mankind:
Whatever she says is with Spirit and Fire;
Every Word I attend, but I only admire.

Prudentia, as vainly too, puts in her Claim;
Ever gazing on Heaven, tho' Man is her Aim.
'Tis Love, not Devotion, that turns up her Eyes:
Those Stars of the World are too good for the Skies.

But my *Chloe*, so lovely, so easy, so fair;
Her Wit so genteel, without Art, without Care;
When she comes in my Way, Oh! the Motion and Pain,
The Leapings and Achings, they return all again.

Thou wonderful Creature! A Woman of Reason!
Never grave out of Pride, never gay out of Season!
When so easy to guess, who this Angel should be,
Would one think that my *Chloe* ne'er thought it was she.

ANNE FINCH, COUNTESS OF WINCHILSEA

1661–1720

279   *A Nocturnal Reverie*

In such a *Night*, when every louder Wind
Is to its distant Cavern safe confin'd;
And only gentle *Zephyr* fans his Wings,
And lonely *Philomel*, still waking, sings;
Or from some Tree, fam'd for the *Owl's* delight,
She, hollowing clear, directs the Wand'rer right:
In such a *Night*, when passing Clouds give place,
Or thinly vail the Heav'ns mysterious Face;
When in some River, overhung with Green,
The waving Moon and trembling Leaves are seen;
When freshen'd Grass now bears it self upright,
And makes cool Banks to pleasing Rest invite,
Whence springs the *Woodbind*, and the *Bramble*-Rose,
And where the sleepy *Cowslip* shelter'd grows;
Whilst now a paler Hue the *Foxglove* takes,
Yet checquers still with Red the dusky brakes

When scatter'd *Glow-worms*, but in Twilight fine,
Shew trivial Beauties watch their Hour to shine;
Whilst *Salisb'ry* stands the Test of every Light,
In perfect Charms, and perfect Virtue bright:
When Odours, which declin'd repelling Day,
Thro' temp'rate Air uninterrupted stray;
When darken'd Groves their softest Shadows wear,
And falling Waters we distinctly hear;
When thro' the Gloom more venerable shows
Some ancient Fabrick, awful in Repose,
While Sunburnt Hills their swarthy Looks conceal,
And swelling Haycocks thicken up the Vale:
When the loos'd *Horse* now, as his Pasture leads,
Comes slowly grazing thro' th' adjoining Meads,
Whose stealing Pace, and lengthen'd Shade we fear,
Till torn up Forage in his Teeth we hear:
When nibbling *Sheep* at large pursue their Food,
And unmolested Kine rechew the Cud;
When *Curlews* cry beneath the Village-walls,
And to her straggling Brood the *Partridge* calls;
Their shortliv'd Jubilee the Creatures keep,
Which but endures, whilst Tyrant-*Man* do's sleep;
When a sedate Content the Spirit feels,
And no fierce Light disturb, whilst it reveals;
But silent Musings urge the Mind to seek
Something, too high for Syllables to speak;
Till the free Soul to a compos'dness charm'd,
Finding the Elements of Rage disarm'd,
O'er all below a solemn Quiet grown,
Joys in th' inferiour World, and thinks it like her Own:
In such a *Night* let Me abroad remain,
Till Morning breaks, and All's confus'd again;
Our Cares, our Toils, our Clamours are renew'd,
Or Pleasures, seldom reach'd, again pursu'd.

280   *Glass*

O Man! what Inspiration was thy Guide,
Who taught thee Light and Air thus to divide;
To let in all the useful Beams of Day,
Yet force, as subtil Winds, without thy Sash to stay;
T'extract from Embers by a strange Device,
Then polish fair these Flakes of solid Ice;
Which, silver'd o'er, redouble all in place,
And give thee back thy well or ill-complexion'd Face.

To Vessels blown exceed the gloomy Bowl,
Which did the Wine's full excellence controul,
These shew the Body, whilst you taste the Soul.
Its colour sparkles Motion, lets thee see,
Tho' yet th' Excess the Preacher warns to flee,
Lest Men at length as clearly spy through Thee.

281   *A Sigh*

  Gentlest Air thou breath of Lovers
    Vapour from a secret fire
  Which by thee itts self discovers
    E're yett daring to aspire.

  Softest Noat of whisper'd anguish
    Harmony's refindest part
  Striking whilst thou seem'st to languish
    Full upon the list'ners heart.

  Safest Messenger of Passion
    Stealing through a crou'd of spys
  Which constrain the outward fassion
    Close the Lips and guard the Eyes.

  Shapelesse Sigh we ne're can show thee
    Form'd but to assault the Ear
  Yett e're to their cost they know thee
    Ev'ry Nymph may read thee here.

282   *The Unequal Fetters*

  Cou'd we stop the time that's flying
    Or recall itt when 'tis past
  Put far off the day of Dying
    Or make Youth for ever last
  To Love wou'd then be worth our cost.

  But since we must loose those Graces
    Which at first your hearts have wonne
  And you seek for in new Faces
    When our Spring of Life is done
  It wou'd but urdge our ruine on

  Free as Nature's first intention
    Was to make us, I'll be found
  Nor by subtle Man's invention
    Yeild to be in Fetters bound
  By one that walks a freer round.

Mariage does but slightly tye Men
　　Whil'st close Pris'ners we remain
They the larger Slaves of Hymen
　　Still are begging Love again
At the full length of all their chain.

TOM BROWN

1663–1704

283

I do not love thee, Doctor *Fell*;
The reason why I cannot tell.
But this I'm sure I know full well,
I do not love thee, Doctor *Fell*.

[after the Latin of Martial]

MATTHEW PRIOR

1664–1721

284

To a Child of Quality of Five Years Old, the Author suppos'd Forty

Lords, Knights, and Squires, the num'rous Band
　　That wear the Fair Miss *Mary*'s Fetters,
Were summon'd, by her high Command,
　　To show their Passion by their Letters.

My Pen amongst the rest I took,
　　Least those bright Eyes that cannot read
Shou'd dart their kindling Fires, and look
　　The Pow'r they have to be obey'd.

Nor Quality, nor Reputation,
　　Forbid me yet my Flame to tell,
Dear Five Years old befriends my Passion,
　　And I may Write 'till she can Spell.

For while she makes her Silk-worms Beds
　　With all the tender things I swear,
Whilst all the House my Passion reads,
　　In Papers round her Baby's Hair,

She may receive and own my Flame,
　　For tho' the strictest *Prudes* shou'd know it,
She'll pass for a most virtuous Dame,
　　And I for an unhappy Poet.

Then too, alas, when she shall tear
  The Lines some younger Rival sends,
She'll give me leave to Write, I fear,
  And we shall still continue Friends.

For as our diff'rent Ages move,
  'Tis so ordain'd, wou'd Fate but mend it,
That I shall be past making Love,
  When she begins to comprehend it.

285   *In Imitation of Anacreon*

  Let 'em Censure: what care I?
The Herd of Criticks I defie.
Let the Wretches know, I write
Regardless of their Grace, or Spight.
No, no: the Fair, the Gay, the Young
Govern the Numbers of my Song.
All that They approve is sweet:
And All is Sense, that They repeat.

  Bid the warbling Nine retire:
Venus, String thy Servant's Lyre:
Love shall be my endless Theme:
Pleasure shall triumph over Fame:
And when these Maxims I decline,
Apollo, may Thy Fate be Mine:
May I grasp at empty Praise;
And lose the Nymph, to gain the Bays.

[after the Greek of Anacreon]

286   *The Lady who offers her Looking-Glass to Venus*

  Venus, take my Votive Glass:
Since I am not what I was;
What from this Day I shall be,
Venus, let Me never see.

[after the Greek of Plato]

287   *A Better Answer [to Cloe Jealous]*

Dear CLOE, how blubber'd is that pretty Face?
    Thy Cheek all on Fire, and Thy Hair all uncurl'd:
Pr'ythee quit this Caprice; and (as Old FALSTAF says)
    Let Us e'en talk a little like Folks of This World.

How can'st Thou presume, Thou hast leave to destroy
    The Beauties, which VENUS but lent to Thy keeping?
Those Looks were design'd to inspire Love and Joy:
    More ord'nary Eyes may serve People for weeping.

To be vext at a Trifle or two that I writ,
    Your Judgment at once, and my Passion You wrong:
You take that for Fact, which will scarce be found Wit:
    Od's Life! must One swear to the Truth of a Song?

What I speak, my fair CLOE, and what I write, shews
    The Diff'rence there is betwixt Nature and Art:
I court others in Verse; but I love Thee in Prose:
    And They have my Whimsies; but Thou hast my Heart.

The God of us Verse-men (You know Child) the SUN,
    How after his Journeys He sets up his Rest:
If at Morning o'er Earth 'tis his Fancy to run;
    At Night he reclines on his THETIS's Breast.

So when I am weary'd with wand'ring all Day;
    To Thee my Delight in the Evening I come:
No Matter what Beauties I saw in my Way:
    They were but my Visits; but Thou art my Home.

Then finish, Dear CLOE, this Pastoral War;
    And let us like HORACE and LYDIA agree:
For Thou art a Girl as much brighter than Her,
    As He was a Poet sublimer than Me.

288   *Epigram*

To JOHN I ow'd great Obligation;
    But JOHN, unhappily, thought fit
To publish it to all the Nation:
    Sure JOHN and I are more than Quit.

                        [after the Latin of Martial]

289   *Human Life*

What trifling coil do we poor mortals keep;
Wake, eat, and drink, evacuate, and sleep.

GEORGE GRANVILLE, LORD LANSDOWNE

1667–1735

290   *Cloe*

Bright as the day, and like the morning, fair,
Such Cloe is—and common as the air.

291   *Cloe*

Cloe's the wonder of her sex,
   'Tis well her heart is tender,
How might such killing eyes perplex,
   With virtue to defend her?

But Nature graciously inclin'd
   With liberal hand to please us,
Has to her boundless beauty join'd
   A boundless bent to ease us.

JONATHAN SWIFT

1667–1745

292   *To their Excellencies the Lords Justices of Ireland*
       The Humble Petition of Frances Harris,
   Who must Starve, and Die a Maid if it miscarries

Anno. 1700

Humbly Sheweth.
That I went to warm my self in Lady *Betty*'s Chamber, because I was cold,
And I had in a Purse, seven Pound, four Shillings and six Pence, besides
   Farthings, in Money, and Gold;

So because I had been buying things for my *Lady* last Night,
I was resolved to tell my Money, to see if it was right:
Now you must know, because my Trunk has a very bad Lock,
Therefore all the Money, I have, which, *God* knows, is a very small Stock,
I keep in a Pocket ty'd about my Middle, next my Smock.
So when I went to put up my Purse, as *God* would have it, my Smock was
    unript,
And, instead of putting it into my Pocket, down it slipt:
Then the Bell rung, and I went down to put my *Lady* to Bed,
And, *God* knows, I thought my Money was as safe as my Maidenhead.
So when I came up again, I found my Pocket feel very light,
But when I search'd, and miss'd my Purse, *Lord!* I thought I should have
    sunk outright:
Lord! Madam, says *Mary*, how d'ye do? Indeed, says I, never worse;
But pray, *Mary*, can you tell what I have done with my Purse!
Lord help me, said *Mary*, I never stirr'd out of this Place!
Nay, said I, I had it in Lady *Betty*'s Chamber, that's a plain Case.
So *Mary* got me to Bed, and cover'd me up warm,
However, she stole away my Garters, that I might do my self no Harm:
So I tumbl'd and toss'd all Night, as you may very well think,
But hardly ever set my Eyes together, or slept a Wink.
So I was a-dream'd, methought, that we went and search'd the Folks
    round,
And in a Corner of Mrs. *Dukes*'s Box, ty'd in a Rag, the Money was
    found.
So next Morning we told *Whittle*, and he fell a Swearing;
Then my Dame *Wadgar* came, and she, you know, is thick of Hearing;
Dame, said I, as loud as I could bawl, do you know what a Loss I have had?
Nay, said she, my Lord *Collway*'s Folks are all very sad,
For my Lord *Dromedary* comes a *Tuesday* without fail;
Pugh! said I, but that's not the Business that I ail.
Says *Cary*, says he, I have been a Servant this Five and Twenty Years, come
    Spring,
And in all the Places I liv'd, I never heard of such a Thing.
Yes, says the *Steward*, I remember when I was at my Lady *Shrewsbury*'s,
Such a thing as this happen'd, just about the time of *Goosberries*.
So I went to the Party suspected, and I found her full of Grief;
(Now you must know, of all Things in the World, I hate a Thief.)
However, I was resolv'd to bring the Discourse slily about,
Mrs. *Dukes*, said I, here's an ugly Accident has happen'd out;
'Tis not that I value the Money three Skips of a Louse;
But the Thing I stand upon, is the Credit of the House;
'Tis true, seven Pound, four Shillings, and six Pence, makes a great Hole in
    my Wages,
Besides, as they say, Service is no Inheritance in these Ages.
Now, Mrs. *Dukes*, you know, and every Body understands,
That tho' 'tis hard to judge, yet Money can't go without Hands.

The *Devil* take me, said she, (blessing her self,) if I ever saw't!
So she roar'd like a *Bedlam*, as tho' I had call'd her all to naught;
So you know, what could I say to her any more,
I e'en left her, and came away as wise as I was before.
Well: But then they would have had me gone to the Cunning Man;
No, said I, 'tis the same Thing, the *Chaplain* will be here anon.
So the *Chaplain* came in; now the Servants say, he is my Sweet-heart,
Because he's always in my Chamber, and I always take his Part;
So, as the *Devil* would have it, before I was aware, out I blunder'd,
Parson, said I, can you cast a *Nativity*, when a Body's plunder'd?
(Now you must know, he hates to be call'd *Parson*, like the *Devil*.)
Truly, says he, Mrs. *Nab*, it might become you to be more civil:
If your Money be gone, as a Learned *Divine* says, d'ye see,
You are no *Text* for my Handling, so take that from me:
I was never taken for a *Conjurer* before, I'd have you to know.
Lord, said I, don't be angry, I'm sure I never thought you so;
You know, I honour the Cloth, I design to be a *Parson*'s Wife,
I never took one in *Your Coat* for a *Conjurer* in all my Life.
With that, he twisted his Girdle at me like a Rope, as who should say,
Now you may go hang your self for me, and so went away.
Well; I thought I should have swoon'd; *Lord*, said I, what shall I do?
I have lost my *Money*, and shall lose my *True-Love* too.
Then my *Lord* call'd me; *Harry*, said my *Lord*, don't cry,
I'll give something towards thy Loss; and says my *Lady*, so will I.
Oh but, said I, what if after all my Chaplain won't *come to*?
For that, he said, (an't please your *Excellencies*) I must Petition You.
The Premises tenderly consider'd, I desire your *Excellencies* Protection,
And that I may have a Share in next *Sunday*'s Collection:
And over and above, that I may have your *Excellencies* Letter,
With an Order for the *Chaplain* aforesaid; or instead of Him, a Better:
And then your poor *Petitioner*, both Night and Day,
Or the *Chaplain*, (for 'tis his *Trade*) as in Duty bound, shall ever *Pray*.

293   *A Description of the Morning*

Now hardly here and there an Hackney-Coach
Appearing, show'd the Ruddy Morns Approach.
Now *Betty* from her Masters Bed had flown,
And softly stole to discompose her own.
The Slipshod Prentice from his Masters Door,
Had par'd the Dirt, and Sprinkled round the Floor.
Now *Moll* had whirl'd her Mop with dext'rous Airs,
Prepar'd to Scrub the Entry and the Stairs.
The Youth with Broomy Stumps began to trace
The Kennel-Edge, where Wheels had worn the Place.

The Smallcoal-Man was heard with Cadence deep,
'Till drown'd in Shriller Notes of Chimney-Sweep,
Duns at his Lordships Gate began to meet,
And Brickdust *Moll* had Scream'd through half the Street,
The Turnkey now his Flock returning sees,
Duly let out a Nights to Steal for Fees.
The watchful Bailiffs take their silent Stands,
And School-Boys lag with Satchels in their Hands.

294–6   from *Verses on the Death of Dr. Swift*

294   [lines 73–164]

  The Time is not remote, when I
Must by the Course of Nature dye:
When I foresee my special Friends,
Will try to find their private Ends:
Tho' it is hardly understood,
Which way my Death can do them good;
Yet, thus methinks, I hear 'em speak;
See, how the Dean begins to break:
Poor Gentleman, he droops apace,
You plainly find it in his Face:
That old Vertígo in his Head,
Will never leave him, till he's dead:
Besides, his Memory decays,
He recollects not what he says;
He cannot call his Friends to Mind;
Forgets the Place where last he din'd:
Plyes you with Stories o'er and o'er,
He told them fifty Times before.
How does he fancy we can sit,
To hear his out-of-fashion'd Wit?
But he takes up with younger Fokes,
Who for his Wine will bear his Jokes:
Faith, he must make his Stories shorter,
Or change his Comrades once a Quarter:
In half the Time, he talks them round;
There must another Sett be found.

  For Poetry, he's past his Prime,
He takes an Hour to find a Rhime:
His Fire is out, his Wit decay'd,
His Fancy sunk, his Muse a Jade.
I'd have him throw away his Pen;
But there's no talking to some Men.

And, then their Tenderness appears,
By adding largely to my Years:
'He's older than he would be reckon'd,
'And well remembers *Charles* the Second.

'He hardly drinks a Pint of Wine;
'And that, I doubt, is no good Sign.
'His Stomach too begins to fail:
'Last Year we thought him strong and hale;
'But now, he's quite another Thing;
'I wish he may hold out till Spring.'

Then hug themselves, and reason thus;
'It is not yet so bad with us.'

In such a Case they talk in Tropes,
And, by their Fears express their Hopes:
Some great Misfortune to portend,
No Enemy can match a Friend;
With all the Kindness they profess,
The Merit of a lucky Guess,
(When daily Howd'y's come of Course,
And Servants answer; *Worse and Worse*)
Wou'd please 'em better than to tell,
That, GOD be prais'd, the Dean is well.
Then he who prophecy'd the best,
Approves his Foresight to the rest:
'You know, I always fear'd the worst,
'And often told you so at first:'
He'd rather chuse that I should dye,
Than his Prediction prove a Lye.
Not one foretels I shall recover;
But, all agree, to give me over.

Yet shou'd some Neighbour feel a Pain,
Just in the Parts, where I complain;
How many a Message would he send?
What hearty Prayers that I should mend?
Enquire what Regimen I kept;
What gave me Ease, and how I slept?
And more lament, when I was dead,
Than all the Sniv'llers round my Bed.

My good Companions, never fear,
For though you may mistake a Year;
Though your Prognosticks run too fast,
They must be verify'd at last.

'Behold the fatal Day arrive!
'How is the Dean? He's just alive.

'Now the departing Prayer is read:
'He hardly breathes. The Dean is dead.
'Before the Passing-Bell begun,
'The News thro' half the Town has run.
'O, may we all for Death prepare!
'What has he left? And who's his Heir?
'I know no more than what the News is,
'' Tis all bequeath'd to publick Uses.
'To publick Use! A perfect Whim!
'What had the Publick done for him!
'Meer Envy, Avarice, and Pride!
'He gave it all:—But first he dy'd.
'And had the Dean, in all the Nation,
'No worthy Friend, no poor Relation?
'So ready to do Strangers good,
'Forgetting his own Flesh and Blood?'

295   [lines 205–42]

Here shift the Scene, to represent
How those I love, my Death lament.
Poor POPE will grieve a Month; and GAY
A Week; and ARBUTHNOTT a Day.

ST. JOHN himself will scarce forbear,
To bite his Pen, and drop a Tear.
The rest will give a Shrug and cry,
I'm sorry; but we all must dye.
Indifference clad in Wisdom's Guise,
All Fortitude of Mind supplies:
For how can stony Bowels melt,
In those who never Pity felt;
When *We* are lash'd, *They* kiss the Rod;
Resigning to the Will of God.

The Fools, my Juniors by a Year,
Are tortur'd with Suspence and Fear.
Who wisely thought my Age a Screen,
When Death approach'd, to stand between:
The Screen remov'd, their Hearts are trembling,
They mourn for me without dissembling.

My female Friends, whose tender Hearts
Have better learn'd to act their Parts,
Receive the News in *doleful Dumps*,
'The Dean is dead, (*and what is Trumps?*)

'Then Lord have Mercy on his Soul.
'(Ladies I'll venture for the *Vole*.)
'Six Deans they say must bear the Pall.
'(I wish I knew what *King* to call.)
'Madam, your Husband will attend
'The Funeral of so good a Friend.
'No Madam, 'tis a shocking Sight,
'And he's engag'd To-morrow Night!
'My Lady *Club* wou'd take it ill,
'If he shou'd fail her at *Quadrill*.
'He lov'd the Dean. (*I lead a Heart*.)
'But dearest Friends, they say, must part.
'His Time was come, he ran his Race;
'We hope he's in a better Place.'

296   [line 455–end]

'Perhaps I may allow, the Dean
'Had too much Satyr in his Vein;
'And seem'd determin'd not to starve it,
'Because no Age could more deserve it.
'Yet, Malice never was his Aim;
'He lash'd the Vice but spar'd the Name.
'No Individual could resent,
'Where Thousands equally were meant.
'His Satyr points at no Defect,
'But what all Mortals may correct;
'For he abhorr'd that senseless Tribe,
'Who call it Humour when they jibe:
'He spar'd a Hump or crooked Nose,
'Whose Owners set not up for Beaux.
'True genuine Dulness mov'd his Pity,
'Unless it offer'd to be witty.
'Those, who their Ignorance confess'd,
'He ne'er offended with a Jest;
'But laugh'd to hear an Idiot quote,
'A Verse from *Horace*, learn'd by Rote.

'He knew an hundred pleasant Stories,
'With all the Turns of *Whigs* and *Tories*:
'Was chearful to his dying Day,
'And Friends would let him have his Way.

'He gave the little Wealth he had,
'To build a House for Fools and Mad:

'And shew'd by one satyric Touch,
'No Nation wanted it so much:
'That Kingdom he hath left his Debtor,
'I wish it soon may have a Better.'

297   *The Day of Judgement*

With a Whirl of Thought oppress'd,
I sink from Reverie to Rest.
An horrid Vision seiz'd my Head,
I saw the Graves give up their Dead.
Jove, arm'd with Terrors, burst the Skies,
And Thunder roars, and Light'ning flies!
Amaz'd, confus'd, its Fate unknown,
The World stands trembling at his Throne.
While each pale Sinner hangs his Head,
Jove, nodding, shook the Heav'ns, and said,
'Offending Race of Human Kind,
By Nature, Reason, Learning, blind;
You who thro' Frailty step'd aside,
And you who never fell—*thro*' *Pride*;
You who in different Sects have shamm'd,
And come to see each other damn'd;
(So some Folks told you, but they knew
No more of Jove's Designs than you)
The World's mad Business now is o'er,
And I resent these Pranks no more.
I to such Blockheads set my Wit!
I damn such Fools!—Go, go, you're bit.'

298   *A Beautiful Young Nymph Going to Bed*

Corinna, Pride of *Drury-Lane*,
For whom no Shepherd sighs in vain;
Never did *Covent Garden* boast
So bright a batter'd, strolling Toast;
No drunken Rake to pick her up,
No Cellar where on Tick to sup;
Returning at the Midnight Hour;
Four Stories climbing to her Bow'r;
Then, seated on a three-legg'd Chair,
Takes off her artificial Hair:
Now, picking out a Crystal Eye,
She wipes it clean, and lays it by.

Her Eye-Brows from a Mouse's Hyde,
Stuck on with Art on either Side,
Pulls off with Care, and first displays 'em,
Then in a Play-Book smoothly lays 'em.
Now dextrously her Plumpers draws,
That serve to fill her hollow Jaws.
Untwists a Wire; and from her Gums
A Set of Teeth completely comes.
Pulls out the Rags contriv'd to prop
Her flabby Dugs and down they drop.
Proceeding on, the lovely Goddess
Unlaces next her Steel-Rib'd Bodice;
Which by the Operator's Skill,
Press down the Lumps, the Hollows fill,
Up goes her Hand, and off she slips
The Bolsters that supply her Hips.
With gentlest Touch, she next explores
Her Shankers, Issues, running Sores,
Effects of many a sad Disaster;
And then to each applies a Plaister.
But must, before she goes to Bed,
Rub off the Dawbs of White and Red;
And smooth the Furrows in her Front,
With greasy Paper stuck upon't.
She takes a *Bolus* e'er she sleeps;
And then between two Blankets creeps.
With Pains of Love tormented lies;
Or if she chance to close her Eyes,
Of *Bridewell* and the *Compter* dreams,
And feels the Lash, and faintly screams;
Or, by a faithless Bully drawn,
At some Hedge-Tavern lies in Pawn;
Or to *Jamaica* seems transported,
Alone, and by no Planter courted;
Or, near *Fleet-Ditch*'s oozy Brinks,
Surrounded with a Hundred Stinks,
Belated, seems on watch to lye,
And snap some Cully passing by;
Or, struck with Fear, her Fancy runs
On Watchmen, Constables and Duns,
From whom she meets with frequent Rubs;
But, never from Religious Clubs;
Whose Favour she is sure to find,
Because she pays 'em all in Kind.
　　CORINNA wakes. A dreadful Sight!
Behold the Ruins of the Night!

A wicked Rat her Plaister stole,
Half eat, and dragg'd it to his Hole.
The Crystal Eye, alas, was miss't;
And *Puss* had on her Plumpers p—st.
A Pigeon pick'd her Issue-Peas;
And *Shock* her Tresses fill'd with Fleas.
   The Nymph, tho' in this mangled Plight,
Must ev'ry Morn her Limbs unite.
But how shall I describe her Arts
To recollect the scatter'd Parts?
Or shew the Anguish, Toil, and Pain,
Of gath'ring up herself again?
The bashful Muse will never bear
In such a Scene to interfere.
Corinna in the Morning dizen'd,
Who sees, will spew; who smells, be poison'd.

WILLIAM CONGREVE

1670–1729

299   *A Hue and Cry after Fair Amoret*

Fair *Amoret* is gone astray;
   Pursue and seek her, ev'ry Lover;
I'll tell the Signs, by which you may
   The wand'ring Shepherdess discover.

Coquet and Coy at once her Air,
   Both study'd, tho' both seem neglected;
Careless she is with artful Care,
   Affecting to seem unaffected.

With Skill her Eyes dart ev'ry Glance,
   Yet change so soon you'd ne'er suspect 'em;
For she'd persuade they wound by chance,
   Tho' certain Aim and Art direct 'em.

She likes her self, yet others hates
   For that which in her self she prizes;
And while she Laughs at them, forgets
   She is the Thing that she despises.

300   *Song*

 False though she be to me and Love,
  I'll ne'er pursue Revenge;
 For still the Charmer I approve,
  Tho' I deplore her Change.

 In Hours of Bliss we oft have met,
  They could not always last;
 And though the present I regret,
  I'm grateful for the past.

301   *Song*

 Pious *Selinda* goes to Pray'rs,
  If I but ask the Favour;
 And yet the tender Fool's in Tears,
  When she believes I'll leave her.

 Wou'd I were free from this Restraint,
  Or else had Hopes to win her;
 Wou'd she cou'd make of me a Saint,
  Or I of her a Sinner.

JOSEPH ADDISON

1672–1719

302   *Ode*

The Spacious Firmament on high,
With all the blue Etherial Sky,
And spangled Heav'ns, a Shining Frame,
Their great Original proclaim:
Th' unwearied Sun, from Day to Day,
Does his Creator's Power display,
And publishes to every Land
The Work of an Almighty Hand.

Soon as the Evening Shades prevail,
The Moon takes up the wondrous Tale,
And nightly to the listning Earth
Repeats the Story of her Birth:

Whilst all the Stars that round her burn,
And all the Planets, in their turn,
Confirm the Tidings as they rowl,
And spread the Truth from Pole to Pole.

What though, in solemn Silence, all
Move round the dark terrestrial Ball?
What tho' nor real Voice nor Sound
Amid their radiant Orbs be found?
In Reason's Ear they all rejoice,
And utter forth a glorious Voice,
For ever singing, as they shine,
'The Hand that made us is Divine.'

ISAAC WATTS

1674–1748

303   *The Day of Judgment*
                      An Ode

          Attempted in English Sapphick

When the fierce Northwind with his airy Forces
Rears up the *Baltick* to a foaming Fury;
And the red Lightning with a Storm of Hail comes
                              Rushing amain down,

How the poor Sailors stand amaz'd and tremble!
While the hoarse Thunder like a bloody Trumpet
Roars a loud Onset to the gaping Waters
                              Quick to devour them.

Such shall the Noise be, and the wild Disorder,
(If things Eternal may be like these Earthly)
Such the dire Terror when the great Archangel
                              Shakes the Creation;

Tears the strong Pillars of the Vault of Heaven,
Breaks up old Marble the Repose of Princes;
See the Graves open, and the Bones arising,
                              Flames all around 'em.

Hark the shrill Outcries of the guilty Wretches!
Lively bright Horror and amazing Anguish
Stare thro' their Eye-lids, while the living Worm lies
                              Gnawing within them.

Thoughts like old Vultures prey upon their Heartstrings,
And the Smart twinges, when their Eye beholds the
Lofty Judge frowning, and a Flood of Vengeance
                                        Rolling afore him.

Hopeless Immortals! how they scream and shiver
While Devils push them to the Pit wide yawning
Hideous and gloomy, to receive them headlong
                                        Down to the Centre.

Stop here my Fancy: (all away ye horrid
Doleful Ideas) come arise to *Jesus,*
How he sits God-like! and the Saints around him
                                        Thron'd, yet adoring!

O may I sit there when he comes Triumphant
Dooming the Nations: then ascend to Glory,
While our *Hosannahs* all along the Passage
                                        Shout the Redeemer.

304   *Crucifixion to the World by the Cross of Christ*

When I survey the wond'rous Cross
On which the Prince of Glory dy'd,
My richest Gain I count but Loss,
And pour Contempt on all my Pride.

Forbid it, Lord, that I should boast
Save in the Death of *Christ* my God;
All the vain things that charm me most,
I sacrifice them to his Blood.

See from his Head, his Hands, his Feet,
Sorrow and Love flow mingled down;
Did e'er such Love and Sorrow meet?
Or Thorns compose so rich a Crown?

His dying Crimson like a Robe
Spreads o'er his Body on the Tree,
Then am I dead to all the Globe,
And all the Globe is dead to me.

Were the whole Realm of Nature mine,
That were a Present far too small;
Love so amazing, so divine
Demands my Soul, my Life, my All.

305   *Man Frail, and God Eternal*

Our God, our Help in Ages past,
  Our Hope for Years to come,
Our Shelter from the Stormy Blast,
  And our eternal Home.

Under the Shadow of thy Throne
  Thy Saints have dwelt secure;
Sufficient is thine Arm alone,
  And our Defence is sure.

Before the Hills in order stood,
  Or Earth receiv'd her Frame,
From everlasting Thou art God,
  To endless Years the same.

Thy Word commands our Flesh to Dust,
  Return, ye Sons of Men:
All Nations rose from Earth at first,
  And turn to Earth again.

A thousand Ages in thy Sight
  Are like an Evening gone;
Short as the Watch that ends the Night
  Before the rising Sun.

The busy Tribes of Flesh and Blood
  With all their Lives and Cares
Are carried downwards by thy Flood,
  And lost in following Years.

Time like an ever-rolling Stream
  Bears all its Sons away;
They fly forgotten as a Dream
  Dies at the opening Day.

Like flow'ry Fields the Nations stand
  Pleas'd with the Morning-light;
The Flowers beneath the Mower's Hand
  Ly withering e'er 'tis Night.

Our God, our Help in Ages past,
  Our Hope for Years to come,
Be thou our Guard while Troubles last,
  And our eternal Home.

306   *Against Idleness and Mischief*

How doth the little busy Bee
   Improve each shining Hour,
And gather Honey all the Day
   From ev'ry op'ning Flow'r!

How skilfully she builds her Cell!
   How neat she spreads the Wax!
And labours hard to store it well
   With the sweet Food she makes.

In Works of Labour or of Skill
   I would be busy too:
For *Satan* finds some Mischief still
   For idle Hands to do.

In Books, or Work, or healthful Play,
   Let my first Years be past,
That I may give for every Day
   Some good Account at last.

307   *The Sluggard*

'Tis the Voice of the Sluggard; I heard him complain,
'You have wak'd me too soon, I must slumber again.'
As the Door on its Hinges, so he on his Bed,
Turns his Sides and his Shoulders and his heavy Head.

'A little more Sleep, and a little more Slumber;'
Thus he wastes half his Days and his Hours without Number;
And when he gets up, he sits folding his Hands,
Or walks about sauntring, or trifling he stands.

I pass'd by his Garden, and saw the wild Brier,
The Thorn and the Thistle grow broader and higher;
The Clothes that hang on him are turning to Rags;
And his Money still wastes, till he starves or he begs.

I made him a Visit, still hoping to find
He had took better Care for improving his Mind:
He told me his Dreams, talk'd of Eating and Drinking;
But he scarce reads his Bible, and never loves Thinking.

Said I then to my Heart, 'Here's a Lesson for me;'
That Man's but a Picture of what I might be:
But thanks to my Friends for their Care in my Breeding,
Who taught me betimes to love Working and Reading.

JOSEPH TRAPP

1679–1747

308a   *On His late Majesty's Gracious Gift*
        to the Universities

The King surveying, with judicious Eyes,
The State of both his Universities,
To one a *Troop* of *Horse* he sent; for why?
'Cause that *learn'd Body* wanted *Loyalty*:
To th'other he sent *Books*, as well discerning
How much that *loyal Body* wanted Learning.

SIR WILLIAM BROWNE

1692–1774

308b   The King to Oxford sent a troop of horse,
        For Tories own no argument but force;
        With equal skill to Cambridge books he sent,
        For Whigs admit no force but argument.

GEORGE BERKELEY

1685–1753

309   *Verses on the Prospect of planting Arts*
        and Learning in America

The Muse, disgusted at an age and clime
    Barren of every glorious theme,
In distant lands now waits a better time,
    Producing subjects worthy fame:

In happy climes, where from the genial sun
    And virgin earth such scenes ensue,
The force of art by nature seems outdone,
    And fancied beauties by the true:

In happy climes the seat of innocence,
    Where nature guides and virtue rules,
Where men shall not impose for truth and sense,
    The pedantry of courts and schools:

There shall be sung another golden age,
   The rise of empire and of arts,
The good and great inspiring epic rage,
   The wisest heads and noblest hearts.

Not such as Europe breeds in her decay;
   Such as she bred when fresh and young,
When heav'nly flame did animate her clay,
   By future poets shall be sung.

Westward the course of empire takes its way;
   The four first acts already past,
A fifth shall close the drama with the day;
   Time's noblest offspring is the last.

JOHN GAY

1685–1732

310   from *Trivia* [Book III, lines 185–204]

Of Oysters   Be sure observe where brown *Ostrea* stands,
Who boasts her shelly Ware from *Wallfleet* Sands;
There may'st thou pass, with safe unmiry Feet,
Where the rais'd Pavement leads athwart the Street.
If where *Fleet-Ditch* with muddy Current flows,
You chance to roam; where Oyster-Tubs in Rows
Are rang'd beside the Posts; there stay thy Haste,
And with the sav'ry Fish indulge thy Taste:
The Damsel's Knife the gaping Shell commands,
While the salt Liquor streams between her Hands.
   The Man had sure a Palate cover'd o'er
With Brass or Steel, that on the rocky Shore
First broke the oozy Oyster's pearly Coat,
And risqu'd the living Morsel down his Throat.
What will not Lux'ry taste? Earth, Sea, and Air
Are daily ransack'd for the Bill of Fare.
Blood stuff'd in Skins is *British* Christians Food,
And *France* robs Marshes of the croaking Brood;
Spungy *Morells* in strong *Ragousts* are found,
And in the *Soupe* the slimy Snail is drown'd.

311   *My own Epitaph*

    Life is a jest; and all things show it,
    I thought so once; but now I know it.

312   from *The Beggar's Opera*

Macheath. Were I laid on *Greenland*'s Coast,
      And in my Arms embrac'd my Lass;
      Warm amidst eternal Frost,
      Too soon the Half Year's Night would pass.
Polly. Were I sold on *Indian* Soil,
      Soon as the burning Day was clos'd,
      I could mock the sultry Toil
      When on my Charmer's Breast repos'd.
Macheath. And I would love you all the Day,
Polly. Every Night would kiss and play,
Macheath. If with me you'd fondly stray
Polly. Over the Hills and far away.

ANONYMOUS
1734

313   In good King *Charles*'s golden days,
    When Loyalty no harm meant;
  A Furious High-Church Man I was,
    And so I gain'd Preferment.
  Unto my Flock I daily Preach'd,
  . Kings are by God appointed,
  And Damn'd are those who dare resist,
    Or touch the Lord's Anointed.
      And this is Law, I will maintain
        Unto my Dying Day, Sir,
      That whatsoever King shall Reign,
        I will be Vicar of *Bray*, Sir!

  When Royal *James* possest the Crown,
    And Popery grew in fashion;
  The Penal Law I houted down,
    And read the Declaration:
  The Church of *Rome*, I found would fit,
    Full well my Constitution,

And I had been a Jesuit,
  But for the Revolution.
    And this is Law, &c.

When *William* our Deliverer came,
  To heal the Nation's Grievance,
I turned the Cat in Pan again,
  And swore to him Allegiance:
Old Principles I did revoke,
  Set Conscience at a distance,
Passive Obedience is a Joke,
  A Jest is Non-resistance.
    And this is Law, &c.

When glorious *Ann* became our Queen,
  The Church of *England*'s Glory,
Another face of things was seen,
  And I became a Tory:
Occasional Conformists base,
  I Damn'd, and Moderation,
And thought the Church in danger was,
  From such Prevarication.
    And this is Law, &c.

When *George* in Pudding time came o'er,
  And Moderate Men looked big, Sir,
My Principles I chang'd once more,
  And so became a Whig, Sir:
And thus Preferment I procur'd,
  From our Faith's Great Defender,
And almost every day abjur'd
  The Pope, and the Pretender.
    And this is Law, &c.

The Illustrious House of *Hannover*,
  And Protestant Succession,
To these I lustily will swear,
  Whilst they can keep possession:
For in my Faith, and Loyalty,
  I never once will faulter,
But *George*, my Lawful King shall be,
  Except the Times shou'd alter.
    And this is Law, I will maintain
      Unto my Dying Day, Sir,
    That whatsoever King shall Reign,
      I will be Vicar of *Bray*, Sir!

ALLAN RAMSAY
1686–1758

314   *Polwart on the Green*

> At Polwart on the Green
> If you'll meet me the morn,
> Where lasses do convene
> To dance about the thorn;
> A kindly welcome you shall meet   5
> Frae her wha likes to view
> A lover and a lad complete,
> The lad and lover you.
>
> Let dorty dames say na,
> As lang as e'er they please,   10
> Seem caulder than the sna',
> While inwardly they bleeze;
> But I will frankly shaw my mind,
> And yield my heart to thee;
> Be ever to the captive kind,   15
> That langs na to be free.
>
> At Polwart on the Green,
> Among the new-mawn hay,
> With sangs and dancing keen
> We'll pass the heartsome day,   20
> *At night if beds be o'er thrang laid,*
> *And thou be twin'd of thine,*
> *Thou shalt be welcome, my dear lad,*
> *To take a part of mine.*

315   *Up in the Air*

> Now the sun's gane out o' sight,
> Beet the ingle and snuff the light:
> In glens the fairies skip and dance,
> And witches wallop o'er to France,
>   Up in the air   5
>   On my bonny grey mare.

314: 9 *dorty*] haughty   12 *bleeze*] blaze   21 *o'er thrang*] overcrowded (throng)
22 *twin'd of*] parted from

315: 2 *ingle*] fire

And I see her yet, and I see her yet,
      Up in the air
    On my bonny grey mare.

The wind's drifting hail and sna'   10
O'er frozen hags like a foot ba',
Nae starns keek throw the azure slit,
'Tis cauld and mirk as ony pit,
      The man i' the moon
      Is carowsing aboon,   15
D'ye see, d'ye see, d'ye see him yet?
      The man, &c.

Take your glass to clear your een,
'Tis the elixir hales the spleen,
Baith wit and mirth it will inspire,   20
And gently puffs the lover's fire,
      Up in the air,
      It drives away care,
Ha'e wi' ye, ha'e wi' ye, and ha'e wi' ye lads yet,
      Up in, &c.   25

Steek the doors, keep out the frost,
Come, Willy, gi'es about ye'r tost,
Til't lads, and lilt it out,
And let us ha'e a blythsom bowt,
      Up wi't there, there,   30
      Dinna cheat, but drink fair,
Huzza, huzza, and huzza lads yet,
      Up wi't there, there,
      Dinna cheat, but drink fair.

316   *Sang*

My Peggy is a young thing,
    Just enter'd in her teens,
Fair as the day, and sweet as May,
Fair as the day, and always gay.
My Peggy is a young thing,   5
    And I'm not very auld,
Yet well I like to meet her at
    The wawking of the fauld.

---

11 *hags*] pits   12 *starns keek*] stars peep   18 *een*] eyes   26 *Steek*] shut
27 *gi'es*] give us   *tost*] toast   28 *Til't*] to it
316: 8 *wawking*] watching   *fauld*] fold

My Peggy speaks sae sweetly,
 When'er we meet alane,   10
I wish nae mair to lay my care,
I wish nae mair of a' that's rare.
 My Peggy speaks sae sweetly,
  To a' the lave I'm cauld;
But she gars a' my spirits glow   15
 At wawking of the fauld.

My Peggy smiles sae kindly,
 Whene'er I whisper love,
That I look down on a' the town,
That I look down upon a crown.   20
 My Peggy smiles sae kindly,
  It makes me blythe and bauld,
And naithing gi'es me sic delight,
 As wawking of the fauld.

My Peggy sings sae saftly,   25
 When on my pipe I play;
By a' the rest it is confest,
By a' the rest, that she sings best.
 My Peggy sings sae saftly,
  And in her sangs are tald,   30
With innocence, the wale of sense,
 At wawking of the fauld.

317   *Lass with a Lump of Land*

Gi'e me a lass with a lump of land,
 And we for life shall gang thegither;
Tho' daft or wise I'll never demand,
 Or black or fair it maksna whether.
I'm aff with wit, and beauty will fade,   5
 And blood alane is no worth a shilling;
But she that's rich, her market's made,
 For ilka charm about her is killing.

Gi'e me a lass with a lump of land,
 And in my bosom I'll hug my treasure; 10
Gin I had anes her gear in my hand,
 Should love turn dowf, it will find pleasure.

14 *lave*] rest   15 *gars*] makes   31 *wale*] choice
      317: 12 *dowf*] dull

Laugh on wha likes, but there's my hand,
   I hate with poortith, though bonny, to meddle;
Unless they bring cash, or a lump of land,   15
   They'se never get me to dance to their fiddle.

There's meikle good love in bands and bags,
   And siller and gowd's a sweet complexion;
But beauty, and wit, and vertue in rags,
   Have tint the art of gaining affection.   20
Love tips his arrows with woods and parks,
   And castles, and riggs, and moors, and meadows;
And nathing can catch our modern sparks,
   But well tochered lasses, or jointured widows.

ALEXANDER POPE

1688–1744

318   from *An Essay on Criticism* [lines 215–42]

A *little Learning* is a dang'rous Thing;
Drink deep, or taste not the *Pierian* Spring:
There *shallow Draughts* intoxicate the Brain,
And drinking *largely* sobers us again.
Fir'd at first Sight with what the *Muse* imparts,
In *fearless Youth* we tempt the Heights of Arts,
While from the bounded *Level* of our Mind,
Short Views we take, nor see the *Lengths behind*,
But *more advanc'd*, behold with strange Surprize
New, distant Scenes of *endless* Science rise!
So pleas'd at first, the towring *Alps* we try,
Mount o'er the Vales, and seem to tread the Sky;
Th' Eternal Snows appear already past,
And the first *Clouds* and *Mountains* seem the last:
But *those attain'd*, we tremble to survey
The growing Labours of the lengthen'd Way,
Th' *increasing* Prospect *tires* our wandring Eyes,
Hills peep o'er Hills, and *Alps* on *Alps* arise!
  A perfect Judge will *read* each Work of Wit
With the same Spirit that its Author *writ*,
Survey the *Whole*, nor seek slight Faults to find,
Where *Nature moves*, and *Rapture warms* the Mind;

---

14 *poortith*] poverty   20 *tint*] lost   22 *riggs*] ridges (as a measure of land)
24 *tochered*] dowried

Nor lose, for that malignant dull Delight,
The *gen'rous Pleasure* to be charm'd with Wit.
But in such Lays as neither *ebb*, nor *flow*,
Correctly cold, and *regularly low*,
That shunning Faults, one quiet *Tenour* keep;
We cannot *blame* indeed—but we may *sleep*.

319–20   from *The Rape of the Lock*

319   [Canto I, lines 121–48]

And now, unveil'd, the *Toilet* stands display'd,
Each Silver Vase in mystic Order laid.
First, rob'd in White, the Nymph intent adores
With Head uncover'd, the *Cosmetic* Pow'rs.
A heav'nly Image in the Glass appears,
To that she bends, to that her Eyes she rears;
Th'inferior Priestess, at her Altar's side,
Trembling, begins the sacred Rites of Pride.
Unnumber'd Treasures ope at once, and here
The various Off'rings of the World appear;
From each she nicely culls with curious Toil,
And decks the Goddess with the glitt'ring Spoil.
This Casket *India's* glowing Gems unlocks,
And all *Arabia* breathes from yonder Box.
The Tortoise here and Elephant unite,
Transform'd to *Combs*, the speckled and the white.
Here Files of Pins extend their shining Rows,
Puffs, Powders, Patches, Bibles, Billet-doux.
Now awful Beauty puts on all its Arms;
The Fair each moment rises in her Charms,
Repairs her Smiles, awakens ev'ry Grace,
And calls forth all the Wonders of her Face;
Sees by Degrees a purer Blush arise,
And keener Lightnings quicken in her Eyes.
The busy *Sylphs* surround their darling Care;
These set the Head, and those divide the Hair,
Some fold the Sleeve, whilst others plait the Gown;
And *Betty's* prais'd for Labours not her own.

320   [Canto V, lines 7–36]

Then grave *Clarissa* graceful wav'd her Fan;
Silence ensu'd, and thus the Nymph began.

Say, why are Beauties prais'd and honour'd most,
The wise Man's Passion, and the vain Man's Toast?
Why deck'd with all that Land and Sea afford,
Why Angels call'd, and Angel-like ador'd?
Why round our Coaches crowd the white-glov'd Beaus,
Why bows the Side-box from its inmost Rows?
How vain are all these Glories, all our Pains,
Unless good Sense preserve what Beauty gains:
That Men may say, when we the Front-box grace,
Behold the first in Virtue, as in Face!
Oh! if to dance all Night, and dress all Day,
Charm'd the Small-pox, or chas'd old Age away;
Who would not scorn what Huswife's Cares produce,
Or who would learn one earthly Thing of Use?
To patch, nay ogle, might become a Saint,
Nor could it sure be such a Sin to paint.
But since, alas! frail Beauty must decay,
Curl'd or uncurl'd, since Locks will turn to grey,
Since painted, or not painted, all shall fade,
And she who scorns a Man, must die a Maid;
What then remains, but well our Pow'r to use,
And keep good Humour still whate'er we lose?
And trust me, Dear! good Humour can prevail,
When Airs, and Flights, and Screams, and Scolding fail.
Beauties in vain their pretty Eyes may roll;
Charms strike the Sight, but Merit wins the Soul.
So spoke the Dame, but no Applause ensu'd;
Belinda frown'd, *Thalestris* call'd her Prude.

321   from *Epistle to a Lady: Of the Characters of Women*
[lines 215–48]

Men, some to Bus'ness, some to Pleasure take;
But ev'ry Woman is at heart a Rake:
Men, some to Quiet, some to public Strife;
But ev'ry Lady would be Queen for life.
  Yet mark the fate of a whole Sex of Queens!
Pow'r all their end, but Beauty all the means.
In Youth they conquer, with so wild a rage,
As leaves them scarce a Subject in their Age:
For foreign glory, foreign joy, they roam;
No thought of Peace or Happiness at home.
But Wisdom's Triumph is well-tim'd Retreat,
As hard a science to the Fair as Great!

Beauties, like Tyrants, old and friendless grown,
Yet hate to rest, and dread to be alone,
Worn out in public, weary ev'ry eye,
Nor leave one sigh behind them when they die.
     Pleasures the sex, as children Birds, pursue,
Still out of reach, yet never out of view,
Sure, if they catch, to spoil the Toy at most,
To covet flying, and regret when lost:
At last, to follies Youth could scarce defend,
'Tis half their Age's prudence to pretend;
Asham'd to own they gave delight before,
Reduc'd to feign it, when they give no more:
As Hags hold Sabbaths, less for joy than spight,
So these their merry, miserable Night;
Still round and round the Ghosts of Beauty glide,
And haunt the places where their Honour dy'd.
     See how the World its Veterans rewards!
A Youth of frolicks, an old Age of Cards,
Fair to no purpose, artful to no end,
Young without Lovers, old without a Friend,
A Fop their Passion, but their Prize a Sot,
Alive, ridiculous, and dead, forgot!

322   from *Epistle to Bathurst: Of the Use of Riches*
                      [lines 297–314]

Behold what blessings Wealth to life can lend!
And see, what comfort it affords our end.
     In the worst inn's worst room, with mat half-hung,
The floors of plaister, and the walls of dung,
On once a flock-bed, but repair'd with straw,
With tape-ty'd curtains, never meant to draw,
The George and Garter dangling from that bed
Where tawdry yellow strove with dirty red,
Great Villers lies—alas! how chang'd from him,
That life of pleasure, and that soul of whim!
Gallant and gay, in Cliveden's proud alcóve,
The bow'r of wanton Shrewsbury and love;
Or just as gay, at Council, in a ring
Of mimick'd Statesmen, and their merry King.
No Wit to flatter, left of all his store!
No Fool to laugh at, which he valu'd more.
There, Victor of his health, of fortune, friends,
And fame; this lord of useless thousands ends.

323   from *Epistle to Burlington: Of the Use of Riches*
[lines 99–176]

At Timon's Villa let us pass a day,
Where all cry out, 'What sums are thrown away!'
So proud, so grand, of that stupendous air,
Soft and Agreeable come never there.
Greatness, with Timon, dwells in such a draught
As brings all Brobdignag before your thought.
To compass this, his building is a Town,
His pond an Ocean, his parterre a Down:
Who but must laugh, the Master when he sees,
A puny insect, shiv'ring at a breeze!
Lo, what huge heaps of littleness around!
The whole, a labour'd Quarry above ground.
Two Cupids squirt before: a Lake behind
Improves the keenness of the Northern wind.
His Gardens next your admiration call,
On ev'ry side you look, behold the Wall!
No pleasing Intricacies intervene,
No artful wildness to perplex the scene;
Grove nods at grove, each Alley has a brother,
And half the platform just reflects the other.
The suff'ring eye inverted Nature sees,
Trees cut to Statues, Statues thick as trees,
With here a Fountain, never to be play'd,
And there a Summer-house, that knows no shade;
Here Amphitrite sails thro' myrtle bow'rs;
There Gladiators fight, or die, in flow'rs;
Un-water'd see the drooping sea-horse mourn,
And swallows roost in Nilus' dusty Urn.
My Lord advances with majestic mien,
Smit with the mighty pleasure, to be seen:
But soft—by regular approach—not yet—
First thro' the length of yon hot Terrace sweat,
And when up ten steep slopes you've dragg'd your thighs,
Just at his Study-door he'll bless your eyes.
His Study! with what Authors is it stor'd?
In Books, not Authors, curious is my Lord;
To all their dated Backs he turns you round,
These Aldus printed, those Du Suëil has bound.
Lo some are Vellom, and the rest as good
For all his Lordship knows, but they are Wood.
For Locke or Milton 'tis in vain to look,
These shelves admit not any modern book.

And now the Chapel's silver bell you hear,
That summons you to all the Pride of Pray'r:
Light quirks of Musick, broken and uneven,
Make the soul dance upon a Jig to Heaven.
On painted Cielings you devoutly stare,
Where sprawl the Saints of Verrio or Laguerre,
On gilded clouds in fair expansion lie,
And bring all Paradise before your eye.
To rest, the Cushion and soft Dean invite,
Who never mentions Hell to ears polite.
But hark! the chiming Clocks to dinner call;
A hundred footsteps scrape the marble Hall:
The rich Buffet well-colour'd Serpents grace,
And gaping Tritons spew to wash your face.
Is this a dinner? this a Genial room?
No, 'tis a Temple, and a Hecatomb.
A solemn Sacrifice, perform'd in state,
You drink by measure, and to minutes eat.
So quick retires each flying course, you'd swear
Sancho's dread Doctor and his Wand were there.
Between each Act the trembling salvers ring,
From soup to sweet-wine, and God bless the King.
In plenty starving, tantaliz'd in state,
And cómplaisantly help'd to all I hate,
Treated, caress'd, and tir'd, I take my leave,
Sick of his civil Pride from Morn to Eve;
I curse such lavish cost, and little skill,
And swear no Day was ever past so ill.
Yet hence the Poor are cloath'd, the Hungry fed;
Health to himself, and to his Infants bread
The Lab'rer bears: What his hard Heart denies,
His charitable Vanity supplies.
Another age shall see the golden Ear
Imbrown the Slope, and nod on the Parterre,
Deep Harvests bury all his pride has plann'd,
And laughing Ceres re-assume the land.

324–5   from *An Epistle from Mr. Pope, to Dr. Arbuthnot*

324   [lines 193–214]

Peace to all such! but were there One whose fires
True Genius kindles, and fair Fame inspires,
Blest with each Talent and each Art to please,
And born to write, converse, and live with ease:

Shou'd such a man, too fond to rule alone,
Bear, like the *Turk*, no brother near the throne,
View him with scornful, yet with jealous eyes,
And hate for Arts that caus'd himself to rise;
Damn with faint praise, assent with civil leer,
And without sneering, teach the rest to sneer;
Willing to wound, and yet afraid to strike,
Just hint a fault, and hesitate dislike;
Alike reserv'd to blame, or to commend,
A tim'rous foe, and a suspicious friend,
Dreading ev'n fools, by Flatterers besieg'd,
And so obliging that he ne'er oblig'd;
Like *Cato*, give his little Senate laws,
And sit attentive to his own applause;
While Wits and Templers ev'ry sentence raise,
And wonder with a foolish face of praise.
Who but must laugh, if such a man there be?
Who would not weep, if *Atticus* were he!

325   [lines 305–33]

Let *Sporus* tremble—'What? that Thing of silk,
Sporus, that mere white Curd of Ass's milk?
Satire or Sense alas! can *Sporus* feel?
Who breaks a Butterfly upon a Wheel?'
Yet let me flap this Bug with gilded wings,
This painted Child of Dirt that stinks and stings;
Whose Buzz the Witty and the Fair annoys,
Yet Wit ne'er tastes, and Beauty ne'er enjoys,
So well-bred Spaniels civilly delight
In mumbling of the Game they dare not bite.
Eternal Smiles his Emptiness betray,
As shallow streams run dimpling all the way.
Whether in florid Impotence he speaks,
And, as the Prompter breathes, the Puppet squeaks;
Or at the Ear of *Eve*, familiar Toad,
Half Froth, half Venom, spits himself abroad,
In Puns, or Politicks, or Tales, or Lyes,
Or Spite, or Smut, or Rymes, or Blasphemies.
His Wit all see-saw between *that* and *this*,
Now high, now low, now Master up, now Miss,
And he himself one vile Antithesis.
Amphibious Thing! that acting either Part,
The trifling Head, or the corrupted Heart!

Fop at the Toilet, Flatt'rer at the Board,
Now trips a Lady, and now struts a Lord.
Eve's Tempter thus the Rabbins have exprest,
A Cherub's face, a Reptile all the rest;
Beauty that shocks you, Parts that none will trust,
Wit that can creep, and Pride that licks the dust.

326   from *The Dunciad* [Book IV, line 619–end]

O Muse! relate (for you can tell alone,
Wits have short Memories, and Dunces none)
Relate, who first, who last resign'd to rest;
Whose Heads she partly, whose completely blest;
What Charms could Faction, what Ambition lull,
The Venal quiet, and intrance the Dull;
'Till drown'd was Sense, and Shame, and Right, and Wrong—
O sing, and hush the Nations with thy Song!

                        *   *   *

In vain, in vain,—the all-composing Hour
Resistless falls: The Muse obeys the Pow'r.
She comes! she comes! the sable Throne behold
Of *Night* Primæval, and of *Chaos* old!
Before her, *Fancy*'s gilded clouds decay,
And all its varying Rain-bows die away.
Wit shoots in vain its momentary fires,
The meteor drops, and in a flash expires.
As one by one, at dread Medea's strain,
The sick'ning stars fade off th' ethereal plain;
As Argus' eyes by Hermes' wand opprest,
Clos'd one by one to everlasting rest;
Thus at her felt approach, and secret might,
Art after *Art* goes out, and all is Night.
See skulking *Truth* to her old Cavern fled,
Mountains of Casuistry heap'd o'er her head!
Philosophy, that lean'd on Heav'n before,
Shrinks to her second cause, and is no more.
Physic of *Metaphysic* begs defence,
And *Metaphysic* calls for aid on *Sense*!
See *Mystery* to *Mathematics* fly!
In vain! they gaze, turn giddy, rave, and die.
Religion blushing veils her sacred fires,
And unawares *Morality* expires.
Nor *public* Flame, nor *private*, dares to shine;
Nor *human* Spark is left, nor Glimpse *divine*!

Lo! thy dread Empire, CHAOS! is restor'd;
Light dies before thy uncreating word:
Thy hand, great Anarch! lets the curtain fall;
And Universal Darkness buries All.

327   *Epitaph. Intended for Sir Isaac Newton,*
                 In Westminster-Abbey

Nature, and Nature's Laws lay hid in Night.
God said, *Let Newton be!* and All was *Light.*

328   *Epigram. Engraved on the Collar of a Dog*
              which I gave to his Royal Highness

I am his Highness' Dog at *Kew*;
Pray tell me Sir, whose Dog are you?

LADY MARY WORTLEY MONTAGU

1689–1762

329   *The Lover: a ballad*

At length by so much Importunity press'd,
Take (Molly) at once the Inside of my Breast,
This stupid Indifference so often you blame
Is not owing to Nature, to fear, or to Shame,
I am not as cold as a Virgin in Lead
Nor is Sunday's Sermon so strong in my Head,
I know but too well how Time flys along,
That we live but few Years and yet fewer are young.

But I hate to be cheated, and never will buy
Long years of Repentance for moments of Joy,
Oh was there a Man (but where shall I find
Good sense, and good Nature so equally joyn'd?)
Would value his pleasure, contribute to mine,
Not meanly would boast, nor lewdly design,
Not over severe, yet not stupidly vain,
For I would have the power thô not give the pain.

No Pedant yet learnèd, not rakehelly Gay
Or laughing because he has nothing to say,
To all my whole sex, obliging and Free,
Yet never be fond of any but me.
In public preserve the Decorums are just
And shew in his Eyes he is true to his Trust,
Then rarely approach, and respectfully Bow,
Yet not fulsomely pert, nor yet foppishly low.

But when the long hours of Public are past
And we meet with Champaign and a Chicken at last,
May every fond Pleasure that hour endear,
Be banish'd afar both Discretion and Fear,
Forgetting or scorning the Airs of the Croud
He may cease to be formal, and I to be proud,
Till lost in the Joy we confess that we live
And he may be rude, and yet I may forgive.

And that my Delight may be solidly fix'd
Let the Freind, and the Lover be handsomly mix'd,
In whose tender Bosom my Soul might confide,
Whose kindness can sooth me, whose Councel could guide,
From such a dear Lover as here I describe
No danger should fright me, no Millions should bribe,
But till this astonishing Creature I know
As I long have liv'd Chaste I will keep my selfe so.

I never will share with the wanton Coquette
Or be caught by a vain affectation of Wit.
The Toasters, and Songsters may try all their Art
But never shall enter the pass of my Heart;
I loath the Lewd Rake, the dress'd Fopling despise,
Before such persuers the nice Virgin flys,
And as Ovid has sweetly in Parables told
We harden like Trees, and like Rivers are cold.

330   *A Receipt to Cure the Vapours*

          Why will Delia thus retire
               And languish Life away?
          While the sighing Crowds admire
               'Tis too soon for Hartshorn Tea.

          All these dismal looks and fretting
               Cannot Damon's life restore,
          Long ago the Worms have eat him,
               You can never see him more.

Once again consult your Toilet,
  In the Glass your Face review,
So much weeping soon will spoil it
  And no Spring your Charms renew.

I like you was born a Woman—
  Well I know what Vapours mean,
The Disease alas! is common,
  Single we have all the Spleen.

All the Morals that they tell us
  Never cur'd Sorrow yet,
Chuse among the pretty Fellows
  One of humour, Youth, and Wit.

Prithee hear him ev'ry Morning
  At least an hour or two,
Once again at Nights returning,
  I beleive the Dose will do.

331   [*On Lord Lyttelton's 'Advice to a Lady'*]

Be plain in Dress and sober in your Diet;
In short my Dearee, kiss me, and be quiet.

WILLIAM OLDYS

1696–1761

332   *The Fly*

Busy, curious, thirsty Fly,
Gently drink, and drink as I;
Freely welcome to my Cup,
Could'st thou sip, and sip it up;
Make the most of Life you may,
Life is short and wears away.

Just alike, both mine and thine,
Hasten quick to their Decline;
Thine's a Summer, mine's no more,
Though repeated to threescore;
Threescore Summers when they're gone,
Will appear as short as one.

[after the Greek of Anacreon]

SAMUEL JOHNSON
1709–1784

333–8   from *The Vanity of Human Wishes*, the Tenth
          Satire of Juvenal Imitated

333   [lines 1–28]

Let Observation with extensive View,
Survey Mankind, from *China* to *Peru*;
Remark each anxious Toil, each eager Strife,
And watch the busy Scenes of crouded Life;
Then say how Hope and Fear, Desire and Hate,
O'erspread with Snares the clouded Maze of Fate,
Where wav'ring Man, betray'd by vent'rous Pride,
To tread the dreary Paths without a guide,
As treach'rous Phantoms in the Mist delude,
Shuns fancied Ills, or chases airy Good.
How rarely Reason guides the stubborn Choice,
Rules the bold Hand, or prompts the suppliant Voice,
How Nations sink, by darling Schemes oppres'd,
When Vengeance listens to the Fool's Request.
Fate wings with ev'ry Wish th' afflictive Dart,
Each Gift of Nature, and each Grace of Art,
With fatal Heat impetuous Courage glows,
With fatal Sweetness Elocution flows,
Impeachment stops the Speaker's pow'rful Breath,
And restless Fire precipitates on Death.
   But scarce observ'd the Knowing and the Bold
Fall in the gen'ral Massacre of Gold;
Wide-wasting Pest! that rages unconfin'd,
And crouds with Crimes the Records of Mankind,
For Gold his Sword the hireling Ruffian draws,
For Gold the hireling Judge distorts the Laws;
Wealth heap'd on Wealth, nor Truth nor Safety buys,
The Dangers gather as the Treasures rise.

334   [lines 73–90]

Unnumber'd Suppliants croud Preferment's Gate,
Athirst for Wealth, and burning to be great;
Delusive Fortune hears th' incessant Call,
They mount, they shine, evaporate, and fall.

On ev'ry Stage the Foes of Peace attend,
Hate dogs their Flight, and Insult mocks their End.
Love ends with Hope, the sinking Statesman's Door
Pours in the Morning Worshiper no more;
For growing Names the weekly Scribbler lies,
To growing Wealth the Dedicator flies,
From every Room descends the painted Face,
That hung the bright *Palladium* of the Place,
And smoak'd in Kitchens, or in Auctions sold,
To better Features yields the Frame of Gold;
For now no more we trace in ev'ry Line
Heroic Worth, Benevolence Divine:
The Form distorted justifies the Fall,
And Detestation rids th' indignant Wall.

335   [lines 99–160]

   In full-blown Dignity, see *Wolsey* stand,
Law in his Voice, and Fortune in his Hand:
To him the Church, the Realm, their Pow'rs consign,
Thro' him the Rays of regal Bounty shine,
Turn'd by his Nod the Stream of Honour flows,
His Smile alone Security bestows:
Still to new Heights his restless Wishes tow'r,
Claim leads to Claim, and Pow'r advances Pow'r;
Till Conquest unresisted ceas'd to please,
And Rights submitted, left him none to seize.
At length his Sov'reign frowns—the Train of State
Mark the keen Glance, and watch the Sign to hate.
Where-e'er he turns he meets a Stranger's Eye,
His Suppliants scorn him, and his Followers fly;
At once is lost the Pride of aweful State,
The golden Canopy, the glitt'ring Plate,
The regal Palace, the luxurious Board,
The liv'ried Army, and the menial Lord.
With Age, with Cares, with Maladies oppress'd,
He seeks the Refuge of Monastic Rest.
Grief aids Disease, remember'd Folly stings,
And his last Sighs reproach the Faith of Kings.
   Speak thou, whose Thoughts at humble Peace repine,
Shall *Wolsey*'s Wealth, with *Wolsey*'s End be thine?
Or liv'st thou now, with safer Pride content,
The wisest Justice on the Banks of *Trent*?
For why did *Wolsey* near the Steeps of Fate,
On weak Foundations raise th' enormous Weight?

Why but to sink beneath Misfortune's Blow,
With louder Ruin to the Gulphs below?
  What gave great *Villiers* to th' Assassin's Knife,
And fixed Disease on *Harley's* closing life?
What murder'd *Wentworth*, and what exil'd *Hyde*,
By Kings protected, and to Kings ally'd?
What but their Wish indulg'd in Courts to shine,
And Pow'r too great to keep or to resign?
  When first the College Rolls receive his Name,
The young Enthusiast quits his Ease for Fame;
Through all his Veins the fever of Renown
Burns from the strong Contagion of the Gown;
O'er *Bodley's* Dome his future Labours spread,
And *Bacon's* Mansion trembles o'er his Head;
Are these thy Views? proceed, illustrious Youth,
And Virtue guard thee to the Throne of Truth,
Yet should thy Soul indulge the gen'rous Heat,
Till captive Science yields her last Retreat;
Should Reason guide thee with her brightest Ray,
And pour on misty Doubt resistless Day;
Should no false Kindness lure to loose Delight,
Nor Praise relax, nor Difficulty fright;
Should tempting Novelty thy Cell refrain,
And Sloth effuse her opiate Fumes in vain;
Should Beauty blunt on Fops her fatal Dart,
Nor claim the triumph of a letter'd Heart;
Should no Disease thy torpid Veins invade,
Nor Melancholy's Phantoms haunt thy Shade;
Yet hope not Life from Grief or Danger free,
Nor think the Doom of Man revers'd for thee:
Deign on the passing World to turn thine Eyes,
And pause awhile from Letters to be wise;
There mark what Ills the Scholar's Life assail,
Toil, Envy, Want, the Patron, and the Jail.

336   [lines 191–222]

  On what Foundation stands the Warrior's Pride?
How just his Hopes let *Swedish Charles* decide;
A Frame of Adamant, a Soul of Fire,
No Dangers fright him, and no Labours tire;
O'er Love, o'er Fear, extends his wide Domain,
Unconquer'd Lord of Pleasure and of Pain;
No Joys to him pacific Scepters yield,
War sounds the Trump, he rushes to the Field;

Behold surrounding Kings their Pow'r combine,
And One capitulate, and One resign;
Peace courts his Hand, but spreads her Charms in vain;
'Think Nothing gain'd, he cries, till nought remain,
'On *Moscow*'s Walls till *Gothic* Standards fly,
'And all be Mine beneath the Polar Sky.'
The March begins in Military State,
And Nations on his Eye suspended wait;
Stern Famine guards the solitary Coast,
And Winter barricades the Realms of Frost;
He comes, not Want and Cold his Course delay;—
Hide, blushing Glory, hide *Pultowa*'s Day:
The vanquish'd Hero leaves his broken Bands,
And shews his Miseries in distant Lands;
Condemn'd a needy Supplicant to wait,
While Ladies interpose, and Slaves debate.
But did not Chance at length her Error mend?
Did no subverted Empire mark his End?
Did rival Monarchs give the fatal Wound?
Or hostile Millions press him to the Ground?
His Fall was destin'd to a barren Strand,
A petty Fortress, and a dubious Hand;
He left the Name, at which the World grew pale,
To point a Moral, or adorn a Tale.

337   [lines 255–310]

Enlarge my Life with Multitude of Days,
In Health, in Sickness, thus the Suppliant prays;
Hides from himself his State, and shuns to know,
That Life protracted is protracted Woe.
Time hovers o'er, impatient to destroy,
And shuts up all the Passages of Joy:
In vain their Gifts the bounteous Seasons pour,
The Fruit autumnal, and the vernal Flow'r,
With listless Eyes the Dotard views the Store,
He views, and wonders that they please no more;
Now pall the tastless Meats, and joyless Wines,
And Luxury with Sighs her Slave resigns.
Approach, ye Minstrels, try the soothing Strain,
Diffuse the tuneful Lenitives of Pain:
No Sounds alas would touch th' impervious Ear,
Though dancing Mountains witness'd *Orpheus* near;
Nor Lute nor Lyre his feeble Pow'rs attend,
Nor sweeter Musick of a virtuous Friend,

But everlasting Dictates croud his Tongue,
Perversely grave, or positively wrong.
The still returning Tale, and ling'ring Jest,
Perplex the fawning Niece and pamper'd Guest,
While growing Hopes scarce awe the gath'ring Sneer,
And scarce a Legacy can bribe to hear;
The watchful Guests still hint the last Offence,
The Daughter's Petulance, the Son's Expence,
Improve his heady Rage with treach'rous Skill,
And mould his Passions till they make his Will.

    Unnumber'd Maladies his Joints invade,
Lay Siege to Life and press the dire Blockade;
But unextinguish'd Av'rice still remains,
And dreaded Losses aggravate his Pains;
He turns, with anxious Heart and cripled Hands,
His Bonds of Debt, and Mortgages of Lands;
Or views his Coffers with suspicious Eyes,
Unlocks his Gold, and counts it till he dies.

    But grant, the Virtues of a temp'rate Prime
Bless with an Age exempt from Scorn or Crime;
An Age that melts with unperceiv'd Decay,
And glides in modest Innocence away;
Whose peaceful Day Benevolence endears,
Whose Night congratulating Conscience cheers;
The gen'ral Fav'rite as the gen'ral Friend:
Such Age there is, and who shall wish its end?

    Yet ev'n on this her Load Misfortune flings,
To press the weary Minutes flagging Wings:
New Sorrow rises as the Day returns,
A Sister sickens, or a Daughter mourns.
Now kindred Merit fills the sable Bier,
Now lacerated Friendship claims a Tear.
Year chases Year, Decay pursues Decay,
Still drops some Joy from with'ring Life away;
New Forms arise, and diff'rent Views engage,
Superfluous lags the Vet'ran on the Stage,
Till pitying Nature signs the last Release,
And bids afflicted Worth retire to Peace.

338   **[line 343–end]**

    Where then shall Hope and Fear their Objects find?
Must dull Suspence corrupt the stagnant Mind?
Must helpless Man, in Ignorance sedate,
Roll darkling down the Torrent of his fate?

Must no Dislike alarm, no Wishes rise,
No Cries attempt the Mercies of the Skies?
Enquirer, cease, Petitions yet remain,
Which Heav'n may hear, nor deem Religion vain.
Still raise for Good the supplicating Voice,
But leave to Heav'n the Measure and the Choice,
Safe in his Pow'r, whose Eyes discern afar
The secret Ambush of a specious Pray'r.
Implore his Aid, in his Decisions rest,
Secure whate'er he gives, he gives the best.
Yet when the Sense of sacred Presence fires,
And strong Devotion to the Skies aspires,
Pour forth thy Fervours for a healthful Mind,
Obedient Passions, and a Will resign'd;
For Love, which scarce collective Man can fill;
For Patience sov'reign o'er transmuted Ill;
For Faith, that panting for a happier Seat,
Counts Death kind Nature's Signal of Retreat:
These Goods for Man the Laws of Heav'n ordain,
These Goods he grants, who grants the Pow'r to gain;
With these celestial Wisdom calms the Mind,
And makes the Happiness she does not find.

[after the Latin of Juvenal]

339 *A Short Song of Congratulation*

Long-expected one and twenty
Ling'ring year, at last is flown,
Pomp and Pleasure, Pride and Plenty
Great Sir John, are all your own.

Loosen'd from the Minor's tether,
Free to mortgage or to sell,
Wild as wind, and light as feather
Bid the slaves of thrift farewel.

Call the Bettys, Kates, and Jennys
Ev'ry name that laughs at Care,
Lavish of your Grandsire's guineas,
Show the Spirit of an heir.

All that prey on vice and folly
Joy to see their quarry fly,
Here the Gamester light and jolly,
There the Lender grave and sly.

Wealth, Sir John, was made to wander,
Let it wander as it will;
See the Jocky, see the Pander,
Bid them come, and take their fill.

When the bonny Blade carouses,
Pockets full, and Spirits high,
What are acres? What are houses?
Only dirt, or wet or dry.

If the Guardian or the Mother
Tell the woes of wilful waste,
Scorn their counsel and their pother,
You can hang or drown at last.

340   *On the Death of Dr. Robert Levet*

Condemn'd to hope's delusive mine,
    As on we toil from day to day,
By sudden blasts, or slow decline,
    Our social comforts drop away.

Well tried through many a varying year,
    See LEVET to the grave descend;
Officious, innocent, sincere,
    Of ev'ry friendless name the friend.

Yet still he fills affection's eye,
    Obscurely wise, and coarsely kind;
Nor, letter'd arrogance, deny
    Thy praise to merit unrefin'd.

When fainting nature call'd for aid,
    And hov'ring death prepar'd the blow,
His vig'rous remedy display'd
    The power of art without the show.

In misery's darkest caverns known,
    His useful care was ever nigh,
Where hopeless anguish pour'd his groan,
    And lonely want retir'd to die.

No summons mock'd by chill delay,
    No petty gain disdain'd by pride,
The modest wants of ev'ry day
    The toil of ev'ry day supplied.

His virtues walk'd their narrow round,
　　Nor made a pause, nor left a void;
And sure th' Eternal Master found
　　The single talent well employ'd.

The busy day, the peaceful night,
　　Unfelt, uncounted, glided by;
His frame was firm, his powers were bright,
　　Tho' now his eightieth year was nigh.

Then with no throbbing fiery pain,
　　No cold gradations of decay,
Death broke at once the vital chain,
　　And free'd his soul the nearest way.

WILLIAM SHENSTONE

1714–1763

341　　　*Written at an Inn at Henley*

To thee, fair freedom! I retire
　　From flattery, cards, and dice, and din:
Nor art thou found in mansions higher
　　Than the low cott, or humble inn.

'Tis here with boundless pow'r, I reign;
　　And ev'ry health which I begin,
Converts dull port to bright champaigne;
　　Such freedom crowns it, at an inn.

I fly from pomp, I fly from plate!
　　I fly from falsehood's specious grin!
Freedom I love, and form I hate,
　　And chuse my lodgings at an inn.

Here, waiter! take my sordid ore,
　　Which lacqueys else might hope to win;
It buys, what courts have not in store;
　　It buys me freedom, at an inn.

And now once more I shape my way
　　Thro' rain or shine, thro' thick or thin,
Secure to meet, at close of day,
　　With kind reception, at an inn.

Whoe'er has travell'd life's dull round,
　　Where'er his stages may have been,
May sigh to think he still has found
　　The warmest welcome, at an inn.

THOMAS GRAY

1716–1771

342   *Ode on the Death of a Favourite Cat,*
       Drowned in a Tub of Gold Fishes

'Twas on a lofty vase's side,
Where China's gayest art had dy'd
   The azure flowers, that blow;
Demurest of the tabby kind,
The pensive Selima reclin'd,
   Gazed on the lake below.

Her conscious tail her joy declar'd;
The fair round face, the snowy beard,
   The velvet of her paws,
Her coat, that with the tortoise vies,
Her ears of jet, and emerald eyes,
   She saw; and purr'd applause.

Still had she gaz'd; but 'midst the tide
Two angel forms were seen to glide,
   The Genii of the stream:
Their scaly armour's Tyrian hue
Thro' richest purple to the view
   Betray'd a golden gleam.

The hapless Nymph with wonder saw:
A whisker first and then a claw,
   With many an ardent wish,
She stretch'd in vain to reach the prize.
What female heart can gold despise?
   What Cat's averse to fish?

Presumptuous Maid! with looks intent
Again she stretch'd, again she bent,
   Nor knew the gulf between.
(Malignant Fate sat by, and smil'd)
The slipp'ry verge her feet beguil'd,
   She tumbled headlong in.

Eight times emerging from the flood
She mew'd to ev'ry watry God,
   Some speedy aid to send.
No Dolphin came, no Nereid stirr'd:
Nor cruel *Tom*, nor *Susan* heard.
   A Fav'rite has no friend!

From hence, ye Beauties, undeceiv'd,
Know, one false step is ne'er retriev'd,
   And be with caution bold.
Not all that tempts your wand'ring eyes
And heedless hearts, is lawful prize;
   Nor all, that glisters, gold.

343   *Elegy Written in a Country Church Yard*

The Curfew tolls the knell of parting day,
The lowing herd wind slowly o'er the lea,
The plowman homeward plods his weary way,
And leaves the world to darkness and to me.

Now fades the glimmering landscape on the sight,
And all the air a solemn stillness holds,
Save where the beetle wheels his droning flight,
And drowsy tinklings lull the distant folds;

Save that from yonder ivy-mantled tow'r
The mopeing owl does to the moon complain
Of such, as wand'ring near her secret bow'r,
Molest her ancient solitary reign.

Beneath those rugged elms, that yew-tree's shade,
Where heaves the turf in many a mould'ring heap,
Each in his narrow cell for ever laid,
The rude Forefathers of the hamlet sleep.

The breezy call of incense-breathing Morn,
The swallow twitt'ring from the straw-built shed,
The cock's shrill clarion, or the ecchoing horn,
No more shall rouse them from their lowly bed.

For them no more the blazing hearth shall burn,
Or busy houswife ply her evening care:
No children run to lisp their sire's return,
Or climb his knees the envied kiss to share.

Oft did the harvest to their sickle yield,
Their furrow oft the stubborn glebe has broke;
How jocund did they drive their team afield!
How bow'd the woods beneath their sturdy stroke!

Let not Ambition mock their useful toil,
Their homely joys, and destiny obscure;
Nor Grandeur hear with a disdainful smile,
The short and simple annals of the poor.

The boast of heraldry, the pomp of pow'r,
And all that beauty, all that wealth e'er gave,
Awaits alike th' inevitable hour.
The paths of glory lead but to the grave.

Nor you, ye Proud, impute to These the fault,
If Mem'ry o'er their Tomb no Trophies raise,
Where thro' the long-drawn isle and fretted vault
The pealing anthem swells the note of praise.

Can storied urn or animated bust
Back to its mansion call the fleeting breath?
Can Honour's voice provoke the silent dust,
Or Flatt'ry sooth the dull cold ear of Death?

Perhaps in this neglected spot is laid
Some heart once pregnant with celestial fire,
Hands, that the rod of empire might have sway'd,
Or wak'd to extasy the living lyre.

But Knowledge to their eyes her ample page
Rich with the spoils of time did ne'er unroll;
Chill Penury repress'd their noble rage,
And froze the genial current of the soul.

Full many a gem of purest ray serene,
The dark unfathom'd caves of ocean bear:
Full many a flower is born to blush unseen,
And waste its sweetness on the desert air.

Some village-Hampden, that with dauntless breast
The little Tyrant of his fields withstood;
Some mute inglorious Milton here may rest,
Some Cromwell guiltless of his country's blood.

Th' applause of list'ning senates to command,
The threats of pain and ruin to despise,
To scatter plenty o'er a smiling land,
And read their hist'ry in a nation's eyes

Their lot forbad: nor circumscrib'd alone
Their growing virtues, but their crimes confin'd;
Forbad to wade through slaughter to a throne,
And shut the gates of mercy on mankind,

The struggling pangs of conscious truth to hide,
To quench the blushes of ingenuous shame,
Or heap the shrine of Luxury and Pride
With incense kindled at the Muse's flame.

Far from the madding crowd's ignoble strife,
Their sober wishes never learn'd to stray;
Along the cool sequester'd vale of life
They kept the noiseless tenor of their way.

Yet ev'n these bones from insult to protect
Some frail memorial still erected nigh,
With uncouth rhimes and shapeless sculpture deck'd,
Implores the passing tribute of a sigh.

Their name, their years, spelt by th' unletter'd muse,
The place of fame and elegy supply:
And many a holy text around she strews,
That teach the rustic moralist to die.

For who to dumb Forgetfulness a prey,
This pleasing anxious being e'er resign'd,
Left the warm precincts of the chearful day,
Nor cast one longing ling'ring look behind?

On some fond breast the parting soul relies,
Some pious drops the closing eye requires;
Ev'n from the tomb the voice of Nature cries,
Ev'n in our Ashes live their wonted Fires.

For thee, who mindful of th' unhonour'd Dead
Dost in these lines their artless tale relate;
If chance, by lonely contemplation led,
Some kindred Spirit shall inquire thy fate,

Haply some hoary-headed Swain may say,
'Oft have we seen him at the peep of dawn
'Brushing with hasty steps the dews away
'To meet the sun upon the upland lawn.

'There at the foot of yonder nodding beech
'That wreathes its old fantastic roots so high,
'His listless length at noontide wou'd he stretch,
'And pore upon the brook that babbles by.

'Hard by yon wood, now smiling as in scorn,
'Mutt'ring his wayward fancies he wou'd rove,
'Now drooping, woeful wan, like one forlorn,
'Or craz'd with care, or cross'd in hopeless love.

'One morn I miss'd him on the custom'd hill,
'Along the heath and near his fav'rite tree;
'Another came; nor yet beside the rill,
'Nor up the lawn, nor at the wood was he,

'The next with dirges due in sad array
'Slow thro' the church-way path we saw him borne.
'Approach and read (for thou can'st read) the lay,
'Grav'd on the stone beneath yon agèd thorn.'

The Epitaph

Here rests his head upon the lap of Earth
A Youth to Fortune and to Fame unknown,
Fair Science frown'd not on his humble birth,
And Melancholy mark'd him for her own.

Large was his bounty, and his soul sincere,
Heav'n did a recompence as largely send:
He gave to Mis'ry all he had, a tear,
He gain'd from Heav'n ('twas all he wish'd) a friend.

No farther seek his merits to disclose,
Or draw his frailties from their dread abode,
(There they alike in trembling hope repose)
The bosom of his Father and his God.

WILLIAM COLLINS

1721–1759

344   *Ode, Written in the beginning of the Year 1746*

How sleep the Brave, who sink to Rest,
By all their Country's Wishes blest!
When *Spring*, with dewy Fingers cold,
Returns to deck their hallow'd Mold,
She there shall dress a sweeter Sod,
Than *Fancy*'s Feet have ever trod.

By Fairy Hands their Knell is rung,
By Forms unseen their Dirge is sung;
There *Honour* comes, a Pilgrim grey,
To bless the Turf that wraps their Clay,
And *Freedom* shall a-while repair,
To dwell a weeping Hermit there!

345   *Ode to Evening*

If ought of Oaten Stop, or Pastoral Song,
May hope, chaste *Eve*, to sooth thy modest Ear,

Like thy own solemn Springs,
  Thy Springs, and dying Gales,
O *Nymph* reserv'd, while now the bright-hair'd Sun
Sits in yon western Tent, whose cloudy Skirts,
  With Brede ethereal wove,
  O'erhang his wavy Bed:
Now Air is hush'd, save where the weak-ey'd Bat,
With short shrill Shriek flits by on leathern Wing,
  Or where the Beetle winds
  His small but sullen Horn,
As oft he rises 'midst the twilight Path,
Against the Pilgrim borne in heedless Hum:
  Now teach me, *Maid* compos'd,
  To breathe some soften'd Strain,
Whose Numbers stealing thro' thy darkning Vale,
May not unseemly with its Stillness suit,
  As musing slow, I hail
  Thy genial lov'd Return!
For when thy folding Star arising shews
His paly Circlet, at his warning Lamp
  The fragrant *Hours*, and *Elves*
  Who slept in Flow'rs the Day,
And many a *Nymph* who wreaths her Brows with Sedge,
And sheds the fresh'ning Dew, and lovelier still,
  The *Pensive Pleasures* sweet
  Prepare thy shadowy Car.
Then lead, calm *Vot'ress*, where some sheety Lake
Cheers the lone Heath, or some time-hallow'd Pile,
  Or up-land Fallows grey
  Reflect it's last cool Gleam.
But when chill blustring Winds, or driving Rain,
Forbid my willing Feet, be mine the Hut,
  That from the Mountain's Side,
  Views Wilds, and swelling Floods,
And Hamlets brown, and dim-discover'd Spires,
And hears their simple Bell, and marks o'er all
  Thy Dewy Fingers draw
  The gradual dusky Veil.
While *Spring* shall pour his Show'rs, as oft he wont,
And bathe thy breathing Tresses, meekest *Eve!*
  While *Summer* loves to sport,
  Beneath thy ling'ring Light:
While sallow *Autumn* fills thy Lap with Leaves,
Or *Winter* yelling thro' the troublous Air,
  Affrights thy shrinking Train,
  And rudely rends thy Robes.

So long, sure-found beneath the Sylvan Shed,
Shall *Fancy, Friendship, Science*, rose-lip'd *Health*,
   Thy gentlest Influence own,
   And hymn thy fav'rite Name!

MARY LEAPOR

1722–1746

346   *Mira's Will*

Imprimis—My departed Shade I trust
To Heav'n—My Body to the silent Dust;
My Name to publick Censure I submit,
To be dispos'd of as the World thinks fit;
My Vice and Folly let Oblivion close,
The World already is o'erstock'd with those;
My Wit I give, as Misers give their Store,
To those who think they had enough before.
Bestow my Patience to compose the Lives
Of slighted Virgins and neglected Wives;
To modish Lovers I resign my Truth,
My cool Reflexion to unthinking Youth;
And some Good-nature give ('tis my Desire)
To surly Husbands, as their Needs require;
And first discharge my Funeral—and then
To the small Poets I bequeath my Pen.
    Let a small Sprig (true Emblem of my Rhyme)
Of blasted Laurel on my Hearse recline;
Let some grave Wight, that struggles for Renown,
By chanting Dirges through a Market-Town,
With gentle Step precede the solemn Train;
A broken Flute upon his Arm shall lean.
Six comick Poets may the Corse surround,
And All Free-holders, if they can be found:
Then follow next the melancholy Throng,
As shrewd Instructors, who themselves are wrong.
The Virtuoso, rich in Sun-dry'd Weeds,
The Politician, whom no Mortal heeds,
The silent Lawyer, chamber'd all the Day,
And the stern Soldier that receives no Pay.
But stay—the Mourners shou'd be first our Care,
Let the freed Prentice lead the Miser's Heir;
Let the young Relict wipe her mournful Eye,
And widow'd Husbands o'er their Garlick cry.

All this let my Executors fulfil,
And rest assured that this is *Mira*'s Will,
Who was, when she these Legacies design'd,
In Body healthy, and compos'd in Mind.

CHRISTOPHER SMART

1722–1771

347   from *A Song to David* [stanzas XLIX–LXIII]

O DAVID, highest in the list
Of worthies, on God's ways insist,
      The genuine word repeat:
Vain are the documents of men,
And vain the flourish of the pen
      That keeps the fool's conceit.

PRAISE above all—for praise prevails;
Heap up the measure, load the scales,
      And good to goodness add:
The gen'rous soul her Saviour aids,
But peevish obloquy degrades;
      The Lord is great and glad.

For ADORATION all the ranks
Of angels yield eternal thanks,
      And DAVID in the midst;
With God's good poor, which, last and least
In man's esteem, thou to thy feast,
      O blessèd bride-groom, bidst.

For ADORATION seasons change,
And order, truth, and beauty range,
      Adjust, attract, and fill:
The grass the polyanthus cheques;
And polish'd porphyry reflects,
      By the descending rill.

Rich almonds colour to the prime
For ADORATION; tendrils climb,
      And fruit-trees pledge their gems;
And *Ivis with her gorgeous vest
Builds for her eggs her cunning nest,
      And bell-flowers bow their stems.

* Humming-bird.

With vinous syrup cedars spout;
From rocks pure honey gushing out,
  For ADORATION springs:
All scenes of painting croud the map
Of nature; to the mermaid's pap
  The scalèd infant clings.

The spotted ounce and playsome cubs
Run rustling 'mongst the flow'ring shrubs,
  And lizards feed the moss;
For ADORATION beasts embark,
While waves upholding halcyon's ark
  No longer roar and toss.

While Israel sits beneath his fig,
With coral root and amber sprig
  The wean'd advent'rer sports;
Where to the palm the jasmin cleaves,
For ADORATION 'mongst the leaves
  The gale his peace reports.

Increasing days their reign exalt,
Nor in the pink and mottled vault
  Th' opposing spirits tilt;
And, by the coasting reader spied,
The silverlings and crusions glide
  For ADORATION gilt.

For ADORATION rip'ning canes
And cocoa's purest milk detains
  The western pilgrim's staff;
Where rain in clasping boughs inclos'd,
And vines with oranges dispos'd,
  Embow'r the social laugh.

Now labour his reward receives,
For ADORATION counts his sheaves
  To peace, her bounteous prince;
The nectarine his strong tint imbibes,
And apples of ten thousand tribes,
  And quick peculiar quince.

The wealthy crops of whit'ning rice,
'Mongst thyine woods and groves of spice,
  For ADORATION grow;
And, marshall'd in the fencèd land,
The peaches and pomegranates stand,
  Where wild carnations blow.

The laurels with the winter strive;
The crocus burnishes alive
 Upon the snow-clad earth:
For ADORATION myrtles stay
To keep the garden from dismay,
 And bless the sight from dearth.

The pheasant shows his pompous neck;
And ermine, jealous of a speck,
 With fear eludes offence:
The sable, with his glossy pride,
For ADORATION is descried,
 Where frosts the wave condense.

The chearful holly, pensive yew,
And holy thorn, their trim renew;
 The squirrel hoards his nuts:
All creatures batten o'er their stores,
And careful nature all her doors
 For ADORATION shuts.

348   from *Jubilate Agno* [Fragment B, lines 695–768]

For I will consider my Cat Jeoffry.
For he is the servant of the Living God duly and daily serving him.
For at the first glance of the glory of God in the East he worships in his way.
For is this done by wreathing his body seven times round with elegant
    quickness.
For then he leaps up to catch the musk, which is the blessing of God upon his
    prayer.
For he rolls upon prank to work it in.
For having done duty and received blessing he begins to consider himself.
For this he performs in ten degrees.
For first he looks upon his fore-paws to see if they are clean.
For secondly he kicks up behind to clear away there.
For thirdly he works it upon stretch with the fore paws extended.
For fourthly he sharpens his paws by wood.
For fifthly he washes himself.
For Sixthly he rolls upon wash.
For Seventhly he fleas himself, that he may not be interrupted upon the beat.
For Eighthly he rubs himself against a post.
For Ninthly he looks up for his instructions.
For Tenthly he goes in quest of food.
For having consider'd God and himself he will consider his neighbour.
For if he meets another cat he will kiss her in kindness.

For when he takes his prey he plays with it to give it chance.
For one mouse in seven escapes by his dallying.
For when his day's work is done his business more properly begins.
For he keeps the Lord's watch in the night against the adversary.
For he counteracts the powers of darkness by his electrical skin and glaring eyes.
For he counteracts the Devil, who is death, by brisking about the life.
For in his morning orisons he loves the sun and the sun loves him.
For he is of the tribe of Tiger.
For the Cherub Cat is a term of the Angel Tiger.
For he has the subtlety and hissing of a serpent, which in goodness he suppresses.
For he will not do destruction, if he is well-fed, neither will he spit without provocation.
For he purrs in thankfulness, when God tells him he's a good Cat.
For he is an instrument for the children to learn benevolence upon.
For every house is incompleat without him and a blessing is lacking in the spirit.
For the Lord commanded Moses concerning the cats at the departure of the Children of Israel from Egypt.
For every family had one cat at least in the bag.
For the English Cats are the best in Europe.
For he is the cleanest in the use of his fore-paws of any quadrupede.
For the dexterity of his defence is an instance of the love of God to him exceedingly.
For he is the quickest to his mark of any creature.
For he is tenacious of his point.
For he is a mixture of gravity and waggery.
For he knows that God is his Saviour.
For there is nothing sweeter than his peace when at rest.
For there is nothing brisker than his life when in motion.
For he is of the Lord's poor and so indeed is he called by benevolence perpetually—Poor Jeoffry! poor Jeoffry! the rat has bit thy throat.
For I bless the name of the Lord Jesus that Jeoffry is better.
For the divine spirit comes about his body to sustain it in compleat cat.
For his tongue is exceeding pure so that it has in purity what it wants in musick.
For he is docile and can learn certain things.
For he can set up with gravity which is patience upon approbation.
For he can fetch and carry, which is patience in employment.
For he can jump over a stick which is patience upon proof positive.
For he can spraggle upon waggle at the word of command.
For he can jump from an eminence into his master's bosom.
For he can catch the cork and toss it again.
For he is hated by the hypocrite and miser.
For the former is affraid of detection.
For the latter refuses the charge.

For he camels his back to bear the first notion of business.
For he is good to think on, if a man would express himself neatly.
For he made a great figure in Egypt for his signal services.
For he killed the Ichneumon-rat very pernicious by land.
For his ears are so acute that they sting again.
For from this proceeds the passing quickness of his attention.
For by stroaking of him I have found out electricity.
For I perceived God's light about him both wax and fire.
For the Electrical fire is the spiritual substance, which God sends from
    heaven to sustain the bodies both of man and beast.
For God has blessed him in the variety of his movements.
For, tho he cannot fly, he is an excellent clamberer.
For his motions upon the face of the earth are more than any other
    quadrupede.
For he can tread to all the measures upon the musick.
For he can swim for life.
For he can creep.

349   *The Nativity of Our Lord and Saviour Jesus Christ*

Where is this stupendous stranger,
    Swains of Solyma, advise,
Lead me to my Master's manger,
    Shew me where my Saviour lies?

O Most Mighty! O Most Holy!
    Far beyond the seraph's thought,
Art thou then so mean and lowly
    As unheeded prophets taught?

O the magnitude of meekness!
    Worth from worth immortal sprung;
O the strength of infant weakness,
    If eternal is so young!

If so young and thus eternal,
    Michael tune the shepherd's reed,
Where the scenes are ever vernal,
    And the loves be love indeed!

See the God blasphem'd and doubted
    In the schools of Greece and Rome;
See the pow'rs of darkness routed,
    Taken at their utmost gloom.

Nature's decorations glisten
    Far above their usual trim;
Birds on box and laurels listen,
    As so near the cherubs hymn.

Boreas now no longer winters
    On the desolated coast;
Oaks no more are riv'n in splinters
    By the whirlwind and his host.

Spinks and ouzles sing sublimely,
    'We too have a Saviour born;'
Whiter blossoms burst untimely
    On the blest Mosaic thorn.

God all-bounteous, all-creative,
    Whom no ills from good dissuade,
Is incarnate, and a native
    Of the very world he made.

FRANCES GREVILLE

1724?–1789

350   *A Prayer for Indifference*

Oft I've implor'd the Gods in vain,
    And pray'd till I've been weary;
For once I'll try my wish to gain
    Of Oberon, the fairy.

Sweet airy being, wanton sprite,
    That lurk'st in woods unseen,
And oft by Cynthia's silver light
    Tripst gaily o'er the green;

If e'er thy pitying heart was mov'd,
    As ancient stories tell,
And for th' Athenian maid, who lov'd,
    Thou sought'st a wondrous spell,

Oh! deign once more t' exert thy power;
    Haply some herb or tree,
Sov'reign as juice from western flower,
    Conceals a balm for me.

I ask no kind return in love,
    No tempting charm to please;
Far from the heart such gifts remove,
    That sighs for peace and ease.

Nor ease nor peace that heart can know,
　　Which, like the needle true,
Turns at the touch of joy or woe,
　　But, turning, trembles too.

Far as distress the soul can wound,
　　'Tis pain in each degree;
Bliss goes but to a certain bound,
　　Beyond is agony.

Take then this treacherous sense of mine,
　　Which dooms me still to smart;
Which pleasure can to pain refine,
　　To pain new pangs impart.

Oh! haste to shed the sovereign balm
　　My shatter'd nerves new string;
And for my guest, serenely calm,
　　The nymph, Indifference, bring.

At her approach, see Hope, see Fear,
　　See Expectation fly;
With Disappointment, in the rear,
　　That blasts the promis'd joy.

The tears which pity taught to flow,
　　My eyes shall then disown;
The heart which throbb'd at other's woe,
　　Shall then scarce feel its own.

The wounds which now each moment bleed,
　　Each moment then shall close,
And peaceful days shall still succeed
　　To nights of sweet repose.

Oh, fairy elf! but grant me this,
　　This one kind comfort send;
And so may never-fading bliss
　　Thy flowery paths attend!

So may the glow-worm's glimmering light
　　Thy tiny footsteps lead
To some new region of delight,
　　Unknown to mortal tread.

And be thy acorn goblets fill'd
　　With heaven's ambrosial dew,
From sweetest, freshest flowers distill'd,
　　That shed fresh sweets for you.

And what of life remains for me
   I'll pass in sober ease,
Half-pleas'd, contented will I be,
   Contented, half to please.

ANONYMOUS

[EIGHTEENTH CENTURY]

351   *Edward*

'Why dois your brand sae drap wi bluid,
               Edward, Edward,
Why dois your brand sae drap wi bluid,
   And why sae sad gang yee O?'
'O I hae killed my hauke sae guid,   5
               Mither, mither,
O I hae killed my hauke sae guid,
   And I had nae mair bot hee O.'

'Your haukis bluid was nevir sae reid,
               Edward, Edward,   10
Your haukis bluid was nevir sae reid,
   My deir son I tell thee O.'
'O I hae killed my reid-roan steid,
               Mither, mither,
O I hae killed my reid-roan steid,   15
   That erst was sae fair and frie O.'

'Your steid was auld, and ye hae gat mair,
               Edward, Edward,
Your steid was auld, and ye hae gat mair,
   Sum other dule ye drie O.'   20
'O I hae killed my fadir deir,
               Mither, mither,
O I hae killed my fadir deir,
   Alas, and wae is mee O!'

'And whatten penance wul ye drie for that,   25
               Edward, Edward?
And whatten penance will ye drie for that?
   My deir son, now tell me O.'

351: 20 *dule ye drie*] sorrow you suffer

'Ile set my feit in yonder boat,
        Mither, mither,   30
Ile set my feit in yonder boat,
    And Ile fare ovir the sea O.'

'And what wul ye doe wi your towirs and your ha,
        Edward, Edward?
And what wul ye doe wi your towirs and your ha,   35
    That were sae fair to see O?'
'Ile let thame stand tul they doun fa,
        Mither, mither,
Ile let thame stand tul they doun fa,
    For here nevir mair maun I bee O.'   40

'And what wul ye leive to your bairns and your wife,
        Edward, Edward?
And what wul ye leive to your bairns and your wife,
    When ye gang ovir the sea O?'
'The warldis room, late them beg thrae life,   45
        Mither, mither,
The warldis room, late them beg thrae life,
    For thame nevir mair wul I see O.'

'And what wul ye leive to your ain mither deir,
        Edward, Edward?   50
And what wul ye leive to your ain mither deir?
    My deir son, now tell me O.'
'The curse of hell frae me sall ye beir,
        Mither, mither,
The curse of hell frae me sall ye beir,   55
    Sic counseils ye gave to me O.'

352   *Helen of Kirconnell*

I wish I were where Helen lies,
Night and day on me she cries;
O that I were where Helen lies,
    On fair Kirconnell lea!

Curst be the heart that thought the thought,
And curst the hand that fired the shot,
When in my arms burd Helen dropt,
    And died to succour me!

33 *ha*] hall

O think na ye my heart was sair,
When my Love dropp'd and spak nae mair!
There did she swoon wi' meikle care,
   On fair Kirconnell lea.

As I went down the water side,
None but my foe to be my guide,
None but my foe to be my guide,
   On fair Kirconnell lea;

I lighted down my sword to draw,
I hackèd him in pieces sma',
I hackèd him in pieces sma',
   For her sake that died for me.

O Helen fair, beyond compare!
I'll mak a garland o' thy hair,
Shall bind my heart for evermair,
   Until the day I die!

O that I were where Helen lies!
Night and day on me she cries;
Out of my bed she bids me rise,
   Says, 'Haste, and come to me!'

O Helen fair! O Helen chaste!
If I were with thee, I'd be blest,
Where thou lies low and taks thy rest,
   On fair Kirconnell lea.

I wish my grave were growing green,
A winding-sheet drawn owre my e'en,
And I in Helen's arms lying,
   On fair Kirconnell lea.

I wish I were where Helen lies!
Night and day on me she cries;
And I am weary of the skies,
   For her sake that died for me.

353   Says Tweed to Till—
         'What gars ye rin sae still?'
         Says Till to Tweed—
         'Though ye rin with speed
          And I rin slaw,
        For ae man that ye droon   5
          I droon twa.'

353: 2 *gars*] makes   6 *droon*] drown

354   *Sir Patrick Spens*

The king sits in Dumferling toune,
   Drinking the blude-reid wine:
'O whar will I get guid sailor,
   To sail this schip of mine?'

Up and spak an eldern knicht,   5
   Sat at the kings richt kne:
'Sir Patrick Spence is the best sailor
   That sails upon the se.'

The king has written a braid letter,
   And signd it wi his hand,   10
And sent it to Sir Patrick Spence,
   Was walking on the sand.

The first line that Sir Patrick red,
   A loud lauch lauched he;
The next line that Sir Patrick red,   15
   The teir blinded his ee.

'O wha is this has don this deid,
   This ill deid don to me,
To send me out this time o' the yeir,
   To sail upon the se!   20

'Mak hast, mak haste, my mirry men all,
   Our guid schip sails the morne:'
'O say na sae, my master deir,
   For I feir a deadlie storme.

'Late late yestreen I saw the new moone,   25
   Wi the auld moone in hir arme,
And I feir, I feir, my deir master,
   That we will cum to harme.'

O our Scots nobles wer richt laith
   To weet their cork-heild schoone;   30
Bot lang owre a' the play wer playd,
   Thair hats they swam aboone.

O lang, lang may their ladies sit,
   Wi thair fans into their hand,
Or eir they se Sir Patrick Spence   35
   Cum sailing to the land.

354: 9 *braid*] informal   29 *laith*] loath   32 *aboone*] above

O lang, lang may the ladies stand,
  Wi thair gold kems in their hair,
Waiting for thair ain deir lords,
  For they'll se thame na mair.   40

Haf owre, haf owre to Aberdour,
  It's fiftie fadom deip,
And thair lies guid Sir Patrick Spence,
  Wi the Scots lords at his feit.

355   *The Twa Corbies*

As I was walking all alane,
I heard twa corbies making a mane;
The tane unto the t'other say,
'Where sall we gang and dine to-day?'

'In behint yon auld fail dyke,   5
I wot there lies a new slain knight;
And naebody kens that he lies there,
But his hawk, his hound, and lady fair.

'His hound is to the hunting gane,
His hawk to fetch the wild-fowl hame,   10
His lady's ta'en another mate,
So we may mak our dinner sweet.

'Ye'll sit on his white hause-bane,
And I'll pike out his bonny blue een;
Wi ae lock o his gowden hair   15
We'll theek our nest when it grows bare.

'Mony a one for him makes mane,
But nane sall ken where he is gane;
Oer his white banes, when they are bare,
The wind sall blaw for evermair.'   20

---

38 *kems*] combs

355: *Corbies*] carrion crows   2 *mane*] moan   5 *fail dyke*] wall built of sods
13 *hause-bane*] neck bone   16 *theek*] thatch

JEAN ELLIOT

1727–1805

356   *The Flowers of the Forest*

I've heard them lilting, at the ewe milking,
  Lasses a' lilting, before dawn of day;
But now they are moaning, on ilka green loaning;
  The flowers of the forest are a' wede awae.

At bughts in the morning, nae blithe lads are scorning;   5
  Lasses are lonely, and dowie and wae;
Nae daffing, nae gabbing, but sighing and sabbing;
  Ilk ane lifts her leglin, and hies her awae.

At har'st at the shearing, nae youths now are jearing;
  Bandsters are runkled, and lyart or gray;   10
At fair, or at preaching, nae wooing, nae fleeching;
  The flowers of the forest are a' wede awae.

At e'en in the gloaming, nae younkers are roaming,
  'Bout stacks, with the lasses at bogle to play;
But ilk maid sits dreary, lamenting her deary—   15
  The flowers of the forest are weded awae.

Dool and wae for the order, sent our lads to the border!
  The English, for ance, by guile wan the day;
The flowers of the forest, that fought aye the foremost,
  The prime of our land are cauld in the clay.   20

We'll hae nae mair lilting at the ewe milking;
  Women and bairns are heartless and wae:
Sighing and moaning, on ilka green loaning—
  The flowers of the forest are a' wede away.

OLIVER GOLDSMITH

1730?–1774

357   When lovely woman stoops to folly,
             And finds too late that men betray,
           What charm can soothe her melancholy,
             What art can wash her guilt away?

356: 3 *loaning*] open ground   4 *wede*] cleared, taken out   5 *bughts*] pens
6 *dowie and wae*] glum and woeful   7 *daffing*] frolicking   8 *leglin*] pail   9 *har'st*]
harvest   10 *Bandsters*] those who bind the sheaves   *lyart*] hoary   11 *fleeching*]
cajoling   14 *bogle*] goblin, scary game   17 *Dool*] dole, sorrow

    The only art her guilt to cover,
        To hide her shame from every eye,
    To give repentance to her lover,
        And wring his bosom, is—to die.

358   from *Retaliation* [lines 29–42, 93–124, 137–46]

    [Each of them was to write the other's epitaph. Mr. Garrick
    immediately said that his epitaph was finished, and spoke
    the following distich extempore:—

        Here lies NOLLY Goldsmith, for shortness call'd Noll,
        Who wrote like an angel, but talk'd like poor Poll.]

                    [*Edmund Burke*]

    Here lies our good Edmund, whose genius was such,
    We scarcely can praise it, or blame it too much;
    Who, born for the Universe, narrow'd his mind,
    And to party gave up what was meant for mankind.
    Though fraught with all learning, yet straining his throat
    To persuade Tommy Townshend to lend him a vote;
    Who, too deep for his hearers, still went on refining,
    And thought of convincing, while they thought of dining;
    Though equal to all things, for all things unfit,
    Too nice for a statesman, too proud for a wit:
    For a patriot, too cool; for a drudge, disobedient;
    And too fond of the *right* to pursue the *expedient*.
    In short, 'twas his fate, unemploy'd, or in place, Sir,
    To eat mutton cold, and cut blocks with a razor.

                    [*David Garrick*]

    Here lies David Garrick, describe me, who can,
    An abridgment of all that was pleasant in man;
    As an actor, confess'd without rival to shine:
    As a wit, if not first, in the very first line:
    Yet, with talents like these, and an excellent heart,
    The man had his failings, a dupe to his art.
    Like an ill-judging beauty, his colours he spread,
    And beplaster'd with rouge his own natural red.
    On the stage he was natural, simple, affecting;
    'Twas only that when he was off he was acting.

With no reason on earth to go out of his way,
He turn'd and he varied full ten times a day.
Though secure of our hearts, yet confoundedly sick
If they were not his own by finessing and trick,
He cast off his friends, as a huntsman his pack,
For he knew when he pleas'd he could whistle them back.
Of praise a mere glutton, he swallow'd what came,
And the puff of a dunce he mistook it for fame;
Till his relish grown callous, almost to disease,
Who pepper'd the highest was surest to please.
But let us be candid, and speak out our mind,
If dunces applauded, he paid them in kind.
Ye Kenricks, ye Kellys, and Woodfalls so grave,
What a commerce was yours, while you got and you gave!
How did Grub-street re-echo the shouts that you rais'd,
While he was be-Roscius'd, and you were be-prais'd!
But peace to his spirit, wherever it flies,
To act as an angel, and mix with the skies:
Those poets, who owe their best fame to his skill,
Shall still be his flatterers, go where he will.
Old Shakespeare, receive him, with praise and with love,
And Beaumonts and Bens be his Kellys above.

[*Sir Joshua Reynolds*]

Here Reynolds is laid, and, to tell you my mind,
He has not left a better or wiser behind:
His pencil was striking, resistless, and grand;
His manners were gentle, complying, and bland;
Still born to improve us in every part,
His pencil our faces, his manners our heart:
To coxcombs averse, yet most civilly steering,
When they judg'd without skill he was still hard of hearing:
When they talk'd of their Raphaels, Correggios, and stuff,
He shifted his trumpet, and only took snuff.

WILLIAM COWPER
1731–1800

359   *The Poplar-Field*

The Poplars are fell'd, farewell to the shade
And the whispering sound of the cool colonnade,
The winds play no longer and sing in the leaves,
Nor Ouse on his bosom their image receives.

Twelve years have elapsed since I last took a view
Of my favourite field and the bank where they grew,
And now in the grass behold they are laid,
And the tree is my seat that once lent me a shade.

The black-bird has fled to another retreat
Where the hazels afford him a screen from the heat,
And the scene where his melody charm'd me before,
Resounds with his sweet-flowing ditty no more.

My fugitive years are all hasting away,
And I must e'er long lie as lowly as they,
With a turf on my breast and a stone at my head
E'er another such grove shall arise in its stead.

'Tis a sight to engage me if any thing can
To muse on the perishing pleasures of Man;
Though his life be a dream, his enjoyments, I see,
Have a Being less durable even than he.

360   *The Cast-Away*

Obscurest night involved the sky,
    Th' Atlantic billows roar'd,
When such a destin'd wretch as I
    Wash'd headlong from on board
Of friends, of hope, of all bereft,
His floating home for ever left.

No braver Chief could Albion boast
    Than He with whom he went,
Nor ever ship left Albion's coast
    With warmer wishes sent,
He loved them both, but both in vain,
Nor Him beheld, nor Her again.

Not long beneath the whelming brine
    Expert to swim, he lay,
Nor soon he felt his strength decline
    Or courage die away;
But waged with Death a lasting strife
Supported by despair of life.

He shouted, nor his friends had fail'd
    To check the vessels' course,
But so the furious blast prevail'd
    That, pitiless perforce,
They left their outcast mate behind,
And scudded still before the wind.

Some succour yet they could afford,
    And, such as storms allow,
The cask, the coop, the floated cord
    Delay'd not to bestow;
But He, they knew, nor ship nor shore,
Whate'er they gave, should visit more.

Nor, cruel as it seem'd, could He
    Their haste, himself, condemn,
Aware that flight in such a sea
    Alone could rescue *them*;
Yet bitter felt it still to die
Deserted, and his friends so nigh.

He long survives who lives an hour
    In ocean, self-upheld,
And so long he with unspent pow'r
    His destiny repell'd,
And ever, as the minutes flew,
Entreated help, or cried, Adieu!

At length, his transient respite past,
    His comrades, who before
Had heard his voice in ev'ry blast,
    Could catch the sound no more;
For then, by toil subdued, he drank
The stifling wave, and then he sank.

No poet wept him, but the page
    Of narrative sincere
That tells his name, his worth, his age,
    Is wet with Anson's tear,
And tears by bards or heroes shed
Alike immortalize the Dead.

I, therefore, purpose not or dream,
  Descanting on his fate,
To give the melancholy theme
  A more enduring date,
But Mis'ry still delights to trace
Its semblance in another's case.

No voice divine the storm allay'd,
  No light propitious shone,
When, snatch'd from all effectual aid,
  We perish'd, each, alone;
But I, beneath a rougher sea,
And whelm'd in deeper gulphs than he.

361   *Light Shining out of Darkness*

God moves in a mysterious way,
His wonders to perform,
He plants his footsteps in the Sea,
And rides upon the Storm.

Deep in unfathomable Mines,
Of never failing Skill,
He treasures up his bright designs,
And works his Sovereign Will.

Ye fearfull Saints fresh courage take,
The clouds ye so much dread,
Are big with Mercy, and shall break
In blessings on your head.

Judge not the Lord by feeble sense,
But trust him for his Grace,
Behind a frowning Providence
He hides a Smiling face.

His purposes will ripen fast,
Unfolding every hour,
The Bud may have a bitter taste,
But *wait*, to *Smell the flower*.

Blind unbelief is sure to err,
And scan his work in vain,
God is his own Interpreter,
And he will make it plain.

362   Hatred and vengeance, my eternal portion,
Scarce can endure delay of execution:—

Wait, with impatient readiness, to seize my
      Soul in a moment.
Damn'd below Judas; more abhorr'd than he was,
Who, for a few pence, sold his holy master.
Twice betray'd, Jesus me, the last delinquent,
      Deems the profanest.
Man disavows, and Deity disowns me.
Hell might afford my miseries a shelter;
Therefore hell keeps her everhungry mouths all
      Bolted against me.
Hard lot! Encompass'd with a thousand dangers,
Weary, faint, trembling with a thousand terrors,
Fall'n, and if vanquish'd, to receive a sentence
      Worse than Abiram's:
Him, the vindictive rod of angry justice
Sent, quick and howling, to the centre headlong;
I, fed with judgments, in a fleshly tomb, am
      Buried above ground.

NURSERY RHYMES

[MOSTLY EIGHTEENTH AND NINETEENTH CENTURY]

363   Baa, baa, black sheep,
              Have you any wool?
           Yes, sir, yes, sir,
              Three bags full;
           One for the master,
              And one for the dame,
           And one for the little boy
              Who lives down the lane.

364   Boys and girls come out to play,
           The moon doth shine as bright as day.
           Leave your supper and leave your sleep,
           And join your playfellows in the street.
           Come with a whoop and come with a call,
           Come with a good will or not at all.
           Up the ladder and down the wall,
           A half-penny loaf will serve us all;
           You find milk, and I'll find flour,
           And we'll have a pudding in half an hour.

365   Bye, baby bunting,
Daddy's gone a-hunting,
Gone to get a rabbit skin
To wrap the baby bunting in.

366   Ding, dong, bell,
Pussy's in the well.
Who put her in?
Little Johnny Green.
Who pulled her out?
Little Tommy Stout.
What a naughty boy was that,
To try to drown poor pussy cat,
Who never did him any harm,
And killed the mice in his father's barn.

367   Doctor Foster went to Gloucester
In a shower of rain;
He stepped in a puddle,
Right up to his middle,
And never went there again.

368   Hey diddle diddle,
The cat and the fiddle,
The cow jumped over the moon;
The little dog laughed
To see such sport,
And the dish ran away with the spoon.

369   Humpty Dumpty sat on a wall,
Humpty Dumpty had a great fall.
  All the king's horses,
  And all the king's men,
Couldn't put Humpty together again.

370   Hush-a-bye, baby, on the tree top,
When the wind blows the cradle will rock;
When the bough breaks the cradle will fall,
Down will come baby, cradle, and all.

371

I saw a fishpond all on fire
I saw a house bow to a squire
I saw a parson twelve feet high
I saw a cottage near the sky
I saw a balloon made of lead
I saw a coffin drop down dead
I saw two sparrows run a race
I saw two horses making lace
I saw a girl just like a cat
I saw a kitten wear a hat
I saw a man who saw these too
And said though strange they all were true.

372

Jack and Jill went up the hill
    To fetch a pail of water;
Jack fell down and broke his crown,
    And Jill came tumbling after.

Up Jack got, and home did trot,
    As fast as he could caper,
To old Dame Dob, who patched his nob
    With vinegar and brown paper.

373

Oranges and lemons,
Say the bells of St. Clement's.

You owe me five farthings,
Say the bells of St. Martin's.

When will you pay me?
Say the bells of Old Bailey.

When I grow rich,
Say the bells of Shoreditch.

When will that be?
Say the bells of Stepney.

I'm sure I don't know,
Says the great bell at Bow.

Here comes a candle to light you to bed,
Here comes a chopper to chop off your head.

374

Ride a cock-horse to Banbury Cross,
To see a fine lady upon a white horse;
Rings on her fingers and bells on her toes,
And she shall have music wherever she goes.

375
See-saw, Margery Daw,
Jacky shall have a new master;
Jacky shall have but a penny a day,
Because he can't work any faster.

376
Sing a song of sixpence,
    A pocket full of rye;
Four and twenty blackbirds,
    Baked in a pie.

When the pie was opened,
    The birds began to sing;
Was not that a dainty dish,
    To set before the king?

The king was in his counting-house,
    Counting out his money;
The queen was in the parlour,
    Eating bread and honey.

The maid was in the garden,
    Hanging out the clothes,
There came a little blackbird,
    And snapped off her nose.

377
This is the house that Jack built.

This is the malt
That lay in the house that Jack built.

This is the rat,
That ate the malt
That lay in the house that Jack built.

This is the cat,
That killed the rat,
That ate the malt
That lay in the house that Jack built.

This is the dog,
That worried the cat,
That killed the rat,
That ate the malt
That lay in the house that Jack built.

This is the cow with the crumpled horn,
That tossed the dog,

That worried the cat,
That killed the rat,
That ate the malt
That lay in the house that Jack built.

This is the maiden all forlorn,
That milked the cow with the crumpled horn,
That tossed the dog,
That worried the cat,
That killed the rat,
That ate the malt
That lay in the house that Jack built.

This is the man all tattered and torn,
That kissed the maiden all forlorn,
That milked the cow with the crumpled horn,
That tossed the dog,
That worried the cat,
That killed the rat,
That ate the malt
That lay in the house that Jack built.

This is the priest all shaven and shorn,
That married the man all tattered and torn,
That kissed the maiden all forlorn,
That milked the cow with the crumpled horn,
That tossed the dog,
That worried the cat,
That killed the rat,
That ate the malt
That lay in the house that Jack built.

This is the cock that crowed in the morn,
That waked the priest all shaven and shorn,
That married the man all tattered and torn,
That kissed the maiden all forlorn,
That milked the cow with the crumpled horn,
That tossed the dog,
That worried the cat,
That killed the rat,
That ate the malt
That lay in the house that Jack built.

This is the farmer sowing his corn,
That kept the cock that crowed in the morn,
That waked the priest all shaven and shorn,
That married the man all tattered and torn,

That kissed the maiden all forlorn,
That milked the cow with the crumpled horn,
That tossed the dog,
That worried the cat,
That killed the rat,
That ate the malt
That lay in the house that Jack built.

378 This little pig went to market,
This little pig stayed at home,
This little pig had roast beef,
This little pig had none,
And this little pig cried, Wee-wee-wee-wee-wee,
  I can't find my way home.

379 Three blind mice, see how they run!
They all ran after the farmer's wife,
Who cut off their tails with a carving knife,
Did you ever see such a thing in your life,
  As three blind mice?

380 White bird featherless
Flew from Paradise,
Pitched on the castle wall;
Along came Lord Landless,
Took it up handless,
And rode away horseless to the King's white hall.

381 Who killed Cock Robin?
I, said the Sparrow,
With my bow and arrow,
I killed Cock Robin.

Who saw him die?
I, said the Fly,
With my little eye,
I saw him die.

Who caught his blood?
I, said the Fish,
With my little dish,
I caught his blood.

Who'll make the shroud?
I, said the Beetle,
With my thread and needle,
I'll make the shroud.

Who'll dig his grave?
I, said the Owl,
With my pick and shovel,
I'll dig his grave.

Who'll be the parson?
I, said the Rook,
With my little book,
I'll be the parson.

Who'll be the clerk?
I, said the Lark,
If it's not in the dark,
I'll be the clerk.

Who'll carry the link?
I, said the Linnet,
I'll fetch it in a minute,
I'll carry the link.

Who'll be chief mourner?
I, said the Dove,
I mourn for my love,
I'll be chief mourner.

Who'll carry the coffin?
I, said the Kite,
If it's not through the night,
I'll carry the coffin.

Who'll bear the pall?
We, said the Wren,
Both the cock and the hen,
We'll bear the pall.

Who'll sing a psalm?
I, said the Thrush,
As she sat on a bush,
I'll sing a psalm.

Who'll toll the bell?
I, said the Bull,
Because I can pull,
I'll toll the bell.

All the birds of the air
Fell a-sighing and a-sobbing,
When they heard the bell toll
For poor Cock Robin.

ANNA SEWARD

1747–1809

382   *An Old Cat's Dying Soliloquy*

Years saw me still Acasto's mansion grace,
The gentlest, fondest of the tabby race;
Before him frisking thro' the garden glade,
Or at his feet, in quiet slumber laid;
Prais'd for my glossy back, of zebra streak,
And wreaths of jet encircling round my neck;
Soft paws, that ne'er extend the clawing nail,
The snowy whisker, and the sinuous tail;
Now feeble age each glazing eye-ball dims,
And pain has stiffen'd these once supple limbs;
Fate of eight lives the forfeit gasp obtains,
And e'en the ninth creeps languid thro' my veins.
   Much sure of good the future has in store,
When on my master's hearth I bask no more,
In those blest climes, where fishes oft forsake
The winding river, and the glassy lake,
There, as our silent-footed race behold
The crimson spots, and fins of lucid gold,
Venturing without the shielding waves to play,
They gasp on shelving banks, our easy prey:
While birds unwing'd hop careless o'er the ground,
And the plump mouse incessant trots around,
Near wells of cream, that mortals never skim,
Warm marum creeping round their shallow brim;
Where green valerian tufts, luxuriant spread,
Cleanse the sleek hide, and form the fragrant bed.
   Yet, stern dispenser of the final blow,
Before thou lay'st an ag'd grimalkin low,
Bend to her last request a gracious ear,
Some days, some few short days to linger here;
So to the guardian of his tabby's weal
Shall softest purrs these tender truths reveal:
   'Ne'er shall thy now expiring puss forget
To thy kind care her long enduring debt,

Nor shall the joys that painless realms decree
Efface the comforts once bestow'd by thee;
To countless mice thy chicken-bones preferred,
Thy toast to golden fish, and wingless bird;
O'er marum borders, and valerian bed,
Thy Selima shall bend her moping head,
Sigh that no more she climbs, with grateful glee,
Thy downy sofa, and thy cradling knee,
Nay e'en at founts of cream shall sullen swear,
Since thou her more loved master, art not there.'

ROBERT FERGUSSON

1750–1774

383   *The Daft-Days*

Now mirk December's dowie face
Glours owr the rigs wi' sour grimace,
While, thro' his minimum of space,
              The bleer-eyed sun,
Wi' blinkin light and stealing pace,   5
              His race doth run.

From naked groves nae birdie sings,
To shepherd's pipe nae hillock rings,
The breeze nae od'rous flavour brings
              From Borean cave,   10
And dwyning nature droops her wings,
              Wi' visage grave.

Mankind but scanty pleasure glean
Frae snawy hill or barren plain,
Whan Winter, midst his nipping train,   15
              Wi' frozen spear,
Sends drift owr a' his bleak domain,
              And guides the weir.

Auld Reikie! thou'rt the canty hole,
A bield for mony caldrife soul,   20
Wha snugly at thine ingle loll,
              Baith warm and couth;
While round they gar the bicker roll
              To weet their mouth.

383: 1 *dowie*] glum   2 *rigs*] ridges   11 *dwyning*] pining   19 *Auld*
Reikie] Edinburgh (smoky)   *canty*] merry   20 *bield*] haven   *caldrife*] cold
21 *ingle*] hearth-fire   23 *bicker*] cup

When merry Yule-day comes, I trow   25
You'll scantlins find a hungry mou';
Sma' are our cares, our stamacks fou
   O' gusty gear,
And kickshaws, strangers to our view,
   Sin fairn-year.   30

Ye browster wives, now busk ye bra,
And fling your sorrows far awa';
Then come and gie's the tither blaw
   Of reaming ale,
Mair precious than the well of Spa,   35
   Our hearts to heal.

Then, tho' at odds wi' a' the warl',
Amang oursells we'll never quarrel;
Tho' Discord gie a cankered snarl
   To spoil our glee,   40
As lang's there's pith into the barrel
   We'll drink and 'gree.

Fidlers, your pins in temper fix,
And roset weel your fiddle-sticks,
And banish vile Italian tricks   45
   From out your quorum,
Nor *fortes* wi' *pianos* mix,
   Gie's *Tulloch Gorum.*

For nought can cheer the heart sae weil
As can a canty Highland reel,   50
It even vivifies the heel
   To skip and dance:
Lifeless is he wha canna feel
   Its influence.

Let mirth abound, let social cheer   55
Invest the dawning of the year;
Let blithesome innocence appear
   To crown our joy,
Nor envy wi' sarcastic sneer
   Our bliss destroy.   60

And thou, great god of Aqua Vitae!
Wha sways the empire of this city,
When fou we're sometimes capernoity,

26 *scantlins*] scarcely   28 *gusty gear*] tasty stuff   29 *kickshaws*] fancy dishes
30 *fairn-year*] yesteryear   31 *browster*] brewer   *busk ye bra*] dress yourselves handsomely
33 *blaw*] blow, stroke   34 *reaming*] foaming   44 *roset*] put rosin on
63 *capernoity*] quarrelsome

Be thou prepared
To hedge us frae that black banditti,   65
The City-Guard.

384   *Braid Claith*

Ye wha are fain to hae your name
Wrote i' the bonny book o' Fame,
Let Merit nae pretension claim
          To laurel'd wreath,
But hap ye weel, baith back and wame,   5
          In gude Braid Claith.

He that some ells o' this may fa',
An' slae-black hat on pow like snaw,
Bids bauld to bear the gree awa',
          Wi' a' this graith,   10
Whan beinly clad wi' shell fu' braw
          O' gude Braid Claith.

Waesuck for him wha has nae feck o't!
For he's a gowk they're sure to geck at,
A chiel that ne'er will be respekit,   15
          While he draws breath,
Till his four quarters are bedeckit
          Wi' gude Braid Claith.

On Sabbath-days the barber spark,
Whan he has done wi' scrapin wark,   20
Wi' siller broachie in his sark,
          Gangs trigly, faith!
Or to the Meadow, or the Park,
          In gude Braid Claith.

Weel might ye trow, to see them there,   25
That they to shave your haffits bare,
Or curl an' sleek a pickle hair,
          Would be right laith,
Whan pacing wi' a gawsy air
          In gude Braid Claith.   30

384: 5 *hap*] wrap   *wame*] belly   7 *fa'*] lay claim to   8 *pow*] poll, head
9 *gree*] prize   10 *graith*] gear   11 *beinly*] snugly   *braw*] brave   13 *Waesuck for*]
woe to   *feck*] plenty   14 *gowk*] dimwit   21 *sark*] shirt   22 *trigly*] neatly
26 *haffits*] cheeks   27 *pickle*] little   28 *laith*] loath   29 *gawsy*] well dressed and
jolly-looking

If ony mettl'd stirrah green
For favour frae a lady's een,
He maunna care for bein' seen
    Before he shcath
His body in a scabbard clean   35
    O' gude Braid Claith.

For, gin he come wi' coat thread-bare,
A feg for him she winna care,
But crook her bonny mou' fu' sair,
    And scald him baith: 40
Wooers shou'd ay their travel spare,
    Without Braid Claith.

Braid Claith lends fock an unco heese;
Makes mony kail-worms butterflies;
Gies mony a doctor his degrees   45
    For little skaith:
In short, you may be what you please
    Wi' gude Braid Claith.

For tho' ye had as wise a snout on
As Shakespeare or Sir Isaac Newton,   50
Your judgment fock would hae a doubt on,
    I'll tak my aith,
Till they cou'd see ye wi' a suit on
    O' gude Braid Claith.

LADY ANNE LINDSAY

1750–1825

385   *Auld Robin Gray*

When the sheep are in the fauld, when the cows come hame,
When a' the weary world to quiet rest are gane,
The woes of my heart fa' in showers frae my ee,
Unken'd by my gudeman, who soundly sleeps by me.

Young Jamie loo'd me weel, and sought me for his bride;
But saving ae crown-piece, he'd naething else beside,
To make the crown a pound, my Jamie gaed to sea;
And the crown and the pound, oh! they were baith for me!

---

31 *stirrah*] sirrah   *green*] crave   38 *feg*] fig   43 *fock*] folk   *unco heese*] great lift
46 *skaith*] pains

Before he had been gane a twelvemonth and a day,
My father brak his arm, our cow was stown away;
My mother she fell sick—my Jamie was at sea—
And Auld Robin Gray, oh! he came a-courting me.

My father cou'dna work—my mother cou'dna spin;
I toil'd day and night, but their bread I cou'dna win;
Auld Rob maintain'd them baith, and, wi' tears in his ee,
Said, 'Jenny, oh! for their sakes, will you marry me?'

My heart it said na, and I look'd for Jamie back;
But hard blew the winds, and his ship was a wrack:
His ship it was a wrack! Why didna Jenny dee?
Or, wherefore am I spared to cry out, Woe is me!

My father argued sair—my mother didna speak,
But she look'd in my face till my heart was like to break:
They gied him my hand, but my heart was in the sea;
And so Auld Robin Gray, he was gudeman to me.

I hadna been his wife, a week but only four
When mournfu' as I sat on the stane at my door,
I saw my Jamie's ghaist—I cou'dna think it he,
Till he said, 'I'm come hame, my love, to marry thee!'

O sair, sair did we greet, and mickle say of a';
Ae kiss we took, nae mair—I bad him gang awa.
I wish that I were dead, but I'm no like to dee;
For O, I am but young to cry out, Woe is me!

I gang like a ghaist, and I carena much to spin;
I darena think o' Jamie, for that wad be a sin.
But I will do my best a gude wife aye to be,
For auld Robin Gray, oh! he is sae kind to me.

RICHARD BRINSLEY SHERIDAN

1751–1816

386   from *The School for Scandal* [Act III, scene iii]

Song and Chorus

Here's to the maiden of Bashful fifteen
    Here's to the Widow of Fifty
Here's to the flaunting, Extravagant Quean,
    And here's to the House Wife that's thrifty.

Chorus.   Let the toast pass—
             Drink to the Lass—
             I'll warrant She'll prove an Excuse for the Glass!

             Here's to the Charmer whose Dimples we Prize!
               Now to the Maid who has none Sir;
             Here's to the Girl with a pair of blue Eyes,
               —And Here's to the Nymph with but one Sir!
Chorus.   Let the Toast pass etc.

             Here's to the Maid with a Bosom of Snow,
               Now to her that's as brown as a berry:
             Here's to the Wife with a face full of Woe,
               And now for the Damsel that's Merry.
Chorus.   Let the Toast pass etc.

             For let 'Em be Clumsy or let 'Em be Slim
               Young or Ancient, I care not a Feather:
             —So fill a Pint Bumper Quite up to the Brim
               —And let us E'en toast 'Em together!
Chorus.   Let the toast pass—
             Drink to the Lass—
             I'll warrant She'll prove an Excuse for the Glass!

PHILIP FRENEAU

1752–1832

387   *Libera nos, Domine—Deliver Us, O Lord.*

    From a junto that labour for absolute power,
    Whose schemes disappointed have made them look sowr,
    From the lords of the council, who fight against freedom,
    Who still follow on where the devil shall lead 'em.

    From the group at St. James's, that slight our Petitions,
    And fools that are waiting for further submissions—
    From a nation whose manners are rough and abrupt,
    From scoundrels and rascals whom gold can corrupt,

    From pirates sent out by command of the king
    To murder and plunder, but never to swing,
    From *Wallace* and *Greaves*, and *Vipers* and *Roses**
    Whom, if heaven pleases, we'll give bloody noses.

  * Captains and Ships of the British navy then employed on our coasts.

From the valiant Dunmore, with his crew of banditti,
Who plunder Virginians at Williamsburg city,
From hot-headed Montague, mighty to swear,
The little fat man with his pretty white hair.

From bishops in Britain, who butchers are grown,
From slaves that would die for a smile from the throne,
From assemblies that vote against Congress proceedings,
(Who now see the fruit of their stupid misleadings).

From Tryon the mighty, who flies from our city,
And, swell'd with importance, disdains the committee;
(But since he is pleas'd to proclaim us his foes,
What the devil care we where the devil he goes).

From the scoundrel, lord *North*, who would bind us in chains,
From a dunce of a king who was born without brains,
The utmost extent of whose sense is to see
That reigning and making of buttons agree.

From an island that bullies, and hectors, and swears,
I send up to heaven my wishes and prayers
That we, disunited, may freemen be still,
And Britain go on—to be damn'd, if she will.

WILLIAM ROSCOE

1753–1831

388   *The Butterfly's Ball and the Grasshopper's Feast*

Come take up your Hats, and away let us haste
To the *Butterfly's* Ball, and the *Grasshopper's* Feast.
The Trumpeter, *Gad-fly*, has summon'd the Crew,
And the Revels are now only waiting for you.

So said little Robert, and pacing along,
His merry Companions came forth in a Throng.
And on the smooth Grass, by the side of a Wood,
Beneath a broad Oak that for Ages had stood,

Saw the Children of Earth, and the Tenants of Air,
For an Evening's Amusement together repair.
And there came the *Beetle*, so blind and so black,
Who carried the *Emmet*, his Friend, on his Back.

And there was the *Gnat* and the *Dragon-fly* too,
With all their Relations, Green, Orange, and Blue.
And there came the *Moth*, with his Plumage of Down,
And the *Hornet* in Jacket of Yellow and Brown;

Who with him the *Wasp*, his Companion, did bring,
But they promis'd, that Evening, to lay by their Sting.
And the sly little *Dormouse* crept out of his Hole,
And brought to the Feast his blind Brother, the *Mole*.

And the *Snail*, with his Horns peeping out of his Shell,
Came from a great Distance, the Length of an Ell.
A Mushroom their Table, and on it was laid
A Water-dock Leaf, which a Table-cloth made.

The Viands were various, to each of their Taste,
And the *Bee* brought her Honey to crown the Repast.
Then close on his Haunches, so solemn and wise,
The *Frog* from a Corner, look'd up to the Skies.

And the *Squirrel* well pleas'd such Diversions to see,
Mounted high over Head, and look'd down from a Tree.
Then out came the *Spider*, with Finger so fine,
To shew his Dexterity on the tight Line.

From one Branch to another, his Cobwebs he slung,
Then quick as an Arrow he darted along,
But just in the Middle,—Oh! shocking to tell,
From his Rope, in an Instant, poor Harlequin fell.

Yet he touch'd not the Ground, but with Talons outspread,
Hung suspended in Air, at the End of a Thread.
Then the *Grasshopper* came with a Jerk and a Spring,
Very long was his Leg, though but short was his Wing;

He took but three Leaps, and was soon out of Sight,
Then chirp'd his own Praises the rest of the Night.
With Step so majestic the *Snail* did advance,
And promis'd the Gazers a Minuet to dance.

But they all laugh'd so loud that he pull'd in his Head,
And went in his own little Chamber to Bed.
Then, as Evening gave Way to the Shadows of Night,
Their Watchman, the *Glow-worm*, came out with a Light.

Then Home let us hasten, while yet we can see,
For no Watchman is waiting for you and for me.
So said little Robert, and pacing along,
His merry Companions returned in a Throng.

PHILLIS WHEATLEY
1753–1784

389   *On being brought from Africa to America*

'Twas mercy brought me from my *Pagan* land,
Taught my benighted soul to understand
That there's a GOD, that there's a *Saviour* too:
Once I redemption neither sought nor knew.
Some view our sable race with scornful eye,
'Their colour is a diabolic die.'
Remember, *Christians*, *Negroes*, black as *Cain*,
May be refin'd, and join th' angelic train.

GEORGE CRABBE
1754–1832

390   from *The Borough: Peter Grimes* [lines 165–204]

Alas! for *Peter* not an helping Hand,
So was he hated, could he now command;
Alone he row'd his Boat, alone he cast
His Nets beside, or made his Anchor fast;
To hold a Rope or hear a Curse was none,—
He toil'd and rail'd; he groan'd and swore alone.

Thus by himself compell'd to live each day,
To wait for certain hours the Tide's delay;
At the same times the same dull views to see,
The bounding Marsh-bank and the blighted Tree;
The Water only, when the Tides were high,
When low, the Mud half-cover'd and half-dry;
The Sun-burnt Tar that blisters on the Planks,
And Bank-side Stakes in their uneven ranks;
Heaps of entangled Weeds that slowly float,
As the Tide rolls by the impeded Boat.

When Tides were neap, and, in the sultry day,
Through the tall bounding Mud-banks made their way,
Which on each side rose swelling, and below
The dark warm Flood ran silently and slow;
There anchoring, *Peter* chose from Man to hide,
There hang his Head, and view the lazy Tide
In its hot slimy Channel slowly glide;

Where the small Eels that left the deeper way
For the warm Shore, within the Shallows play;
Where gaping Muscles, left upon the Mud,
Slope their slow passage to the fallen Flood;—
Here dull and hopeless he'd lie down and trace
How sidelong Crabs had scrawl'd their crooked race;
Or sadly listen to the tuneless cry
Of fishing *Gull* or clanging *Golden-eye*;
What time the Sea-birds to the Marsh would come,
And the loud *Bittern*, from the Bull-rush home,   )
Gave from the Salt-ditch side the bellowing Boom: }
He nurst the Feelings these dull Scenes produce,   )
And lov'd to stop beside the opening Sluice;
Where the small Stream, confin'd in narrow bound,
Ran with a dull, unvaried, sad'ning sound;
Where all presented to the Eye or Ear,
Oppress'd the Soul! with Misery, Grief, and Fear.

391   The ring so worn, as you behold,
           So thin, so pale, is yet of gold:
           The passion such it was to prove;
           Worn with life's cares, love yet was love.

WILLIAM BLAKE

1757–1827

392   from *An Island in the Moon*

           Hail Matrimony made of Love
           To thy wide gates how great a drove
           On purpose to be yok'd do come
           Widows and maids and Youths also
           That lightly trip on beauty's toe
           Or sit on beauty's bum

           Hail fingerfooted lovely Creatures
           The females of our human Natures
           Formed to suckle all Mankind
           Tis you that come in time of need
           Without you we shoud never Breed
           Or any Comfort find

For if a Damsel's blind or lame
Or Nature's hand has crooked her frame
Or if she's deaf or is wall eyed
Yet if her heart is well inclined
Some tender lover she shall find
That panteth for a Bride

The universal Poultice this
To cure whatever is amiss
In damsel or in Widow gay
It makes them smile it makes them skip
Like Birds just cured of the pip
They chirp and hop away

Then come ye Maidens come ye Swains
Come and be eased of all your pains
In Matrimony's Golden cage—

393   from *The Book of Thel*

IV

The eternal gates terrific porter lifted the northern bar:
Thel enter'd in and saw the secrets of the land unknown;
She saw the couches of the dead, and where the fibrous roots
Of every heart on earth infixes deep its restless twists:
A land of sorrows and of tears where never smile was seen.

She wanderd in the land of clouds thro' valleys dark, listning
Dolours and lamentations: waiting oft beside a dewy grave
She stood in silence. listning to the voices of the ground,
Till to her own grave plot she came. and there she sat down.
And heard this voice of sorrow breathed from the hollow pit.

Why cannot the Ear be closed to its own destruction?
Or the glistning Eye to the poison of a smile!
Why are Eyelids stord with arrows ready drawn,
Where a thousand fighting men in ambush lie?
Or an Eye of gifts and graces, show'ring fruits and coined gold!
Why a Tongue impress'd with honey from every wind?
Why an Ear, a whirlpool fierce to draw creations in?
Why a Nostril wide inhaling terror trembling and affright
Why a tender curb upon the youthful burning boy!
Why a little curtain of flesh on the bed of our desire?

The Virgin started from her seat, and with a shriek
Fled back unhinderd till she came into the vales of Har

from *Songs of Innocence*

394   *The Divine Image*

To Mercy Pity Peace and Love,
All pray in their distress:
And to these virtues of delight
Return their thankfulness.

For Mercy Pity Peace and Love,
Is God our father dear:
And Mercy Pity Peace and Love,
Is Man his child and care.

For Mercy has a human heart
Pity, a human face:
And Love, the human form divine,
And Peace, the human dress.

Then every man of every clime,
That prays in his distress,
Prays to the human form divine
Love Mercy Pity Peace.

And all must love the human form,
In heathen, turk or jew.
Where Mercy, Love and Pity dwell
There God is dwelling too.

395–402   from *Songs of Experience*

395   *Introduction*

Hear the voice of the Bard!
Who Present, Past, and Future sees
Whose ears have heard,
The Holy Word,
That walk'd among the ancient trees.

Calling the lapsed Soul
And weeping in the evening dew:
That might controll,
The starry pole;
And fallen fallen light renew!

O Earth O Earth return!
Arise from out the dewy grass;
Night is worn,
And the morn
Rises from the slumberous mass.

Turn away no more:
Why wilt thou turn away
The starry floor
The watry shore
Is giv'n thee till the break of day.

396   *The Clod and the Pebble*

Love seeketh not Itself to please,
Nor for itself hath any care;
But for another gives its ease,
And builds a Heaven in Hells despair.

So sang a little Clod of Clay,
Trodden with the cattles feet:
But a Pebble of the brook,
Warbled out these metres meet.

Love seeketh only Self to please,
To bind another to its delight;
Joys in anothers loss of ease,
And builds a Hell in Heavens despite.

397   *The Sick Rose*

O Rose thou art sick.
The invisible worm,
That flies in the night
In the howling storm:

Has found out thy bed
Of crimson joy:
And his dark secret love
Does thy life destroy.

398   *The Tyger*

> Tyger Tyger, burning bright,
> In the forests of the night:
> What immortal hand or eye,
> Could frame thy fearful symmetry?
>
> In what distant deeps or skies
> Burnt the fire of thine eyes!
> On what wings dare he aspire?
> What the hand, dare sieze the fire?
>
> And what shoulder, and what art,
> Could twist the sinews of thy heart?
> And when thy heart began to beat,
> What dread hand? and what dread feet?
>
> What the hammer? what the chain,
> In what furnace was thy brain?
> What the anvil? what dread grasp,
> Dare its deadly terrors clasp?
>
> When the stars threw down their spears
> And water'd heaven with their tears:
> Did he smile his work to see?
> Did he who made the Lamb make thee?
>
> Tyger, Tyger burning bright,
> In the forests of the night:
> What immortal hand or eye,
> Dare frame thy fearful symmetry?

399   *The Garden of Love*

> I went to the Garden of Love.
> And saw what I never had seen:
> A Chapel was built in the midst,
> Where I used to play on the green.
>
> And the gates of this Chapel were shut,
> And Thou shalt not. writ over the door;
> So I turn'd to the Garden of Love,
> That so many sweet flowers bore.
>
> And I saw it was filled with graves,
> And tomb-stones where flowers should be:
> And Priests in black gowns, were walking their rounds,
> And binding with briars, my joys and desires.

400   *London*

I wander thro' each charter'd street,
Near where the charter'd Thames does flow.
And mark in every face I meet
Marks of weakness, marks of woe.

In every cry of every Man,
In every Infants cry of fear,
In every voice: in every ban,
The mind-forg'd manacles I hear

How the Chimney-sweepers cry
Every blackning Church appalls,
And the hapless Soldiers sigh,
Runs in blood down Palace walls

But most thro' midnight streets I hear
How the youthful Harlots curse
Blasts the new-born Infants tear
And blights with plagues the Marriage hearse

401   *Infant Sorrow*

My mother groand! my father wept.
Into the dangerous world I leapt:
Helpless, naked, piping loud;
Like a fiend hid in a cloud.

Struggling in my fathers hands:
Striving against my swadling bands:
Bound and weary I thought best
To sulk upon my mothers breast.

402   *A Poison Tree*

I was angry with my friend:
I told my wrath, my wrath did end.
I was angry with my foe:
I told it not, my wrath did grow.

And I watered it in fears.
Night and morning with my tears:
And I sunned it with smiles.
And with soft deceitful wiles.

And it grew both day and night.
Till it bore an apple bright.
And my foe beheld it shine.
And he knew that it was mine.

And into my garden stole.
When the night had veild the pole;
In the morning glad I see;
My foe outstretchd beneath the tree.

403   Never seek to tell thy love
Love that never told can be
For the gentle wind does move
Silently invisibly

I told my love I told my love
I told her all my heart
Trembling cold in ghastly fears
Ah she doth depart

Soon as she was gone from me
A traveller came by
Silently invisibly
He took her with a sigh

[first version]

404   I told my love I told my love
I told her all my heart
Trembling cold in ghastly fears
Ah she doth depart

Soon as she was gone from me
A traveller came by
Silently invisibly
O was no deny

[last version]

405   Abstinence sows sand all over
The ruddy limbs and flaming hair
But Desire Gratified
Plants fruits of life and beauty there

406   *The Question Answerd*

What is it men in women do require?
The lineaments of Gratified Desire.
What is it women do in men require?
The lineaments of Gratified Desire.

407–8   from *Visions of the Daughters of Albion*

407   [Plate 6, lines 2–13]

With what sense is it that the chicken shuns the ravenous hawk?
With what sense does the tame pigeon measure out the expanse?
With what sense does the bee form cells? have not the mouse and frog
Eyes and ears and sense of touch? yet are their habitations.
And their pursuits, as different as their forms and as their joys:
Ask the wild ass why he refuses burdens: and the meek camel
Why he loves man: is it because of eye ear mouth or skin
Or breathing nostrils? No. for these the wolf and tyger have.
Ask the blind worm the secrets of the grave, and why her spires
Love to curl round the bones of death; and ask the rav'nous snake
Where she gets poison: and the wing'd eagle why he loves the sun
And then tell me the thoughts of man, that have been hid of old.

408   [Plate 10, lines 3–29]

The moment of desire! the moment of desire! The virgin
That pines for man; shall awaken her womb to enormous joys
In the secret shadows of her chamber; the youth shut up from
The lustful joy. shall forget to generate. and create an amorous image
In the shadows of his curtains and in the folds of his silent pillow.
Are not these the places of religion? the rewards of continence?
The self enjoyings of self denial? Why dost thou seek religion?
Is it because acts are not lovely, that thou seekest solitude,
Where the horrible darkness is impressed with reflections of desire.

Father of Jealousy. be thou accursed from the earth!
Why hast thou taught my Theotormon this accursed thing?
Till beauty fades from off my shoulders darken'd and cast out,
A solitary shadow wailing on the margin of non-entity.

I cry, Love! Love! Love! happy happy Love! free as the mountain wind!
Can that be Love, that drinks another as a sponge drinks water?
That clouds with jealousy his nights, with weepings all the day:

To spin a web of age around him. grey and hoary! dark!
Till his eyes sicken at the fruit that hangs. before his sight.
Such is self-love that envies all! a creeping skeleton
With lamplike eyes watching around the frozen marriage bed.

But silken nets and traps of adamant will Oothoon spread,
And catch for thee girls of mild silver, or of furious gold;
I'll lie beside thee on a bank and view their wanton play
In lovely copulation bliss on bliss with Theotormon:
Red as the rosy morning, lustful as the first born beam,
Oothoon shall view his dear delight, nor e'er with jealous cloud
Come in the heaven of generous love; nor selfish blightings bring.

409   from *Auguries of Innocence* [lines 1–54]

                To see a World in a Grain of Sand
                And a Heaven in a Wild Flower
                Hold Infinity in the palm of your hand
                And Eternity in an hour
                A Robin Red breast in a Cage
                Puts all Heaven in a Rage
                A dove house filld with doves and Pigeons
                Shudders Hell thro all its regions
                A dog starvd at his Masters Gate
                Predicts the ruin of the State
                A Horse misusd upon the Road
                Calls to Heaven for Human blood
                Each outcry of the hunted Hare
                A fibre from the Brain does tear
                A Skylark wounded in the wing
                A Cherubim does cease to sing
                The Game Cock clipd and armd for fight
                Does the Rising Sun affright
                Every Wolfs and Lions howl
                Raises from Hell a Human Soul
                The wild deer wandring here and there
                Keeps the Human Soul from Care
                The Lamb misusd breeds Public strife
                And yet forgives the Butchers Knife
                The Bat that flits at close of Eve
                Has left the Brain that wont Believe
                The Owl that calls upon the Night
                Speaks the Unbelievers fright
                He who shall hurt the little Wren
                Shall never be belovd by Men

He who the Ox to wrath has movd
Shall never be by Woman lovd
The wanton Boy that kills the Fly
Shall feel the Spiders enmity
He who torments the Chafers sprite
Weaves a Bower in endless Night
The Catterpiller on the Leaf
Repeats to thee thy Mothers grief
Kill not the Moth nor Butterfly
For the Last Judgment draweth nigh
He who shall train the Horse to War
Shall never pass the Polar Bar
The Beggers Dog & Widows Cat
Feed them and thou wilt grow fat
The Gnat that sings his Summers song
Poison gets from Slanders tongue
The poison of the Snake and Newt
Is the sweat of Envys Foot
The Poison of the Honey Bee
Is the Artists Jealousy
The Princes Robes and Beggars Rags
Are Toadstools on the Misers Bags
A truth thats told with bad intent
Beats all the Lies you can invent

410   from *Milton*

And did those feet in ancient time.
Walk upon Englands mountains green:
And was the holy Lamb of God,
On Englands pleasant pastures seen!

And did the Countenance Divine,
Shine forth upon our clouded hills?
And was Jerusalem builded here,
Among these dark Satanic Mills?

Bring me my Bow of burning gold:
Bring me my Arrows of desire:
Bring me my Spear: O clouds unfold!
Bring me my Chariot of fire!

I will not cease from Mental Fight,
Nor shall my Sword sleep in my hand:
Till we have built Jerusalem,
In Englands green and pleasant Land.

411   *To the Accuser who is the God of this World*

> Truly My Satan thou art but a Dunce
> And dost not know the Garment from the Man
> Every Harlot was a Virgin once
> Nor canst thou ever change Kate into Nan
>
> Tho thou art Worshipd by the Names Divine
> Of Jesus and Jehovah: thou art still
> The Son of Morn in weary Nights decline
> The lost Travellers Dream under the Hill

MARY ROBINSON

1758–1800

412   *January, 1795*

> Pavement slipp'ry, people sneezing,
> Lords in ermine, beggars freezing;
> Titled gluttons dainties carving,
> Genius in a garret starving.
>
> Lofty mansions, warm and spacious;
> Courtiers cringing and voracious;
> Misers scarce the wretched heeding;
> Gallant soldiers fighting, bleeding.
>
> Wives who laugh at passive spouses;
> Theatres, and meeting-houses;
> Balls, where simp'ring misses languish;
> Hospitals, and groans of anguish.
>
> Arts and sciences bewailing;
> Commerce drooping, credit failing;
> Placemen mocking subjects loyal;
> Separations, weddings royal.
>
> Authors who can't earn a dinner;
> Many a subtle rogue a winner;
> Fugitives for shelter seeking;
> Misers hoarding, tradesmen breaking.
>
> Taste and talents quite deserted;
> All the laws of truth perverted;
> Arrogance o'er merit soaring;
> Merit silently deploring.

Ladies gambling night and morning;
Fools the works of genius scorning;
Ancient dames for girls mistaken,
Youthful damsels quite forsaken.

Some in luxury delighting;
More in talking than in fighting;
Lovers old, and beaux decrepid;
Lordlings empty and insipid.

Poets, painters, and musicians;
Lawyers, doctors, politicians:
Pamphlets, newspapers, and odes,
Seeking fame by diff 'rent roads.

Gallant souls with empty purses,
Gen'rals only fit for nurses;
School-boys, smit with martial spirit,
Taking place of vet'ran merit.

Honest men who can't get places,
Knaves who shew unblushing faces;
Ruin hasten'd, peace retarded;
Candour spurn'd, and art rewarded.

ROBERT BURNS
1759–1796

413   *Address to the Unco Guid, or the Rigidly Righteous*

> *My son, these maxims make a rule,*
> *And lump them ay thegither;*
> *The* Rigid Righteous *is a fool,*
> *The* Rigid Wise *anither;*
> *The cleanest corn that e'er was dights*   5
> *May hae some pyles o' caff in;*
> *So ne'er a fellow-creature slight*
> *For random fits o' daffin.*
>   Solomon. Eccles. 7: 1–6

O ye wha are sae guid yoursel,
    Sae pious and sae holy,
Ye've nought to do but mark and tell
    Your neebours' fauts and folly!

413: Epigraph 5 *dight*] cleaned from chaff   Epigraph 8 *daffin*] merriment

Thy voice, nor catch from thy wild eyes these gleams
Of past existence—wilt thou then forget
That on the banks of this delightful stream
We stood together; and that I, so long
A worshipper of Nature, hither came
Unwearied in that service: rather say
With warmer love—oh! with far deeper zeal
Of holier love. Nor wilt thou then forget,
That after many wanderings, many years
Of absence, these steep woods and lofty cliffs,
And this green pastoral landscape, were to me
More dear, both for themselves and for thy sake!

429   A slumber did my spirit seal;
            I had no human fears:
        She seemed a thing that could not feel
            The touch of earthly years.

        No motion has she now, no force;
            She neither hears nor sees;
        Rolled round in earth's diurnal course,
            With rocks, and stones, and trees.

430   *Influence of Natural Objects in Calling Forth*
    and Strengthening the Imagination in Boyhood
                and Early Youth

        Wisdom and Spirit of the universe!
        Thou Soul, that art the Eternity of thought!
        And giv'st to forms and images a breath
        And everlasting motion! not in vain,
        By day or star-light, thus from my first dawn
        Of childhood didst thou intertwine for me
        The passions that build up our human soul;
        Not with the mean and vulgar works of Man;
        But with high objects, with enduring things,
        With life and nature; purifying thus
        The elements of feeling and of thought,
        And sanctifying by such discipline
        Both pain and fear,—until we recognize
        A grandeur in the beatings of the heart.

Nor was this fellowship vouchsafed to me
With stinted kindness. In November days,
When vapours rolling down the valleys made
A lonely scene more lonesome; among woods
At noon; and 'mid the calm of summer nights,
When, by the margin of the trembling lake,
Beneath the gloomy hills, homeward I went
In solitude, such intercourse was mine:
Mine was it in the fields both day and night,
And by the waters, all the summer long.
And in the frosty season, when the sun
Was set, and, visible for many a mile,
The cottage-windows through the twilight blazed,
I heeded not the summons: happy time
It was indeed for all of us; for me
It was a time of rapture! Clear and loud
The village-clock tolled six—I wheeled about,
Proud and exulting like an untired horse
That cares not for his home.—All shod with steel
We hissed along the polished ice, in games
Confederate, imitative of the chase
And woodland pleasures,—the resounding horn,
The pack loud-chiming, and the hunted hare.
So through the darkness and the cold we flew,
And not a voice was idle: with the din
Smitten, the precipices rang aloud;
The leafless trees and every icy crag
Tinkled like iron; while far-distant hills
Into the tumult sent an alien sound
Of melancholy, not unnoticed while the stars,
Eastward, were sparkling clear, and in the west
The orange sky of evening died away.

Not seldom from the uproar I retired
Into a silent bay, or sportively
Glanced sideway, leaving the tumultuous throng,
To cut across the reflex of a star;
Image, that, flying still before me, gleamed
Upon the glassy plain: and oftentimes,
When we had given our bodies to the wind,
And all the shadowy banks on either side
Came sweeping through the darkness, spinning still
The rapid line of motion, then at once
Have I, reclining back upon my heels,
Stopped short; yet still the solitary cliffs
Wheeled by me—even as if the earth had rolled
With visible motion her diurnal round!

Behind me did they stretch in solemn train,
Feebler and feebler, and I stood and watched
Till all was tranquil as a summer sea.

431

Composed Upon Westminster Bridge, September 3, 1802

Earth has not anything to show more fair:
Dull would he be of soul who could pass by
A sight so touching in its majesty:
This City now doth, like a garment, wear
The beauty of the morning; silent, bare,
Ships, towers, domes, theatres, and temples lie
Open unto the fields, and to the sky;
All bright and glittering in the smokeless air.
Never did sun more beautifully steep
In his first splendour, valley, rock, or hill;
Ne'er saw I, never felt, a calm so deep!
The river glideth at his own sweet will:
Dear God! the very houses seem asleep;
And all that mighty heart is lying still!

432

Ode: Intimations of Immortality from Recollections of Early Childhood

The Child is Father of the Man;
And I could wish my days to be
Bound each to each by natural piety.

I

There was a time when meadow, grove, and stream,
The earth, and every common sight,
To me did seem
Apparelled in celestial light,
The glory and the freshness of a dream.
It is not now as it hath been of yore;—
Turn wheresoe'er I may,
By night or day,
The things which I have seen I now can see no more.

II

The Rainbow comes and goes,
And lovely is the Rose;
The Moon doth with delight

Look round her when the heavens are bare;
   Waters on a starry night
   Are beautiful and fair;
The sunshine is a glorious birth;
But yet I know, where'er I go,
That there hath past away a glory from the earth.

III

Now, while the birds thus sing a joyous song,
   And while the young lambs bound
   As to the tabor's sound,
To me alone there came a thought of grief:
A timely utterance gave that thought relief,
   And I again am strong:
The cataracts blow their trumpets from the steep;
No more shall grief of mine the season wrong;
I hear the Echoes through the mountains throng,
The Winds come to me from the fields of sleep,
      And all the earth is gay;
         Land and sea
      Give themselves up to jollity,
      And with the heart of May
      Doth every Beast keep holiday;—
         Thou Child of Joy,
Shout round me, let me hear thy shouts, thou happy
         Shepherd-boy!

IV

Ye blessèd Creatures, I have heard the call
   Ye to each other make; I see
The heavens laugh with you in your jubilee;
   My heart is at your festival,
   My head hath its coronal,
The fulness of your bliss, I feel—I feel it all.
   Oh evil day! if I were sullen
   While Earth herself is adorning,
      This sweet May-morning,
   And the Children are culling
      On every side,
   In a thousand valleys far and wide,
   Fresh flowers; while the sun shines warm,
And the Babe leaps up on his Mother's arm:—
   I hear, I hear, with joy I hear!
   —But there's a Tree, of many, one,
A single Field which I have looked upon,
Both of them speak of something that is gone:

The Pansy at my feet
Doth the same tale repeat:
Whither is fled the visionary gleam?
Where is it now, the glory and the dream?

V

Our birth is but a sleep and a forgetting:
The Soul that rises with us, our life's Star,
    Hath had elsewhere its setting,
        And cometh from afar:
    Not in entire forgetfulness,
    And not in utter nakedness,
But trailing clouds of glory do we come
    From God, who is our home:
Heaven lies about us in our infancy!
Shades of the prison-house begin to close
    Upon the growing Boy,
But He beholds the light, and whence it flows,
    He sees it in his joy;
The Youth, who daily farther from the east
    Must travel, still is Nature's Priest,
    And by the vision splendid
    Is on his way attended;
At length the Man perceives it die away,
And fade into the light of common day.

VI

Earth fills her lap with pleasures of her own;
Yearnings she hath in her own natural kind,
And, even with something of a Mother's mind,
    And no unworthy aim,
    The homely Nurse doth all she can
To make her Foster-child, her Inmate Man,
    Forget the glories he hath known,
And that imperial palace whence he came.

VII

Behold the Child among his new-born blisses,
A six years' Darling of a pigmy size!
See, where 'mid work of his own hand he lies,
Fretted by sallies of his mother's kisses,
With light upon him from his father's eyes!
See, at his feet, some little plan or chart,
Some fragment from his dream of human life,
Shaped by himself with newly-learnèd art;
    A wedding or a festival,

A mourning or a funeral;
   And this hath now his heart,
And unto this he frames his song:
   Then will he fit his tongue
To dialogues of business, love, or strife;
   But it will not be long
   Ere this be thrown aside,
   And with new joy and pride
The little Actor cons another part;
Filling from time to time his 'humorous stage'
With all the Persons, down to palsied Age,
That Life brings with her in her equipage;
   As if his whole vocation
   Were endless imitation.

VIII

Thou, whose exterior semblance doth belie
   Thy Soul's immensity;
Thou best Philosopher, who yet dost keep
Thy heritage, thou Eye among the blind,
That, deaf and silent, read'st the eternal deep,
Haunted for ever by the eternal mind,—
   Mighty Prophet! Seer blest!
   On whom those truths do rest,
Which we are toiling all our lives to find,
In darkness lost, the darkness of the grave;
Thou, over whom thy Immortality
Broods like the Day, a Master o'er a Slave,
A Presence which is not to be put by;
Thou little Child, yet glorious in the might
Of heaven-born freedom on thy being's height,
Why with such earnest pains dost thou provoke
The years to bring the inevitable yoke,
Thus blindly with thy blessedness at strife?
Full soon thy Soul shall have her earthly freight,
And custom lie upon thee with a weight,
Heavy as frost, and deep almost as life!

IX

   O joy! that in our embers
   Is something that doth live,
   That nature yet remembers
   What was so fugitive!
The thought of our past years in me doth breed
Perpetual benediction: not indeed
For that which is most worthy to be blest;

Delight and liberty, the simple creed
Of Childhood, whether busy or at rest,
With new-fledged hope still fluttering in his breast:—
    Not for these I raise
    The song of thanks and praise;
   But for those obstinate questionings
   Of sense and outward things,
   Fallings from us, vanishings;
   Blank misgivings of a Creature
Moving about in worlds not realized,
High instincts before which our mortal Nature
Did tremble like a guilty Thing surprised:
    But for those first affections,
    Those shadowy recollections,
   Which, be they what they may,
Are yet the fountain light of all our day,
Are yet a master light of all our seeing;
   Uphold us, cherish, and have power to make
Our noisy years seem moments in the being
Of the eternal Silence: truths that wake,
    To perish never;
Which neither listlessness, nor mad endeavour,
    Nor Man nor Boy,
Nor all that is at enmity with joy,
Can utterly abolish or destroy!
    Hence in a season of calm weather
    Though inland far we be,
Our Souls have sight of that immortal sea
    Which brought us hither,
    Can in a moment travel thither,
And see the Children sport upon the shore,
And hear the mighty waters rolling evermore.

X

Then sing, ye Birds, sing, sing a joyous song!
    And let the young Lambs bound
    As to the tabor's sound!
We in thought will join your throng,
    Ye that pipe and ye that play,
    Ye that through your hearts today
    Feel the gladness of the May!
What though the radiance which was once so bright
Be now for ever taken from my sight,
    Though nothing can bring back the hour
Of splendour in the grass, of glory in the flower;
    We will grieve not, rather find
    Strength in what remains behind;

In the primal sympathy
Which having been must ever be;
In the soothing thoughts that spring
Out of human suffering;
In the faith that looks through death,
In years that bring the philosophic mind.

XI

And O, ye Fountains, Meadows, Hills, and Groves,
Forebode not any severing of our loves!
Yet in my heart of hearts I feel your might;
I only have relinquished one delight
To live beneath your more habitual sway.
I love the Brooks which down their channels fret,
Even more than when I tripped lightly as they;
The innocent brightness of a new-born Day
        Is lovely yet;
The Clouds that gather round the setting sun
Do take a sober colouring from an eye
That hath kept watch o'er man's mortality;
Another race hath been, and other palms are won.
Thanks to the human heart by which we live,
Thanks to its tenderness, its joys, and fears,
To me the meanest flower that blows can give
Thoughts that do often lie too deep for tears.

433

I wandered lonely as a cloud
That floats on high o'er vales and hills,
When all at once I saw a crowd,
A host, of golden daffodils;
Beside the lake, beneath the trees,
Fluttering and dancing in the breeze.

Continuous as the stars that shine
And twinkle on the milky way,
They stretched in never-ending line
Along the margin of a bay:
Ten thousand saw I at a glance,
Tossing their heads in sprightly dance.

The waves beside them danced; but they
Out-did the sparkling waves in glee:
A poet could not but be gay,
In such a jocund company:
I gazed—and gazed—but little thought
What wealth the show to me had brought:

For oft, when on my couch I lie
In vacant or in pensive mood,
They flash upon that inward eye
Which is the bliss of solitude;
And then my heart with pleasure fills,
And dances with the daffodils.

434   *The Solitary Reaper*

Behold her, single in the field,
Yon solitary Highland Lass!
Reaping and singing by herself;
Stop here, or gently pass!
Alone she cuts and binds the grain,
And sings a melancholy strain;
O listen! for the Vale profound
Is overflowing with the sound.

No Nightingale did ever chaunt
More welcome notes to weary bands
Of travellers in some shady haunt,
Among Arabian sands:
A voice so thrilling ne'er was heard
In spring-time from the Cuckoo-bird,
Breaking the silence of the seas
Among the farthest Hebrides.

Will no one tell me what she sings?—
Perhaps the plaintive numbers flow
For old, unhappy, far-off things,
And battles long ago:
Or is it some more humble lay,
Familiar matter of today?
Some natural sorrow, loss, or pain,
That has been, and may be again?

Whate'er the theme, the Maiden sang
As if her song could have no ending;
I saw her singing at her work,
And o'er the sickle bending;—
I listened, motionless and still;
And, as I mounted up the hill,
The music in my heart I bore,
Long after it was heard no more.

SIR WALTER SCOTT
1771–1832

435　　　　from *The Lay of the Last Minstrel*
　　　　　　[Canto Sixth, lines 1–16]

Breathes there the man with soul so dead,
Who never to himself hath said,
　　　This is my own, my native land!
Whose heart hath ne'er within him burn'd,
As home his footsteps he hath turn'd
　　　From wandering on a foreign strand!
If such there breathe, go, mark him well;
For him no Minstrel raptures swell;
High though his titles, proud his name,
Boundless his wealth as wish can claim;
Despite those titles, power, and pelf,
The wretch, concentred all in self,
Living, shall forfeit fair renown,
And, doubly dying, shall go down
To the vile dust, from whence he sprung,
Unwept, unhonour'd, and unsung.

436　　　　　　　Proud Maisie is in the wood,
　　　　　　　　　Walking so early;
　　　　　　　Sweet Robin sits on the bush,
　　　　　　　　　Singing so rarely.

　　　　　　　'Tell me, thou bonny bird,
　　　　　　　　　When shall I marry me?'
　　　　　　　'When six braw gentlemen
　　　　　　　　　Kirkward shall carry ye.'

　　　　　　　'Who makes the bridal bed,
　　　　　　　　　Birdie, say truly?'
　　　　　　　'The grey-headed sexton
　　　　　　　　　That delves the grave duly.

　　　　　　　'The glow-worm o'er grave and stone
　　　　　　　　　Shall light thee steady.
　　　　　　　The owl from the steeple sing,
　　　　　　　　　"Welcome, proud lady".'

437

Look not thou on beauty's charming,
Sit thou still when kings are arming,
Taste not when the wine-cup glistens,
Speak not when the people listens,
Stop thine ear against the singer,
From the red gold keep thy finger;
Vacant heart and hand and eye,
Easy live and quiet die.

SAMUEL TAYLOR COLERIDGE

1772–1834

438 *The Rime of the Ancient Mariner*

PART I

It is an ancient Mariner,
And he stoppeth one of three.
'By thy long grey beard and glittering eye,
Now wherefore stopp'st thou me?

The Bridegroom's doors are opened wide,
And I am next of kin;
The guests are met, the feast is set:
May'st hear the merry din.'

He holds him with his skinny hand,
'There was a ship,' quoth he.
'Hold off! unhand me, grey-beard loon!'
Eftsoons his hand dropt he.

He holds him with his glittering eye—
The Wedding-Guest stood still,
And listens like a three years' child:
The Mariner hath his will.

The Wedding-Guest sat on a stone:
He cannot choose but hear;
And thus spake on that ancient man,
The bright-eyed Mariner.

'The ship was cheered, the harbour cleared,
Merrily did we drop
Below the kirk, below the hill,
Below the lighthouse top.

The Sun came up upon the left,
Out of the sea came he!
And he shone bright, and on the right
Went down into the sea.

Higher and higher every day,
Till over the mast at noon—'
The Wedding-Guest here beat his breast,
For he heard the loud bassoon.

The bride hath paced into the hall,
Red as a rose is she;
Nodding their heads before her goes
The merry minstrelsy.

The Wedding-Guest he beat his breast,
Yet he cannot choose but hear;
And thus spake on that ancient man,
The bright-eyed Mariner.

'And now the Storm-blast came, and he
Was tyrannous and strong:
He struck with his o'ertaking wings,
And chased us south along.

With sloping masts and dipping prow,
As who pursued with yell and blow
Still treads the shadow of his foe,
And forward bends his head,
The ship drove fast, loud roared the blast,
And southward aye we fled.

And now there came both mist and snow,
And it grew wondrous cold:
And ice, mast-high, came floating by,
As green as emerald.

And through the drifts the snowy clifts
Did send a dismal sheen:
Nor shapes of men nor beasts we ken—
The ice was all between.

The ice was here, the ice was there,
The ice was all around:
It cracked and growled, and roared and howled,
Like noises in a swound!

At length did cross an Albatross,
Thorough the fog it came;
As if it had been a Christian soul,
We hailed it in God's name.

It ate the food it ne'er had eat,
And round and round it flew.
The ice did split with a thunder-fit;
The helmsman steered us through!

And a good south wind sprung up behind;
The Albatross did follow,
And every day, for food or play,
Came to the mariner's hollo!

In mist or cloud, on mast or shroud,
It perched for vespers nine;
Whiles all the night, through fog-smoke white,
Glimmered the white Moon-shine.'

'God save thee, ancient Mariner!
From the fiends, that plague thee thus!—
Why look'st thou so?'—With my cross-bow
I shot the ALBATROSS.

PART II

The Sun now rose upon the right:
Out of the sea came he,
Still hid in mist, and on the left
Went down into the sea.

And the good south wind still blew behind,
But no sweet bird did follow,
Nor any day for food or play
Came to the mariners' hollo!

And I had done a hellish thing,
And it would work 'em woe:
For all averred, I had killed the bird
That made the breeze to blow.
Ah wretch! said they, the bird to slay,
That made the breeze to blow!

Nor dim nor red, like God's own head,
The glorious Sun uprist:
Then all averred, I had killed the bird
That brought the fog and mist.
'Twas right, said they, such birds to slay,
That bring the fog and mist.

The fair breeze blew, the white foam flew,
The furrow followed free;
We were the first that ever burst
Into that silent sea.

Down dropt the breeze, the sails dropt down,
'Twas sad as sad could be;
And we did speak only to break
The silence of the sea!

All in a hot and copper sky,
The bloody Sun, at noon,
Right up above the mast did stand,
No bigger than the Moon.

Day after day, day after day,
We stuck, nor breath nor motion;
As idle as a painted ship
Upon a painted ocean.

Water, water, every where,
And all the boards did shrink;
Water, water, every where,
Nor any drop to drink.

The very deep did rot: O Christ!
That ever this should be!
Yea, slimy things did crawl with legs
Upon the slimy sea.

About, about, in reel and rout
The death-fires danced at night;
The water, like a witch's oils,
Burnt green, and blue and white.

And some in dreams assurèd were
Of the Spirit that plagued us so;
Nine fathom deep he had followed us
From the land of mist and snow.

And every tongue, through utter drought,
Was withered at the root;
We could not speak, no more than if
We had been choked with soot.

Ah! well a-day! what evil looks
Had I from old and young!
Instead of the cross, the Albatross
About my neck was hung.

PART III

There passed a weary time. Each throat
Was parched, and glazed each eye.

A weary time! a weary time!
How glazed each weary eye,
When looking westward, I beheld
A something in the sky.

At first it seemed a little speck,
And then it seemed a mist;
It moved and moved, and took at last
A certain shape, I wist.

A speck, a mist, a shape, I wist!
And still it neared and neared:
As if it dodged a water-sprite,
It plunged and tacked and veered.

With throats unslaked, with black lips baked,
We could nor laugh nor wail;
Through utter drought all dumb we stood!
I bit my arm, I sucked the blood,
And cried, A sail! a sail!

With throats unslaked, with black lips baked,
Agape they heard me call:
Gramercy! they for joy did grin,
And all at once their breath drew in,
As they were drinking all.

See! see! (I cried) she tacks no more!
Hither to work us weal;
Without a breeze, without a tide,
She steadies with upright keel!

The western wave was all a-flame.
The day was well nigh done!
Almost upon the western wave
Rested the broad bright Sun;
When that strange shape drove suddenly
Betwixt us and the Sun.

And straight the Sun was flecked with bars,
(Heaven's Mother send us grace!)
As if through a dungeon-grate he peered
With broad and burning face.

Alas! (thought I, and my heart beat loud)
How fast she nears and nears!
Are those *her* sails that glance in the Sun,
Like restless gossameres?

Are those *her* ribs through which the Sun
Did peer, as through a grate?
And is that Woman all her crew?
Is that a DEATH? and are there two?
Is DEATH that woman's mate?

Her lips were red, *her* looks were free,
Her locks were yellow as gold:
Her skin was as white as leprosy,
The Night-mare LIFE-IN-DEATH was she,
Who thicks man's blood with cold.

The naked hulk alongside came,
And the twain were casting dice;
'The game is done! I've won! I've won!'
Quoth she, and whistles thrice.

The Sun's rim dips; the stars rush out:
At one stride comes the dark;
With far-heard whisper, o'er the sea,
Off shot the spectre-bark.

We listened and looked sideways up!
Fear at my heart, as at a cup,
My life-blood seemed to sip!
The stars were dim, and thick the night,
The steersman's face by his lamp gleamed white;
From the sails the dew did drip—
Till clomb above the eastern bar
The hornèd Moon, with one bright star
Within the nether tip.

One after one, by the star-dogged Moon,
Too quick for groan or sigh,
Each turned his face with a ghastly pang,
And cursed me with his eye.

Four times fifty living men,
(And I heard nor sigh nor groan)
With heavy thump, a lifeless lump,
They dropped down one by one.

The souls did from their bodies fly,—
They fled to bliss or woe!
And every soul, it passed me by,
Like the whizz of my cross-bow!

Part IV

'I fear thee, ancient Mariner!
I fear thy skinny hand!
And thou art long, and lank, and brown,
As is the ribbed sea-sand.

I fear thee and thy glittering eye,
And thy skinny hand, so brown.'—
Fear not, fear not, thou Wedding-Guest!
This body dropt not down.

Alone, alone, all, all alone,
Alone on a wide wide sea!
And never a saint took pity on
My soul in agony.

The many men, so beautiful!
And they all dead did lie:
And a thousand thousand slimy things
Lived on; and so did I.

I looked upon the rotting sea,
And drew my eyes away;
I looked upon the rotting deck,
And there the dead men lay.

I looked to heaven, and tried to pray;
But or ever a prayer had gusht,
A wicked whisper came, and made
My heart as dry as dust.

I closed my lids, and kept them close,
And the balls like pulses beat;
For the sky and the sea, and the sea and the sky
Lay like a load on my weary eye,
And the dead were at my feet.

The cold sweat melted from their limbs,
Nor rot nor reek did they:
The look with which they looked on me
Had never passed away.

An orphan's curse would drag to hell
A spirit from on high;
But oh! more horrible than that
Is the curse in a dead man's eye!
Seven days, seven nights, I saw that curse,
And yet I could not die.

The moving Moon went up the sky,
And no where did abide:
Softly she was going up,
And a star or two beside—

Her beams bemocked the sultry main,
Like April hoar-frost spread;
But where the ship's huge shadow lay,
The charmèd water burnt alway
A still and awful red.

Beyond the shadow of the ship,
I watched the water-snakes:
They moved in tracks of shining white,
And when they reared, the elfish light
Fell off in hoary flakes.

Within the shadow of the ship
I watched their rich attire:
Blue, glossy green, and velvet black,
They coiled and swam; and every track
Was a flash of golden fire.

O happy living things! no tongue
Their beauty might declare:
A spring of love gushed from my heart,
And I blessed them unaware:
Sure my kind saint took pity on me,
And I blessed them unaware.

The self-same moment I could pray;
And from my neck so free
The Albatross fell off, and sank
Like lead into the sea.

PART V

Oh sleep! it is a gentle thing,
Beloved from pole to pole!
To Mary Queen the praise be given!
She sent the gentle sleep from Heaven,
That slid into my soul.

The silly buckets on the deck,
That had so long remained,
I dreamt that they were filled with dew;
And when I awoke, it rained.

My lips were wet, my throat was cold,
My garments all were dank;
Sure I had drunken in my dreams,
And still my body drank.

I moved, and could not feel my limbs:
I was so light—almost
I thought that I had died in sleep,
And was a blessèd ghost.

And soon I heard a roaring wind:
It did not come anear;
But with its sound it shook the sails,
That were so thin and sere.

The upper air burst into life!
And a hundred fire-flags sheen,
To and fro they were hurried about!
And to and fro, and in and out,
The wan stars danced between.

And the coming wind did roar more loud,
And the sails did sigh like sedge;
And the rain poured down from one black cloud;
The Moon was at its edge.

The thick black cloud was cleft, and still
The Moon was at its side:
Like waters shot from some high crag,
The lightning fell with never a jag,
A river steep and wide.

The loud wind never reached the ship,
Yet now the ship moved on!
Beneath the lightning and the Moon
The dead men gave a groan.

They groaned, they stirred, they all uprose,
Nor spake, nor moved their eyes;
It had been strange, even in a dream,
To have seen those dead men rise.

The helmsman steered, the ship moved on;
Yet never a breeze up-blew;
The mariners all 'gan work the ropes,
Where they were wont to do;
They raised their limbs like lifeless tools—
We were a ghastly crew.

The body of my brother's son
Stood by me, knee to knee:
The body and I pulled at one rope,
But he said nought to me.

'I fear thee, ancient Mariner!'
Be calm, thou Wedding-Guest!
'Twas not those souls that fled in pain,
Which to their corses came again,
But a troop of spirits blest:

For when it dawned—they dropped their arms,
And clustered round the mast;
Sweet sounds rose slowly through their mouths,
And from their bodies passed.

Around, around, flew each sweet sound,
Then darted to the Sun;
Slowly the sounds came back again,
Now mixed, now one by one.

Sometimes a-dropping from the sky
I heard the sky-lark sing;
Sometimes all little birds that are,
How they seemed to fill the sea and air
With their sweet jargoning!

And now 'twas like all instruments,
Now like a lonely flute;
And now it is an angel's song,
That makes the heavens be mute.

It ceased; yet still the sails made on
A pleasant noise till noon,
A noise like of a hidden brook
In the leafy month of June,
That to the sleeping woods all night
Singeth a quiet tune.

Till noon we quietly sailed on,
Yet never a breeze did breathe:
Slowly and smoothly went the ship,
Moved onward from beneath.

Under the keel nine fathom deep,
From the land of mist and snow,
The spirit slid: and it was he
That made the ship to go.
The sails at noon left off their tune,
And the ship stood still also.

The Sun, right up above the mast,
Had fixed her to the ocean:
But in a minute she 'gan stir,
With a short uneasy motion—
Backwards and forwards half her length
With a short uneasy motion.

Then like a pawing horse let go,
She made a sudden bound:
It flung the blood into my head,
And I fell down in a swound.

How long in that same fit I lay,
I have not to declare;
But ere my living life returned,
I heard and in my soul discerned
Two voices in the air.

'Is it he?' quoth one, 'Is this the man?
By him who died on cross,
With his cruel bow he laid full low
The harmless Albatross.

The spirit who bideth by himself
In the land of mist and snow,
He loved the bird that loved the man
Who shot him with his bow.'

The other was a softer voice,
As soft as honey-dew:
Quoth he, 'The man hath penance done,
And penance more will do.'

PART VI

FIRST VOICE
'But tell me, tell me! speak again,
Thy soft response renewing—
What makes that ship drive on so fast?
What is the ocean doing?'

SECOND VOICE
'Still as a slave before his lord,
The ocean hath no blast;
His great bright eye most silently
Up to the Moon is cast—

If he may know which way to go;
For she guides him smooth or grim.
See, brother, see! how graciously
She looketh down on him.'

FIRST VOICE

'But why drives on that ship so fast,
Without or wave or wind?'

SECOND VOICE

'The air is cut away before,
And closes from behind.

Fly, brother, fly! more high, more high!
Or we shall be belated:
For slow and slow that ship will go,
When the Mariner's trance is abated.'

I woke, and we were sailing on
As in a gentle weather:
'Twas night, calm night, the moon was high;
The dead men stood together.

All stood together on the deck,
For a charnel-dungeon fitter:
All fixed on me their stony eyes,
That in the Moon did glitter.

The pang, the curse, with which they died,
Had never passed away:
I could not draw my eyes from theirs,
Nor turn them up to pray.

And now this spell was snapt: once more
I viewed the ocean green,
And looked far forth, yet little saw
Of what had else been seen—

Like one, that on a lonesome road
Doth walk in fear and dread,
And having once turned round walks on,
And turns no more his head;
Because he knows, a frightful fiend
Doth close behind him tread.

But soon there breathed a wind on me,
Nor sound nor motion made:
Its path was not upon the sea,
In ripple or in shade.

It raised my hair, it fanned my cheek
Like a meadow-gale of spring—
It mingled strangely with my fears,
Yet it felt like a welcoming.

Swiftly, swiftly flew the ship,
Yet she sailed softly too:
Sweetly, sweetly blew the breeze—
On me alone it blew.

Oh! dream of joy! is this indeed
The light-house top I see?
Is this the hill? is this the kirk?
Is this mine own countree?

We drifted o'er the harbour-bar,
And I with sobs did pray—
O let me be awake, my God!
Or let me sleep alway.

The harbour-bay was clear as glass,
So smoothly it was strewn!
And on the bay the moonlight lay,
And the shadow of the Moon.

The rock shone bright, the kirk no less,
That stands above the rock:
The moonlight steeped in silentness
The steady weathercock.

And the bay was white with silent light,
Till rising from the same,
Full many shapes, that shadows were,
In crimson colours came.

A little distance from the prow
Those crimson shadows were:
I turned my eyes upon the deck—
Oh, Christ! what saw I there!

Each corse lay flat, lifeless and flat,
And, by the holy rood!
A man all light, a seraph-man,
On every corse there stood.

This seraph-band, each waved his hand:
It was a heavenly sight!
They stood as signals to the land,
Each one a lovely light;

This seraph-band, each waved his hand,
No voice did they impart—
No voice; but oh! the silence sank
Like music on my heart.

But soon I heard the dash of oars,
I heard the Pilot's cheer;
My head was turned perforce away
And I saw a boat appear.

The Pilot and the Pilot's boy,
I heard them coming fast:
Dear Lord in Heaven! it was a joy
The dead men could not blast.

I saw a third—I heard his voice:
It is the Hermit good!
He singeth loud his godly hymns
That he makes in the wood.
He'll shrieve my soul, he'll wash away
The Albatross's blood.

Part VII

This Hermit good lives in that wood
Which slopes down to the sea.
How loudly his sweet voice he rears!
He loves to talk with marineres
That come from a far countree.

He kneels at morn, and noon, and eve—
He hath a cushion plump:
It is the moss that wholly hides
The rotted old oak-stump.

The skiff-boat neared: I heard them talk,
'Why, this is strange, I trow!
Where are those lights so many and fair,
That signal made but now?'

'Strange, by my faith!' the Hermit said—
'And they answered not our cheer!
The planks looked warped! and see those sails,
How thin they are and sere!
I never saw aught like to them,
Unless perchance it were

Brown skeletons of leaves that lag
My forest-brook along;
When the ivy-tod is heavy with snow,
And the owlet whoops to the wolf below,
That eats the she-wolf's young.'

'Dear Lord! it hath a fiendish look—
(The Pilot made reply)
I am a-feared'—'Push on, push on!'
Said the Hermit cheerily.

The boat came closer to the ship,
But I nor spake nor stirred;
The boat came close beneath the ship,
And straight a sound was heard.

Under the water it rumbled on,
Still louder and more dread:
It reached the ship, it split the bay;
The ship went down like lead.

Stunned by that loud and dreadful sound,
Which sky and ocean smote,
Like one that hath been seven days drowned
My body lay afloat;
But swift as dreams, myself I found
Within the Pilot's boat.

Upon the whirl, where sank the ship,
The boat spun round and round;
And all was still, save that the hill
Was telling of the sound.

I moved my lips—the Pilot shrieked
And fell down in a fit;
The holy Hermit raised his eyes,
And prayed where he did sit.

I took the oars: the Pilot's boy,
Who now doth crazy go,
Laughed loud and long, and all the while
His eyes went to and fro.
'Ha! ha!' quoth he, 'full plain I see,
The Devil knows how to row.'

And now, all in my own countree,
I stood on the firm land!
The Hermit stepped forth from the boat,
And scarcely he could stand.

'O shrieve me, shrieve me, holy man!'
The Hermit crossed his brow.
'Say quick,' quoth he, 'I bid thee say—
What manner of man art thou?'

Forthwith this frame of mine was wrenched
With a woful agony,
Which forced me to begin my tale;
And then it left me free.

Since then, at an uncertain hour,
That agony returns:
And till my ghastly tale is told,
This heart within me burns.

I pass, like night, from land to land;
I have strange power of speech;
That moment that his face I see,
I know the man that must hear me:
To him my tale I teach.

What loud uproar bursts from that door!
The wedding-guests are there:
But in the garden-bower the bride
And bride-maids singing are:
And hark the little vesper bell,
Which biddeth me to prayer!

O Wedding-Guest! this soul hath been
Alone on a wide wide sea:
So lonely 'twas, that God himself
Scarce seemèd there to be.

O sweeter than the marriage-feast,
'Tis sweeter far to me,
To walk together to the kirk
With a goodly company!—

To walk together to the kirk,
And all together pray,
While each to his great Father bends,
Old men, and babes, and loving friends
And youths and maidens gay!

Farewell, farewell! but this I tell
To thee, thou Wedding-Guest!
He prayeth well, who loveth well
Both man and bird and beast.

He prayeth best, who loveth best
All things both great and small;
For the dear God who loveth us,
He made and loveth all.

The Mariner, whose eye is bright,
Whose beard with age is hoar,
Is gone: and now the Wedding-Guest
Turned from the bridegroom's door.

He went like one that hath been stunned,
And is of sense forlorn:
A sadder and a wiser man,
He rose the morrow morn.

439 *Kubla Khan*

In Xanadu did Kubla Khan
A stately pleasure-dome decree:
Where Alph, the sacred river, ran
Through caverns measureless to man
 Down to a sunless sea.
So twice five miles of fertile ground
With walls and towers were girdled round:
And there were gardens bright with sinuous rills,
Where blossomed many an incense-bearing tree;
And here were forests ancient as the hills,
Enfolding sunny spots of greenery.
But oh! that deep romantic chasm which slanted
Down the green hill athwart a cedarn cover!
A savage place! as holy and enchanted
As e'er beneath a waning moon was haunted
By woman wailing for her demon-lover!
And from this chasm, with ceaseless turmoil seething,
As if this earth in fast thick pants were breathing,
A mighty fountain momently was forced:
Amid whose swift half-intermitted burst
Huge fragments vaulted like rebounding hail,
Or chaffy grain beneath the thresher's flail:
And 'mid these dancing rocks at once and ever
It flung up momently the sacred river.
Five miles meandering with a mazy motion
Through wood and dale the sacred river ran,
Then reached the caverns measureless to man,
And sank in tumult to a lifeless ocean:
And 'mid this tumult Kubla heard from far
Ancestral voices prophesying war!
 The shadow of the dome of pleasure
 Floated midway on the waves;
 Where was heard the mingled measure
 From the fountain and the caves.
It was a miracle of rare device,
A sunny pleasure-dome with caves of ice!

 A damsel with a dulcimer
 In a vision once I saw:

It was an Abyssinian maid,
And on her dulcimer she played,
Singing of Mount Abora.
Could I revive within me
Her symphony and song,
To such a deep delight 'twould win me,
That with music loud and long,
I would build that dome in air,
That sunny dome! those caves of ice!
And all who heard should see them there,
And all should cry, Beware! Beware!
His flashing eyes, his floating hair!
Weave a circle round him thrice,
And close your eyes with holy dread,
For he on honey-dew hath fed,
And drunk the milk of Paradise.

WALTER SAVAGE LANDOR

1775–1864

440   Stand close around, ye Stygian set,
              With Dirce in one boat conveyed!
        Or Charon, seeing, may forget
              That he is old and she a shade.

441   Past ruin'd Ilion Helen lives,
              Alcestis rises from the shades;
        Verse calls them forth; 'tis verse that gives
              Immortal youth to mortal maids.

        Soon shall Oblivion's deepening veil
              Hide all the peopled hills you see,
        The gay, the proud, while lovers hail
              In distant ages you and me.

        The tear for fading beauty check,
              For passing glory cease to sigh;
        One form shall rise above the wreck,
              One name, Ianthe, shall not die.

442   Yes; I write verses now and then,
            But blunt and flaccid is my pen,
            No longer talkt of by young men
                As rather clever:

In the last quarter are my eyes,
You see it by their form and size;
Is it not time then to be wise?
    Or now or never.

Fairest that ever sprang from Eve!
While Time allows the short reprieve,
Just look at me! would you believe
    'Twas once a lover?

I can not clear the five-bar gate,
But, trying first its timber's state,
Climb stiffly up, take breath, and wait
    To trundle over.

Thro' gallopade I can not swing
The entangling blooms of Beauty's spring:
I can not say the tender thing,
    Be 't true or false,

And am beginning to opine
Those girls are only half-divine
Whose waists yon wicked boys entwine
    In giddy waltz.

I fear that arm above that shoulder,
I wish them wiser, graver, older,
Sedater, and no harm if colder
    And panting less.

Ah! people were not half so wild
In former days, when, starchly mild,
Upon her high-heel'd Essex smiled
    The brave Queen Bess.

443   *Dying Speech of an Old Philosopher*

I strove with none, for none was worth my strife:
    Nature I loved, and, next to Nature, Art:
I warm'd both hands before the fire of Life;
    It sinks; and I am ready to depart.

444   *Age*

Death, tho I see him not, is near
And grudges me my eightieth year.

Now, I would give him all these last
For one that fifty have run past.
Ah! he strikes all things, all alike,
But bargains: those he will not strike.

445   *Hearts-Ease*

There is a flower I wish to wear,
   But not until first worne by you . . .
Hearts-ease . . . of all Earth's flowers most rare;
   Bring it; and bring enough for two.

446   *A Foreign Ruler*

He says, *My reign is peace,* so slays
   A thousand in the dead of night.
Are you all happy now? he says,
   And those he leaves behind cry *quite.*
He swears he will have no contention,
   And sets all nations by the ears;
He shouts aloud, *No intervention!*
   Invades, and drowns them all in tears.

CHARLES LAMB

1775–1834

447   *The Old Familiar Faces*

Where are they gone, the old familiar faces?

I had a mother, but she died, and left me,
Died prematurely in a day of horrors—
All, all are gone, the old familiar faces.

I have had playmates, I have had companions,
In my days of childhood, in my joyful school-days,
All, all are gone, the old familiar faces.

I have been laughing, I have been carousing,
Drinking late, sitting late, with my bosom cronies,
All, all are gone, the old familiar faces.

I loved a love once, fairest among women;
Closed are her doors on me, I must not see her—
All, all are gone, the old familiar faces.

I have a friend, a kinder friend has no man;
Like an ingrate, I left my friend abruptly;
Left him, to muse on the old familiar faces.

Ghost-like, I paced round the haunts of my childhood.
Earth seemed a desert I was bound to traverse,
Seeking to find the old familiar faces.

Friend of my bosom, thou more than a brother,
Why wert not thou born in my father's dwelling?
So might we talk of the old familiar faces—

How some they have died, and some they have left me,
And some are taken from me; all are departed;
All, all are gone, the old familiar faces.

448   *Parental Recollections*

A child's a plaything for an hour;
    Its pretty tricks we try
For that or for a longer space;
    Then tire, and lay it by.

But I knew one, that to itself
    All seasons could controul;
That would have mock'd the sense of pain
    Out of a grieved soul.

Thou straggler into loving arms,
    Young climber up of knees,
When I forget thy thousand ways,
    Then life and all shall cease.

JANE TAYLOR

1783–1824

449   *The Star*

Twinkle, twinkle, little star,
How I wonder what you are!
Up above the world so high,
Like a diamond in the sky.

When the blazing sun is gone,
When he nothing shines upon,
Then you show your little light,
Twinkle, twinkle, all the night.

Then the traveller in the dark,
Thanks you for your tiny spark!
He could not see which way to go,
If you did not twinkle so.

In the dark blue sky you keep,
And often through my curtains peep,
For you never shut your eye,
Till the sun is in the sky.

As your bright and tiny spark
Lights the traveller in the dark,
Though I know not what you are,
Twinkle, twinkle, little star.

LEIGH HUNT

1784–1859

450   *Rondeau*

Jenny kissed me when we met,
    Jumping from the chair she sat in;
Time, you thief, who love to get
    Sweets into your list, put that in:
Say I'm weary, say I'm sad,
    Say that health and wealth have missed me,
Say I'm growing old, but add,
    Jenny kissed me.

THOMAS LOVE PEACOCK

1785–1866

451   *Rich and Poor*
            or, Saint and Sinner

The poor man's sins are glaring;
In the face of ghostly warning
        He is caught in the fact
        Of an overt act—
Buying greens on Sunday morning.

The rich man's sins are hidden
In the pomp of wealth and station;
 And escape the sight
 Of the children of light,
Who are wise in their generation.

The rich man has a kitchen,
And cooks to dress his dinner;
 The poor who would roast
 To the baker's must post,
And thus becomes a sinner.

The rich man has a cellar,
And a ready butler by him;
 The poor must steer
 For his pint of beer
Where the saint can't choose but spy him.

The rich man's painted windows
Hide the concerts of the quality;
 The poor can but share
 A crack'd fiddle in the air,
Which offends all sound morality.

The rich man is invisible
In the crowd of his gay society;
 But the poor man's delight
 Is a sore in the sight,
And a stench in the nose of piety.

The rich man has a carriage
Where no rude eye can flout him;
 The poor man's bane
 Is a third-class train,
With the day-light all about him.

The rich man goes out yachting
Where sanctity can't pursue him;
 The poor goes afloat
 In a fourpenny boat,
Where the bishops groan to view him.

GEORGE GORDON, LORD BYRON

1788–1824

452 *She Walks in Beauty*

She walks in beauty, like the night
　Of cloudless climes and starry skies;
And all that's best of dark and bright
　Meet in her aspect and her eyes:
Thus mellow'd to that tender light
　Which heaven to gaudy day denies.

One shade the more, one ray the less,
　Had half impair'd the nameless grace
Which waves in every raven tress,
　Or softly lightens o'er her face;
Where thoughts serenely sweet express
　How pure, how dear their dwelling place.

And on that cheek, and o'er that brow,
　So soft, so calm, yet eloquent,
The smiles that win, the tints that glow,
　But tell of days in goodness spent,
A mind at peace with all below,
　A heart whose love is innocent!

453 So, we'll go no more a roving
　So late into the night,
Though the heart be still as loving,
　And the moon be still as bright.

For the sword outwears its sheath,
　And the soul wears out the breast,
And the heart must pause to breathe,
　And love itself have rest.

Though the night was made for loving,
　And the day returns too soon,
Yet we'll go no more a roving
　By the light of the moon.

454–6   from *Don Juan*

454   [unincorporated stanza; headpiece, 1832]

    I would to Heaven that I were so much Clay—
      As I am blood—bone—marrow, passion—feeling—
    Because at least the past were past away—
      And for the future—(but I write this reeling
    Having got drunk exceedingly to day
      So that I seem to stand upon the ceiling)
    I say—the future is a serious matter—
    And so—for Godsake—Hock and Soda water.

455   [Canto II, stanzas 61–78]

    Nine souls more went in her: the long-boat still
      Kept above water, with an oar for mast,
    Two blankets stitch'd together, answering ill
      Instead of sail, were to the oar made fast:
    Though every wave roll'd menacing to fill,
      And present peril all before surpass'd,
    They grieved for those who perish'd with the cutter,
    And also for the biscuit casks and butter.

    The sun rose red and fiery, a sure sign
      Of the continuance of the gale: to run
    Before the sea, until it should grow fine,
      Was all that for the present could be done:
    A few tea-spoonfuls of their rum and wine
      Was served out to the people, who begun
    To faint, and damaged bread wet through the bags,
    And most of them had little clothes but rags.

    They counted thirty, crowded in a space
      Which left scarce room for motion or exertion;
    They did their best to modify their case,
      One half sate up, though numb'd with the immersion,
    While t'other half were laid down in their place,
      At watch and watch; thus, shivering like the tertian
    Ague in its cold fit, they fill'd their boat,
    With nothing but the sky for a great coat.

    'Tis very certain the desire of life
      Prolongs it; this is obvious to physicians,
    When patients, neither plagued with friends nor wife,
      Survive through very desperate conditions,

Because they still can hope, nor shines the knife
   Nor shears of Atropos before their visions:
Despair of all recovery spoils longevity,
And makes men's miseries of alarming brevity.

'Tis said that persons living on annuities
   Are longer lived than others,—God knows why,
Unless to plague the grantors,—yet so true it is,
   That some, I really think, *do* never die;
Of any creditors the worst a Jew it is,
   And *that's* their mode of furnishing supply:
In my young days they lent me cash that way,
Which I found very troublesome to pay.

'Tis thus with people in an open boat,
   They live upon the love of life, and bear
More than can be believed, or even thought,
   And stand like rocks the tempest's wear and tear;
And hardship still has been the sailor's lot,
   Since Noah's ark went cruising here and there;
She had a curious crew as well as cargo,
Like the first old Greek privateer, the Argo.

But man is a carnivorous production,
   And must have meals, at least one meal a day;
He cannot live, like woodcocks, upon suction,
   But, like the shark and tiger, must have prey:
Although his anatomical construction
   Bears vegetables in a grumbling way,
Your labouring people think beyond all question,
Beef, veal, and mutton, better for digestion.

And thus it was with this our hapless crew,
   For on the third day there came on a calm,
And though at first their strength it might renew,
   And lying on their weariness like balm,
Lull'd them like turtles sleeping on the blue
   Of ocean, when they woke they felt a qualm,
And fell all ravenously on their provision,
Instead of hoarding it with due precision.

The consequence was easily foreseen—
   They ate up all they had, and drank their wine,
In spite of all remonstrances, and then
   On what, in fact, next day were they to dine?
They hoped the wind would rise, these foolish men!
   And carry them to shore; these hopes were fine,
But as they had but one oar, and that brittle,
It would have been more wise to save their victual.

The fourth day came, but not a breath of air,
   And Ocean slumber'd like an unwean'd child:
The fifth day, and their boat lay floating there,
   The sea and sky were blue, and clear, and mild—
With their one oar (I wish they had had a pair)
   What could they do? and hunger's rage grew wild:
So Juan's spaniel, spite of his entreating,
Was kill'd, and portion'd out for present eating.

On the sixth day they fed upon his hide,
   And Juan, who had still refused, because
The creature was his father's dog that died,
   Now feeling all the vulture in his jaws,
With some remorse received (though first denied)
   As a great favour one of the fore-paws,
Which he divided with Pedrillo, who
Devour'd it, longing for the other too.

The seventh day, and no wind—the burning sun
   Blister'd and scorch'd, and, stagnant on the sea,
They lay like carcases; and hope was none,
   Save in the breeze that came not; savagely
They glared upon each other—all was done,
   Water, and wine, and food,—and you might see
The longings of the cannibal arise
(Although they spoke not) in their wolfish eyes.

At length one whisper'd his companion, who
   Whisper'd another, and thus it went round,
And then into a hoarser murmur grew,
   An ominous, and wild, and desperate sound,
And when his comrade's thought each sufferer knew,
   'Twas but his own, suppress'd till now, he found:
And out they spoke of lots for flesh and blood,
And who should die to be his fellow's food.

But ere they came to this, they that day shared
   Some leathern caps, and what remain'd of shoes;
And then they look'd around them, and despair'd,
   And none to be the sacrifice would choose;
At length the lots were torn up, and prepared,
   But of materials that much shock the Muse—
Having no paper, for the want of better,
They took by force from Juan Julia's letter.

The lots were made, and mark'd, and mix'd, and handed,
   In silent horror, and their distribution
Lull'd even the savage hunger which demanded,
   Like the Promethean vulture, this pollution;

None in particular had sought or plann'd it,
    'Twas nature gnaw'd them to this resolution,
By which none were permitted to be neuter—
And the lot fell on Juan's luckless tutor.

He but requested to be bled to death:
    The surgeon had his instruments, and bled
Pedrillo, and so gently ebb'd his breath,
    You hardly could perceive when he was dead.
He died as born, a Catholic in faith,
    Like most in the belief in which they're bred,
And first a little crucifix he kiss'd,
And then held out his jugular and wrist.

The surgeon, as there was no other fee,
    Had his first choice of morsels for his pains;
But being thirstiest at the moment, he
    Preferr'd a draught from the fast-flowing veins:
Part was divided, part thrown in the sea,
    And such things as the entrails and the brains
Regaled two sharks, who follow'd o'er the billow—
The sailors ate the rest of poor Pedrillo.

The sailors ate him, all save three or four,
    Who were not quite so fond of animal food;
To these was added Juan, who, before
    Refusing his own spaniel, hardly could
Feel now his appetite increased much more;
    'Twas not to be expected that he should,
Even in extremity of their disaster,
Dine with them on his pastor and his master.

456   [Canto II, stanzas 192–7]

Alas! they were so young, so beautiful,
    So lonely, loving, helpless, and the hour
Was that in which the heart is always full,
    And, having o'er itself no further power,
Prompts deeds eternity can not annul,
    But pays off moments in an endless shower
Of hell-fire—all prepared for people giving
Pleasure or pain to one another living.

Alas! for Juan and Haidee! they were
    So loving and so lovely—till then never,
Excepting our first parents, such a pair
    Had run the risk of being damn'd for ever;

And Haidee, being devout as well as fair,
   Had, doubtless, heard about the Stygian river,
And hell and purgatory—but forgot
Just in the very crisis she should not.

They look upon each other, and their eyes
   Gleam in the moonlight; and her white arm clasps
Round Juan's head, and his around hers lies
   Half buried in the tresses which it grasps;
She sits upon his knee, and drinks his sighs,
   He hers, until they end in broken gasps;
And thus they form a group that's quite antique,
Half naked, loving, natural, and Greek.

And when those deep and burning moments pass'd,
   And Juan sunk to sleep within her arms,
She slept not, but all tenderly, though fast,
   Sustain'd his head upon her bosom's charms;
And now and then her eye to heaven is cast,
   And then on the pale cheek her breast now warms,
Pillow'd on her o'erflowing heart, which pants
With all it granted, and with all it grants.

An infant when it gazes on a light,
   A child the moment when it drains the breast,
A devotee when soars the Host in sight,
   An Arab with a stranger for a guest,
A sailor when the prize has struck in fight,
   A miser filling his most hoarded chest,
Feel rapture; but not such true joy are reaping
As they who watch o'er what they love while sleeping.

For there it lies so tranquil, so beloved,
   All that it hath of life with us is living;
So gentle, stirless, helpless, and unmoved,
   And all unconscious of the joy 'tis giving;
All it hath felt, inflicted, pass'd, and proved,
   Hush'd into depths beyond the watcher's diving;
There lies the thing we love with all its errors
And all its charms, like death without its terrors.

CHARLES WOLFE
1791–1823

457   *The Burial of Sir John Moore*

Not a drum was heard, not a funeral note,
    As his corse to the rampart we hurried;
Not a soldier discharged his farewell shot
    O'er the grave where our hero we buried.

We buried him darkly at dead of night,
    The sods with our bayonets turning;
By the struggling moonbeam's misty light,
    And the lantern dimly burning.

No useless coffin enclosed his breast,
    Not in sheet or in shroud we wound him;
But he lay like a warrior taking his rest,
    With his martial cloak around him.

Few and short were the prayers we said,
    And we spoke not a word of sorrow;
But we steadfastly gazed on the face that was dead,
    And we bitterly thought of the morrow.

We thought, as we hollowed his narrow bed,
    And smoothed down his lonely pillow,
That the foe and the stranger would tread o'er his head,
    And we far away on the billow!

Lightly they'll talk of the spirit that's gone,
    And o'er his cold ashes upbraid him,—
But little he'll reck, if they let him sleep on
    In the grave where a Briton has laid him.

But half of our heavy task was done,
    When the clock struck the hour for retiring;
And we heard the distant and random gun
    That the foe was sullenly firing.

Slowly and sadly we laid him down,
    From the field of his fame fresh and gory;
We carved not a line, and we raised not a stone—
    But we left him alone with his glory!

PERCY BYSSHE SHELLEY

1792–1822

458   from *Hellas*

Chorus

The world's great age begins anew,
    The golden years return,
The earth doth like a snake renew
    Her winter weeds outworn:
Heaven smiles, and faiths and empires gleam,
Like wrecks of a dissolving dream.

A brighter Hellas rears its mountains
    From waves serener far;
A new Peneus rolls his fountains
    Against the morning star.
Where fairer Tempes bloom, there sleep
Young Cyclads on a sunnier deep.

A loftier Argo cleaves the main,
    Fraught with a later prize;
Another Orpheus sings again,
    And loves, and weeps, and dies.
A new Ulysses leaves once more
Calypso for his native shore.

Oh, write no more the tale of Troy,
    If earth Death's scroll must be!
Nor mix with Laian rage the joy
    Which dawns upon the free:
Although a subtler Sphinx renew
Riddles of death Thebes never knew.

Another Athens shall arise,
    And to remoter time
Bequeath, like sunset to the skies,
    The splendour of its prime;
And leave, if nought so bright may live,
All earth can take or Heaven can give.

Saturn and Love their long repose
    Shall burst, more bright and good
Than all who fell, than One who rose,
    Than many unsubdued:
Not gold, not blood, their altar dowers,
But votive tears and symbol flowers.

Oh, cease! must hate and death return?
  Cease! must men kill and die?
Cease! drain not to its dregs the urn
  Of bitter prophecy.
The world is weary of the past,
Oh, might it die or rest at last!

459   from *The Triumph of Life* [lines 176–215]

Struck to the heart by this sad pageantry,
Half to myself I said—'And what is this?
Whose shape is that within the car? And why—'

I would have added—'is all here amiss?—'
But a voice answered—'Life!'—I turned, and knew
(O Heaven, have mercy on such wretchedness!)

That what I thought was an old root which grew
To strange distortion out of the hill side,
Was indeed one of those deluded crew,

And that the grass, which methought hung so wide
And white, was but his thin discoloured hair,
And that the holes he vainly sought to hide,

Were or had been eyes:—'If thou canst, forbear
To join the dance, which I had well forborne!'
Said the grim Feature (of my thought aware).

'I will unfold that which to this deep scorn
Led me and my companions, and relate
The progress of the pageant since the morn;

'If thirst of knowledge shall not then abate,
Follow it thou even to the night, but I
Am weary.'—Then like one who with the weight

Of his own words is staggered, wearily
He paused; and ere he could resume, I cried:
'First, who art thou?'—'Before thy memory,

'I feared, loved, hated, suffered, did and died,
And if the spark with which Heaven lit my spirit
Had been with purer nutriment supplied,

'Corruption would not now thus much inherit
Of what was once Rousseau,—nor this disguise
Stain that which ought to have disdained to wear it;

'If I have been extinguished, yet there rise
A thousand beacons from the spark I bore'—
'And who are those chained to the car?'—'The wise,

'The great, the unforgotten,—they who wore
Mitres and helms and crowns, or wreaths of light,
Signs of thought's empire over thought—their lore

'Taught them not this, to know themselves; their might
Could not repress the mystery within,
And for the morn of truth they feigned, deep night

'Caught them ere evening.'—

460   *Ozymandias*

I met a traveller from an antique land
Who said: Two vast and trunkless legs of stone
Stand in the desert . . . Near them, on the sand,
Half sunk, a shattered visage lies, whose frown,
And wrinkled lip, and sneer of cold command,
Tell that its sculptor well those passions read
Which yet survive, stamped on these lifeless things,
The hand that mocked them, and the heart that fed:
And on the pedestal these words appear:
'My name is Ozymandias, king of kings;
Look on my works, ye Mighty, and despair!'
Nothing beside remains. Round the decay
Of that colossal wreck, boundless and bare
The lone and level sands stretch far away.

461   *Sonnet: England in 1819*

An old, mad, blind, despised, and dying king,—
Princes, the dregs of their dull race, who flow
Through public scorn,—mud from a muddy spring,—
Rulers who neither see, nor feel, nor know,
But leech-like to their fainting country cling,
Till they drop, blind in blood, without a blow,—
A people starved and stabbed in the untilled field,—
An army, which liberticide and prey
Makes as a two-edged sword to all who wield,—
Golden and sanguine laws which tempt and slay;

Religion Christless, Godless—a book sealed;
A Senate,—Time's worst statute unrepealed,—
Are graves, from which a glorious Phantom may
Burst, to illumine our tempestuous day.

462   *Ode to the West Wind*

I

O wild West Wind, thou breath of Autumn's being,
Thou, from whose unseen presence the leaves dead
Are driven, like ghosts from an enchanter fleeing,

Yellow, and black, and pale, and hectic red,
Pestilence-stricken multitudes: O thou,
Who chariotest to their dark wintry bed

The wingèd seeds, where they lie cold and low,
Each like a corpse within its grave, until
Thine azure sister of the Spring shall blow

Her clarion o'er the dreaming earth, and fill
(Driving sweet buds like flocks to feed in air)
With living hues and odours plain and hill:

Wild Spirit, which art moving everywhere;
Destroyer and preserver; hear, oh, hear!

II

Thou on whose stream, mid the steep sky's commotion,
Loose clouds like earth's decaying leaves are shed,
Shook from the tangled boughs of Heaven and Ocean,

Angels of rain and lightning: there are spread
On the blue surface of thine aëry surge,
Like the bright hair uplifted from the head

Of some fierce Maenad, even from the dim verge
Of the horizon to the zenith's height,
The locks of the approaching storm. Thou dirge

Of the dying year, to which this closing night
Will be the dome of a vast sepulchre,
Vaulted with all thy congregated might

Of vapours, from whose solid atmosphere
Black rain, and fire, and hail will burst: oh, hear!

III

Thou who didst waken from his summer dreams
The blue Mediterranean, where he lay,
Lulled by the coil of his crystálline streams,

Beside a pumice isle in Baiae's bay,
And saw in sleep old palaces and towers
Quivering within the wave's intenser day,

All overgrown with azure moss and flowers
So sweet, the sense faints picturing them! Thou
For whose path the Atlantic's level powers

Cleave themselves into chasms, while far below
The sea-blooms and the oozy woods which wear
The sapless foliage of the ocean, know

Thy voice, and suddenly grow gray with fear,
And tremble and despoil themselves: oh, hear!

IV

If I were a dead leaf thou mightest bear;
If I were a swift cloud to fly with thee;
A wave to pant beneath thy power, and share

The impulse of thy strength, only less free
Than thou, O uncontrollable! If even
I were as in my boyhood, and could be

The comrade of thy wanderings over Heaven,
As then, when to outstrip thy skiey speed
Scarce seemed a vision; I would ne'er have striven

As thus with thee in prayer in my sore need.
Oh, lift me as a wave, a leaf, a cloud!
I fall upon the thorns of life! I bleed!

A heavy weight of hours has chained and bowed
One too like thee: tameless, and swift, and proud.

V

Make me thy lyre, even as the forest is:
What if my leaves are falling like its own!
The tumult of thy mighty harmonies

Will take from both a deep, autumnal tone,
Sweet though in sadness. Be thou, Spirit fierce,
My spirit! Be thou me, impetuous one!

Drive my dead thoughts over the universe
Like withered leaves to quicken a new birth!
And, by the incantation of this verse,

Scatter, as from an unextinguished hearth
Ashes and sparks, my words among mankind!
Be through my lips to unawakened earth

The trumpet of a prophecy! O, Wind,
If Winter comes, can Spring be far behind?

463   *The Question*

I dreamed that, as I wandered by the way,
    Bare Winter suddenly was changed to Spring,
And gentle odours led my steps astray,
    Mixed with a sound of waters murmuring
Along a shelving bank of turf, which lay
    Under a copse, and hardly dared to fling
Its green arms round the bosom of the stream,
But kissed it and then fled, as thou mightest in dream.

There grew pied wind-flowers and violets,
    Daisies, those pearled Arcturi of the earth,
The constellated flower that never sets;
    Faint oxslips; tender bluebells, at whose birth
The sod scarce heaved; and that tall flower that wets—
    Like a child, half in tenderness and mirth—
Its mother's face with Heaven's collected tears,
When the low wind, its playmate's voice, it hears.

And in the warm hedge grew lush eglantine,
    Green cowbind and the moonlight-coloured may,
And cherry-blossoms, and white cups, whose wine
    Was the bright dew, yet drained not by the day;
And wild roses, and ivy serpentine,
    With its dark buds and leaves, wandering astray;
And flowers azure, black, and streaked with gold,
Fairer than any wakened eyes behold.

And nearer to the river's trembling edge
    There grew broad flag-flowers, purple pranked with white,
And starry river buds among the sedge,
    And floating water-lilies, broad and bright,
Which lit the oak that overhung the hedge
    With moonlight beams of their own watery light;
And bulrushes, and reeds of such deep green
As soothed the dazzled eye with sober sheen.

Methought that of these visionary flowers
  I made a nosegay, bound in such a way
That the same hues, which in their natural bowers
  Were mingled or opposed, the like array
Kept these imprisoned children of the Hours
  Within my hand,—and then, elate and gay,
I hastened to the spot whence I had come,
That I might there present it!—Oh! to whom?

464   *To* ——

        Music, when soft voices die,
        Vibrates in the memory—
        Odours, when sweet violets sicken,
        Live within the sense they quicken.

        Rose leaves, when the rose is dead,
        Are heaped for the belovèd's bed;
        And so thy thoughts, when thou art gone,
        Love itself shall slumber on.

465   *Lines: 'When the Lamp is Shattered'*

          When the lamp is shattered
        The light in the dust lies dead—
          When the cloud is scattered
        The rainbow's glory is shed.
          When the lute is broken,
        Sweet tones are remembered not;
          When the lips have spoken,
        Loved accents are soon forgot.

          As music and splendour
        Survive not the lamp and the lute,
          The heart's echoes render
        No song when the spirit is mute:—
          No song but sad dirges,
        Like the wind through a ruined cell,
          Or the mournful surges
        That ring the dead seaman's knell.

          When hearts have once mingled
        Love first leaves the well-built nest;
          The weak one is singled
        To endure what it once possessed.

O Love! who bewailest
The frailty of all things here,
   Why choose you the frailest
For your cradle, your home, and your bier?

   Its passions will rock thee
As the storms rock the ravens on high;
   Bright reason will mock thee,
Like the sun from a wintry sky.
   From thy nest every rafter
Will rot, and thine eagle home
   Leave thee naked to laughter,
When leaves fall and cold winds come.

JOHN CLARE

1793–1864

466   *A Vision*

I lost the love, of heaven above;
I spurn'd the lust, of earth below;
I felt the sweets of fancied love,—
And hell itself my only foe.

I lost earths joys, but felt the glow,
Of heaven's flame abound in me:
'Till loveliness, and I did grow,
The bard of immortality.

I loved, but woman fell away;
I hid me, from her faded fame:
I snatch'd the sun's eternal ray,—
And wrote 'till earth was but a name.

In every language upon earth,
On every shore, o'er every sea;
I gave my name immortal birth,
And kep't my spirit with the free.

467   *'I Am'*

I am—yet what I am, none cares or knows;
   My friends forsake me like a memory lost:—

I am the self-consumer of my woes;—
  They rise and vanish in oblivion's host,
Like shadows in love's frenzied stifled throes:—
And yet I am, and live—like vapours tost

Into the nothingness of scorn and noise,—
  Into the living sea of waking dreams,
Where there is neither sense of life or joys,
  But the vast shipwreck of my lifes esteems;
Even the dearest, that I love the best
Are strange—nay, rather stranger than the rest.

I long for scenes, where man hath never trod
  A place where woman never smiled or wept
There to abide with my Creator, God;
  And sleep as I in childhood, sweetly slept,
Untroubling, and untroubled where I lie,
The grass below—above the vaulted sky.

468   *Song*

    I hid my love when young while I
    Coud'nt bear the buzzing of a flye
    I hid my love to my despite
    Till I could not bear to look at light
    I dare not gaze upon her face
    But left her memory in each place
    Where ere I saw a wild flower lye
    I kissed and bade my love good bye

    I met her in the greenest dells
    Where dew drops pearl the wood blue bells
    The lost breeze kissed her bright blue eye
    The Bee kissed and went singing bye
    A sun beam found a passage there
    A gold chain round her neck so fair
    As secret as the wild bees song
    She lay there all the summer long

    I hid my love in field and town
    Till e'en the breeze would knock me down
    The Bees seemed singing ballads oe'r
    The flyes buzz turned a Lions roar
    And even silence found a tongue
    To haunt me all the summer long
    The Riddle nature could not prove
    Was nothing else but secret love

469   I found a ball of grass among the hay
           And proged it as I passed and went away
           And when I looked I fancied somthing stirred
           And turned agen and hoped to catch the bird
           When out an old mouse bolted in the wheat   5
           With all her young ones hanging at her teats
           She looked so odd and so grotesque to me
           I ran and wondered what the thing could be
           And pushed the knapweed bunches where I stood
           When the mouse hurried from the crawling brood   10
           The young ones squeaked and when I went away
           She found her nest again among the hay
           The water oer the pebbles scarce could run
           And broad old cesspools glittered in the sun

470   The sheep get up and make their many tracks
           And bear a load of snow upon their backs
           And gnaw the frozen turnip to the ground
           With sharp quick bite and then go noising round
           The boy that pecks the turnips all the day
           And knocks his hands to keep the cold away
           And laps his legs in straw to keep them warm
           And hides behind the hedges from the storm
           The sheep as tame as dogs go where he goes
           And try to shake their fleeces from the snows
           Then leave their frozen meal and wander round
           The stubble stack that stands beside the ground
           And lye all night and face the drizzling storm
           And shun the hovel where they might be warm

471   The wild duck startles like a sudden thought
           And heron slow as if it might be caught
           The flopping crows on weary wing go bye
           And grey beard jackdaws noising as they flye
           The crowds of starnels wiz and hurry bye   5
           And darken like a cloud the evening sky
           The larks like thunder rise and suthy round
           Then drop and nestle in the stubble ground
           The wild swan hurrys high and noises loud
           With white necks peering to the evening cloud   10

         469: 2 *proged*] prodded
      471: 5 *starnels*] starlings   7 *suthy*] sigh, whistle

The weary rooks to distant woods are gone
With length of tail the magpie winnows on
To neighbouring tree and leaves the distant crow
While small birds nestle in the hedge below

JOHN KEATS

1795–1821

472   *On First Looking into Chapman's Homer*

Much have I travelled in the realms of gold,
    And many goodly states and kingdoms seen;
    Round many western islands have I been
Which bards in fealty to Apollo hold.
Oft of one wide expanse had I been told
    That deep-browed Homer ruled as his demesne;
    Yet did I never breathe its pure serene
Till I heard Chapman speak out loud and bold:
Then felt I like some watcher of the skies
    When a new planet swims into his ken;
Or like stout Cortez when with eagle eyes
    He stared at the Pacific—and all his men
Looked at each other with a wild surmise—
    Silent, upon a peak in Darien.

473   from *Endymion* [Book I, lines 1–24]

A thing of beauty is a joy for ever:
Its loveliness increases; it will never
Pass into nothingness; but still will keep
A bower quiet for us, and a sleep
Full of sweet dreams, and health, and quiet breathing.
Therefore, on every morrow, are we wreathing
A flowery band to bind us to the earth,
Spite of despondence, of the inhuman dearth
Of noble natures, of the gloomy days,
Of all the unhealthy and o'er-darkened ways
Made for our searching: yes, in spite of all,
Some shape of beauty moves away the pall
From our dark spirits. Such the sun, the moon,
Trees old, and young, sprouting a shady boon
For simple sheep; and such are daffodils
With the green world they live in; and clear rills

That for themselves a cooling covert make
'Gainst the hot season; the mid forest brake,
Rich with a sprinkling of fair musk-rose blooms:
And such too is the grandeur of the dooms
We have imagined for the mighty dead;
All lovely tales that we have heard or read—
An endless fountain of immortal drink,
Pouring unto us from the heaven's brink.

474   from *Hyperion: A Fragment* [Book I, lines 1–21]

Deep in the shady sadness of a vale
Far sunken from the healthy breath of morn,
Far from the fiery noon, and eve's one star,
Sat grey-haired Saturn, quiet as a stone,
Still as the silence round about his lair;
Forest on forest hung above his head
Like cloud on cloud. No stir of air was there,
Not so much life as on a summer's day
Robs not one light seed from the feathered grass,
But where the dead leaf fell, there did it rest.
A stream went voiceless by, still deadened more
By reason of his fallen divinity
Spreading a shade: the Naiad 'mid her reeds
Pressed her cold finger closer to her lips.

Along the margin-sand large foot-marks went,
No further than to where his feet had strayed,
And slept there since. Upon the sodden ground
His old right hand lay nerveless, listless, dead,
Unsceptred; and his realmless eyes were closed;
While his bowed head seemed listening to the Earth,
His ancient mother, for some comfort yet.

475   from *The Eve of St Agnes* [stanzas XXII–XXX]

Her faltering hand upon the balustrade,
Old Angela was feeling for the stair,
When Madeline, St Agnes' charmèd maid,
Rose, like a missioned spirit, unaware:
With silver taper's light, and pious care,
She turned, and down the agèd gossip led
To a safe level matting. Now prepare,
Young Porphyro, for gazing on that bed—
She comes, she comes again, like ring-dove frayed and fled.

Out went the taper as she hurried in;
Its little smoke, in pallid moonshine, died:
She closed the door, she panted, all akin
To spirits of the air, and visions wide—
No uttered syllable, or, woe betide!
But to her heart, her heart was voluble,
Paining with eloquence her balmy side;
As though a tongueless nightingale should swell
Her throat in vain, and die, heart-stiflèd, in her dell.

A casement high and triple-arched there was,
All garlanded with carven imag'ries
Of fruits, and flowers, and bunches of knot-grass,
And diamonded with panes of quaint device,
Innumerable of stains and splendid dyes,
As are the tiger-moth's deep-damasked wings;
And in the midst, 'mong thousand heraldries,
And twilight saints, and dim emblazonings,
A shielded scutcheon blushed with blood of queens and kings.

Full on this casement shone the wintry moon,
And threw warm gules on Madeline's fair breast,
As down she knelt for heaven's grace and boon;
Rose-bloom fell on her hands, together pressed,
And on her silver cross soft amethyst,
And on her hair a glory, like a saint:
She seemed a splendid angel, newly dressed,
Save wings, for Heaven—Porphyro grew faint;
She knelt, so pure a thing, so free from mortal taint.

Anon his heart revives; her vespers done,
Of all its wreathèd pearls her hair she frees;
Unclasps her warmèd jewels one by one;
Loosens her fragrant bodice; by degrees
Her rich attire creeps rustling to her knees:
Half-hidden, like a mermaid in sea-weed,
Pensive awhile she dreams awake, and sees,
In fancy, fair St Agnes in her bed,
But dares not look behind, or all the charm is fled.

Soon, trembling in her soft and chilly nest,
In sort of wakeful swoon, perplexed she lay,
Until the poppied warmth of sleep oppressed
Her soothèd limbs, and soul fatigued away—
Flown, like a thought, until the morrow-day;
Blissfully havened both from joy and pain;
Clasped like a missal where swart Paynims pray;
Blinded alike from sunshine and from rain,
As though a rose should shut, and be a bud again.

Stolen to this paradise, and so entranced,
Porphyro gazed upon her empty dress,
And listened to her breathing, if it chanced
To wake into a slumbrous tenderness;
Which when he heard, that minute did he bless,
And breathed himself: then from the closet crept,
Noiseless as fear in a wide wilderness,
And over the hushed carpet, silent, stepped,
And 'tween the curtains peeped, where, lo!—how fast she slept.

Then by the bed-side, where the faded moon
Made a dim, silver twilight, soft he set
A table, and, half anguished, threw thereon
A cloth of woven crimson, gold, and jet—
O for some drowsy Morphean amulet!
The boisterous, midnight, festive clarion,
The kettle-drum, and far-heard clarinet,
Affray his ears, though but in dying tone;
The hall door shuts again, and all the noise is gone.

And still she slept an azure-lidded sleep,
In blanchèd linen, smooth, and lavendered,
While he from forth the closet brought a heap
Of candied apple, quince, and plum, and gourd,
With jellies soother than the creamy curd,
And lucent syrups, tinct with cinnamon;
Manna and dates, in argosy transferred
From Fez; and spicèd dainties, every one,
From silken Samarkand to cedared Lebanon.

476   *La Belle Dame sans Merci: A Ballad*

O what can ail thee, knight-at-arms,
    Alone and palely loitering?
The sedge has withered from the lake,
    And no birds sing.

O what can ail thee, knight-at-arms,
    So haggard and so woe-begone?
The squirrel's granary is full,
    And the harvest's done.

I see a lily on thy brow,
    With anguish moist and fever-dew,
And on thy cheeks a fading rose
    Fast withereth too.

I met a lady in the meads,
   Full beautiful—a faery's child,
Her hair was long, her foot was light,
   And her eyes were wild.

I made a garland for her head,
   And bracelets too, and fragrant zone;
She looked at me as she did love,
   And made sweet moan.

I set her on my pacing steed,
   And nothing else saw all day long,
For sidelong would she bend, and sing
   A faery's song.

She found me roots of relish sweet,
   And honey wild, and manna-dew,
And sure in language strange she said—
   'I love thee true'.

She took me to her elfin grot,
   And there she wept and sighed full sore,
And there I shut her wild wild eyes
   With kisses four.

And there she lullèd me asleep
   And there I dreamed—Ah! woe betide!—
The latest dream I ever dreamt
   On the cold hill side.

I saw pale kings and princes too,
   Pale warriors, death-pale were they all;
They cried—'La Belle Dame sans Merci
   Thee hath in thrall!'

I saw their starved lips in the gloam,
   With horrid warning gapèd wide,
And I awoke and found me here,
   On the cold hill's side.

And this is why I sojourn here
   Alone and palely loitering,
Though the sedge is withered from the lake,
   And no birds sing.

477   *Ode on a Grecian Urn*

Thou still unravished bride of quietness,
   Thou foster-child of silence and slow time,
Sylvan historian, who canst thus express
   A flowery tale more sweetly than our rhyme:

What leaf-fringed legend haunts about thy shape
  Of deities or mortals, or of both,
    In Tempe or the dales of Arcady?
  What men or gods are these? What maidens loth?
What mad pursuit? What struggle to escape?
    What pipes and timbrels? What wild ecstasy?

Heard melodies are sweet, but those unheard
  Are sweeter; therefore, ye soft pipes, play on;
Not to the sensual ear, but, more endeared,
  Pipe to the spirit ditties of no tone:
Fair youth, beneath the trees, thou canst not leave
  Thy song, nor ever can those trees be bare;
    Bold Lover, never, never canst thou kiss,
Though winning near the goal—yet, do not grieve:
    She cannot fade, though thou hast not thy bliss,
  For ever wilt thou love, and she be fair!

Ah, happy, happy boughs! that cannot shed
  Your leaves, nor ever bid the Spring adieu;
And, happy melodist, unwearièd,
  For ever piping songs for ever new;
More happy love! more happy, happy love!
  For ever warm and still to be enjoyed,
    For ever panting, and for ever young—
All breathing human passion far above,
  That leaves a heart high-sorrowful and cloyed,
    A burning forehead, and a parching tongue.

Who are these coming to the sacrifice?
  To what green altar, O mysterious priest,
Lead'st thou that heifer lowing at the skies,
  And all her silken flanks with garlands dressed?
What little town by river or sea shore,
  Or mountain-built with peaceful citadel,
    Is emptied of this folk, this pious morn?
And, little town, thy streets for evermore
  Will silent be; and not a soul to tell
    Why thou art desolate, can e'er return.

O Attic shape! Fair attitude! with brede
  Of marble men and maidens overwrought,
With forest branches and the trodden weed;
  Thou, silent form, dost tease us out of thought
As doth eternity: Cold Pastoral!
  When old age shall this generation waste,
    Thou shalt remain, in midst of other woe

Than ours, a friend to man, to whom thou say'st,
'Beauty is truth, truth beauty,—that is all
    Ye know on earth, and all ye need to know.'

478   *Ode to a Nightingale*

My heart aches, and a drowsy numbness pains
  My sense, as though of hemlock I had drunk,
Or emptied some dull opiate to the drains
  One minute past, and Lethe-wards had sunk:
'Tis not through envy of thy happy lot,
  But being too happy in thine happiness—
    That thou, light-wingèd Dryad of the trees,
      In some melodious plot
  Of beechen green, and shadows numberless,
    Singest of summer in full-throated ease.

O, for a draught of vintage! that hath been
  Cooled a long age in the deep-delvèd earth,
Tasting of Flora and the country green,
  Dance, and Provençal song, and sunburnt mirth!
O for a beaker full of the warm South,
  Full of the true, the blushful Hippocrene,
    With beaded bubbles winking at the brim,
      And purple-stainèd mouth,
  That I might drink, and leave the world unseen,
    And with thee fade away into the forest dim—

Fade far away, dissolve, and quite forget
  What thou among the leaves hast never known,
The weariness, the fever, and the fret
  Here, where men sit and hear each other groan;
Where palsy shakes a few, sad, last grey hairs,
  Where youth grows pale, and spectre-thin, and dies;
    Where but to think is to be full of sorrow
      And leaden-eyed despairs;
  Where Beauty cannot keep her lustrous eyes,
    Or new Love pine at them beyond to-morrow.

Away! away! for I will fly to thee,
  Not charioted by Bacchus and his pards,
But on the viewless wings of Poesy,
  Though the dull brain perplexes and retards.
Already with thee! tender is the night,
  And haply the Queen-Moon is on her throne,

Clustered around by all her starry Fays;
   But here there is no light,
Save what from heaven is with the breezes blown
   Through verdurous glooms and winding mossy ways.

I cannot see what flowers are at my feet,
   Nor what soft incense hangs upon the boughs,
But, in embalmèd darkness, guess each sweet
   Wherewith the seasonable month endows
The grass, the thicket, and the fruit-tree wild—
   White hawthorn, and the pastoral eglantine;
     Fast fading violets covered up in leaves;
      And mid-May's eldest child,
   The coming musk-rose, full of dewy wine,
     The murmurous haunt of flies on summer eves.

Darkling I listen; and, for many a time
   I have been half in love with easeful Death,
Called him soft names in many a musèd rhyme,
   To take into the air my quiet breath;
Now more than ever seems it rich to die,
   To cease upon the midnight with no pain,
     While thou art pouring forth thy soul abroad
      In such an ecstasy!
   Still wouldst thou sing, and I have ears in vain—
     To thy high requiem become a sod.

Thou wast not born for death, immortal Bird!
   No hungry generations tread thee down;
The voice I hear this passing night was heard
   In ancient days by emperor and clown:
Perhaps the self-same song that found a path
   Through the sad heart of Ruth, when, sick for home,
     She stood in tears amid the alien corn;
      The same that oft-times hath
   Charmed magic casements, opening on the foam
     Of perilous seas, in faery lands forlorn.

Forlorn! the very word is like a bell
   To toll me back from thee to my sole self!
Adieu! the fancy cannot cheat so well
   As she is famed to do, deceiving elf.
Adieu! adieu! thy plaintive anthem fades
   Past the near meadows, over the still stream,
     Up the hill-side; and now 'tis buried deep
      In the next valley-glades:
   Was it a vision, or a waking dream?
     Fled is that music—Do I wake or sleep?

479   *Ode on Melancholy*

No, no, go not to Lethe, neither twist
   Wolf's-bane, tight-rooted, for its poisonous wine:
Nor suffer thy pale forehead to be kissed
   By nightshade, ruby grape of Proserpine;
Make not your rosary of yew-berries,
   Nor let the beetle, nor the death-moth be
     Your mournful Psyche, nor the downy owl
A partner in your sorrow's mysteries;
   For shade to shade will come too drowsily,
     And drown the wakeful anguish of the soul.

But when the melancholy fit shall fall
   Sudden from heaven like a weeping cloud,
That fosters the droop-headed flowers all,
   And hides the green hill in an April shroud;
Then glut thy sorrow on a morning rose,
   Or on the rainbow of the salt sand-wave,
     Or on the wealth of globèd peonies;
Or if thy mistress some rich anger shows,
   Emprison her soft hand, and let her rave,
     And feed deep, deep upon her peerless eyes.

She dwells with Beauty—Beauty that must die;
   And Joy, whose hand is ever at his lips
Bidding adieu; and aching Pleasure nigh,
   Turning to poison while the bee-mouth sips:
Ay, in the very temple of Delight
   Veiled Melancholy has her sovran shrine,
     Though seen of none save him whose strenuous tongue
Can burst Joy's grape against his palate fine;
   His soul shall taste the sadness of her might,
     And be among her cloudy trophies hung.

480   *To Autumn*

Season of mists and mellow fruitfulness,
   Close bosom-friend of the maturing sun,
Conspiring with him how to load and bless
   With fruit the vines that round the thatch-eves run;
To bend with apples the mossed cottage-trees,
   And fill all fruit with ripeness to the core;
     To swell the gourd, and plump the hazel shells
With a sweet kernel; to set budding more,

And still more, later flowers for the bees,
Until they think warm days will never cease,
    For Summer has o'er-brimmed their clammy cells.

Who hath not seen thee oft amid thy store?
    Sometimes whoever seeks abroad may find
Thee sitting careless on a granary floor,
    Thy hair soft-lifted by the winnowing wind;
Or on a half-reaped furrow sound asleep,
    Drowsed with the fume of poppies, while thy hook
        Spares the next swath and all its twinèd flowers;
And sometimes like a gleaner thou dost keep
    Steady thy laden head across a brook;
    Or by a cider-press, with patient look,
        Thou watchest the last oozings hours by hours.

Where are the songs of Spring? Ay, where are they?
    Think not of them, thou hast thy music too—
While barrèd clouds bloom the soft-dying day,
    And touch the stubble-plains with rosy hue:
Then in a wailful choir the small gnats mourn
    Among the river sallows, borne aloft
        Or sinking as the light wind lives or dies;
And full-grown lambs loud bleat from hilly bourn;
    Hedge-crickets sing; and now with treble soft
    The red-breast whistles from a garden-croft;
        And gathering swallows twitter in the skies.

481   from *The Fall of Hyperion: A Dream* [lines 216–71]

            Then the tall shade, in drooping linens veiled,
        Spake out, so much more earnest, that her breath
        Stirred the thin folds of gauze that drooping hung
        About a golden censer from her hand
        Pendant; and by her voice I knew she shed
        Long-treasured tears. 'This temple, sad and lone,
        Is all spared from the thunder of a war
        Foughten long since by giant hierarchy
        Against rebellion; this old Image here,
        Whose carvèd features wrinkled as he fell,
        Is Saturn's; I Moneta, left supreme
        Sole Priestess of his desolation.'
        I had no words to answer, for my tongue,
        Useless, could find about its roofèd home

No syllable of a fit majesty
To make rejoinder to Moneta's mourn.
There was a silence, while the altar's blaze
Was fainting for sweet food: I looked thereon,
And on the pavèd floor, where nigh were piled
Faggots of cinnamon, and many heaps
Of other crispèd spice-wood—then again
I looked upon the altar, and its horns
Whitened with ashes, and its languorous flame,
And then upon the offerings again;
And so by turns—till sad Moneta cried:
'The sacrifice is done, but not the less
Will I be kind to thee for thy goodwill.
My power, which to me is still a curse,
Shall be to thee a wonder; for the scenes
Still swooning vivid through my globèd brain,
With an electral changing misery,
Thou shalt with those dull mortal eyes behold,
Free from all pain, if wonder pain thee not.'
As near as an immortal's spherèd words
Could to a mother's soften, were these last:
But yet I had a terror of her robes,
And chiefly of the veils, that from her brow
Hung pale, and curtained her in mysteries
That made my heart too small to hold its blood.
This saw that Goddess, and with sacred hand
Parted the veils. Then saw I a wan face,
Not pined by human sorrows, but bright-blanched
By an immortal sickness which kills not;
It works a constant change, which happy death
Can put no end to; deathwards progressing
To no death was that visage; it had passed
The lily and the snow; and beyond these
I must not think now, though I saw that face—
But for her eyes I should have fled away.
They held me back, with a benignant light,
Soft-mitigated by divinest lids
Half-closed, and visionless entire they seemed
Of all external things—they saw me not,
But in blank splendour beamed like the mild moon,
Who comforts those she sees not, who knows not
What eyes are upward cast.

JAMES HENRY
1798–1876

482   *Very Old Man*

I well remember how some threescore years
And ten ago, a helpless babe, I toddled
From chair to chair about my mother's chamber,
Feeling, as 'twere, my way in the new world
And foolishly afraid of, or, as 't might be,
Foolishly pleased with, th' unknown objects round me.
And now with stiffened joints I sit all day
In one of those same chairs, as foolishly
Hoping or fearing something from me hid
Behind the thick, dark veil which I see hourly
And minutely on every side round closing
And from my view all objects shutting out.

483   Another and another and another
And still another sunset and sunrise,
The same yet different, different yet the same,
Seen by me now in my declining years
As in my early childhood, youth and manhood;
And by my parents and my parents' parents,
And by the parents of my parents' parents,
And by their parents counted back for ever,
Seen, all their lives long, even as now by me;
And by my children and my children's children
And by the children of my children's children
And by their children counted on for ever
Still to be seen as even now seen by me;
Clear and bright sometimes, sometimes dark and clouded
But still the same sunsetting and sunrise;
The same for ever to the never ending
Line of observers, to the same observer
Through all the changes of his life the same:
Sunsetting and sunrising and sunsetting,
And then again sunrising and sunsetting,
Sunrising and sunsetting evermore.

THOMAS HOOD

1799–1845

484   *I Remember, I Remember*

I remember, I remember,
The house where I was born,
The little window where the sun
Came peeping in at morn;
He never came a wink too soon,
Nor brought too long a day,
But now I often wish the night
Had borne my breath away!

I remember, I remember,
The roses, red and white,
The vi'lets, and the lily-cups,
Those flowers made of light!
The lilacs where the robin built,
And where my brother set
The laburnum on his birthday,—
The tree is living yet!

I remember, I remember,
Where I was used to swing,
And thought the air must rush as fresh
To swallows on the wing;
My spirit flew in feathers then,
That is so heavy now,
And summer pools could hardly cool
The fever on my brow!

I remember, I remember,
The fir trees dark and high;
I used to think their slender tops
Were close against the sky:
It was a childish ignorance,
But now 'tis little joy
To know I'm farther off from heav'n
Than when I was a boy.

WILLIAM BARNES
1801–1886

485   *My Orcha'd in Linden Lea*

'Ithin the woodlands, flow'ry gleäded,
    By the woak tree's mossy moot,
The sheenen grass-bleädes, timber-sheäded,
    Now do quiver under voot;
An' birds do whissle over head,   5
An' water's bubblen in its bed,
An' there vor me the apple tree
Do leän down low in Linden Lea.

When leaves that leätely wer a-springen
    Now do feäde 'ithin the copse,   10
An' païnted birds do hush their zingen
    Up upon the timber's tops;
An' brown-leav'd fruit's a-turnen red,
In cloudless zunsheen, over head,
Wi' fruit vor me, the apple tree   15
Do leän down low in Linden Lea.

Let other vo'k meäke money vaster
    In the aïr o' dark-room'd towns,
I don't dread a peevish meäster;
    Though noo man do heed my frowns,   20
I be free to goo abrode,
Or teäke ageän my homeward road
To where, vor me, the apple tree
Do leän down low in Linden Lea.

486   *The Turnstile*

Ah! sad wer we as we did peäce
The wold church road, wi' downcast feäce,
The while the bells, that mwoan'd so deep
Above our child a-left asleep,
Wer now a-zingen all alive   5
Wi' tother bells to meäke the vive.
But up at woone pleäce we come by,
'Twer hard to keep woone's two eyes dry:

485: 2 *moot*] bottom and roots of a felled tree

On Steän-cliff road, 'ithin the drong,
Up where, as vo'k do pass along,   10
The turnen stile, a-païnted white,
Do sheen by day an' show by night.
Vor always there, as we did goo
To church, thik stile did let us drough,
Wi' spreaden eärms that wheel'd to guide   15
Us each in turn to tother zide.
An' vu'st ov all the traïn he took
My wife, wi' winsome gaït an' look;
An' then zent on my little maïd,
A-skippen onward, overjaÿ'd   20
To reach ageän the pleäce o' pride,
Her comely mother's left han' zide.
An' then, a-wheelen roun', he took
On me, 'ithin his third white nook.
An' in the fourth, a-sheäkèn wild,   25
He zent us on our giddy child.
But eesterday he guided slow
My downcast Jenny, vull o' woe,
An' then my little maïd in black,
A-walken softly on her track: 30
An' after he'd a-turn'd ageän,
To let me goo along the leäne,
He had noo little bwoy to vill
His last white eärms, an' they stood still.

487   *Lwonesomeness*

As I do zew, wi' nimble hand,
    In here avore the window's light,
How still do all the housegear stand
    Around my lwonesome zight.
How still do all the housegear stand
Since Willie now 've a-left the land.

The rwose-tree's window-sheäden bow
    Do hang in leaf, an' win'-blow'd flow'rs
Avore my lwonesome eyes do show
    Theäse bright November hours.
Avore my lwonesome eyes do show
Wi' nwone but I to zee em blow.

The sheädes o' leafy buds, avore
    The peänes, do sheäke upon the glass,
An' stir in light upon the vloor,
    Where now vew veet do pass.
An' stir in light upon the vloor
Where there's a-stirren nothen mwore.

This win' mid dreve upon the maïn,
    My brother's ship, a-plowen foam,
But not bring mother, cwold, nor raïn,
    At her now happy hwome.
But not bring mother, cwold, nor raïn,
Where she is out o' païn.

Zoo now that I'm a-mwopen dumb,
    A-keepen father's house, do you
Come of 'en wi' your work vrom hwome,
    Vor company. Now do.
Come of 'en wi' your work vrom hwome,
Up here a while. Do come.

488   *Shellbrook*

When out by Shellbrook, round by stile and tree,
With longer days and sunny hours come on,
With spring and all its sunny showers come on,
With May and all its shining flowers come on,
How merry, young with young would meet in glee.

And there, how we in merry talk went by
The foam below the river bay, all white,
And blossom on the green-leav'd may, all white,
And chalk beside the dusty way, all white,
Where glittering water match'd with blue the sky.

Or else in winding paths and lanes, along
The timbry hillocks, sloping steep, we roam'd;
Or down the dells and dingles deep we roam'd;
Or by the bending brook's wide sweep we roam'd
On holidays, with merry laugh or song.

But now, the frozen churchyard wallings keep
The patch of tower-shaded ground, all white,
Where friends can find the frosted mound, all white
With turfy sides upswelling round, all white
With young offsunder'd from the young in sleep.

489   *Sister Gone*

When Mary on her wedding day,
At last a bride, had gone away
From all her friends that there had spent
The happy day in merriment,
And ringers rang, at evenfall,
Their peals of bells, from great to small,
Within the tower's mossy wall
So high against the evening sky,

Then Jane, that there throughout the day
Had been the gayest of the gay,
At last began to hang her head
And ponder on her sister fled,
And days that seem'd too quickly flown,
To leave her now at home alone,
With no one's life to match her own,
So sad, though hitherto so glad.

It saddened me that moonpaled night
To see her by the wall, in white,
While friends departed mate with mate
Beyond the often-swinging gate,
As there beside the lilac shade,
Where golden-chained laburnum sway'd,
Around her face her hairlocks play'd,
All black with light behind her back.

490   *The Hill-Shade*

At such a time, of year and day,
      In ages gone, that steep hill-brow
Cast down an evening shade, that lay
      In shape the same as lies there now;
Though then no shadows wheel'd around
The things that now are on the ground.

The hill's high shape may long outstand
      The house, of slowly-wasting stone;
The house may longer shade the land
      Than man's on-gliding shade is shown;
The man himself may longer stay
Than stands the summer's rick of hay.

The trees that rise, with boughs o'er boughs,
    To me for trees long-fall'n may pass;
And I could take those red-hair'd cows
    For those that pull'd my first-known grass;
Our flow'rs seem yet on ground and spray,
But oh, our people; where are they?

WINTHROP MACKWORTH PRAED

1802–1839

491   *Good-night to the Season*

Thus runs the world away.
                        HAMLET

Good-night to the Season! 'tis over!
    Gay dwellings no longer are gay;
The courtier, the gambler, the lover,
    Are scatter'd like swallows away:
There's nobody left to invite one,
    Except my good uncle and spouse;
My mistress is bathing at Brighton,
    My patron is sailing at Cowes:
For want of a better employment,
    Till Ponto and Don can get out,
I'll cultivate rural enjoyment,
    And angle immensely for trout.

Good-night to the Season!—the lobbies,
    Their changes, and rumours of change,
Which startled the rustic Sir Bobbies,
    And made all the Bishops look strange:
The breaches, and battles, and blunders,
    Perform'd by the Commons and Peers;
The Marquis's eloquent thunders,
    The Baronet's eloquent ears:
Denouncings of Papists and treasons,
    Of foreign dominion and oats;
Misrepresentations of reasons,
    And misunderstandings of notes.

Good-night to the Season!—the buildings
    Enough to make Inigo sick;
The paintings, and plasterings, and gildings
    Of stucco, and marble, and brick;
The orders deliciously blended,
    From love of effect, into one;

The club-houses only intended,
   The palaces only begun;
The hell where the fiend, in his glory,
   Sits staring at putty and stones,
And scrambles from story to story,
   To rattle at midnight his bones.

Good-night to the Season!—the dances,
   The fillings of hot little rooms,
The glancings of rapturous glances,
   The fancyings of fancy costumes;
The pleasures which Fashion makes duties,
   The praisings of fiddles and flutes,
The luxury of looking at beauties,
   The tedium of talking to mutes;
The female diplomatists, planners
   Of matches for Laura and Jane,
The ice of her Ladyship's manners,
   The ice of his Lordship's champagne.

Good-night to the Season!—the rages
   Led off by the chiefs of the throng,
The Lady Matilda's new pages,
   The Lady Eliza's new song;
Miss Fennel's macaw, which at Boodle's
   Is held to have something to say;
Mrs. Splenetic's musical poodles,
   Which bark 'Batti Batti' all day;
The pony Sir Araby sported,
   As hot and as black as a coal,
And the Lion his mother imported,
   In bearskins and grease, from the Pole.

Good-night to the Season!—the Toso,
   So very majestic and tall;
Miss Ayton, whose singing was so-so,
   And Pasta, divinest of all;
The labour in vain of the Ballet,
   So sadly deficient in stars;
The foreigners thronging the Alley,
   Exhaling the breath of cigars;
The 'loge' where some heiress, how killing,
   Environ'd with Exquisites sits,
The lovely one out of her drilling,
   The silly ones out of their wits.

Good-night to the Season!—the splendour
   That beam'd in the Spanish Bazaar;

Where I purchased—my heart was so tender—
  A card-case,—a pasteboard guitar,—
A bottle of perfume,—a girdle,—
  A lithograph'd Riego full-grown,
Whom Bigotry drew on a hurdle
  That artists might draw him on stone,—
A small panorama of Seville,—
  A trap for demolishing flies,—
A caricature of the Devil,—
  And a look from Miss Sheridan's eyes.

Good-night to the Season!—the flowers
  Of the grand horticultural fête,
When boudoirs were quitted for bowers,
  And the fashion was not to be late;
When all who had money and leisure
  Grew rural o'er ices and wines,
All pleasantly toiling for pleasure,
  All hungrily pining for pines,
And making of beautiful speeches,
  And marring of beautiful shows,
And feeding on delicate peaches,
  And treading on delicate toes.

Good-night to the Season!—another
  Will come with its trifles and toys,
And hurry away, like its brother,
  In sunshine, and odour, and noise.
Will it come with a rose or a briar?
  Will it come with a blessing or curse?
Will its bonnets be lower or higher?
  Will its morals be better or worse?
Will it find me grown thinner or fatter,
  Or fonder of wrong or of right,
Or married,—or buried?—no matter,
  Good-night to the Season, Good-night!

JAMES CLARENCE MANGAN

1803–1849

492   *Twenty Golden Years Ago*

O, the rain, the weary, dreary rain,
  How it plashes on the window-sill!
Night, I guess too, must be on the wane,
  Strass and Gass around are grown so still.

Here I sit, with coffee in my cup—
   Ah! 'twas rarely I beheld it flow
In the taverns where I loved to sup
   Twenty golden years ago!

Twenty years ago, alas!—but stay,
   On my life, 'tis half-past twelve o'clock!
After all, the hours *do* slip away—
   Come, here goes to burn another block!
For the night, or morn, is wet and cold,
   And my fire is dwindling rather low:—
I had fire enough, when young and bold,
   Twenty golden years ago!

Dear! I don't feel well at all, somehow:
   Few in Weimar dream how bad I am;
Floods of tears grow common with me now,
   High-Dutch floods, that Reason cannot dam.
Doctors think I'll neither live nor thrive
   If I mope at home so—I don't know—
Am I living *now?* I *was* alive
   Twenty golden years ago.

Wifeless, friendless, flagonless, alone,
   Not quite bookless, though, unless I chuse,
Left with nought to do, except to groan,
   Not a soul to woo, except the Muse—
O! this, this is hard for *me* to bear,
   Me, who whilome lived so much *en haut*,
Me, who broke all hearts like chinaware
   Twenty golden years ago!

P'rhaps 'tis better:—Time's defacing waves
   Long have quenched the radiance of my brow—
They who curse me nightly from their graves
   Scarce could love me were they living now;
But my loneliness hath darker ills—
   Such dun-duns as Conscience, Thought and Co.,
Awful Gorgons! worse than tailors' bills
   Twenty golden years ago!

Did I paint a fifth of what I feel,
   O, how plaintive you would ween I was!
But I won't, albeit I have a deal
   More to wail about than Kerner has!
Kerner's tears are wept for withered flowers,
   Mine for withered hopes; my Scroll of Woe
Dates, alas! from Youth's deserted bowers,
   Twenty golden years ago!

Yet may Deutschland's bardlings flourish long!
　　Me, I tweak no beak among them;—hawks
Must not pounce on hawks; besides, in song
　　I could once beat all of them by chalks.
Though you find me, as I near my goal,
　　Sentimentalising like Rousseau,
Oh! I had a grand Byronian soul
　　　　Twenty golden years ago!

Tick-tick, tick-tick!—Not a sound save Time's,
　　And the windgust, as it drives the rain—
Tortured torturer of reluctant rhymes,
　　Go to bed, and rest thine aching brain!
Sleep!—no more the dupe of hopes or schemes;
　　Soon thou sleepest where the thistles blow—
Curious anticlimax to thy dreams
　　　　Twenty golden years ago!

THOMAS LOVELL BEDDOES
1803–1849

493   *A Crocodile*

Hard by the lilied Nile I saw
A duskish river-dragon stretched along,
The brown habergeon of his limbs enamelled
With sanguine almandines and rainy pearl:
And on his back there lay a young one sleeping,
No bigger than a mouse; with eyes like beads,
And a small fragment of its speckled egg
Remaining on its harmless, pulpy snout;
A thing to laugh at, as it gaped to catch
The baulking merry flies. In the iron jaws
Of the great devil-beast, like a pale soul
Fluttering in rocky hell, lightsomely flew
A snowy trochilus, with roseate beak
Tearing the hairy leeches from his throat.

494–5   from *Death's Jest-Book*

494   *Song by Isbrand* [Act III, scene iii]

　　Squats on a toad-stool under a tree
　　　　A bodiless childfull of life in the gloom,

Crying with frog voice, 'What shall I be?
Poor unborn ghost, for my mother killed me
  Scarcely alive in her wicked womb.
What shall I be? shall I creep to the egg
  That's cracking asunder yonder by Nile,
    And with eighteen toes,
    And a snuff-taking nose,
  Make an Egyptian crocodile?
Sing, "Catch a mummy by the leg
And crunch him with an upper jaw,
Wagging tail and clenching claw;
Take a bill-full from my craw,
Neighbour raven, caw, O caw,
Grunt, my crocky, pretty maw!"

'Swine, shall I be one? 'Tis a dear dog;
  But for a smile, and kiss, and pout,
  I much prefer *your* black-lipped snout,
    Little, gruntless, fairy hog,
    Godson of the hawthorn hedge.
For, when Ringwood snuffs me out,
    And 'gins my tender paunch to grapple,
    Sing, "'Twixt your ancles visage wedge,
      And roll up like an apple."

'Serpent Lucifer, how do you do?
Of your worms and your snakes I'd be one or two
  For in this dear planet of wool and of leather
'Tis pleasant to need no shirt, breeches or shoe,
  And have arm, leg, and belly together.
  Then aches your head, or are you lazy?
  Sing, "Round your neck your belly wrap,
  Tail-a-top, and make your cap
    Any bee and daisy."

'I'll not be a fool, like the nightingale
Who sits up all midnight without any ale,
  Making a noise with his nose;
Nor a camel, although 'tis a beautiful back;
Nor a duck, notwithstanding the music of quack
  And the webby, mud-patting toes.
I'll be a new bird with the head of an ass,
    Two pigs' feet, two men's feet, and two of a hen;
Devil-winged; dragon-bellied; grave-jawed, because grass
  Is a beard that's soon shaved, and grows seldom again
    Before it is summer; so cow all the rest;
    The new Dodo is finished. O! come to my nest.'

495   *Dirge* [Act V, scene iv]

We do lie beneath the grass
  In the moonlight, in the shade
Of the yew-tree. They that pass
  Hear us not. We are afraid
    They would envy our delight,
    In our graves by glow-worm night.
Come follow us, and smile as we;
    We sail to the rock in the ancient waves,
Where the snow falls by thousands into the sea,
    And the drowned and the shipwrecked have happy graves.

ELIZABETH BARRETT BROWNING

1806–1861

496   from *Sonnets from the Portuguese*

XXIV

Let the world's sharpness, like a clasping knife,
Shut in upon itself and do no harm
In this close hand of Love, now soft and warm,
And let us hear no sound of human strife
After the click of the shutting. Life to life—
I lean upon thee, Dear, without alarm,
And feel as safe as guarded by a charm
Against the stab of worldlings, who if rife
Are weak to injure. Very whitely still
The lilies of our lives may reassure
Their blossoms from their roots, accessible
Alone to heavenly dews that drop not fewer,
Growing straight, out of man's reach, on the hill.
God only, who made us rich, can make us poor.

497   *The Best Thing in the World*

What's the best thing in the world?
June-rose, by May-dew impearled;
Sweet south-wind, that means no rain;
Truth, not cruel to a friend;
Pleasure, not in haste to end;

Beauty, not self-decked and curled
Till its pride is over-plain;
Light, that never makes you wink;
Memory, that gives no pain;
Love, when, *so*, you're loved again.
What's the best thing in the world?
—Something out of it, I think.

CHARLES TURNER

[formerly TENNYSON]

1808–1879

498   *Letty's Globe*

When Letty had scarce pass'd her third glad year,
And her young, artless words began to flow,
One day we gave the child a colour'd sphere
Of the wide earth, that she might mark and know,
By tint and outline, all its sea and land.
She patted all the world; old empires peep'd
Between her baby fingers; her soft hand
Was welcome at all frontiers. How she leap'd,
And laugh'd, and prattled in her world-wide bliss;
But when we turned her sweet unlearnèd eye
On our own isle, she raised a joyous cry,
'Oh! yes, I see it, Letty's home is there!'
And, while she hid all England with a kiss,
Bright over Europe fell her golden hair.

499   *A Country Dance*

He has not woo'd, but he has lost his heart.
That country dance is a sore test for him;
He thinks her cold; his hopes are faint and dim;
But though with seeming mirth she takes her part
In all the dances and the laughter there,
And though to many a youth, on brief demand,
She gives a kind assent and courteous hand,
She loves but him, for him is all her care.
With jealous heed her lessening voice he hears
Down that long vista, where she seems to move

Among fond faces and relays of love,
And sweet occasion, full of tender fears:
Down those long lines he watches from above,
Till with the refluent dance she reappears.

EDWARD FitzGERALD

1809–1883

500–1   from *Rubáiyát of Omar Khayyám*

500   [stanzas I–XI]

Awake! for Morning in the Bowl of Night
Has flung the Stone that puts the Stars to Flight:
    And Lo! the Hunter of the East has caught
The Sultán's Turret in a Noose of Light.

Dreaming when Dawn's Left Hand was in the Sky
I heard a Voice within the Tavern cry,
    'Awake, my Little ones, and fill the Cup
'Before Life's Liquor in its Cup be dry.'

And, as the Cock crew, those who stood before
The Tavern shouted—'Open then the Door!
    'You know how little while we have to stay,
'And, once departed, may return no more.'

Now the New Year reviving old Desires,
The thoughtful Soul to Solitude retires,
    Where the WHITE HAND OF MOSES on the Bough
Puts out, and Jesus from the Ground suspires.

Irám indeed is gone with all its Rose,
And Jamshýd's Sev'n-ring'd Cup where no one knows;
    But still the Vine her ancient Ruby yields,
And still a Garden by the Water blows.

And David's Lips are lock't; but in divine
High piping Péhlevi, with 'Wine! Wine! Wine!
    '*Red* Wine!'—the Nightingale cries to the Rose
That yellow Cheek of her's to'incarnadine.

Come, fill the Cup, and in the Fire of Spring
The Winter Garment of Repentance fling:
    The Bird of Time has but a little way
To fly—and Lo! the Bird is on the Wing.

And look—a thousand Blossoms with the Day
Woke—and a thousand scatter'd into Clay;
   And this first Summer Month that brings the Rose
Shall take Jamshýd and Kaikobád away.

But come with old Khayyám, and leave the Lot
Of Kaikobád and Kaikhosrú forgot:
   Let Rustum lay about him as he will,
Or Hátim Tai cry Supper—heed them not.

With me along some Strip of Herbage strown
That just divides the desert from the sown,
   Where name of Slave and Sultán scarce is known,
And pity Sultán Máhmúd on his Throne.

Here with a Loaf of Bread beneath the Bough,
A Flask of Wine, a Book of Verse—and Thou
   Beside me singing in the Wilderness—
And Wilderness is Paradise enow.

501   [stanzas XLV–LII]

But leave the Wise to wrangle, and with me
The Quarrel of the Universe let be:
   And, in some corner of the Hubbub coucht,
Make Game of that which makes as much of Thee.

For in and out, above, about, below,
'Tis nothing but a Magic Shadow-show,
   Play'd in a Box whose Candle is the Sun,
Round which we Phantom Figures come and go.

And if the Wine you drink, the Lip you press,
End in the Nothing all Things end in—Yes—
   Then fancy while Thou art, Thou art but what
Thou shalt be—Nothing—Thou shalt not be less.

While the Rose blows along the River Brink,
With old Khayyám the Ruby Vintage drink:
   And when the Angel with his darker Draught
Draws up to Thee—take that, and do not shrink.

'Tis all a Chequer-board of Nights and Days
Where Destiny with Men for Pieces plays:
   Hither and thither moves, and mates, and slays,
And one by one back in the Closet lays.

The Ball no Question makes of Ayes and Noes,
But Right or Left as strikes the Player goes;
   And He that toss'd Thee down into the Field,
He knows about it all—HE knows—HE knows!

The Moving Finger writes; and, having writ,
Moves on: nor all thy Piety nor Wit
   Shall lure it back to cancel half a Line,
Nor all thy Tears wash out a Word of it.

And that inverted Bowl we call The Sky,
Whereunder crawling coop't we live and die,
   Lift not thy hands to *It* for help—for It
Rolls impotently on as Thou or I.

ALFRED, LORD TENNYSON

1809–1892

502   *Ulysses*

It little profits that an idle king,
By this still hearth, among these barren crags,
Match'd with an aged wife, I mete and dole
Unequal laws unto a savage race,
That hoard, and sleep, and feed, and know not me.

I cannot rest from travel: I will drink
Life to the lees: all times I have enjoy'd
Greatly, have suffer'd greatly, both with those
That loved me, and alone; on shore, and when
Thro' scudding drifts the rainy Hyades
Vext the dim sea: I am become a name;
For always roaming with a hungry heart
Much have I seen and known; cities of men
And manners, climates, councils, governments,
Myself not least, but honour'd of them all;
And drunk delight of battle with my peers,
Far on the ringing plains of windy Troy.
I am a part of all that I have met;
Yet all experience is an arch wherethro'
Gleams that untravell'd world, whose margin fades
For ever and for ever when I move.
How dull it is to pause, to make an end,
To rust unburnish'd, not to shine in use!
As tho' to breathe were life. Life piled on life

Were all too little, and of one to me
Little remains: but every hour is saved
From that eternal silence, something more,
A bringer of new things; and vile it were
For some three suns to store and hoard myself,
And this gray spirit yearning in desire
To follow knowledge like a sinking star,
Beyond the utmost bound of human thought.

    This is my son, mine own Telemachus,
To whom I leave the sceptre and the isle—
Well-loved of me, discerning to fulfil
This labour, by slow prudence to make mild
A rugged people, and thro' soft degrees
Subdue them to the useful and the good.
Most blameless is he, centred in the sphere
Of common duties, decent not to fail
In offices of tenderness, and pay
Meet adoration to my household gods,
When I am gone. He works his work, I mine.

    There lies the port; the vessel puffs her sail:
There gloom the dark broad seas. My mariners,
Souls that have toil'd, and wrought, and thought with me—
That ever with a frolic welcome took
The thunder and the sunshine, and opposed
Free hearts, free foreheads—you and I are old;
Old age hath yet his honour and his toil;
Death closes all: but something ere the end,
Some work of noble note, may yet be done,
Not unbecoming men that strove with Gods.
The lights begin to twinkle from the rocks:
The long day wanes: the slow moon climbs: the deep
Moans round with many voices. Come, my friends,
'Tis not too late to seek a newer world.
Push off, and sitting well in order smite
The sounding furrows; for my purpose holds
To sail beyond the sunset, and the baths
Of all the western stars, until I die.
It may be that the gulfs will wash us down:
It may be we shall touch the Happy Isles,
And see the great Achilles, whom we knew.
Tho' much is taken, much abides; and tho'
We are not now that strength which in old days
Moved earth and heaven; that which we are, we are;
One equal temper of heroic hearts,
Made weak by time and fate, but strong in will
To strive, to seek, to find, and not to yield.

503   Break, break, break,
            On thy cold gray stones, O Sea!
        And I would that my tongue could utter
            The thoughts that arise in me.

        O well for the fisherman's boy,
            That he shouts with his sister at play!
        O well for the sailor lad,
            That he sings in his boat on the bay!

        And the stately ships go on
            To their haven under the hill;
        But O for the touch of a vanish'd hand,
            And the sound of a voice that is still!

        Break, break, break,
            At the foot of thy crags, O Sea!
        But the tender grace of a day that is dead
            Will never come back to me.

504–6   from *The Princess*

504   [from section IV]

        Tears, idle tears, I know not what they mean,
        Tears from the depth of some divine despair
        Rise in the heart, and gather to the eyes,
        In looking on the happy Autumn-fields,
        And thinking of the days that are no more.

        Fresh as the first beam glittering on a sail,
        That brings our friends up from the underworld,
        Sad as the last which reddens over one
        That sinks with all we love below the verge;
        So sad, so fresh, the days that are no more.

        Ah, sad and strange as in dark summer dawns
        The earliest pipe of half-awaken'd birds
        To dying ears, when unto dying eyes
        The casement slowly grows a glimmering square;
        So sad, so strange, the days that are no more.

        Dear as remember'd kisses after death,
        And sweet as those by hopeless fancy feign'd
        On lips that are for others; deep as love,
        Deep as first love, and wild with all regret;
        O Death in Life, the days that are no more.

505 [from section VII]

Now sleeps the crimson petal, now the white;
Nor waves the cypress in the palace walk;
Nor winks the gold fin in the porphyry font:
The fire-fly wakens: waken thou with me.

Now droops the milkwhite peacock like a ghost,
And like a ghost she glimmers on to me.

Now lies the Earth all Danaë to the stars,
And all thy heart lies open unto me.

Now slides the silent meteor on, and leaves
A shining furrow, as thy thoughts in me.

Now folds the lily all her sweetness up,
And slips into the bosom of the lake:
So fold thyself, my dearest, thou, and slip
Into my bosom and be lost in me.

506 [from section VII]

Come down, O maid, from yonder mountain height:
What pleasure lives in height (the shepherd sang)
In height and cold, the splendour of the hills?
But cease to move so near the Heavens, and cease
To glide a sunbeam by the blasted Pine,
To sit a star upon the sparkling spire;
And come, for Love is of the valley, come,
For Love is of the valley, come thou down
And find him; by the happy threshold, he,
Or hand in hand with Plenty in the maize,
Or red with spirted purple of the vats,
Or foxlike in the vine; nor cares to walk
With Death and Morning on the silver horns,
Nor wilt thou snare him in the white ravine,
Nor find him dropt upon the firths of ice,
That huddling slant in furrow-cloven falls
To roll the torrent out of dusky doors:
But follow; let the torrent dance thee down
To find him in the valley; let the wild
Lean-headed Eagles yelp alone, and leave
The monstrous ledges there to slope, and spill

Their thousand wreaths of dangling water-smoke,
That like a broken purpose waste in air:
So waste not thou; but come; for all the vales
Await thee; azure pillars of the hearth
Arise to thee; the children call, and I
Thy shepherd pipe, and sweet is every sound,
Sweeter thy voice, but every sound is sweet;
Myriads of rivulets hurrying thro' the lawn,
The moan of doves in immemorial elms,
And murmuring of innumerable bees.

507–8   from *In Memoriam A.H.H.*

507   VII

    Dark house, by which once more I stand
       Here in the long unlovely street,
       Doors, where my heart was used to beat
    So quickly, waiting for a hand,

    A hand that can be clasp'd no more—
       Behold me, for I cannot sleep,
       And like a guilty thing I creep
    At earliest morning to the door.

    He is not here; but far away
       The noise of life begins again,
       And ghastly thro' the drizzling rain
    On the bald street breaks the blank day.

508   XI

    Calm is the morn without a sound,
       Calm as to suit a calmer grief,
       And only thro' the faded leaf
    The chestnut pattering to the ground:

    Calm and deep peace on this high wold,
       And on these dews that drench the furze,
       And all the silvery gossamers
    That twinkle into green and gold:

    Calm and still light on yon great plain
       That sweeps with all its autumn bowers,
       And crowded farms and lessening towers,
    To mingle with the bounding main:

Calm and deep peace in this wide air,
   These leaves that redden to the fall;
   And in my heart, if calm at all,
If any calm, a calm despair:

Calm on the seas, and silver sleep,
   And waves that sway themselves in rest,
   And dead calm in that noble breast
Which heaves but with the heaving deep.

509   *The Charge of the Light Brigade*

Half a league, half a league,
   Half a league onward,
All in the valley of Death
   Rode the six hundred.
'Forward, the Light Brigade!
Charge for the guns!' he said:
Into the valley of Death
   Rode the six hundred.

'Forward, the Light Brigade!'
Was there a man dismay'd?
Not tho' the soldier knew
   Some one had blunder'd:
Their's not to make reply,
Their's not to reason why,
Their's but to do and die:
Into the valley of Death
   Rode the six hundred.

Cannon to right of them,
Cannon to left of them,
Cannon in front of them
   Volley'd and thunder'd;
Storm'd at with shot and shell,
Boldly they rode and well,
Into the jaws of Death,
Into the mouth of Hell
   Rode the six hundred.

Flash'd all their sabres bare,
Flash'd as they turn'd in air
Sabring the gunners there,
Charging an army, while
   All the world wonder'd:

Plunged in the battery-smoke
Right thro' the line they broke;
Cossack and Russian
Reel'd from the sabre-stroke
    Shatter'd and sunder'd.
Then they rode back, but not
    Not the six hundred.

Cannon to right of them,
Cannon to left of them,
Cannon behind them
    Volley'd and thunder'd;
Storm'd at with shot and shell,
While horse and hero fell,
They that had fought so well
Came thro' the jaws of Death,
Back from the mouth of Hell,
All that was left of them,
    Left of six hundred.

When can their glory fade?
O the wild charge they made!
    All the world wonder'd.
Honour the charge they made!
Honour the Light Brigade,
    Noble six hundred!

510   from *Maud*

I. xxii

Come into the garden, Maud,
    For the black bat, night, has flown,
Come into the garden, Maud,
    I am here at the gate alone;
And the woodbine spices are wafted abroad,
    And the musk of the rose is blown.

For a breeze of morning moves,
    And the planet of Love is on high,
Beginning to faint in the light that she loves
    On a bed of daffodil sky,
To faint in the light of the sun she loves,
    To faint in his light, and to die.

All night have the roses heard
    The flute, violin, bassoon;

All night has the casement jessamine stirr'd
　　To the dancers dancing in tune;
Till a silence fell with the waking bird,
　　And a hush with the setting moon.

I said to the lily, 'There is but one
　　With whom she has heart to be gay.
When will the dancers leave her alone?
　　She is weary of dance and play.'
Now half to the setting moon are gone,
　　And half to the rising day;
Low on the sand and loud on the stone
　　The last wheel echoes away.

I said to the rose, 'The brief night goes
　　In babble and revel and wine.
O young lord-lover, what sighs are those,
　　For one that will never be thine?
But mine, but mine,' so I sware to the rose,
　　'For ever and ever, mine.'

And the soul of the rose went into my blood,
　　As the music clash'd in the hall;
And long by the garden lake I stood,
　　For I heard your rivulet fall
From the lake to the meadow and on to the wood,
　　Our wood, that is dearer than all;

From the meadow your walks have left so sweet
　　That whenever a March-wind sighs
He sets the jewel-print of your feet
　　In violets blue as your eyes,
To the woody hollows in which we meet
　　And the valleys of Paradise.

The slender acacia would not shake
　　One long milk-bloom on the tree;
The white lake-blossom fell into the lake
　　As the pimpernel dozed on the lea;
But the rose was awake all night for your sake,
　　Knowing your promise to me;
The lilies and roses were all awake,
　　They sigh'd for the dawn and thee.

Queen rose of the rosebud garden of girls,
　　Come hither, the dances are done,
In gloss of satin and glimmer of pearls,
　　Queen lily and rose in one;
Shine out, little head, sunning over with curls,
　　To the flowers, and be their sun.

There has fallen a splendid tear
   From the passion-flower at the gate.
She is coming, my dove, my dear;
   She is coming, my life, my fate;
The red rose cries, 'She is near, she is near;'
   And the white rose weeps, 'She is late;'
The larkspur listens, 'I hear, I hear;'
   And the lily whispers, 'I wait.'

She is coming, my own, my sweet;
   Were it ever so airy a tread,
My heart would hear her and beat,
   Were it earth in an earthy bed;
My dust would hear her and beat,
   Had I lain for a century dead;
Would start and tremble under her feet,
   And blossom in purple and red.

511   *Tithonus*

The woods decay, the woods decay and fall,
The vapours weep their burthen to the ground,
Man comes and tills the field and lies beneath,
And after many a summer dies the swan.
Me only cruel immortality
Consumes: I wither slowly in thine arms,
Here at the quiet limit of the world,
A white-hair'd shadow roaming like a dream
The ever-silent spaces of the East,
Far-folded mists, and gleaming halls of morn.

   Alas! for this gray shadow, once a man—
So glorious in his beauty and thy choice,
Who madest him thy chosen, that he seem'd
To his great heart none other than a God!
I ask'd thee, 'Give me immortality.'
Then didst thou grant mine asking with a smile,
Like wealthy men, who care not how they give.
But thy strong Hours indignant work'd their wills,
And beat me down and marr'd and wasted me,
And tho' they could not end me, left me maim'd
To dwell in presence of immortal youth,
Immortal age beside immortal youth,
And all I was, in ashes. Can thy love,
Thy beauty, make amends, tho' even now,

Close over us, the silver star, thy guide,
Shines in those tremulous eyes that fill with tears
To hear me? Let me go: take back thy gift:
Why should a man desire in any way
To vary from the kindly race of men
Or pass beyond the goal of ordinance
Where all should pause, as is most meet for all?

    A soft air fans the cloud apart; there comes
A glimpse of that dark world where I was born.
Once more the old mysterious glimmer steals
From thy pure brows, and from thy shoulders pure,
And bosom beating with a heart renew'd.
Thy cheek begins to redden thro' the gloom,
Thy sweet eyes brighten slowly close to mine,
Ere yet they blind the stars, and the wild team
Which love thee, yearning for thy yoke, arise,
And shake the darkness from their loosen'd manes,
And beat the twilight into flakes of fire.

    Lo! ever thus thou growest beautiful
In silence, then before thine answer given
Departest, and thy tears are on my cheek.

    Why wilt thou ever scare me with thy tears,
And make me tremble lest a saying learnt,
In days far-off, on that dark earth, be true?
'The Gods themselves cannot recall their gifts.'

    Ay me! ay me! with what another heart
In days far-off, and with what other eyes
I used to watch—if I be he that watch'd—
The lucid outline forming round thee; saw
The dim curls kindle into sunny rings;
Changed with thy mystic change, and felt my blood
Glow with the glow that slowly crimson'd all
Thy presence and thy portals, while I lay,
Mouth, forehead, eyelids, growing dewy-warm
With kisses balmier than half-opening buds
Of April, and could hear the lips that kiss'd
Whispering I knew not what of wild and sweet,
Like that strange song I heard Apollo sing,
While Ilion like a mist rose into towers.

    Yet hold me not for ever in thine East:
How can my nature longer mix with thine?
Coldly thy rosy shadows bathe me, cold
Are all thy lights, and cold my wrinkled feet

Upon thy glimmering thresholds, when the steam
Floats up from those dim fields about the homes
Of happy men that have the power to die,
And grassy barrows of the happier dead.
Release me, and restore me to the ground;
Thou seëst all things, thou wilt see my grave:
Thou wilt renew thy beauty morn by morn;
I earth in earth forget these empty courts,
And thee returning on thy silver wheels.

WILLIAM MILLER

1810–1872

512 Wee Willie Winkie rins through the town,
Up stairs and doon stairs in his nicht-gown,
Tirling at the window, crying at the lock,
Are the weans in their bed, for it's now ten o'clock?

Hey, Willie Winkie, are ye coming ben?   5
The cat's singing grey thrums to the sleeping hen,
The dog's spelder'd on the floor, and disna gi'e a cheep,
But here's a waukrife laddie! that winna fa' asleep.

Onything but sleep, you rogue! glow'ring like the moon,
Rattling in an airn jug wi' an airn spoon,   10
Rumbling, tumbling round about, crawing like a cock,
Skirling like a kenna-what, wauk'ning sleeping fock.

Hey, Willie Winkie—the wean's in a creel!
Wambling aff a bodie's knee like a very eel,
Rugging at the cat's lug, and raveling a' her thrums— 15
Hey, Willie Winkie—see, there he comes!

Wearied is the mither that has a stoorie wean,
A wee stumpie stoussie, that canna rin his lane,
That has a battle aye wi' sleep before he'll close an ee—
But a kiss frae aff his rosy lips gi'es strength anew to me. 20

512: 3 *Tirling*] rapping   4 *weans*] young children (wee anes)   5 *ben*] in
6 *thrums*] purrings 7 *spelder'd*] stretched out 8 *waukrife*] indisposed to sleep
10 *airn*] iron 12 *kenna-what*] don't know what *fock*] folk 13 *creel*] state of
temporary mental aberration 17 *stoorie*] restless 18 *stumpie stoussie*] plump sturdy
child *rin his lane*] go on his own

ROBERT BROWNING

1812–1889

513   *My Last Duchess*

Ferrara

That's my last Duchess painted on the wall,
Looking as if she were alive. I call
That piece a wonder, now: Frà Pandolf's hands
Worked busily a day, and there she stands.
Will't please you sit and look at her? I said
'Frà Pandolf' by design, for never read
Strangers like you that pictured countenance,
The depth and passion of its earnest glance,
But to myself they turned (since none puts by
The curtain I have drawn for you, but I)
And seemed as they would ask me, if they durst,
How such a glance came there; so, not the first
Are you to turn and ask thus. Sir, 't was not
Her husband's presence only, called that spot
Of joy into the Duchess' cheek: perhaps
Frà Pandolf chanced to say 'Her mantle laps
'Over my lady's wrist too much,' or 'Paint
'Must never hope to reproduce the faint
'Half-flush that dies along her throat:' such stuff
Was courtesy, she thought, and cause enough
For calling up that spot of joy. She had
A heart—how shall I say?—too soon made glad,
Too easily impressed; she liked whate'er
She looked on, and her looks went everywhere.
Sir, 't was all one! My favour at her breast,
The dropping of the daylight in the West,
The bough of cherries some officious fool
Broke in the orchard for her, the white mule
She rode with round the terrace—all and each
Would draw from her alike the approving speech,
Or blush, at least. She thanked men,—good! but thanked
Somehow—I know not how—as if she ranked
My gift of a nine-hundred-years-old name
With anybody's gift. Who'd stoop to blame
This sort of trifling? Even had you skill
In speech—(which I have not)—to make your will
Quite clear to such an one, and say, 'Just this
'Or that in you disgusts me; here you miss,

'Or there exceed the mark'—and if she let
Herself be lessoned so, nor plainly set
Her wits to yours, forsooth, and made excuse,
—E'en then would be some stooping; and I choose
Never to stoop. Oh sir, she smiled, no doubt,
Whene'er I passed her; but who passed without
Much the same smile? This grew; I gave commands;
Then all smiles stopped together. There she stands
As if alive. Will't please you rise? We'll meet
The company below, then. I repeat,
The Count your master's known munificence
Is ample warrant that no just pretence
Of mine for dowry will be disallowed;
Though his fair daughter's self, as I avowed
At starting, is my object. Nay, we'll go
Together down, sir. Notice Neptune, though,
Taming a sea-horse, thought a rarity,
Which Claus of Innsbruck cast in bronze for me!

514   *Soliloquy of the Spanish Cloister*

Gr-r-r—there go, my heart's abhorrence!
    Water your damned flower-pots, do!
If hate killed men, Brother Lawrence,
    God's blood, would not mine kill you!
What? your myrtle-bush wants trimming?
    Oh, that rose has prior claims—
Needs its leaden vase filled brimming?
    Hell dry you up with its flames!

At the meal we sit together:
    Salve tibi! I must hear
Wise talk of the kind of weather,
    Sort of season, time of year:
Not a plenteous cork-crop: scarcely
    Dare we hope oak-galls, I doubt:
What's the Latin name for 'parsley'?
    What's the Greek name for Swine's Snout?

Whew! We'll have our platter burnished,
    Laid with care on our own shelf!
With a fire-new spoon we're furnished,
    And a goblet for ourself,
Rinsed like something sacrificial
    Ere 't is fit to touch our chaps—
Marked with L. for our initial!
    (He-he! There his lily snaps!)

Saint, forsooth! While brown Dolores
   Squats outside the Convent bank
With Sanchicha, telling stories,
   Steeping tresses in the tank,
Blue-black, lustrous, thick like horsehairs,
   —Can't I see his dead eye glow,
Bright as 't were a Barbary corsair's?
   (That is, if he'd let it show!)

When he finishes refection,
   Knife and fork he never lays
Cross-wise, to my recollection,
   As do I, in Jesu's praise.
I the Trinity illústrate,
   Drinking watered orange-pulp—
In three sips the Arian frustrate;
   While he drains his at one gulp.

Oh, those melons? If he's able
   We're to have a feast! so nice!
One goes to the Abbot's table,
   All of us get each a slice.
How go on your flowers? None double?
   Not one fruit-sort can you spy?
Strange!—And I, too, at such trouble,
   Keep them close-nipped on the sly!

There's a great text in Galatians,
   Once you trip on it, entails
Twenty-nine distinct damnations,
   One sure, if another fails:
If I trip him just a-dying,
   Sure of heaven as sure can be,
Spin him round and send him flying
   Off to hell, a Manichee?

Or, my scrofulous French novel
   On grey paper with blunt type!
Simply glance at it, you grovel
   Hand and foot in Belial's gripe:
If I double down its pages
   At the woeful sixteenth print,
When he gathers his greengages,
   Ope a sieve and slip it in 't?

Or, there's Satan!—one might venture
   Pledge one's soul to him, yet leave
Such a flaw in the indenture
   As he'd miss till, past retrieve,

Blasted lay that rose-acacia
　　We're so proud of! *Hy, Zy, Hine* ...
'St, there's Vespers! *Plena gratiâ*
　　Ave, Virgo! Gr-r-r—you swine!

515   *Meeting at Night*

The grey sea and the long black land;
And the yellow half-moon large and low;
And the startled little waves that leap
In fiery ringlets from their sleep,
As I gain the cove with pushing prow,
And quench its speed i' the slushy sand.

Then a mile of warm sea-scented beach;
Three fields to cross till a farm appears;
A tap at the pane, the quick sharp scratch
And blue spurt of a lighted match,
And a voice less loud, thro' its joys and fears,
Than the two hearts beating each to each!

516   *Memorabilia*

Ah, did you once see Shelley plain,
　　And did he stop and speak to you
And did you speak to him again?
　　How strange it seems and new!

But you were living before that,
　　And also you are living after;
And the memory I started at—
　　My starting moves your laughter.

I crossed a moor, with a name of its own
　　And a certain use in the world no doubt,
Yet a hand's-breadth of it shines alone
　　'Mid the blank miles round about:

For there I picked up on the heather
　　And there I put inside my breast
A moulted feather, an eagle-feather!
　　Well, I forget the rest.

517   *Two in the Campagna*

I wonder do you feel to-day
    As I have felt since, hand in hand,
We sat down on the grass, to stray
    In spirit better through the land,
This morn of Rome and May?

For me, I touched a thought, I know,
    Has tantalized me many times,
(Like turns of thread the spiders throw
    Mocking across our path) for rhymes
To catch at and let go.

Help me to hold it! First it left
    The yellowing fennel, run to seed
There, branching from the brickwork's cleft,
    Some old tomb's ruin: yonder weed
Took up the floating weft,

Where one small orange cup amassed
    Five beetles,—blind and green they grope
Among the honey-meal: and last,
    Everywhere on the grassy slope
I traced it. Hold it fast!

The champaign with its endless fleece
    Of feathery grasses everywhere!
Silence and passion, joy and peace,
    An everlasting wash of air—
Rome's ghost since her decease.

Such life here, through such lengths of hours,
    Such miracles performed in play,
Such primal naked forms of flowers,
    Such letting nature have her way
While heaven looks from its towers!

How say you? Let us, O my dove,
    Let us be unashamed of soul,
As earth lies bare to heaven above!
    How is it under our control
To love or not to love?

I would that you were all to me,
    You that are just so much, no more.
Nor yours nor mine, nor slave nor free!
    Where does the fault lie? What the core
O' the wound, since wound must be?

I would I could adopt your will,
   See with your eyes, and set my heart
Beating by yours, and drink my fill
   At your soul's springs,—your part my part
In life, for good and ill.

No. I yearn upward, touch you close,
   Then stand away. I kiss your cheek,
Catch your soul's warmth,—I pluck the rose
   And love it more than tongue can speak—
Then the good minute goes.

Already how am I so far
   Out of that minute? Must I go
Still like the thistle-ball, no bar,
   Onward, whenever light winds blow
Fixed by no friendly star?

Just when I seemed about to learn!
   Where is the thread now? Off again!
The old trick! Only I discern—
   Infinite passion, and the pain
Of finite hearts that yearn.

518   *Love in a Life*

Room after room,
I hunt the house through
We inhabit together.
Heart, fear nothing, for, heart, thou shalt find her—
Next time, herself!—not the trouble behind her
Left in the curtain, the couch's perfume!
As she brushed it, the cornice-wreath blossomed anew:
Yon looking-glass gleamed at the wave of her feather.

Yet the day wears,
And door succeeds door;
I try the fresh fortune—
Range the wide house from the wing to the centre.
Still the same chance! she goes out as I enter.
Spend my whole day in the quest,—who cares?
But 't is twilight, you see,—with such suites to explore,
Such closets to search, such alcóves to importune!

EDWARD LEAR

1812–1888

519   There was an Old Man on some rocks,
    Who shut his wife up in a box,
    When she said, 'Let me out,' he exclaimed, 'Without doubt,
    You will pass all your life in that box.'

520   There was an old man who screamed out
    Whenever they knocked him about;
    So they took off his boots, And fed him with fruits,
    And continued to knock him about.

521   *The Dong with a Luminous Nose*

    When awful darkness and silence reign
    Over the great Gromboolian plain,
      Through the long, long wintry nights;—
    When the angry breakers roar
    As they beat on the rocky shore;—
      When Storm-clouds brood on the towering heights
    Of the Hills of the Chankly Bore:—

    Then, through the vast and gloomy dark,
    There moves what seems a fiery spark,
      A lonely spark with silvery rays
      Piercing the coal-black night,—
    A Meteor strange and bright:—
    Hither and thither the vision strays,
      A single lurid light.

    Slowly it wanders,—pauses,—creeps,—
    Anon it sparkles,—flashes and leaps;
    And ever as onward it gleaming goes
    A light on the Bong-tree stems it throws.
    And those who watch at that midnight hour
    From Hall or Terrace, or lofty Tower,
    Cry, as the wild light passes along,—
        'The Dong!—the Dong!
      'The wandering Dong through the forest goes!
        'The Dong! the Dong!
      'The Dong with a luminous Nose!'

Long years ago
The Dong was happy and gay,
Till he fell in love with a Jumbly Girl
Who came to those shores one day,
For the Jumblies came in a sieve, they did,—
Landing at eve near the Zemmery Fidd
Where the Oblong Oysters grow,
And the rocks are smooth and gray.
And all the woods and the valleys rang
With the Chorus they daily and nightly sang,—
    'Far and few, far and few,
    Are the lands where the Jumblies live;
    Their heads are green, and their hands are blue
    And they went to sea in a sieve.'

Happily, happily passed those days!
While the cheerful Jumblies staid;
They danced in circlets all night long,
To the plaintive pipe of the lively Dong,
In moonlight, shine, or shade.
For day and night he was always there
By the side of the Jumbly Girl so fair,
With her sky-blue hands, and her sea-green hair.
Till the morning came of that hateful day
When the Jumblies sailed in their sieve away,
And the Dong was left on the cruel shore
Gazing—gazing for evermore,—
Ever keeping his weary eyes on
That pea-green sail on the far horizon,—
Singing the Jumbly Chorus still
As he sate all day on the grassy hill,—
    'Far and few, far and few,
    Are the lands where the Jumblies live;
    Their heads are green, and their hands are blue,
    And they went to sea in a sieve.'

But when the sun was low in the West,
The Dong arose and said,—
—'What little sense I once possessed
Has quite gone out of my head!'—
And since that day he wanders still
By lake and forest, marsh and hill,
Singing—'O somewhere, in valley or plain
'Might I find my Jumbly Girl again!
'For ever I'll seek by lake and shore
'Till I find my Jumbly Girl once more!'

    Playing a pipe with silvery squeaks,
    Since then his Jumbly Girl he seeks,

And because by night he could not see,
He gathered the bark of the Twangum Tree
  On the flowery plain that grows.
  And he wove him a wondrous Nose,—
  A Nose as strange as a Nose could be!
Of vast proportions and painted red,
And tied with cords to the back of his head.
  —In a hollow rounded space it ended
  With a luminous Lamp within suspended,
    All fenced about
    With a bandage stout
    To prevent the wind from blowing it out;—
  And with holes all round to send the light,
  In gleaming rays on the dismal night.

And now each night, and all night long,
Over those plains still roams the Dong;
And above the wail of the Chimp and Snipe
You may hear the squeak of his plaintive pipe
While ever he seeks, but seeks in vain
To meet with his Jumbly Girl again;
Lonely and wild—all night he goes,—
The Dong with a luminous Nose!
And all who watch at the midnight hour,
From Hall or Terrace, or lofty Tower,
Cry, as they trace the Meteor bright,
Moving along through the dreary night,—
  'This is the hour when forth he goes,
  'The Dong with a luminous Nose!
  'Yonder—over the plain he goes;
    'He goes!
    'He goes;
  'The Dong with a luminous Nose!'

522   'How pleasant to know Mr Lear!'
    Who has written such volumes of stuff!
Some think him ill-tempered and queer,
    But a few think him pleasant enough.

His mind is concrete and fastidious,
    His nose is remarkably big;
His visage is more or less hideous,
    His beard it resembles a wig.

He has ears, and two eyes, and ten fingers,
    Leastways if you reckon two thumbs;
Long ago he was one of the singers,
    But now he is one of the dumbs.

He sits in a beautiful parlour,
    With hundreds of books on the wall;
He drinks a great deal of Marsala,
    But never gets tipsy at all.

He has many friends, laymen and clerical,
    Old Foss is the name of his cat:
His body is perfectly spherical,
    He weareth a runcible hat.

When he walks in a waterproof white,
    The children run after him so!
Calling out, 'He's come out in his night-
    gown, that crazy old Englishman, oh!'

He weeps by the side of the ocean,
    He weeps on the top of the hill;
He purchases pancakes and lotion,
    And chocolate shrimps from the mill.

He reads but he cannot speak Spanish,
    He cannot abide ginger-beer:
Ere the days of his pilgrimage vanish,
    How pleasant to know Mr Lear!

CHARLOTTE BRONTË

1816–1855

(perhaps EMILY JANE BRONTË)

523   Often rebuked, yet always back returning
    To those first feelings that were born with me,
And leaving busy chase of wealth and learning
    For idle dreams of things which cannot be:

Today, I will seek not the shadowy region;
    Its unsustaining vastness waxes drear;
And visions rising, legion after legion,
    Bring the unreal world too strangely near.

I'll walk, but not in old heroic traces,
    And not in paths of high morality,
And not among the half-distinguished faces,
    The clouded forms of long-past history.

I'll walk where my own nature would be leading:
    It vexes me to choose another guide:
Where the grey flocks in ferny glens are feeding;
    Where the wild wind blows on the mountain side.

What have those lonely mountains worth revealing?
    More glory and more grief than I can tell:
The earth that wakes *one* human heart to feeling
    Can centre both the worlds of Heaven and Hell.

EMILY JANE BRONTË

1818–1848

524   What winter floods what showers of spring
Have drenched the grass by night and day
And yet beneath that spectre ring
Unmoved and undiscovered lay

A mute remembrancer of crime
Long lost concealed forgot for years
It comes at last to cancel time
And waken unavailing tears

525   The night is darkening round me
The wild winds coldly blow
But a tyrant spell has bound me
And I cannot cannot go

The giant trees are bending
Their bare boughs weighed with snow
And the storm is fast descending
And yet I cannot go

Clouds beyond clouds above me
Wastes beyond wastes below
But nothing drear can move me
I will not cannot go

526   All hushed and still within the house
Without—all wind and driving rain
But something whispers to my mind
Through rain and through the wailing wind
            —Never again
Never again? Why not again?
Memory has power as real as thine

527　　　　Long neglect has worn away
　　　　　Half the sweet enchanting smile
　　　　　Time has turned the bloom to grey
　　　　　Mould and damp the face defile

　　　　　But that lock of silky hair
　　　　　Still beneath the picture twined
　　　　　Tells what once those features were
　　　　　Paints their image on the mind

　　　　　Fair the hand that traced that line
　　　　　'Dearest ever deem me true'
　　　　　Swiftly flew the fingers fine
　　　　　When the pen that motto drew

528　　　　I know not how it falls on me
　　　　　This summer evening, hushed and lone
　　　　　Yet the faint wind comes soothingly
　　　　　With something of an olden tone

　　　　　Forgive me if I've shunned so long
　　　　　Your gentle greeting earth and air
　　　　　But sorrow withers even the strong
　　　　　And who can fight against despair

529　　　　　　　　*Remembrance*

　　　　Cold in the earth—and the deep snow piled above thee,
　　　　Far, far, removed, cold in the dreary grave!
　　　　Have I forgot, my only Love, to love thee,
　　　　Severed at last by Time's all-severing wave?

　　　　Now, when alone, do my thoughts no longer hover
　　　　Over the mountains, on that northern shore,
　　　　Resting their wings where heath and fern-leaves cover
　　　　Thy noble heart for ever, ever more?

　　　　Cold in the earth—and fifteen wild Decembers,
　　　　From those brown hills, have melted into spring:
　　　　Faithful, indeed, is the spirit that remembers
　　　　After such years of change and suffering!

　　　　Sweet Love of youth, forgive, if I forget thee,
　　　　While the world's tide is bearing me along;
　　　　Other desires and other hopes beset me,
　　　　Hopes which obscure, but cannot do thee wrong!

No later light has lightened up my heaven,
No second morn has ever shone for me;
All my life's bliss from thy dear life was given,
All my life's bliss is in the grave with thee.

But, when the days of golden dreams had perished,
And even Despair was powerless to destroy;
Then did I learn how existence could be cherished,
Strengthened, and fed without the aid of joy.

Then did I check the tears of useless passion—
Weaned my young soul from yearning after thine;
Sternly denied its burning wish to hasten
Down to that tomb already more than mine.

And, even yet, I dare not let it languish,
Dare not indulge in memory's rapturous pain;
Once drinking deep of that divinest anguish,
How could I seek the empty world again?

EMILY JANE BRONTË
and CHARLOTTE BRONTË

530   *The Visionary*

Silent is the house: all are laid asleep:
One alone looks out o'er the snow-wreaths deep;
Watching every cloud, dreading every breeze
That whirls the wildering drift, and bends the groaning trees.

Cheerful is the hearth, soft the matted floor;
Not one shivering gust creeps through pane or door;
The little lamp burns straight, its rays shoot strong and far:
I trim it well, to be the wanderer's guiding-star.

Frown, my haughty sire! chide, my angry dame;
Set your slaves to spy; threaten me with shame:
But neither sire nor dame, nor prying serf shall know,
What angel nightly tracks that waste of frozen snow.

What I love shall come like visitant of air,
Safe in secret power from lurking human snare;
What loves me, no word of mine shall e'er betray,
Though for faith unstained my life must forfeit pay.

Burn, then, little lamp; glimmer straight and clear—
Hush! a rustling wing stirs, methinks, the air:
He for whom I wait, thus ever comes to me;
Strange Power! I trust thy might; trust thou my constancy.

ARTHUR HUGH CLOUGH

1819–1861

531   Say not the struggle nought availeth,
              The labour and the wounds are vain,
         The enemy faints not, nor faileth,
              And as things have been, things remain.

         If hopes were dupes, fears may be liars;
              It may be, in yon smoke concealed,
         Your comrades chase e'en now the fliers,
              And, but for you, possess the field.

         For while the tired waves, vainly breaking,
              Seem here no painful inch to gain,
         Far back through creeks and inlets making
              Came, silent, flooding in, the main,

         And not by eastern windows only,
              When daylight comes, comes in the light,
         In front the sun climbs slow, how slowly,
              But westward, look, the land is bright.

532   *The Latest Decalogue*

         Thou shalt have one God only; who
         Would be at the expense of two?
         No graven images may be
         Worshipped, except the currency:
         Swear not at all; for for thy curse
         Thine enemy is none the worse:
         At church on Sunday to attend
         Will serve to keep the world thy friend:
         Honour thy parents; that is, all
         From whom advancement may befall:
         Thou shalt not kill; but needst not strive
         Officiously to keep alive:

Do not adultery commit;
Advantage rarely comes of it:
Thou shalt not steal; an empty feat,
When it's so lucrative to cheat:
Bear not false witness; let the lie
Have time on its own wings to fly:
Thou shalt not covet; but tradition
Approves all forms of competition.

The sum of all is, thou shalt love,
If any body, God above:
At any rate shall never labour
More than thyself to love thy neighbour.

533   from *Dipsychus* [Scene VI]

'There is no God,' the wicked saith,
  'And truly it's a blessing,
For what he might have done with us
  It's better only guessing.'

'There is no God,' a youngster thinks,
  'Or really, if there may be,
He surely didn't mean a man
  Always to be a baby.'

'There is no God, or if there is,'
  The tradesman thinks, ''twere funny
If he should take it ill in me
  To make a little money.'

'Whether there be,' the rich man says,
  'It matters very little,
For I and mine, thank somebody,
  Are not in want of victual.'

Some others, also, to themselves
  Who scarce so much as doubt it,
Think there is none, when they are well,
  And do not think about it.

But country folks who live beneath
  The shadow of the steeple;
The parson and the parson's wife,
  And mostly married people;

Youths green and happy in first love,
　　So thankful for illusion;
And men caught out in what the world
　　Calls guilt, in first confusion;

And almost every one when age,
　　Disease, or sorrows strike him,
Inclines to think there is a God,
　　Or something very like Him.

JEAN INGELOW

1820–1897

534　　　　　*The Long White Seam*

As I came round the harbour buoy,
　　The lights began to gleam,
No wave the land-locked water stirred,
　　The crags were white as cream;
And I marked my love by candle-light
　　Sewing her long white seam.
　　　　It's aye sewing ashore, my dear,
　　　　　Watch and steer at sea,
　　　　It's reef and furl, and haul the line,
　　　　　Set sail and think of thee.

I climbed to reach her cottage door;
　　O sweetly my love sings!
Like a shaft of light her voice breaks forth,
　　My soul to meet it springs
As the shining water leaped of old,
　　When stirred by angel wings.
　　　　Aye longing to list anew,
　　　　　Awake and in my dream,
　　　　But never a song she sang like this,
　　　　　Sewing her long white seam.

Fair fall the lights, the harbour lights,
　　That brought me in to thee,
And peace drop down on that low roof
　　For the sight that I did see,
And the voice, my dear, that rang so clear
　　All for the love of me.
　　　　For O, for O, with brows bent low
　　　　　By the candle's flickering gleam,
　　　　Her wedding gown it was she wrought,
　　　　　Sewing the long white seam.

MATTHEW ARNOLD
1822–1888

535   *To Marguerite—Continued*

Yes! in the sea of life enisled,
With echoing straits between us thrown,
Dotting the shoreless watery wild,
We mortal millions live *alone*.
The islands feel the enclasping flow,
And then their endless bounds they know.

But when the moon their hollows lights,
And they are swept by balms of spring,
And in their glens, on starry nights,
The nightingales divinely sing;
And lovely notes, from shore to shore,
Across the sounds and channels pour—

Oh! then a longing like despair
Is to their farthest caverns sent;
For surely once, they feel, we were
Parts of a single continent!
Now round us spreads the watery plain—
Oh might our marges meet again!

Who order'd, that their longing's fire
Should be, as soon as kindled, cool'd?
Who renders vain their deep desire?—
A God, a God their severance ruled!
And bade betwixt their shores to be
The unplumb'd, salt, estranging sea.

536   from *Sohrab and Rustum* [line 865–end]

And night came down over the solemn waste,
And the two gazing hosts, and that sole pair,
And darken'd all; and a cold fog, with night,
Crept from the Oxus. Soon a hum arose,
As of a great assembly loosed, and fires
Began to twinkle through the fog; for now
Both armies moved to camp, and took their meal;
The Persians took it on the open sands

Southward, the Tartars by the river marge;
And Rustum and his son were left alone.
   But the majestic river floated on,
Out of the mist and hum of that low land,
Into the frosty starlight, and there moved,
Rejoicing, through the hush'd Chorasmian waste,
Under the solitary moon;—he flow'd
Right for the polar star, past Orgunjè,
Brimming, and bright, and large; then sands begin
To hem his watery march, and dam his streams,
And split his currents; that for many a league
The shorn and parcell'd Oxus strains along
Through beds of sand and matted rushy isles—
Oxus, forgetting the bright speed he had
In his high mountain-cradle in Pamere,
A foil'd circuitous wanderer—till at last
The long'd-for dash of waves is heard, and wide
His luminous home of waters opens, bright
And tranquil, from whose floor the new-bathed stars
Emerge, and shine upon the Aral Sea.

537   from *The Scholar-Gipsy* [line 201–end]

O born in days when wits were fresh and clear,
   And life ran gaily as the sparkling Thames;
      Before this strange disease of modern life,
   With its sick hurry, its divided aims,
         Its heads o'ertax'd, its palsied hearts, was rife—
            Fly hence, our contact fear!
   Still fly, plunge deeper in the bowering wood!
      Averse, as Dido did with gesture stern
      From her false friend's approach in Hades turn,
   Wave us away, and keep thy solitude!

Still nursing the unconquerable hope,
   Still clutching the inviolable shade,
      With a free, onward impulse brushing through,
   By night, the silver'd branches of the glade—
         Far on the forest-skirts, where none pursue,
            On some mild pastoral slope
   Emerge, and resting on the moonlit pales
      Freshen thy flowers as in former years
      With dew, or listen with enchanted ears,
   From the dark dingles, to the nightingales!

But fly our paths, our feverish contact fly!
   For strong the infection of our mental strife,
      Which, though it gives no bliss, yet spoils for rest;
   And we should win thee from thy own fair life,
      Like us distracted, and like us unblest.
       Soon, soon, thy cheer would die,
   Thy hopes grow timorous, and unfix'd thy powers,
      And thy clear aims be cross and shifting made;
   And then thy glad perennial youth would fade,
Fade, and grow old at last, and die like ours.

Then fly our greetings, fly our speech and smiles!
   —As some grave Tyrian trader, from the sea,
      Descried at sunrise an emerging prow
   Lifting the cool-hair'd creepers stealthily,
      The fringes of a southward-facing brow
       Among the Ægæan isles;
   And saw the merry Grecian coaster come,
      Freighted with amber grapes, and Chian wine,
      Green, bursting figs, and tunnies steep'd in brine—
   And knew the intruders on his ancient home,

The young light-hearted masters of the waves—
   And snatch'd his rudder, and shook out more sail;
      And day and night held on indignantly
O'er the blue Midland waters with the gale,
      Betwixt the Syrtes and soft Sicily,
       To where the Atlantic raves
Outside the western straits; and unbent sails
      There, where down cloudy cliffs, through sheets of foam,
      Shy traffickers, the dark Iberians come;
   And on the beach undid his corded bales.

538   *Dover Beach*

     The sea is calm to-night.
     The tide is full, the moon lies fair
     Upon the straits;—on the French coast the light
     Gleams and is gone; the cliffs of England stand,
     Glimmering and vast, out in the tranquil bay.
     Come to the window, sweet is the night-air!

     Only, from the long line of spray
     Where the sea meets the moon-blanch'd land,
     Listen! you hear the grating roar
     Of pebbles which the waves draw back, and fling,

At their return, up the high strand,
Begin, and cease, and then again begin,
With tremulous cadence slow, and bring
The eternal note of sadness in.

Sophocles long ago
Heard it on the Ægæan, and it brought
Into his mind the turbid ebb and flow
Of human misery; we
Find also in the sound a thought,
Hearing it by this distant northern sea.

The Sea of Faith
Was once, too, at the full, and round earth's shore
Lay like the folds of a bright girdle furl'd.
But now I only hear
Its melancholy, long, withdrawing roar,
Retreating, to the breath
Of the night-wind, down the vast edges drear
And naked shingles of the world.

Ah, love, let us be true
To one another! for the world, which seems
To lie before us like a land of dreams,
So various, so beautiful, so new,
Hath really neither joy, nor love, nor light,
Nor certitude, nor peace, nor help for pain;
And we are here as on a darkling plain
Swept with confused alarms of struggle and flight,
Where ignorant armies clash by night.

COVENTRY PATMORE

1823–1896

539   *Magna est Veritas*

Here, in this little Bay,
Full of tumultuous life and great repose,
Where, twice a day,
The purposeless, glad ocean comes and goes,
Under high cliffs, and far from the huge town,
I sit me down.
For want of me the world's course will not fail:
When all its work is done, the lie shall rot;
The truth is great, and shall prevail,
When none cares whether it prevail or not.

540   *Arbor Vitæ*

With honeysuckle, over-sweet, festoon'd;
With bitter ivy bound;
Terraced with funguses unsound;
Deform'd with many a boss
And closed scar, o'ercushion'd deep with moss;
Bunch'd all about with pagan mistletoe;
And thick with nests of the hoarse bird
That talks, but understands not his own word;
Stands, and so stood a thousand years ago,
A single tree.
Thunder has done its worst among its twigs,
Where the great crest yet blackens, never pruned,
But in its heart, alway
Ready to push new verdurous boughs, whene'er
The rotting saplings near it fall and leave it air,
Is all antiquity and no decay.
Rich, though rejected by the forest-pigs,
Its fruit, beneath whose rough, concealing rind
They that will break it find
Heart-succouring savour of each several meat,
And kernell'd drink of brain-renewing power,
With bitter condiment and sour,
And sweet economy of sweet,
And odours that remind
Of haunts of childhood and a different day.
Beside this tree,
Praising no Gods nor blaming, sans a wish,
Sits, Tartar-like, the Time's civility,
And eats its dead-dog off a golden dish.

WILLIAM ALLINGHAM
1824–1889

541   Everything passes and vanishes;
                  Everything leaves its trace;
              And often you see in a footstep
                  What you could not see in a face.

542   No funeral gloom, my dears, when I am gone,
           Corpse-gazing, tears, black raiment, graveyard grimness;
           Think of me as withdrawn into the dimness,

Yours still, you mine; remember all the best
Of our past moments, and forget the rest;
And so, to where I wait, come gently on.

GEORGE MEREDITH

1828–1909

543–5   from *Modern Love*

543   XXXIV

Madam would speak with me. So, now it comes:
The Deluge or else Fire! She's well; she thanks
My husbandship. Our chain on silence clanks.
Time leers between, above his twiddling thumbs.
Am I quite well? Most excellent in health!
The journals, too, I diligently peruse.
Vesuvius is expected to give news:
Niagara is no noisier. By stealth
Our eyes dart scrutinizing snakes. She's glad
I'm happy, says her quivering under-lip.
'And are not you?' 'How can I be?' 'Take ship!
For happiness is somewhere to be had.'
'Nowhere for me!' Her voice is barely heard.
I am not melted, and make no pretence.
With commonplace I freeze her, tongue and sense.
Niagara or Vesuvius is deferred.

544   XLVII

We saw the swallows gathering in the sky,
And in the osier-isle we heard them noise.
We had not to look back on summer joys,
Or forward to a summer of bright dye:
But in the largeness of the evening earth
Our spirits grew as we went side by side.
The hour became her husband and my bride.
Love that had robbed us so, thus blessed our dearth!
The pilgrims of the year waxed very loud
In multitudinous chatterings, as the flood
Full brown came from the West, and like pale blood
Expanded to the upper crimson cloud.

Love that had robbed us of immortal things,
This little moment mercifully gave,
Where I have seen across the twilight wave
The swan sail with her young beneath her wings.

545   L

Thus piteously Love closed what he begat:
The union of this ever-diverse pair!
These two were rapid falcons in a snare,
Condemned to do the flitting of the bat.
Lovers beneath the singing sky of May,
They wandered once; clear as the dew on flowers:
But they fed not on the advancing hours:
Their hearts held cravings for the buried day.
Then each applied to each that fatal knife,
Deep questioning, which probes to endless dole.
Ah, what a dusty answer gets the soul
When hot for certainties in this our life!—
In tragic hints here see what evermore
Moves dark as yonder midnight ocean's force,
Thundering like ramping hosts of warrior horse,
To throw that faint thin line upon the shore!

546   *Lucifer in Starlight*

On a starred night Prince Lucifer uprose.
Tired of his dark dominion swung the fiend
Above the rolling ball in cloud part screened,
Where sinners hugged their spectre of repose.
Poor prey to his hot fit of pride were those.
And now upon his western wing he leaned,
Now his huge bulk o'er Afric's sands careened,
Now the black planet shadowed Arctic snows.
Soaring through wider zones that pricked his scars
With memory of the old revolt from Awe,
He reached a middle height, and at the stars,
Which are the brain of heaven, he looked, and sank.
Around the ancient track marched, rank on rank,
The army of unalterable law.

DANTE GABRIEL ROSSETTI
1828–1882

547 *A Half-Way Pause*

The turn of noontide has begun.
  In the weak breeze the sunshine yields.
  There is a bell upon the fields.
On the long hedgerow's tangled run
  A low white cottage intervenes:
  Against the wall a blind man leans,
And sways his face to have the sun.

Our horses' hoofs stir in the road,
  Quiet and sharp. Light hath a song
  Whose silence, being heard, seems long.
The point of noon maketh abode,
  And will not be at once gone through.
  The sky's deep colour saddens you,
And the heat weighs a dreamy load.

548 *Sudden Light*

I have been here before,
  But when or how I cannot tell:
I know the grass beyond the door,
  The sweet, keen smell,
The sighing sound, the lights around the shore.

You have been mine before,—
  How long ago I may not know:
But just when at that swallow's soar
  Your neck turned so,
Some veil did fall,—I knew it all of yore.

Has this been thus before?
  And shall not thus time's eddying flight
Still with our lives our love restore
  In death's despite,
And day and night yield one delight once more?

549 ## *A Match with the Moon*

Weary already, weary miles to-night
 I walked for bed: and so, to get some ease,
 I dogged the flying moon with similes.
And like a wisp she doubled on my sight
In ponds; and caught in tree-tops like a kite;
 And in a globe of film all liquorish
 Swam full-faced like a silly silver fish;—
Last like a bubble shot the welkin's height
Where my road turned, and got behind me, and sent
 My wizened shadow craning round at me,
 And jeered, 'So, step the measure,—one two three!'
And if I faced on her, looked innocent.
But just at parting, halfway down a dell,
She kissed me for good-night. So you'll not tell.

550 ## *The Woodspurge*

The wind flapped loose, the wind was still,
Shaken out dead from tree and hill:
I had walked on at the wind's will,—
I sat now, for the wind was still.

Between my knees my forehead was,—
My lips drawn in, said not Alas!
My hair was over in the grass,
My naked ears heard the day pass.

My eyes, wide open, had the run
Of some ten weeds to fix upon;
Among those few, out of the sun,
The woodspurge flowered, three cups in one.

From perfect grief there need not be
Wisdom or even memory:
One thing then learnt remains to me,—
The woodspurge has a cup of three.

CHRISTINA G. ROSSETTI
1830–1894

551   *Goblin Market*

Morning and evening
Maids heard the goblins cry:
'Come buy our orchard fruits,
Come buy, come buy:
Apples and quinces,
Lemons and oranges,
Plump unpecked cherries,
Melons and raspberries,
Bloom-down-cheeked peaches,
Swart-headed mulberries,
Wild free-born cranberries,
Crab-apples, dewberries,
Pine-apples, blackberries,
Apricots, strawberries;—
All ripe together
In summer weather,—
Morns that pass by,
Fair eves that fly;
Come buy, come buy:
Our grapes fresh from the vine,
Pomegranates full and fine,
Dates and sharp bullaces,
Rare pears and greengages,
Damsons and bilberries,
Taste them and try:
Currants and gooseberries,
Bright-fire-like barberries,
Figs to fill your mouth,
Citrons from the South,
Sweet to tongue and sound to eye;
Come buy, come buy.'

Evening by evening
Among the brookside rushes,
Laura bowed her head to hear,
Lizzie veiled her blushes:
Crouching close together
In the cooling weather,
With clasping arms and cautioning lips,
With tingling cheeks and finger tips.

'Lie close,' Laura said,
Pricking up her golden head:
'We must not look at goblin men,
We must not buy their fruits:
Who knows upon what soil they fed
Their hungry thirsty roots?'
'Come buy,' call the goblins
Hobbling down the glen.
'Oh,' cried Lizzie, 'Laura, Laura,
You should not peep at goblin men.'
Lizzie covered up her eyes,
Covered close lest they should look;
Laura reared her glossy head,
And whispered like the restless brook:
'Look, Lizzie, look, Lizzie,
Down the glen tramp little men.
One hauls a basket,
One bears a plate,
One lugs a golden dish
Of many pounds weight.
How fair the vine must grow
Whose grapes are so luscious;
How warm the wind must blow
Thro' those fruit bushes.'
'No,' said Lizzie: 'No, no, no;
Their offers should not charm us,
Their evil gifts would harm us.'
She thrust a dimpled finger
In each ear, shut eyes and ran:
Curious Laura chose to linger
Wondering at each merchant man.
One had a cat's face,
One whisked a tail,
One tramped at a rat's pace,
One crawled like a snail,
One like a wombat prowled obtuse and furry,
One like a ratel tumbled hurry skurry.
She heard a voice like voice of doves
Cooing all together:
They sounded kind and full of loves
In the pleasant weather.

Laura stretched her gleaming neck
Like a rush-imbedded swan,
Like a lily from the beck,
Like a moonlit poplar branch,
Like a vessel at the launch

When its last restraint is gone.
Backwards up the mossy glen
Turned and trooped the goblin men,
With their shrill repeated cry,
'Come buy, come buy.'
When they reached where Laura was
They stood stock still upon the moss,
Leering at each other,
Brother with queer brother;
Signalling each other,
Brother with sly brother.
One set his basket down,
One reared his plate;
One began to weave a crown
Of tendrils, leaves and rough nuts brown
(Men sell not such in any town);
One heaved the golden weight
Of dish and fruit to offer her:
'Come buy, come buy,' was still their cry.

Laura stared but did not stir,
Longed but had no money:
The whisk-tailed merchant bade her taste
In tones as smooth as honey,
The cat-faced purr'd,
The rat-paced spoke a word
Of welcome, and the snail-paced even was heard;
One parrot-voiced and jolly
Cried 'Pretty Goblin' still for 'Pretty Polly;'—
One whistled like a bird.

But sweet-tooth Laura spoke in haste:
'Good folk, I have no coin;
To take were to purloin:
I have no copper in my purse,
I have no silver either,
And all my gold is on the furze
That shakes in windy weather
Above the rusty heather.'
'You have much gold upon your head,'
They answered all together:
'Buy from us with a golden curl.'
She clipped a precious golden lock,
She dropped a tear more rare than pearl,
Then sucked their fruit globes fair or red:
Sweeter than honey from the rock,
Stronger than man-rejoicing wine,

Clearer than water flowed that juice;
She never tasted such before,
How should it cloy with length of use?
She sucked and sucked and sucked the more
Fruits which that unknown orchard bore;
She sucked until her lips were sore;
Then flung the emptied rinds away
But gathered up one kernel-stone,
And knew not was it night or day
As she turned home alone.

Lizzie met her at the gate
Full of wise upbraidings:
'Dear, you should not stay so late,
Twilight is not good for maidens;
Should not loiter in the glen
In the haunts of goblin men.
Do you not remember Jeanie,
How she met them in the moonlight,
Took their gifts both choice and many,
Ate their fruits and wore their flowers
Plucked from bowers
Where summer ripens at all hours?
But ever in the noonlight
She pined and pined away;
Sought them by night and day,
Found them no more but dwindled and grew grey;
Then fell with the first snow,
While to this day no grass will grow
Where she lies low:
I planted daisies there a year ago
That never blow.
You should not loiter so.'
'Nay, hush,' said Laura:
'Nay, hush, my sister:
I ate and ate my fill,
Yet my mouth waters still;
Tomorrow night I will
Buy more:' and kissed her:
'Have done with sorrow;
I'll bring you plums tomorrow
Fresh on their mother twigs,
Cherries worth getting;
You cannot think what figs
My teeth have met in,
What melons icy-cold
Piled on a dish of gold

Too huge for me to hold,
What peaches with a velvet nap,
Pellucid grapes without one seed:
Odorous indeed must be the mead
Whereon they grow, and pure the wave they drink
With lilies at the brink,
And sugar-sweet their sap.'

Golden head by golden head,
Like two pigeons in one nest
Folded in each other's wings,
They lay down in their curtained bed:
Like two blossoms on one stem,
Like two flakes of new-fall'n snow,
Like two wands of ivory
Tipped with gold for awful kings.
Moon and stars gazed in at them,
Wind sang to them lullaby,
Lumbering owls forbore to fly,
Not a bat flapped to and fro
Round their rest:
Cheek to cheek and breast to breast
Locked together in one nest.

Early in the morning
When the first cock crowed his warning,
Neat like bees, as sweet and busy,
Laura rose with Lizzie:
Fetched in honey, milked the cows,
Aired and set to rights the house,
Kneaded cakes of whitest wheat,
Cakes for dainty mouths to eat,
Next churned butter, whipped up cream,
Fed their poultry, sat and sewed;
Talked as modest maidens should:
Lizzie with an open heart,
Laura in an absent dream,
One content, one sick in part;
One warbling for the mere bright day's delight,
One longing for the night.

At length slow evening came:
They went with pitchers to the reedy brook;
Lizzie most placid in her look,
Laura most like a leaping flame.
They drew the gurgling water from its deep;
Lizzie plucked purple and rich golden flags,

Then turning homewards said: 'The sunset flushes
Those furthest loftiest crags;
Come, Laura, not another maiden lags,
No wilful squirrel wags,
The beasts and birds are fast asleep.'
But Laura loitered still among the rushes
And said the bank was steep.

And said the hour was early still,
The dew not fall'n, the wind not chill:
Listening ever, but not catching
The customary cry,
'Come buy, come buy,'
With its iterated jingle
Of sugar-baited words:
Not for all her watching
Once discerning even one goblin
Racing, whisking, tumbling, hobbling;
Let alone the herds
That used to tramp along the glen,
In groups or single,
Of brisk fruit-merchant men.
Till Lizzie urged, 'O Laura, come;
I hear the fruit-call but I dare not look:
You should not loiter longer at this brook:
Come with me home.
The stars rise, the moon bends her arc,
Each glowworm winks her spark,
Let us get home before the night grows dark:
For clouds may gather
Tho' this is summer weather,
Put out the lights and drench us thro';
Then if we lost our way what should we do?'

Laura turned cold as stone
To find her sister heard that cry alone,
That goblin cry,
'Come buy our fruits, come buy.'
Must she then buy no more such dainty fruit?
Must she no more such succous pasture find,
Gone deaf and blind?
Her tree of life drooped from the root:
She said not one word in her heart's sore ache;
But peering thro' the dimness, nought discerning,
Trudged home, her pitcher dripping all the way;
So crept to bed, and lay

Silent till Lizzie slept;
Then sat up in a passionate yearning,
And gnashed her teeth for baulked desire, and wept
As if her heart would break.

Day after day, night after night,
Laura kept watch in vain
In sullen silence of exceeding pain.
She never caught again the goblin cry:
'Come buy, come buy;'—
She never spied the goblin men
Hawking their fruits along the glen:
But when the noon waxed bright
Her hair grew thin and gray;
She dwindled, as the fair full moon doth turn
To swift decay and burn
Her fire away.

One day remembering her kernel-stone
She set it by a wall that faced the south;
Dewed it with tears, hoped for a root,
Watched for a waxing shoot,
But there came none;
It never saw the sun,
It never felt the trickling moisture run:
While with sunk eyes and faded mouth
She dreamed of melons, as a traveller sees
False waves in desert drouth
With shade of leaf-crowned trees,
And burns the thirstier in the sandful breeze.

She no more swept the house,
Tended the fowls or cows,
Fetched honey, kneaded cakes of wheat,
Brought water from the brook:
But sat down listless in the chimney-nook
And would not eat.

Tender Lizzie could not bear
To watch her sister's cankerous care
Yet not to share.
She night and morning
Caught the goblins' cry:
'Come buy our orchard fruits,
Come buy, come buy:'—
Beside the brook, along the glen,
She heard the tramp of goblin men,
The voice and stir
Poor Laura could not hear;

Longed to buy fruit to comfort her,
But feared to pay too dear.
She thought of Jeanie in her grave,
Who should have been a bride;
But who for joys brides hope to have
Fell sick and died
In her gay prime,
In earliest Winter time,
With the first glazing rime,
With the first snow-fall of crisp Winter time.

Till Laura dwindling
Seemed knocking at Death's door:
Then Lizzie weighed no more
Better and worse;
But put a silver penny in her purse,
Kissed Laura, crossed the heath with clumps of furze
At twilight, halted by the brook:
And for the first time in her life
Began to listen and look.

Laughed every goblin
When they spied her peeping:
Came towards her hobbling,
Flying, running, leaping,
Puffing and blowing,
Chuckling, clapping, crowing,
Clucking and gobbling,
Mopping and mowing,
Full of airs and graces,
Pulling wry faces,
Demure grimaces,
Cat-like and rat-like,
Ratel- and wombat-like,
Snail-paced in a hurry,
Parrot-voiced and whistler,
Helter skelter, hurry skurry,
Chattering like magpies,
Fluttering like pigeons,
Gliding like fishes,—
Hugged her and kissed her,
Squeezed and caressed her:
Stretched up their dishes,
Panniers, and plates:
'Look at our apples
Russet and dun,
Bob at our cherries,

Bite at our peaches,
Citrons and dates,
Grapes for the asking,
Pears red with basking
Out in the sun,
Plums on their twigs;
Pluck them and suck them,
Pomegranates, figs.'—

'Good folk,' said Lizzie,
Mindful of Jeanie:
'Give me much and many:'—
Held out her apron,
Tossed them her penny.
'Nay, take a seat with us,
Honour and eat with us,'
They answered grinning:
'Our feast is but beginning.
Night yet is early,
Warm and dew-pearly,
Wakeful and starry:
Such fruits as these
No man can carry;
Half their bloom would fly,
Half their dew would dry,
Half their flavour would pass by.
Sit down and feast with us,
Be welcome guest with us,
Cheer you and rest with us.'—
'Thank you,' said Lizzie: 'But one waits
At home alone for me:
So without further parleying,
If you will not sell me any
Of your fruits tho' much and many,
Give me back my silver penny
I tossed you for a fee.'—
They began to scratch their pates,
No longer wagging, purring,
But visibly demurring,
Grunting and snarling.
One called her proud,
Cross-grained, uncivil;
Their tones waxed loud,
Their looks were evil.
Lashing their tails
They trod and hustled her,
Elbowed and jostled her,

Clawed with their nails,
Barking, mewing, hissing, mocking,
Tore her gown and soiled her stocking,
Twitched her hair out by the roots,
Stamped upon her tender feet,
Held her hands and squeezed their fruits
Against her mouth to make her eat.

White and golden Lizzie stood,
Like a lily in a flood,—
Like a rock of blue-veined stone
Lashed by tides obstreperously,—
Like a beacon left alone
In a hoary roaring sea,
Sending up a golden fire,—
Like a fruit-crowned orange-tree
White with blossoms honey-sweet
Sore beset by wasp and bee,—
Like a royal virgin town
Topped with gilded dome and spire
Close beleaguered by a fleet
Mad to tug her standard down.

One may lead a horse to water,
Twenty cannot make him drink.
Tho' the goblins cuffed and caught her,
Coaxed and fought her,
Bullied and besought her,
Scratched her, pinched her black as ink,
Kicked and knocked her,
Mauled and mocked her,
Lizzie uttered not a word;
Would not open lip from lip
Lest they should cram a mouthful in:
But laughed in heart to feel the drip
Of juice that syrupped all her face,
And lodged in dimples of her chin,
And streaked her neck which quaked like curd.
At last the evil people
Worn out by her resistance
Flung back her penny, kicked their fruit
Along whichever road they took,
Not leaving root or stone or shoot;
Some writhed into the ground,
Some dived into the brook
With ring and ripple,
Some scudded on the gale without a sound,
Some vanished in the distance.

In a smart, ache, tingle,
Lizzie went her way;
Knew not was it night or day;
Sprang up the bank, tore thro' the furze,
Threaded copse and dingle,
And heard her penny jingle
Bouncing in her purse,
Its bounce was music to her ear.
She ran and ran
As if she feared some goblin man
Dogged her with gibe or curse
Or something worse:
But not one goblin skurried after,
Nor was she pricked by fear;
The kind heart made her windy-paced
That urged her home quite out of breath with haste
And inward laughter.

She cried 'Laura,' up the garden,
'Did you miss me?
Come and kiss me.
Never mind my bruises,
Hug me, kiss me, suck my juices
Squeezed from goblin fruits for you,
Goblin pulp and goblin dew.
Eat me, drink me, love me;
Laura, make much of me:
For your sake I have braved the glen
And had to do with goblin merchant men.'

Laura started from her chair,
Flung her arms up in the air,
Clutched her hair:
'Lizzie, Lizzie, have you tasted
For my sake the fruit forbidden?
Must your light like mine be hidden,
Your young life like mine be wasted,
Undone in mine undoing
And ruined in my ruin,
Thirsty, cankered, goblin-ridden?'—
She clung about her sister,
Kissed and kissed and kissed her:
Tears once again
Refreshed her shrunken eyes,
Dropping like rain
After long sultry drouth;
Shaking with aguish fear, and pain,
She kissed and kissed her with a hungry mouth.

Her lips began to scorch,
That juice was wormwood to her tongue,
She loathed the feast:
Writhing as one possessed she leaped and sung,
Rent all her robe, and wrung
Her hands in lamentable haste,
And beat her breast.
Her locks streamed like the torch
Borne by a racer at full speed,
Or like the mane of horses in their flight,
Or like an eagle when she stems the light
Straight toward the sun,
Or like a caged thing freed,
Or like a flying flag when armies run.

Swift fire spread thro' her veins, knocked at her heart,
Met the fire smouldering there
And overbore its lesser flame;
She gorged on bitterness without a name:
Ah! fool, to choose such part
Of soul-consuming care!
Sense failed in the mortal strife:
Like the watch-tower of a town
Which an earthquake shatters down,
Like a lightning-stricken mast,
Like a wind-uprooted tree
Spun about,
Like a foam-topped waterspout
Cast down headlong in the sea,
She fell at last;
Pleasure past and anguish past,
Is it death or is it life?

Life out of death.
That night long Lizzie watched by her,
Counted her pulse's flagging stir,
Felt for her breath,
Held water to her lips, and cooled her face
With tears and fanning leaves:
But when the first birds chirped about their eaves,
And early reapers plodded to the place
Of golden sheaves,
And dew-wet grass
Bowed in the morning winds so brisk to pass,
And new buds with new day
Opened of cup-like lilies on the stream,
Laura awoke as from a dream,
Laughed in the innocent old way,

472

CHRISTINA G. ROSSETTI

Hugged Lizzie but not twice or thrice;
Her gleaming locks showed not one thread of grey,
Her breath was sweet as May
And light danced in her eyes.

Days, weeks, months, years
Afterwards, when both were wives
With children of their own;
Their mother-hearts beset with fears,
Their lives bound up in tender lives;
Laura would call the little ones
And tell them of her early prime,
Those pleasant days long gone
Of not-returning time:
Would talk about the haunted glen,
The wicked, quaint fruit-merchant men,
Their fruits like honey to the throat
But poison in the blood;
(Men sell not such in any town:)
Would tell them how her sister stood
In deadly peril to do her good,
And win the fiery antidote:
Then joining hands to little hands
Would bid them cling together,
'For there is no friend like a sister
In calm or stormy weather;
To cheer one on the tedious way,
To fetch one if one goes astray,
To lift one if one totters down,
To strengthen whilst one stands.'

552   *From the Antique*

It's a weary life, it is, she said:—
    Doubly blank in a woman's lot:
I wish and I wish I were a man:
    Or, better than any being, were not:

Were nothing at all in all the world,
    Not a body and not a soul:
Not so much as a grain of dust
    Or drop of water from pole to pole.

Still the world would wag on the same,
    Still the seasons go and come:
Blossoms bloom as in days of old,
    Cherries ripen and wild bees hum.

None would miss me in all the world,
　How much less would care or weep:
I should be nothing, while all the rest
　Would wake and weary and fall asleep.

553 ### *May*

I cannot tell you how it was;
But this I know: it came to pass
Upon a bright and breezy day
When May was young; ah pleasant May!
As yet the poppies were not born
Between the blades of tender corn;
The last eggs had not hatched as yet,
Nor any bird foregone its mate.

I cannot tell you what it was;
But this I know: it did but pass.
It passed away with sunny May,
With all sweet things it passed away,
And left me old, and cold, and grey.

554 ### *Somewhere or Other*

Somewhere or other there must surely be
　The face not seen, the voice not heard,
The heart that not yet—never yet— ah me!
　Made answer to my word.

Somewhere or other, may be near or far;
　Past land and sea, clean out of sight;
Beyond the wandering moon, beyond the star
　That tracks her night by night.

Somewhere or other, may be far or near;
　With just a wall, a hedge, between;
With just the last leaves of the dying year
　Fallen on a turf grown green.

555 ### *A Dirge*

Why were you born when the snow was falling?
You should have come to the cuckoo's calling,
Or when grapes are green in the cluster,
Or, at least, when lithe swallows muster
　　For their far off flying
　　From summer dying.

Why did you die when the lambs were cropping?
You should have died at the apples' dropping,
When the grasshopper comes to trouble,
And the wheat-fields are sodden stubble,
      And all winds go sighing
      For sweet things dying.

556   *A Christmas Carol*

In the bleak mid-winter
   Frosty wind made moan,
Earth stood hard as iron,
   Water like a stone;
Snow had fallen, snow on snow,
   Snow on snow,
In the bleak mid-winter
   Long ago.

Our God, Heaven cannot hold Him
   Nor earth sustain;
Heaven and earth shall flee away
   When He comes to reign:
In the bleak mid-winter
   A stable-place sufficed
The Lord God Almighty
   Jesus Christ.

Enough for Him whom cherubim
   Worship night and day,
A breastful of milk
   And a mangerful of hay;
Enough for Him whom angels
   Fall down before,
The ox and ass and camel
   Which adore.

Angels and archangels
   May have gathered there,
Cherubim and seraphim
   Throng'd the air,
But only His mother
   In her maiden bliss
Worshipped the Beloved
   With a kiss.

What can I give Him,
    Poor as I am?
If I were a shepherd
    I would bring a lamb,
If I were a wise man
    I would do my part,—
Yet what I can I give Him,
    Give my heart.

557   *'Summer is Ended'*

To think that this meaningless thing was ever a rose,
    Scentless, colourless, *this*!
  Will it ever be thus (who knows?)
    Thus with our bliss,
  If we wait till the close?

Tho' we care not to wait for the end, there comes the end
    Sooner, later, at last,
  Which nothing can mar, nothing mend:
    An end locked fast,
  Bent we cannot re-bend.

LEWIS CARROLL
[CHARLES LUTWIDGE DODGSON]
1832–1898

558   How doth the little crocodile
    Improve his shining tail,
And pour the waters of the Nile
    On every golden scale!

How cheerfully he seems to grin,
    How neatly spreads his claws,
And welcomes little fishes in,
    With gently smiling jaws!

559   'You are old, Father William,' the young man said
    'And your hair has become very white;
And yet you incessantly stand on your head—
    Do you think, at your age, it is right?'

'In my youth', Father William replied to his son,
   'I feared it might injure the brain;
But, now that I'm perfectly sure I have none,
   Why, I do it again and again.'

'You are old,' said the youth, 'as I mentioned before,
   And have grown most uncommonly fat;
Yet you turned a back-somersault in at the door—
   Pray, what is the reason of that?'

'In my youth', said the sage, as he shook his grey locks,
   'I kept all my limbs very supple
By the use of this ointment—one shilling the box—
   Allow me to sell you a couple?'

'You are old,' said the youth, 'and your jaws are too weak
   For anything tougher than suet;
Yet you finished the goose, with the bones and the beak—
   Pray, how did you manage to do it?'

'In my youth', said his father, 'I took to the law,
   And argued each case with my wife;
And the muscular strength, which it gave to my jaw
   Has lasted the rest of my life.'

'You are old,' said the youth, 'one would hardly suppose
   That your eye was as steady as ever;
Yet you balanced an eel on the end of your nose—
   What made you so awfully clever?'

'I have answered three questions, and that is enough,'
   Said his father, 'Don't give yourself airs!
Do you think I can listen all day to such stuff?
   Be off, or I'll kick you down-stairs!'

560   *Jabberwocky*

'Twas brillig, and the slithy toves
   Did gyre and gimble in the wabe:
All mimsy were the borogoves,
   And the mome raths outgrabe.

'Beware the Jabberwock, my son!
   The jaws that bite, the claws that catch!
Beware the Jubjub bird, and shun
   The frumious Bandersnatch!'

He took his vorpal sword in hand:
   Long time the manxome foe he sought—
So rested he by the Tumtum tree,
   And stood awhile in thought.

And, as in uffish thought he stood,
   The Jabberwock, with eyes of flame,
Came whiffling through the tulgey wood,
   And burbled as it came!

One, two! One, two! And through and through
   The vorpal blade went snicker-snack!
He left it dead, and with its head
   He went galumphing back.

'And hast thou slain the Jabberwock?
   Come to my arms, my beamish boy!
O frabjous day! Callooh! Callay!'
   He chortled in his joy.

'Twas brillig, and the slithy toves
   Did gyre and gimble in the wabe:
All mimsy were the borogoves,
   And the mome raths outgrabe.

RICHARD WATSON DIXON

1833–1900

561   *Dream*

I

With camel's hair I clothed my skin,
   I fed my mouth with honey wild;
And set me scarlet wool to spin,
   And all my breast with hyssop filled;
Upon my brow and cheeks and chin
   A bird's blood spilled.

I took a broken reed to hold,
   I took a sponge of gall to press;
I took weak water-weeds to fold
   About my sacrificial dress.

I took the grasses of the field,
   The flax was bolled upon my crine;
And ivy thorn and wild grapes healed
   To make good wine.

I took my scrip of manna sweet,
   My cruse of water did I bless;
I took the white dove by the feet,
   And flew into the wilderness.

II

The tiger came and played;
Uprose the lion in his mane;
The jackal's tawny nose
And sanguine dripping tongue
Out of the desert rose
And plunged its sands among;
The bear came striding o'er the desert plain.

Uprose the horn and eyes
And quivering flank of the great unicorn,
And galloped round and round;
Uprose the gleaming claw
Of the leviathan, and wound
In steadfast march did draw
Its course away beyond the desert's bourn.

I stood within a maze
Woven round about me by a magic art,
And ordered circle-wise:
The bear more near did tread,
And with two fiery eyes,
And with a wolfish head,
Did close the circle round in every part.

III

With scarlet corded horn,
With frail wrecked knees and stumbling pace,
The scapegoat came:
His eyes took flesh and spirit dread in flame
At once, and he died looking towards my face.

WILLIAM MORRIS

1834–1896

562   *Summer Dawn*

Pray but one prayer for me 'twixt thy closed lips,
   Think but one thought of me up in the stars.
The summer night waneth, the morning light slips,
   Faint & grey 'twixt the leaves of the aspen, betwixt the cloud-bars,

That are patiently waiting there for the dawn:
   Patient and colourless, though Heaven's gold
Waits to float through them along with the sun.
Far out in the meadows, above the young corn,
   The heavy elms wait, and restless and cold
The uneasy wind rises; the roses are dun;
Through the long twilight they pray for the dawn,
Round the lone house in the midst of the corn.
   Speak but one word to me over the corn,
   Over the tender, bow'd locks of the corn.

563   *Another for the Briar Rose*

O treacherous scent, O thorny sight,
O tangle of world's wrong and right,
What art thou 'gainst my armour's gleam
But dusky cobwebs of a dream?

Beat down, deep sunk from every gleam
Of hope, they lie and dully dream;
Men once, but men no more, that Love
Their waste defeated hearts should move.

Here sleeps the world that would not love!
Let it sleep on, but if He move
Their hearts in humble wise to wait
On his new-wakened fair estate.

O won at last is never late!
Thy silence was the voice of fate;
Thy still hands conquered in the strife;
Thine eyes were light; thy lips were life.

564   *Pomona*

I am the ancient Apple-Queen,
As once I was so am I now.
For evermore a hope unseen,
Betwixt the blossom and the bough.

Ah, where's the river's hidden Gold!
And where the windy grave of Troy?
Yet come I as I came of old,
From out the heart of Summer's joy.

JAMES THOMSON
1834–1882

565   *In the Room*

'*Ceste insigne fable et tragicque comedie*'
                                  —RABELAIS

The sun was down, and twilight grey
    Filled half the air; but in the room,
Whose curtain had been drawn all day,
    The twilight was a dusky gloom:
Which seemed at first as still as death,
    And void; but was indeed all rife
With subtle thrills, the pulse and breath
    Of multitudinous lower life.

In their abrupt and headlong way
    Bewildered flies for light had dashed
Against the curtain all the day,
    And now slept wintrily abashed;
And nimble mice slept, wearied out
    With such a double night's uproar;
But solid beetles crawled about
    The chilly hearth and naked floor.

And so throughout the twilight hour
    That vaguely murmurous hush and rest
There brooded; and beneath its power
    Life throbbing held its throbs supprest:
Until the thin-voiced mirror sighed,
    I am all blurred with dust and damp,
So long ago the clear day died,
    So long has gleamed nor fire nor lamp.

Whereon the curtain murmured back,
    Some change is on us, good or ill;
Behind me and before is black
    As when those human things lie still:
But I have seen the darkness grow
    As grows the daylight every morn;
Have felt out there long shine and glow,
    In here long chilly dusk forlorn.

The cupboard grumbled with a groan,
    Each new day worse starvation brings:
Since *he* came here I have not known
    Or sweets or cates or wholesome things:

But now! a pinch of meal, a crust,
  Throughout the week is all I get.
I am so empty; it is just
  As when they said we were to let.

What is become, then, of our Man?
  The petulant old glass exclaimed;
If all this time he slumber can,
  He really ought to be ashamed.
I wish we had our Girl again,
  So gay and busy, bright and fair:
The girls are better than these men,
  Who only for their dull selves care.

It is so many hours ago—
  The lamp and fire were both alight—
I saw him pacing to and fro,
  Perturbing restlessly the night.
His face was pale to give one fear,
  His eyes when lifted looked too bright;
He muttered; what, I could not hear:
  Bad words though; something was not right.

The table said, He wrote so long
  That I grew weary of his weight;
The pen kept up a cricket song,
  It ran and ran at such a rate:
And in the longer pauses he
  With both his folded arms downpressed
And stared as one who does not see,
  Or sank his head upon his breast.

The fire-grate said, I am as cold
  As if I never had a blaze;
The few dead cinders here I hold,
  I held unburned for days and days.
Last night he made them flare; but still
  What good did all his writing do?
Among my ashes curl and thrill
  Thin ghosts of all those papers too.

The table answered, Not quite all;
  He saved and folded up one sheet,
And sealed it fast, and let it fall;
  And here it lies now white and neat.
Whereon the letter's whisper came,
  My writing is closed up too well;
Outside there's not a single name,
  And who should read me I can't tell.

The mirror sneered with scornful spite,
  (That ancient crack which spoiled her looks
Had marred her temper), Write and write!
  And read those stupid, worn-out books!
That's all he does, read, write, and read,
  And smoke that nasty pipe which stinks:
He never takes the slightest heed
  How any of us feels or thinks.

But Lucy fifty times a day
  Would come and smile here in my face,
Adjust a tress that curled astray,
  Or tie a ribbon with more grace:
She looked so young and fresh and fair,
  She blushed with such a charming bloom,
It did one good to see her there,
  And brightened all things in the room.

She did not sit hours stark and dumb
  As pale as moonshine by the lamp;
To lie in bed when day was come,
  And leave us curtained chill and damp.
She slept away the dreary dark,
  And rose to greet the pleasant morn;
And sang as gaily as a lark
  While busy as the flies sun-born.

And how she loved us every one;
  And dusted this and mended that,
With trills and laughs and freaks of fun,
  And tender scoldings in her chat!
And then her bird, that sang as shrill
  As she sang sweet; her darling flowers
That grew there in the window-sill,
  Where she would sit at work for hours.

It was not much she ever wrote;
  Her fingers had good work to do;
Say, once a week a pretty note;
  And very long it took her too.
And little more she read, I wis;
  Just now and then a pictured sheet,
Besides those letters she would kiss
  And croon for hours, they were so sweet.

She had her friends too, blithe young girls,
  Who whispered, babbled, laughed, caressed,
And romped and danced with dancing curls,
  And gave our life a joyous zest.

But with this dullard, glum and sour,
    Not one of all his fellow-men
Has ever passed a social hour;
    We might be in some wild beast's den.

This long tirade aroused the bed,
    Who spoke in deep and ponderous bass,
Befitting that calm life he led,
    As if firm-rooted in his place:
In broad majestic bulk alone,
    As in thrice venerable age,
He stood at once the royal throne,
    The monarch, the experienced sage:

I know what is and what has been;
    Not anything to me comes strange,
Who in so many years have seen
    And lived through every kind of change.
I know when men are good or bad,
    When well or ill, he slowly said;
When sad or glad, when sane or mad,
    And when they sleep alive or dead.

At this last word of solemn lore
    A tremor circled through the gloom,
As if a crash upon the floor
    Had jarred and shaken all the room:
For nearly all the listening things
    Were old and worn, and knew what curse
Of violent change death often brings,
    From good to bad, from bad to worse;

They get to know each other well,
    To feel at home and settled down;
Death bursts among them like a shell,
    And strews them over all the town.
The bed went on, This man who lies
    Upon me now is stark and cold;
He will not any more arise,
    And do the things he did of old.

But we shall have short peace or rest;
    For soon up here will come a rout,
And nail him in a queer long chest,
    And carry him like luggage out.
They will be muffled all in black,
    And whisper much, and sigh and weep:
But he will never more come back,
    And some one else in me must sleep.

Thereon a little phial shrilled,
   Here empty on the chair I lie:
I heard one say, as I was filled,
   With half of this a man would die.
The man there drank me with slow breath,
   And murmured, Thus ends barren strife:
O sweeter, thou cold wine of death,
   Than ever sweet warm wine of life.

One of my cousins long ago,
   A little thing, the mirror said,
Was carried to a couch to show,
   Whether a man was really dead.
Two great improvements marked the case:
   He did not blur her with his breath,
His many-wrinkled, twitching face
   Was smooth old ivory: verdict, Death.—

It lay, the lowest thing there, lulled
   Sweet-sleep-like in corruption's truce;
The form whose purpose was annulled,
   While all the other shapes meant use.
It lay, the *he* become now *it*,
   Unconscious of the deep disgrace,
Unanxious how its parts might flit
   Through what new forms in time and space.

It lay and preached, as dumb things do,
   More powerfully than tongues can prate;
Though life be torture through and through,
   Man is but weak to plain of fate:
The drear path crawls on drearier still
   To wounded feet and hopeless breast?
Well, he can lie down when he will,
   And straight all ends in endless rest.

And while the black night nothing saw,
   And till the cold morn came at last,
That old bed held the room in awe
   With tales of its experience vast.
It thrilled the gloom; it told such tales
   Of human sorrows and delights,
Of fever moans and infant wails,
   Of births and deaths and bridal nights.

ALGERNON CHARLES SWINBURNE

1837–1909

566   *A Leave-Taking*

Let us go hence, my songs; she will not hear.
Let us go hence together without fear;
Keep silence now, for singing-time is over,
And over all old things and all things dear.
She loves not you nor me as all we love her.
Yea, though we sang as angels in her ear,
          She would not hear.

Let us rise up and part; she will not know.
Let us go seaward as the great winds go,
Full of blown sand and foam; what help is here?
There is no help, for all these things are so,
And all the world is bitter as a tear.
And how these things are, though ye strove to show,
          She would not know.

Let us go home and hence; she will not weep.
We gave love many dreams and days to keep,
Flowers without scent, and fruits that would not grow,
Saying 'If thou wilt, thrust in thy sickle and reap.'
All is reaped now; no grass is left to mow;
And we that sowed, though all we fell on sleep,
          She would not weep.

Let us go hence and rest; she will not love.
She shall not hear us if we sing hereof,
Nor see love's ways, how sore they are and steep.
Come hence, let be, lie still; it is enough.
Love is a barren sea, bitter and deep;
And though she saw all heaven in flower above,
          She would not love.

Let us give up, go down; she will not care.
Though all the stars made gold of all the air,
And the sea moving saw before it move
One moon-flower making all the foam-flowers fair;
Though all those waves went over us, and drove
Deep down the stifling lips and drowning hair,
          She would not care.

Let us go hence, go hence; she will not see.
Sing all once more together; surely she,
She too, remembering days and words that were,

Will turn a little toward us, sighing; but we,
We are hence, we are gone, as though we had not been there.
Nay, and though all men seeing had pity on me,
    She would not see.

567 *The Leper*

Nothing is better, I well think,
    Than love; the hidden well-water
Is not so delicate to drink:
    This was well seen of me and her.

I served her in a royal house;
    I served her wine and curious meat.
For will to kiss between her brows,
    I had no heart to sleep or eat.

Mere scorn God knows she had of me,
    A poor scribe, nowise great or fair,
Who plucked his clerk's hood back to see
    Her curled-up lips and amorous hair.

I vex my head with thinking this.
    Yea, though God always hated me,
And hates me now that I can kiss
    Her eyes, plait up her hair to see

How she then wore it on the brows,
    Yet am I glad to have her dead
Here in this wretched wattled house
    Where I can kiss her eyes and head.

Nothing is better, I well know,
    Than love; no amber in cold sea
Or gathered berries under snow:
    That is well seen of her and me.

Three thoughts I make my pleasure of:
    First I take heart and think of this:
That knight's gold hair she chose to love,
    His mouth she had such will to kiss.

Then I remember that sundawn
    I brought him by a privy way
Out at her lattice, and thereon
    What gracious words she found to say.

(Cold rushes for such little feet—
  Both feet could lie into my hand.
A marvel was it of my sweet
  Her upright body could so stand.)

'Sweet friend, God give you thank and grace;
  Now am I clean and whole of shame,
Nor shall men burn me in the face
  For my sweet fault that scandals them.'

I tell you over word by word.
  She, sitting edgewise on her bed,
Holding her feet, said thus. The third,
  A sweeter thing than these, I said.

God, that makes time and ruins it
  And alters not, abiding God,
Changed with disease her body sweet,
  The body of love wherein she abode.

Love is more sweet and comelier
  Than a dove's throat strained out to sing.
All they spat out and cursed at her
  And cast her forth for a base thing.

They cursed her, seeing how God had wrought
  This curse to plague her, a curse of his.
Fools were they surely, seeing not
  How sweeter than all sweet she is.

He that had held her by the hair,
  With kissing lips blinding her eyes,
Felt her bright bosom, strained and bare,
  Sigh under him, with short mad cries

Out of her throat and sobbing mouth
  And body broken up with love,
With sweet hot tears his lips were loth
  Her own should taste the savour of,

Yea, he inside whose grasp all night
  Her fervent body leapt or lay,
Stained with sharp kisses red and white,
  Found her a plague to spurn away.

I hid her in this wattled house,
  I served her water and poor bread.
For joy to kiss between her brows
  Time upon time I was nigh dead.

Bread failed; we got but well-water
　　And gathered grass with dropping seed.
I had such joy of kissing her,
　　I had small care to sleep or feed.

Sometimes when service made me glad
　　The sharp tears leapt between my lids,
Falling on her, such joy I had
　　To do the service God forbids.

'I pray you let me be at peace,
　　Get hence, make room for me to die.'
She said that: her poor lip would cease,
　　Put up to mine, and turn to cry.

I said, 'Bethink yourself how love
　　Fared in us twain, what either did;
Shall I unclothe my soul thereof?
　　That I should do this, God forbid.'

Yea, though God hateth us, he knows
　　That hardly in a little thing
Love faileth of the work it does
　　Till it grow ripe for gathering.

Six months, and now my sweet is dead
　　A trouble takes me; I know not
If all were done well, all well said,
　　No word or tender deed forgot.

Too sweet, for the least part in her,
　　To have shed life out by fragments; yet,
Could the close mouth catch breath and stir,
　　I might see something I forget.

Six months, and I sit still and hold
　　In two cold palms her cold two feet.
Her hair, half grey half ruined gold,
　　Thrills me and burns me in kissing it.

Love bites and stings me through, to see
　　Her keen face made of sunken bones.
Her worn-off eyelids madden me,
　　That were shot through with purple once.

She said, 'Be good with me; I grow
　　So tired for shame's sake, I shall die
If you say nothing:' even so.
　　And she is dead now, and shame put by.

Yea, and the scorn she had of me
   In the old time, doubtless vexed her then.
I never should have kissed her. See
   What fools God's anger makes of men!

She might have loved me a little too,
   Had I been humbler for her sake.
But that new shame could make love new
   She saw not—yet her shame did make.

I took too much upon my love,
   Having for such mean service done
Her beauty and all the ways thereof,
   Her face and all the sweet thereon.

Yea, all this while I tended her,
   I know the old love held fast his part:
I know the old scorn waxed heavier,
   Mixed with sad wonder, in her heart.

It may be all my love went wrong—
   A scribe's work writ awry and blurred,
Scrawled after the blind evensong—
   Spoilt music with no perfect word.

But surely I would fain have done
   All things the best I could. Perchance
Because I failed, came short of one,
   She kept at heart that other man's.

I am grown blind with all these things:
   It may be now she hath in sight
Some better knowledge; still there clings
   The old question. Will not God do right?

568   *The Garden of Proserpine*

Here, where the world is quiet;
Here, where all trouble seems
Dead winds' and spent waves' riot
In doubtful dreams of dreams;
I watch the green field growing
For reaping folk and sowing,
For harvest-time and mowing,
A sleepy world of streams.

I am tired of tears and laughter,
And men that laugh and weep;
Of what may come hereafter
For men that sow to reap:
I am weary of days and hours,
Blown buds of barren flowers,
Desires and dreams and powers
And everything but sleep.

Here life has death for neighbour,
And far from eye or ear
Wan waves and wet winds labour,
Weak ships and spirits steer;
They drive adrift, and whither
They wot not who make thither;
But no such winds blow hither,
And no such things grow here.

No growth of moor or coppice,
No heather-flower or vine,
But bloomless buds of poppies,
Green grapes of Proserpine,
Pale beds of blowing rushes
Where no leaf blooms or blushes
Save this whereout she crushes
For dead men deadly wine.

Pale, without name or number,
In fruitless fields of corn,
They bow themselves and slumber
All night till light is born;
And like a soul belated,
In hell and heaven unmated,
By cloud and mist abated
Comes out of darkness morn.

Though one were strong as seven,
He too with death shall dwell,
Nor wake with wings in heaven,
Nor weep for pains in hell;
Though one were fair as roses,
His beauty clouds and closes;
And well though love reposes,
In the end it is not well.

Pale, beyond porch and portal,
Crowned with calm leaves, she stands
Who gathers all things mortal
With cold immortal hands;

Her languid lips are sweeter
Than love's who fears to greet her
To men that mix and meet her
From many times and lands.

She waits for each and other,
She waits for all men born;
Forgets the earth her mother,
The life of fruits and corn;
And spring and seed and swallow
Take wing for her and follow
Where summer song rings hollow
And flowers are put to scorn.

There go the loves that wither,
The old loves with wearier wings;
And all dead years draw thither,
And all disastrous things;
Dead dreams of days forsaken,
Blind buds that snows have shaken,
Wild leaves that winds have taken,
Red strays of ruined springs.

We are not sure of sorrow,
And joy was never sure;
To-day will die to-morrow;
Time stoops to no man's lure;
And love, grown faint and fretful,
With lips but half regretful
Sighs, and with eyes forgetful
Weeps that no loves endure.

From too much love of living,
From hope and fear set free,
We thank with brief thanksgiving
Whatever gods may be
That no life lives for ever;
That dead men rise up never;
That even the weariest river
Winds somewhere safe to sea.

Then star nor sun shall waken,
Nor any change of light:
Nor sound of waters shaken,
Nor any sound or sight:
Nor wintry leaves nor vernal,
Nor days nor things diurnal;
Only the sleep eternal
In an eternal night.

569   from *Atalanta in Calydon*

Chorus

When the hounds of spring are on winter's traces,
   The mother of months in meadow or plain
Fills the shadows and windy places
   With lisp of leaves and ripple of rain;
And the brown bright nightingale amorous
Is half assuaged for Itylus,
For the Thracian ships and the foreign faces,
   The tongueless vigil, and all the pain.

Come with bows bent and with emptying of quivers,
   Maiden most perfect, lady of light,
With a noise of winds and many rivers,
   With a clamour of waters, and with might;
Bind on thy sandals, O thou most fleet,
Over the splendour and speed of thy feet;
For the faint east quickens, the wan west shivers,
   Round the feet of the day and the feet of the night.

Where shall we find her, how shall we sing to her,
   Fold our hands round her knees, and cling?
O that man's heart were as fire and could spring to her,
   Fire, or the strength of the streams that spring!
For the stars and the winds are unto her
As raiment, as songs of the harp-player;
For the risen stars and the fallen cling to her,
   And the southwest-wind and the west-wind sing.

For winter's rains and ruins are over,
   And all the season of snows and sins;
The days dividing lover and lover,
   The light that loses, the night that wins;
And time remembered is grief forgotten,
And frosts are slain and flowers begotten,
And in green underwood and cover
   Blossom by blossom the spring begins.

The full streams feed on flower of rushes,
   Ripe grasses trammel a travelling foot,
The faint fresh flame of the young year flushes
   From leaf to flower and flower to fruit;
And fruit and leaf are as gold and fire,
And the oat is heard above the lyre,
And the hoofèd heel of a satyr crushes
   The chestnut-husk at the chestnut-root.

And Pan by noon and Bacchus by night,
  Fleeter of foot than the fleet-foot kid,
Follows with dancing and fills with delight
  The Mænad and the Bassarid;
And soft as lips that laugh and hide
The laughing leaves of the trees divide,
And screen from seeing and leave in sight
  The god pursuing, the maiden hid.

The ivy falls with the Bacchanal's hair
  Over her eyebrows hiding her eyes;
The wild vine slipping down leaves bare
  Her bright breast shortening into sighs;
The wild vine slips with the weight of its leaves,
But the berried ivy catches and cleaves
To the limbs that glitter, the feet that scare
  The wolf that follows, the fawn that flies.

COSMO MONKHOUSE

1840–1901

570   *Any Soul to Any Body*

So we must part, my body, you and I
  Who've spent so many pleasant years together.
'Tis sorry work to lose your company
  Who clove to me so close, whate'er the weather,
From winter unto winter, wet or dry;
  But you have reached the limit of your tether,
And I must journey on my way alone,
And leave you quietly beneath a stone.

They say that you are altogether bad
  (Forgive me, 'tis not my experience),
And think me very wicked to be sad
  At leaving you, a clod, a prison, whence
To get quite free I should be very glad.
  Perhaps I may be so, some few days hence,
But now, methinks, 'twere graceless not to spend
A tear or two on my departing friend.

Now our long partnership is near completed,
  And I look back upon its history;
I greatly fear I have not always treated
  You with the honesty you showed to me.

And I must own that you have oft defeated
   Unworthy schemes by your sincerity,
And by a blush or stammering tongue have tried
To make me think again before I lied.

'Tis true you're not so handsome as you were,
   But that's not your fault and is partly mine.
You might have lasted longer with more care,
   And still looked something like your first design;
And even now, with all your wear and tear,
   'Tis pitiful to think I must resign
You to the friendless grave, the patient prey
Of all the hungry legions of Decay.

But you must stay, dear body, and I go.
   And I was once so very proud of you:
You made my mother's eyes to overflow
   When first she saw you, wonderful and new.
And now, with all your faults, 'twere hard to find
   A slave more willing or a friend more true.
Ay—even they who say the worst about you
Can scarcely tell what I shall do without you.

THOMAS HARDY

1840–1928

571   *The Darkling Thrush*

I leant upon a coppice gate
   When Frost was spectre-gray,
And Winter's dregs made desolate
   The weakening eye of day.
The tangled bine-stems scored the sky
   Like strings of broken lyres,
And all mankind that haunted nigh
   Had sought their household fires.

The land's sharp features seemed to be
   The Century's corpse outleant,
His crypt the cloudy canopy,
   The wind his death-lament.
The ancient pulse of germ and birth
   Was shrunken hard and dry,
And every spirit upon earth
   Seemed fervourless as I.

At once a voice arose among
   The bleak twigs overhead
In a full-hearted evensong
   Of joy illimited;
An aged thrush, frail, gaunt, and small,
   In blast-beruffled plume,
Had chosen thus to fling his soul
   Upon the growing gloom.

So little cause for carolings
   Of such ecstatic sound
Was written on terrestrial things
   Afar or nigh around,
That I could think there trembled through
   His happy good-night air
Some blessed Hope, whereof he knew
   And I was unaware.

572 ## The Self-Unseeing

Here is the ancient floor,
Footworn and hollowed and thin,
Here was the former door
Where the dead feet walked in.

She sat here in her chair,
Smiling into the fire;
He who played stood there,
Bowing it higher and higher.

Childlike, I danced in a dream;
Blessings emblazoned that day;
Everything glowed with a gleam;
Yet we were looking away!

573 ## Channel Firing

That night your great guns, unawares,
Shook all our coffins as we lay,
And broke the chancel window-squares,
We thought it was the Judgment-day

And sat upright. While drearisome
Arose the howl of wakened hounds:
The mouse let fall the altar-crumb,
The worms drew back into the mounds,

The glebe cow drooled. Till God called, 'No;
It's gunnery practice out at sea
Just as before you went below;
The world is as it used to be:

'All nations striving strong to make
Red war yet redder. Mad as hatters
They do no more for Christés sake
Than you who are helpless in such matters.

'That this is not the judgment-hour
For some of them's a blessed thing,
For if it were they'd have to scour
Hell's floor for so much threatening. . . .

'Ha, ha. It will be warmer when
I blow the trumpet (if indeed
I ever do; for you are men,
And rest eternal sorely need).'

So down we lay again. 'I wonder,
Will the world ever saner be',
Said one, 'than when He sent us under
In our indifferent century!'

And many a skeleton shook his head.
'Instead of preaching forty year,'
My neighbour Parson Thirdly said,
'I wish I had stuck to pipes and beer.'

Again the guns disturbed the hour,
Roaring their readiness to avenge,
As far inland as Stourton Tower,
And Camelot, and starlit Stonehenge.

574   *The Convergence of the Twain*

(Lines on the loss of the *Titanic*)

In a solitude of the sea
Deep from human vanity,
And the Pride of Life that planned her, stilly couches she.

Steel chambers, late the pyres
Of her salamandrine fires,
Cold currents thrid, and turn to rhythmic tidal lyres.

Over the mirrors meant
To glass the opulent
The sea-worm crawls—grotesque, slimed, dumb, indifferent.

Jewels in joy designed
To ravish the sensuous mind
Lie lightless, all their sparkles bleared and black and blind.

Dim moon-eyed fishes near
Gaze at the gilded gear
And query: 'What does this vaingloriousness down here?' . . .

Well: while was fashioning
This creature of cleaving wing,
The Immanent Will that stirs and urges everything

Prepared a sinister mate
For her—so gaily great—
A Shape of Ice, for the time far and dissociate.

And as the smart ship grew
In stature, grace, and hue,
In shadowy silent distance grew the Iceberg too.

Alien they seemed to be:
No mortal eye could see
The intimate welding of their later history,

Or sign that they were bent
By paths coincident
On being anon twin halves of one august event,

Till the Spinner of the Years
Said 'Now!' And each one hears,
And consummation comes, and jars two hemispheres.

575   *The Walk*

You did not walk with me
Of late to the hill-top tree
By the gated ways,
As in earlier days;
You were weak and lame,
So you never came,
And I went alone, and I did not mind,
Not thinking of you as left behind.

I walked up there to-day
Just in the former way:
Surveyed around
The familiar ground

By myself again:
What difference, then?
Only that underlying sense
Of the look of a room on returning thence.

576   *The Voice*

Woman much missed, how you call to me, call to me,
Saying that now you are not as you were
When you had changed from the one who was all to me,
But as at first, when our day was fair.

Can it be you that I hear? Let me view you, then,
Standing as when I drew near to the town
Where you would wait for me: yes, as I knew you then,
Even to the original air-blue gown!

Or is it only the breeze, in its listlessness
Travelling across the wet mead to me here,
You being ever dissolved to wan wistlessness,
Heard no more again far or near?

        Thus I; faltering forward,
        Leaves around me falling,
Wind oozing thin through the thorn from norward
        And the woman calling.

577   *After a Journey*

Hereto I come to view a voiceless ghost;
    Whither, O whither will its whim now draw me?
Up the cliff, down, till I'm lonely, lost,
    And the unseen waters' ejaculations awe me.
Where you will next be there's no knowing,
    Facing round about me everywhere,
        With your nut-coloured hair,
And gray eyes, and rose-flush coming and going.

Yes: I have re-entered your olden haunts at last;
    Through the years, through the dead scenes I have tracked you;
What have you now found to say of our past—
    Scanned across the dark space wherein I have lacked you?
Summer gave us sweets, but autumn wrought division?
    Things were not lastly as firstly well
        With us twain, you tell?
But all's closed now, despite Time's derision.

I see what you are doing: you are leading me on
　　To the spots we knew when we haunted here together,
The waterfall, above which the mist-bow shone
　　At the then fair hour in the then fair weather,
And the cave just under, with a voice still so hollow
　　That it seems to call out to me from forty years ago,
　　　　When you were all aglow,
And not the thin ghost that I now frailly follow!

Ignorant of what there is flitting here to see,
　　The waked birds preen and the seals flop lazily,
Soon you will have, Dear, to vanish from me,
　　For the stars close their shutters and the dawn whitens hazily.
Trust me, I mind not, though Life lours,
　　The bringing me here; nay, bring me here again!
　　　　I am just the same as when
Our days were a joy, and our paths through flowers.

578   *At Castle Boterel*

　　As I drive to the junction of lane and highway,
　　　　And the drizzle bedrenches the waggonette,
　　I look behind at the fading byway,
　　　　And see on its slope, now glistening wet,
　　　　　　Distinctly yet

　　Myself and a girlish form benighted
　　　　In dry March weather. We climb the road
　　Beside a chaise. We had just alighted
　　　　To ease the sturdy pony's load
　　　　　　When he sighed and slowed.

　　What we did as we climbed, and what we talked of
　　　　Matters not much, nor to what it led,—
　　Something that life will not be balked of
　　　　Without rude reason till hope is dead,
　　　　　　And feeling fled.

　　It filled but a minute. But was there ever
　　　　A time of such quality, since or before,
　　In that hill's story? To one mind never,
　　　　Though it has been climbed, foot-swift, foot-sore,
　　　　　　By thousands more.

　　Primaeval rocks form the road's steep border,
　　　　And much have they faced there, first and last,
　　Of the transitory in Earth's long order;
　　　　But what they record in colour and cast
　　　　　　Is—that we two passed.

And to me, though Time's unflinching rigour,
　　In mindless rote, has ruled from sight
The substance now, one phantom figure
　　Remains on the slope, as when that night
　　　　Saw us alight.

I look and see it there, shrinking, shrinking,
　　I look back at it amid the rain
For the very last time; for my sand is sinking,
　　And I shall traverse old love's domain
　　　　Never again.

579   *During Wind and Rain*

They sing their dearest songs—
He, she, all of them—yea,
Treble and tenor and bass,
　　And one to play;
With the candles mooning each face....
　　Ah, no; the years O!
How the sick leaves reel down in throngs!

They clear the creeping moss—
Elders and juniors—aye,
Making the pathways neat
　　And the garden gay:
And they build a shady seat....
　　Ah, no; the years, the years;
See, the white storm-birds wing across.

They are blithely breakfasting all—
Men and maidens—yea,
Under the summer tree,
　　With a glimpse of the bay,
While pet fowl come to the knee....
　　Ah, no; the years O!
And the rotten rose is ript from the wall.

They change to a high new house,
He, she, all of them—aye,
Clocks and carpets and chairs
　　On the lawn all day,
And brightest things that are theirs....
　　Ah, no; the years, the years;
Down their carved names the rain-drop ploughs.

580   *Afterwards*

When the Present has latched its postern behind my tremulous stay,
    And the May month flaps its glad green leaves like wings,
Delicate-filmed as new-spun silk, will the neighbours say,
    'He was a man who used to notice such things'?

If it be in the dusk when, like an eyelid's soundless blink,
    The dewfall-hawk comes crossing the shades to alight
Upon the wind-warped upland thorn, a gazer may think,
    'To him this must have been a familiar sight'.

If I pass during some nocturnal blackness, mothy and warm,
    When the hedgehog travels furtively over the lawn,
One may say, 'He strove that such innocent creatures should come to no harm,
    But he could do little for them; and now he is gone'.

If, when hearing that I have been stilled at last, they stand at the door,
    Watching the full-starred heavens that winter sees,
Will this thought rise on those who will meet my face no more,
    'He was one who had an eye for such mysteries'?

And will any say when my bell of quittance is heard in the gloom,
    And a crossing breeze cuts a pause in its outrollings,
Till they swell again, as they were a new bell's boom,
    'He hears it not now, but used to notice such things'?

GERARD M. HOPKINS
1844–1889

581   *The Wreck of the Deutschland*

To the
happy memory of five Franciscan nuns
exiles by the Falck Laws
drowned between midnight and morning of
Dec. 7th, 1875

PART THE FIRST

Thou mastering me
God! giver of breath and bread;
World's strand, sway of the sea;
Lord of living and dead;
Thou hast bound bones and veins in me, fastened me flesh,

And after it almost unmade, what with dread,
    Thy doing: and dost thou touch me afresh?
Over again I feel thy finger and find thee.

        I did say yes
    O at lightning and lashed rod;
Thou heardst me truer than tongue confess
    Thy terror, O Christ, O God;
Thou knowest the walls, altar and hour and night:
The swoon of a heart that the sweep and the hurl of thee trod
    Hard down with a horror of height:
And the midriff astrain with leaning of, laced with fire of stress.

      The frown of his face
    Before me, the hurtle of hell
Behind, where, where was a, where was a place?
    I whirled out wings that spell
And fled with a fling of the heart to the heart of the Host.
My heart, but you were dovewinged, I can tell,
    Carrier-witted, I am bold to boast,
To flash from the flame to the flame then, tower from the grace to the grace.

       I am soft sift
    In an hourglass—at the wall
Fast, but mined with a motion, a drift,
    And it crowds and it combs to the fall;
I steady as a water in a well, to a poise, to a pane,
But roped with, always, all the way down from the tall
    Fells or flanks of the voel, a vein
Of the gospel proffer, a pressure, a principle, Christ's gift.

      I kiss my hand
    To the stars, lovely-asunder
Starlight, wafting him out of it; and
    Glow, glory in thunder;
Kiss my hand to the dappled-with-damson west:
Since, tho' he is under the world's splendour and wonder,
    His mystery must be instressed, stressed;
For I greet him the days I meet him, and bless when I understand.

      Not out of his bliss
    Springs the stress felt
Nor first from heaven (and few know this)
    Swings the stroke dealt—
Stroke and a stress that stars and storms deliver,
That guilt is hushed by, hearts are flushed by and melt—
    But it rides time like riding a river
(And here the faithful waver, the faithless fable and miss).

It dates from day
Of his going in Galilee;
Warm-laid grave of a womb-life grey;
Manger, maiden's knee;
The dense and the driven Passion, and frightful sweat:
Thence the discharge of it, there its swelling to be,
Though felt before, though in high flood yet—
What none would have known of it, only the heart, being hard at bay,

Is out with it! Oh,
We lash with the best or worst
Word last! How a lush-kept plush-capped sloe
Will, mouthed to flesh-burst,
Gush!—flush the man, the being with it, sour or sweet,
Brim, in a flash, full!—Hither then, last or first,
To hero of Calvary, Christ,'s feet—
Never ask if meaning it, wanting it, warned of it—men go.

Be adored among men,
God, three-numberèd form;
Wring thy rebel, dogged in den,
Man's malice, with wrecking and storm.
Beyond saying sweet, past telling of tongue,
Thou art lightning and love, I found it, a winter and warm;
Father and fondler of heart thou hast wrung:
Hast thy dark descending and most art merciful then.

With an anvil-ding
And with fire in him forge thy will
Or rather, rather then, stealing as Spring
Through him, melt him but master him still:
Whether at once, as once at a crash Paul,
Or as Austin, a lingering-out swéet skíll,
Make mercy in all of us, out of us all
Mastery, but be adored, but be adored King.

PART THE SECOND

'Some find me a sword; some
The flange and the rail; flame,
Fang, or flood' goes Death on drum,
And storms bugle his fame.
But wé dream we are rooted in earth—Dust!
Flesh falls within sight of us, we, though our flower the same,
Wave with the meadow, forget that there must
The sour scythe cringe, and the blear share come.

On Saturday sailed from Bremen,
American-outward-bound,

Take settler and seamen, tell men with women,
    Two hundred souls in the round—
O Father, not under thy feathers nor ever as guessing
    The goal was a shoal, of a fourth the doom to be drowned;
        Yet did the dark side of the bay of thy blessing
Not vault them, the million of rounds of thy mercy not reeve even them in?

        Into the snows she sweeps,
            Hurling the haven behind,
        The Deutschland, on Sunday; and so the sky keeps,
            For the infinite air is unkind,
        And the sea flint-flake, black-backed in the regular blow,
        Sitting Eastnortheast, in cursed quarter, the wind;
            Wiry and white-fiery and whirlwind-swivellèd snow
        Spins to the widow-making unchilding unfathering deeps.

        She drove in the dark to leeward,
            She struck—not a reef or a rock
        But the combs of a smother of sand: night drew her
            Dead to the Kentish Knock;
        And she beat the bank down with her bows and the ride of her keel:
        The breakers rolled on her beam with ruinous shock;
            And canvas and compass, the whorl and the wheel
        Idle for ever to waft her or wind her with, these she endured.

        Hope had grown grey hairs,
            Hope had mourning on,
        Trenched with tears, carved with cares,
            Hope was twelve hours gone;
        And frightful a nightfall folded rueful a day
        Nor rescue, only rocket and lightship, shone,
            And lives at last were washing away:
        To the shrouds they took,—they shook in the hurling and horrible airs.

        One stirred from the rigging to save
            The wild woman-kind below,
        With a rope's end round the man, handy and brave—
            He was pitched to his death at a blow,
        For all his dreadnought breast and braids of thew:
        They could tell him for hours, dandled the to and fro
            Through the cobbled foam-fleece. What could he do
        With the burl of the fountains of air, buck and the flood of the wave?

        They fought with God's cold—
            And they could not and fell to the deck
        (Crushed them) or water (and drowned them) or rolled
            With the sea-romp over the wreck.
        Night roared, with the heart-break hearing a heart-broke rabble,
        The woman's wailing, the crying of child without check—
            Till a lioness arose breasting the babble,
        A prophetess towered in the tumult, a virginal tongue told.

Ah, touched in your bower of bone,
Are you! turned for an exquisite smart,
Have you! make words break from me here all alone,
Do you!—mother of being in me, heart.
O unteachably after evil, but uttering truth,
Why, tears! is it? tears; such a melting, a madrigal start!
Never-eldering revel and river of youth,
What can it be, this glee? the good you have there of your own?

Sister, a sister calling
A master, her master and mine!—
And the inboard seas run swirling and hawling;
The rash smart sloggering brine
Blinds her; but she that weather sees one thing, one;
Has one fetch in her: she rears herself to divine
Ears, and the call of the tall nun
To the men in the tops and the tackle rode over the storm's brawling.

She was first of a five and came
Of a coifèd sisterhood.
(O Deutschland, double a desperate name!
O world wide of its good!
But Gertrude, lily, and Luther, are two of a town,
Christ's lily and beast of the waste wood:
From life's dawn it is drawn down,
Abel is Cain's brother and breasts they have sucked the same.)

Loathed for a love men knew in them,
Banned by the land of their birth,
Rhine refused them, Thames would ruin them;
Surf, snow, river and earth
Gnashed: but thou art above, thou Orion of light;
Thy unchancelling poising palms were weighing the worth,
Thou martyr-master: in thy sight
Storm flakes were scroll-leaved flowers, lily showers—sweet heaven was
astrew in them.

Five! the finding and sake
And cipher of suffering Christ.
Mark, the mark is of man's make
And the word of it Sacrificed.
But he scores it in scarlet himself on his own bespoken,
Before-time-taken, dearest prizèd and priced—
Stigma, signal, cinquefoil token
For lettering of the lamb's fleece, ruddying of the rose-flake.

Joy fall to thee, father Francis,
Drawn to the Life that died;
With the gnarls of the nails in thee, niche of the lance, his
Lovescape crucified

And seal of his seraph-arrival! and these thy daughters
And five-livèd and leavèd favour and pride,
    Are sisterly sealed in wild waters,
To bathe in his fall-gold mercies, to breathe in his all-fire glances.

    Away in the loveable west,
      On a pastoral forehead of Wales,
    I was under a roof here, I was at rest,
      And they the prey of the gales;
She to the black-about air, to the breaker, the thickly
Falling flakes, to the throng that catches and quails
    Was calling 'O Christ, Christ, come quickly':
The cross to her she calls Christ to her, christens her wild-worst Best.

    The majesty! what did she mean?
      Breathe, arch and original Breath.
    Is it love in her of the being as her lover had been?
      Breathe, body of lovely Death.
They were else-minded then, altogether, the men
Woke thee with a *We are perishing* in the weather of Gennesareth.
    Or is it that she cried for the crown then,
The keener to come at the comfort for feeling the combating keen?

    For how to the heart's cheering
      The down-dugged ground-hugged grey
    Hovers off, the jay-blue heavens appearing
      Of pied and peeled May!
Blue-beating and hoary-glow height; or night, still higher,
With belled fire and the moth-soft Milky Way,
    What by your measure is the heaven of desire,
The treasure never eyesight got, nor was ever guessed what for the hearing?

    No, but it was not these.
      The jading and jar of the cart,
    Time's tasking, it is fathers that asking for ease
      Of the sodden-with-its-sorrowing heart,
Not danger, electrical horror; then further it finds
The appealing of the Passion is tenderer in prayer apart:
    Other, I gather, in measure her mind's
Burden, in wind's burly and beat of endragonèd seas.

    But how shall I . . . make me room there:
      Reach me a . . . Fancy, come faster—
    Strike you the sight of it? look at it loom there,
      Thing that she . . . There then! the Master,
Ipse, the only one, Christ, King, Head:
He was to cure the extremity where he had cast her;
    Do, deal, lord it with living and dead;
Let him ride, her pride, in his triumph, despatch and have done with his
    doom there.

Ah! there was a heart right!
There was single eye!
Read the unshapeable shock night
And knew the who and the why;
Wording it how but by him that present and past,
Heaven and earth are word of, worded by?—
The Simon Peter of a soul! to the blast
Tarpeïan-fast, but a blown beacon of light.

Jesu, heart's light,
Jesu, maid's son,
What was the feast followed the night
Thou hadst glory of this nun?—
Feast of the one woman without stain.
For so conceivèd, so to conceive thee is done;
But here was heart-throe, birth of a brain,
Word, that heard and kept thee and uttered thee outright.

Well, she has thee for the pain, for the
Patience; but pity of the rest of them!
Heart, go and bleed at a bitterer vein for the
Comfortless unconfessed of them—
No not uncomforted: lovely-felicitous Providence
Finger of a tender of, O of a feathery delicacy, the breast of the
Maiden could obey so, be a bell to, ring of it, and
Startle the poor sheep back! is the shipwrack then a harvest, does tempest
carry the grain for thee?

I admire thee, master of the tides,
Of the Yore-flood, of the year's fall;
The recurb and the recovery of the gulf's sides,
The girth of it and the wharf of it and the wall;
Stanching, quenching ocean of a motionable mind;
Ground of being, and granite of it: past all
Grasp God, throned behind
Death with a sovereignty that heeds but hides, bodes but abides;

With a mercy that outrides
The all of water, an ark
For the listener; for the lingerer with a love glides
Lower than death and the dark;
A vein for the visiting of the past-prayer, pent in prison,
The-last-breath penitent spirits—the uttermost mark
Our passion-plungèd giant risen,
The Christ of the Father compassionate, fetched in the storm of his strides.

Now burn, new born to the world,
Double-naturèd name,
The heaven-flung, heart-fleshed, maiden-furled
Miracle-in-Mary-of-flame,

Mid-numberèd he in three of the thunder-throne!
Not a dooms-day dazzle in his coming nor dark as he came;
        Kind, but royally reclaiming his own;
A released shower, let flash to the shire, not a lightning of fire hard-hurled.

            Dame, at our door
            Drowned, and among our shoals,
        Remember us in the roads, the heaven-haven of the reward:
            Our King back, Oh, upon English souls!
Let him easter in us, be a dayspring to the dimness of us, be a
        crimson-cresseted east,
More brightening her, rare-dear Britain, as his reign rolls,
        Pride, rose, prince, hero of us, high-priest,
Our heart's charity's hearth's fire, our thoughts' chivalry's throng's Lord.

582   *God's Grandeur*

    The world is charged with the grandeur of God.
        It will flame out, like shining from shook foil;
        It gathers to a greatness, like the ooze of oil
    Crushed. Why do men then now not reck his rod?
    Generations have trod, have trod, have trod;
        And all is seared with trade; bleared, smeared with toil;
        And wears man's smudge and shares man's smell: the soil
    Is bare now, nor can foot feel, being shod.

    And for all this, nature is never spent;
        There lives the dearest freshness deep down things;
    And though the last lights off the black West went
        Oh, morning, at the brown brink eastwards, springs—
    Because the Holy Ghost over the bent
        World broods with warm breast and with ah! bright wings.

583   *The Windhover*

                    To Christ our Lord

    I caught this morning morning's minion, king-
        dom of daylight's dauphin, dapple-dawn-drawn Falcon, in his riding
        Of the rolling level underneath him steady air, and striding
    High there, how he rung upon the rein of a wimpling wing
    In his ecstasy! then off, off forth on swing,
        As a skate's heel sweeps smooth on a bow-bend: the hurl and gliding
        Rebuffed the big wind. My heart in hiding
    Stirred for a bird,—the achieve of, the mastery of the thing!

Brute beauty and valour and act, oh, air, pride, plume, here
  Buckle! AND the fire that breaks from thee then, a billion
Times told lovelier, more dangerous, O my chevalier!

  No wonder of it: shéer plód makes plough down sillion
Shine, and blue-bleak embers, ah my dear,
  Fall, gall themselves, and gash gold-vermilion.

584   *Pied Beauty*

Glory be to God for dappled things—
  For skies of couple-colour as a brinded cow;
    For rose-moles all in stipple upon trout that swim;
Fresh-firecoal chestnut-falls; finches' wings;
  Landscape plotted and pieced—fold, fallow, and plough;
    And áll trádes, their gear and tackle and trim.

All things counter, original, spare, strange;
  Whatever is fickle, freckled (who knows how?)
    With swift, slow; sweet, sour; adazzle, dim;
He fathers-forth whose beauty is past change:
                         Praise him.

585   As kingfishers catch fire, dragonflies draw flame;
  As tumbled over rim in roundy wells
    Stones ring; like each tucked string tells, each hung bell's
Bow swung finds tongue to fling out broad its name;
Each mortal thing does one thing and the same:
  Deals out that being indoors each one dwells;
    Selves—goes its self; *myself* it speaks and spells,
Crying *What I do is me: for that I came.*

Í say more: the just man justices;
  Keeps gráce: thát keeps all his goings graces;
Acts in God's eye what in God's eye he is—
  Chríst. For Christ plays in ten thousand places,
Lovely in limbs, and lovely in eyes not his
  To the Father through the features of men's faces.

586   *Spelt from Sibyl's Leaves*

Earnest, earthless, equal, attuneable, ¦ vaulty, voluminous, . . . stupendous
Evening strains to be tíme's vást, ¦ womb-of-all, home-of-all, hearse-of-all
  night.

Her fond yellow hornlight wound to the west, ' her wild hollow hoarlight
    hung to the height
Waste; her earliest stars, earlstars, ' stárs principal, overbend us,
Fíre-féaturing heaven. For earth ' her being has unbound; her dapple is at an
    end, as-
tray or aswarm, all throughther, in throngs; ' self ín self steepèd and páshed—
    qúite
Disremembering, dísmémbering ' áll now. Heart, you round me right
With: Óur évening is over us; óur night ' whélms, whélms, ánd will end us.
Only the beakleaved boughs dragonish ' damask the tool-smooth bleak light;
    black,
Ever so black on it. Óur tale, O óur oracle! ' Lét life, wáned, ah lét life wind
Off hér once skéined stained véined varíety ' upon, áll on twó spools; párt,
    pen, páck
Now her áll in twó flocks, twó folds—black, white; ' right, wrong; reckon but,
    reck but, mind
But thése two; wáre of a wórld where bút these ' twó tell, each off the óther; of
    a rack
Where, selfwrung, selfstrung, sheathe- and shelterless, ' thóughts agaínst
    thoughts ín groans grínd.

587   I wake and feel the fell of dark, not day.
          What hours, O what black hoürs we have spent
          This night! what sights you, heart, saw; ways you went!
          And more must, in yet longer light's delay.

          With witness I speak this. But where I say
          Hours I mean years, mean life. And my lament
          Is cries countless, cries like dead letters sent
          To dearest him that lives alas! away.

          I am gall, I am heartburn. God's most deep decree
          Bitter would have me taste: my taste was me;
          Bones built in me, flesh filled, blood brimmed the curse.

          Selfyeast of spirit a dull dough sours. I see
          The lost are like this, and their scourge to be
          As I am mine, their sweating selves; but worse.

588   *Justus quidem tu es, Domine, si disputem tecum; verumtamen*
          justa loquar ad te: Quare via impiorum prosperatur? &c.

          Thou art indeed just, Lord, if I contend
          With thee; but, sir, so what I plead is just.
          Why do sinners' ways prosper? and why must
          Disappointment all I endeavour end?

Wert thou my enemy, O thou my friend,
How wouldst thou worse, I wonder, than thou dost
Defeat, thwart me? Oh, the sots and thralls of lust
Do in spare hours more thrive than I that spend,

Sir, life upon thy cause. See, banks and brakes
Now, leavèd how thick! lacèd they are again
With fretty chervil, look, and fresh wind shakes

Them; birds build—but not I build; no, but strain,
Time's eunuch, and not breed one work that wakes.
Mine, O thou lord of life, send my roots rain.

ROBERT BRIDGES

1844–1930

589 *Ghosts*

Mazing around my mind like moths at a shaded candle.
In my heart like lost bats in a cave fluttering,
Mock ye the charm whereby I thought reverently to lay you,
When to the wall I nail'd your reticent effigys?

590 Ἐτώσιον ἄχθος ἀρούρης

Who goes there? God knows. I'm nobody. How should I answer?
Can't jump over a gate nor run across the meadow.
I'm but an old whitebeard of inane identity. Pass on!
What's left of me to-day will very soon be nothing.

WILLIAM ERNEST HENLEY

1849–1903

591 *To W.R.*

Madam Life's a piece in bloom
   Death goes dogging everywhere:
She's the tenant of the room,
   He's the ruffian on the stair.

You shall see her as a friend,
   You shall bilk him once and twice;
But he'll trap you in the end,
   And he'll stick you for her price.

With his kneebones at your chest,
   And his knuckles in your throat,
You would reason—plead—protest!
   Clutching at her petticoat;

But she's heard it all before,
   Well she knows you've had your fun,
Gingerly she gains the door,
   And your little job is done.

ROBERT LOUIS STEVENSON

1850–1894

592   *Requiem*

Under the wide and starry sky,
Dig the grave and let me lie.
Glad did I live and gladly die,
   And I laid me down with a will.

This be the verse you grave for me:
Here he lies where he longed to be;
Home is the sailor, home from sea,
   And the hunter home from the hill.

593   *A Mile an' a Bittock*

A mile an' a bittock, a mile or twa,
Abüne, the burn, ayont the law,
Davie an' Donal' an' Cherlie an' a',
   An' the müne was shinin' clearly!

Ane went hame wi' the ither, an' then   5
The ither went hame wi' the ither twa men,
An' baith wad return him the service again,
   An' the müne was shinin' clearly!

The clocks were chappin' in house an' ha',
Eleeven, twal an' ane an' twa;   10
An' the guidman's face was turnt to the wa',
   An' the müne was shinin' clearly!

A wind got up frae affa the sea,
It blew the stars as clear's could be,

593: 2 *ayont the law*] beyond, the low hill

It blew in the een of a' o' the three,   15
 An' the müne was shinin' clearly!

Noo, Davie was first to get sleep in his head,
'The best o' frien's maun twine,' he said;
'I'm weariet, an' here I'm awa' to my bed.'
 An' the müne was shinin' clearly!   20

Twa o' them walkin' an' crackin' their lane,
The mornin' licht cam gray an' plain,
An' the birds they yammert on stick an' stane,
 An' the müne was shinin' clearly!

O years ayont, O years awa',   25
My lads, ye'll mind whate'er befa'—
My lads, ye'll mind on the bield o' the law,
 When the müne was shinin' clearly.

594 *My house*, I say. But hark to the sunny doves
That make my roof the arena of their loves,
That gyre about the gable all day long
And fill the chimneys with their murmurous song:
Our house, they say; and *mine*, the cat declares
And spreads his golden fleece upon the chairs;
And *mine* the dog, and rises stiff with wrath
If any alien foot profane the path.
So too the buck that trimmed my terraces,
Our whilome gardener, called the garden his;
Who now, deposed, surveys my plain abode
And his late kingdom, only from the road.

595 It's an owercome sooth for age an' youth
  And it brooks wi' nae denial,
That the dearest friends are the auldest friends
  And the young are just on trial.

There's a rival bauld wi' young an' auld
  And it's him that has bereft me;
For the sürest friends are the auldest friends
  And the maist o' mines hae left me.

There are kind hearts still, for friends to fill
  And fools to take and break them;
But the nearest friends are the auldest friends
  And the grave's the place to seek them.

18 *twine*] separate 21 *crackin' their lane*] talking on their own 27 *bield o' the law*]
shelter of the hill

596 I have trod the upward and the downward slope;
 I have endured and done in days before;
 I have longed for all, and bid farewell to hope;
 And I have lived and loved, and closed the door.

OSCAR WILDE
1854–1900

597 from *The Ballad of Reading Gaol*

I

He did not wear his scarlet coat,
 For blood and wine are red,
And blood and wine were on his hands
 When they found him with the dead,
The poor dead woman whom he loved,
 And murdered in her bed.

He walked amongst the Trial Men
 In a suit of shabby gray;
A cricket cap was on his head,
 And his step seemed light and gay;
But I never saw a man who looked
 So wistfully at the day.

I never saw a man who looked
 With such a wistful eye
Upon that little tent of blue
 Which prisoners call the sky,
And at every drifting cloud that went
 With sails of silver by.

I walked, with other souls in pain,
 Within another ring,
And was wondering if the man had done
 A great or little thing,
When a voice behind me whispered low,
 '*That fellow's got to swing.*'

Dear Christ! the very prison walls
 Suddenly seemed to reel,
And the sky above my head became
 Like a casque of scorching steel;
And, though I was a soul in pain,
 My pain I could not feel.

I only knew what hunted thought
  Quickened his step, and why
He looked upon the garish day
  With such a wistful eye;
The man had killed the thing he loved,
  And so he had to die.

     *   *   *

Yet each man kills the thing he loves,
  By each let this be heard,
Some do it with a bitter look,
  Some with a flattering word,
The coward does it with a kiss,
  The brave man with a sword!

Some kill their love when they are young,
  And some when they are old;
Some strangle with the hands of Lust,
  Some with the hands of Gold:
The kindest use a knife, because
  The dead so soon grow cold.

Some love too little, some too long,
  Some sell, and others buy;
Some do the deed with many tears,
  And some without a sigh:
For each man kills the thing he loves,
  Yet each man does not die.

He does not die a death of shame
  On a day of dark disgrace,
Nor have a noose about his neck,
  Nor a cloth upon his face,
Nor drop feet foremost through the floor
  Into an empty space.

     *   *   *

He does not sit with silent men
  Who watch him night and day;
Who watch him when he tries to weep,
  And when he tries to pray;
Who watch him lest himself should rob
  The prison of its prey.

He does not wake at dawn to see
  Dread figures throng his room,
The shivering Chaplain robed in white,
  The Sheriff stern with gloom,

And the Governor all in shiny black,
  With the yellow face of Doom.

He does not rise in piteous haste
  To put on convict-clothes,
While some coarse-mouthed Doctor gloats, and notes
  Each new and nerve-twitched pose,
Fingering a watch whose little ticks
  Are like horrible hammer-blows.

He does not know that sickening thirst
  That sands one's throat, before
The hangman with his gardener's gloves
  Slips through the padded door,
And binds one with three leathern thongs,
  That the throat may thirst no more.

He does not bend his head to hear
  The Burial Office read,
Nor, while the terror of his soul
  Tells him he is not dead,
Cross his own coffin, as he moves
  Into the hideous shed.

He does not stare upon the air
  Through a little roof of glass:
He does not pray with lips of clay
  For his agony to pass;
Nor feel upon his shuddering cheek
  The kiss of Caiaphas.

JOHN DAVIDSON

1857–1909

598   *Thirty Bob a Week*

I couldn't touch a stop and turn a screw,
  And set the blooming world a-work for me,
Like such as cut their teeth—I hope, like you—
  On the handle of a skeleton gold key;
I cut mine on a leek, which I eat it every week:
  I'm a clerk at thirty bob as you can see.

But I don't allow it's luck and all a toss;
  There's no such thing as being starred and crossed;
It's just the power of some to be a boss,

And the bally power of others to be bossed:
I face the music, sir; you bet I ain't a cur;
  Strike me lucky if I don't believe I'm lost!

For like a mole I journey in the dark,
  A-travelling along the underground
From my Pillar'd Halls and broad Suburbean Park,
  To come the daily dull official round;
And home again at night with my pipe all alight,
  A-scheming how to count ten bob a pound.

And it's often very cold and very wet,
  And my missis stitches towels for a hunks;
And the Pillar'd Halls is half of it to let—
  Three rooms about the size of travelling trunks.
And we cough, my wife and I, to dislocate a sigh,
  When the noisy little kids are in their bunks.

But you never hear her do a growl or whine,
  For she's made of flint and roses, very odd;
And I've got to cut my meaning rather fine,
  Or I'd blubber, for I'm made of greens and sod:
So p'r'aps we are in Hell for all that I can tell,
  And lost and damn'd and served up hot to God.

I ain't blaspheming, Mr Silver-tongue;
  I'm saying things a bit beyond your art:
Of all the rummy starts you ever sprung,
  Thirty bob a week's the rummiest start!
With your science and your books and your the'ries about spooks,
  Did you ever hear of looking in your heart?

I didn't mean your pocket, Mr, no:
  I mean that having children and a wife,
With thirty bob on which to come and go,
  Isn't dancing to the tabor and the fife:
When it doesn't make you drink, by Heaven! it makes you think,
  And notice curious items about life.

I step into my heart and there I meet
  A god-almighty devil singing small,
Who would like to shout and whistle in the street,
  And squelch the passers flat against the wall;
If the whole world was a cake he had the power to take,
  He would take it, ask for more, and eat them all.

And I meet a sort of simpleton beside,
  The kind that life is always giving beans;
With thirty bob a week to keep a bride

He fell in love and married in his teens:
At thirty bob he stuck; but he knows it isn't luck:
He knows the seas are deeper than tureens.

And the god-almighty devil and the fool
    That meet me in the High Street on the strike,
When I walk about my heart a-gathering wool,
    Are my good and evil angels if you like.
And both of them together in every kind of weather
    Ride me like a double-seated bike.

That's rough a bit and needs its meaning curled.
    But I have a high old hot un in my mind—
A most engrugious notion of the world,
    That leaves your lightning 'rithmetic behind:
I give it at a glance when I say 'There ain't no chance,
    Nor nothing of the lucky-lottery kind.'

And it's this way that I make it out to be:
    No fathers, mothers, countries, climates—none;
No Adam was responsible for me,
    Nor society, nor systems, nary one:
A little sleeping seed, I woke—I did, indeed—
    A million years before the blooming sun.

I woke because I thought the time had come;
    Beyond my will there was no other cause;
And everywhere I found myself at home,
    Because I chose to be the thing I was;
And in whatever shape of mollusc or of ape
    I always went according to the laws.

I was the love that chose my mother out;
    I joined two lives and from the union burst;
My weakness and my strength without a doubt
    Are mine alone for ever from the first:
It's just the very same with a difference in the name
    As 'Thy will be done.' You say it if you durst!

They say it daily up and down the land
    As easy as you take a drink, it's true;
But the difficultest go to understand,
    And the difficultest job a man can do,
Is to come it brave and meek with thirty bob a week,
    And feel that that's the proper thing for you.

It's a naked child against a hungry wolf;
    It's playing bowls upon a splitting wreck;
It's walking on a string across a gulf

With millstones fore-and-aft about your neck;
But the thing is daily done by many and many a one;
And we fall, face forward, fighting, on the deck.

DOLLIE RADFORD

1858–1920

599   *Soliloquy of a Maiden Aunt*

The ladies bow, and partners set,
And turn around and pirouette
            And trip the Lancers.

But no one seeks my ample chair,
Or asks me with persuasive air
            To join the dancers.

They greet me, as I sit alone
Upon my solitary throne,
            And pass politely.

Yet mine could keep the measured beat,
As surely as the youngest feet,
            And tread as lightly.

No other maiden had my skill
In our old homestead on the hill—
            That merry May-time

When Allan closed the flagging ball,
And danced with me before them all,
            Until the day-time.

Again I laugh, and step alone,
And curtsey low as on my own
            His strong hand closes.

But Allan now seeks staid delight,
His son there, brought my niece to-night
            These early roses.

Time orders well, we have our Spring,
Our songs, and may-flower gathering,
            Our love and laughter.

And children chatter all the while,
And leap the brook and climb the stile
            And follow after.

And yet—the step of Allan's son,
Is not as light as was the one
    That went before it.

And that old lace, I think, falls down
Less softly on Priscilla's gown
    Than when I wore it.

A. E. HOUSMAN
1859–1936

600–1   from *A Shropshire Lad*

600   XVI

It nods and curtseys and recovers
    When the wind blows above,
The nettle on the graves of lovers
    That hanged themselves for love.

The nettle nods, the wind blows over,
    The man, he does not move,
The lover of the grave, the lover
    That hanged himself for love.

601   XL

Into my heart an air that kills
    From yon far country blows:
What are those blue remembered hills,
    What spires, what farms are those?

That is the land of lost content,
    I see it shining plain,
The happy highways where I went
    And cannot come again.

602–5   from *Last Poems*

602   III

Her strong enchantments failing,
    Her towers of fear in wreck,
Her limbecks dried of poisons
    And the knife at her neck,

The Queen of air and darkness
    Begins to shrill and cry,
'O young man, O my slayer,
    To-morrow you shall die.'

O Queen of air and darkness,
    I think 'tis truth you say,
And I shall die to-morrow;
    But you will die to-day.

603   XXVII

The sigh that heaves the grasses
    Whence thou wilt never rise
Is of the air that passes
    And knows not if it sighs.

The diamond tears adorning
    Thy low mound on the lea,
Those are the tears of morning,
    That weeps, but not for thee.

604   XXXVII

EPITAPH ON AN ARMY OF MERCENARIES

These, in the day when heaven was falling,
    The hour when earth's foundations fled,
Followed their mercenary calling
    And took their wages and are dead.

Their shoulders held the sky suspended;
    They stood, and earth's foundations stay;
What God abandoned, these defended,
    And saved the sum of things for pay.

605   XL

Tell me not here, it needs not saying,
    What tune the enchantress plays
In aftermaths of soft September
    Or under blanching mays,
For she and I were long acquainted
    And I knew all her ways.

On russet floors, by waters idle,
    The pine lets fall its cone;
The cuckoo shouts all day at nothing
    In leafy dells alone;
And traveller's joy beguiles in autumn
    Hearts that have lost their own.

On acres of the seeded grasses
    The changing burnish heaves;
Or marshalled under moons of harvest
    Stand still all night the sheaves;
Or beeches strip in storms for winter
    And stain the wind with leaves.

Possess, as I possessed a season,
    The countries I resign,
Where over elmy plains the highway
    Would mount the hills and shine,
And full of shade the pillared forest
    Would murmur and be mine.

For nature, heartless, witless nature,
    Will neither care nor know
What stranger's feet may find the meadow
    And trespass there and go,
Nor ask amid the dews of morning
    If they are mine or no.

606   I to my perils
                                Of cheat and charmer
                                Came clad in armour
                           By stars benign.
                           Hope lies to mortals
                                And most believe her,
                                But man's deceiver
                           Was never mine.

The thoughts of others
  Were light and fleeting,
  Of lovers' meeting
Or luck or fame.
Mine were of trouble,
  And mine were steady;
  So I was ready
When trouble came.

607

Crossing alone the nighted ferry
  With the one coin for fee,
Whom, on the far quayside in waiting,
  Count you to find? not me.

The fond lackey to fetch and carry,
  The true, sick-hearted slave,
Expect him not in the just city
  And free land of the grave.

608

Because I liked you better
  Than suits a man to say,
It irked you and I promised
  I'd throw the thought away.

To put the world between us
  We parted stiff and dry:
'Farewell,' said you, 'forget me.'
  'Fare well, I will,' said I.

If e'er, where clover whitens
  The dead man's knoll, you pass,
And no tall flower to meet you
  Starts in the trefoiled grass,

Halt by the headstone shading
  The heart you have not stirred,
. And say the lad that loved you
  Was one that kept his word.

609

Here dead lie we because we did not choose
  To live and shame the land from which we sprung.
Life, to be sure, is nothing much to lose,
  But young men think it is, and we were young.

610
> When the bells justle in the tower
> The hollow night amid,
> Then on my tongue the taste is sour
> Of all I ever did.

611
> Some can gaze and not be sick
> But I could never learn the trick.
> There's this to say for blood and breath,
> They give a man a taste for death.

W. B. YEATS
1865–1939

612
The Sorrow of Love

> The quarrel of the sparrows in the eaves,
> The full round moon and the star-laden sky,
> And the loud song of the ever-singing leaves
> Had hid away earth's old and weary cry.
>
> And then you came with those red mournful lips,
> And with you came the whole of the world's tears,
> And all the sorrows of her labouring ships,
> And all the burden of her myriad years.
>
> And now the sparrows warring in the eaves,
> The crumbling moon, the white stars in the sky,
> And the loud chanting of the unquiet leaves,
> Are shaken with earth's old and weary cry.

[1892, with 'the', line 8, supplied from 1895]

613
The Sorrow of Love

> The brawling of a sparrow in the eaves,
> The brilliant moon and all the milky sky,
> And all that famous harmony of leaves,
> Had blotted out man's image and his cry.
>
> A girl arose that had red mournful lips
> And seemed the greatness of the world in tears,
> Doomed like Odysseus and the labouring ships
> And proud as Priam murdered with his peers;

Arose, and on the instant clamorous eaves,
A climbing moon upon an empty sky,
And all that lamentation of the leaves,
Could but compose man's image and his cry.

[1925]

614   *When You Are Old*

When you are old and grey and full of sleep,
And nodding by the fire, take down this book,
And slowly read, and dream of the soft look
Your eyes had once, and of their shadows deep;

How many loved your moments of glad grace,
And loved your beauty with love false or true,
But one man loved the pilgrim soul in you,
And loved the sorrows of your changing face;

And bending down beside the glowing bars,
Murmur, a little sadly, how Love fled
And paced upon the mountains overhead
And hid his face amid a crowd of stars.

[after Ronsard]

615   *The Second Coming*

Turning and turning in the widening gyre
The falcon cannot hear the falconer;
Things fall apart; the centre cannot hold;
Mere anarchy is loosed upon the world,
The blood-dimmed tide is loosed, and everywhere
The ceremony of innocence is drowned;
The best lack all conviction, while the worst
Are full of passionate intensity.

Surely some revelation is at hand;
Surely the Second Coming is at hand.
The Second Coming! Hardly are those words out
When a vast image out of *Spiritus Mundi*
Troubles my sight: somewhere in sands of the desert
A shape with lion body and the head of a man,
A gaze blank and pitiless as the sun,

Is moving its slow thighs, while all about it
Reel shadows of the indignant desert birds.
The darkness drops again; but now I know
That twenty centuries of stony sleep
Were vexed to nightmare by a rocking cradle,
And what rough beast, its hour come round at last,
Slouches towards Bethlehem to be born?

616   *Sailing to Byzantium*

That is no country for old men. The young
In one another's arms, birds in the trees
—Those dying generations—at their song,
The salmon-falls, the mackerel-crowded seas,
Fish, flesh, or fowl, commend all summer long
Whatever is begotten, born, and dies.
Caught in that sensual music all neglect
Monuments of unageing intellect.

An aged man is but a paltry thing,
A tattered coat upon a stick, unless
Soul clap its hands and sing, and louder sing
For every tatter in its mortal dress,
Nor is there singing school but studying
Monuments of its own magnificence;
And therefore I have sailed the seas and come
To the holy city of Byzantium.

O sages standing in God's holy fire
As in the gold mosaic of a wall,
Come from the holy fire, perne in a gyre,
And be the singing-masters of my soul.
Consume my heart away; sick with desire
And fastened to a dying animal
It knows not what it is; and gather me
Into the artifice of eternity.

Once out of nature I shall never take
My bodily form from any natural thing,
But such a form as Grecian goldsmiths make
Of hammered gold and gold enamelling
To keep a drowsy Emperor awake;
Or set upon a golden bough to sing
To lords and ladies of Byzantium
Of what is past, or passing, or to come.

617   *Leda and the Swan*

A sudden blow: the great wings beating still
Above the staggering girl, her thighs caressed
By the dark webs, her nape caught in his bill,
He holds her helpless breast upon his breast.

How can those terrified vague fingers push
The feathered glory from her loosening thighs?
And how can body, laid in that white rush,
But feel the strange heart beating where it lies?

A shudder in the loins engenders there
The broken wall, the burning roof and tower
And Agamemnon dead.
                                Being so caught up,
So mastered by the brute blood of the air,
Did she put on his knowledge with his power
Before the indifferent beak could let her drop?

618   *Among School Children*

I walk through the long schoolroom questioning;
A kind old nun in a white hood replies;
The children learn to cipher and to sing,
To study reading books and histories,
To cut and sew, be neat in everything
In the best modern way—the children's eyes
In momentary wonder stare upon
A sixty-year-old smiling public man.

I dream of a Ledaean body, bent
Above a sinking fire, a tale that she
Told of a harsh reproof, or trivial event
That changed some childish day to tragedy—
Told, and it seemed that our two natures blent
Into a sphere from youthful sympathy,
Or else, to alter Plato's parable,
Into the yolk and white of the one shell.

And thinking of that fit of grief or rage
I look upon one child or t'other there
And wonder if she stood so at that age—
For even daughters of the swan can share

Something of every paddler's heritage—
And had that colour upon cheek or hair,
And thereupon my heart is driven wild:
She stands before me as a living child.

Her present image floats into the mind—
Did Quattrocento finger fashion it
Hollow of cheek as though it drank the wind
And took a mess of shadows for its meat?
And I though never of Ledaean kind
Had pretty plumage once—enough of that,
Better to smile on all that smile, and show
There is a comfortable kind of old scarecrow.

What youthful mother, a shape upon her lap
Honey of generation had betrayed,
And that must sleep, shriek, struggle to escape
As recollection or the drug decide,
Would think her son, did she but see that shape
With sixty or more winters on its head,
A compensation for the pang of his birth,
Or the uncertainty of his setting forth?

Plato thought nature but a spume that plays
Upon a ghostly paradigm of things;
Solider Aristotle played the taws
Upon the bottom of a king of kings;
World-famous golden-thighed Pythagoras
Fingered upon a fiddle-stick or strings
What a star sang and careless Muses heard:
Old clothes upon old sticks to scare a bird.

Both nuns and mothers worship images,
But those the candles light are not as those
That animate a mother's reveries,
But keep a marble or a bronze repose.
And yet they too break hearts—O Presences
That passion, piety or affection knows,
And that all heavenly glory symbolise—
O self-born mockers of man's enterprise;

Labour is blossoming or dancing where
The body is not bruised to pleasure soul,
Nor beauty born out of its own despair,
Nor blear-eyed wisdom out of midnight oil.
O chestnut-tree, great-rooted blossomer,
Are you the leaf, the blossom or the bole?
O body swayed to music, O brightening glance,
How can we know the dancer from the dance?

619   *Byzantium*

The unpurged images of day recede;
The Emperor's drunken soldiery are abed;
Night resonance recedes, night-walkers' song
After great cathedral gong;
A starlit or a moonlit dome disdains
All that man is,
All mere complexities,
The fury and the mire of human veins.

Before me floats an image, man or shade,
Shade more than man, more image than a shade;
For Hades' bobbin bound in mummy-cloth
May unwind the winding path;
A mouth that has no moisture and no breath
Breathless mouths may summon;
I hail the superhuman;
I call it death-in-life and life-in-death.

Miracle, bird or golden handiwork,
More miracle than bird or handiwork,
Planted on the star-lit golden bough,
Can like the cocks of Hades crow,
Or, by the moon embittered, scorn aloud
In glory of changeless metal
Common bird or petal
And all complexities of mire or blood.

At midnight on the Emperor's pavement flit
Flames that no faggot feeds, nor steel has lit,
Nor storm disturbs, flames begotten of flame,
Where blood-begotten spirits come
And all complexities of fury leave,
Dying into a dance,
An agony of trance,
An agony of flame that cannot singe a sleeve.

Astraddle on the dolphin's mire and blood,
Spirit after spirit! The smithies break the flood,
The golden smithies of the Emperor!
Marbles of the dancing floor
Break bitter furies of complexity,
Those images that yet
Fresh images beget,
That dolphin-torn, that gong-tormented sea.

RUDYARD KIPLING
1865–1936

620   *The Story of Uriah*

'Now there were two men in one city; the one rich, and the other poor.'

Jack Barrett went to Quetta
  Because they told him to.
He left his wife at Simla
  On three-fourths his monthly screw.
Jack Barrett died at Quetta
  Ere the next month's pay he drew.

Jack Barrett went to Quetta.
  He didn't understand
The reason of his transfer
  From the pleasant mountain-land.
The season was September,
  And it killed him out of hand.

Jack Barrett went to Quetta
  And there gave up the ghost,
Attempting two men's duty
  In that very healthy post;
And Mrs. Barrett mourned for him
  Five lively months at most.

Jack Barrett's bones at Quetta
  Enjoy profound repose;
But I shouldn't be astonished
  If *now* his spirit knows
The reason of his transfer
  From the Himalayan snows.

And, when the Last Great Bugle Call
  Adown the Hurnai throbs,
And the last grim joke is entered
  In the big black Book of Jobs,
And Quetta graveyards give again
  Their victims to the air,
I shouldn't like to be the man
  Who sent Jack Barrett there.

621 *The Vampire*

A fool there was and he made his prayer
(Even as you and I!)
To a rag and a bone and a hank of hair
(We called her the woman who did not care)
But the fool he called her his lady fair—
(Even as you and I!)

Oh, the years we waste and the tears we waste
And the work of our head and hand
Belong to the woman who did not know
(And now we know that she never could know)
And did not understand!

A fool there was and his goods he spent
(Even as you and I!)
Honour and faith and a sure intent
(And it wasn't the least what the lady meant)
But a fool must follow his natural bent
(Even as you and I!)

Oh, the toil we lost and the spoil we lost
And the excellent things we planned
Belong to the woman who didn't know why
(And now we know that she never knew why)
And did not understand!

The fool was stripped to his foolish hide
(Even as you and I!)
Which she might have seen when she threw him aside—
(But it isn't on record the lady tried)
So some of him lived but the most of him died—
(Even as you and I!)

And it isn't the shame and it isn't the blame
That stings like a white hot brand—
It's coming to know that she never knew why
(Seeing, at last, she could never know why)
And never could understand!

622 *A Death-Bed*

'This is the State above the Law.
    The State exists for the State alone.'
[*This is a gland at the back of the jaw,*
    And an answering lump by the collar-bone.]

Some die shouting in gas or fire;
  Some die silent, by shell and shot.
Some die desperate, caught on the wire;
  Some die suddenly. This will not.

'Regis suprema voluntas Lex'
  [*It will follow the regular course of—throats.*]
Some die pinned by the broken decks,
  Some die sobbing between the boats.

Some die eloquent, pressed to death
  By the sliding trench, as their friends can hear.
Some die wholly in half a breath.
    Some—give trouble for half a year.

'There is neither Evil nor Good in life
  Except as the needs of the State ordain.'
[*Since it is rather too late for the knife,
  All we can do is to mask the pain.*]

Some die saintly in faith and hope—
  One died thus in a prison-yard—
Some die broken by rape or the rope;
  Some die easily. This dies hard.

'I will dash to pieces who bar my way.
  Woe to the traitor! Woe to the weak!'
[*Let him write what he wishes to say.
  It tires him out if he tries to speak.*]

Some die quietly. Some abound
  In loud self-pity. Others spread
Bad morale through the cots around . . .
  This is a type that is better dead.

'The war was forced on me by my foes.
  All that I sought was the right to live.'
[*Don't be afraid of a triple dose;
  The pain will neutralize half we give.*

*Here are the needles. See that he dies
  While the effects of the drug endure. . . .
What is the question he asks with his eyes?—
  Yes, All-Highest, to God, be sure.*]

623   *Recessional*

        God of our fathers, known of old,
          Lord of our far-flung battle-line,
        Beneath whose awful Hand we hold
          Dominion over palm and pine—

Lord God of Hosts, be with us yet,
Lest we forget—lest we forget!

The tumult and the shouting dies;
    The Captains and the Kings depart:
Still stands Thine ancient sacrifice,
    An humble and a contrite heart.
Lord God of Hosts, be with us yet,
Lest we forget—lest we forget!

Far-called, our navies melt away;
    On dune and headland sinks the fire:
Lo, all our pomp of yesterday
    Is one with Nineveh and Tyre!
Judge of the Nations, spare us yet,
Lest we forget—lest we forget!

If, drunk with sight of power, we loose
    Wild tongues that have not Thee in awe,
Such boastings as the Gentiles use,
    Or lesser breeds without the Law—
Lord God of Hosts, be with us yet,
Lest we forget—lest we forget!

For heathen heart that puts her trust
    In reeking tube and iron shard,
All valiant dust that builds on dust,
    And guarding, calls not Thee to guard,
For frantic boast and foolish word —
Thy mercy on Thy People, Lord!

624   *Danny Deever*

'What are the bugles blowin' for?' said Files-on-Parade.
'To turn you out, to turn you out,' the Colour-Sergeant said.
'What makes you look so white, so white?' said Files-on-Parade.
'I'm dreadin' what I've got to watch,' the Colour-Sergeant said.
    For they're hangin' Danny Deever, you can hear the Dead March play,
    The regiment's in 'ollow square—they're hangin' him to-day;
    They've taken of his buttons off an' cut his stripes away,
    An' they're hangin' Danny Deever in the mornin'.

'What makes the rear-rank breathe so 'ard?' said Files-on-Parade.
'It's bitter cold, it's bitter cold,' the Colour-Sergeant said.
'What makes that front-rank man fall down?' said Files-on-Parade.
'A touch o' sun, a touch o' sun,' the Colour-Sergeant said.

They are hangin' Danny Deever, they are marchin' of 'im round,
They 'ave 'alted Danny Deever by 'is coffin on the ground;
An' 'e'll swing in 'arf a minute for a sneakin' shootin' hound—
O they're hangin' Danny Deever in the mornin'!

''Is cot was right-'and cot to mine,' said Files-on-Parade.
''E's sleepin' out an' far to-night,' the Colour-Sergeant said.
'I've drunk 'is beer a score o' times,' said Files-on-Parade.
''E's drinkin' bitter beer alone,' the Colour-Sergeant said.
    They are hangin' Danny Deever, you must mark 'im to 'is place,
    For 'e shot a comrade sleepin'—you must look 'im in the face;
    Nine 'undred of 'is county an' the Regiment's disgrace,
    While they're hangin' Danny Deever in the mornin'.

'What's that so black agin the sun?' said Files-on-Parade.
'It's Danny fightin' 'ard for life,' the Colour-Sergeant said.
'What's that that whimpers over'ead?' said Files-on-Parade.
'It's Danny's soul that's passin' now,' the Colour-Sergeant said.
    For they're done with Danny Deever, you can 'ear the quickstep play,
    The regiment's in column, an' they're marchin' us away;
    Ho! the young recruits are shakin', an' they'll want their beer to-day,
    After hangin' Danny Deever in the mornin'!

625   *The Fabulists*

When all the world would keep a matter hid,
    Since Truth is seldom friend to any crowd,
Men write in fable, as old Æsop did,
    Jesting at that which none will name aloud.
And this they needs must do, or it will fall
Unless they please they are not heard at all.

When desperate Folly daily laboureth
    To work confusion upon all we have,
When diligent Sloth demandeth Freedom's death,
    And banded Fear commandeth Honour's grave—
Even in that certain hour before the fall,
Unless men please they are not heard at all.

Needs must all please, yet some not all for need,
    Needs must all toil, yet some not all for gain,
But that men taking pleasure may take heed,
    Whom present toil shall snatch from later pain.
Thus some have toiled but their reward was small
Since, though they pleased, they were not heard at all.

This was the lock that lay upon our lips,
    This was the yoke that we have undergone,
Denying us all pleasant fellowships
    As in our time and generation.
Our pleasures unpursued age past recall.
And for our pains—we are not heard at all.

What man hears aught except the groaning guns?
    What man heeds aught save what each instant brings?
When each man's life all imaged life outruns,
    What man shall pleasure in imaginings?
So it hath fallen, as it was bound to fall,
We are not, nor we were not, heard at all.

ERNEST DOWSON

1867–1900

626   *Vitae summa brevis spem nos vetat incohare longam.*

They are not long, the weeping and the laughter,
    Love and desire and hate:
I think they have no portion in us after
    We pass the gate.

They are not long, the days of wine and roses:
    Out of a misty dream
Our path emerges for a while, then closes
    Within a dream.

CHARLOTTE MEW

1869–1928

627   *Sea Love*

Tide be runnin' the great world over.
    'Twas only last June month I mind that we
Was thinkin' the toss and the call in the breast of the lover
    So everlastin' as the sea.

Heer's the same little fishes that sputter and swim,
    Wi' the moon's old glim on the grey, wet sand;
An' him no more to me nor me to him
    Than the wind goin' over my hand.

628   *I so liked Spring*

I so liked Spring last year
    Because you were here;—
        The thrushes too—
Because it was these you so liked to hear—
        I so liked you.

    This year's a different thing,—
        I'll not think of you.
But I'll like Spring because it is simply Spring
        As the thrushes do.

629   *A Quoi Bon Dire*

Seventeen years ago you said
    Something that sounded like Good-bye;
    And everybody thinks that you are dead,
        But I.

    So I, as I grow stiff and cold
To this and that say Good-bye too;
    And everybody sees that I am old
        But you.

    And one fine morning in a sunny lane
Some boy and girl will meet and kiss and swear
    That nobody can love their way again
        While over there
You will have smiled, I shall have tossed your hair.

HILAIRE BELLOC

1870–1953

630   *On a General Election*

The accursèd power which stands on Privilege
(And goes with Women, and Champagne and Bridge)
Broke—and Democracy resumed her reign:
(Which goes with Bridge, and Women and Champagne).

J. M. SYNGE

1871–1909

631   *On an Island*

You've plucked a curlew, drawn a hen,
Washed the shirts of seven men,
You've stuffed my pillow, stretched the sheet,
And filled the pan to wash your feet,
You've cooped the pullets, wound the clock,
And rinsed the young men's drinking crock;
And now we'll dance to jigs and reels,
Nailed boots chasing girls' naked heels,
Until your father'll start to snore,
And Jude, now you're married, will stretch on the floor.

632   *He Understands the Great Cruelty of Death*

My flowery and green age was passing away, and I feeling a chill
in the fires had been wasting my heart, for I was drawing near the
hillside above the grave.

Then my sweet enemy was making a start, little by little, to give
over her great wariness, the way she was wringing a sweet thing
out of my sharp sorrow. The time was coming when Love and
Decency can keep company, and Lovers may sit together and say
out all things are in their hearts. But Death had his grudge against
me, and he got up in the way, like an armed robber, with a pike in
his hand.

[after the Italian of Petrarch]

WALTER DE LA MARE

1873–1956

633   *Napoleon*

'What is the world, O soldiers?
        It is I:
I, this incessant snow,
        This northern sky;

Soldiers, this solitude
Through which we go
Is I.'

634　　　　　　　　*Fare Well*

When I lie where shades of darkness
Shall no more assail mine eyes,
Nor the rain make lamentation
　　When the wind sighs;
How will fare the world whose wonder
Was the very proof of me?
Memory fades, must the remembered
　　Perishing be?

Oh, when this my dust surrenders
Hand, foot, lip, to dust again,
May these loved and loving faces
　　Please other men!
May the rusting harvest hedgerow
Still the Traveller's Joy entwine,
And as happy children gather
　　Posies once mine.

Look thy last on all things lovely,
Every hour. Let no night
Seal thy sense in deathly slumber
　　Till to delight
Thou have paid thy utmost blessing;
Since that all things thou wouldst praise
Beauty took from those who loved them
　　In other days.

E. C. BENTLEY

1875–1956

635　　　　Sir Humphry Davy
Abominated gravy.
He lived in the odium
Of having discovered Sodium.

636   George the Third
            Ought never to have occurred.
            One can only wonder
            At so grotesque a blunder.

637   Sir Christopher Wren
            Said, 'I am going to dine with some men.
            If anybody calls
            Say I am designing St. Paul's.'

EDWARD THOMAS

1878–1917

638   *Old Man*

Old Man, or Lad's-love,—in the name there's nothing
To one that knows not Lad's-love, or Old Man,
The hoar-green feathery herb, almost a tree,
Growing with rosemary and lavender.
Even to one that knows it well, the names
Half decorate, half perplex, the thing it is:
At least, what that is clings not to the names
In spite of time. And yet I like the names.

The herb itself I like not, but for certain
I love it, as some day the child will love it
Who plucks a feather from the door-side bush
Whenever she goes in or out of the house.
Often she waits there, snipping the tips and shrivelling
The shreds at last on to the path, perhaps
Thinking, perhaps of nothing, till she sniffs
Her fingers and runs off. The bush is still
But half as tall as she, though it is as old;
So well she clips it. Not a word she says;
And I can only wonder how much hereafter
She will remember, with that bitter scent,
Of garden rows, and ancient damson-trees
Topping a hedge, a bent path to a door,
A low thick bush beside the door, and me
Forbidding her to pick.
                    As for myself,
Where first I met the bitter scent is lost.

I, too, often shrivel the grey shreds,
Sniff them and think and sniff again and try
Once more to think what it is I am remembering,
Always in vain. I cannot like the scent,
Yet I would rather give up others more sweet,
With no meaning, than this bitter one.

I have mislaid the key. I sniff the spray
And think of nothing; I see and I hear nothing;
Yet seem, too, to be listening, lying in wait
For what I should, yet never can, remember:
No garden appears, no path, no hoar-green bush
Of Lad's-love, or Old Man, no child beside,
Neither father nor mother, nor any playmate;
Only an avenue, dark, nameless, without end.

639   *The Barn and the Down*

It stood in the sunset sky
Like the straight-backed down,
Many a time—the barn
At the edge of the town,

So huge and dark that it seemed
It was the hill
Till the gable's precipice proved
It impossible.

Then the great down in the west
Grew into sight,
A barn stored full to the ridge
With black of night;

And the barn fell to a barn
Or even less
Before critical eyes and its own
Late mightiness.

But far down and near barn and I
Since then have smiled,
Having seen my new cautiousness
By itself beguiled

To disdain what seemed the barn
Till a few steps changed
It past all doubt to the down;
So the barn was avenged.

640   *A Tale*

There once the walls
Of the ruined cottage stood.
The periwinkle crawls
With flowers in its hair into the wood.

In flowerless hours
Never will the bank fail,
With everlasting flowers
On fragments of blue plates, to tell the tale.

[published 1918; MS cancelled by Thomas]

641

Here once flint walls,
Pump, orchard and wood pile stood.
Blue periwinkle crawls
From the lost garden down into the wood.

The flowerless hours
Of Winter cannot prevail
To blight these other flowers,
Blue china fragments scattered, that tell the tale.

[published 1978; revised version]

642   *Aspens*

All day and night, save winter, every weather,
Above the inn, the smithy, and the shop,
The aspens at the cross-roads talk together
Of rain, until their last leaves fall from the top.

Out of the blacksmith's cavern comes the ringing
Of hammer, shoe, and anvil; out of the inn
The clink, the hum, the roar, the random singing—
The sounds that for these fifty years have been.

The whisper of the aspens is not drowned,
And over lightless pane and footless road,
Empty as sky, with every other sound
Not ceasing, calls their ghosts from their abode,

A silent smithy, a silent inn, nor fails
In the bare moonlight or the thick-furred gloom,
In tempest or the night of nightingales,
To turn the cross-roads to a ghostly room.

And it would be the same were no house near.
Over all sorts of weather, men, and times,
Aspens must shake their leaves and men may hear
But need not listen, more than to my rhymes.

Whatever wind blows, while they and I have leaves
We cannot other than an aspen be
That ceaselessly, unreasonably grieves,
Or so men think who like a different tree.

643   *Rain*

Rain, midnight rain, nothing but the wild rain
On this bleak hut, and solitude, and me
Remembering again that I shall die
And neither hear the rain nor give it thanks
For washing me cleaner than I have been
Since I was born into this solitude.
Blessed are the dead that the rain rains upon:
But here I pray that none whom once I loved
Is dying tonight or lying still awake
Solitary, listening to the rain,
Either in pain or thus in sympathy
Helpless among the living and the dead,
Like a cold water among broken reeds,
Myriads of broken reeds all still and stiff,
Like me who have no love which this wild rain
Has not dissolved except the love of death,
If love it be towards what is perfect and
Cannot, the tempest tells me, disappoint.

644   *Thaw*

Over the land freckled with snow half-thawed
The speculating rooks at their nests cawed
And saw from elm-tops, delicate as flower of grass,
What we below could not see, Winter pass.

645 *Tall Nettles*

Tall nettles cover up, as they have done
These many springs, the rusty harrow, the plough
Long worn out, and the roller made of stone:
Only the elm butt tops the nettles now.

This corner of the farmyard I like most:
As well as any bloom upon a flower
I like the dust on the nettles, never lost
Except to prove the sweetness of a shower.

646 *It rains*

It rains, and nothing stirs within the fence
Anywhere through the orchard's untrodden, dense
Forest of parsley. The great diamonds
Of rain on the grassblades there is none to break,
Or the fallen petals further down to shake.

And I am nearly as happy as possible
To search the wilderness in vain though well,
To think of two walking, kissing there,
Drenched, yet forgetting the kisses of the rain:
Sad, too, to think that never, never again,

Unless alone, so happy shall I walk
In the rain. When I turn away, on its fine stalk
Twilight has fined to naught, the parsley flower
Figures, suspended still and ghostly white,
The past hovering as it revisits the light.

647 Out in the dark over the snow
The fallow fawns invisible go
With the fallow doe;
And the winds blow
Fast as the stars are slow.

Stealthily the dark haunts round
And, when a lamp goes, without sound
At a swifter bound
Than the swiftest hound,
Arrives, and all else is drowned;

And I and star and wind and deer
Are in the dark together,—near,
Yet far,—and fear
Drums on my ear
In that sage company drear.

How weak and little is the light,
All the universe of sight,
Love and delight,
Before the might,
If you love it not, of night.

JOHN MASEFIELD
1878–1967

648   *Sonnet*

I saw the ramparts of my native land,
One time so strong, now dropping in decay,
Their strength destroyed by this new age's way,
That has worn out and rotted what was grand.

I went into the fields: there I could see
The sun drink up the waters newly thawed,
And on the hills the moaning cattle pawed;
Their miseries robbed the day of light for me.

I went into my house: I saw how spotted,
Decaying things made that old home their prize.
My withered walking-staff had come to bend.
I felt the age had won; my sword was rotted,
And there was nothing on which to set my eyes
That was not a reminder of the end.

[after the Spanish of Quevedo]

649   *Autumn Ploughing*

After the ranks of stubble have lain bare,
And field mice and the finches' beaks have found
The last spilled seed corn left upon the ground;
And no more swallows miracle in air;

When the green tuft no longer hides the hare,
And dropping starling flights at evening come;
When birds, except the robin, have gone dumb,
And leaves are rustling downwards everywhere;

Then out, with the great horses, come the ploughs,
And all day long the slow procession goes,
Darkening the stubble fields with broadening strips.

Gray sea-gulls settle after to carouse:
Harvest prepares upon the harvest's close,
Before the blackbird pecks the scarlet hips.

650   *An Epilogue*

I have seen flowers come in stony places
And kind things done by men with ugly faces,
And the gold cup won by the worst horse at the races,
So I trust, too.

JAMES STEPHENS

1882–1950

651   *The Cage*

It tried to get from out the cage;
    Here and there it ran, and tried
    At the edges and the side,
In a busy, timid rage.

Trying yet to find the key
    Into freedom, trying yet,
    In a timid rage, to get
To its old tranquillity.

It did not know, it did not see,
    It did not turn an eye, or care
    That a man was watching there
While it raged so timidly.

It ran without a sound, it tried,
    In a busy, timid rage,
    To escape from out the cage
By the edges and the side.

652   *A Glass of Beer*

The lanky hank of a she in the inn over there
Nearly killed me for asking the loan of a glass of beer;
May the devil grip the whey-faced slut by the hair,
And beat bad manners out of her skin for a year.

That parboiled ape, with the toughest jaw you will see
On virtue's path, and a voice that would rasp the dead,
Came roaring and raging the minute she looked at me,
And threw me out of the house on the back of my head!

If I asked her master he'd give me a cask a day;
But she, with the beer at hand, not a gill would arrange!
May she marry a ghost and bear him a kitten, and may
The High King of Glory permit her to get the mange.

D. H. LAWRENCE
1885–1930

653   *Snake*

A snake came to my water-trough
On a hot, hot day, and I in pyjamas for the heat,
To drink there.

In the deep, strange-scented shade of the great dark carob-tree
I came down the steps with my pitcher
And must wait, must stand and wait, for there he was at the trough
        before me.

He reached down from a fissure in the earth-wall in the gloom
And trailed his yellow-brown slackness soft-bellied down, over the edge of
        the stone trough
And rested his throat upon the stone bottom,
And where the water had dripped from the tap, in a small clearness,
He sipped with his straight mouth,
Softly drank through his straight gums, into his slack long body,
Silently.

Someone was before me at my water-trough,
And I, like a second comer, waiting.

He lifted his head from his drinking, as cattle do,
And looked at me vaguely, as drinking cattle do,

And flickered his two-forked tongue from his lips, and mused a moment,
And stooped and drank a little more,
Being earth-brown, earth-golden from the burning bowels of the earth
On the day of Sicilian July, with Etna smoking.

The voice of my education said to me
He must be killed,
For in Sicily the black, black snakes are innocent, the gold are venomous.

And voices in me said, If you were a man
You would take a stick and break him now, and finish him off.

But must I confess how I liked him,
How glad I was he had come like a guest in quiet, to drink at my water-
        trough
And depart peaceful, pacified, and thankless,
Into the burning bowels of this earth?

Was it cowardice, that I dared not kill him?
Was it perversity, that I longed to talk to him?
Was it humility, to feel so honoured?
I felt so honoured.

And yet those voices:
If you were not afraid, you would kill him!

And truly I was afraid, I was most afraid,
But even so, honoured still more
That he should seek my hospitality
From out the dark door of the secret earth.

He drank enough
And lifted his head, dreamily, as one who has drunken,
And flickered his tongue like a forked night on the air, so black;
Seeming to lick his lips,
And looked around like a god, unseeing, into the air,
And slowly turned his head,
And slowly, very slowly, as if thrice adream,
Proceeded to draw his slow length curving round
And climb again the broken bank of my wall-face.

And as he put his head into that dreadful hole,
And as he slowly drew up, snake-easing his shoulders, and entered farther,
A sort of horror, a sort of protest against his withdrawing into that horrid
        black hole,
Deliberately going into the blackness, and slowly drawing himself after,
Overcame me now his back was turned.

I looked round, I put down my pitcher,
I picked up a clumsy log
And threw it at the water-trough with a clatter.

I think it did not hit him,
But suddenly that part of him that was left behind convulsed in undignified
    haste,
Writhed like lightning, and was gone
Into the black hole, the earth-lipped fissure in the wall-front,
At which, in the intense still noon, I stared with fascination.

And immediately I regretted it.
I thought how paltry, how vulgar, what a mean act!
I despised myself and the voices of my accursed human education.

And I thought of the albatross,
And I wished he would come back, my snake.

For he seemed to me again like a king,
Like a king in exile, uncrowned in the underworld,
Now due to be crowned again.

And so, I missed my chance with one of the lords
Of life.
And I have something to expiate;
A pettiness.

654   *Humming-Bird*

    I can imagine, in some otherworld
    Primeval-dumb, far back
    In that most awful stillness, that only gasped and hummed,
    Humming-birds raced down the avenues.

    Before anything had a soul,
    While life was a heave of Matter, half inanimate,
    This little bit chipped off in brilliance
    And went whizzing through the slow, vast, succulent stems.

    I believe there were no flowers then,
    In the world where the humming-bird flashed ahead of creation.
    I believe he pierced the slow vegetable veins with his long beak.

    Probably he was big
    As mosses, and little lizards, they say, were once big.
    Probably he was a jabbing, terrifying monster.

    We look at him through the wrong end of the long telescope of Time,
    Luckily for us.

655   *Thought*

Thought, I love thought.
But not the jaggling and twisting of already existent ideas
I despise that self-important game.
Thought is the welling up of unknown life into consciousness,
Thought is the testing of statements on the touchstone of the conscience,
Thought is gazing on to the face of life, and reading what can be read,
Thought is pondering over experience, and coming to conclusion.
Thought is not a trick, or an exercise, or a set of dodges,
Thought is a man in his wholeness wholly attending.

656   *Bavarian Gentians*

Not every man has gentians in his house
in Soft September, at slow, sad Michaelmas.

Bavarian gentians, big and dark, only dark
darkening the day-time, torch-like with the smoking blueness of Pluto's
      gloom,
ribbed and torch-like, with their blaze of darkness spread blue
down flattening into points, flattened under the sweep of white day
torch-flower of the blue-smoking darkness, Pluto's dark-blue daze,
black lamps from the halls of Dis, burning dark blue,
giving off darkness, blue darkness, as Demeter's pale lamps give off light,
lead me then, lead the way.

Reach me a gentian, give me a torch!
let me guide myself with the blue, forked torch of this flower
down the darker and darker stairs, where blue is darkened on blueness
even where Persephone goes, just now, from the frosted September
to the sightless realm where darkness is awake upon the dark
and Persephone herself is but a voice
or a darkness invisible enfolded in the deeper dark
of the arms Plutonic, and pierced with the passion of dense gloom,
among the splendour of torches of darkness, shedding darkness on the lost
      bride and her groom.

657   *The Ship of Death*

I

Now it is autumn and the falling fruit
and the long journey towards oblivion.

The apples falling like great drops of dew
to bruise themselves an exit from themselves.

And it is time to go, to bid farewell
to one's own self, and find an exit
from the fallen self.

II

Have you built your ship of death, O have you?
O build your ship of death, for you will need it.

The grim frost is at hand, when the apples will fall
thick, almost thundrous, on the hardened earth.

And death is on the air like a smell of ashes!
Ah! can't you smell it?

And in the bruised body, the frightened soul
finds itself shrinking, wincing from the cold
that blows upon it through the orifices.

III

And can a man his own quietus make
with a bare bodkin?

With daggers, bodkins, bullets, man can make
a bruise or break of exit for his life;
but is that a quietus, O tell me, is it quietus?

Surely not so! for how could murder, even self-murder
ever a quietus make?

IV

O let us talk of quiet that we know,
that we can know, the deep and lovely quiet
of a strong heart at peace!

How can we this, our own quietus, make?

V

Build then the ship of death, for you must take
the longest journey, to oblivion.

And die the death, the long and painful death
that lies between the old self and the new.

Already our bodies are fallen, bruised, badly bruised,
already our souls are oozing through the exit
of the cruel bruise.

Already the dark and endless ocean of the end
is washing in through the breaches of our wounds,
already the flood is upon us.

Oh build your ship of death, your little ark
and furnish it with food, with little cakes, and wine
for the dark flight down oblivion.

VI

Piecemeal the body dies, and the timid soul
has her footing washed away, as the dark flood rises.

We are dying, we are dying, we are all of us dying
and nothing will stay the death-flood rising within us
and soon it will rise on the world, on the outside world.

We are dying, we are dying, piecemeal our bodies are dying
and our strength leaves us,
and our soul cowers naked in the dark rain over the flood,
cowering in the last branches of the tree of our life.

VII

We are dying, we are dying, so all we can do
is now to be willing to die, and to build the ship
of death to carry the soul on the longest journey.

A little ship, with oars and food
and little dishes, and all accoutrements
fitting and ready for the departing soul.

Now launch the small ship, now as the body dies
and life departs, launch out, the fragile soul
in the fragile ship of courage, the ark of faith
with its store of food and little cooking pans
and change of clothes,
upon the flood's black waste
upon the waters of the end
upon the sea of death, where still we sail
darkly, for we cannot steer, and have no port.

There is no port, there is nowhere to go
only the deepening blackness darkening still
blacker upon the soundless, ungurgling flood
darkness at one with darkness, up and down
and sideways utterly dark, so there is no direction any more,
and the little ship is there; yet she is gone.
She is not seen, for there is nothing to see her by.

She is gone! gone! and yet
somewhere she is there.
Nowhere!

VIII

And everything is gone, the body is gone
completely under, gone, entirely gone.
The upper darkness is heavy as the lower,
between them the little ship
is gone
she is gone.

It is the end, it is oblivion.

IX

And yet out of eternity, a thread
separates itself on the blackness,
a horizontal thread
that fumes a little with pallor upon the dark.

Is it illusion? or does the pallor fume
A little higher?
Ah wait, wait, for there's the dawn,
the cruel dawn of coming back to life
out of oblivion.

Wait, wait, the little ship
drifting, beneath the deathly ashy grey
of a flood-dawn.

Wait, wait! even so, a flush of yellow
and strangely, O chilled wan soul, a flush of rose.

A flush of rose, and the whole thing starts again.

X

The flood subsides, and the body, like a worn sea-shell
emerges strange and lovely.
And the little ship wings home, faltering and lapsing
on the pink flood,
and the frail soul steps out, into her house again
filling the heart with peace.

Swings the heart renewed with peace
even of oblivion.

Oh build your ship of death, oh build it!
for you will need it.
For the voyage of oblivion awaits you.

HUMBERT WOLFE

1886–1940

658
You cannot hope
  to bribe or twist,
thank God! the
  British journalist.

But, seeing what
  the man will do
unbribed, there's
  no occasion to.

FRANCES CORNFORD

1886–1960

659
Childhood

I used to think that grown-up people chose
To have stiff backs and wrinkles round their nose,
And veins like small fat snakes on either hand,
On purpose to be grand.
Till through the banisters I watched one day
My great-aunt Etty's friend who was going away,
And how her onyx beads had come unstrung.
I saw her grope to find them as they rolled;
And then I knew that she was helplessly old,
As I was helplessly young.

660
To a Fat Lady Seen from the Train

TRIOLET

O why do you walk through the fields in gloves,
  Missing so much and so much?
O fat white woman whom nobody loves,
Why do you walk through the fields in gloves,
When the grass is soft as the breast of doves
  And shivering-sweet to the touch?
O why do you walk through the fields in gloves,
  Missing so much and so much?

SIEGFRIED SASSOON

1886–1967

661 *'Blighters'*

The House is crammed: tier beyond tier they grin
And cackle at the Show, while prancing ranks
Of harlots shrill the chorus, drunk with din;
'We're sure the Kaiser loves our dear old Tanks!'

I'd like to see a Tank come down the stalls,
Lurching to rag-time tunes, or 'Home, sweet Home',
And there'd be no more jokes in Music-halls
To mock the riddled corpses round Bapaume.

662 *Base Details*

If I were fierce, and bald, and short of breath,
    I'd live with scarlet Majors at the Base,
And speed glum heroes up the line to death.
    You'd see me with my puffy petulant face,
Guzzling and gulping in the best hotel,
    Reading the Roll of Honour. 'Poor young chap,'
I'd say—'I used to know his father well;
    Yes, we've lost heavily in this last scrap.'
And when the war is done and youth stone dead,
I'd toddle safely home and die—in bed.

663 *The General*

'Good-morning; good-morning!' the General said
When we met him last week on our way to the line.
Now the soldiers he smiled at are most of 'em dead,
And we're cursing his staff for incompetent swine.
'He's a cheery old card,' grunted Harry to Jack
As they slogged up to Arras with rifle and pack.

* * *

But he did for them both by his plan of attack.

EDWIN MUIR

1887–1959

664   *Then*

There were no men and women then at all,
But the flesh lying alone,
And angry shadows fighting on a wall
That now and then sent out a groan
Buried in lime and stone,
And sweated now and then like tortured wood
Big drops that looked yet did not look like blood.

And yet as each drop came a shadow faded
And left the wall.
There was a lull
Until another in its shadow arrayed it,
Came, fought and left a blood-mark on the wall;
And that was all; the blood was all.

If there had been women there they might have wept
For the poor blood, unowned, unwanted,
Blank as forgotten script.
The wall was haunted
By mute maternal presences whose sighing
Fluttered the fighting shadows and shook the wall
As if that fury of death itself were dying.

RUPERT BROOKE

1887–1915

665   *Heaven*

Fish (fly-replete, in depth of June,
Dawdling away their wat'ry noon)
Ponder deep wisdom, dark or clear,
Each secret fishy hope or fear.
Fish say, they have their Stream and Pond;
But is there anything Beyond?
This life cannot be All, they swear,
For how unpleasant, if it were!
One may not doubt that, somehow, Good
Shall come of Water and of Mud;

And, sure, the reverent eye must see
A Purpose in Liquidity.
We darkly know, by Faith we cry,
The future is not Wholly Dry.
Mud unto mud!—Death eddies near—
Not here the appointed End, not here!
But somewhere, beyond Space and Time,
Is wetter water, slimier slime!
And there (they trust) there swimmeth One
Who swam ere rivers were begun,
Immense, of fishy form and mind,
Squamous, omnipotent, and kind;
And under that Almighty Fin,
The littlest fish may enter in.
Oh! never fly conceals a hook,
Fish say, in the Eternal Brook,
But more than mundane weeds are there,
And mud, celestially fair;
Fat caterpillars drift around,
And Paradisal grubs are found;
Unfading moths, immortal flies,
And the worm that never dies.
And in that Heaven of all their wish,
There shall be no more land, say fish.

ELIZABETH DARYUSH

1887–1977

666   Children of wealth in your warm nursery,
        Set in the cushioned window-seat to watch
        The volleying snow, guarded invisibly
        By the clear double pane through which no touch
        Untimely penetrates, you cannot tell
        What winter means; its cruel truths to you
        Are only sound and sight; your citadel
        Is safe from feeling, and from knowledge too.

        Go down, go out to elemental wrong,
        Waste your too round limbs, tan your skin too white;
        The glass of comfort, ignorance, seems strong
        Today, and yet perhaps this very night

        You'll wake to horror's wrecking fire—your home
        Is wired within for this, in every room.

667   *Still-Life*

Through the open French window the warm sun
lights up the polished breakfast-table, laid
round a bowl of crimson roses, for one—
a service of Worcester porcelain, arrayed
near it a melon, peaches, figs, small hot
rolls in a napkin, fairy rack of toast,
butter in ice, high silver coffee pot,
and, heaped on a salver, the morning's post.

She comes over the lawn, the young heiress,
from her early walk in her garden-wood
feeling that life's a table set to bless
her delicate desires with all that's good,

that even the unopened future lies
like a love-letter, full of sweet surprise.

                          R. A. KNOX
                          1888–1957

668a   There once was a man who said 'God
                 Must think it exceedingly odd
                     If he finds that this tree
                     Continues to be
                 When there's no one about in the Quad.'

                        ANONYMOUS

668b   Dear Sir, Your astonishment's odd:
                 I am always about in the Quad.
                     And that's why the tree
                     Will continue to be,
                 Since observed by Yours faithfully, God.

                         T. S. ELIOT
                          1888–1965

669   *The Love Song of J. Alfred Prufrock*

                 S'io credessi che mia risposta fosse
                 a persona che mai tornasse al mondo,

questa fiamma staria senza più scosse.
Ma per ciò che giammai di questo fondo
non tornò vivo alcun, s'i' odo il vero,
senza tema d'infamia ti rispondo.

Let us go then, you and I,
When the evening is spread out against the sky
Like a patient etherised upon a table;
Let us go, through certain half-deserted streets,
The muttering retreats
Of restless nights in one-night cheap hotels
And sawdust restaurants with oyster-shells:
Streets that follow like a tedious argument
Of insidious intent
To lead you to an overwhelming question . . .
Oh, do not ask, 'What is it?'
Let us go and make our visit.

In the room the women come and go
Talking of Michelangelo.

The yellow fog that rubs its back upon the window-panes,
The yellow smoke that rubs its muzzle on the window-panes,
Licked its tongue into the corners of the evening,
Lingered upon the pools that stand in drains,
Let fall upon its back the soot that falls from chimneys,
Slipped by the terrace, made a sudden leap,
And seeing that it was a soft October night,
Curled once about the house, and fell asleep.

And indeed there will be time
For the yellow smoke that slides along the street
Rubbing its back upon the window-panes;
There will be time, there will be time
To prepare a face to meet the faces that you meet;
There will be time to murder and create,
And time for all the works and days of hands
That lift and drop a question on your plate;
Time for you and time for me,
And time yet for a hundred indecisions,
And for a hundred visions and revisions,
Before the taking of a toast and tea.

In the room the women come and go
Talking of Michelangelo.

And indeed there will be time
To wonder, 'Do I dare?' and, 'Do I dare?'
Time to turn back and descend the stair,
With a bald spot in the middle of my hair—

(They will say: 'How his hair is growing thin!')
My morning coat, my collar mounting firmly to the chin,
My necktie rich and modest, but asserted by a simple pin—
(They will say: 'But how his arms and legs are thin!')
Do I dare
Disturb the universe?
In a minute there is time
For decisions and revisions which a minute will reverse.

    For I have known them all already, known them all—
Have known the evenings, mornings, afternoons,
I have measured out my life with coffee spoons;
I know the voices dying with a dying fall
Beneath the music from a farther room.
      So how should I presume?

    And I have known the eyes already, known them all—
The eyes that fix you in a formulated phrase,
And when I am formulated, sprawling on a pin,
When I am pinned and wriggling on the wall,
Then how should I begin
To spit out all the butt-ends of my days and ways?
      And how should I presume?

    And I have known the arms already, known them all—
Arms that are braceleted and white and bare
(But in the lamplight, downed with light brown hair!)
Is it perfume from a dress
That makes me so digress?
Arms that lie along a table, or wrap about a shawl.
      And should I then presume?
      And how should I begin?

*　*　*

    Shall I say, I have gone at dusk through narrow streets
And watched the smoke that rises from the pipes
Of lonely men in shirt-sleeves, leaning out of windows? . . .

    I should have been a pair of ragged claws
Scuttling across the floors of silent seas.

*　*　*

    And the afternoon, the evening, sleeps so peacefully!
Smoothed by long fingers,
Asleep . . . tired . . . or it malingers,
Stretched on the floor, here beside you and me.

Should I, after tea and cakes and ices,
Have the strength to force the moment to its crisis?
But though I have wept and fasted, wept and prayed,
Though I have seen my head (grown slightly bald) brought in upon a platter,
I am no prophet—and here's no great matter;
I have seen the moment of my greatness flicker,
And I have seen the eternal Footman hold my coat, and snicker,
And in short, I was afraid.

And would it have been worth it, after all,
After the cups, the marmalade, the tea,
Among the porcelain, among some talk of you and me,
Would it have been worth while,
To have bitten off the matter with a smile,
To have squeezed the universe into a ball
To roll it towards some overwhelming question,
To say: 'I am Lazarus, come from the dead,
Come back to tell you all, I shall tell you all'—
If one, settling a pillow by her head,
    Should say: 'That is not what I meant at all.
    That is not it, at all.'

And would it have been worth it, after all,
Would it have been worth while,
After the sunsets and the dooryards and the sprinkled streets,
After the novels, after the teacups, after the skirts that trail along the floor—
And this, and so much more?—
It is impossible to say just what I mean!
But as if a magic lantern threw the nerves in patterns on a screen:
Would it have been worth while
If one, settling a pillow or throwing off a shawl,
And turning toward the window, should say:
    'That is not it at all,
    That is not what I meant, at all.'

                    *   *   *

No! I am not Prince Hamlet, nor was meant to be;
Am an attendant lord, one that will do
To swell a progress, start a scene or two,
Advise the prince; no doubt, an easy tool,
Deferential, glad to be of use,
Politic, cautious, and meticulous;
Full of high sentence, but a bit obtuse;
At times, indeed, almost ridiculous—
Almost, at times, the Fool.

    I grow old . . . I grow old . . .
I shall wear the bottoms of my trousers rolled.

Shall I part my hair behind? Do I dare to eat a peach?
I shall wear white flannel trousers, and walk upon the beach.
I have heard the mermaids singing, each to each.

I do not think that they will sing to me.

I have seen them riding seaward on the waves
Combing the white hair of the waves blown back
When the wind blows the water white and black.

We have lingered in the chambers of the sea
By sea-girls wreathed with seaweed red and brown
Till human voices wake us, and we drown.

670 *Morning at the Window*

They are rattling breakfast plates in basement kitchens,
And along the trampled edges of the street
I am aware of the damp souls of housemaids
Sprouting despondently at area gates.

The brown waves of fog toss up to me
Twisted faces from the bottom of the street,
And tear from a passer-by with muddy skirts
An aimless smile that hovers in the air
And vanishes along the level of the roofs.

671 *Hysteria*

As she laughed I was aware of becoming involved in her laughter
and being part of it, until her teeth were only accidental stars
with a talent for squad-drill. I was drawn in by short gasps,
inhaled at each momentary recovery, lost finally in the dark
caverns of her throat, bruised by the ripple of unseen muscles.
An elderly waiter with trembling hands was hurriedly spreading
a pink and white checked cloth over the rusty green iron table,
saying: 'If the lady and gentleman wish to take their tea in the
garden, if the lady and gentleman wish to take their tea in
the garden . . .' I decided that if the shaking of her breasts could
be stopped, some of the fragments of the afternoon might be
collected, and I concentrated my attention with careful subtlety
to this end.

672   *La Figlia Che Piange*

                       O quam te memorem virgo . . .

Stand on the highest pavement of the stair—
Lean on a garden urn—
Weave, weave the sunlight in your hair—
Clasp your flowers to you with a pained surprise—
Fling them to the ground and turn
With a fugitive resentment in your eyes:
But weave, weave the sunlight in your hair.

So I would have had him leave,
So I would have had her stand and grieve,
So he would have left
As the soul leaves the body torn and bruised,
As the mind deserts the body it has used.
I should find
Some way incomparably light and deft,
Some way we both should understand,
Simple and faithless as a smile and shake of the hand.

She turned away, but with the autumn weather
Compelled my imagination many days,
Many days and many hours:
Her hair over her arms and her arms full of flowers.
And I wonder how they should have been together!
I should have lost a gesture and a pose.
Sometimes these cogitations still amaze
The troubled midnight and the noon's repose.

673   *Sweeney Among the Nightingales*

          ὤμοι, πέπληγμαι καιρίαν πληγὴν ἔσω.

Apeneck Sweeney spreads his knees
Letting his arms hang down to laugh,
The zebra stripes along his jaw
Swelling to maculate giraffe.

The circles of the stormy moon
Slide westward toward the River Plate,
Death and the Raven drift above
And Sweeney guards the hornèd gate.

Gloomy Orion and the Dog
Are veiled; and hushed the shrunken seas;
The person in the Spanish cape
Tries to sit on Sweeney's knees

Slips and pulls the table cloth
Overturns a coffee-cup,
Reorganised upon the floor
She yawns and draws a stocking up;

The silent man in mocha brown
Sprawls at the window-sill and gapes;
The waiter brings in oranges
Bananas figs and hothouse grapes;

The silent vertebrate in brown
Contracts and concentrates, withdraws;
Rachel *née* Rabinovitch
Tears at the grapes with murderous paws;

She and the lady in the cape
Are suspect, thought to be in league;
Therefore the man with heavy eyes
Declines the gambit, shows fatigue,

Leaves the room and reappears
Outside the window, leaning in,
Branches of wistaria
Circumscribe a golden grin;

The host with someone indistinct
Converses at the door apart,
The nightingales are singing near
The Convent of the Sacred Heart,

And sang within the bloody wood
When Agamemnon cried aloud
And let their liquid siftings fall
To stain the stiff dishonoured shroud.

674   from *The Waste Land*

IV. *Death by Water*

Phlebas the Phoenician, a fortnight dead,
Forgot the cry of gulls, and the deep sea swell
And the profit and loss.
                    A current under sea

Picked his bones in whispers. As he rose and fell
He passed the stages of his age and youth
Entering the whirlpool.

                Gentile or Jew
O you who turn the wheel and look to windward,
Consider Phlebas, who was once handsome and tall as you.

675   *Marina*

        Quis hic locus, quae
        regio, quae mundi plaga?

What seas what shores what grey rocks and what islands
What water lapping the bow
And scent of pine and the woodthrush singing through the fog
What images return
O my daughter.

Those who sharpen the tooth of the dog, meaning
Death
Those who glitter with the glory of the hummingbird, meaning
Death
Those who sit in the sty of contentment, meaning
Death
Those who suffer the ecstasy of the animals, meaning
Death

Are become unsubstantial, reduced by a wind,
A breath of pine, and the woodsong fog
By this grace dissolved in place

What is this face, less clear and clearer
The pulse in the arm, less strong and stronger—
Given or lent? more distant than stars and nearer than the eye

Whispers and small laughter between leaves and hurrying feet
Under sleep, where all the waters meet.

Bowsprit cracked with ice and paint cracked with heat.
I made this, I have forgotten
And remember.
The rigging weak and the canvas rotten
Between one June and another September.
Made this unknowing, half conscious, unknown, my own.
The garboard strake leaks, the seams need caulking.
This form, this face, this life
Living to live in a world of time beyond me; let me
Resign my life for this life, my speech for that unspoken,
The awakened, lips parted, the hope, the new ships.

What seas what shores what granite islands towards my timbers
And woodthrush calling through the fog
My daughter.

676   from *Four Quartets: Little Gidding*

II

Ash on an old man's sleeve
Is all the ash the burnt roses leave.
Dust in the air suspended
Marks the place where a story ended.
Dust inbreathed was a house—
The wall, the wainscot and the mouse.
The death of hope and despair,
        This is the death of air.

There are flood and drouth
Over the eyes and in the mouth,
Dead water and dead sand
Contending for the upper hand.
The parched eviscerate soil
Gapes at the vanity of toil,
Laughs without mirth.
        This is the death of earth.

Water and fire succeed
The town, the pasture and the weed.
Water and fire deride
The sacrifice that we denied.
Water and fire shall rot
The marred foundations we forgot,
Of sanctuary and choir.
        This is the death of water and fire.

In the uncertain hour before the morning
    Near the ending of interminable night
    At the recurrent end of the unending
After the dark dove with the flickering tongue
    Had passed below the horizon of his homing
    While the dead leaves still rattled on like tin
Over the asphalt where no other sound was
    Between three districts whence the smoke arose
    I met one walking, loitering and hurried
As if blown towards me like the metal leaves
    Before the urban dawn wind unresisting.
    And as I fixed upon the down-turned face

That pointed scrutiny with which we challenge
   The first-met stranger in the waning dusk
   I caught the sudden look of some dead master
Whom I had known, forgotten, half recalled
   Both one and many; in the brown baked features
   The eyes of a familiar compound ghost
Both intimate and unidentifiable.
   So I assumed a double part, and cried
   And heard another's voice cry: 'What! are *you* here?'
Although we were not. I was still the same,
   Knowing myself yet being someone other—
   And he a face still forming; yet the words sufficed
To compel the recognition they preceded.
   And so, compliant to the common wind,
   Too strange to each other for misunderstanding,
In concord at this intersection time
   Of meeting nowhere, no before and after,
   We trod the pavement in a dead patrol.
I said: 'The wonder that I feel is easy,
   Yet ease is cause of wonder. Therefore speak:
   I may not comprehend, may not remember.'
And he: 'I am not eager to rehearse
   My thoughts and theory which you have forgotten.
   These things have served their purpose: let them be.
So with your own, and pray they be forgiven
   By others, as I pray you to forgive
   Both bad and good. Last season's fruit is eaten
And the fullfed beast shall kick the empty pail.
   For last year's words belong to last year's language
   And next year's words await another voice.
But, as the passage now presents no hindrance
   To the spirit unappeased and peregrine
   Between two worlds become much like each other,
So I find words I never thought to speak
   In streets I never thought I should revisit
   When I left my body on a distant shore.
Since our concern was speech, and speech impelled us
   To purify the dialect of the tribe
   And urge the mind to aftersight and foresight,
Let me disclose the gifts reserved for age
   To set a crown upon your lifetime's effort.
   First, the cold friction of expiring sense
Without enchantment, offering no promise
   But bitter tastelessness of shadow fruit
   As body and soul begin to fall asunder.
Second, the conscious impotence of rage
   At human folly, and the laceration
   Of laughter at what ceases to amuse.

And last, the rending pain of re-enactment
  Of all that you have done, and been; the shame
  Of motives late revealed, and the awareness
Of things ill done and done to others' harm
  Which once you took for exercise of virtue.
  Then fools' approval stings, and honour stains.
From wrong to wrong the exasperated spirit
  Proceeds, unless restored by that refining fire
  Where you must move in measure, like a dancer.'
The day was breaking. In the disfigured street
  He left me, with a kind of valediction,
  And faded on the blowing of the horn.

ARTHUR WALEY
1889–1966

677   *The Ejected Wife*

Entering the Hall, she meets the new wife;
Leaving the gate, she runs into former husband.
Words stick; does not manage to say anything,
Presses hands together: stands hesitating.
Agitates moon-like fan, sheds pearl-like tears,
Realises she loves him as much as ever—
Present pain never come to an end.

      [after the Chinese of Yüan-ti]

678   Yellow dusk: messenger fails to appear.
Restraining anger, heart sick and sad.
Turn candle towards bed-foot;
Averting face—sob in darkness.

      [after the Chinese, Anon.]

679   In her boudoir, the young lady,—unacquainted with grief.
Spring day,—best clothes, mounts shining tower.
Suddenly sees at the dyke's head, the changed colour of the
    willows.
Regrets she made her dear husband go to win a fief.

      [after the Chinese, Anon.]

IVOR GURNEY
1890–1937

680   *La Gorgue*

The long night, the short sleep, and La Gorgue to wander,
So be the Fates were kind and our Commander;
With a mill, and still canal, and like-Stroudway bridges.
One looks back on these as Time's truest riches
Which were so short an escape, so perilous a joy
Since fatigues, weather, line trouble or any whimsical ploy
Division might hatch out would have finished peace.

There was a house there, (I tell the noted thing)
The kindest woman kept, and an unending string
Of privates as wasps to sugar went in and out.
Friendliness sanctified all there without doubt,
As lovely as the mill above the still green
Canal where the dark fishes went almost unseen.
B Company had come down from Tilleloy
Lousy, thirsty, avid of any employ
Of peace; and this woman in leanest times had plotted
A miracle to amaze the army-witted.
And this was café-au-lait as princes know it,
And fasting, and poor-struck; dead but not to show it.
A drink of edicts, dooms, a height of tales.
Heat, cream, coffee; the maker tries and fails,
The poet too, where such thirst such mate had.
A campaign thing that makes remembrance sad.

There was light there, too, in the clear North French way.
It blessed the room, and bread, and the mistress giver,
The husband for his wife's sake, and both for a day
Were blessed by many soldiers tired however;
A mark in Time, a Peace, a Making-delay.

681   *The Soaking*

The rain has come, and the earth must be very glad
Of its moisture, and the made roads all dust clad;
It lets a friendly veil down on the lucent dark,
And not of any bright ground thing shows any spark.

Tomorrow's grey morning will show cow-parsley,
Hung all with shining drops, and the river will be
Duller because of the all soddenness of things,
Till the skylark breaks his reluctance, hangs shaking, and sings.

682 *First March*

It was first marching, hardly we had settled yet
To think of England, or escaped body pain—
Flat country going leaves but small chance for
The mind to escape to any resort but its vain
Own circling greyness and stain.
First halt, second halt, and then to spoiled country again.
There were unknown kilometres to march, one must settle
To play chess or talk home-talk or think as might happen.
After three weeks of February frost few were in fettle,
Barely frostbite the most of us had escapen.
To move, then to go onward, at least to be moved.
Myself had revived and then dulled down, it was I
Who stared for body-ease at the grey sky
And watched in grind of pain the monotony
Of grit, road metal, slide underneath by.
To get there being the one way not to die.
Suddenly a road's turn brought the sweet unexpected
Balm. Snowdrops bloomed in a ruined garden neglected:
Roman the road as of Birdlip we were on the verge,
And this west country thing so from chaos to emerge.
One gracious touch the whole wilderness corrected.

683 *Behind the Line*

I suppose France this morning is as white as here
High white clouds veiling the sun, and the mere
Cabbage fields and potato plants lovely to see,
Back behind at Robecq there with the day free.

In the estaminets I suppose the air as cool, and the floor
Grateful dark red; the beer and the different store
Of citron, grenadine, red wine as surely delectable
As in Nineteen Sixteen; with the round stains on the dark table.

Journals Français tell the same news and the queer
Black printed columns give news, but no longer the fear
Of shrapnel or any evil metal torments.
High white morning as here one is sure is on France.

684   *To God*

Why have you made life so intolerable
And set me between four walls, where I am able
Not to escape meals without prayer, for that is possible
Only by annoying an attendant. And tonight a sensual
Hell has been put on me, so that all has deserted me
And I am merely crying and trembling in heart
For death, and cannot get it. And gone out is part
Of sanity. And there is dreadful hell within me.
And nothing helps. Forced meals there have been and electricity
And weakening of sanity by influence
That's dreadful to endure. And there is Orders
And I am praying for death, death, death,
And dreadful is the indrawing or out-breathing of breath
Because of the intolerable insults put on my whole soul,
Of the soul loathed, loathed, loathed of the soul.
Gone out every bright thing from my mind.
All lost that ever God himself designed.
Not half can be written of cruelty of man, on man,
Not often such evil guessed as between man and man.

                               ISAAC ROSENBERG
                                    1890–1918

685   *God*

In his malodorous brain what slugs and mire,
Lanthorned in his oblique eyes, guttering burned!
His body lodged a rat where men nursed souls.
The world flashed grape-green eyes of a foiled cat
To him. On fragments of an old shrunk power,
On shy and maimed, on women wrung awry,
He lay, a bullying hulk, to crush them more.
But when one, fearless, turned and clawed like bronze,
Cringing was easy to blunt these stern paws,
And he would weigh the heavier on those after.

Who rests in God's mean flattery now? Your wealth
Is but his cunning to make death more hard.
Your iron sinews take more pain in breaking.
And he has made the market for your beauty
Too poor to buy, although you die to sell.

Only that he has never heard of sleep;
And when the cats come out the rats are sly.
Here we are safe till he slinks in at dawn.

But he has gnawed a fibre from strange roots,
And in the morning some pale wonder ceases.
Things are not strange and strange things are forgetful.
Ah! if the day were arid, somehow lost
Out of us, but it is as hair of us,
And only in the hush no wind stirs it.
And in the light vague trouble lifts and breathes,
And restlessness still shadows the lost ways.
The fingers shut on voices that pass through,
Where blind farewells are taken easily....

Ah! this miasma of a rotting God!

686   *The Troop Ship*

Grotesque and queerly huddled
Contortionists to twist
The sleepy soul to a sleep,
We lie all sorts of ways
And cannot sleep.
The wet wind is so cold,
And the lurching men so careless,
That, should you drop to a doze,
Winds' fumble or men's feet
Are on your face.

687   *August 1914*

What in our lives is burnt
In the fire of this?
The heart's dear granary?
The much we shall miss?

Three lives hath one life—
Iron, honey, gold.
The gold, the honey gone—
Left is the hard and cold.

Iron are our lives
Molten right through our youth.
A burnt space through ripe fields,
A fair mouth's broken tooth.

688   *Break of Day in the Trenches*

The darkness crumbles away.
It is the same old druid Time as ever,
Only a live thing leaps my hand,
A queer sardonic rat,
As I pull the parapet's poppy
To stick behind my ear.
Droll rat, they would shoot you if they knew
Your cosmopolitan sympathies.
Now you have touched this English hand
You will do the same to a German
Soon, no doubt, if it be your pleasure
To cross the sleeping green between.
It seems you inwardly grin as you pass
Strong eyes, fine limbs, haughty athletes,
Less chanced than you for life,
Bonds to the whims of murder,
Sprawled in the bowels of the earth,
The torn fields of France.
What do you see in our eyes
At the shrieking iron and flame
Hurled through still heavens?
What quaver—what heart aghast?
Poppies whose roots are in man's veins
Drop, and are ever dropping;
But mine in my ear is safe—
Just a little white with the dust.

689   *Louse Hunting*

Nudes—stark and glistening,
Yelling in lurid glee. Grinning faces
And raging limbs
Whirl over the floor one fire.
For a shirt verminously busy
Yon soldier tore from his throat, with oaths
Godhead might shrink at, but not the lice.
And soon the shirt was aflare
Over the candle he'd lit while we lay.

Then we all sprang up and stript
To hunt the verminous brood.
Soon like a demons' pantomime

The place was raging.
See the silhouettes agape,
See the gibbering shadows
Mixed with the battled arms on the wall.
See gargantuan hooked fingers
Pluck in supreme flesh
To smutch supreme littleness.
See the merry limbs in hot Highland fling
Because some wizard vermin
Charmed from the quiet this revel
When our ears were half lulled
By the dark music
Blown from Sleep's trumpet.

HUGH MacDIARMID
[CHRISTOPHER MURRAY GRIEVE]
1892–1978

690   *Empty Vessel*

I met ayont the cairney
A lass wi' tousie hair
Singin' till a bairnie
That was nae langer there.

Wunds wi warlds to swing   5
Dinna sing sae sweet,
The licht that bends owre a' thing
Is less ta'en up wi't.

691   *A Vision of Myself*

I maun feed frae the common trough ana'
Whaur a' the lees o' hope are jumbled up;
While centuries like pigs are slorpin' owre't
Sall my wee 'oor be cryin': 'Let pass this cup?'

690: 1 *ayont*] beyond   *cairney*] hillock   5 *Wunds*] winds
691: 1 *ana'*] as well   4 *'oor*] hour

In wi' your gruntle then, puir wheengin' saul,   5
Lap up the ugsome aidle wi' the lave,
What gin it's your ain vomit that you swill
And frae Life's gantin' and unfaddomed grave?

I doot I'm geylies mixed, like Life itsel',
But I was never ane that thocht to pit   10
An ocean in a mutchkin. As the haill's
Mair than the pairt sae I than reason yet.

I dinna haud the warld's end in my heid
As maist folk think they dae; nor filter truth
In fishy gills through which its tides may poor   15
For ony *animalculae* forsooth.

I lauch to see my crazy little brain
—And ither folks'—tak'n itsel' seriously,
And in a sudden lowe o' fun my saul
Blinks dozent as the owl I ken't to be.   20

I'll ha'e nae hauf-way hoose, but aye be whaur
Extremes meet—it's the only way I ken
To dodge the curst conceit o' bein' richt
That damns the vast majority o' men.

I'll bury nae heid like an ostrich's,   25
Nor yet believe my een and naething else.
My senses may advise me, but I'll be
Mysel' nae maitter what they tell's. . . .

I ha'e nae doot some foreign philosopher
Has wrocht a system oot to justify   30
A' this: but I'm a Scot wha blin'ly follows
Auld Scottish instincts, and I winna try.

For I've nae faith in ocht I can explain,
And stert whaur the philosophers leave aff,
Content to glimpse its loops I dinna ettle   35
To land the sea serpent's sel' wi' ony gaff.

Like staundin' water in a pocket o'
Impervious clay I'pray I'll never be,
Cut aff and self-sufficient, but let reenge
Heichts o' the lift and benmaist deeps o' sea.   40

---

5 *gruntle*] pig's nose   6 *ugsome aidle*] horrible slop   *lave*] rest   7 *gin*] if
8 *gantin'*] yawning   9 *geylies*] very much   11 *mutchkin*] half-bottle   *haill*] whole
13 *haud*] hold   17 *lauch*] laugh   19 *lowe*] flame   20 *dozent*] stupid
35 *ettle*] aspire   36 *gaff*] hook   40 *lift*] sky   *benmaist*] inmost

Water! Water! There was owre muckle o't
In yonder whisky, sae I'm in deep water
(And gin I could wun hame I'd be in het,
For even Jean maun natter, natter, natter)....

And in the toon that I belang tae   45
—What tho'ts Montrose or Nazareth?—
Helplessly the folk continue
To lead their livin' death!...

692   *O Wha's the Bride?*

O wha's the bride that cairries the bunch
O' thistles blinterin' white?
Her cuckold bridegroom little dreids
What he sall ken this nicht.

For closer than gudeman can come   5
And closer to'r than hersel',
Wha didna need her maidenheid
Has wrocht his purpose fell.

O wha's been here afore me, lass,
And hoo did he get in?   10
—*A man that deed or was I born*
This evil thing has din.

And left, as it were on a corpse,
Your maidenheid to me?
—*Nae lass, gudeman, sin' Time began*   15
'S hed ony mair to gi'e.

But I can gi'e ye kindness, lad,
And a pair o' willin' hands,
And you sall ha'e my breists like stars,
My limbs like willow wands.   20

And on my lips ye'll heed nae mair,
And in my hair forget,
The seed o' a' the men that in
My virgin womb ha'e met....

41 *owre muckle*] over-much   43 *het*] hot (water)
692: 2 *blinterin'*] gleaming   11 *deed or*] died before

693   *The Spur of Love*

The munelicht is my knowledge o' mysel',
Mysel' the thistle in the munelicht seen,
And hauf my shape has fund itsel' in thee
And hauf my knowledge in your piercin' een.

E'en as the munelicht's borrowed frae the sun   5
I ha'e my knowledge o' mysel' frae thee,
And much that nane but thee can e'er mak' clear,
Save my licht's frae the source, is dark to me.

Your acid tongue, vieve lauchter, and hawk's een,
And bluid that drobs like haill to quicken me,   10
Can turn the mid-day black or midnicht bricht,
Lowse me frae licht or eke frae darkness free.

Bite into me forever mair and lift
Me clear o' chaos in a great relief
Till, like this thistle in the munelicht growin',   15
I brak' in roses owre a hedge o' grief. . . .

694   *Cattle Show*

I shall go among red faces and virile voices,
See stylish sheep, with fine heads and well-wooled,
And great bulls mellow to the touch,
Brood mares of marvellous approach, and geldings
With sharp and flinty bones and silken hair.

And through th'enclosure draped in red and gold
I shall pass on to spheres more vivid yet
Where countesses' coque feathers gleam and glow
And, swathed in silks, the painted ladies are
Whose laughter plays like summer lightning there.

695   *Of John Davidson* *

I remember one death in my boyhood
That next to my father's, and darker, endures;
Not Queen Victoria's, but Davidson, yours,
And something in me has always stood

693: 3 *hauf*] half   9 *vieve*] vivid   12 *Lowse*] loosen

* Scottish poet who committed suicide in 1909.

Since then looking down the sandslope
On your small black shape by the edge of the sea,
—A bullet-hole through a great scene's beauty,
God through the wrong end of a telescope.

696 ## *Perfect*

On the Western Seaboard of South Uist

Los muertos abren los ojos a los que viven

I found a pigeon's skull on the machair,
All the bones pure white and dry, and chalky,
But perfect,
Without a crack or a flaw anywhere.

At the back, rising out of the beak,
Were domes like bubbles of thin bone,
Almost transparent, where the brain had been
That fixed the tilt of the wings.

697 ## *The Caledonian Antisyzygy*

I write now in English and now in Scots
To the despair of friends who plead
For consistency; sometimes achieve the true lyric cry,
Next but chopped-up prose; and write whiles
In traditional forms, next in a mixture of styles.
So divided against myself, they ask:
How can I stand (or they understand) indeed?

Fatal division in my thought they think
Who forget that although the thrush
Is more cheerful and constant, the lark
More continuous and celestial, and, after all,
The irritating cuckoo unique
In singing a true musical interval,
Yet the nightingale remains supreme,
The nightingale whose thin high call
And that deep throb,
Which seem to come from different birds
In different places, find an emotion
And vibrate in the memory as the song
Of no other bird—not even—
The love-note of the curlew—
      can do!

WILFRED OWEN

1893–1918

698   *Anthem for Doomed Youth*

What passing-bells for these who die as cattle?
    —Only the monstrous anger of the guns.
    Only the stuttering rifles' rapid rattle
Can patter out their hasty orisons.
No mockeries now for them; no prayers nor bells;
    Nor any voice of mourning save the choirs,—
The shrill, demented choirs of wailing shells;
    And bugles calling for them from sad shires.

What candles may be held to speed them all?
    Not in the hands of boys but in their eyes
Shall shine the holy glimmers of goodbyes.
    The pallor of girls' brows shall be their pall;
Their flowers the tenderness of patient minds,
And each slow dusk a drawing-down of blinds.

699   *Dulce et Decorum Est*

Bent double, like old beggars under sacks,
Knock-kneed, coughing like hags, we cursed through sludge,
Till on the haunting flares we turned our backs
And towards our distant rest began to trudge.
Men marched asleep. Many had lost their boots
But limped on, blood-shod. All went lame; all blind;
Drunk with fatigue; deaf even to the hoots
Of tired, outstripped Five-Nines that dropped behind.

Gas! Gas! Quick, boys!—An ecstasy of fumbling,
Fitting the clumsy helmets just in time;
But someone still was yelling out and stumbling,
And flound'ring like a man in fire or lime . . .
Dim, through the misty panes and thick green light,
As under a green sea, I saw him drowning.

In all my dreams, before my helpless sight,
He plunges at me, guttering, choking, drowning.

If in some smothering dreams you too could pace
Behind the wagon that we flung him in,
And watch the white eyes writhing in his face,
His hanging face, like a devil's sick of sin;

If you could hear, at every jolt, the blood
Come gargling from the froth-corrupted lungs,
Obscene as cancer, bitter as the cud
Of vile, incurable sores on innocent tongues,—
My friend, you would not tell with such high zest
To children ardent for some desperate glory,
The old Lie: Dulce et decorum est
Pro patria mori.

700 *Strange Meeting*

It seemed that out of battle I escaped
Down some profound dull tunnel, long since scooped
Through granites which titanic wars had groined.

Yet also there encumbered sleepers groaned,
Too fast in thought or death to be bestirred.
Then, as I probed them, one sprang up, and stared
With piteous recognition in fixed eyes,
Lifting distressful hands, as if to bless.
And by his smile, I knew that sullen hall,—
By his dead smile I knew we stood in Hell.

With a thousand pains that vision's face was grained;
Yet no blood reached there from the upper ground,
And no guns thumped, or down the flues made moan.
'Strange friend,' I said, 'here is no cause to mourn.'
'None,' said that other, 'save the undone years,
The hopelessness. Whatever hope is yours,
Was my life also; I went hunting wild
After the wildest beauty in the world,
Which lies not calm in eyes, or braided hair,
But mocks the steady running of the hour,
And if it grieves, grieves richlier than here.
For by my glee might many men have laughed,
And of my weeping something had been left,
Which must die now. I mean the truth untold,
The pity of war, the pity war distilled.
Now men will go content with what we spoiled,
Or, discontent, boil bloody, and be spilled.
They will be swift with swiftness of the tigress.
None will break ranks, though nations trek from progress.
Courage was mine, and I had mystery,
Wisdom was mine, and I had mastery:
To miss the march of this retreating world
Into vain citadels that are not walled.

Then, when much blood had clogged their chariot-wheels,
I would go up and wash them from sweet wells,
Even with truths that lie too deep for taint.
I would have poured my spirit without stint
But not through wounds; not on the cess of war.
Foreheads of men have bled where no wounds were.

'I am the enemy you killed, my friend.
I knew you in this dark: for so you frowned
Yesterday through me as you jabbed and killed.
I parried; but my hands were loath and cold.
Let us sleep now. . . .'

701   *Arms and the Boy*

Let the boy try along this bayonet-blade
How cold steel is, and keen with hunger of blood;
Blue with all malice, like a madman's flash;
And thinly drawn with famishing for flesh.

Lend him to stroke these blind, blunt bullet-leads,
Which long to nuzzle in the hearts of lads,
Or give him cartridges whose fine zinc teeth
Are sharp with sharpness of grief and death.

For his teeth seem for laughing round an apple.
There lurk no claws behind his fingers supple;
And God will grow no talons at his heels,
Nor antlers through the thickness of his curls.

702   *The Show*

We have fallen in the dreams the ever-living
Breathe on the tarnished mirror of the world,
And then smooth out with ivory hands and sigh.
                                W. B. YEATS

My soul looked down from a vague height, with Death,
As unremembering how I rose or why,
And saw a sad land, weak with sweats of dearth,
Grey, cratered like the moon with hollow woe,
And pitted with great pocks and scabs of plagues.

Across its beard, that horror of harsh wire,
There moved thin caterpillars, slowly uncoiled.
It seemed they pushed themselves to be as plugs
Of ditches, where they writhed and shrivelled, killed.

By them had slimy paths been trailed and scraped
Round myriad warts that might be little hills.

From gloom's last dregs these long-strung creatures crept,
And vanished out of dawn down hidden holes.

(And smell came up from those foul openings
As out of mouths, or deep wounds deepening.)

On dithering feet upgathered, more and more,
Brown strings, towards strings of grey, with bristling spines,
All migrants from green fields, intent on mire.

Those that were grey, of more abundant spawns,
Ramped on the rest and ate them and were eaten.

I saw their bitten backs curve, loop, and straighten.
I watched those agonies curl, lift, and flatten.

Whereat, in terror what that sight might mean,
I reeled and shivered earthward like a feather.

And Death fell with me, like a deepening moan.
And He, picking a manner of worm, which half had hid
Its bruises in the earth, but crawled no further,
Showed me its feet, the feet of many men,
And the fresh-severed head of it, my head.

703   *The Send-Off*

Down the close darkening lanes they sang their way
    To the siding-shed,
And lined the train with faces grimly gay.

Their breasts were stuck all white with wreath and spray
    As men's are, dead.

Dull porters watched them, and a casual tramp
    Stood staring hard,
Sorry to miss them from the upland camp.

Then, unmoved, signals nodded, and a lamp
    Winked to the guard.

So secretly, like wrongs hushed-up, they went.
They were not ours:
We never heard to which front these were sent;

Nor there if they yet mock what women meant
Who gave them flowers.

Shall they return to beating of great bells
In wild train-loads?
A few, a few, too few for drums and yells,

May creep back, silent, to village wells,
Up half-known roads.

ROBERT GRAVES

1895–1985

704   *A False Report*

Are they blind, the lords of Gaza,
That each his fellow urges
'Samson the proud is pillow-smothered,'
They raise mock dirges?

Philistines and dullards,
Turn, look with amaze
At my foxes running in your cornfields
With their tails ablaze,

At bloody jawbone, at bees flitting
From the stark lion's hide,
At these, the gates of well-walled Gaza
Clanking to my stride.

[1923]

705   *Angry Samson*

Are they blind, the lords of Gaza
    In their strong towers,
Who declare Samson pillow-smothered
    And stripped of his powers?

O stolid Philistines,
    Stare now in amaze
At my foxes running in your cornfields
    With their tails ablaze,

At swung jaw-bone, at bees swarming
  In the stark lion's hide,
At these, the gates of well-walled Gaza
  A-clank to my stride.

[1975]

706   *Love without Hope*

Love without hope, as when the young bird-catcher
Swept off his tall hat to the Squire's own daughter,
So let the imprisoned larks escape and fly
Singing about her head, as she rode by.

707   *The Cool Web*

Children are dumb to say how hot the day is,
How hot the scent is of the summer rose,
How dreadful the black wastes of evening sky,
How dreadful the tall soldiers drumming by.

But we have speech, to chill the angry day,
And speech, to dull the rose's cruel scent.
We spell away the overhanging night,
We spell away the soldiers and the fright.

There's a cool web of language winds us in,
Retreat from too much joy or too much fear:
We grow sea-green at last and coldly die
In brininess and volubility.

But if we let our tongues lose self-possession,
Throwing off language and its watery clasp
Before our death, instead of when death comes,
Facing the wide glare of the children's day,
Facing the rose, the dark sky and the drums,
We shall go mad no doubt and die that way.

708   *Warning to Children*

Children, if you dare to think
Of the greatness, rareness, muchness,

Fewness of this precious only
Endless world in which you say
You live, you think of things like this:
Blocks of slate enclosing dappled
Red and green, enclosing tawny
Yellow nets, enclosing white
And black acres of dominoes,
Where a neat brown paper parcel
Tempts you to untie the string.
In the parcel a small island,
On the island a large tree,
On the tree a husky fruit.
Strip the husk and pare the rind off:
In the kernel you will see
Blocks of slate enclosed by dappled
Red and green, enclosed by tawny
Yellow nets, enclosed by white
And black acres of dominoes,
Where the same brown paper parcel—
Children, leave the string alone!
For who dares undo the parcel
Finds himself at once inside it,
On the island, in the fruit,
Blocks of slate about his head,
Finds himself enclosed by dappled
Green and red, enclosed by yellow
Tawny nets, enclosed by black
And white acres of dominoes,
With the same brown paper parcel
Still unopened on his knee.
And, if he then should dare to think
Of the fewness, muchness, rareness,
Greatness of this endless only
Precious world in which he says
He lives—he then unties the string.

709   *Welsh Incident*

'But that was nothing to what things came out
From the sea-caves of Criccieth yonder.'
'What were they? Mermaids? dragons? ghosts?'
'Nothing at all of any things like that.'
'What were they, then?'
                        'All sorts of queer things,

Things never seen or heard or written about,
Very strange, un-Welsh, utterly peculiar
Things. Oh, solid enough they seemed to touch,
Had anyone dared it. Marvellous creation,
All various shapes and sizes, and no sizes,
All new, each perfectly unlike his neighbour,
Though all came moving slowly out together.'
'Describe just one of them.'
      'I am unable.'
'What were their colours?'
      'Mostly nameless colours,
Colours you'd like to see; but one was puce
Or perhaps more like crimson, but not purplish.
Some had no colour.'
     'Tell me, had they legs?'
'Not a leg or foot among them that I saw.'
'But did these things come out in any order?
What o'clock was it? What was the day of the week?
Who else was present? What was the weather?'
'I was coming to that. It was half-past three
On Easter Tuesday last. The sun was shining.
The Harlech Silver Band played *Marchog Jesu*
On thirty-seven shimmering instruments,
Collecting for Carnarvon's (Fever) Hospital Fund.
The populations of Pwlheli, Criccieth,
Portmadoc, Borth, Tremadoc, Penrhyndeudraeth,
Were all assembled. Criccieth's mayor addressed them
First in good Welsh and then in fluent English,
Twisting his fingers in his chain of office,
Welcoming the things. They came out on the sand,
Not keeping time to the band, moving seaward
Silently at a snail's pace. But at last
The most odd, indescribable thing of all,
Which hardly one man there could see for wonder,
Did something recognizably a something.'
'Well, what?'
   'It made a noise.'
      'A frightening noise?'
'No, no.'
   'A musical noise? A noise of scuffling?'
'No, but a very loud, respectable noise—
Like groaning to oneself on Sunday morning
In Chapel, close before the second psalm.'
'What did the mayor do?'
     'I was coming to that.'

710   *To Juan at the Winter Solstice*

There is one story and one story only
That will prove worth your telling,
Whether as learned bard or gifted child;
To it all lines or lesser gauds belong
That startle with their shining
Such common stories as they stray into.

Is it of trees you tell, their months and virtues,
Of strange beasts that beset you,
Of birds that croak at you the Triple will?
Or of the Zodiac and how slow it turns
Below the Boreal Crown,
Prison of all true kings that ever reigned?

Water to water, ark again to ark,
From woman back to woman:
So each new victim treads unfalteringly
The never altered circuit of his fate,
Bringing twelve peers as witness
Both to his starry rise and starry fall.

Or is it of the Virgin's silver beauty,
All fish below the thighs?
She in her left hand bears a leafy quince;
When with her right she crooks a finger, smiling,
How may the King hold back?
Royally then he barters life for love.

Or of the undying snake from chaos hatched,
Whose coils contain the ocean,
Into whose chops with naked sword he springs,
Then in black water, tangled by the reeds,
Battles three days and nights,
To be spewed up beside her scalloped shore?

Much snow is falling, winds roar hollowly,
The owl hoots from the elder,
Fear in your heart cries to the loving-cup:
Sorrow to sorrow as the sparks fly upward.
The log groans and confesses:
There is one story and one story only.

Dwell on her graciousness, dwell on her smiling,
Do not forget what flowers
The great boar trampled down in ivy time.

Her brow was creamy as the crested wave,
Her sea-grey eyes were wild
But nothing promised that is not performed.

AUSTIN CLARKE

1896–1974

711   *The Planter's Daughter*

When night stirred at sea
And the fire brought a crowd in,
They say that her beauty
Was music in mouth
And few in the candlelight
Thought her too proud,
For the house of the planter
Is known by the trees.

Men that had seen her
Drank deep and were silent,
The women were speaking
Wherever she went—
As a bell that is rung
Or a wonder told shyly,
And O she was the Sunday
In every week.

712   *Martha Blake*

Before the day is everywhere
And the timid warmth of sleep
Is delicate on limb, she dares
The silence of the street
Until the double bells are thrown back
For Mass and echoes bound
In the chapel yard, O then her soul
Makes bold in the arms of sound.

But in the shadow of the nave
Her well-taught knees are humble,
She does not see through any saint
That stands in the sun

With veins of lead, with painful crown;
She waits that dreaded coming,
When all the congregation bows
And none may look up.

The word is said, the Word sent down,
The miracle is done
Beneath those hands that have been rounded
Over the embodied cup,
And with a few, she leaves her place
Kept by an east-filled window
And kneels at the communion rail
Starching beneath her chin.

She trembles for the Son of Man,
While the priest is murmuring
What she can scarcely tell, her heart
Is making such a stir;
But when he picks a particle
And she puts out her tongue,
That joy is the glittering of candles
And benediction sung.

Her soul is lying in the Presence
Until her senses, one
By one, desiring to attend her,
Come as for feast and run
So fast to share the sacrament,
Her mouth must mother them:
'Sweet tooth grow wise, lip, gum be gentle,
I touch a purple hem.'

Afflicted by that love she turns
To multiply her praise,
Goes over all the foolish words
And finds they are the same;
But now she feels within her breast
Such calm that she is silent,
For soul can never be immodest
Where body may not listen.

On a holy day of obligation
I saw her first in prayer,
But mortal eye had been too late
For all that thought could dare.
The flame in heart is never grieved
That pride and intellect
Were cast below, when God revealed
A heaven for this earth.

So to begin the common day
She needs a miracle,
Knowing the safety of angels
That see her home again,
Yet ignorant of all the rest,
The hidden grace that people
Hurrying to business
Look after in the street.

713 *Penal Law*

Burn Ovid with the rest. Lovers will find
A hedge-school for themselves and learn by heart
All that the clergy banish from the mind,
When hands are joined and head bows in the dark.

714 *Miss Marnell*

No bells rang in her house. The silver plate
Was gone. She scarcely had a candle-wick,
Though old, to pray by, ne'er a maid to wait
At all. She had become a Catholic
So long ago, we smiled, did good by stealth,
Bade her good-day, invited her to tea
With deep respect. Forgetting her loss of wealth,
She took barmbrack and cake so hungrily,
We pitied her, wondered about her past.
But her poor mind had not been organized;
She was taken away, fingering to the last
Her ivory decades. Every room surprised:
Wardrobes of bombazine, silk dresses, stank:
Cobwebby shrouds, pantries, cupboard, bone-bare.
Yet she had prospering money in the bank,
Admiring correspondents everywhere,
In Ireland, Wales, the Far East, India;
Her withered hand was busy doing good
Against our older missions in Africa.
False teeth got little acid from her food:
But scribble helped to keep much mortar wet
For convent, college, higher institution,
To build new churches or reduce their debt.
The figure on her cross-cheque made restitution
For many sins. Piled on her escritoire

Were necessary improvements, paint-pot, ladder
And new coats for Maynooth, in a world at war,
Circulars, leaflets, pleas that made her madder
To comfort those who need for holy living
Their daily post: litterings, flyblown, miced
In corners, faded notes of thanksgiving,
All signed—'Yours Gratefully, in Jesus Christ.'

715–17 *Eighteenth Century Harp Songs*

715 I

Mabel Kelly

Lucky the husband
Who puts his hand beneath her head.
They kiss without scandal
Happiest two near feather-bed.
He sees the tumble of brown hair
Unplait, the breasts, pointed and bare
When nightdress shows
From dimple to toe-nail,
All Mabel glowing in it, here, there, everywhere.

Music might listen
To her least whisper,
Learn every note, for all are true.
While she is speaking,
Her voice goes sweetly
To charm the herons in their musing.
Her eyes are modest, blue, their darkness
Small rooms of thought, but when they sparkle
Upon a feast-day,
Glasses are meeting,
Each raised to Mabel Kelly, our toast and darling.

Gone now are many Irish ladies
Who kissed and fondled, their very pet-names
Forgotten, their tibia degraded.
She takes their sky. Her smile is famed.
Her praise is scored by quill and pencil.
Harp and spinet
Are in her debt
And when she plays or sings, melody is content.

No man who sees her
Will feel uneasy.

He goes his way, head high, however tired.
    Lamp loses light
    When placed beside her.
She is the pearl and being of all Ireland
Foot, hand, eye, mouth, breast, thigh and instep, all that we desire.
Tresses that pass small curls as if to touch the ground;
    So many prizes
    Are not divided.
Her beauty is her own and she is not proud.

716   II
Gracey Nugent

I drink, wherever I go, to the charms
Of Gracey Nugent in whose white arms
I dare not look for more. Enraptured
By a kiss or two, a little slap,
    Her virtue cannot harm me.

Delightful to share her company
Even with others. While she is speaking,
Music goes by and what she smiles at,
Would bring the swan back to the tide.
    Was ever plight so pleasing?

Her graceful walk, her pearly neck-lace,
And bosom so near, have made me reckless.
I want to sit, clasping her waist,
Upon her boudoir sofa, waste
    Hope. Days are only seconds.

Happy the young fellow, who wins
And can enjoy her without sinning.
Close in the darkness, they will rest
Together and when her fears are less,
    She'll take his meaning in

And know at last why he is seeking
Shoulder and breast, her shapely cheeks,
All that I must not try to sing of.
The modest may not point a finger
    Or mention what is best.

And so I raise my glass, content
To drink a health to Gracey Nugent,
Her absence circles around the table.
Empty the rummer while you are able,
    Two Sundays before Lent.

III

717 *Peggy Browne*

The dark-haired girl, who holds my thought entirely
Yet keeps me from her arms and what I desire,
Will never take my word for she is proud
And none may have his way with Peggy Browne.

Often I dream that I am in the woods
At Westport House. She strays alone, blue-hooded,
Then lifts her flounces, hurries from a shower,
But sunlight stays all day with Peggy Browne.

Her voice is music, every little echo
My pleasure and O her shapely breasts, I know,
Are white as her own milk, when taffeta gown
Is let out, inch by inch, for Peggy Browne.

A lawless dream comes to me in the night-time,
That we are stretching together side by side,
Nothing I want to do can make her frown.
I wake alone, sighing for Peggy Browne.

[after the Gaelic of Turlough O'Carolan]

EDMUND BLUNDEN

1896–1974

718 *Report on Experience*

I have been young, and now am not too old;
And I have seen the righteous forsaken,
His health, his honour and his quality taken.
    This is not what we were formerly told.

I have seen a green country, useful to the race,
Knocked silly with guns and mines, its villages vanished,
Even the last rat and last kestrel banished—
    God bless us all, this was peculiar grace.

I knew Seraphina; Nature gave her hue,
Glance, sympathy, note, like one from Eden.
I saw her smile warp, heard her lyric deaden;
    She turned to harlotry;—this I took to be new.

Say what you will, our God sees how they run.
These disillusions are his curious proving
That he loves humanity and will go on loving;
    Over there are faith, life, virtue in the sun.

BASIL BUNTING

1900–1985

719   from *Villon*

Remember, imbeciles and wits,
sots and ascetics, fair and foul,
young girls with little tender tits,
that DEATH is written over all.

Worn hides that scarcely clothe the soul
they are so rotten, old and thin,
or firm and soft and warm and full—
fellmonger Death gets every skin.

All that is piteous, all that's fair,
all that is fat and scant of breath,
Elisha's baldness, Helen's hair,
is Death's collateral:

Three score and ten years after sight
of this pay me your pulse and breath
value received. And who dare cite,
as we forgive our debtors, Death?

Abelard and Eloise,
Henry the Fowler, Charlemagne,
Genée, Lopokova, all these
die, die in pain.

And General Grant and General Lee,
Patti and Florence Nightingale,
like Tyro and Antiope
drift among ghosts in Hell,

know nothing, are nothing, save a fume
driving across a mind
preoccupied with this: our doom
is, to be sifted by the wind,

heaped up, smoothed down like silly sands.
We are less permanent than thought.
The Emperor with the Golden Hands

is still a word, a tint, a tone,
insubstantial-glorious,
when we ourselves are dead and gone
and the green grass growing over us.

[after the French of Villon]

720   Came to me—
                                    Who?
                       She.
                                    When?
                       In the dawn, afraid.

                                    What of?
                       Anger.
                                    Whose?
                       Her father's.
                                    Confide!

                       I kissed her twice.
                                    Where?
                       On her moist mouth.
                                    Mouth?

                       No.
                                    What, then?
                       Cornelian.
                                    How was it?
                       Sweet.

                            [after the Persian of Rudaki]

STEVIE SMITH
1902–1971

721   *Pad, pad*

I always remember your beautiful flowers
And the beautiful kimono you wore
When you sat on the couch
With that tigerish crouch
And told me you loved me no more.

What I cannot remember is how I felt when you were unkind
All I know is, if you were unkind now I should not mind.
Ah me, the power to feel exaggerated, angry and sad
The years have taken from me. Softly I go now, pad pad.

722 *Not Waving but Drowning*

Nobody heard him, the dead man,
But still he lay moaning:
I was much further out than you thought
And not waving but drowning.

Poor chap, he always loved larking
And now he's dead
It must have been too cold for him his heart gave way,
They said.

Oh, no no no, it was too cold always
(Still the dead one lay moaning)
I was much too far out all my life
And not waving but drowning.

723 *Songe d'Athalie*

It was a dream and shouldn't I bother about a dream?
But it goes on you know, tears me rather.
Of course I try to forget it but it will not let me.
Well it was on an extraordinarily dark night at midnight
My mother Queen Jezebel appeared suddenly before me
Looking just as she did the day she died, dressed grandly.
It was her pride you noticed, nothing she had gone through touched that
And she still had the look of being most carefully made up
She always made up a lot she didn't want people to know how old she was.
She spoke: Be warned my daughter, true girl to me, she said,
Do not suppose the cruel God of the Jews has finished with you,
I am come to weep your falling into his hands, my child.
With these appalling words my mother,
This ghost, leant over me stretching out her hands
And I stretched out my hands too to touch her
But what was it, oh this is horrible, what did I touch?
Nothing but the mangled flesh and the breaking bones
Of a body that the dogs tearing quarrelled over.

[after the French of Racine]

724 *Magna est Veritas*

With my looks I am bound to look simple or fast I would rather look
    simple
So I wear a tall hat on the back of my head that is rather a temple

And I walk rather queerly and comb my long hair
And people say, Don't bother about her.
So in my time I have picked up a good many facts,
Rather more than the people do who wear smart hats
And I do not deceive because I am rather simple too
And although I collect facts I do not always know what they amount to.
I regard them as a contribution to almighty Truth, magna est veritas et
　　　praevalebit,
Agreeing with that Latin writer, Great is Truth and will prevail in a bit.

725　　　　　　　　　　*Was it not curious?*

　　　Was it not curious of Aúgustin
　　　Saint Aúgustin, Saint Aúgustin,
　　　When he saw the beautiful British children
　　　To say such a curious thing?

　　　He said he must send the gospel, the gospel,
　　　At once to them over the waves
　　　He never said he thought it was wicked
　　　To steal them away for slaves

　　　To steal the children away
　　　To buy and have slavery at all
　　　Oh no, oh no, it was not a thing
　　　That caused him any appal.

　　　Was it not curious of *Gregory*
　　　Rather more than of Aúgustin?
　　　It was not curious so much
　　　As it was wicked of them.

ROY CAMPBELL

1902–1957

726　　　　　*On Some South African Novelists*

　　　You praise the firm restraint with which they write—
　　　I'm with you there, of course:
　　　They use the snaffle and the curb all right,
　　　But where's the bloody horse?

727   *On a Shipmate, Pero Moniz, dying at Sea*

My years on earth were short, but long for me,
And full of bitter hardship at the best:
My light of day sinks early in the sea:
Five lustres from my birth I took my rest.
Through distant lands and seas I was a ranger
Seeking some cure or remedy for life,
Which he whom Fortune loves not as a wife,
Will seek in vain through strife, and toil, and danger.
Portugal reared me in my green, my darling
Alanguer, but the dank, corrupted air
That festers in the marshes around there
Has made me food for fish here in the snarling,
Fierce seas that dark the Abyssinian shore,
Far from the happy homeland I adore.

[after the Portuguese of Camoëns]

NORMAN CAMERON

1905–1953

728   *Naked among the Trees*

Formerly he had been a well-loved god,
Each visit from him a sweet episode,
Not like the outrageous Pentecostal rush
Or wilful Jahveh shrieking from a bush.

He bloomed in our bodies to the finger-tips
And rose like barley-sugar round the lips,
Then unawares was cleanly gone away,
With no relapse or aftertaint to pay.

We've forced the burgeoned lust he gave to us
Into a thousand manners of misuse,
Into the hot alarms, wishes and frets,
The drinking-bouts, the boasting and the bets.

And these have made his cult degenerate,
So that the booted Puritan magistrate
Did right to spur down on the devotees,
Catch them and whip them naked among the trees.

729   *Forgive me, Sire*

Forgive me, Sire, for cheating your intent,
That I, who should command a regiment,
Do amble amiably here, O God,
One of the neat ones in your awkward squad.

SAMUEL BECKETT
1906–1989

730   *Something there*

something there
where
out there
out where
outside
what
the head what else
something there somewhere outside
the head

at the faint sound so brief
it is gone and the whole globe
not yet bare
the eye
opens wide
wide
till in the end
nothing more
shutters it again

so the odd time
out there
somewhere out there
like as if
as if
something
not life
necessarily

731   *Roundelay*

on all that strand
at end of day
steps sole sound
long sole sound
until unbidden stay
then no sound
on all that strand
long no sound
until unbidden go
steps sole sound
long sole sound
on all that strand
at end of day

732   *What is the word*

folly —
folly for to —
for to —
what is the word —
folly from this —
all this —
folly from all this —
given —
folly given all this —
seeing —
folly seeing all this —
this —
what is the word —
this this —
this this here —
all this this here —
folly given all this —
seeing —
folly seeing all this this here —
for to —
what is the word —
see —
glimpse —
seem to glimpse —
need to seem to glimpse —
folly for to need to seem to glimpse —
what —

what is the word —
and where —
folly for to need to seem to glimpse what where —
where —
what is the word —
there —
over there —
away over there —
afar —
afar away over there —
afaint —
afaint afar away over there what —
what —
what is the word —
seeing all this —
all this this —
all this this here —
folly for to see what —
glimpse —
seem to glimpse —
need to seem to glimpse —
afaint afar away over there what —
folly for to need to seem to glimpse afaint afar away over there what —
what —
what is the word —

what is the word

SIR JOHN BETJEMAN

1906–1984

733   *Death of King George V*

> 'New King arrives in his capital by air . . .'
> *Daily Newspaper*

Spirits of well-shot woodcock, partridge, snipe
    Flutter and bear him up the Norfolk sky:
In that red house in a red mahogany book-case
    The stamp collection waits with mounts long dry.

The big blue eyes are shut which saw wrong clothing
    And favourite fields and coverts from a horse;
Old men in country houses hear clocks ticking
    Over thick carpets with a deadened force;

Old men who never cheated, never doubted,
   Communicated monthly, sit and stare
At the new suburb stretched beyond the run-way
   Where a young man lands hatless from the air.

734   *On Seeing an Old Poet in the Café Royal*

   I saw him in the Café Royal,
      Very old and very grand.
   Modernistic shone the lamplight
      There in London's fairyland.
   'Devilled chicken. Devilled whitebait.
      Devil if I understand.

   Where is Oscar? Where is Bosie?
      Have I seen that man before?
   And the old one in the corner,
      Is it really Wratislaw?'
   Scent of Tutti-Frutti-Sen-Sen
      And cheroots upon the floor.

SIR WILLIAM EMPSON

1906–1984

735   *To an Old Lady*

Ripeness is all; her in her cooling planet
Revere; do not presume to think her wasted.
Project her no projectile, plan nor man it;
Gods cool in turn, by the sun long outlasted.

Our earth alone given no name of god
Gives, too, no hold for such a leap to aid her;
Landing, you break some palace and seem odd;
Bees sting their need, the keeper's queen invader.

No, to your telescope; spy out the land;
Watch while her ritual is still to see,
Still stand her temples emptying in the sand
Whose waves o'erthrew their crumbled tracery;

Still stand uncalled-on her soul's appanage;
Much social detail whose successor fades,
Wit used to run a house and to play Bridge,
And tragic fervour, to dismiss her maids.

Years her precession do not throw from gear.
She reads a compass certain of her pole;
Confident, finds no confines on her sphere,
Whose failing crops are in her sole control.

Stars how much further from me fill my night,
Strange that she too should be inaccessible,
Who shares my sun. He curtains her from sight,
And but in darkness is she visible.

736   *Homage to the British Museum*

There is a Supreme God in the ethnological section;
A hollow toad shape, faced with a blank shield.
He needs his belly to include the Pantheon,
Which is inserted through a hole behind.
At the navel, at the points formally stressed, at the organs of sense,
Lice glue themselves, dolls, local deities,
His smooth wood creeps with all the creeds of the world.

Attending there let us absorb the cultures of nations
And dissolve into our judgement all their codes.
Then, being clogged with a natural hesitation
(People are continually asking one the way out),
Let us stand here and admit that we have no road.
Being everything, let us admit that is to be something,
Or give ourselves the benefit of the doubt;
Let us offer our pinch of dust all to this God,
And grant his reign over the entire building.

737   *Note on Local Flora*

There is a tree native in Turkestan,
Or further east towards the Tree of Heaven,
Whose hard cold cones, not being wards to time,
Will leave their mother only for good cause;
Will ripen only in a forest fire;
Wait, to be fathered as was Bacchus once,
Through men's long lives, that image of time's end.
I knew the Phoenix was a vegetable.
So Semele desired her deity
As this in Kew thirsts for the Red Dawn.

738 *Aubade*

Hours before dawn we were woken by the quake.
My house was on a cliff. The thing could take
Bookloads off shelves, break bottles in a row.
Then the long pause and then the bigger shake.
It seemed the best thing to be up and go.

And far too large for my feet to step by.
I hoped that various buildings were brought low.
The heart of standing is you cannot fly.

It seemed quite safe till she got up and dressed.
The guarded tourist makes the guide the test.
Then I said The Garden? Laughing she said No.
Taxi for her and for me healthy rest.
It seemed the best thing to be up and go.

The language problem but you have to try.
Some solid ground for lying could she show?
The heart of standing is you cannot fly.

None of these deaths were her point at all.
The thing was that being woken he would bawl
And finding her not in earshot he would know.
I tried saying Half an Hour to pay this call.
It seemed the best thing to be up and go.

I slept, and blank as that I would yet lie.
Till you have seen what a threat holds below,
The heart of standing is you cannot fly.

Tell me again about Europe and her pains,
Who's tortured by the drought, who by the rains.
Glut me with floods where only the swine can row
Who cuts his throat and let him count his gains.
It seemed the best thing to be up and go.

A bedshift flight to a Far Eastern sky.
Only the same war on a stronger toe.
The heart of standing is you cannot fly.

Tell me more quickly what I lost by this,
Or tell me with less drama what they miss
Who call no die a god for a good throw,
Who say after two aliens had one kiss
It seemed the best thing to be up and go.

But as to risings, I can tell you why.
It is on contradiction that they grow.
It seemed the best thing to be up and go.
Up was the heartening and the strong reply.
The heart of standing is we cannot fly.

739   *Missing Dates*

Slowly the poison the whole blood stream fills.
It is not the effort nor the failure tires.
The waste remains, the waste remains and kills.

It is not your system or clear sight that mills
Down small to the consequence a life requires;
Slowly the poison the whole blood stream fills.

They bled an old dog dry yet the exchange rills
Of young dog blood gave but a month's desires;
The waste remains, the waste remains and kills.

It is the Chinese tombs and the slag hills
Usurp the soil, and not the soil retires.
Slowly the poison the whole blood stream fills.

Not to have fire is to be a skin that shrills.
The complete fire is death. From partial fires
The waste remains, the waste remains and kills.

It is the poems you have lost, the ills
From missing dates, at which the heart expires.
Slowly the poison the whole blood stream fills.
The waste remains, the waste remains and kills.

740   *Let it go*

It is this deep blankness is the real thing strange.
    The more things happen to you the more you can't
        Tell or remember even what they were.

The contradictions cover such a range.
    The talk would talk and go so far aslant.
        You don't want madhouse and the whole thing there.

741   *Chinese Ballad*

Now he has seen the girl Hsiang-Hsiang,
    Now back to the guerrilla band;
And she goes with him down the vale
    And pauses at the strand.

The mud is yellow, deep, and thick,
    And their feet stick, where the stream turns.
'Make me two models out of this,
    That clutches as it yearns.

'Make one of me and one of you,
    And both shall be alive.
Were there no magic in the dolls
    The children could not thrive.

'When you have made them smash them back:
    They yet shall live again.
Again make dolls of you and me
    But mix them grain by grain.

'So your flesh shall be part of mine
    And part of mine be yours.
Brother and sister we shall be
    Whose unity endures.

'Always the sister doll will cry,
    Made in these careful ways,
Cry on and on, Come back to me,
    Come back, in a few days.'

                    [after the Chinese of Li Chi]

W. H. AUDEN

1907–1973

742   'O where are you going?' said reader to rider,
             'That valley is fatal when furnaces burn,
             Yonder's the midden whose odours will madden,
             That gap is the grave where the tall return.'

             'O do you imagine,' said fearer to farer,
             'That dusk will delay on your path to the pass,
             Your diligent looking discover the lacking,
             Your footsteps feel from granite to grass?'

'O what was that bird,' said horror to hearer,
'Did you see that shape in the twisted trees?
Behind you swiftly the figure comes softly,
The spot on your skin is a shocking disease.'

'Out of this house'—said rider to reader,
'Yours never will'—said farer to fearer,
'They're looking for you'—said hearer to horror,
As he left them there, as he left them there.

743   *Adolescence*

By landscape reminded once of his mother's figure
The mountain heights he remembers get bigger and bigger:
With the finest of mapping pens he fondly traces
All the family names on the familiar places.

In a green pasture straying, he walks by still waters;
Surely a swan he seems to earth's unwise daughters,
Bending a beautiful head, worshipping not lying
'Dear' the dear beak in the dear concha crying.

Under the trees the summer bands were playing;
'Dear boy, be brave as these roots,' he heard them saying:
Carries the good news gladly to a world in danger,
Is ready to argue, he smiles, with any stranger.

And yet this prophet, homing the day is ended,
Receives odd welcome from the country he so defended:
The band roars 'Coward, Coward,' in his human fever,
The giantess shuffles nearer, cries 'Deceiver'.

744   *On This Island*

Look, stranger, on this island now
The leaping light for your delight discovers,
Stand stable here
And silent be
That through the channels of the ear
May wander like a river
The swaying sound of the sea.

Here at the small field's ending pause
When the chalk wall falls to the foam and its tall ledges
Oppose the pluck
And knock of the tide,

And the shingle scrambles after the suck-
-ing surf,
And the gull lodges
A moment on its sheer side.

Far off like floating seeds the ships
Diverge on urgent voluntary errands,
And the full view
Indeed may enter
And move in memory as now these clouds do,
That pass the harbour mirror
And all the summer through the water saunter.

745   *Lullaby*

Lay your sleeping head, my love,
Human on my faithless arm;
Time and fevers burn away
Individual beauty from
Thoughtful children, and the grave
Proves the child ephemeral:
But in my arms till break of day
Let the living creature lie,
Mortal, guilty, but to me
The entirely beautiful.

Soul and body have no bounds:
To lovers as they lie upon
Her tolerant enchanted slope
In their ordinary swoon,
Grave the vision Venus sends
Of supernatural sympathy,
Universal love and hope;
While an abstract insight wakes
Among the glaciers and the rocks
The hermit's carnal ecstasy.

Certainty, fidelity
On the stroke of midnight pass
Like vibrations of a bell
And fashionable madmen raise
Their pedantic boring cry:
Every farthing of the cost,
All the dreaded cards foretell,
Shall be paid, but from this night
Not a whisper, not a thought,
Not a kiss nor look be lost.

Beauty, midnight, vision dies:
Let the winds of dawn that blow
Softly round your dreaming head
Such a day of welcome show
Eye and knocking heart may bless,
Find our mortal world enough;
Noons of dryness find you fed
By the involuntary powers,
Nights of insult let you pass
Watched by every human love.

746   *Musée des Beaux Arts*

About suffering they were never wrong,
The Old Masters: how well they understood
Its human position: how it takes place
While someone else is eating or opening a window or just walking
      dully along;
How, when the aged are reverently, passionately waiting
For the miraculous birth, there always must be
Children who did not specially want it to happen, skating
On a pond at the edge of the wood:
They never forgot
That even the dreadful martyrdom must run its course
Anyhow in a corner, some untidy spot
Where the dogs go on with their doggy life and the torturer's horse
Scratches its innocent behind on a tree.

In Breughel's *Icarus*, for instance: how everything turns away
Quite leisurely from the disaster; the ploughman may
Have heard the splash, the forsaken cry,
But for him it was not an important failure; the sun shone
As it had to on the white legs disappearing into the green
Water; and the expensive delicate ship that must have seen
Something amazing, a boy falling out of the sky,
Had somewhere to get to and sailed calmly on.

747   *Epitaph on a Tyrant*

Perfection, of a kind, was what he was after,
And the poetry he invented was easy to understand;
He knew human folly like the back of his hand,
And was greatly interested in armies and fleets;
When he laughed, respectable senators burst with laughter,
And when he cried the little children died in the streets.

748 ## The Fall of Rome

The piers are pummelled by the waves;
In a lonely field the rain
Lashes an abandoned train;
Outlaws fill the mountain caves.

Fantastic grow the evening gowns;
Agents of the Fisc pursue
Absconding tax-defaulters through
The sewers of provincial towns.

Private rites of magic send
The temple prostitutes to sleep;
All the literati keep
An imaginary friend.

Cerebrotonic Cato may
Extol the Ancient Disciplines,
But the muscle-bound Marines
Mutiny for food and pay.

Caesar's double-bed is warm
As an unimportant clerk
Writes *I DO NOT LIKE MY WORK*
On a pink official form.

Unendowed with wealth or pity,
Little birds with scarlet legs,
Sitting on their speckled eggs,
Eye each flu-infected city.

Altogether elsewhere, vast
Herds of reindeer move across
Miles and miles of golden moss,
Silently and very fast.

749 ## The Shield of Achilles

She looked over his shoulder
        For vines and olive trees,
Marble well-governed cities
        And ships upon untamed seas,
But there on the shining metal
        His hands had put instead
An artificial wilderness
        And a sky like lead.

A plain without a feature, bare and brown,
   No blade of grass, no sign of neighborhood,
Nothing to eat and nowhere to sit down,
   Yet, congregated on its blankness, stood
   An unintelligible multitude,
A million eyes, a million boots in line,
Without expression, waiting for a sign.

Out of the air a voice without a face
   Proved by statistics that some cause was just
In tones as dry and level as the place:
   No one was cheered and nothing was discussed;
   Column by column in a cloud of dust
They marched away enduring a belief
Whose logic brought them, somewhere else, to grief.

     She looked over his shoulder
       For ritual pieties,
     White flower-garlanded heifers,
       Libation and sacrifice,
     But there on the shining metal
       Where the altar should have been,
     She saw by his flickering forge-light
       Quite another scene.

Barbed wire enclosed an arbitrary spot
   Where bored officials lounged (one cracked a joke)
And sentries sweated for the day was hot:
   A crowd of ordinary decent folk
   Watched from without and neither moved nor spoke
As three pale figures were led forth and bound
To three posts driven upright in the ground.

The mass and majesty of this world, all
   That carries weight and always weighs the same
Lay in the hands of others; they were small
   And could not hope for help and no help came:
   What their foes liked to do was done, their shame
Was all the worst could wish; they lost their pride
And died as men before their bodies died.

     She looked over his shoulder
       For athletes at their games,
     Men and women in a dance
       Moving their sweet limbs
     Quick, quick, to music,
       But there on the shining shield
     His hands had set no dancing-floor
       But a weed-choked field.

A ragged urchin, aimless and alone,
  Loitered about that vacancy; a bird
Flew up to safety from his well-aimed stone:
  That girls are raped, that two boys knife a third,
  Were axioms to him, who'd never heard
Of any world where promises were kept,
Or one could weep because another wept.

        The thin-lipped armorer,
          Hephaestos, hobbled away,
        Thetis of the shining breasts
          Cried out in dismay
        At what the god had wrought
          To please her son, the strong
        Iron-hearted man-slaying Achilles
          Who would not live long.

LOUIS MacNEICE

1907–1963

750   *Snow*

The room was suddenly rich and the great bay-window was
Spawning snow and pink roses against it
Soundlessly collateral and incompatible:
World is suddener than we fancy it.

World is crazier and more of it than we think,
Incorrigibly plural. I peel and portion
A tangerine and spit the pips and feel
The drunkenness of things being various.

And the fire flames with a bubbling sound for world
Is more spiteful and gay than one supposes—
On the tongue on the eyes on the ears in the palms of one's hands—
There is more than glass between the snow and the huge roses.

751   *Bagpipe music*

It's no go the merrygoround, it's no go the rickshaw,
All we want is a limousine and a ticket for the peepshow.
Their knickers are made of crêpe-de-chine, their shoes are made of
    python,
Their halls are lined with tiger rugs and their walls with heads of bison.

John MacDonald found a corpse, put it under the sofa,
Waited till it came to life and hit it with a poker,
Sold its eyes for souvenirs, sold its blood for whisky,
Kept its bones for dumb-bells to use when he was fifty.

It's no go the Yogi-Man, it's no go Blavatsky,
All we want is a bank balance and a bit of skirt in a taxi.

Annie MacDougall went to milk, caught her foot in the heather,
Woke to hear a dance record playing of Old Vienna.
It's no go your maidenheads, it's no go your culture,
All we want is a Dunlop tyre and the devil mend the puncture.

The Laird o' Phelps spent Hogmanay declaring he was sober,
Counted his feet to prove the fact and found he had one foot over.
Mrs. Carmichael had her fifth, looked at the job with repulsion,
Said to the midwife 'Take it away; I'm through with over-production'.

It's no go the gossip column, it's no go the ceilidh,
All we want is a mother's help and a sugar-stick for the baby.

Willie Murray cut his thumb, couldn't count the damage,
Took the hide of an Ayrshire cow and used it for a bandage.
His brother caught three hundred cran when the seas were lavish,
Threw the bleeders back in the sea and went upon the parish.

It's no go the Herring Board, it's no go the Bible,
All we want is a packet of fags when our hands are idle.

It's no go the picture palace, it's no go the stadium,
It's no go the country cot with a pot of pink geraniums,
It's no go the Government grants, it's no go the elections,
Sit on your arse for fifty years and hang your hat on a pension.

It's no go my honey love, it's no go my poppet;
Work your hands from day to day, the winds will blow the profit.
The glass is falling hour by hour, the glass will fall for ever,
But if you break the bloody glass you won't hold up the weather.

752   *Château Jackson*

Where is the Jack that built the house
That housed the folk that tilled the field
That filled the bags that brimmed the mill
That ground the flour that browned the bread
That fed the serfs that scrubbed the floors

That wore the mats that kissed the feet
That bore the bums that raised the heads
That raised the eyes that eyed the glass
That sold the pass that linked the lands
That sink the sands that told the time
That stopped the clock that guards the shelf
That shrines the frame that lacks the face
That mocked the man that sired the Jack
That chanced the arm that bought the farm
That caught the wind that skinned the flocks
That raised the rocks that sunk the ship
That rode the tide that washed the bank
That grew the flowers that brewed the red
That stained the page that drowned the loan
That built the house that Jack built?

Here, to begin with, is the world
That breeds the race that claims the right
That makes the pace that makes the race
That bursts the tape that rings the bell
That drees the weird that scoops the news
That stews the tea that stales the smut
That gluts the guts that loathe the lights
That light the path that probes the maze
That traps the days that dodge the wolf
That haunts the door that bears the box
That gulped the bills that swelled the debt
That bent the back that caused the pain
That warped the mind that steered the feet
That took the road that climbed the hill
That boasts the yew that chills the ground
That grows the grass that chokes the flowers
That brewed the red that decked the bank
That bears the slab that wears the words
That tell the truth that ends the quest:
Where is the Jack that built the house?

753   *Charon*

The conductor's hands were black with money:
Hold on to your ticket, he said, the inspector's
Mind is black with suspicion, and hold on to
That dissolving map. We moved through London,
We could see the pigeons through the glass but failed
To hear their rumours of wars, we could see
The lost dog barking but never knew

That his bark was as shrill as a cock crowing,
We just jogged on, at each request
Stop there was a crowd of aggressively vacant
Faces, we just jogged on, eternity
Gave itself airs in revolving lights
And then we came to the Thames and all
The bridges were down, the further shore
Was lost in fog, so we asked the conductor
What we should do. He said: Take the ferry
Faute de mieux. We flicked the flashlight
And there was the ferryman just as Virgil
And Dante had seen him. He looked at us coldly
And his eyes were dead and his hands on the oar
Were black with obols and varicose veins
Marbled his calves and he said to us coldly:
If you want to die you will have to pay for it.

F. T. PRINCE
1912–

754   *An Epistle to a Patron*

My lord, hearing lately of your opulence in promises and your house
Busy with parasites, of your hands full of favours, your statutes
Admirable as music, and no fear of your arms not prospering, I have
Considered how to serve you and breed from my talents
These few secrets which I shall make plain
To your intelligent glory. You should understand that I have plotted,
Being in command of all the ordinary engines
Of defence and offence, a hundred and fifteen buildings
Less others less complete: complete, some are courts of serene stone,
Some the civil structures of a war-like elegance as bridges,
Sewers, aqueducts and citadels of brick, with which I declare the fact
That your nature is to vanquish. For these I have acquired a knowledge
Of the habits of numbers and of various tempers, and skill in setting
Firm sets of pure bare members which will rise, hanging together
Like an argument, with beams, ties and sistering pilasters:
The lintels and windows with mouldings as round as a girl's chin; thresholds
To libraries; halls that cannot be entered without a sensation as of myrrh
By your vermilion officers, your sages and dancers. There will be chambers
Like the recovery of a sick man, your closet waiting not
Less suitably shadowed than the heart, and the coffers of a ceiling
To reflect your diplomatic taciturnities. You may commission
Hospitals, huge granaries that will smile to bear your filial plunders,
And stables washed with a silver lime in whose middle tower seated

In the slight acridity you may watch
The copper thunder kept in the sulky flanks of your horse, a rolling field
Of necks glad to be groomed, the strong crupper, the edged hoof
And the long back, seductive and rebellious to saddles.
And barracks, fortresses, in need of no vest save light, light
That to me is breath, food and drink, I live by effects of light, I live
To catch it, to break it, as an orator plays off
Against each other and his theme his casual gems, and so with light,
Twisted in strings, plucked, crossed or knotted or crumbled
As it may be allowed to be by leaves,
Or clanged back by lakes and rocks or otherwise beaten,
Or else spilt and spread like a feast of honey, dripping
Through delightful voids and creeping along long fractures, brimming
Carved canals, bowls and lachrymatories with pearls: all this the work
Of now advancing, now withdrawing faces, whose use I know.
I know what slabs thus will be soaked to a thumb's depth by the sun,
And where to rob them, what colour stifles in your intact quarries, what
Sand silted in your river-gorges will well mix with the dust of flint; I know
What wood to cut by what moon in what weather
Of your sea-winds, your hill-wind: therefore tyrant, let me learn
Your high-ways, ways of sandstone, roads of the oakleaf, and your sea-ways.
Send me to dig dry graves, exposing what you want: I must
Attend your orgies and debates (let others apply for austerities), admit me
To your witty table, stuff me with urban levities, feed me, bind me
To a prudish luxury, free me thus, and with a workshop
From my household consisting
Of a pregnant wife, one female and one boy child and an elder bastard
With other properties; these let me regard, let me neglect, and let
What I begin be finished. Save me, noble sir, from the agony
Of starved and privy explorations such as those I stumble
From a hot bed to make, to follow lines to which the night-sky
Holds only faint contingencies. These flights with no end but failure,
And failure not to end them, these palliate or prevent.
I wish for liberty, let me then be tied: and seeing too much
I aspire to be constrained by your emblems of birth and triumph,
And between the obligations of your future and the checks of actual state
To flourish, adapt the stubs of an interminable descent, and place
The crested key to confident vaults; with a placid flurry of petals,
And bosom and lips, will stony functionaries support
The persuasion, so beyond proof, of your power. I will record
In peculiar scrolls your alien alliances,
Fit an apartment for your eastern hostage, extol in basalt
Your father, praise with white festoons the goddess your lady;
And for your death which will be mine prepare
An encasement as if of solid blood. And so let me
Forget, let me remember, that this is stone, stick, metal, trash
Which I will pile and hack, my hands will stain and bend

(None better knowing how to gain from the slow pains of a marble
Bruised, breathing strange climates). Being pressed as I am, being broken
By wealth and poverty, torn between strength and weakness, take me, choose
To relieve me, to receive of me, and must you not agree
As you have been to some—a great giver of banquets, of respite from swords,
Who shook out figured cloths, who rained coin,
A donor of laurel and of grapes, a font of profuse intoxicants—and so,
To be so too for me? And none too soon, since the panting mind
Rather than barren will be prostitute, and once
I served a herd of merchants; but since I will be faithful
And my virtue is such, though far from home let what is yours be mine, and
     this be a match
As many have been proved, enduring exiles and blazed
Not without issue in returning shows: your miserly freaks
Your envies, racks and poisons not out of mind
Although not told, since often borne—indeed how should it be
That you employed them less than we? but now be flattered a little
To indulge the extravagant gist of this communication,
For my pride puts all in doubt and at present I have no patience,
I have simply hope, and I submit me
To your judgement which will be just.

ANNE RIDLER

1912–

755   *Now Philippa Is Gone*

          Now Philippa is gone, that so divinely
          Could strum and sing, and is rufus and gay,
          Have we the heart to sing, or at midday
          Dive under Trotton Bridge? We shall only
          Doze in the yellow spikenard by the wood
          And take our tea and melons in the shade.

R. S. THOMAS

1913–

756   *On the Farm*

          There was Dai Puw. He was no good.
          They put him in the fields to dock swedes,
          And took the knife from him, when he came home

At late evening with a grin
Like the slash of a knife on his face.

There was Llew Puw, and he was no good.
Every evening after the ploughing
With the big tractor he would sit in his chair,
And stare into the tangled fire garden,
Opening his slow lips like a snail.

There was Huw Puw, too. What shall I say?
I have heard him whistling in the hedges
On and on, as though winter
Would never again leave those fields,
And all the trees were deformed.

And lastly there was the girl:
Beauty under some spell of the beast.
Her pale face was the lantern
By which they read in life's dark book
The shrill sentence: God is love.

757   *A Peasant*

Iago Prytherch his name, though, be it allowed,
Just an ordinary man of the bald Welsh hills,
Who pens a few sheep in a gap of cloud.
Docking mangels, chipping the green skin
From the yellow bones with a half-witted grin
Of satisfaction, or churning the crude earth
To a stiff sea of clods that glint in the wind—
So are his days spent, his spittled mirth
Rarer than the sun that cracks the cheeks
Of the gaunt sky perhaps once in a week.
And then at night see him fixed in his chair
Motionless, except when he leans to gob in the fire.
There is something frightening in the vacancy of his mind.
His clothes, sour with years of sweat
And animal contact, shock the refined,
But affected, sense with their stark naturalness.
Yet this is your prototype, who, season by season
Against siege of rain and the wind's attrition,
Preserves his stock, an impregnable fortress
Not to be stormed even in death's confusion.
Remember him then, for he, too, is a winner of wars,
Enduring like a tree under the curious stars.

758   *January*

    The fox drags its wounded belly
    Over the snow, the crimson seeds
    Of blood burst with a mild explosion,
    Soft as excrement, bold as roses.
    Over the snow that feels no pity,
    Whose white hands can give no healing,
    The fox drags its wounded belly.

759   *Evans*

    Evans? Yes, many a time
    I came down his bare flight
    Of stairs into the gaunt kitchen
    With its wood fire, where crickets sang
    Accompaniment to the black kettle's
    Whine, and so into the cold
    Dark to smother in the thick tide
    Of night that drifted about the walls
    Of his stark farm on the hill ridge.

    It was not the dark filling my eyes
    And mouth appalled me; not even the drip
    Of rain like blood from the one tree
    Weather-tortured. It was the dark
    Silting the veins of that sick man
    I left stranded upon the vast
    And lonely shore of his bleak bed.

HENRY REED
1914–1986

760   *Dull Sonnet*

    I have always been remarkably impressed
    By the various sights and sounds of trees and birds
    Respectively; have always thought that words
    Could not express the beauties of the West
    With much exactitude. Yet in my breast,
    When pondering on the ruminating herds,
    I have (not seldom) felt like one who girds

His spiritual loins; and have confessed
That it is clear that those restrictive laws
Which tie the tongues of men of meaner clay
Do not apply to Me: that I have cause
To assume, without compunction or delay,
A just complacency, that scorns to hide
In (a) mock modesty, or (b) false pride.

761–2   from *Lessons of the War*

761   1 *Naming of Parts*

Today we have naming of parts. Yesterday,
We had daily cleaning. And tomorrow morning,
We shall have what to do after firing. But today,
Today we have naming of parts. Japonica
Glistens like coral in all of the neighbouring gardens,
        And today we have naming of parts.

This is the lower sling swivel. And this
Is the upper sling swivel, whose use you will see,
When you are given your slings. And this is the piling swivel,
Which in your case you have not got. The branches
Hold in the gardens their silent, eloquent gestures,
        Which in our case we have not got.

This is the safety-catch, which is always released
With an easy flick of the thumb. And please do not let me
See anyone using his finger. You can do it quite easy
If you have any strength in your thumb. The blossoms
Are fragile and motionless, never letting anyone see
        Any of them using their finger.

And this you can see is the bolt. The purpose of this
Is to open the breech, as you see. We can slide it
Rapidly backwards and forwards: we call this
Easing the spring. And rapidly backwards and forwards
The early bees are assaulting and fumbling the flowers:
        They call it easing the Spring.

They call it easing the Spring: it is perfectly easy
If you have any strength in your thumb: like the bolt,
And the breech, and the cocking-piece, and the point of balance,
Which in our case we have not got; and the almond-blossom
Silent in all of the gardens and the bees going backwards and forwards,
        For today we have naming of parts.

762   2 *Judging Distances*

Not only how far away, but the way that you say it
Is very important. Perhaps you may never get
The knack of judging a distance, but at least you know
How to report on a landscape: the central sector,
The right of arc and that, which we had last Tuesday,
        And at least you know

That maps are of time, not place, so far as the army
Happens to be concerned—the reason being,
Is one which need not delay us. Again, you know
There are three kinds of tree, three only, the fir and the poplar,
And those which have bushy tops to; and lastly
        That things only seem to be things.

A barn is not called a barn, to put it more plainly,
Or a field in the distance, where sheep may be safely grazing.
You must never be over-sure. You must say, when reporting:
At five o'clock in the central sector is a dozen
Of what appear to be animals; whatever you do,
        Don't call the bleeders *sheep*.

I am sure that's quite clear; and suppose, for the sake of example,
The one at the end, asleep, endeavours to tell us
What he sees over there to the west, and how far away,
After first having come to attention. There to the west,
On the fields of summer the sun and the shadows bestow
        Vestments of purple and gold.

The still white dwellings are like a mirage in the heat,
And under the swaying elms a man and a woman
Lie gently together. Which is, perhaps, only to say
That there is a row of houses to the left of arc,
And that under some poplars a pair of what appear to be humans
        Appear to be loving.

Well that, for an answer, is what we might rightly call
Moderately satisfactory only, the reason being,
Is that two things have been omitted, and those are important.
The human beings, now: in what direction are they,
And how far away, would you say? And do not forget
        There may be dead ground in between.

There may be dead ground in between; and I may not have got
The knack of judging a distance; I will only venture
A guess that perhaps between me and the apparent lovers
(Who, incidentally, appear by now to have finished)
At seven o'clock from the houses, is roughly a distance
        Of about one year and a half.

DYLAN THOMAS

1914–1953

763
The force that through the green fuse
drives the flower

The force that through the green fuse drives the flower
Drives my green age; that blasts the roots of trees
Is my destroyer.
And I am dumb to tell the crooked rose
My youth is bent by the same wintry fever.

The force that drives the water through the rocks
Drives my red blood; that dries the mouthing streams
Turns mine to wax.
And I am dumb to mouth unto my veins
How at the mountain spring the same mouth sucks.

The hand that whirls the water in the pool
Stirs the quicksand; that ropes the blowing wind
Hauls my shroud sail.
And I am dumb to tell the hanging man
How of my clay is made the hangman's lime.

The lips of time leech to the fountain head;
Love drips and gathers, but the fallen blood
Shall calm her sores.
And I am dumb to tell a weather's wind
How time has ticked a heaven round the stars.

And I am dumb to tell the lover's tomb
How at my sheet goes the same crooked worm.

764
Light breaks where no sun shines

Light breaks where no sun shines;
Where no sea runs, the waters of the heart
Push in their tides;
And, broken ghosts with glow-worms in their heads,
The things of light
File through the flesh where no flesh decks the bones.

A candle in the thighs
Warms youth and seed and burns the seeds of age;

Where no seed stirs,
The fruit of man unwrinkles in the stars,
Bright as a fig;
Where no wax is, the candle shows its hairs.

Dawn breaks behind the eyes;
From poles of skull and toe the windy blood
Slides like a sea;
Nor fenced, nor staked, the gushers of the sky
Spout to the rod
Divining in a smile the oil of tears.

Night in the sockets rounds,
Like some pitch moon, the limit of the globes;
Day lights the bone;
Where no cold is, the skinning gales unpin
The winter's robes;
The film of spring is hanging from the lids.

Light breaks on secret lots,
On tips of thought where thoughts smell in the rain;
When logics die,
The secret of the soil grows through the eye,
And blood jumps in the sun;
Above the waste allotments the dawn halts.

765   *Should lanterns shine*

Should lanterns shine, the holy face,
Caught in an octagon of unaccustomed light,
Would wither up, and any boy of love
Look twice before he fell from grace.
The features in their private dark
Are formed of flesh, but let the false day come
And from her lips the faded pigments fall,
The mummy cloths expose an ancient breast.

I have been told to reason by the heart,
But heart, like head, leads helplessly;
I have been told to reason by the pulse,
And, when it quickens, alter the actions' pace
Till field and roof lie level and the same
So fast I move defying time, the quiet gentleman
Whose beard wags in Egyptian wind.

I have heard many years of telling,
And many years should see some change.

The ball I threw while playing in the park
Has not yet reached the ground.

766   *I have longed to move away*

I have longed to move away
From the hissing of the spent lie
And the old terrors' continual cry
Growing more terrible as the day
Goes over the hill into the deep sea;
I have longed to move away
From the repetition of salutes,
For there are ghosts in the air
And ghostly echoes on paper,
And the thunder of calls and notes.

I have longed to move away but am afraid;
Some life, yet unspent, might explode
Out of the old lie burning on the ground,
And, crackling into the air, leave me half-blind.
Neither by night's ancient fear,
The parting of hat from hair,
Pursed lips at the receiver,
Shall I fall to death's feather.
By these I would not care to die,
Half convention and half lie.

767   *Twenty-four years*

Twenty-four years remind the tears of my eyes.
(Bury the dead for fear that they walk to the grave in labour.)
In the groin of the natural doorway I crouched like a tailor
Sewing a shroud for a journey
By the light of the meat-eating sun.
Dressed to die, the sensual strut begun,
With my red veins full of money,
In the final direction of the elementary town
I advance for as long as forever is.

768 *The Hunchback in the Park*

The hunchback in the park
A solitary mister
Propped between trees and water
From the opening of the garden lock
That lets the trees and water enter
Until the Sunday sombre bell at dark

Eating bread from a newspaper
Drinking water from the chained cup
That the children filled with gravel
In the fountain basin where I sailed my ship
Slept at night in a dog kennel
But nobody chained him up.

Like the park birds he came early
Like the water he sat down
And Mister they called Hey mister
The truant boys from the town
Running when he had heard them clearly
On out of sound

Past lake and rockery
Laughing when he shook his paper
Hunchbacked in mockery
Through the loud zoo of the willow groves
Dodging the park keeper
With his stick that picked up leaves.

And the old dog sleeper
Alone between nurses and swans
While the boys among willows
Made the tigers jump out of their eyes
To roar on the rockery stones
And the groves were blue with sailors

Made all day until bell time
A woman figure without fault
Straight as a young elm
Straight and tall from his crooked bones
That she might stand in the night
After the locks and chains

All night in the unmade park
After the railings and shrubberies
The birds the grass the trees the lake

And the wild boys innocent as strawberries
Had followed the hunchback
To his kennel in the dark.

ALUN LEWIS

1915–1944

769   *The Peasants*

The dwarf barefooted, chanting
Behind the oxen by the lake,
Stepping lightly and lazily among the thorntrees
Dusky and dazed with sunlight, half awake;

The women breaking stones upon the highway,
Walking erect with burdens on their heads,
One body growing in another body,
Creation touching verminous straw beds.

Across scorched hills and trampled crops
The soldiers straggle by.
History staggers in their wake.
The peasants watch them die.

TOM SCOTT

1918–1995

770   *Ballat O the Leddies O Langsyne*

Tell me whaur, in whit countrie
Bides Flora nou, yon Roman belle?
Whaur Thais, Alcibiades be,
Thon sibbit cuisins. Can ye tell
Whaur clettaran echo draws pell-mell   5
Abuin some burn owrehung wi bine
Her beautie's mair nor human spell—
Ay, whaur's the snaws o langsyne?

Whaur's Heloise, yon wyce abbess
For wham Pete Abelard manless fell,   10

770: 4 *Thon sibbit cuisins*] those cousins by blood

Yet lovin aye, at Sanct Denys
Wrocht out his days in cloistrit cell?
And say whaur yon queen is as well
That ordrit Buridan ae dine
Be seckt and cuist in the Seine to cool—   15
Ay, whaur's the snaws o langsyne?

Queen Blanche, as pure's the flour-de-lys,
Whase voice nae siren's could excel,
Bertha Braidfuit, Beatrice, Alys,
Ermbourg that hent the maine hersel?   20
Guid Joan of Arc, the lass they tell
The English brunt at Rouen hyne—
Whaur are they, Lady, I appeal?
Ay, whaur's the snaws o langsyne?

Prince, this week I cannae well,   25
Nor this year, whaur they aa nou shine.
Speir, ye's but hear the owrecome swell—
Ay, whaur's the snaws o langsyne?

[after the French of Villon]

KEITH DOUGLAS

1920–1944

771   *Sportsmen*

'I think I am becoming a God.'

The noble horse with courage in his eye,
clean in the bone, looks up at a shellburst:
away fly the images of the shires
but he puts the pipe back in his mouth.

Peter was unfortunately killed by an 88;
it took his leg off; he died in the ambulance.
When I saw him crawling, he said:
It's most unfair, they've shot my foot off.

How then can I live among this gentle
obsolescent breed of heroes, and not weep?

14 *ae dine*] one dinner-time   15 *seckt and cuist*] sacked and cast   22 *hyne*] afar
27 *Speir*] ask   *owrecome*] refrain

Unicorns, almost. For they are fading into two legends
in which their stupidity and chivalry are celebrated;
the fool and the hero will be immortals.

These plains were a cricket pitch
and in the hills the tremendous drop fences
brought down some of the runners, who
under these stones and earth lounge still
in famous attitudes of unconcern. Listen
against the bullet cries the simple horn.

772   *Vergissmeinnicht*

Three weeks gone and the combatants gone
returning over the nightmare ground
we found the place again, and found
the soldier sprawling in the sun.

The frowning barrel of his gun
overshadowing. As we came on
that day, he hit my tank with one
like the entry of a demon.

Look. Here in the gunpit spoil
the dishonoured picture of his girl
who has put: *Steffi. Vergissmeinnicht*
in a copybook gothic script.

We see him almost with content,
abased, and seeming to have paid
and mocked at by his own equipment
that's hard and good when he's decayed.

But she would weep to see today
how on his skin the swart flies move;
the dust upon the paper eye
and the burst stomach like a cave.

For here the lover and killer are mingled
who had one body and one heart.
And death who had the soldier singled
has done the lover mortal hurt.

EDWIN MORGAN

1920–

773   *The Computer's First Christmas Card*

```
j o l l y m e r r y
h o l l y b e r r y
j o l l y b e r r y
m e r r y h o l l y
h a p p y j o l l y
j o l l y j e l l y
j e l l y b e l l y
b e l l y m e r r y
h o l l y h e p p y
j o l l y M o l l y
m a r r y J e r r y
m e r r y H a r r y
h o p p y B a r r y
h e p p y J a r r y
b o p p y h e p p y
b e r r y j o r r y
j o r r y j o l l y
m o p p y j e l l y
M o l l y m e r r y
J e r r y j o l l y
b e l l y b o p p y
j o r r y h o p p y
h o l l y m o p p y
B a r r y m e r r y
J a r r y h a p p y
h a p p y b o p p y
b o p p y j o l l y
j o l l y m e r r y
m e r r y m e r r y
m e r r y m e r r y
m e r r y C h r i s
a m m e r r y a s a
C h r i s m e r r y
a s M E R R Y C H R
Y S A N T H E M U M
```

DONALD DAVIE

1922–1995

774   *The Garden Party*

Above a stretch of still unravaged weald
In our Black Country, in a cedar-shade,
I found, shared out in tennis courts, a field
Where children of the local magnates played.

And I grew envious of their moneyed ease
In Scott Fitzgerald's unembarrassed vein.
Let prigs, I thought, fool others as they please,
I only wish I had my time again.

To crown a situation as contrived
As any in 'The Beautiful and Damned',
The phantom of my earliest love arrived;
I shook absurdly as I shook her hand.

As dusk drew in on cultivated cries,
Faces hung pearls upon a cedar-bough;
And gin could blur the glitter of her eyes,
But it's too late to learn to tango now.

My father, of a more submissive school,
Remarks the rich themselves are always sad.
There is that sort of equalizing rule;
But theirs is all the youth we might have had.

775   *The Mushroom Gatherers*

Strange walkers! See their processional
Perambulations under low boughs,
The birches white, and the green turf under.
These should be ghosts by moonlight wandering.

Their attitudes strange: the human tree
Slowly revolves on its bole. All around
Downcast looks; and the direct dreamer
Treads out in trance his lane, unwavering.

Strange decorum: so prodigal of bows,
Yet lost in thought and self-absorbed, they meet
Impassively, without acknowledgment.
A courteous nation, but unsociable.

Field full of folk, in their immunity
From human ills, crestfallen and serene.
Who would have thought these shades our lively friends?
Surely these acres are Elysian Fields.

[after the Polish of Mickiewicz]

776   *Tunstall Forest*

Stillness! Down the dripping ride,
    The firebreak avenue
Of Tunstall Forest, at the side
    Of which we sought for you,
You did not come. The soft rain dropped,
    And quiet indeed we found:
No cars but ours, and ours was stopped,
    Rainfall the only sound.

And quiet is a lovely essence;
    Silence is of the tomb,
Austere though happy; but the tense
    Stillness did not come,
The deer did not, although they fed
    Perhaps nearby that day,
The liquid eye and elegant head
    No more than a mile away.

PHILIP LARKIN

1922–1985

777   *At Grass*

The eye can hardly pick them out
From the cold shade they shelter in,
Till wind distresses tail and mane;
Then one crops grass, and moves about
—The other seeming to look on—
And stands anonymous again.

Yet fifteen years ago, perhaps
Two dozen distances sufficed
To fable them: faint afternoons
Of Cups and Stakes and Handicaps,
Whereby their names were artificed
To inlay faded, classic Junes—

Silks at the start: against the sky
Numbers and parasols: outside,
Squadrons of empty cars, and heat,
And littered grass: then the long cry
Hanging unhushed till it subside
To stop-press columns on the street.

Do memories plague their ears like flies?
They shake their heads. Dusk brims the shadows.
Summer by summer all stole away,
The starting-gates, the crowds and cries—
All but the unmolesting meadows.
Almanacked, their names live; they

Have slipped their names, and stand at ease,
Or gallop for what must be joy,
And not a fieldglass sees them home,
Or curious stop-watch prophesies:
Only the groom, and the groom's boy,
With bridles in the evening come.

778   *Absences*

Rain patters on a sea that tilts and sighs.
Fast-running floors, collapsing into hollows,
Tower suddenly, spray-haired. Contrariwise,
A wave drops like a wall: another follows,
Wilting and scrambling, tirelessly at play
Where there are no ships and no shallows.

Above the sea, the yet more shoreless day,
Riddled by wind, trails lit-up galleries:
They shift to giant ribbing, sift away.

Such attics cleared of me! Such absences!

779   *Days*

What are days for?
Days are where we live.
They come, they wake us
Time and time over.
They are to be happy in:
Where can we live but days?

Ah, solving that question
Brings the priest and the doctor
In their long coats
Running over the fields.

780   *Age*

My age fallen away like white swaddling
Floats in the middle distance, becomes
An inhabited cloud. I bend closer, discern
A lighted tenement scuttling with voices.
O you tall game I tired myself with joining!
Now I wade through you like knee-level weeds,

And they attend me, dear translucent bergs:
Silence and space. By now so much has flown
From the nest here of my head that I needs must turn
To know what prints I leave, whether of feet,
Or spoor of pads, or a bird's adept splay.

781   *Mr Bleaney*

'This was Mr Bleaney's room. He stayed
The whole time he was at the Bodies, till
They moved him.' Flowered curtains, thin and frayed,
Fall to within five inches of the sill,

Whose window shows a strip of building land,
Tussocky, littered. 'Mr Bleaney took
My bit of garden properly in hand.'
Bed, upright chair, sixty-watt bulb, no hook

Behind the door, no room for books or bags—
'I'll take it.' So it happens that I lie
Where Mr Bleaney lay, and stub my fags
On the same saucer-souvenir, and try

Stuffing my ears with cotton-wool, to drown
The jabbering set he egged her on to buy.
I know his habits—what time he came down,
His preference for sauce to gravy, why

He kept on plugging at the four aways—
Likewise their yearly frame: the Frinton folk
Who put him up for summer holidays,
And Christmas at his sister's house in Stoke.

But if he stood and watched the frigid wind
Tousling the clouds, lay on the fusty bed
Telling himself that this was home, and grinned,
And shivered, without shaking off the dread

That how we live measures our own nature,
And at his age having no more to show
Than one hired box should make him pretty sure
He warranted no better, I don't know.

782   *Afternoons*

Summer is fading:
The leaves fall in ones and twos
From trees bordering
The new recreation ground.
In the hollows of afternoons
Young mothers assemble
At swing and sandpit
Setting free their children.

Behind them, at intervals,
Stand husbands in skilled trades,
An estateful of washing,
And the albums, lettered
Our Wedding, lying
Near the television:
Before them, the wind
Is ruining their courting-places

That are still courting-places
(But the lovers are all in school),
And their children, so intent on
Finding more unripe acorns,
Expect to be taken home.
Their beauty has thickened.
Something is pushing them
To the side of their own lives.

783   *Love Songs in Age*

She kept her songs, they took so little space,
    The covers pleased her:
One bleached from lying in a sunny place,
One marked in circles by a vase of water,

One mended, when a tidy fit had seized her,
    And coloured, by her daughter—
So they had waited, till in widowhood
She found them, looking for something else, and stood

Relearning how each frank submissive chord
    Had ushered in
Word after sprawling hyphenated word,
And the unfailing sense of being young
Spread out like a spring-woken tree, wherein
    That hidden freshness sung,
That certainty of time laid up in store
As when she played them first. But, even more,

The glare of that much-mentioned brilliance, love,
    Broke out, to show
Its bright incipience sailing above,
Still promising to solve, and satisfy,
And set unchangeably in order. So
    To pile them back, to cry,
Was hard, without lamely admitting how
It had not done so then, and could not now.

784   *As Bad as a Mile*

Watching the shied core
Striking the basket, skidding across the floor,
Shows less and less of luck, and more and more

Of failure spreading back up the arm
Earlier and earlier, the unraised hand calm,
The apple unbitten in the palm.

785   *Faith Healing*

Slowly the women file to where he stands
Upright in rimless glasses, silver hair,
Dark suit, white collar. Stewards tirelessly
Persuade them onwards to his voice and hands,
Within whose warm spring rain of loving care
Each dwells some twenty seconds. *Now, dear child,
What's wrong*, the deep American voice demands,
And, scarcely pausing, goes into a prayer
Directing God about this eye, that knee.
Their heads are clasped abruptly; then, exiled

Like losing thoughts, they go in silence; some
Sheepishly stray, not back into their lives
Just yet; but some stay stiff, twitching and loud
With deep hoarse tears, as if a kind of dumb
And idiot child within them still survives
To re-awake at kindness, thinking a voice
At last calls them alone, that hands have come
To lift and lighten; and such joy arrives
Their thick tongues blort, their eyes squeeze grief, a crowd
Of huge unheard answers jam and rejoice—

What's wrong! Moustached in flowered frocks they shake:
By now, all's wrong. In everyone there sleeps
A sense of life lived according to love.
To some it means the difference they could make
By loving others, but across most it sweeps
As all they might have done had they been loved.
That nothing cures. An immense slackening ache,
As when, thawing, the rigid landscape weeps,
Spreads slowly through them—that, and the voice above
Saying *Dear child*, and all time has disproved.

786   *Homage to a Government*

Next year we are to bring the soldiers home
For lack of money, and it is all right.
Places they guarded, or kept orderly,
Must guard themselves, and keep themselves orderly.
We want the money for ourselves at home
Instead of working. And this is all right.

It's hard to say who wanted it to happen,
But now it's been decided nobody minds.
The places are a long way off, not here,
Which is all right, and from what we hear
The soldiers there only made trouble happen.
Next year we shall be easier in our minds.

Next year we shall be living in a country
That brought its soldiers home for lack of money.
The statues will be standing in the same
Tree-muffled squares, and look nearly the same.
Our children will not know it's a different country.
All we can hope to leave them now is money.

                                        1969

CHARLES TOMLINSON
1927–

787   *At Vshchizh*

After the tumult and the blood
Had died, had dried,
Silence unmade its history:
A group of mounds; on them
A group of oaks. They spread
Their broad unmindful glories
Over the unheard rumour of those dead
And rustle there, rooted on ruin.
All nature's knowledge
Is to stay unknowing—
Ours, to confess confusion:
Dreamt-out by her,
Our years are apparitions in their coming-going.
Her random seed
Spread to their fruitless feat, she then
Regathers them
Into that peace all history must feed.

[after the Russian of Tyutchev; with Henry Gifford]

788   *To His Wife*

Punishing God has taken all content
Of day and dark, of health and open air:
You he has left for my encouragement,
That, robbed of will, I am not robbed of prayer.

[after the Russian of Tyutchev; with Henry Gifford]

789   *The Door*

Too little
has been said
of the door, its one
face turned to the night's
downpour and its other
to the shift and glisten of firelight.

Air, clasped
by this cover
into the room's book,
is filled by the turning
pages of dark and fire
as the wind shoulders the panels, or unsteadies that burning.

Not only
the storm's
breakwater, but the sudden
frontier to our concurrences, appearances,
and as full of the offer of space
as the view through a cromlech is.

For doors
are both frame and monument
to our spent time,
and too little
has been said
of our coming through and leaving by them.

790   *Saving the Appearances*

The horse is white. Or it
appears to be under this
November light that could
well be October. It goes
as nimbly as a spider does
but it is gainly: the great
field makes it small
so that it seems
to crawl out of the distance
and to grow not larger
but less slow. Stains
on its sides show where
the mud is and the power
now overmasters the fragility
of its earlier bearing. Tall
it shudders over one and bends
a full neck, cropping
the foreground, blotting
the whole space back
behind those pounding feet.
Mounted, one feels the sky
as much the measure of the event

as the field had been, and all
the divisions of the indivisible
unite again, or seem
to do as when the approaching
horse was white, on this
November unsombre day
where what appears, is.

IAIN CRICHTON SMITH

1928–1998

791   *Old Woman*

And she, being old, fed from a mashed plate
as an old mare might droop across a fence
to the dull pastures of its ignorance.
Her husband held her upright while he prayed

to God who is all-forgiving to send down
some angel somewhere who might land perhaps
in his foreign wings among the gradual crops.
She munched, half dead, blindly searching the spoon.

Outside, the grass was raging. There I sat
imprisoned in my pity and my shame
that men and women having suffered time
should sit in such a place, in such a state

and wished to be away, yes, to be far away
with athletes, heroes, Greeks or Roman men
who pushed their bitter spears into a vein
and would not spend an hour with such decay.

'Pray God,' he said, 'we ask you, God,' he said.
The bowed back was quiet. I saw the teeth
tighten their grip around a delicate death.
And nothing moved within the knotted head

but only a few poor veins as one might see
vague wishless seaweed floating on a tide
of all the salty waters where had died
too many waves to mark two more or three.

THOMAS KINSELLA

1928–

792   *Ancestor*

I was going up to say something,
and stopped. Her profile against the curtains
was old, and dark like a hunting bird's.

It was the way she perched on the high stool,
staring into herself, with one fist
gripping the side of the barrier around her desk
—or her head held by something, from inside.
And not caring for anything around her
or anyone there by the shelves.
I caught a faint smell, musky and queer.

I may have made some sound—she stopped rocking
and pressed her fist in her lap; then she stood up
and shut down the lid of the desk, and turned the key.
She shoved a small bottle under her aprons
and came toward me, darkening the passageway.

Ancestor . . . among sweet- and fruit-boxes.
Her black heart . . .
                        Was that a sigh?
—brushing by me in the shadows,
with her heaped aprons, through the red hangings
to the scullery, and down to the back room.

793   *Tear*

I was sent in to see her.
A fringe of jet drops
chattered at my ear
as I went in through the hangings.

I was swallowed in chambery dusk.
My heart shrank
at the smell of disused
organs and sour kidney.

The black aprons I used to
bury my face in
were folded at the foot of the bed
in the last watery light from the window

(Go in and say goodbye to her)
and I was carried off
to unfathomable depths.
I turned to look at her.

She stared at the ceiling
and puffed her cheek, distracted,
propped high in the bed
resting for the next attack.

The covers were gathered close
up to her mouth,
that the lines of ill-temper still
marked. Her grey hair

was loosened out like
a young woman's all over
the pillow, mixed with the shadows
criss-crossing her forehead

and at her mouth and eyes,
like a web of strands tying down her head
and tangling down toward the shadow
eating away the floor at my feet.

I couldn't stir at first, nor wished to,
for fear she might turn and tempt me
(my own father's mother)
with open mouth

—with some fierce wheedling whisper—
to hide myself one last time
against her, and bury my
self in her drying mud.

Was I to kiss her? As soon
kiss the damp that crept
in the flowered walls
of this pit.

Yet I had to kiss.
I knelt by the bulk of the death bed
and sank my face in the chill
and smell of her black aprons.

Snuff and musk, the folds against my eyelids,
carried me into a derelict place
smelling of ash: unseen walls and roofs
rustled like breathing.

I found myself disturbing
dead ashes for any trace

of warmth, when far off
in the vaults a single drop

splashed. And I found
what I was looking for
—not heat nor fire,
not any comfort,

but her voice, soft, talking to someone
about my father: 'God help him, he cried
big tears over there by the machine
for the poor little thing.' Bright

drops on the wooden lid for
my infant sister. My own
wail of child-animal grief
was soon done, with any early guess

at sad dullness and tedious pain
and lives bitter with hard bondage.
How I tasted it now—
her heart beating in my mouth!

She drew an uncertain breath
and pushed at the clothes
and shuddered tiredly.
I broke free

and left the room
promising myself
when she was really dead
I would really kiss.

My grandfather half looked up
from the fireplace as I came out,
and shrugged and turned back
with a deaf stare to the heat.

I fidgeted beside him for a minute
and went out to the shop.
It was still bright there
and I felt better able to breathe.

Old age can digest
anything: the commotion
at Heaven's gate—the struggle
in store for you all your life.

How long and hard it is
before you get to Heaven,
unless like little Agnes
you vanish with early tears.

PETER PORTER

1929–

794   *Epigrams*, Book IV, xviii

Near the Vipsanian columns where the aqueduct
   drips down the side of its dark arch,
the stone is a green and pulsing velvet
   and the air is powdered with sweat
from the invisible faucet: there winter
   shaped a dagger of ice, waiting till
a boy looked up at the quondam stalactites,
   threw it like a gimlet through his throat
and as in a murder in a paperback the clever
   weapon melted away in its own hole. Where
have blood and water flowed before from one wound?
   The story is trivial and the instance holy—
what portion of power has violent fortune
   ever surrendered, what degraded circumstance
will she refuse? Death is everywhere
   if water, the life-giving element,
will descend to cutting throats.

       [after the Latin of Martial]

U. A. FANTHORPE

1929–

795   *BC:AD*

This was the moment when Before
Turned into After, and the future's
Uninvented timekeepers presented arms.

This was the moment when nothing
Happened. Only dull peace
Sprawled boringly over the earth.

This was the moment when even energetic Romans
Could find nothing better to do
Than counting heads in remote provinces.

And this was the moment
When a few farm workers and three
Members of an obscure Persian sect

Walked haphazard by starlight straight
Into the kingdom of heaven.

796   *Portraits of Tudor Statesmen*

Surviving is keeping your eyes open,
Controlling the twitchy apparatus
Of iris, white, cornea, lash and lid.

So the literal painter set it down—
The sharp raptorial look; strained eyeball;
And mail, ruff, bands, beard, anything, to hide
The violently vulnerable neck.

THOM GUNN

1929–

797   *The Feel of Hands*

The hands explore tentatively,
two small live entities whose shapes
I have to guess at. They touch me
all, with the light of fingertips

testing each surface of each thing
found, timid as kittens with it.
I connect them with amusing
hands I have shaken by daylight.

There is a sudden transition:
they plunge together in a full
formed single fury; they are grown
to cats, hunting without scruple;

they are expert but desperate.
I am in the dark. I wonder
when they grew up. It strikes me that
I do not know whose hands they are.

798   *Considering the Snail*

The snail pushes through a green
night, for the grass is heavy
with water and meets over
the bright path he makes, where rain
has darkened the earth's dark. He
moves in a wood of desire,

pale antlers barely stirring
as he hunts. I cannot tell
what power is at work, drenched there
with purpose, knowing nothing.
What is a snail's fury? All
I think is that if later

I parted the blades above
the tunnel and saw the thin
trail of broken white across
litter, I would never have
imagined the slow passion
to that deliberate progress.

799   *Terminal*

The eight years difference in age seems now
Disparity so wide between the two
That when I see the man who armoured stood
Resistant to all help however good
Now helped through day itself, eased into chairs,
Or else led step by step down the long stairs
With firm and gentle guidance by his friend,
Who loves him, through each effort to descend,
Each wavering, each attempt made to complete
An arc of movement and bring down the feet
As if with that spare strength he used to enjoy,
I think of Oedipus, old, led by a boy.

DEREK WALCOTT

1930–

800   *Missing the Sea*

Something removed roars in the ears of this house,
Hangs its drapes windless, stuns mirrors
Till reflections lack substance.

Some sound like the gnashing of windmills ground
To a dead halt;
A deafening absence, a blow.

It hoops this valley, weighs this mountain,
Estranges gesture, pushes this pencil
Through a thick nothing now,

Freights cupboards with silence, folds sour laundry
Like the clothes of the dead left exactly
As the dead behaved by the beloved,

Incredulous, expecting occupancy.

ANTHONY THWAITE

1930–

801   Clouds now and then
             Giving men relief
             From moon-viewing.

                    [after the Japanese of Bashō;
                       with Geoffrey Bownas]

802   Girls planting paddy:
             Only their song
             Free of the mud.

                    [after the Japanese of Konishi Raizan;
                       with Geoffrey Bownas]

803   Winter withering:
             Sparrows strut
             In the guttering.

                    [after the Japanese of Tan Taigi;
                       with Geoffrey Bownas]

804 *On Consulting 'Contemporary Poets*
of the English Language'

Dannie Abse, Douglas Dunn,
Andrew Waterman, Thom Gunn,
Peter Redgrove, Gavin Ewart,
Susan Fromberg Schaeffer, Stewart
Conn, Pete Brown, Elizabeth
Jennings, Jim Burns, George MacBeth,
Vernon Scannell, Edwin Brock,
Philip Hobsbaum, Fleur Adcock,
Brian Patten, Patricia Beer,
Colin Falck, David Rokeah,
Peter Dale and David Gill,
David Holbrook, Geoffrey Hill,
David Gascoyne and John Hewitt,
William Empson and Frank Prewett,
Norman Hidden, David Wright,
Philip Larkin, Ivan White,
Stephen Spender, Tom McGrath,
dom silvester houédard,
A. Alvarez, Herbert Lomas,
D.M., R.S., Donald Thomas,
Causley, Cunningham, Wes Magee,
Silkin, Simmons, Laurie Lee,
Peter Jay, Laurence Lerner,
David Day, W. Price Turner,
Peter Porter, Seamus Deane,
Hugo Williams, Seamus Heane-
y, Jonathan Green, Nina Steane,
C. Busby Smith and F. Pratt Green,
Fullers both and Joneses all,
Donald Davie, Donald Hall,
Muldoon, Middleton, Murphy, Miller,
Tomlinson, Tonks, Turnbull, Tiller,
Barker, Brownjohn, Blackburn, Bell,
Kirkup, Kavanagh, Kendrick, Kell,
McGough, Maclean, MacSweeney, Schmidt,
Hughes (of Crow) and (of *Millstone Grit*),
Sir John Waller Bt. and Major Rook,
Ginsberg, Corso, Stanley Cook,
Peter Scupham, John Heath-Stubbs,
Fenton, Feinstein, both the Grubbs,
Holloway G., Holloway J.,
Anselm Hollo and Peter Way,

Logue, O'Connor, Kevin Crossley-
Holland, Hollander, Keith Bosley,
Matthew Mead and Erica Jong,
Henry Reed and Patience Strong,
Kunitz, Kizer, Kops, Mark Strand,
Creeley, Merwin, Dickey and
The other Dickeys, Eberhart,
Bunting, Wantling, Pilling, Mart-
in Booth, a Dorn and then a Knight,
A Comfort following on a Blight,
Skelton (not the Rector of Diss—
The Poet's Calling Robin, this),
Alistair Elliot, Alastair Reid,
Michael Longley, Michael Fried,
Ian Hamilton (twice—the Scot
With 'Finlay' at the end, and the other not),
Adrians Henri, Mitchell, Stokes,
Lucie-Smith and Philip Oakes,
Father Levi of the Soc-
iety of Jesus, Alan Ross,
Betjeman, Nicholson, Grigson, Walker,
Pitter, Amis, Hilary Corke, a
Decad of Smiths, a Potts and a Black,
Roberts Conquest, Mezey, Graves and Pack,
Hugh MacDiarmid (C. M. Grieve's
His real name, of course), James Reeves,
Hamburger, Stallworthy, Dickinson, Prynne,
Jeremy Hooker, Bartholomew Quinn,
Durrell, Gershon, Harwood, Mahon,
Edmond Wright, Nathaniel Tarn,
Sergeant, Snodgrass, C. K. Stead,
William Shakespeare (no, he's dead),
Cole and Mole and Lowell and Bly,
Robert Nye and Atukwei Okai,
Christopher Fry and George Mackay
Brown, Wayne Brown, John Wain, K. Raine,
Jenny Joseph, Jeni Couzyn,
D. J. Enright, J. C. Hall,
C. H. Sisson and all and all . . .
What is it, you may ask, that Thwaite's
Up to in this epic? Yeats'
Remark in the Cheshire Cheese one night
With poets so thick they blocked the light:
'No one can tell who has talent, if any.
Only one thing is certain. We are too many.'

805 *At Evening*

They were always there, at the end of the garden or elsewhere
Talking unfathomably about whatever it was
In a way that even in childhood I could understand
Enough, at any rate, to feel frightened of.
And here they all are again, as I stoop to brush off
Four or five grey hairs from the arm of the chair—still talking,
Their heads close together, familiar faces in congress,
Knowing I'm there, not afraid to talk when I'm there,
But secret too, surreptitious. I wish I could hear.
The shadows move down the garden, the bonfire smoke
Drifts across hedges, the smell of the smoke pricks my nose,
The hairs on my arm stand up as evening comes on:
And still they are talking, talking, and I want to go in,
Into the house where I know I have always been.

TED HUGHES

1930–1998

806 *View of a Pig*

The pig lay on a barrow dead.
It weighed, they said, as much as three men.
Its eyes closed, pink-white eyelashes.
Its trotters stuck straight out.

Such weight and thick pink bulk
Set in death seemed not just dead.
It was less than lifeless, further off.
It was like a sack of wheat.

I thumped it without feeling remorse.
One feels guilty insulting the dead,
Walking on graves. But this pig
Did not seem able to accuse.

It was too dead. Just so much
A poundage of lard and pork.
Its last dignity had entirely gone.
It was not a figure of fun.

Too dead now to pity.
To remember its life, din, stronghold
Of earthly pleasure as it had been,
Seemed a false effort, and off the point.

Too deadly factual. Its weight
Oppressed me—how could it be moved?
And the trouble of cutting it up!
The gash in its throat was shocking, but not pathetic.

Once I ran at a fair in the noise
To catch a greased piglet
That was faster and nimbler than a cat;
Its squeal was the rending of metal.

Pigs must have hot blood, they feel like ovens.
Their bite is worse than a horse's—
They chop a half-moon clean out.
They eat cinders, dead cats.

Distinctions and admirations such
As this one was long finished with.
I stared at it a long time. They were going to scald it,
Scald it and scour it like a doorstep.

807   *Hawk Roosting*

I sit in the top of the wood, my eyes closed.
Inaction, no falsifying dream
Between my hooked head and hooked feet:
Or in sleep rehearse perfect kills and eat.

The convenience of the high trees!
The air's buoyancy and the sun's ray
Are of advantage to me;
And the earth's face upward for my inspection.

My feet are locked upon the rough bark.
It took the whole of Creation
To produce my foot, my each feather:
Now I hold Creation in my foot

Or fly up, and revolve it all slowly—
I kill where I please because it is all mine.
There is no sophistry in my body:
My manners are tearing off heads—

The allotment of death.
For the one path of my flight is direct
Through the bones of the living.
No arguments assert my right:

The sun is behind me.
Nothing has changed since I began.
My eye has permitted no change.
I am going to keep things like this.

808   *Esther's Tomcat*

Daylong this tomcat lies stretched flat
As an old rough mat, no mouth and no eyes,
Continual wars and wives are what
Have tattered his ears and battered his head.

Like a bundle of old rope and iron
Sleeps till blue dusk. Then reappear
His eyes, green as ringstones: he yawns wide red,
Fangs fine as a lady's needle and bright.

A tomcat sprang at a mounted knight,
Locked round his neck like a trap of hooks
While the knight rode fighting its clawing and bite.
After hundreds of years the stain's there

On the stone where he fell, dead of the tom:
That was at Barnborough. The tomcat still
Grallochs odd dogs on the quiet,
Will take the head clean off your simple pullet,

Is unkillable. From the dog's fury,
From gunshot fired point-blank he brings
His skin whole, and whole
From owlish moons of bekittenings

Among ashcans. He leaps and lightly
Walks upon sleep, his mind on the moon.
Nightly over the round world of men,
Over the roofs go his eyes and outcry.

809   *Pike*

Pike, three inches long, perfect
Pike in all parts, green tigering the gold.
Killers from the egg: the malevolent aged grin.
They dance on the surface among the flies.

Or move, stunned by their own grandeur,
Over a bed of emerald, silhouette
Of submarine delicacy and horror.
A hundred feet long in their world.

In ponds, under the heat-struck lily pads—
Gloom of their stillness:
Logged on last year's black leaves, watching upwards.
Or hung in an amber cavern of weeds

The jaws' hooked clamp and fangs
Not to be changed at this date;
A life subdued to its instrument;
The gills kneading quietly, and the pectorals.

Three we kept behind glass,
Jungled in weed: three inches, four,
And four and a half: fed fry to them—
Suddenly there were two. Finally one.

With a sag belly and the grin it was born with.
And indeed they spare nobody.
Two, six pounds each, over two feet long,
High and dry and dead in the willow-herb—

One jammed past its gills down the other's gullet:
The outside eye stared: as a vice locks—
The same iron in this eye
Though its film shrank in death.

A pond I fished, fifty yards across,
Whose lilies and muscular tench
Had outlasted every visible stone
Of the monastery that planted them—

Stilled legendary depth:
It was as deep as England. It held
Pike too immense to stir, so immense and old
That past nightfall I dared not cast

But silently cast and fished
With the hair frozen on my head
For what might move, for what eye might move.
The still splashes on the dark pond,

Owls hushing the floating woods
Frail on my ear against the dream
Darkness beneath night's darkness had freed,
That rose slowly toward me, watching.

ELAINE FEINSTEIN

1930–

810   from *Insomnia*

3

In my enormous city it is—night,
as from my sleeping house I go—out,
and people think perhaps I'm a daughter or wife
but in my mind is one thought only: night.

The July wind now sweeps a way for—me.
From somewhere, some window, music though—faint.
The wind can blow until the dawn—today,
in through the fine walls of the breast rib-cage.

Black poplars, windows, filled with—light.
Music from high buildings, in my hand a flower.
Look at my steps—following—nobody
Look at my shadow, nothing's here of me.

The lights—are like threads of golden beads
in my mouth is the taste of the night—leaf.
Liberate me from the bonds of—day,
my friends, understand: I'm nothing but your dream.

[after the Russian of Tsvetayeva]

811   *An Attempt at Jealousy*

How is your life with the other one,
    simpler, isn't it? One   stroke of the oar
then a long coastline, and soon
    even the memory of me

will be a floating island
    (in the sky, not on the waters):
spirits, spirits, you will be
    sisters, and never lovers.

How is your life with an ordinary
    woman?   without godhead?
Now that your sovereign has
    been deposed (and you have stepped down).

How is your life? Are you fussing?
    flinching? How   do you get up?
The tax of deathless vulgarity
    can you cope with it, poor man?

'Scenes and hysterics   I've had
    enough! I'll rent my own house.'
How is your life with the other one
    now, you that I chose for my own?

More to your taste, more delicious
    is it, your food? Don't moan if you sicken.
How is your life with an *image*
    you, who walked on Sinai?

How is your life with a stranger
    from this world? Can you (be frank)
love her? Or do you   feel shame
    like Zeus' reins on your forehead?

How is your life? Are you
    healthy? How do you   sing?
How do you deal with the pain
    of an undying conscience, poor man?

How is your life with a piece of market
    stuff, at a steep price.
After Carrara marble,
    how is your life with the dust of

plaster now? (God was hewn from
    stone, but he is smashed to bits.)
How do you live with one of a
    thousand women   after Lilith?

Sated with newness, are you?
    Now you are grown cold to magic,
how is your life with an
    earthly woman, without a sixth

sense? Tell me: are you happy?
    Not? In a shallow pit How is
your life, my love? Is it as
    hard as mine with another man?

        [after the Russian of Tsvetayeva]

GEOFFREY HILL

1932–

812   *The Turtle Dove*

Love that drained her drained him she'd loved, though each
For the other's sake forged passion upon speech,
Bore their close days through sufferance towards night
Where she at length grasped sleep and he lay quiet

As though needing no questions, now, to guess
What her secreting heart could not well hide.
Her caught face flinched in half-sleep at his side.
Yet she, by day, modelled her real distress,

Poised, turned her cheek to the attending world
Of children and intriguers and the old;
Conversed freely, exercised, was admired,
Being strong to dazzle. All this she endured

To affront him. He watched her rough grief work
Under the formed surface of habit. She spoke
Like one long undeceived but she was hurt.
She denied more love, yet her starved eyes caught

His, devouring, at times. Then, as one self-dared,
She went to him, plied there; like a furious dove
Bore down with visitations of such love
As his lithe, fathoming heart absorbed and buried.

813   *Ovid in the Third Reich*

non peccat, quaecumque potest peccasse negare,
solaque famosam culpa professa facit
AMORES, III. xiv

I love my work and my children. God
Is distant, difficult. Things happen.
Too near the ancient troughs of blood
Innocence is no earthly weapon.

I have learned one thing: not to look down
So much upon the damned. They, in their sphere,
Harmonize strangely with the divine
Love. I, in mine, celebrate the love-choir.

814 *September Song*

born 19.6.32–deported 24.9.42

Undesirable you may have been, untouchable
you were not. Not forgotten
or passed over at the proper time.

As estimated, you died. Things marched,
sufficient, to that end.
Just so much Zyklon and leather, patented
terror, so many routine cries.

(I have made
an elegy for myself it
is true)

September fattens on vines. Roses
flake from the wall. The smoke
of harmless fires drifts to my eyes.

This is plenty. This is more than enough.

815 from *Mercian Hymns*

XXI

Cohorts of charabancs fanfared Offa's province and
his concern, negotiating the by-ways from Teme
to Trent. Their windshields dripped butterflies.
Stranded on hilltops they signalled with plumes
of steam. Twilight menaced the land. The young
women wept and surrendered.

Still, everyone was cheerful, heedless in such days:
at summer weekends dipping into valleys beyond
Mercia's dyke. Tea was enjoyed, by lakesides where
all might fancy carillons of real Camelot vi-
brating through the silent water.

Gradually, during the years, deciduous velvet peeled
from evergreen albums and during the years more
treasures were mislaid: the harp-shaped brooches,
the nuggets of fool's gold.

816   from *The Pentecost Castle*

8

And you my spent heart's treasure
my yet unspent desire
measurer past all measure
cold paradox of fire

as seeker so forsaken
consentingly denied
your solitude a token
the sentries at your side

fulfilment to my sorrow
indulgence of your prey
the sparrowhawk the sparrow
the nothing that you say

817   from *An Apology for the Revival of Christian*
                    Architecture in England

12 *The Eve of St Mark*

Stroke the small silk with your whispering hands,
godmother; nod and nod from the half-gloom;
broochlight intermittent between the fronds,
the owl immortal in its crystal dome.

Along the mantelpiece veined lustres trill,
the clock discounts us with a telling chime.
Familiar ministrants, clerks-of-appeal,
burnish upon the threshold of the dream:

churchwardens in wing-collars bearing scrolls
of copyhold well-tinctured and well-tied.
Your photo-albums loved by the boy-king

preserve in sepia waterglass the souls
of distant cousins, virgin till they died,
and the lost delicate suitors who could sing.

818   *To the High Court of Parliament*

November 1994

—who could outbalance poised
                              Marvell; balk the strength
of Gillray's unrelenting, unreconciling mind;
grandees risen from scavenge; to whom Milton
                              addressed his ideal censure:
once more, singular, ill-attended,
staid and bitter Commedia—as she is called—
delivers to your mirth her veiled presence.

None the less amazing: Barry's and Pugin's grand
dark-lantern above the incumbent Thames.
You: as by custom unillumined
                              masters of servile counsel.
Who can now speak for despoiled merit,
                              the fouled catchments of Demos,
as 'thy' high lamp presides with sovereign
equity, over against us, across this
densely reflective, long-drawn, procession of waters?

SEAMUS HEANEY

1939–

819   *Death of a Naturalist*

All year the flax-dam festered in the heart
Of the townland; green and heavy headed
Flax had rotted there, weighted down by huge sods.
Daily it sweltered in the punishing sun.
Bubbles gargled delicately, bluebottles
Wove a strong gauze of sound around the smell.
There were dragon-flies, spotted butterflies,
But best of all was the warm thick slobber
Of frogspawn that grew like clotted water
In the shade of the banks. Here, every spring
I would fill jampotfuls of the jellied
Specks to range on window-sills at home,
On shelves at school, and wait and watch until
The fattening dots burst into nimble-
Swimming tadpoles. Miss Walls would tell us how
The daddy frog was called a bullfrog

And how he croaked and how the mammy frog
Laid hundreds of little eggs and this was
Frogspawn. You could tell the weather by frogs too
For they were yellow in the sun and brown
In rain.

   Then one hot day when fields were rank
With cowdung in the grass the angry frogs
Invaded the flax-dam; I ducked through hedges
To a coarse croaking that I had not heard
Before. The air was thick with a bass chorus.
Right down the dam gross-bellied frogs were cocked
On sods; their loose necks pulsed like sails. Some hopped:
The slap and plop were obscene threats. Some sat
Poised like mud grenades, their blunt heads farting.
I sickened, turned, and ran. The great slime kings
Were gathered there for vengeance and I knew
That if I dipped my hand the spawn would clutch it.

820   *Ugolino*

We had already left him. I walked the ice
And saw two soldered in a frozen hole
On top of other, one's skull capping the other's,
Gnawing at him where the neck and head
Are grafted to the sweet fruit of the brain,
Like a famine victim at a loaf of bread.
So the berserk Tydeus gnashed and fed
Upon the severed head of Menalippus
As if it were some spattered carnal melon.
'You,' I shouted, 'you on top, what hate
Makes you so ravenous and insatiable?
What keeps you so monstrously at rut?
Is there any story I can tell
For you, in the world above, against him?
If my tongue by then's not withered in my throat
I will report the truth and clear your name.'

That sinner eased his mouth up off his meal
To answer me, and wiped it with the hair
Left growing on his victim's ravaged skull,
Then said, 'Even before I speak
The thought of having to relive all that
Desperate time makes my heart sick;
Yet while I weep to say them, I would sow

My words like curses—that they might increase
And multiply upon this head I gnaw.
I know you come from Florence by your accent
But I have no idea who you are
Nor how you ever managed your descent.
Still, you should know my name, for I was Count
Ugolino, this was Archbishop Roger,
And why I act the jockey to his mount
Is surely common knowledge; how my good faith
Was easy prey to his malignancy,
How I was taken, held, and put to death.
But you must hear something you cannot know
If you're to judge him—the cruelty
Of my death at his hands. So listen now.

Others will pine as I pined in that jail
Which is called Hunger after me, and watch
As I watched through a narrow hole
Moon after moon, bright and somnambulant,
Pass overhead, until that night I dreamt
The bad dream and my future's veil was rent.
I saw a wolf-hunt: this man rode the hill
Between Pisa and Lucca, hounding down
The wolf and wolf-cubs. He was lordly and masterful,
His pack in keen condition, his company
Deployed ahead of him, Gualandi
And Sismundi as well, and Lanfranchi,
Who soon wore down wolf-father and wolf-sons
And my hallucination
Was all sharp teeth and bleeding flanks ripped open.
When I awoke before the dawn, my head
Swam with cries of my sons who slept in tears
Beside me there, crying out for bread.
(If your sympathy has not already started
At all that my heart was foresuffering
And if you are not crying, you are hardhearted.)

They were awake now, it was near the time
For food to be brought in as usual,
Each one of them disturbed after his dream,
When I heard the door being nailed and hammered
Shut, far down in the nightmare tower.
I stared in my sons' faces and spoke no word.
My eyes were dry and my heart was stony.
They cried and my little Anselm said,
"What's wrong? Why are you staring, daddy?"
But I shed no tears, I made no reply
All through that day, all through the night that followed

Until another sun blushed in the sky
And sent a small beam probing the distress
Inside those prison walls. Then when I saw
The image of my face in their four faces
I bit on my two hands in desperation
And they, since they thought hunger drove me to it,
Rose up suddenly in agitation
Saying, "Father, it will greatly ease our pain
If you eat us instead, and you who dressed us
In this sad flesh undress us here again."
So then I calmed myself to keep them calm.
We hushed. That day and the next stole past us
And earth seemed hardened against me and them.
For four days we let the silence gather.
Then, throwing himself flat in front of me,
Gaddo said, "Why don't you help me, father?"
He died like that, and surely as you see
Me here, one by one I saw my three
Drop dead during the fifth day and the sixth day
Until I saw no more. Searching, blinded,
For two days I groped over them and called them.
Then hunger killed where grief had only wounded.'
When he had said all this, his eyes rolled
And his teeth, like a dog's teeth clamping round a bone,
Bit into the skull and again took hold.

Pisa! Pisa, your sounds are like a hiss
Sizzling in our country's grassy language.
And since the neighbour states have been remiss
In your extermination, let a huge
Dyke of islands bar the Arno's mouth, let
Capraia and Gorgona dam and deluge
You and your population. For the sins
Of Ugolino, who betrayed your forts,
Should never have been visited on his sons.
Your atrocity was Theban. They were young
And innocent: Hugh and Brigata
And the other two whose names are in my song.

from Dante, *Inferno*, xxxii *and* xxxiii

821   *The Grauballe Man*

              As if he had been poured
              in tar, he lies
              on a pillow of turf
              and seems to weep

the black river of himself.
The grain of his wrists
is like bog oak,
the ball of his heel

like a basalt egg.
His instep has shrunk
cold as a swan's foot
or a wet swamp root.

His hips are the ridge
and purse of a mussel,
his spine an eel arrested
under a glisten of mud.

The head lifts,
the chin is a visor
raised above the vent
of his slashed throat

that has tanned and toughened.
The cured wound
opens inwards to a dark
elderberry place.

Who will say 'corpse'
to his vivid cast?
Who will say 'body'
to his opaque repose?

And his rusted hair,
a mat unlikely
as a foetus's.
I first saw his twisted face

in a photograph,
a head and shoulder
out of the peat,
bruised like a forceps baby,

but now he lies
perfected in my memory,
down to the red horn
of his nails,

hung in the scales
with beauty and atrocity:
with the Dying Gaul
too strictly compassed

on his shield,
with the actual weight
of each hooded victim,
slashed and dumped.

822   *The Pitchfork*

Of all implements, the pitchfork was the one
That came near to an imagined perfection:
When he tightened his raised hand and aimed with it,
It felt like a javelin, accurate and light.

So whether he played the warrior or the athlete
Or worked in earnest in the chaff and sweat,
He loved its grain of tapering, dark-flecked ash
Grown satiny from its own natural polish.

Riveted steel, turned timber, burnish, grain,
Smoothness, straightness, roundness, length and sheen.
Sweat-cured, sharpened, balanced, tested, fitted.
The springiness, the clip and dart of it.

And then when he thought of probes that reached the farthest,
He would see the shaft of a pitchfork sailing past
Evenly, imperturbably through space,
Its prongs starlit and absolutely soundless—

But has learned at last to follow that simple lead
Past its own aim, out to an other side
Where perfection—or nearness to it—is imagined
Not in the aiming but the opening hand.

ACKNOWLEDGEMENTS

I am grateful to the friends who gave me advice: Kenneth Haynes, Marcia Karp, Jim McCue, Lisa Rodensky, and Frances Whistler.

W. H. Auden: 'O where are you going?', copyright © 1934 and renewed 1962 by W. H. Auden; 'On This Island', copyright © 1937 and renewed 1965 by W. H. Auden; 'Lullaby', 'Musée des Beaux Arts', and 'Epitaph on a Tyrant', all copyright © 1940 and renewed 1968 by W. H. Auden; 'Adolescence', copyright © 1945 by W. H. Auden; 'The Fall of Rome', copyright © 1947 by W. H. Auden; and 'The Shield of Achilles' copyright © 1952 by W. H. Auden; all from *Collected Poems*, by permission of the publishers, Faber & Faber Ltd. and Random House, Inc.

Samuel Beckett: 'Something there' and 'Roundelay' from *Collected Poems in English and French*, copyright © 1977 by Samuel Beckett, by permission of the publishers, Calder Publications Ltd. and Grove/Atlantic, Inc.; 'What is the word' from *As the Story Was Told*, by permission of the publishers, Calder Publications Ltd.

Hilaire Belloc: 'On a General Election' from *Complete Verse* (Random House), by permission of The Peters Fraser and Dunlop Group Ltd. on behalf of The Estate of Hilaire Belloc.

E. C. Bentley: Three clerihews from *Complete Clerihews* (OUP, 1981), copyright the Estate of E. C. Bentley, by permission of Curtis Brown Ltd., London on behalf of the Estate of E. C. Bentley.

John Betjeman: 'Death of King George V' and 'On Seeing an Old Poet in the Café Royal' from *Collected Poems*, by permission of John Murray (Publishers) Ltd.

Edmund Blunden: 'Report on Experience' from *Collected Poems* (Duckworth), by permission of The Peters Fraser and Dunlop Group Ltd.

Robert Bridges: 'Ghosts' and 'Who goes there?' from *The Poetical Works of Robert Bridges* (OUP, 1936), by permission of Oxford University Press.

Basil Bunting: 'Came to me' (translated from Rudaki) and 'Remember, imbeciles' (translated from Villon) from *The Complete Poems* (OUP, 1994), by permission of Oxford University Press.

Norman Cameron: 'Naked among the Trees' and 'Forgive me, Sire' from Warren Hope and Jonathan Barker (eds.): *Collected Poems and Selected Translations* (Anvil, 1990), by permission of Anvil Press Poetry Ltd.

Roy Campbell: 'On Some South African Novelists' and 'On a Shipmate . . .' from *Collected Works* (Ad Donker) by permission of the publishers, Jonathan Ball Publishers (Pty) Ltd.

John Clare: 'A Vision', 'I Am', 'Song' ('I hid my love when young'), 'The Mouse's Nest' ('I found a ball of grass among the hay'), 'Sheep in Winter' ('The sheep get up and make their many tracks'), and 'Autumn Birds' ('The wild duck startles like a sudden thought') from Eric Robinson and David Powell (eds.): *John Clare* (Oxford Authors), copyright Eric Robinson 1984, by permission of Curtis Brown Ltd., London, on behalf of Eric Robinson.

Austin Clarke: 'Mabel Kelly', 'Gracey Nugent', and 'Peggy Browne' from *Flight to Africa* (Dolmen Press, 1963); 'Martha Blake' and 'Penal Law' from *Night and Morning* (1938); 'The Planter's Daughter' from *Pilgrimage* (1929); and 'Miss Marnell' from *Too Great a Vine* (1957) all by permission of R. Dardis Clarke, 21 Pleasants Street, Dublin 8.

Frances Cornford: 'Childhood' and 'To a Fat Lady . . .' from *Collected Poems* (Cresset Press), by permission of Hutchinson Press, Random House UK Ltd.

Elizabeth Daryush: 'Children of Wealth' and 'Still-Life' from *Collected Poems* (1976), by permission of the publisher, Carcanet Press Ltd.

Donald Davie: 'The Garden Party', 'The Mushroom Gatherers', and 'Tunstall Forest' from *Collected Poems* (1990) by permission of the publisher, Carcanet Press Ltd.

Walter de la Mare: 'Napoleon' and 'Fare Well' from *The Complete Poems of Walter de la Mare* (Faber, 1969), by permission of The Literary Trustees of Walter de la Mare and the Society of Authors as their Representative.

Keith Douglas: 'Sportsmen' and 'Vergissmeinnicht' from Desmond Graham (ed.): *The Complete Poems* (OUP, 3rd edn., 1998), by permission of Oxford University Press.

T. S. Eliot: 'The Love Song of J. Alfred Prufrock', 'Morning at the Window', 'Hysteria', 'La Figlia Che Piange', 'Sweeney Among the Nightingales', 'Marina', 'The Waste Land IV: Death by Water', and 'Little Gidding II' all from *Collected Poems*, by permission of the publisher, Faber & Faber Ltd.; 'Marina' also from *Collected Poems 1909–1962*, copyright 1936 by Harcourt Brace & Company, copyright © 1963, 1964 by T. S. Eliot, and 'Little Gidding II' also from *Four Quartets*, copyright 1943 by T. S. Eliot and renewed 1971 by Esme Valerie Eliot, by permission of Harcourt Brace & Company.

William Empson: 'To an Old Lady', 'Homage to the British Museum', 'Note on Local Flora', 'Aubade', 'Missing Dates', 'Let it go', and 'Chinese Ballad' from *Collected Poems* (Hogarth Press), copyright 1949 and renewed 1977 by William Empson, by permission of Random House UK Ltd. on behalf of Lady Empson, and Harcourt Brace & Company.

U. A. Fanthorpe: 'BC:AD' and 'Portraits of Tudor Statesmen' from *Standing To* (1982), copyright © U. A. Fanthorpe, by permission of the publisher, Peterloo Poets.

Elaine Feinstein: 'In my enormous city' and 'An Attempt at Jealousy' from *Selected Poems of Tsvetayeva* (Oxford Poets, 1993), copyright © Elaine

Feinstein 1971, 1981, 1986, 1993, by permission of the author c/o Rogers, Coleridge & White, 20 Powis Mews, London W11 1JN.

Robert Graves: 'Love without Hope', 'Warning to Children', 'The Cool Web', 'Welsh Incident', 'To Juan at the Winter Solstice', and 'A False Report' from *Complete Poems* (1997), by permission of the publisher, Carcanet Press Ltd.

Thom Gunn: 'The Feel of Hands' and 'Considering the Snail' from *Collected Poems*, copyright © 1994 by Thom Gunn; and 'Terminal' from *The Man with Night Sweats*, all by permission of the publishers, Faber & Faber Ltd. and Farrar, Straus & Giroux, Inc.

Ivor Gurney: 'La Gorgue', 'The Soaking', 'First March', 'Behind the Line', and 'To God' from *Selected Poems* (OUP, 1990), by permission of Oxford University Press.

Seamus Heaney: 'Death of a Naturalist' from *Death of a Naturalist*, 'Ugolino' from *Field Work*, 'The Grauballe Man' from *New and Selected Poems*, and 'The Pitchfork' from *Seeing Things*, all by permission of the publishers, Faber & Faber Ltd.; also from *Opened Ground: Selected Poems 1966–1996*, copyright © 1998 by Seamus Heaney, by permission of the publishers, Farrar, Straus & Giroux, Inc.

Geoffrey Hill: 'The Turtle Dove', 'Ovid in the Third Reich', 'September Song', 'Mercian Hymns XXI', 'The Pentecost Castle: And you . . .', and 'The Eve of St Mark' from *Collected Poems* (Penguin, 1985), © Geoffrey Hill 1959, 1971, 1978, 1985, by permission of Penguin Books Ltd.; also from *New and Collected Poems 1952–1992*, copyright © 1994 by Geoffrey Hill, by permission of Houghton Mifflin Company. All rights reserved. 'To the High Court of Parliament' from *Canaan* (Penguin, 1996), copyright © Geoffrey Hill 1996, by permission of Penguin Books Ltd.

A. E. Housman: 'A Shropshire Lad XVI' and 'XL'; 'Last Poems III', 'XXVII', 'XXXVII', and 'XL'; 'More Poems VI: I to my perils', 'XXIII: Crossing alone the nighted ferry', 'XXXI: Because I liked you better', 'XXXVI: Here dead lie we . . .'; 'Additional Poems IX: When the bells justle . . .', and 'XVI: Some can gaze . . .', all from Archie Burnett (ed.), *The Poems* (OUP, 1997), by permission of the Society of Authors as the Literary Representative of the Estate of A. E. Housman; all 'Last Poems' and 'More Poems' also from *Selected Poetry*, by permission of the publisher, Henry Holt & Company, Inc.; 'Additional Poems' also from *My Brother, A. E. Housman* by Laurence Housman, copyright © 1937, 1938 by Laurence Housman, copyrights renewed © 1965, 1966 by Lloyds Bank Limited, by permission of Scribner, a division of Simon & Schuster, Inc.

Ted Hughes: 'View of a Pig', 'Hawk Roosting', 'Esther's Tomcat', and 'Pike' from *Lupercal*, by permission of the publishers, Faber & Faber Ltd.

Thomas Kinsella: 'Ancestor' and 'Tear' from *New Poems* (Dolmen Press, 1973), by permission of the author.

Rudyard Kipling: 'The Story of Uriah', 'The Vampire', 'The Fabulists', 'Danny Deever', 'Recessional', and 'A Death-Bed', from *Rudyard Kipling's Verse: The Definitive Edition* (Hodder & Stoughton, 1945), by permission of A. P. Watt Ltd. on behalf of The National Trust for Places of Historic Interest or Natural Beauty.

Philip Larkin: 'At Grass', 'Absences', 'Days', 'Age', 'Mr Bleaney', 'Love Songs in Age', 'Afternoons', 'As Bad as a Mile', 'Faith Healing', and 'Homage to a Government' from *Collected Poems*, copyright © 1988, 1989 by The Estate of Philip Larkin, by permission of the publishers, Faber & Faber Ltd. and Farrar, Straus & Giroux, Inc.

D. H. Lawrence: 'Snake', 'Humming-Bird' (may not be photocopied without written permission), 'Thought', 'Bavarian Gentians', and 'The Ship of Death', all copyright © 1964, 1971 by Angelo Ravagli and C. M. Weekley, Executors of the Estate of Frieda Lawrence Ravagli, from V. de Sola Pinto and F. W. Roberts (eds.): *The Complete Poems of D. H. Lawrence*, by permission of Laurence Pollinger Ltd. and the Estate of Frieda Lawrence Ravagli, and Viking Penguin, a division of Penguin Putnam Inc.

Alun Lewis: 'The Peasants' from *Collected Poems*, by permission of Harper-Collins Publishers Ltd.

Hugh MacDiarmid: 'Empty Vessel', 'A Vision of Myself', 'O Wha's the Bride?', 'The Spur of Love', 'Of John Davidson', 'Perfect', 'The Caledonian Antisyzygy', and 'Cattle Show' all from *Collected Poems* (1993), by permission of the publisher, Carcanet Press Ltd.; and from *Selected Poetry*, copyright © 1992 by Michael Grieve, by permission of New Directions Publishing Corp.

Louis MacNeice: 'Snow', 'Bagpipe music', 'Château Jackson', and 'Charon' from *Collected Poems* (Faber & Faber), by permission of David Higham Associates.

John Masefield: 'An Epilogue', 'Autumn Ploughing', and 'Sonnet from Quevedo' from *Collected Poems* (Macmillan), by permission of the Society of Authors as the Literary Representative of the Estate of John Masefield.

Edwin Morgan: 'The Computer's First Christmas Card' from *Collected Poems* (1990), by permission of the publishers, Carcanet Press Ltd.

Edwin Muir: 'Then' from *Collected Poems*, copyright © 1960 by Willa Muir, by permission of the publishers, Faber & Faber Ltd. and Oxford University Press, Inc.

Peter Porter: 'Near the Vipsanian columns' (translated from Martial) from *Collected Poems* (OUP, 1983), by permission of Oxford University Press.

F. T. Prince: 'Epistle to a Patron' from *Collected Poems* (1993), by permission of the publishers, Carcanet Press Ltd. and The Sheep Meadow Press.

Henry Reed: 'Naming of Parts', 'Judging Distances', and 'Dull Sonnet' from Jon Stallworthy (ed.): *Collected Poems* (OUP, 1991), by permission of Oxford University Press.

Anne Ridler: 'Now Philippa Is Gone' from *Selected Poems* (1994), by permission of the publisher, Carcanet Press Ltd.

Siegfried Sassoon: 'Base Details' copyright 1918 by E. P. Dutton, renewed 1946 by Siegfried Sassoon, 'Blighters' and 'The General' both copyright 1918, 1920 by E. P. Dutton, copyright 1936, 1946, 1947, 1948 by Siegfried Sassoon, all from *The Collected Poems of Siegfried Sassoon* (Faber/Viking), by permission of Barbary Levy Literary Agency on behalf of George Sassoon, and Viking Penguin, a division of Penguin Putnam Inc.

Tom Scott: 'Ballat O the Leddies O Langsyne' (translated from Villon) from *The Collected Shorter Poems of Tom Scott* (Agenda/Chapman, 1993), by permission of Mrs Heather Scott and Chapman Publications.

Iain Crichton Smith: 'Old Woman' from *Collected Poems* (1995), by permission of the publisher, Carcanet Press Ltd.

Stevie Smith: 'Pad, pad', 'Not Waving but Drowning', 'Songe d'Athalie', 'Magna est Veritas', and 'Was it not curious?' from *Collected Poems of Stevie Smith* (Allen Lane/New Directions), copyright © 1972 by Stevie Smith, by permission of James MacGibbon and New Directions Publishing Corp.

James Stephens: 'The Cage' and 'A Glass of Beer' from *Collected Poems* (Macmillan), by permission of the Society of Authors as the Literary Representative of the Estate of James Stephens.

Dylan Thomas: 'The force that through the green fuse . . .', 'Light breaks', 'Should lanterns shine', all copyright © 1939 by New Directions Publishing Corp.; 'Twenty-four years', copyright © 1945 by The Trustees for the Copyrights of Dylan Thomas; 'I have longed to move away' and 'The Hunchback in the Park', both copyright © 1943, 1939 by New Directions Publishing Corp.; all from *The Poems of Dylan Thomas*, by permission of the publisher, New Directions Publishing Corp. All poems also from *Collected Poems* (J. M. Dent), by permission of David Higham Associates.

R. S. Thomas: 'On the Farm', 'A Peasant', 'January', and 'Evans' from *Selected Poems 1946–1968* (Bloodaxe Books, 1986) by permission of the publishers.

Anthony Thwaite: 'On Consulting "Contemporary Poets . . ."' and 'At Evening' from *Poems 1953–1983* (Secker & Warburg) copyright © Anthony Thwaite, by permission of Curtis Brown Ltd., London, on behalf of the author; 'Clouds now and then', by Matsuo Bashō, 'Girls planting paddy', by Konishi Raizan, and 'Winter withering' by Tan Taigi, from the *Penguin Book of Japanese Verse* (Penguin, 1964), edited and translated by Geoffrey Bownas and Anthony Thwaite, translation copyright © Geoffrey Bownas and Anthony Thwaite 1964, by permission of Penguin Books Ltd.

Charles Tomlinson: 'Saving the Appearances' and 'The Door' from *Selected Poems* (OUP, 1997); 'At Vshchizh' and 'To His Wife' (translated from Tyutchev) from *Translations* (OUP, 1983), by permission of Oxford University Press.

Derek Walcott: 'Missing the Sea' from *Collected Poems* 1948–1984, copyright © 1986 by Derek Walcott, by permission of the publishers, Faber & Faber Ltd. and Farrar, Straus & Giroux, Inc.

Arthur Waley: poems translated from the Chinese, 'The Ejected Wife' (original 1916 version, later revised as 'The Rejected Wife', copyright 1919 and renewed 1947 by Arthur Waley) from *One Hundred and Seventy Chinese Poems*, by permission of Constable Publishers and Alfred A. Knopf, Inc: 'Yellow dusk' and 'In her boudoir' from *Chinese Poems*, by permission of John Robinson for the Arthur Waley Estate.

W. B. Yeats: 'The Sorrow of Love' (two versions), 'When You Are Old', 'The Second Coming' copyright © 1924 by Macmillan Publishing Company, renewed 1952 by Bertha Georgie Yeats; 'Sailing to Byzantium', 'Among School Children', and 'Leda and the Swan' all copyright 1928 by Macmillan Publishing Company, copyright renewed © 1956 by Bertha Georgie Yeats; and 'Byzantium' copyright 1940 by Georgie Yeats, copyright renewed © 1968 by Bertha Georgie Yeats, Michael Butler Yeats, and Anne Yeats; all from *Collected Poems* (Macmillan), by permission of A. P. Watt on behalf of Michael B. Yeats; all poems also from Richard J. Finneran (ed.): *The Poems of W. B. Yeats: A New Edition*, by permission of the publisher, Simon & Schuster, Inc.

Every effort has been made to trace and contact copyright holders prior to publication. If notified, the publisher undertakes to rectify any errors or omissions at the earliest opportunity.

Endpapers: (*front*) 'By the rushy-fringèd bank' in Milton's hand, from the Trinity Manuscript, by permission of the Master and Fellows of Trinity College, Cambridge.
(*back*) Lines from 'Thou art indeed just, Lord, if I contend' in Hopkins's hand, by permission of the Bodleian Library, University of Oxford; MS. Eng. poet. d. 149, fo. 52r.

INDEX OF AUTHORS

References are by page-number

INDEX OF FOREIGN AUTHORS IN
TRANSLATION OR IMITATION

References are by page-number

INDEX OF TITLES AND FIRST LINES

References are by page-number

; verumtamen justo

impiorum prosper

march 17

hou ast indeed jus
ith thee; but,

just

hy do sinners' wa
isappointment all
Vest thou my enem
low wouldst thou

thou

speat, thwart me?